CREDIT DERIVATIVES

CDOs AND STRUCTURED CREDIT PRODUCTS

CREDIT DERIVATIVES
CDOs AND STRUCTURED CREDIT PRODUCTS

Third Edition

Satyajit Das

John Wiley & Sons (Asia) Pte Ltd

Published in 2005 by John Wiley & Sons (Asia) Pte Ltd
2 Clementi Loop, #02-01, Singapore 129809

Other Wiley Editorial Offices

John Wiley & Sons, Inc., 111 River Street, Hoboken, NJ 07030, USA
John Wiley & Sons Ltd, The Atrium Southern Gate, Chichester P019 8SQ, England
John Wiley & Sons (Canada) Ltd, 22 Worcester Road, Rexdale, Ontario M9W 1L1, Canada
John Wiley & Sons Australia Ltd, 33 Park Road (PO Box 1226), Milton, Queensland 4064, Australia
Wiley-VCH, Pappelallee 3, 69469 Weinheim, Germany

Library of Congress Cataloging-in-Publication Data
0-470-82159-0

Typeset in 10/13 points, Times by Cepha Imaging Pvt Ltd
Printed in Singapore by Saik Wah Press Pte Ltd
10 9 8 7 6 5 4 3 2 1

Contents

Introduction ix

1 Credit Derivative Products 1

2 Structured Credit Products 153

3 Credit Linked Notes 239

4 Collateralised Debt Obligations 305

5 Credit Derivatives Pricing and Valuation 459

6 Credit Modelling/Credit Portfolio Management 533

7 Credit Derivative Applications 611

8 Credit Derivative Markets 709

Profile

Satyajit Das is an international specialist in the area of financial derivatives, risk management, and capital markets. He presents seminars on financial derivatives/risk management and capital markets in Europe, North America, Asia and Australia. He acts as a consultant to financial institutions and corporations on derivatives and financial products, risk management, and capital markets issues.

Between 1988 and 1994, Mr Das was the Treasurer of the TNT Group, an Australian-based international transport and logistics company with responsibility for the Global Treasury function, including liquidity management, corporate finance, funding/capital markets and financial risk management. Between 1977 and 1987, he worked in banking with the Commonwealth Bank of Australia, Citicorp Investment Bank and Merrill Lynch Capital Markets specialising in capital markets and risk management/derivative products.

In 1987, Mr Das was a Visiting Fellow at the Centre for Studies in Money, Banking and Finance, Macquarie University.

Mr Das is the author of *Swaps/Financial Derivatives – Third Edition* (2004, John Wiley & Sons) and *Structured Products & Hybrid Securities – Second Edition* (2001, John Wiley & Sons). He is the major contributor and editor of *Credit Derivatives & Credit Linked Notes – Second Edition* (2001, John Wiley & Sons).

He is also the author of *Swap Financing* (1989, IFR Publishing Limited/ The Law Book Company Limited), *Swaps and Financial Derivatives: The Global Reference to Products, Pricing, Applications and Markets* (1994, IFR Publishing Limited/The Law Book Company Limited/McGraw-Hill), *Exotic Options* (1996, IFR Publishing/The Law Book Company) and *Structured Notes and Derivative Embedded Securities* (1996, Euromoney Publications). He is also the major contributor and editor of *The Global Swaps Market* (1991, IFR Publishing Limited), *Financial Derivatives & Risk Management: A Guide to the Mathematics* (1997, Law Book

Company/McGraw-Hill/MacMillan Publishing) and *Credit Derivatives* (1998, John Wiley & Sons).

He has published on financial derivatives, corporate finance, treasury and risk management issues in professional and applied finance journals (including: Risk, Journal of International Securities Markets, Capital Market Strategies, Euromoney Corporate Finance, Futures & OTC World (FOW), Financial Products and Financial Derivatives & Risk Management).

Mr Das holds Bachelors' degrees in Commerce (Accounting, Finance and Systems) and Law from the University of New South Wales and a Masters degree in Business Administration from the Australian Graduate School of Management.

Introduction

1 Background

Credit derivatives have emerged as a very important and rapidly growing area in global derivatives and risk management practice. These instruments have revolutionised the management of and investment in credit risk in capital markets. Credit derivatives have increased the liquidity of and trading in credit risk. The rapid growth in volumes, the proliferation of products and the wide range of participants are testament to the rapid development of credit derivatives.

The First Edition of **Credit Derivatives** was published in 1998. It was designed to meet the high interest in learning of and gaining familiarity with these instruments. An updated Second Edition of **Credit Derivatives** was released in 2000. This edition – **Credit Derivatives, CDOs & Structured Credit Products 3rd Edition** – is in response to the success of the previous editions. It also reflects the rapid changes in the market for these instruments.

2 Objectives

The major objective of **Credit Derivatives, CDOs & Structured Credit Products 3rd Edition** is to provide comprehensive information on credit derivative products (both standard and structured), documentation issues, pricing/valuation approaches, applications and the market. Its major purpose is to function as a complete reference work on credit derivatives.

Previous editions have consisted of a number of chapters written by the author and a collection of papers from leading market practitioners. This edition departs from the previous format. All chapters have been written by the author.

Key areas of new/enhanced coverage include:

- Inclusion of latest developments in documentation (the 2003 Credit Derivative Definitions and market developments such as Master Confirmations).

- Detailed discussion of practical documentation issues.
- Description of developments in structured credit products including:
    1. Portfolio products
    2. Up-front credit default swaps
    3. Quanto credit default swaps
    4. Credit swaptions
    5. Zero recovery credit default swaps
    6. First-to-default swaps/N^{th}-to-default swaps
    7. Asset swaptions/synthetic lending facilities/structured asset swaps
    8. Constant maturity credit spread products and constant maturity credit default swaps
    9. Credit index products
    10. Equity default swaps
    11. Currency convertibility products
- Increased coverage of credit linked notes including repackaging structures.
- Detailed discussion of the collateralised debt obligations ("CDO") market including:
    1. CDO structures
    2. Pricing and valuation
    3. Rating methodology
    4. CDO variations (including SME CDOs, structured finance/ABS CDOs, collateralised fund obligations ("CFOs")).
    5. Single tranche CDOs
    6. Hedging of CDO tranches (including credit deltas and other greeks and default correlation risk).
    7. Behaviour of CDO tranche (equity, mezzanine, senior and super senior) investments.
- Increased coverage of pricing of credit default swaps (including models and valuation approaches).
- Discussion of cash-synthetic basis and its causes and behaviour.
- Coverage of E2C (equity to credit) hedging.
- Enhanced coverage of credit portfolio management models and approaches to portfolio modelling.
- Detailed examples of applications of credit derivatives by different market participants.
- Discussion of trading in credit derivatives including more complex trading strategies such as basis trading and capital structure arbitrage trades.

- Updated coverage of regulatory framework for credit derivatives.
- Updated discussion of market structures, developments and prospects.

The style of the book remains practical, emphasising examples to convey concepts associated with these instruments.

The target audience for this book includes:

- Banks and dealers active in credit derivative products and capital markets.
- Asset/investment managers who use or are looking at using credit derivatives.
- Service industries, consultants, IT firms, accountants etc, active in advising traders or users of these instruments.
- Regulatory agencies.

The Book can also be used as the basis for practical in-house training programs as well as in post-graduate programs such as MBA or Applied Finance courses in credit risk management, either as the primary text or supplementary reading.

3   Content And Structure

The Book is structured around the following themes:

- **Products and Structures:** *Chapter 1 – Credit Derivative Products* outlines the basic building block instruments – total return loan swaps, credit spread products, and (most importantly) credit default swaps. The Chapter covers documentation and legal issues of credit derivatives, including the revised ISDA standard form confirmation and 2003 ISDA Credit Derivatives definitions. *Chapter 2 – Structured Credit Products* covers structured credit products. *Chapter 3 – Credit Linked Notes* covers credit linked structured notes and synthetic credit linked notes created using special purpose repackaging vehicles. *Chapter 4 – Collateralised Debt Obligations* covers credit risk portfolio securitisation structures.
- **Pricing & Valuation Issues:** *Chapter 5 – Credit Derivatives Pricing And Valuation* covers the pricing, valuation and risk management of credit default swaps and other standard credit derivative structures.
- **Credit Portfolio Management:** *Chapter 6 – Credit Modelling/Credit Portfolio Management* covers credit modelling, credit portfolio models and credit portfolio management.

- **Applications:** *Chapter 7 – Credit Derivative Applications* covers applications of credit derivatives by banks/financial institutions, investors and corporations.
- **Markets:** *Chapter 8 – Credit Derivative Markets* focuses on the market for credit derivatives.

The Book is designed either to be read through from start to finish or operate as a reference source where individual sections are read as required.

4 Acknowledgments

I would like to thank the Publishers – John Wiley (Nick Wallwork) – for agreeing to publish the Book. I would like to thank Malar Manoharan and Karen Noakes who edited the book.

I would like to thank my parents Sukumar and Aparna Das for their continued support and encouragement in my work. In particular, I would like to thank my friend and partner Jade Novakovic. Without her support, help, patience and encouragement this Book like so many others before it would never have been completed. This book is dedicated to these three people.

Satyajit Das
October 2004

This Book is dedicated to

My friend and partner Jade Novakovic

And my parents

Sukumar and Aparna Das

For their support and encouragement

1
Credit Derivative Products[1]

1 Overview

Credit derivatives are traditional derivatives re-engineered to a credit orientation. The underlying asset in credit derivatives is the credit risk on an underlying bond, loan or other financial instrument. The central focus of this book is a description of credit derivatives including the key products, pricing/valuation issues, applications and the structure of the market.

---

[1] There is significant literature on credit derivatives. The references listed here are the ones that the author finds most useful in practice. The list is not comprehensive. See (1998) Credit Derivatives: Applications For Risk Management; Euromoney Books, London; (1998) Credit Derivatives: Applications for Risk Management, Investment and Portfolio Optimisation; Risk Books, London; Tavakoli, Janet M. (1998) Credit Derivatives: A Guide To Instruments And Applications; John Wiley & Sons, Inc., New York; Francis, Jack Clark, Frost, Joyce A., and Whittaker, J. Gregg (Editors) (1999) The Handbook of Credit Derivatives; McGraw-Hill, New York; Nelken, Dr. Israel (1999) Implementing Credit Derivatives; McGraw-Hill, New York; (1999) The J.P. Morgan Guide To Credit Derivatives; Risk Publications, London; Tavakoli, Janet M. (2001) Credit Derivatives & Synthetic Structures – Second Edition; John Wiley & Sons, Inc., New York; Gregory, Jon (Editor) (2003) Credit Derivatives: The Definitive Guide; Risk Publications, London. See also Falloon, William "Credit Where Credit's Due" (March 1994) Risk 9–11; Reoch, Rob and Masters, Blythe "Credit Swaps: An Innovation In Negotiable Exposure" (1995) Capital Market Strategies 7 3–8; Howard, Kerrin "An Introduction To Credit Derivatives" (Winter 1995) Derivatives Quarterly 28–37; Smithson, Charles with Holappa, Hal "Credit Derivatives" (December 1995) Risk 12 38–39; Whittaker, Greg J. and Kumar, Sumita "Credit Derivatives: A Primer" in Konishi, Atsuo and Dattatreya, Ravi (Ed) (1996) The Handbook of Derivative Instruments; Irwin Publishing, Chicago at 595–614; Masters, Blythe and Reoch, Rob (March 1996) Credit Derivatives: Structures And Applications; JP Morgan, New York and London; Masters, Blythe and Reoch, Rob (March 1996) Credit Derivatives: An Innovation in

In this Chapter, the key building block credit derivative instruments are outlined. The structure of this Chapter is as follows:

- The concept of credit derivatives is discussed.
- Credit derivatives are defined.
- The major types of credit derivatives (total return swaps, credit spread forwards/options and credit default swaps) are described.
- Documentation issues are outlined.
- Treatment of credit derivatives for regulatory capital purposes is discussed.

2   Credit Derivatives and Decomposition of Financial Risk[2]

The emergence of credit derivatives must be understood against a background of a progressive re-definition of risk in financial markets. This change may ultimately prove to be as important as the advent of derivatives themselves and their use in capital markets.

The concept of financial derivatives is increasingly becoming one of the trading *attributes* of assets. A simple asset, such as a physical bond, is a

---

Negotiable Exposure; JP Morgan, New York and London; Masters, Blythe "A Credit Derivatives Primer" (May 1996) Derivatives Strategy 42–44; Iacono, Frank "Credit Derivatives" in Schwartz, Robert J. and Smith Jr., Clifford W. (Editors) (1997) Derivatives Handbook: Risk Management and Control; John Wiley & Sons, Inc., New York at Chapter 2; Ghose, Ronit (Editor) (1997) Credit Derivatives: Key Issues; British Bankers' Association, London; Chase Manhattan Bank "Credit Derivatives: A Primer" (April 1997) Asiamoney Derivatives Guide 2–5; BZW "An Investor's Guide to Credit Derivatives" (June 1997) Derivatives Strategy Credit Derivatives Supplement 1–8; Scott-Quinn, Brian and Walmsley, Julian K. (1998) The Impact Of Credit Derivatives On Securities Markets; International Securities Market Association, Zurich; Citibank/Salomon Smith Barney (2001) Credit Derivatives 2001 – Issues and Opportunities; Risk Publications, London; Finnerty, John D. (1999) Credit Derivatives: An Introduction To The Mechanics; PricewaterhouseCoopers, New York; Storrow, Jamie (Editor) (1999) Credit Derivatives: Key Issues – 2nd Edition; British Bankers' Association, London; Francis, Chris, Kakodkar, Atish and Rooney, Mary (31 January 2002) Credit Default Swap Handbook"; Merrill Lynch, London; "Credit Derivatives Update 2002" (March 2002) Euromoney Research Guide; Francis, Chris, Kakodkar, Atish and Martin, Barnaby (16 April 2003) Credit Derivative Handbook"; Merrill Lynch, London.

[2]   For a general description of financial derivatives, see Das, Satyajit (2004) Swaps/ Financial Derivatives – 3rd Edition; John Wiley & Sons, Singapore.

complex bundle of attributes. These attributes include:

- **Liquidity** – represented by the investment of funds and the ultimate return of the investment where the amount and timing of the cash flows (principal and interest) determines the return on or value of the investment.
- **Interest rates/debt prices** – where the return is represented by fluctuations in the asset price representing the present value of cash flows driven by interest rate movements or changes in the discount rate. The discount rate applicable, which combines a risk-free rate and a risk margin (to compensate for credit risk), is used in valuing the cash flows. The risk in this case also includes exposure to a series of discount rates (the zero curve) (in effect the risk of yield curve shape changes) which will interact with the movement of time (maturity and term structure risk).
- **Currency** – reflecting changes in the value of the currency in which the cash flows are paid.
- **Contingent elements** – relating to embedded option features such as embedded prepayment or other rights.
- **Default risk** – relating to the exposure to the potential failure of the issuer to perform its obligations under the contract.

Exhibit 1.1 sets out the process of risk decomposition.

Credit derivatives effectively allow the unbundling of credit risk from other transactions. This allows credit risk to be separately traded in financial markets.

Exhibit 1.1   Risk Decomposition

Assume the following bond:

Issuer	Company A
Amount	Euro 100 million
Maturity	10 Years
Coupon	6.00% pa payable annually on the basis of a 30/360 day year.
Issue Price	100
Yield To Maturity	6.00% pa (equivalent to 100 bps over the equivalent German Risk Free Rate)
Call Option	The bond is redeemable at par after 5 years.
Rating	A

The bond can be decomposed into and reconstructed from a number of distinct and separate transactions. The decomposition set out below is from the perspective of a US\$ investor. The individual steps are as follows:

- **Step 1** – invest the US\$ equivalent of Euro 100 million (US\$110 million assuming a spot exchange rate of Euro 1=US\$1.10) in a risk free 10 year asset yielding floating rate US\$ money market rates.
- **Step 2** – enter into a 10 year cross currency floating-to-floating (basis) swap where the investor receives Euro floating rates (Euro-IBOR) and pays US\$ floating rates (funded by its US\$ investment outlined in Step 1).
- **Step 3** – enter into a Euro interest rate swap where the investor receives fixed rate Euro for 10 years against payment of Euro floating rates (funded by the cross currency basis swap outlined in Step 2).

The above three steps create a Euro 10 year bond. To add the default risk aspect to the transaction, the following additional transaction is needed:

- **Step 4** – the investor enters into a default risk swap where it assumes the default risk of Company A in return for receipt of an annual fee.

The effect of this step is to create a *corporate bond* where the investor suffers a loss of coupon and/or principal (subject to recovery in bankruptcy) upon the default of the issuer. The spread over the equivalent risk free rate that derives from the fee received in exchange for entry into the default swap is designed to compensate for the credit risk assumed.

The call option can also be added by the investor entering into a final transaction:

- **Step 5** – enter into a sale of a European exercise receiver swaption where the counterparty has the right at its option to receive 6.00% pa in Euro against payment of Euro floating rate for a period of 5 years exercisable in 5 years time.

The individual steps are set out in a diagrammatic form below:

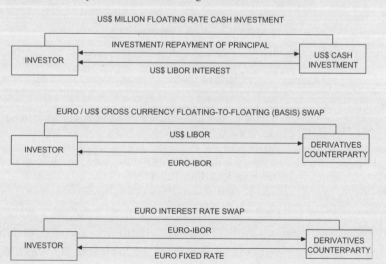

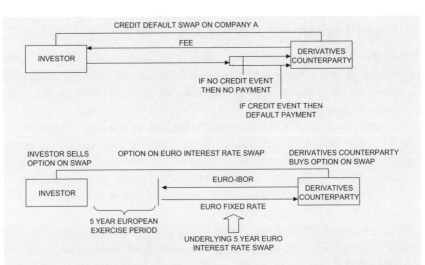

The pricing of the bond should equal the sum of the individual components. This ignores both the transaction costs and additional credit risks assumed in each of the different elements.

The decomposition illustrates the distinct risks that exist in each transaction and the capacity to unbundle the risks and to trade these separately[3]. This is set out in the Table below:

Risk	Source
Liquidity	Floating Rate Investment
Currency Risk	Cross Currency Basis Swap
Interest Rate Risk	Euro Interest Rate Swap
Call or Prepayment Risk	Euro Swaption
Credit/Default Risk	Default Swap

The analysis is designed to highlight that derivative instruments in conjunction with a cash investment, can be used to replicate physical assets. Moreover, reversing the process allows the deconstruction of physical assets into the constituent elements facilitating separate trading in individual risk aspects, including credit risk. This process can be applied to any financial asset.

---

[3] The decomposition is a simplification. For example, the swaps and swaptions need to be capable of termination in the event of default by the underlying credit in order to reflect more accurately the actual underlying transaction.

3   Credit Derivatives – Concept/Definition

Credit derivatives are defined as *a class of financial instrument, the value of which is derived from an underlying market value driven by the credit risk of private or government entities other than the counterparties to the credit derivative transaction itself.*

The last component of the definition is critical. In essence, it captures the role of credit derivatives in trading the credit risk of a particular entity (credit spread or price fluctuations arising from changes in credit quality including default) by two parties. The two parties trading the credit derivative may have no commercial or financial relationship with the entity whose credit risk is being traded.

The principal feature of these instruments is the separation and isolation of credit risk, facilitating the trading of credit risk with the purpose of:

- Replicating credit risk.
- Transferring credit risk.
- Hedging credit risk.

Credit derivatives also create new mechanisms for taking on credit risk in non-traditional formats within defined risk/reward parameters.

The principal demand for credit derivative products has been from banks/financial institutions and institutional investors. The use of credit derivatives by banks has been motivated by the desire to hedge or assume credit risk, improve portfolio diversification (synthetically) and to improve the management of credit portfolios.

Investor demand is motivated by the following factors:

- Ability to add value to portfolios through trading in credit as a separate dimension. This particularly entails assumption of specific types of credit risk *without the acquisition of the credit asset itself.*
- Opportunity to manage the credit risk of investments.
- Inability of traditional institutional investors and asset managers to participate in certain credit markets (for example, loan markets), in part as a result of the absence of the necessary origination and loan administration infrastructure.
- Ability to arbitrage the pricing of credit risk in and between separate market sectors.

In the longer term, it is probable that credit derivatives will dictate a profound change in the activity of both these groups as follows[4]:

- Banks will alter their role into that of the *originator* of credit assets that are then distributed to investors.
- Institutional investors increasingly will regard credit risk as *a separate and distinct* investible asset class that is managed within general asset allocation frameworks.

Corporate use of credit derivatives is also likely to develop as a mechanism for the management of financing risk or project risk (particularly in emerging markets), increasing the range of business counterparties and providing protection against default of major suppliers or purchasers.

Exhibit 1.2 sets out the product groupings of credit derivative instruments.

The principal credit derivative structures encompass three instruments:

- **Total return swaps** – total return swaps are adaptations of the traditional swap format to *synthetically* create bond or credit asset investments for investors and to hedge or short credit risk. The defining characteristic of these structures is that they are off balance sheet and do not necessitate entry into loan or bond purchase arrangements (in the traditional sense) and the concomitant obligation to fund.
- **Credit spread products** – credit spread products are generally forwards or options on the credit spread on credit sensitive assets (bonds, loans or other credit assets). These instruments allow the separate trading of this attribute of assets for the purpose of risk reduction, speculation or return enhancement.
- **Credit default swaps** – credit default swaps are structured as instruments which make an agreed payoff (either fixed or calculated with reference to a specific mechanism) upon the occurrence of a credit event (default of the reference credit). Credit default swaps allow the transfer and assumption of the risk of default of a nominated entity.

Total return swaps and credit spread products are regarded as replication products as they allow the synthetic creation of certain positions. The positions can be created in the physical market but the derivative format

---

[4] See discussion in Chapter 8.

offers significant advantages in terms of increased efficiency and transaction cost savings.

In practice, credit default swaps are the most important credit derivative instrument. Credit default swaps make up the bulk of trading volume in credit derivatives markets.

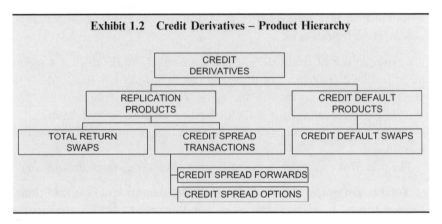

Exhibit 1.2   Credit Derivatives – Product Hierarchy

4   Total Return Swaps

4.1   Structure[5]

The central concept of a total return swap is the replication of *the total performance of a loan asset*. **Exhibit 1.3** sets out the basic structure of a total return swap.

The key elements of the structure include[6]:

- The majority of total return swap transactions are on *traded* bonds and loans (primarily, bonds) as the underlying asset.
- The investor assumes all risk and cash flow of the underlying asset. The dealer passes through all payments of the underlying asset. The investor, in return, effectively makes a payment akin to a funding cost.

---

[5]   See Smith, Bradley E. "Total Return Swaps" (1994) Capital Market Strategies 3 37–39; James, Jessica and Thomas, Phyllis "Total Return Swaps" in (1998) Credit Derivatives: Applications for Risk Management, Investment and Portfolio Optimisation; Risk Books, London at Chapter 7.

[6]   The structure of a total return swap is similar to that of an equity swap, see Das, Satyajit (2004) Swaps/Financial Derivatives – 3rd Edition; John Wiley & Sons, Singapore at Chapter 55.

- The investor bears the full risk of capital price fluctuations on the underlying asset. This requires payments by the investor to the dealer where the price of the underlying asset decreases and payments by the dealer to the investor where the price of the underlying asset increases. This adjustment is made at specified times through the life of the transaction in accordance with an agreed mechanism based on the *actual* market price of the underlying asset.

The quotation convention for total rate of return swaps is for the total return to be paid or received against the payment or receipt of the money market return *plus or minus* a margin. The margin is used to adjust the return to the purchaser of the underlying bond or loan asset.

The investor may fully fund the total return swap (in effect, eliminating all leverage) by investing cash equivalent to the notional principal of the transaction in an asset yielding a return related to money market interest rates which matches its payments to the bank. **Exhibit 1.4** sets out the structure of a fully funded total return swap transaction.

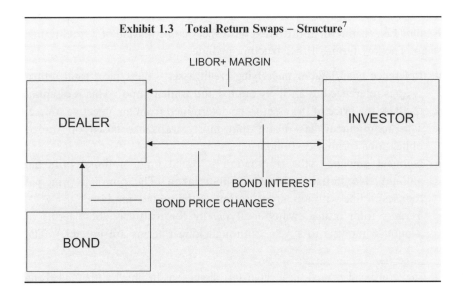

Exhibit 1.3   Total Return Swaps – Structure[7]

LIBOR+ MARGIN

DEALER   INVESTOR

BOND INTEREST

BOND PRICE CHANGES

BOND

---

[7]   The phrase investor is used to merely differentiate the parties; in reality, both parties may well be banks.

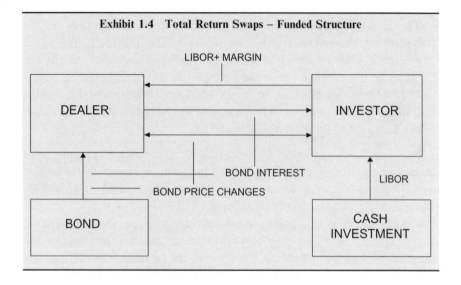

Exhibit 1.4   Total Return Swaps – Funded Structure

4.2   Key Terms/Documentation

4.2.1   Key Terms

Exhibit 1.5 sets out an abbreviated term sheet/confirmation of a total return swap. The key terms of the structure include:

- **Reference bond/loan or underlying credit asset** – the typical total return swap is referenced to a widely quoted and traded bond[8]. This is essential to allow the price of the asset to be determined from an objective source. This requirement has meant that most swaps are based on traded obligations (primarily, bonds).
- **Notional amount** – the transaction is based on a notional principal amount. No initial exchange is undertaken. The notional principal reduces in line with any amortisation of the underlying bond.
- **Term** – total return swaps are typically for relatively short terms of around 6 months to 1 year, although longer terms are possible[9]. The

---

[8]   The term bond is used throughout this discussion. In practice, the underlying asset may also be a tradeable loan as noted above.

[9]   In practice, in some transactions, the documented term may be 3 years, with the provision on each annual anniversary of the transaction for the termination of the swap at the option *of either* party. This type of structure provides the flexibility of a 1 year term renewable annually. It has the added benefit of reducing the documentation costs in such a swap where the transaction is renewed.

term of the total return swap does not need to coincide with the maturity of the underlying asset. The swap also terminates in case of a credit event on the underlying bond, as well as the default by either party to the total return swap itself[10].

- **Asset Price** – the initial price is agreed between the parties based on the current asset price as established by trading. In the case of a new bond, the initial price will be set at or close to 100% or par value. In the case of an existing bond, it will be the prevailing market price (which may be greater than or lower than the face or par value). It will generally be the offered price of the bond. This reflects the fact that the total return payer will need to purchase the bond to hedge its risk under the total return swap. The current price is required to calculate the final settlement under the transaction. This will be at maturity of the total return swap in the absence of default on the underlying bond, or prior to maturity in case of default on the bond or default by either party to the total return swap. It may also be needed to calculate the mark-to-market value of the swap for the purpose of valuation or collateral calculations. The relevant price will generally be the bid price of the bond. This reflects the fact that the total return payer will need to sell the bond held to hedge the position at maturity. The current price is determined in one of the following ways:
  1. *Dealer poll* – independent quotes, obtained from dealers in the asset over an agreed period, which are then averaged.
  2. *Market quotes* – publicly available (screen or quote services) price information on the asset.

  The problem of determination of the bond price is common to both total return swaps and credit default swaps (where cash settlement is used)[11].
- **Payments** – under the total return swap structure, the total return receiver receives the following payments:
  1. Interest payments.
  2. Any fees including commitment etc fees (where the underlying is a loan).

---

[10]   In cases where an illiquid and non-traded asset is used, the term of the asset and the total return swap must coincide. This is designed to avoid the need for price discovery in the market to settle the transaction.

[11]   This matter is discussed later in the context of credit default swaps.

The total return receiver pays:

1. LIBOR (or equivalent money market interest rate in the relevant currency) plus or minus an agreed margin.

All payments are calculated on the notional principal adjusted for any amortisation or repayments on the underlying bond. Payments are usually made quarterly on the floating rate money market side while bond payments are passed through as close as possible to actual receipt. The payments may be netted when they are on the same date.

- **Final (Cash) Settlement** – at maturity, upon default on the underlying asset or default by one of the counterparties to the total return swap, a price settlement based on the change in the value of the bond is made. The price used is that determined in accordance with the relevant price calculation mechanism agreed. In the case of appreciation in the bond price, the total return receiver receives a payment equal to the change in value of the bond. In the case of depreciation in the bond price, the total return receiver *makes* a payment equal to the change in the value of the bond. While it is usual to make the settlement at maturity or default, more frequent adjustments (effectively marking the swap to market) can be made. These more frequent adjustments may be made for the purposes of lodging collateral or notionally in order to mark the position to market for valuation purposes.

- **Physical Settlement** – the final settlement, described above, entails a cash settlement. In practice, physical settlement of the total return swap is also feasible. Physical settlement would take place at maturity, upon default on the underlying asset or default by one of the counterparties to the total return swap. It would entail the total return payer delivering the underlying bond to the total return receiver. In return, the total return payer would receive a cash payment equal to the notional amount (adjusted for any amortisation) from the total return receiver. In economic terms, the cash and physical settlement should result in very similar outcomes. In practice, difficulties in obtaining market prices for the underlying bond may create difficulties in effecting a cash settlement. For example, this may occur where the obligor of the underlying bond has defaulted and trading in the asset is illiquid. In these circumstances, physical settlement may be more practical.

The above structure assumes a total return swap indexed to a single bond. Total return swaps indexed to a basket of assets or a specified loan index are also feasible[12]. A total return swap based on a specific index would be structurally similar to a bond index swap[13]. Total return swaps linked to a loan index are gradually increasing despite some problems, including:

- Illiquidity of the index itself.
- Occasional divergence between bond trading and index values that makes the structure difficult to hedge.
- Issues regarding the transparency of the index and the index calculations.

Index structures have the advantage of creating diversified exposure that may be sought by investors seeking either to hedge or assume exposure to the credit risk of the assets in the index.

Exhibit 1.5   Total Return Swaps – Confirmation/Term Sheet

Underlying Credit Asset	[6.50%] coupon [15 November 2012] final maturity bond issued by [ABC Corporation]
Total Return Payer	[Dealer]
Total Return Receiver	[Investor]
Initial Notional Principal	US$ [20] million times the Initial Price
Current Notional Principal	Initial Notional Principal adjusted pro rata for any principal reductions in the Underlying Credit Asset since the Commencement Date
Commencement Date	3 business days after entry into transaction
Maturity Date	The earlier of:
	1. One (1) year from Commencement Date.
	2. The next succeeding payment date following repayment of the full principal and interest due on the Underlying Credit Asset.
	3. Occurrence of a credit event on the Underlying Credit Asset.
	4. Default or termination event caused by Total Return Payer and Total Return Receiver
Initial Price	[94.00] %

---

[12]   Indexes used include various bond indexes published by other investment banks/ dealers on investment grade, non-investment grade and emerging market bonds. It also increasingly used credit indexes; See Chapter 2.

[13]   See Das, Satyajit (2004) Swaps/Financial Derivatives – 3rd Edition; John Wiley & Sons, Singapore at Chapter 53.

Current Price	The [bid or offer] price of the Underlying Credit Asset expressed as a percentage as calculated by the Calculation Agent in accordance with the Calculation Method at 11.00 AM (New York time) [3] business days prior to the Final Settlement
Total Return Payment	All coupons on the Underlying Credit Asset received by the Total Return Payer
Total Return Payment Date	Two (2) business days after Total Return Payments are received
Floating Rate Payment	3 Month LIBOR plus Floating Rate Margin calculated on the Current Notional Principal. LIBOR is as quoted by the BBA, 2 business days prior to the commencement of each floating rate interest period.
Floating Rate Margin	[0.50] % pa
Floating Rate Payment Date	Quarterly in arrears commencing 3 months after the Commencement Date.
Total Return Payments	The Total Return Payer pays to the Total Return Receiver the Total Return Payment on the Total Return Payment Date
Floating Rate Payments	The Total Return Receiver pays the Floating Rate Payment to the Total Return Payer on the Floating Rate Payment Date
Final Settlement	On Maturity Date, the Total Return Receiver will, at the election of the Total Return Receiver, receive from the Total Return Payer, either:

1. Cash Settlement Amount calculated as:
    (Current Price – Initial Price)/Initial Price times the Current Notional Principal Amount.

    In the event the Cash Settlement Amount is positive then the Total Return Payer will make the payment to the Total Return Receiver. In the event the Cash Settlement Amount is negative then the Total Return Receiver will make the payment to the Total Return Payer.
2. Physical Delivery of the Underlying Credit Asset (including any existing cash or successor debt) in exchange for payment to the Total Return Payer of the Current Notional Principal times the Initial Price.

[Select one of the above Settlement Methods at the time of entry into the transaction.]

Credit Event[14]	[Bankruptcy or insolvency event], [failure to pay or payment default above a nominated minimum amount] or [restructuring event as defined] affecting the Underlying Credit Asset or [ABC Corporation]
Collateral (optional)	10% of the Initial Notional Principal in cash or US government securities. The transaction is to be marked to market and the collateral requirement may be adjusted on a [daily/weekly/monthly] basis.
Calculation Agent	[Dealer]
Calculation Method	1. By dealer poll under which the Calculation Agent will poll at least 4 and no more than 6 dealers in the Underlying Credit Asset on agreed dates and utilise the quoted prices to determine an average price for the Underlying Credit Asset; or 2. By reference to a screen or quote service. [Select one of the above Calculation Methods at the time of entry into the transaction.]

4.2.2 Documentation

The documentation of total return swaps is usually undertaken as a confirmation under an ISDA Master Agreement[15]. However, unlike credit default swaps, there is no standard confirmation. This means that there is no standard market language or documentary format for total return transactions. The total return swap is usually based on a confirmation based on the principal terms of the swap. Total return language is included in the ISDA Equity Derivatives Definitions (the Equity Definitions). This may be used for total return swaps. The total return swap confirmation will also generally use the Credit Derivatives Definitions for credit default swaps where appropriate (for example, in defining credit events or the settlement mechanism).

4.3 Transaction Rationale

The explicit rationale of the total return swap is to facilitate the purchase of or investment in (or sale or divestment of) credit assets (bonds) in a

---

[14] Credit events used are similar to those in credit default swaps; see discussion later in Chapter.

[15] For a discussion of ISDA Master Agreements see Das, Satyajit (2004) Swaps/ Financial Derivatives – 3rd Edition; John Wiley & Sons, Singapore at Chapter 30.

synthetic format. The receiver of the total return under the total return swap structure has full exposure to the underlying credit asset. The payer of the total return under the total return swap structure effectively *short sells* or hedges its exposure to the underlying asset. It is important to note that the total return swap transfers the *full* risk of the underlying asset covering:

- **Credit spread risk** (effectively credit improvement or deterioration short of default) – this is achieved by the final payment mechanism. There is a payment between the counterparties to the transaction, reflecting the price change in the underlying bond. As this price change reflects market changes in credit spread, this risk is effectively assumed and transferred under the structure.
- **Default risk** – this is also achieved through the final payment mechanism. In the event of default, the total return swap will terminate and the final payment will reflect the impact of default through the fall in price of the underlying bond (effectively the expected recovery level on the asset). The final payment mechanism indemnifies the payer under the total return swap against any loss as a result of default. This is the difference between the price at the commencement of the transaction and the price following default. The receiver in the total return swap will, correspondingly, bear the loss upon default through the payment to be made.

The total return swap structure is similar to and achieves the same *economic* outcome as a number of transactions involving the physical asset, including:

- Sale or purchase of the asset.
- A sub-participation transaction[16].
- A repurchase (repo) arrangement

---

[16]   An unfunded sub-participation agreement is used between banks to transfer loan risk on an indemnity basis. A participation agreement is one way in which the parties may arrange for physical settlement of a credit default swap with a Loan as the underlying risk. The protection seller receives payments equal to interest on the loan (adjusted to reflect funding costs) and in return for giving an indemnity if the borrower defaults. If the participation agreement is funded, then the protection seller pays a cash amount equal to the face value of the loan being acquired. The protection seller receives amounts equal to all payments of interest in full and repayment of the cash at maturity to the extent the borrower repays. The difference between a credit derivative and a participation agreement mainly reflects differences in documentation. For example, a participation agreement is generally treated as a banking book product for capital adequacy purposes. In contrast, a credit derivative may be treated as a trading book product.

The advantages of the total return swap include:

- The off-balance-sheet nature of the structure.
- The capacity to short sell the bond to hedge or position credit assets.
- Potential cost of funding advantages.
- The ability to leverage the exposure by using a fraction of asset value as collateral to take advantage of the credit view (because of the off-balance-sheet nature of the structure).
- The separation of the transaction from the underlying security or loan transaction. This effectively allows the de facto transfer of the credit risk to occur without the consent of the issuer or borrower. This also allows the transfer of the economic rights relating to the obligation to be undertaken in complete confidentiality.
- The ability to separate the maturity of the exposure from that of the underlying credit asset.
- Potential tax advantages from separation of the legal and economic ownership of the asset[17].

The off-balance-sheet nature of the transaction and potential funding cost advantages provide significant benefits for banks and investors with lower credit ratings and higher funding costs in certain markets. The structure is attractive to institutional investors seeking to participate in some credit markets (such as loan markets). These investors may lack the essential infrastructure to undertake such transactions or suffer from significant barriers to trading credit assets. Hedge funds are also large users of total return swaps. Total return swaps are used to obtain access to credit assets and create leveraged exposures to credit risk.

The structure of total return swaps also creates certain issues. There is no direct relationship or contractual nexus between the borrower in the underlying transaction and the investor assuming the economic risk exposure to the bond or loan. This means that there may be problems of confidentiality or representation in the case of default, distress short of default requiring restructuring of liabilities, or dispute resolution. This will be a problem specifically where the credit asset is a loan.

Confidentiality issues may arise in respect of confidential financial and other information that is not public. In loan transactions, confidential information may be provided by the borrower to the *lender on record.*

---

[17] See Das, Satyajit (2004) Swaps/Financial Derivatives – 3rd Edition; John Wiley & Sons, Singapore at Chapter 73.

The total return receiver may not be able to access this information without breach of the confidentiality provisions. In the event of default or other matters requiring creditors to meet to agree to a restructuring of the obligation or amendment to the terms of the original bond or borrowing, the investor (via the total return swap) may not be entitled to be directly represented at any such meeting or be able to participate in moves to protect its economic interests. It may be forced to rely on the lender of record to act *on its behalf*, presumably based on its advised intentions and views in relation to the matter[18]. The problems are most relevant to loans. In practice, almost all total return swaps are undertaken on bonds, avoiding some of these problems.

5   Credit Spread Products

5.1   Credit Spreads

The credit spread represents the margin relative to the risk free rate designed to compensate the investor for the risk of default on the underlying security. The credit spread itself is calculated as:

$$\text{Credit spread} = \text{yield of bond or loan minus yield} \\ \text{of a corresponding risk free security}$$

In theoretical terms, the credit spread is the difference between the yield on a risky security and the yield on a *government* security. This reflects the total compensation for credit risk. In practice, it is common to trade the "spread to the swap rate" (generally referred to as the asset swap spread)[19]. The asset swap spread is the credit spread to US$ LIBOR. This is the case despite the fact that LIBOR itself is not strictly a *risk free rate*. **Exhibit 1.6** sets out the structure of credit spreads.

The asset swap spread is frequently used in markets outside the US. This reflects the following factors:

- **Market practice** – the US market is focused on spread to Treasuries as a measure of relative value. In contrast, in many other markets (Europe and Asia) the asset swap spread is used as the primary measure of relative value.

---

[18]   See Whiteley, Christopher "Credit Derivatives: Documentation And Legal Issues" in Das, Satyajit (Editor) (2001) Credit Derivatives & Credit Linked Notes – Second Edition; John Wiley & Sons, Singapore at Chapter 17.

[19]   See Chapter 5. See also Das, Satyajit (2004) Swaps/Financial Derivatives – 3rd Edition; John Wiley & Sons, Singapore at Chapter 38.

- **Availability of benchmark** – the relevant benchmark must be available. In the Euro market, there is difficulty in establishing a single benchmark because of the numerous government bond markets (Germany, France etc). This means that a spread to a government (or risk free) benchmark is more difficult to establish. This makes the asset swap spread more attractive.
- **Liquidity** – the liquidity of and ability to trade in the benchmark is crucial. In markets where the underlying government bond market is illiquid or difficult to trade, the asset swap spread is used.

In practice, credit spread products can be based on both the spread to a government benchmark and asset swap spread[20].

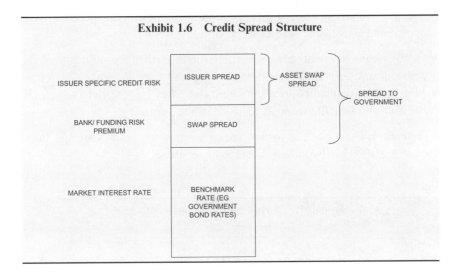

Exhibit 1.6 Credit Spread Structure

5.2 Credit Spread Products

The two general formats of credit spread derivatives are:

- Credit spreads relative to the benchmark (the absolute spread).
- Credit spreads between *two* credit sensitive assets (the relative spread)[21].

---

[20] In this Chapter, the two are treated as being interchangeable.

[21] The relative spread transaction, in reality, is the absolute spread case where the counterparty enters into two credit spread swaps where the benchmark/swap rate component is offset and eliminated.

Linear (forward) and non-linear (option) formats of investments are available.

Exhibit 1.7 sets out the structure of a credit spread swap. In the transaction depicted, the counterparty gains if the spread between the nominated security and either a risk free security or other risky security decreases. If the spread increases, then the counterparty suffers a loss of value. The dealer has opposite exposures.

Structurally, the credit spread swap is a forward on the credit spread. In reality, it does not need to be structured as a swap or exchange of cash flows. It can be structured as a simple forward akin to a Forward Rate Agreement ("FRA") where, at maturity of the contract, there is a net cash settlement based on the difference between the agreed spread and the actual spread.

Options on credit spreads create a non-linear payoff on the underlying credit spread movement. The types of options are:

- **Call options on credit spreads** – where the buyer has the right to buy the spread and benefits from a decreasing spread.
- **Put options on credit spreads** – where the buyer has the right to sell the spread and benefits from an increase in the spread.

Exhibit 1.8 sets out the format for premiums for options on the bond credit spreads for a hypothetical range of securities.

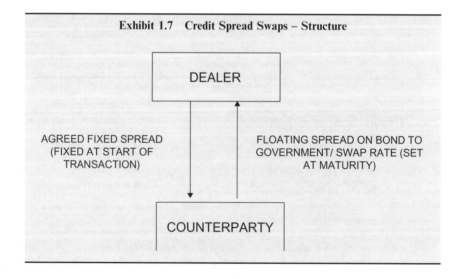

Exhibit 1.7   Credit Spread Swaps – Structure

Exhibit 1.8 One Month Credit Spread Options – Indicative Pricing

Type of Option	European call options on the spreads at the strike spread	European call options on the spreads at the strike spread	European call options on the spreads at the strike spread
Issuer	A Corporation	B Corporation	C Corporation
Rating	Baa3/BBB–	A2/A	Baa2/BBB
Underlying Bond Issue	8.000% 15 July 2031	6.875% 15 January 2006	8.625% 15 April 2012
Reference Treasury	6.25% August 2031	6.25% February 2006	6.25% August 2012
Spot Spread (bps)	180	80	160
Strike Spread (bps)	150	70	140
Premium (bps)	28	6	10

Type of Option	European put options on the spreads at the strike spread	European put options on the spreads at the strike spread	European put options on the spreads at the strike spread
Issuer	A Corporation	B Corporation	C Corporation
Rating	Baa3/BBB–	A2/A	Baa2/BBB
Underlying Bond Issue	8.000% 15 July 2031	6.875% 15 January 2006	8.625% 15 April 2012
Reference Treasury	6.25% August 2031	6.25% February 2006	6.25% August 2012
Spot Spread (bps)	180	80	160
Strike Spread (bps)	220	95	180
Premium (bps)	35	15	40

5.3 Spread Duration

Credit spread products entail the use of the concept of spread duration. Spread duration can be defined as the sensitivity of the capital value of a bond to a movement in the credit spread. It represents the effective change in the capital price of the bond, reflecting the impact of a change in the spread on the discount rate used to calculate the present value of the security. It therefore captures the impact of the spread changes *over the full life of the security* in the present value price of the cash flows. Spread duration is used to scale movements in the credit spread to calculate the settlement amounts under credit spread products.

Spread duration is typically calculated by measuring the change in the value of the underlying bond price for a change in credit spread of, say, 1 bp at current yield levels. **Exhibit 1.9** sets out an example of the calculation of spread duration.

Exhibit 1.9   Spread Duration

Assume the following bond:

Issuer	Company A
Term	10 years
Coupon	7.25% pa payable semi-annually
Yield	7.55% pa (semi-annual)
Spread (to Treasury)	64 bps over reference Treasury bond which is yielding 6.91% pa.

The spread duration of the security is 6.8. This signifies that for 0.01% pa (1 bp pa) change in yield at current yield levels, the value of the underlying bond will change by 0.068% (6.8 bps).

The sensitivity of the spread duration (expressed as bps change in price) to changes in yield and spread levels is summarised in the table below:

Yield Level (% pa Treasury yield) Spread to Treasury (bps pa)	5.91	6.91	7.91
34	7.7	7.0	6.4
64	7.5	6.8	6.3
94	7.3	6.7	6.1

Spread duration is also maturity sensitive as set out in the table below:

Maturity (years)	1	3	5	7	10	20	30
Coupon (% pa semi-annual)	8.00	8.00	8.00	8.00	8.00	8.00	8.00
Yield Level (% pa Treasury yield)	8.00	8.00	8.00	8.00	8.00	8.00	8.00
Spread to Treasury (bps pa)	50	50	50	50	50	50	50
Spread Duration (bps in price)	0.9	2.6	4.0	5.1	6.5	9.2	10.3

It should be noted that spread duration exhibits convexity; that is, the spread duration alters at different yield levels and with changes in the level of credit spread. It is feasible to adjust for the convexity of the credit spread[22].

5.4 Applications

The central concept of credit spread derivatives is the isolation and capture of value from:

- Relative credit value changes independent of changes in interest rates.
- Trading forward credit spread expectations.
- Trading the volatility of credit spreads.

The central concept underlying credit spread products is the ability to use credit spread derivatives to trade, hedge or monetise expectations on *future credit spreads*.

The key dimension related to trading and hedging credit spreads is the term structure and volatility of credit spreads[23]. The forward credit spread is calculated as follows:

- Identify the yield of the bond and the benchmark.
- Forward rates of both securities are calculated.
- The forward credit spread is taken as the forward bond yield minus the forward benchmark rate.

From a theoretical perspective, the credit spread should increase in line with increasing default risk and maturity. In practice, the mathematics of

---

[22] See Chapter 5.
[23] For discussion of credit spreads and the mathematics of credit spreads, see Chapter 5.

the calculation indicates that in the case of a positively sloped yield curve, the forward credit spreads increase. This merely reflects the inherent mathematics of the calculation of forward prices and yields. The slope of the forward rates on the security increases at a faster rate than the forwards on the risk free rate, reflecting the increasing credit spread.

Implied forward credit spreads exhibit the following characteristics in practice:

- Implied forward spreads do not appear to accurately reflect investor expectations.
- Forward credit spreads appear to be poor indicators of future spot spreads.

The forward credit spreads also appear to be more volatile than the underlying securities. This higher spread volatility reflects the following:

- Lower absolute level of spread.
- Imperfect correlation between the security and the risk free rate[24].

The factors allow the use of credit spread forwards or options for the following purposes:

- Trading credit spreads as an isolated variable.
- Trading the credit spread without assuming the interest rate risk.
- Structuring specific risk reward profiles on credit spreads.

In contrast to total return swaps which transfer both the spread risk and the default risk, credit spread forwards and options only transfer the risk of changes in the credit spread. In reality, the transfer of spread risk may provide default protection, as the spread would be expected to increase following default.

The use of credit spread products rather than physical transactions to replicate the positions is favoured by the fact that the transactions are off balance sheet and generally have lower transactional costs.

Exhibit 1.10 and **Exhibit 1.11** set out an example of using credit spread derivatives. **Exhibit 1.12** sets out an example of a credit spread derivative transaction involving emerging market securities.

---

[24] The volatility of credit spreads and their behaviour is discussed in the context of valuation of credit spread transactions in Chapter 5.

Exhibit 1.10   Credit Spread Forwards – Example 1

Assume the credit spreads on bonds issued by ABC Company increase. An investor seeks exposure to the forward credit spread. The following transaction is structured:

Notional Amount	(up to) US$10 million
Termination Date	1 year
Payoff of Spread Rate at Termination Date	4.9 × (Forward Spread – Final Spread) × Notional Principal
Forward Spread	150 bps
Final Spread	Reference Yield at Termination Date minus Reference Treasury Yield at Termination Date
Issuer	ABC Corporation
Reference Yield	Yield to maturity of Issuer's 7.75% of 15 February 2010
Reference Treasury Yield[25]	Yield to maturity of US Treasury 6.00% of 15 May 2010

The investor entering into the transaction effectively receives the fixed spread and pays the floating credit spread on the credit spread swap. The result of the transaction is that the investor receives a fixed percentage of the notional amount for every basis point (the spread duration) that the spread on the Issuer's bonds decreases relative to the forward spread of 150 bps. If the spread increases, then the investor pays a fixed amount per basis point of the widening spread.

The transaction effectively segregates the spread duration of the underlying corporate bond from its interest rate risk. This type of transaction would be undertaken in an environment where spreads for these bonds had increased and were expected to decline over the 1 year time horizon of the transaction.

The return analysis for the investor in this type of transaction is set out below:

Final Spread (bps)	75	100	125	150	175	200	225
Payoff On Spread Agreement (% of notional amount)	3.675	2.45	1.225	0	−1.225	−2.45	−3.675

The investor benefits under the structure as long as the spread on the bond tightens from the forward spread level of 150 bps. The investor would suffer losses where the spread widens.

In a variation, the structures are combined with an option that effectively guarantees the investor a minimum spread on the investment. This is achieved through embedding an option on the spread in the structure, which limits the downside from a continued increase in the credit spread.

---

[25]   In the case of a credit spread transaction on an asset swap spread, the reference benchmark rate is described as the interpolated swap rate to the final maturity of the Issuer's bond at termination of the credit spread forward.

Exhibit 1.11   Credit Spread Options – Example 1

Assume an investor perceives that the credit spread on bonds issued by ABC Company is likely to narrow over a 1 year period. The investor can monetise its expectations by selling the following put option on the credit spread:

Notional Amount	(up to) US$25 million
Expiry Date	1 year
Option Premium	0.75% flat
Current Offer Spread (bps)	85
Strike Spread (bps)	100
Reference Bond	ABC Company's 7.75% 10 year bonds
Reference Treasury	Current US Treasury benchmark 10 year (as agreed by the parties)
Reference Spread	Yield of Reference Bonds minus yield of Reference Treasury
Option Payoff	The purchaser of the option has the right to put the Reference Bonds to the seller of the option at the Strike Spread over the yield on the Reference Treasury at the Expiry Date.

Under the terms of the transaction, the investor is selling an out-of-the-money spread option where the purchaser can sell the reference bonds of the issuer to the investor at a spread of 100 bps over the relevant Treasury benchmark[26]. The investor receives 75 bps in premium for the sale of this option.

Based on the spread duration of the ABC Company bonds at maturity of the option (that is, the price of the bond changes 6.81% for each 100 bps change in the spread), the investor's breakeven level is around 11 bps. This is calculated as the premium divided by the spread duration. This breakeven point is some 26 bps above the spot spread. This means that the spread on the bonds would have to increase in excess of 27 bps above current levels (around a 32% increase *in the spread*) before the investor suffered a loss.

The investors would be seeking to monetise their neutral to positive view on the credit spread outlook through this trade. The sale of the put option may be superior to an outright position in the bonds for the following reasons:

- Absence of direct interest rate risk.
- Capture of return from the high volatility of the spread relative to the volatility on the underlying bonds.

---

[26] It is not strictly correct to view this option as being out-of-the-money. The in or out-of-the-money nature of the option is determined by looking at the implied *forward* credit spread (*not* the current spot spread).

- Ability through the strike level to adjust the spread level at which the bonds are acquired if the put option is exercised.

In this case, the purchaser obtains protection against an increase in the spread on the bonds above the strike level.

Exhibit 1.12   Credit Spread Forwards – Example 2

In the aftermath of the emerging market sell-off in early 1995, the mis-pricing in relative value terms of various emerging market securities created interesting trading opportunities. For example, the following transaction involving a credit spread forward was designed to take advantage of the relative pricing of two types of Brady Bonds of an emerging market issuer. As of early 1995, the following bonds were trading as follows:

Security	Stripped Yield (% pa)	Stripped Spread (bps pa)	Stripped Duration (years)
Bond 1 (around 26 years final maturity)	15.84	943	3.5
Bond 2 (around 9 years final maturity)	14.42	870	4.1

The prevailing spread of 142 bps between the two securities is at the upper end of the range over the past 12 to 24 months. Given the similar stripped duration between the two securities, an investor believes that the two bonds should trade closer together. The investor can monetise this expectation with the following transaction:

Notional Amount	US$10 million
Expiry	6 months
Payment	Notional Amount × (Current Spread – Final Spread) × Average Of Stripped Spread Duration of the two bonds
Payment Flows	If the payment is positive, then the dealer pays the investor. If the payment is negative, then the investor pays the dealer.
Final Spread	Bond 1 Stripped Yield at Expiry minus Bond 2 Stripped Yield at Expiry.
Bond 1	[Issuer; type of bond; coupon; final maturity]
Bond 2	[Issuer; type of bond; coupon; final maturity]
Bond 1 Stripped Yield Calculation	For Bond 1, the stripped yield is the semi-annual yield to maturity of cash flows resulting from a long position in the Bond and a short position in the US Treasury zero coupon bond corresponding to its final maturity.

Bond 2 Stripped Yield Calculation	For Bond 2, the yield to maturity is calculated by using a coupon bond with amortisation similar to the bond and a price which is the sum of the offer price on the bonds and the unwind value of an interest rate swap to pay LIBOR plus an agreed margin and receive the coupon.

The spread indexed swap outlined allows the investor to profit (lose) from a narrowing (widening) of the spread between the two securities.

5.5   Documentation

There is no standard ISDA confirmation for credit spread transactions. In practice, dealers use customised documentation for transactions. The documentation of a credit spread derivative is relatively straightforward. Major issues that need to be addressed include:

- **Price discovery** – the mechanism for establishing the credit spread to allow settlement of the transaction needs to be agreed.
- **Market events** – the document will need to cover adjustments or extraordinary events that may make the relevant credit spread impossible to establish.

6   Credit Default Swaps[27]

6.1   Concept

Credit default swaps are designed to isolate the risk of default on credit obligations. These instruments are referred to as credit default swaps or credit default options. **Exhibit 1.13** sets out the structure of a credit default swap. The transaction would operate as follows:

- The bank seeking protection pays a fee to the bank providing protection on an identified reference entity.

---

[27]   See Francis, Chris, Kakodkar, Atish and Rooney, Mary (31 January 2002) "Credit Default Swap Handbook"; Merrill Lynch, London; Francis, Chris, Kakodkar, Atish and Martin, Barnaby (16 April 2003) "Credit Derivative Handbook"; Merrill Lynch, London.

- If there is a credit event in respect of the reference entity, then the bank providing protection would make an agreed payment to the bank seeking protection to cover any loss suffered because of credit exposure to the reference entity[28].
- If there is no credit event, then there are no payments by the bank selling protection.

In effect, the bank seeking protection has acquired protection from the risk of default of the reference entity in return for the payment of a periodic fee to the bank providing protection. The credit default swap is analogous to the following transactions:

- Guarantees or letters of credit covering the performance of the reference entity.
- Credit insurance covering the performance of the reference entity.

The essential elements of a credit default swap are:

- A series of payments in return for an indemnity against non performance of the reference entity.
- The concept of a credit event (in effect, default) that triggers the payment to cover loss arising from default.
- The default payment itself usually takes one of the following forms:
  1. *Cash settlement* – this entails the seller of protection paying the buyer of protection an amount based on the change in price of a reference asset. The change in price is the difference in the price of the reference asset at the time of entry into the credit default swap and the price of the asset immediately following the credit event.
  2. *Physical settlement or delivery* – this entails the buyer of protection delivering to the seller of protection an agreed asset (generally a bond or loan issued by the reference entity) following a credit event. The seller of protection purchases the (defaulted) security at a pre-agreed value (the face value of the credit default swap).
  3. *Fixed payment* – this entails the seller of protection paying the buyer of protection a pre-agreed fixed amount in the event of default. The amount paid reflects an agreed estimate of loss given

---

[28] This assumes that the buyer of protection is seeking to hedge an existing credit exposure. It is also possible that the bank may buy protection under a credit default swap to short the credit.

default. This structure is also referred to as a binary or digital credit default swap[29].

4. *Actual workout/recovery value* – this entails the seller of protection paying the buyer of protection the full face value amount of the credit default swap where a credit event occurs. The buyer of protection is required to collect and pay through to the seller of protection all actual amounts recovered from the reference entity following the credit event.

   In practice, credit default swaps are settled using physical delivery or (less commonly) cash settlement.

Exhibit 1.14 sets out an example of using a credit default swap. **Exhibit 1.15** sets out quotes for credit default swaps for a range of reference credits.

There are some variations on the standard structure. As noted above, in a conventional credit default swap, the fee for purchasing protection is paid periodically (typically, quarterly or semi-annually) over the term of the transaction. Where the underlying reference entity is of low credit quality (for example, distressed credits), dealers frequently quote on a "points up front" basis. Under this structure, the dealers quote the fee in two components:

- An up-front amount that is paid by the buyer of protection at the time of entry into the credit default swap transaction.
- A periodic fee payable quarterly or semi-annually (this component is the same as in a conventional credit default swap).

The two components together are equivalent to the fee on a conventional credit default swap.

---

[29] For a discussion of the valuation issues presented by binary credit default swaps, see Berd, Arthur and Kapoor, Vivek "Digital Premium" (Spring 2003) Journal of Derivatives 66–76. Binary credit default swaps have become popular as recovery rates for cash settled credit default swaps and synthetic collateralised debt obligations are highly variable. This is especially so relative to corporate bond recoveries (see Chapter 6). The fixed recovery rate implied by a binary credit default swap reduces this variability and risk. This is attractive to both buyers and sellers of protection because of lower cost and more accurate risk provisioning. Binary credit default swaps pose an interesting moral hazard problem. This relates to the fact that binary credit default swaps have identical payouts for all credit events. This means there is a natural incentive for the buyer of protection to trigger a credit event. See "Moody's Warns Investors On Digital CDS 'Moral Hazard'" (August 2004) Risk 8.

The major reason for this structure is to equate the credit default swap to a distressed bond. The distressed bond would trade at a significant discount to face value. The seller of protection under the "points up front" structure receives the discount on the distressed bond upfront via the upfront payment[30].

It is important to note the difference between credit default swaps and total return swaps or credit spread transactions. Credit default swaps transfer price risk on the underlying bond or loan *in the event of a credit event*. The credit default swap does not transfer any price risk arising from *changes in credit quality falling short of default*. This is because there is no settlement between the parties unless there is a credit event. In contrast, both total return swaps and credit spread forwards transfer the risk of price changes as the result of changes in credit quality falling short of default. This reflects the fact that changes in credit spread result in changes in the price of the bond or loan. Total return swap and credit spread transaction settlements are based on changes in the market price or spread.

Despite this fundamental difference, participants in the credit default swap market frequently treat credit default swaps as *credit spread* instruments (analogous to credit spread derivatives). This reflects the fact that the pricing of the credit default swap is related to credit spreads on the reference entity[31]. This means that where there are changes in the credit spread applicable to the underlying reference entity, there will generally be a similar (although not exactly identical) change in the fee on a corresponding credit default swap. This will generally be true where the credit default swap has *significant remaining time to maturity*. As the remaining time to maturity of the credit default swap becomes shorter, the value (that is, mark-to-market) of the credit default swap declines towards zero. This reflects the fact that the credit default swap starts to trade as a binary instrument; that is, the value is driven by the risk that the underlying reference entity will experience a credit event/default rather than changes in *relative* credit valuation. The use of credit default swaps to trade credit spread expectations is most relevant to traders in credit default swaps that are likely to close out their position prior to maturity[32].

---

[30] For a more detailed discussion of this structure, see Chapter 2.
[31] See Chapter 5.
[32] For discussion of trading in credit default swaps, see Chapter 5. For discussion of trading in credit default swaps to hedge credit spread risk, see Chapter 7.

6.2   Applications

The principal application of credit default structures is the transfer of credit risk. It is used primarily by banks/dealers to manage credit risk acquired in the course of financing and trading. Investment applications include the ability to both transfer or more commonly *assume* credit risk synthetically to enhance portfolio return.

Principal applications include:

- Management of concentration risk within credit portfolios, particularly increasing the diversification of portfolios.
- Adjustment of term requirements of credit by aligning supply of credit assets with internal constraints on the maximum term.
- Synthesis of credit risks with highly structured return profiles or to create credit investments that are not directly available.
- Creation of and investment in non-funded and off-balance-sheet credit exposures.
- Pre-determination of and trading in types of credit risks (credit risk layers, default correlation and recovery rates) that are not generally directly available in capital markets.
- Management of return on credit risk, including optimising returns unaffected by funding constraints or balance sheet restrictions.

Exhibit 1.13   Credit Default Swaps – Structure

1.   Credit Default Swap

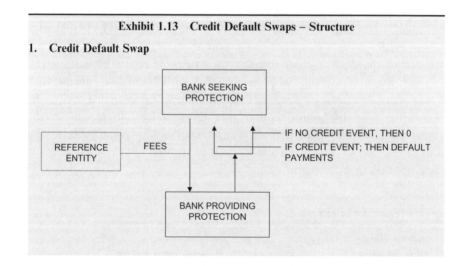

2. Credit Default Swap As Hedge

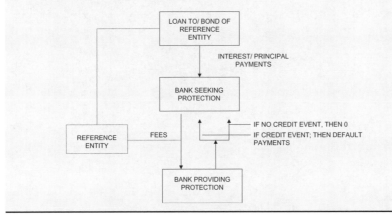

Exhibit 1.14   Credit Default Swaps

Assume an investor has a position in long maturity bonds issued by a company (ABC Company). The credit spread on the bond has widened. 3 year spreads are currently quoted at 115 bps over the swap rate and 10 year spreads at 200 bps over the swap rate. The investor is concerned with short term default risk. The investor hedges the credit risk to ABC Company with the following credit default swap:

Buyer of Protection	Investor
Seller of Protection	Dealer
Maturity	3 years
Reference Entity	ABC Company
Reference Bond	Reference Entity's 10 year 8.50% coupon bond
Credit Event	[Bankruptcy or insolvency event], [failure to pay or payment default above a nominated minimum amount] or [restructuring event as defined]
Default Payment	Notional Amount × [100% − Fair Market value of Reference Bond after Credit Event]
Default Swap Premium	1.25% pa payable by Buyer of Protection to Seller of Protection
Payment of Default Payment	The Default Payment is payable by the Seller of Protection to the Buyer of Protection upon the occurrence of a Credit Event.

The transaction allows the investor to hedge its exposure to default by the Reference Entity for the first three years.

Exhibit 1.15   Credit Default Swaps – Quotations[33]

1. US Credit Default Swap Quotes

Sector	Issuer	Ticker	Deutsche Bank All Liquid US Levels Credit Default Swaps				Moodys	S&P	SharePx Pctg Chg	Earnings Rel	Date/Time (GMT)	
			Maturity	Bid	Ask	Dly Chng						
Aerospace and Defence	BOEING CAPITAL CORP	BA	5Y	43	43	0	A2	A	N/A	N/A	25-May-04	6:20
	GOODRICH CORPORATION	GR	5Y	71	76	0	Baa3	BBB–	–0.8	29/04/2004	02-Jul-04	16:06
	LOCKHEED MARTIN CORP	LMT	5Y	41	46	0	Baa2	BBB	0.8	27/04/2004	02-Jul-04	16:06
	RAYTHEON COMPANY	RTN	5Y	59	64	0	Baa3	BBB–	0.5	21/04/2004	02-Jul-04	16:06
	TEXTRON FINANCIAL CORP	TXT	5Y	36	41	0	A3	A–	–0.7	22/04/2004	02-Jul-04	16:06
Autos	BORGWARNER	BWA	5Y	30	36	0	Baa2	BBB+	1	22/04/2004	07-Apr-04	17:27
	COOPER	COOPER	5Y	51	57	0	Baa2	BBB *_	–1.2	22/04/2004	07-Apr-04	17:27
	DELPHI CORPORATION	DPH	5Y	115	120	0	Baa2	BBB–	1.3	16/04/2004	02-Jul-04	16:06
	FORD MOTOR CREDIT CO	F	5Y	181	185	7.5	A3	BBB–	–0.8	21/04/2004	02-Jul-04	16:06
	GENERAL MOTORS ACCEPTANCE	GM	5Y	177	181	5	A3	BBB	–0.2	20/04/2004	02-Jul-04	16:06
	TRW	TRW	5Y	30	40	0	Baa3	BBB	0.4	N/A	07-Apr-04	17:27
	VISTEON CORPORATION	VC	5Y	230	240	7.5	Ba1	BB+	0.6	22/04/2004	02-Jul-04	16:06
Banks	AMERICAN EXPRESS COMPANY	AXP	5Y	29	33	1	A1	A+	–0.5	23/04/2004	02-Jul-04	16:06
	BANK OF AMERICA	BAC	5Y	23	26	0	Aa2	A+	0.9	14/04/2004	07-Apr-04	17:27
	BEAR STEARNS	BSC	5Y	44	44	0	n/a	n/a	N/A	N/A	25-May-04	6:21

[33] The author would like to thank Deutsche Bank for their consent to include the price quotes. The author would also like to thank Andrew Baume and Jill Edwards for their help in arranging the inclusion of the credit default swap quotations. All quotations are as of July 2004.

Sector	Issuer	Ticker	Maturity	Bid	Ask	Dly Chng	Moodys	S&P	SharePx Pctg Chg	Earnings Rel	Date/Time (GMT)
	COUNTRYWIDE HOME LOANS	CFC	5Y	52	56	0	A3	A	1.2	21/04/2004	02-Jul-04 16:06
	CIT GROUP INC	CIT	5Y	53	58	1	A2	A	-0.1	22/04/2004	02-Jul-04 16:06
	CAPITAL ONE BANK	COF	5Y	64	69	1	Baa2	BBB-	0.8	21/04/2004	02-Jul-04 16:06
	CITIGROUP	C	5Y	23	26	0	Aa1	AA-	-0.1	15/04/2004	07-Apr-04 17:27
	FLEET BOSTON FINANCIAL	FBF	5Y	23	26	0	Aa2	A+	N/A	14/04/2004	07-Apr-04 17:27
	FEDERAL HOME LOAN MORTGAGE	FHLMC	5Y	26	27.5	0.25	Aaa	n/a	0.1	N/A	02-Jul-04 16:06
	FEDERAL NATIONAL MORTGAGE	FNMA	5Y	25	26.5	-0.75	Aaa	AAA	-0.2	14/04/2004	02-Jul-04 16:06
	GENERAL ELECTRIC CAPITAL	GE	5Y	34	34	0	Aaa	AAA	N/A	N/A	25-May-04 6:25
	GOLDMAN	GS	5Y	40	40	0	Aa3	A+	N/A	N/A	25-May-04 6:24
	HOUSEHOLD FINANCE	HI	5Y	31	31	0	A1	A	N/A	N/A	25-May-04 6:17
	JP MORGAN	JPM	5Y	38	38	0	A1	A+	N/A	N/A	25-May-04 6:21
	MBNA CORP.	KRB	5Y	57	62	0	Baa2	BBB	-0.1	22/04/2004	02-Jul-04 16:06
	LEHMAN	LEH	5Y	44	44	0	n/a	A+	N/A	N/A	25-May-04 6:21
	MERRILL	MER	5Y	40	40	0	Aa3	A+	N/A	N/A	25-May-04 6:20
	MORGAN STANLEY	MWD	5Y	35	38	0	Aa3	A+	0.8	18/06/2004	07-Apr-04 17:27
	BANK ONE	ONE	5Y	29	34	0	Aa3	A *+	0	20/04/2004	07-Apr-04 17:27
	SAFECO CORPORATION	SAFC	5Y	32	37	0	Baa1	BBB+	-0.7	20/04/2004	07-Apr-04 17:27
	SIMON PROPERTY GROUP	SPG	5Y	47	52	0	Baa2	BBB	-3.8	07/05/2004	02-Jul-04 16:06
Chemicals	AGRIUM	AGU	5Y	37	42	0	Baa2	BBB	0.5	27/04/2004	07-Apr-04 17:27
	DUPONT, E.I. DE NEMOURS	DD	5Y	15	20	1	Aa3	AA-	0.4	29/04/2004	02-Jul-04 16:06
	DOW CHEMICAL COMPANY	DOW	5Y	47	52	1	A3	A-	0.4	23/04/2004	02-Jul-04 16:06

(continued)

Exhibit 1.15   Continued

Sector	Issuer	Ticker	Maturity	Bid	Ask	Dly Chng	Moodys	S&P	SharePx Pctg Chg	Earnings Rel	Date/Time (GMT)	
	ROHM AND HAAS COMPANY	ROH	5Y	38	36	3.5	A3	BBB+	−0.7	28/04/2004	02-Jul-04	16:06
Consumer Goods	COCA-COLA ENTERPRISES	CCE	5Y	27	32	0	A2	A	−1.3	23/04/2004	07-Apr-04	17:27
	CAMPBELL SOUP CO.	CPB	5Y	24	29	0	A3	A	1.1	24/05/2004	02-Jul-04	16:06
	EASTMAN KODAK COMPANY	EK	5Y	165	170	2	Baa3	BBB−	1.7	21/04/2004	02-Jul-04	16:06
	GENERAL MILLS, INC.	GIS	5Y	35	40	0	Baa2	BBB+	0.3	25/06/2004	02-Jul-04	16:06
	KRAFT FOODS INC	KFT	5Y	40	45	0	A3	BBB+	−1.6	19/04/2004	02-Jul-04	16:06
	MATTEL	MAT	5Y	35	40	0	Baa2	BBB	3.1	20/04/2004	07-Apr-04	17:27
	MCDONALD'S CORP.	MCD	5Y	24	29	0	A2	A	−1.1	13/04/2004	02-Jul-04	16:06
	ALTRIA GROUP, INC.	MO	5Y	180	185	1.5	Baa2	BBB	0.6	20/04/2004	02-Jul-04	16:06
	NEWELL RUBBERMAID INC	NWL	5Y	58	63	0	Baa2	BBB+	−0.2	29/04/2004	02-Jul-04	16:06
	R.J.R.	RJR	5Y	260	265	0	Ba2	BB+	0.7	23/04/2004	07-Apr-04	17:27
Energy & Utilities	AMERICAN ELECTRIC POWER	AEP	5Y	57	62	0	Baa3	BBB	−0.2	29/04/2004	02-Jul-04	16:06
	DUKE ENERGY CORPORATION	DUK	5Y	84	84	0	Baa3	BBB+	N/A	N/A	25-May-04	6:08
	DOMINION RESOURCES, INC	D	5Y	57	63	0	Baa1	BBB+	0.4	21/04/2004	02-Jul-04	16:06
	NATIONAL RURAL UTILITIES	NRUC	5Y	40	45	0	A2	A	N/A	N/A	02-Jul-04	16:06
Industrials (Diversified)	SEMPRA ENERGY	SRE	5Y	40	45	0	Baa1	BBB+	−0.3	29/04/2004	02-Jul-04	16:06
	CATERPILLAR INC	CAT	5Y	26	29	0	A2	A	0.5	22/04/2004	02-Jul-04	16:06
	DEERE & COMPANY	DE	5Y	28	32	0	A3	A−	1.7	13/05/2004	02-Jul-04	16:06
	DANAHER	DHR	5Y	25	30	0	A2	A+	−0.3	16/04/2004	07-Apr-04	17:27

Sector	Issuer	Ticker	Maturity	Bid	Ask	Dly Chng	Moodys	S&P	SharePx Pctg Chg	Earnings Rel	Date/Time (GMT)
	EMERSON	EMR	5Y	21	26	0	A2	A	0.5	06/05/2004	07-Apr-04 17:27
	INGERSOLL-RAND COMPANY	IR	5Y	37	42	0	A3	BBB+	2.4	20/04/2004	02-Jul-04 16:06
	TYCO INTL. LTD.	TYC	5Y	90	95	0	WR	NR	-1.3	04/05/2004	07-Apr-04 17:27
Insurance	ACE LIMITED	ACE	5Y	45	50	0	A3	BBB+	-0.2	27/04/2004	02-Jul-04 16:06
	AETNA INC.	AET	5Y	38	42	0	Baa2	BBB	-1	29/04/2004	02-Jul-04 16:06
	AMERICAN INTERNATIONAL	AIG	5Y	20	24	0	Aaa	AAA	-0.2	23/04/2004	02-Jul-04 16:06
	CHUBB CORPORATION	CB	5Y	31	35	0	A2	A	-0.7	26/04/2004	02-Jul-04 16:06
	CNA FINANCIAL	CNA	5Y	110	110	0	Baa2	BBB-	N/A	N/A	25-May-04 6:21
	MBIA INSURANCE CORPORATION	MBI	5Y	38	43	0	Aaa	AAA	-1.4	06/05/2004	02-Jul-04 16:06
	WASHINGTON MUTUAL INC	WM	5Y	45	49	0	A3	BBB+	0.8	19/04/2004	02-Jul-04 16:06
	XL CAPITAL LTD	XL	5Y	47	52	0	A2	A	0.6	03/05/2004	02-Jul-04 16:06
Leisure	CARNIVAL CORPORATION	CCL	5Y	55	59	0	A3	A-	0.7	25/06/2004	02-Jul-04 16:06
	CENDANT CORPORATION	CD	5Y	52	56	0	Baa1	BBB	0.6	19/04/2004	02-Jul-04 16:06
	HILTON HOTELS	HLT	5Y	140	140	0	n/a	BBB	N/A	N/A	25-May-04 6:28
	MARRIOTT INTERNATIONAL	MAR	5Y	51	55	0	Baa2	BBB+	-0.5	22/04/2004	02-Jul-04 16:06
	MGM MIRAGE	MGG	5Y	175	175	0	Ba1	BB+	N/A	N/A	25-May-04 6:26
	PARK PLACE ENT.	PPE	5Y	150	158	0	Ba1	BB+	N/A	22/04/2004	07-Apr-04 17:27
Media	CLEAR CHANNEL COMMUNICATIONS	CCU	5Y	79	83	0	Baa3	BBB-	0	30/04/2004	02-Jul-04 16:06
	WALT DISNEY COMPANY	DIS	5Y	50	54	0	Baa1 *-	BBB+ *-	0.3	12/05/2004	02-Jul-04 16:06

(continued)

Exhibit 1.15 Continued

Sector	Issuer	Ticker	Maturity	Bid	Ask	Dly Chng	Moodys	S&P	SharePx Pctg Chg	Earnings Rel	Date/Time (GMT)
	NEWS AMERICA INC	NCP	5Y	61	65	0	Baa3	BBB-	-1.2	N/A	02-Jul-04	16:06
	OMNICOM GROUP INC.	OMC	5Y	40	44	0	Baa1	A-	-1	29/04/2004	02-Jul-04	16:06
	TIME WARNER INC	TWX	5Y	81	86	0	Baa1	BBB+	3.6	23/04/2004	02-Jul-04	16:06
	VIACOM INC	VIA	5Y	49	54	0	A3	A-	0.8	22/04/2004	02-Jul-04	16:06
Oil and Gas/Metals	ALCOA INC.	AA	5Y	39	44	3	A2	A-	1.1	06/04/2004	02-Jul-04	16:06
	ANADARKO PETROLEUM CORP	APC	5Y	32	37	0	Baa1	BBB+	-0.7	23/04/2004	02-Jul-04	16:06
	CONOCOPHILLIPS	COP	5Y	22	27	0	A3	A-	0.7	28/04/2004	02-Jul-04	16:06
	DEVON ENERGY CORP	DVN	5Y	65	70	0	Baa2	BBB	-0.1	07/05/2004	02-Jul-04	16:06
	EL PASO	EP	5Y	740	740	-5	Caa1	B+	N/A	N/A	25-May-04	14:42
	NABORS INDUSTRIES	NBR	5Y	33	33	0	n/a	A-	N/A	N/A	25-May-04	6:06
	OCCIDENTAL PETROLEUM	OXY	5Y	34	39	0	Baa1	BBB+	-0.2	23/04/2004	07-Apr-04	17:27
	TRANSOCEAN INC.	RIG	5Y	43	48	0	Baa2	A-	0.3	27/04/2004	02-Jul-04	16:06
	VALERO ENERGY CORPORATION	VLO	5Y	61	66	1	Baa3	BBB	-0.7	22/04/2004	02-Jul-04	16:06
	WEATHERFORD INTERNATIONAL	WFT	5Y	40	45	0	Baa1	BBB+	0.4	21/04/2004	07-Apr-04	17:27
	WILLIAMS	WMB	5Y	245	265	0	B3	B+	-0.2	06/05/2004	07-Apr-04	17:27
Other	ABITIBI	ABY	5Y	289	289	-1	Ba1	BB+	N/A	N/A	25-May-04	14:41
	BOWATER	BOW	5Y	280	280	-3	Ba1	BB+	N/A	N/A	25-May-04	14:40
	CSX CORPORATION	CSX	5Y	59	64	0	Baa2	BBB	0.9	28/04/2004	02-Jul-04	16:06
	GEORGIA PACIFIC	GP	5Y	170	190	0	Ba3	BB+	-0.5	29/04/2004	07-Apr-04	17:27
	MASCO	MAS	5Y	33	38	0	Baa1	BBB+	-2.7	06/05/2004	07-Apr-04	17:27
	MAYTAG CORPORATION	MYG	5Y	82	87	0	Baa2	BBB	0.7	22/04/2004	02-Jul-04	16:06

Sector	Issuer	Ticker	Maturity	Bid	Ask	Dly Chng	Moodys	S&P	SharePx Pctg Chg	Earnings Rel	Date/Time (GMT)	
	NORFOLK SOUTHERN CORPORATION	NSC	5Y	41	46	0	Baa1	BBB	0.8	23/04/2004	02-Jul-04	16:06
	UNION PACIFIC CORP	UNP	5Y	43	48	0	Baa2	BBB	0.3	23/04/2004	02-Jul-04	16:06
	WHIRLPOOL CORPORATION	WHR	5Y	55	60	0	Baa1	BBB+	-0.4	21/04/2004	02-Jul-04	16:06
Pharma-ceuticals	AMGEN INC.	AMGN	5Y	21	24	0	A2	A+	-1.1	22/04/2004	02-Jul-04	16:06
	BAXTER INTERNATIONAL	BAX	5Y	43	48	0	A3 *_	A-	-0.7	22/04/2004	02-Jul-04	16:06
	MEDTRONIC, INC.	MDT	5Y	18	23	0	A1	AA-	-0.3	19/05/2004	07-Apr-04	17:27
Pulp/Paper/ Packaging	INTERNATIONAL PAPER CO	IP	5Y	63	68	0	Baa2	BBB	0.8	23/04/2004	02-Jul-04	16:06
	WEYERHAEUSER CO.	WY	5Y	45	50	0	Baa2	BBB	1	23/04/2004	02-Jul-04	16:06
Retail	ALBERTSONS, INC	ABS	5Y	67	70	1	Baa2	BBB	1.3	04/06/2004	02-Jul-04	16:06
	FEDERATED DEPARTMENT STORES	FD	5Y	58	62	0	Baa1	BBB+	-0.3	14/05/2004	02-Jul-04	16:06
	GAP	GPS	5Y	78	83	0	Ba3 *+	BB+	1.3	20/05/2004	07-Apr-04	17:27
	NORDSTROM INC	JWN	5Y	40	45	0	Baa1	A-	-0.2	19/05/2004	02-Jul-04	16:06
	LOWES COMPANIES	LOW	5Y	20	25	0	A2	A	-0.4	17/05/2004	07-Apr-04	17:27
	MAY DEPARTMENT STORES COMPANY	MAY	5Y	76	79	0	Baa1	BBB+	0.6	11/05/2004	02-Jul-04	16:06
	SAFEWAY INC.	SWY	5Y	69	71	1.5	Baa2	BBB	2.2	30/04/2004	02-Jul-04	16:06
	SEARS ROEBUCK ACCEPTANCE	S	5Y	102	107	0	Baa1	BBB	1.2	22/04/2004	02-Jul-04	16:06
	TARGET CORP	TGT	5Y	25	28	0	A2	A+	1	14/05/2004	02-Jul-04	16:06
	TOYS R US INC.	TOY	5Y	278	283	5	Ba2	BB *_	2.2	19/05/2004	02-Jul-04	16:06

(continued)

Exhibit 1.15 Continued

Sector	Issuer	Ticker	Maturity	Bid	Ask	Dly Chng	Moodys	S&P	SharePx Pctg Chg	Earnings Rel	Date/Time (GMT)	
	WAL-MART STORES INC	WMT	5Y	17	20	0	Aa2	AA	0.7	13/05/2004	02-Jul-04	16:06
Technology	ARROW ELECTRONICS, INC.	ARW	5Y	122	127	0	Baa3	BBB-	-0.9	22/04/2004	02-Jul-04	16:06
	COMPUTER ASSOCIATES INT	CA	5Y	87	92	0	Ba1	BBB+*-	-0.9	14/05/2004	02-Jul-04	16:06
	COMPUTER SCIENCES CORPORATION	CSC	5Y	36	41	0	A3	A	0.8	17/05/2004	02-Jul-04	16:06
	DELL	DELL	5Y	20	25	0	A3	A-	-1	13/05/2004	07-Apr-04	17:27
	ELECTRONIC DATA SYSTEMS	EDS	5Y	195	200	0	Baa3 *-	BBB-	-0.5	07/05/2004	02-Jul-04	16:06
	CORNING INC.	GLW	5Y	170	170	0	Ba2	BB+	N/A	N/A	17-Dec-03	16:14
	HONEYWELL INTERNATIONAL	HON	5Y	30	34	0	A2	A	-0.1	21/04/2004	02-Jul-04	16:06
	HEWLETT-PACKARD COMPANY	HPQ	5Y	24	27	0	A3	A-	-1.3	20/05/2004	02-Jul-04	16:06
	INTERNATIONAL BUSINESS	IBM	5Y	25	30	0	A1	A+	-0.7	15/04/2004	02-Jul-04	16:06
	MOTOROLA INC.	MOT	5Y	70	75	0	Baa3	BBB	-1.6	20/04/2004	02-Jul-04	16:06
	ORACLE	ORCL	5Y	16	21	0	A3 *-	A- *-	-2.2	11/06/2004	07-Apr-04	17:27
	SUN MICROSYSTEMS, INC.	SUNW	5Y	140	145	0	Baa3	BB+	-2.8	15/04/2004	02-Jul-04	16:06
Telecom/ Cable	AT&T WIRELESS SERVICES	AWE	5Y	53	57	0	Baa2 *	BBB *+	0.4	28/04/2004	02-Jul-04	16:06
	BELLSOUTH CORPORATION	BLS	5Y	36	40	0	A1 *-	A+ *-	-1.9	22/04/2004	02-Jul-04	16:06

Sector	Issuer	Ticker	Maturity	Bid	Ask	Dly Chng	Moodys	S&P	SharePx Pctg Chg	Earnings Rel	Date/Time (GMT)	
	COMCAST CABLE COMMUNICATIONS	CMCSA	5Y	65	70	0	Baa3 *+	BBB	0.3	28/04/2004	02-Jul-04	16:06
	CINGULAR WIRELESS LLC	CNG	5Y	46	50	0	A3 *-	A+ *-	N/A	N/A	02-Jul-04	16:06
	COX COMMUNICATIONS, INC	COX	5Y	67	71	0	Baa2	BBB	-0.8	29/04/2004	02-Jul-04	16:06
	CENTURYTEL, INC.	CTL	5Y	130	135	0	Baa2	BBB+	-0.6	30/04/2004	02-Jul-04	16:05
	CITIZENS COMMUNICATIONS	CZN	5Y	280	290	-20	Baa2	BBB *-	0.5	06/05/2004	02-Jul-04	16:06
	SPRINT CORPORATION	FON	5Y	98	103	-2.5	Baa3	BBB-	2.8	20/04/2004	02-Jul-04	16:06
	SBC COMMUNICATIONS INC	SBC	5Y	44	48	0	A1 *-	A+ *-	-1.4	21/04/2004	02-Jul-04	16:06
	AT&T CORP	T	5Y	320	328	-2	Baa2	BBB	0.6	22/04/2004	02-Jul-04	16:06
	VERIZON GLOBAL FUNDING	VZ	5Y	44	48	0	A2	A+ *-	-0.6	27/04/2004	02-Jul-04	16:06

2. European Credit Default Swap Quotes

Sector	Issuer	Ticker	1 Year		3 Year		5 Year		7 Year		10 Year		Time
			Bid	Ask	Bid	Ask	Bid	Ask	Bid	Ask	Bid	Ask	
Aerospace	EADS	EADS	15.5	20.5	23	28	33	36	39.5	44.5	49.5	54.5	43:41.0
Defence	BAE SYSTEMS	BAPLC	27.5	32.5	47.5	52.5	60	64	65.1	70.1	73.5	78.5	00:09.0
	FINMECCANICA	FINMEC	38	43	57	62	62.5	67.5	70.5	75.5	82.5	87.5	43:38.0
	THALES	THALES	10	15	21.5	26.5	30	33	34.5	39.5	40.5	45.5	41:44.0
	ROLLS ROYCE	ROLLS	24.5	29.5	39.5	44.5	53	57	58.5	63.5	67.5	72.5	00:08.0
Airlines	AIR FRANCE	AIRFR	45.5	60.5	81.5	96.5	105	115	114	129	129	144	44:12.0
	BRITISH AIRWAYS	BAB	147	197	229.5	254.5	282	292	291	306	306	326	22:49.0
	LUFTHANSA	LUFTHA	46	51	71	76	87.5	92.5	97	102	106	111	44:08.0
	SAS	SAS	442.5	517.5	550	590	590	630	587	627	580	620	12:50.0
Auto Parts	CONTINENTAL	CONRUB	19	24	38	43	44	49	47	52	55	60	33:05.0
	GKH	GKNLN	73	78	77.5	82.5	82	90	87	92	92	97	21:29.0
Autos	BMW	BMW	9.5	14.5	20.5	25.5	29	31	32.5	37.5	40.6	45.6	51:52.0
	DCX	DCX	26.5	31.5	59.5	64.5	86.5	89.5	95	100	110	115	51:00.0
	FIAT	FIAT	200	260	325	365	380	400	390	410	403	423	40:55.0
	PEUGEOT	PEUGEOT	12	17	27.5	32.5	37.5	40.5	42	47	54	59	51:52.0
	RENAULT	RENAUL	22.5	27.5	37.5	42.5	48.5	51.5	53	58	65	70	51:52.0
	VOLKSWAGEN	VW	29.5	34.5	55.5	60.5	69.5	72.5	76.5	81.5	86.5	91.5	51:51.0
Banking	BCP SENIOR	BCPN	4.5	7.5	11	14	19.5	22.5	21.5	25.5	25.5	30.5	49:06.0
	BNP SENIOR	BNP	3	6	7	10	11	13	13	17	16.5	21.5	51:16.0
	BNROMA SUB	BNROMA_SUB	7.5	12.5	41	46	55.5	60.5	59	65	67	73	46:36.0
	CREDIT SUISSE GROUP SEN	CRDSUI_GROUP	4.5	7.5	14.5	17.5	21	24	24	28	27.5	32.5	48:56.0
	BANCO SANTANDER SENIOR	SANTAN	10	13	12	15	16	18	18	22	21	26	51:15.0
	BANCO SANTANDER SUB	SANTAN_SUB	15	19	25	29	33	37	37	43	40	46	51:11.0
	SOCGEN SENIOR	SOCGEN	7	10	9	12	13	15	15	19	18	23	46:18.0

Sector	Issuer	Ticker	1 Year		3 Year		5 Year		7 Year		10 Year		Time
			Bid	Ask	Bid	Ask	Bid	Ask	Bid	Ask	Bid	Ask	
Chemicals	AKZO	AKZO	18.5	23.5	26.5	31.5	35	40	42.5	47.5	50.5	55.5	04:10.0
	BAYER	BYIF	27.5	32.5	35.5	40.5	45	50	52	57	62	67	04:10.0
	ICI	ICI	61	66	69	74	78	83	85	90	94.5	99.5	41:28.0
	NOVARTIS	NOVART	7	11	9	13	11	15	12	16	15	19	41:27.0
	RHODIA	RHA	315	365	585	615	640	660	636	661	630	660	55:47.0
Construction	HEIDELBERGCEMENT	HEI	83	113	142.5	157.5	200	206	206	216	227	237	41:23.0
	HOLCIM	HOLZSW	24.5	29.5	33.5	38.5	40	45	46	51	53.5	58.5	21:27.0
	LAFARGE	LAFCP	12	17	35.5	40.5	47	52	53	58	61.5	66.5	21:26.0
	ST GOBAIN	STGOBN	10	15	25	30	32	36	36.5	41.5	46.5	51.5	21:18.0
Diversified	INVESTOR AB	INVSA	13.5	18.5	25	30	35	40	42	47	50	55	44:13.0
	LINDE	LINDE	19	24	28	33	35	40	43.5	48.5	55.5	60.5	21:27.0
Energy	BP	BP	4	8	7	11	11	15	15	19	20	24	03:39.0
	EDF	EDF	3.5	6.5	12.5	15.5	23.5	26.5	28.5	33.5	36.5	41.5	01:21.0
	EDP	EDP	5.5	10.5	19.5	24.5	30	34	33.5	38.5	39.5	44.5	01:20.0
	ENDESA	ELESM	13.5	18.5	28.5	33.5	37	41	40.5	45.5	49.5	54.5	01:17.0
	ENBW	ENBW	11	15	22	26	32	36	36	40	44	48	01:13.0
	ENEL	ENEL	10.5	15.5	19.5	24.5	27	31	30.5	35.5	36.5	41.5	01:10.0
	EON	EON	6.5	9.5	14.5	17.5	21.5	24.5	25	29	31	35	00:09.0
	SUEZ	LYOE	17	21	34	38	44	48	47.5	52.5	56.5	61.5	59:07.0
	NATIONAL GRID TRANSCO	NATGRID	18.5	23.5	29.5	34.5	41	45	45.5	50.5	53.5	58.5	58:46.0
	REPSOL	REP	19	23	35	39	51	55	54.5	59.5	64.5	69.5	58:43.0
	RWE	RWE	6.5	9.5	15.5	18.5	23.5	26.5	27	31	36	40	58:41.0
	UNION FENOSA	UNFSM	27.5	32.5	42.5	47.5	52.5	57.5	58.5	63.5	67.5	72.5	03:49.0
	VATTENFALL AB	VATFAL	15.5	20.5	22.5	27.5	33	37	36.5	41.5	44.5	49.5	03:47.0
	VEOLIA ENVIRONNEMENT	VIEFP	16.5	21.5	33.5	38.5	45	49	49.5	54.5	58.5	63.5	03:46.0

(continued)

Exhibit 1.15   Continued

Sector	Issuer	Ticker	1 Year		3 Year		5 Year		7 Year		10 Year		Time
			Bid	Ask	Bid	Ask	Bid	Ask	Bid	Ask	Bid	Ask	
Food Beverage	CADBURY SCHWEPPES	CBRY	19.5	24.5	32.5	37.5	43.5	48.5	48.5	53.5	58.5	63.5	01:40.0
	UNILEVER	ULVR	4	8	13	17	22	26	28	32	34	38	58:48.0
Industrials	ABB	ABB	83.5	98.5	126	136	161	167	164	174	181	191	05:08.0
	CORUS	CORUS	225	275	380	420	480	495	490	515	505	530	22:50.0
	FKI	FKI	69	79	94	104	112	122	122	132	134	144	21:02.0
	INVENSYS	ISYSLN	250	300	445	485	550	565	557	577	571	591	08:47.0
	METSO	METSO	108	118	137.5	147.5	165	175	178	188	190	200	04:09.0
	THYSSENKRUPP	TKAGR	58	88	88.5	103.5	112	118	119	127	128	136	50:05.0
Insurance	AEGON	AEGON	5	8	15	18	23	26	25	29	31	36	51:38.0
	ALLIANZ SENIOR	ALZ	6	9	17	20	25	28	28	32	34	39	51:37.0
	ALLIANZ SUB	ALLIANZ	9	13	22	26	38	42	43	48	57	62	49:13.0
	AVIVA	AVLN	6	9	13	16	21	24	24	28	30	35	46:35.0
	AXA SENIOR	AXASA	6	9	16	19	24	27	27	31	35	40	51:37.0
	AXA SUB	AXASA_SUB	9	13	25	29	40	44	46	51	64	69	49:12.0
	MUNICH RE SENIOR	MUNRE	7	10	16	19	24	27	27	31	34	39	51:19.0
	MUNICH RE SUB	MUNRE_SUB	14	18	29	33	45	49	51	56	68	74	46:29.0
	OLD MUTUAL	OLDMUT	10	16	33	39	42	48	47	55	58	68	46:28.0
	PRUDENTIAL	PRUFIN	7	10	15	18	22	25	25	29	30	35	46:26.0
	SWISS RE SENIOR	SCHREI	6	9	15	18	21	24	23	27	29	34	51:17.0
	SWISS RE SUB	SCHREI_SUB	7	11	22	26	33	37	39	43	48	53	46:20.0
	ZURICH INSURANCE	VERSIC	10	15	21	25	29	33	33	38	40	46	51:17.0
Leisure Hotels	ACCOR	ACCOR	45	55	62	72	80	88	84	94	91	101	01:07.0
	SODEXHO	EXHO	45	55	55	65	69	75	71	81	80	90	58:44.0
	HILTON GROUP	HGLN	40	46	51	57	63	69	69	75	74	80	59:11.0
Media	ADECCO	ADO	50	60	75	85	85	95	91	101	100	110	06:04.0
	BERTELSMAN	BERTEL	17	27	36.5	41.5	46	49	52.5	57.5	60.5	65.5	50:57.0
	COMPASS GROUP	CCMLN	21	31	38	43	51	56	55.5	60.5	63	73	50:58.0

Sector	Issuer	Ticker	1 Year		3 Year		5 Year		7 Year		10 Year		Time
			Bid	Ask	Bid	Ask	Bid	Ask	Bid	Ask	Bid	Ask	
	VIVENDI UNIVERSAL	EAUG	23	33	49	57	76	80	82	90	93	103	50:58.0
	EMI	EMI	100	120	165	175	205	215	213	228	225	245	21:06.0
	PEARSON	PSON	14	24	28.5	33.5	38	41	43.5	48.5	52	62	50:55.0
	PUBLICIS	PUBFP	70	90	115	125	130	140	135	155	150	170	40:54.0
	REUTERS	RTRGRP	18	28	30	35	38	41	40	48	49	59	50:54.0
	UBM	UNWS	39	49	57.5	62.5	68	73	76	84	84	94	50:51.0
	VNU	VNU	24	34	40	45	54	57	59	67	68	78	50:50.0
	WOLTERS KLUWER	WOLKLU	18	28	39	44	51	54	57.5	62.5	67	75	50:49.0
	WPP	WPPLN	27	37	43.5	48.5	56	59	62	70	71	81	51:02.0
Metals Mining	ANGLO AMERICAN	AALLN	22	27	37	42	49	54	55.3	60.3	63	68	21:11.0
	GLENCORE	GLEN	130	135	180	185	195	210	208	213	222	227	41:21.0
	ARCELOR	LORSCA	53	63	62	70	73	78	80	85	85.5	90.5	21:10.0
	PECHINEY	PECFP	28	38	37	47	43	53	48	58	57	67	21:09.0
	XSTRATA	XSTRATA	105	115	115	125	125	135	135	145	150	160	21:05.0
Paper	M-REAL	SOLSM	130	180	222.5	247.5	250	270	258	278	267	287	26:23.0
	STORA	ENSGUT	30	35	38	43	50	55	58	63	66	71	04:08.0
	UPM	UPMKYM	41	46	55	60	61	66	67	72	76	81	41:26.0
Retail	AHOLD	AHOLD	130	160	200	210	240	250	248	258	260	270	21:10.0
	CARREFOUR	CARR	11	15	18	22	27.5	32.5	30.5	35.5	41.5	46.5	01:17.0
	CASINO	GROUPE	32.5	37.5	47.5	52.5	62.5	67.5	68.5	73.5	80.5	85.5	01:12.0
	KINGFISHER	KINGFI	20	24	32	36	45	49	50	54	60	64	01:09.0
	METRO	METFNL	21.5	26.5	39.5	44.5	51	55	56.5	61.5	68.5	73.5	00:37.0
	MARKS & SPENCER	MKS	85	115	180	210	255	275	260	290	272	302	01:41.0
	LVMH	MOET	16.5	21.5	29.5	34.5	40.5	45.5	48.5	53.5	57.5	62.5	59:15.0
	PINAULT	PRTP	60	110	100	130	130	140	133	153	145	165	40:53.0
	SAINSBURY	SBRY	44	54	81	91	106	116	112	122	126	136	59:13.0
	TESCO	TSCO	8	12	12	16	19	23	23	27	30	34	59:09.0

(continued)

Exhibit 1.15 Continued

Sector	Issuer	Ticker	1 Year		3 Year		5 Year		7 Year		10 Year		Time
			Bid	Ask	Bid	Ask	Bid	Ask	Bid	Ask	Bid	Ask	
Technology	CAP GEMINI	CAPGEM	15	65	35	85	75	85	63	113	75	125	51:51.0
	PHILIPS	PHG	16	21	28.5	33.5	38	43	45	53	53	63	50:55.0
	SIEMENS	SIEM	9.5	14.5	17.5	22.5	25	28	31.5	36.5	39	47	50:54.0
	STMICRO	STM	13	23	25.5	30.5	35	40	41	49	48	58	50:52.0
	THOMSON	TMMFP	17	27	27.5	32.5	38	43	42	50	53	63	50:52.0
Telecom Operators	BRITISH TELECOM	BRITEL	18.5	23.5	40.5	45.5	62	65	72.5	77.5	85.5	90.5	51:50.0
	DEUTSCHE TELEKOM	DT	14.5	19.5	33.5	38.5	55	58	63.5	68.5	77.5	82.5	50:53.0
	FRANCE TELECOM	FRTEL	18.5	23.5	40.5	45.5	62	65	70	75	84.5	89.5	51:49.0
	KPN	KPN	16.5	21.5	32.5	37.5	54	57	61.5	66.5	74.5	79.5	51:49.0
	NOKIA	NOKIA	13.5	18.5	24.5	29.5	34	37	38	43	45	55	50:56.0
	MM02	OOMLN	17	27	37	47	53	56	60	70	71	81	51:48.0
	PORTUGAL TELECOM	PLTMPL	15	20	27	32	35	38	41.5	46.5	52.5	57.5	53:25.0
	TELEFONICA	TELEF	17	27	25	33	33	38	41	49	51	61	52:55.0
	TELECOM ITALIA	TITIM	19.5	24.5	42.5	47.5	68	71	77.5	82.5	90.5	95.5	52:56.0
	VODAFONE	VOD	17.5	22.5	28.5	33.5	40	43	45.5	50.5	56.5	61.5	51:54.0
Telecom Suppliers	ALCATEL	ALAFP	70	90	130	140	176	184	187	197	205	215	40:52.0
	CABLE & WIRELESS	CWLN	105	135	212.5	227.5	265	275	272	292	290	310	58:46.0
	ERICSSON	LMTEL	61	81	121	131	162	170	171	181	186	196	40:53.0

Sector	Issuer	Ticker	1 Year		3 Year		5 Year		7 Year		10 Year		Time
			Bid	Ask	Bid	Ask	Bid	Ask	Bid	Ask	Bid	Ask	
Tobacco	BAT	BATSLN	29.5	34.5	55.5	60.5	69.5	74.5	74.5	79.5	84.5	89.5	03:37.0
	IMPERIAL TOBACCO	IMPTOB	29.5	34.5	46.5	51.5	57.5	62.5	61.5	66.5	70.5	75.5	02:10.0
Transportation	BAA	BAA	14.5	19.5	27.5	32.5	35	39	41	46	46	51	21:25.0
	DEUTSCHE POST	DPW	2.5	7.5	18.5	23.5	28.5	33.5	32.5	37.5	40.5	45.5	02:37.0

The Deutsche Bank Group ("DB") is providing the referenced indicative bid/ask price data and related information (collectively "Pricing Data") for informational purposes only and solely for your internal use. Pricing Data represents an indication (determined by DB at its sole discretion) of the spreads at which DB might have paid or charged, as the case may be, to purchase default protection (DB's bid) or sell default protection (DB's ask) as of the time/date indicated. DB's providing Pricing Data does not constitute an offer to sell or a solicitation of an offer to buy any referenced instrument, and DB shall have no obligation to quote to you firm prices or to purchase or sell any referenced instrument.

Among other factors, Pricing Data is based upon a limited transaction size, prevailing market conditions and DB's current appetite for the resulting altered risk profile. Pricing Data does not necessarily represent DB's economic assessment of the referenced instrument. The reliability, accuracy, completeness or timeliness of Pricing Data cannot be guaranteed. Without limitation, you should understand that Pricing Data may be delayed and may not reflect prices at which the referenced instruments may be bought or sold and you should therefore not make any decisions to buy or sell the referenced instruments based on Pricing Data and should not use Pricing Data in preparation of your own financial books and records. DB reserves the right at any time and without notice to you to discontinue its providing of Pricing Data.

DB SPECIFICALLY DISCLAIMS LIABILITY FOR DIRECT, INDIRECT, CONSEQUENTIAL OR OTHER LOSSES OR DAMAGES INCLUDING LOSS OF PROFITS INCURRED BY YOU OR ANY THIRD PARTY THAT MAY ARISE FROM ANY RELIANCE ON PRICING DATA OR FOR THE RELIABILITY, ACCURACY, COMPLETENESS OR TIMELINESS THEREOF, OR FOR ANY DELAYS OR ERRORS IN THE TRANSMISSION OR DELIVERY OF PRICING DATA.

(continued)

3. Japanese Credit Default Swap Quotes

Deutsche Bank Group

Deutsche Securities Limited, Tokyo Branch
Integrated Credit Trading   Phone: 81 (3) 5156-6289
Bankruptcy, Failure to Pay, '99 Restructuring
Roll Date: 20th of Mar, Jun, Sep, and Dec
(* Govt of Japan; 5yr and 10 yr)

Exhibit 1.15   Continued

Tokyo Credit Derivatives Desk Default Swap Indications   http://research.gm.db.com/

Today: 06-Jul-04   As of the close on: 05-Jul-04   To obtain a password, please contact
your sales representatives
Maturity (Quarterly Settlement)   Deutsche Bank Credit Derivatives
5yr   20-Sep-09   DBCD <GO> (Bloomberg)

NO.	INDUSTRY	TSE	TICKER	REFERENCE ENTITY	Moody's	R&I	Crncy	BID	OFFER	5yr MID Chg 1d	5yr MID Chg 5d	5yr MID Chg 20d	5yr MID Chg 60d	5yr MID Chg 120d	Equity Closing Px	Equity Px Chg %	NOTES
1	Automobiles	5108	BSTONE	BRIDGESTONE CORPORATION	Baa2	A+	JPY	10	16	–	–2	–1	–1	–4	2,065	0.00	
2	Automobiles	7270	FUJIHI	FUJI HEAVY INDUSTRIES LTD.		A–	JPY	16	22	–	–2	–3	–5	–8	579	–1.19	
3	Automobiles	7267	HNDA	HONDA MOTOR CO., LTD.	A1	AA	JPY	11	17	–	–2	–2	2	1	5,090	–1.17	CJ50
4	Automobiles	7201	NSANY	NISSAN MOTOR CO., LTD.	Baa1	A–	JPY	17	23	–1	–2	–2	3	–2	1,190	–0.50	CJ50
5	Automobiles	7203	TOYOTA	TOYOTA MOTOR CORPORATION	Aaa	AAA	JPY	5	9	–	–	–1	–	–2	4,350	–1.36	CJ50
6	Automobiles	7272	YAMAHA	YAMAHA MOTOR CO., LTD.	Baa3	A–	JPY	13	19	–	–	–1	4	–3	1,646	–1.79	CJ50

NO.	INDUSTRY	TSE	TICKER	REFERENCE ENTITY	Moody's	R&I	Crncy	BID	OFFER	5yr MID Chg 1d	5yr MID Chg 5d	5yr MID Chg 20d	5yr MID Chg 60d	5yr MID Chg 120d	Equity Closing Px	Equity Px Chg %	NOTES
7	Banks	8315	MTFG	THE BANK OF TOKYO-MITSUBISHI LTD.	A2	AA–	USD	15	22	–	–	–3	1	2	946,000	–1.77	
8	Banks	8318	SUMIBK	SUMITOMO MITSUI BANKING CORPORATION	A3	A	USD	22	32	–	–	–4	2	–8	690,000	–1.57	
9	Banks	8320	UFJ	UFJ BANK	A3	A–	USD	38	48	–	–	–3	8	–3	449,000	1.81	
10	Banks	MIZC	MIZUHO	MIZUHO CORPORATE BANK LTD.	A3	A–	USD	31	41	–	–2	–5	4	–11	460,000	–2.95	
11	Banks	8315	MTFG	THE BANK OF TOKYO-MITSUBISHI LTD.	A2	AA–	JPY	11	20	–	–	–3	2	3	946,000	–1.77	CJ50
12	Banks	8318	SUMIBK	SUMITOMO MITSUI BANKING CORPORATION	A3	A	JPY	18	28	–	–1	–4	2	–7	690,000	–1.57	CJ50
13	Banks	8320	UFJ	UFJ BANK	A3	A–	JPY	33	45	–	–	–4	10	4	449,000	1.81	
14	Banks	MIZC	MIZUHO	MIZUHO CORPORATE BANK LTD.	A3	A–	JPY	27	38	–	–2	–5	4	–3	460,000	–2.95	
15	Banks	DBJZ	DBJIP	DEVELOPMENT BANK OF JAPAN	A2	AAA	JPY	5	8	–	–	–1	1	1			
16	Chemicals	4010	MITCHM	MITSUBISHI CHEMICAL CORPORATION	Baa3	BBB+	JPY	25	32	–	–2	–2	5	–2	281	–2.43	CJ50

(continued)

Exhibit 1.15 Continued

NO.	INDUSTRY	TSE	TICKER	REFERENCE ENTITY	Moody's	R&I	Crncy	BID	OFFER	5yr MID Chg 1d	5yr MID Chg 5d	5yr MID Chg 20d	5yr MID Chg 60d	5yr MID Chg 120d	Equity Closing Px	Equity Px Chg %	NOTES
17	Chemicals	4183	MITTOA	MITSUI CHEMICALS, INC.	Baa2	A	JPY	18	24	–	–1	–	3	–4	539	–2.00	
18	Chemicals	4005	SUMICH	SUMITOMO CHEMICAL COMPANY, LIMITED	Baa1	A+	JPY	12	18	–	–1	–2	1	–4	503	0.20	CJ50
19	Electrical Appliances	7751	CANNY	CANON INC.	Aa3	AA+	JPY	8	13	–	–	–	1	–1	5,690	–0.87	CJ50
20	Electrical Appliances	6952	CASIO	CASIO COMPUTER CO., LTD.	Baa3	A–	JPY	13	21	–	–3	–6	–	–4	1,607	–2.37	
21	Electrical Appliances	7762	CITWAT	CITIZEN WATCH CO., LTD.	A3		JPY	13	20	–	–1	–3	–3	–12	1,218	0.25	
22	Electrical Appliances	6752	MATSEL	MATSUSHITA ELECTRIC INDUSTRIAL CO., LTD.	Aa3	AA+	JPY	8	14	–	–	–	2	–	1,511	–0.53	CJ50
23	Electrical Appliances	6753	SHARP	SHARP CORPORATION	A2	AA	JPY	11	16	–	–1	2	4	4	1,693	–1.86	CJ50
24	Electrical Appliances	6758	SNE	SONY CORPORATION	A1	AA	JPY	24	29	–1	–3	–4	1	–1	4,090	–1.21	CJ50
25	Electronics	6702	FUJITS	FUJITSU LIMITED	Baa2	A	JPY	52	58	–1	–1	–4	–8	–11	733	–2.01	CJ50
26	Electronics	6501	HITACH	HITACHI, LTD.	A2	AA–	JPY	19	24	–	–2	4	6	4	730	–1.75	CJ50
27	Electronics	6503	MITELC	MITSUBISHI ELECTRIC CORPORATION	Baa1	A	JPY	20	26	–	–2	–2	6	2	503	–3.82	CJ50

NO.	INDUSTRY	TSE	TICKER	REFERENCE ENTITY	Moody's	R&I	Crncy	BID	OFFER	5yr MID Chg 1d	5yr MID Chg 5d	5yr MID Chg 20d	5yr MID Chg 60d	5yr MID Chg 120d	Equity Closing Px	Equity Px Chg %	NOTES
28	Electronics	6701	NECORP	NEC CORPORATION	Baa2	A	JPY	35	40	–	–4	–3	8	2	744	–1.20	CJ50
29	Electronics	6502	TOSH	TOSHIBA CORPORATION	Baa1	A	JPY	31	36	–	4	3	5	4	430	–1.15	CJ50
30	Foods; Beverages; Breweries	2502	ASABRE	ASAHI BREWERIES LTD.	Baa3	A+	JPY	13	19	–	–	–1	2	–1	1,179	–1.50	CJ50
31	Foods; Beverages; Breweries	2914	JAPTOB	JAPAN TOBACCO INC.	Aa3	AA+	JPY	7	12	–	–	–	–	–1	848,000	–0.24	
32	Foods; Beverages; Breweries	2501	SAPBRW	SAPPORO HOLDINGS LIMITED	Ba3	BBB–	JPY	47	56	–	–1	–1	4	–14	394	–1.75	
33	General Construction	1812	KAJIMA	KAJIMA CORPORATION	Baa3	A–	JPY	26	32	–1	–2	–3	5	–2	386	–3.98	
34	General Construction	1802	OBACRP	OBAYASHI CORPORATION	Baa2	A	JPY	24	30	–1	–2	–3	4	–2	564	–1.91	
35	General Construction	1801	TAISEI	TAISEI CORPORATION	Ba1	BBB+	JPY	38	48	1	–1	–2	6	–7	393	–2.24	
36	Housing	1928	SEKIS	SEKISUI HOUSE, LTD.	Baa2	AA–	JPY	10	17	–1	–2	–4	–3	–3	1,179	–2.24	CJ50
37	Iron & Steel	5403	JFEHLD	JFE STEEL CORPORATION	Baa3	A–	JPY	26	33	–	–3	–1	13	10	2,625	–1.32	CJ50
38	Iron & Steel	5401	NIPSTL	NIPPON STEEL CORPORATION	Baa2	A+	JPY	18	23	–	–3	–3	7	4	223	–1.76	CJ50

(continued)

Exhibit 1.15   Continued

NO.	INDUSTRY	TSE	TICKER	REFERENCE ENTITY	Moody's	R&I	Crncy	BID	OFFER	5yr MID Chg 1d	5yr MID Chg 5d	5yr MID Chg 20d	5yr MID Chg 60d	5yr MID Chg 120d	Equity Closing Px	Equity Px Chg %	NOTES
39	Life & Non-Life Insurance	8752	TAISHO	MITSUI SUMITOMO INSURANCE COMPANY, LIMITED	Aa3	AA	JPY	8	12	–	–	–	1	–2	976	–1.61	CJ50
40	Life & Non-Life Insurance	8751	MILLEA	THE TOKIO MARINE AND FIRE INSURANCE COMPANY, LIMITED	Aa2	AA+	JPY	8	12	–	–	–	1	–1			CJ50
41	Life & Non-Life Insurance	8755	YASUFI	SOMPO JAPAN INSURANCE INC.	Aa3	AA	JPY	8	12	–	–	–	1	–3	1,075	–2.01	
42	Machinery	6361	EBARA	EBARA CORPORATION	Baa3	BBB	JPY	38	48	–	–1	–5	–3	–32	523	–2.06	CJ50
43	Machinery	7012	KAWHI	KAWASAKI HEAVY INDUSTRIES, LTD.	Baa3	BBB+	JPY	36	43	–	–3	–3	5	–3	171	–1.16	CJ50
44	Machinery	7011	MITHI	MITSUBISHI HEAVY INDUSTRIES, LTD.	Baa1	AA–	JPY	23	29	–	–	1	11	8	290	–0.68	CJ50
45	Media; Publishing & Printing	7911	TOPPAN	TOPPAN PRINTING CO., LTD.	Aa3	AA	JPY	8	13	–	–	–	–	–	1,205	–0.33	

NO.	INDUSTRY	TSE	TICKER	REFERENCE ENTITY	Moody's	R&I	Crncy	BID	OFFER	5yr MID Chg 1d	5yr MID Chg 5d	5yr MID Chg 20d	5yr MID Chg 60d	5yr MID Chg 120d	Equity Closing Px	Equity Px Chg %	NOTES
46	Non-bank Financial Institutions	8572	ACOM	ACOM CO., LTD.	Baa1	A	JPY	32	40	–	–1	–1	11	–29	6,980	–2.51	CJ50
47	Non-bank Financial Institutions	8515	AIFUL	AIFUL CORPORATION	Baa2	A–	JPY	42	50	–	–1	–1	5	–31	11,040	–2.99	
48	Non-bank Financial Institutions	8591	ORIX	ORIX CORPORATION	Baa3	A+	JPY	40	48	–	–3	–3	3	–36	11,850	–2.07	CJ50
49	Non-bank Financial Institutions	8574	PROMIS	PROMISE CO., LTD.	Baa1	A	JPY	33	42	–	–2	–6	7	–27	6,910	–3.63	CJ50
50	Non-bank Financial Institutions	8564	TAKFUJ	TAKEFUJI CORPORATION	Baa2		JPY	58	78	–	–14	–55	–67	–232	7,570	–1.30	
51	Nonferrous Metal Products	5201	ASAGLA	ASAHI GLASS COMPANY, LIMITED	A2	AA	JPY	10	15	–	–2	–3	–2	–4	1,135	–1.05	CJ50
52	Nonferrous Metal Products	5711	MITMAT	MITSUBISHI MATERIALS CORPORATION	Ba1	BBB–	JPY	90	120	–	–	–	–	–25	238	–2.46	
53	Nonferrous Metal Products	5802	SUMIEL	SUMITOMO ELECTRIC INDUSTRIES, LTD.	A2	AA–	JPY	10	16	–	–1	–2	–1	–6	1,090	–0.37	CJ50
54	Oil	5001	NIPOIL	NIPPON OIL CORPORATION	Baa1	A	JPY	14	20	–	–	–2	2	–4	666	–0.45	CJ50

(continued)

Exhibit 1.15 Continued

NO.	INDUSTRY	TSE	TICKER	REFERENCE ENTITY	Moody's	R&I	Crncy	BID	OFFER	5yr MID Chg 1d	5yr MID Chg 5d	5yr MID Chg 20d	5yr MID Chg 60d	5yr MID Chg 120d	Equity Closing Px	Equity Px Chg %	NOTES
55	Private Railways	9020	EJRAIL	EAST JAPAN RAILWAY COMPANY	Aa2	AA+	JPY	7	12	–	–	–	1	1	606,000	–2.73	
56	Private Railways	9042	HANKYU	HANKYU CORPORATION	Baa2	BB+	JPY	41	49	–1	–2	–1	6	–21	428	–1.61	
57	Private Railways	9041	KINKI	KINTETSU CORPORATION	Baa2	BBB+	JPY	37	45	–2	–1	–2	7	–4	404	–1.22	
58	Private Railways	9005	TOKYU	TOKYU CORPORATION	Baa3	BBB+	JPY	28	36	–	–1	–2	5	–7	541	–2.70	CJ50
59	Pulp & Paper	3863	NUNPC	NIPPON PAPER INDUSTRIES CO., LTD.	Baa2	A–	JPY	17	24	–	–	–1	–1	–7	569,000	–2.74	
60	Real Estate	8802	MITEST	MITSUBISHI ESTATE COMPANY, LIMITED	A3	AA–	JPY	12	18	–	–3	–4	2	–3	1,295	–1.75	CJ50
61	Real Estate	8801	MITSRE	MITSUI FUDOSAN CO., LTD.	Baa3	A–	JPY	15	22	–	–4	–4	–2	–9	1,241	–1.90	CJ50
62	Retail	8267	JUSCO	AEON CO., LTD.	Baa3	A+	JPY	17	23	–	–	–2	1	–8	4,140	–4.17	CJ50
63	Securities Companies	8601	DAIWA	DAIWA SECURITIES GROUP INC.	Baa3	A–	JPY	22	33	–	–1	–1	3	–10	746	–0.93	CJ50
64	Securities Companies	8603	NIKKO	NIKKO CORDIAL CORPORATION	Baa3	A–	JPY	25	38	–	–2	–2	1	–10	513	–1.91	
65	Securities Companies	NCLZ	NOMURA	NOMURA SECURITIES CO., LTD.	Baa1	A+	JPY	15	21	–1	–1	–1	2	–2	1,578	–0.94	CJ50

NO.	INDUSTRY	TSE	TICKER	REFERENCE ENTITY	Moody's	R&I	Crncy	BID	OFFER	5yr MID Chg 1d	5yr MID Chg 5d	5yr MID Chg 20d	5yr MID Chg 60d	5yr MID Chg 120d	Equity Closing Px	Equity Px Chg %	NOTES
66	Sovereign			GOVERNMENT OF JAPAN	A2	AAA	USD	6	9	–	1	–1	–	–	–	0.00	
67	Sovereign			GOVERNMENT OF JAPAN	A2	AAA	USD	14.5	17.5	1	–1	–1	–2	–1	–	0.00	
68	Telecommunications	9433	DDI	KDDI CORPORATION		A–	JPY	16	21	–	–	–1	1	–6	611,000	–0.49	CJ50
69	Telecommunications	9432	NTT	NIPPON TELEGRAPH AND TELEPHONE CORPORATION	Aa2		JPY	7	11	–	–	–	–	–1	573,000	–0.17	
70	Telecommunications	9437	NTTDCM	NTT DOCOMO, INC.	Aa1	AA+	JPY	8	12	–	–	–	1	–	191,000	–1.04	CJ50
71	Trading Firms; Wholesalers	8058	MITCO	MITSUBISHI CORPORATION	A3	AA–	JPY	21	27	–1	–1	–1	5	2	1,025	–1.16	CJ50
72	Trading Firms; Wholesalers	8031	MITSCO	MITSUI & CO LTD	A3	AA–	JPY	21	27	–	–	–	5	3	817	–1.92	CJ50
73	Trading Firms; Wholesalers	8053	SUMI	SUMITOMO CORPORATION (SUMITOMO SHOJI KAISHA, LTD.)	Baa1	A+	JPY	21	27	–	–	–	5	3	783	–1.88	CJ50
74	Transportation	9202	ANAIR	ALL NIPPON AIRWAYS CO., LTD.	Ba3	BBB	JPY	80	100	–5	–17	–14	–	–35	350	–1.41	
75	Transportation	9201	JALSTM	JAPAN AIRLINES COMPANY, LTD.	Ba3	BBB	JPY	85	105	–5	–10	–6	–	–10	339	–2.02	CJ50
76	Transportation	9062	NIPEXP	NIPPON EXPRESS CO., LTD.	A2	AA	JPY	8	13	–	–	–	–	–1	614	–2.38	CJ50

(continued)

Exhibit 1.15   Continued

NO.	INDUSTRY	TSE	TICKER	REFERENCE ENTITY	Moody's	R&I	Crncy	BID	OFFER	5yr MID Chg 1d	5yr MID Chg 5d	5yr MID Chg 20d	5yr MID Chg 60d	5yr MID Chg 120d	Equity Closing Px	Equity Px Chg %	NOTES
77	Utilities	9502	CHUBEP	CHUBU ELECTRIC POWER COMPANY INCORPORATED	Aa3	AA+	JPY	7	11	–	–	–	1	–2	2,310	–0.22	CJ50
78	Utilities	9503	KANSEL	THE KANSAI ELECTRIC POWER COMPANY INCORPORATED	Aa3	AA+	JPY	7	11	–	–	–	1	–2	1,973	–0.65	CJ50
79	Utilities	9508	KYUSEL	KYUSHU ELECTRIC POWER COMPANY INCORPORATED	A1	AA+	JPY	7	11	–	–	–	1	–2	2,025	–0.74	CJ50
80	Utilities	9501	TOKELP	THE TOKYO ELECTRIC POWER COMPANY, INCORPORATED	Aa3	AA+	JPY	8	12	–	–	–	1	–3	2,450	–1.80	CJ50

NO.	INDUSTRY	TSE	TICKER	REFERENCE ENTITY	Moody's	R&I	Crncy	BID	OFFER	5yr MID Chg 1d	5yr MID Chg 5d	5yr MID Chg 20d	5yr MID Chg 60d	5yr MID Chg 120d	Equity Closing Px	Equity Px Chg %	NOTES
81	Utilities	9531	TOKGAS	TOKYO GAS CO., LTD.	Aa1	AA+	JPY	7	11	–	–	–	1	–2	384	–0.78	CJ50
	CJ50 Index	22.5/24															
	DB Mkt:																

The above referenced indicative bid/ask price data and related information (collectively "Pricing Data") is provided by Deutsche Securities Limited, Tokyo Branch ("SL") for informational purposes only and solely for your internal use. Pricing Data represents an indication (determined by Deutsche Bank AG ("DB") at its sole discretion) of the spreads at which DB might have paid or charged, as the case may be, to purchase default protection (DB's bid) or sell default protection (DB's ask) as of the time/date indicated, for which transaction DSL may act as agent for and on behalf of DB. The Pricing Data does not constitute an offer, an invitation to offer, or a solicitation or recommendation to sell or buy any referenced instrument, and DB and/or DSL shall have no obligation to quote to you firm prices or to purchase or sell any referenced instrument. Among other factors, Pricing Data is based upon a limited transaction size, prevailing market conditions and DB's current appetite for the resulting altered risk profile. Pricing Data does not necessarily represent DB's economic assessment of the referenced instrument. The reliability, accuracy, completeness or timeliness of Pricing Data cannot be guaranteed. Without limitation, you should understand that Pricing Data may be delayed and may not reflect prices at which the referenced instruments may be bought or sold and you should therefore not make any decisions to buy or sell the referenced instruments based on Pricing Data and should not use Pricing Data in preparation of your own financial books and records. DB and DSL reserve the right at any time and without notice to you to discontinue its providing of Pricing Data. DB AND DSL SPECIFICALLY DISCLAIM LIABILITY FOR DIRECT, INDIRECT, CONSEQUENTIAL OR OTHER LOSSES OR DAMAGES INCLUDING LOSS OF PROFITS INCURRED BY YOU OR ANY THIRD PARTY THAT MAY ARISE FROM ANY RELIANCE ON PRICING DATA OR FOR THE RELIABILITY, ACCURACY, COMPLETENESS OR TIMELINESS THEREOF, OR FOR ANY DELAYS OR ERRORS IN THE TRANSMISSION OR DELIVERY OF PRICING DATA.

Source : **Deutsche Bank Group**

7 Credit Default Swaps – Documentation Issues[34]

7.1 Documentation Approach[35]

The documentation of credit default swaps seeks to give effect to the basic underlying commercial intent of the transaction. The primary objective is the transfer of the risk of a specific entity defaulting and any consequent loss. The ability to achieve this objective is dependent on the efficacy of the documentation[36].

The documentation of credit default swaps must deal with several complexities, including:

- The credit default swap does not entail a direct contractual relationship with the reference entity. This creates significant difficulties in structuring the arrangements.

---

[34] The author would like to thank Christopher Whiteley and Benjamin Bowden for their comments on an earlier draft of this Chapter.

[35] The description of the documentary and legal aspects of credit default swaps is in general terms only. There are significant differences between jurisdictions and the specific circumstances of each transaction are different. This discussion does not purport to provide professional advice or counsel. Participants in credit derivatives transactions should seek full and comprehensive legal/documentation advice from suitably qualified and experienced professionals in the relevant jurisdiction prior to entering into transactions or undertaking any action in relation to such transactions.

[36] For discussion of the documentation of credit default swaps, see William, Jeevan, Espinelli, Ray and Reoch, Robert "Keeping The Books" (February 1998) Asia Risk 27–29; Roberts, Samantha and Mahrotri, Tarun "Is It Time For A Change?" (April 1999) Asia Risk 12–15; Bennett, Oliver "Documentation Dilemmas" (March 2001) Risk – Credit Risk Special Report S6–S7; Tolk, Jeffrey S. "Understanding The Risks in Credit Default Swaps" (May 2001) Credit 40–43; Tolk, Jeffrey S. "Understanding The Risks in Credit Default Swaps" (Spring 2001) FOW/Credit Derivatives 26–30; Francis, Chris, Kakodkar, Atish and Rooney, Mary (31 January 2002) Credit Default Swap Handbook"; Merrill Lynch, London; "2001: The Year That Tested The Credit Swap Contract" in "Credit Derivatives Update 2002" (March 2002) Euromoney Research Guide 14–16; (16 October 2002) Standardised Documentation For Credit Derivatives Growth; Fitch Ratings; New York; Francis, Chris, Kakodkar, Atish and Martin, Barnaby (16 April 2003) Credit Derivative Handbook"; Merrill Lynch, London; Tierney, John F. (13 June 2003) 2003 ISDA Credit Definitions; Deutsche Bank, Global Markets Research – Credit Derivatives, New York; Harding, Paul C. (2004) A Practical Guide to the 2003 Credit Derivatives Definition; Euromoney Books, London. For a discussion of ISDA derivatives documentation more generally, see Gooch, Anthony C. and Klein, Linda B. (2004) Documentation For Derivatives 4th Edition Volumes 1 and 2; Euromoney Books, London.

- Under a credit default swap, losses and payments in compensation for the loss are calculated synthetically. There are inherent difficulties in establishing the event of default and the value of a defaulted credit. This difficulty may be because of liquidity, market conditions and absence of price discovery. There may also be inherent conflicts of interest and moral hazards that affect this process.
- There may be a need to match any underlying credit exposure being hedged/transferred through the credit default swap. This is to ensure that the transaction operates as an effective hedge. The complexity derives from the fact that the documentation of the underlying transaction may differ significantly from the terms of the credit default swap. This would expose the hedger to basis risk – referred to as "documentary asymmetry". In practice, the non-standard nature of credit documentation creates significant complexity in this regard.
- Where a dealer trades credit default swaps, a key concern will be to ensure that offsetting trades/hedges are identical. This requires that the terms and conditions of the credit default swaps and/or instruments used to hedge positions are substantially identical. This is designed to ensure that the dealer is not exposed to any residual risk from documentary mismatches.

In practice, the documentation of credit default swaps is complex. This reflects the obvious tension between the desire/need for standardisation and the capacity to accommodate the complexity identified.

In the development period of the market, dealers documented credit default swaps using specifically developed confirmations within an ISDA Master documentation framework. This created problems in negotiating transactions, as different dealers used different confirmations. Delays in confirming/documenting transactions became problematic. The dealers recognised the need for standardisation of documentation. Leading dealers worked with ISDA to develop a standard documentary format for credit default swaps.

The first attempt to standardise documentation resulted in the development of the Confirmation for an OTC Credit Swap Transaction (Single Reference Entity, Non Sovereign). This confirmation (the Long Form Confirmation) was published in 1998. This document was about 20 pages in length. The length reflected, in part, the fact that the definitions of required terms were contained in the confirmation itself. The Long Form Confirmation created operational problems. The structure of the confirmation required dealers transacting a credit default swap to make a large number of choices/selections. This caused delays and confusion. It also increased the risk of operational errors. The problems led a number of leading dealers to amend the Long Form Confirmation. This entailed eliminating certain choices and/or amending some provisions. This detracted from the objective of standardisation and ease of documentation. The problems identified resulted in an expansion and revision of the Long Form Confirmation.

In July 1999, ISDA published the revised standard documentary framework for privately negotiated credit default swaps. The revised format consisted of two separate components:

- Standard definitions for credit default swap transactions (the "1999 Definitions").
- A shorter confirmation for individual credit default swaps ("the Short Form Confirmation").

The structure of the revised documentary format relies on the parties to the transaction nominating a limited range of terms. The agreed terms, in turn, rely on the detailed standard definitions being incorporated by reference.

The structure relies on the concept of fall back provisions whereby certain terms are assumed to apply if the parties fail to make a specific election in the Short Form Confirmation. This is designed to minimise the risk that important terms are inadvertently omitted.

Current market practice is for the Short Form Confirmation to be used in documentation of the majority of credit default swap transactions. ISDA also subsequently announced a number of supplements clarifying a number of issues.

In 2002, ISDA reviewed the 1999 Credit Definitions. The primary objective was to publish new Credit Definitions that incorporated the supplements and refined a number of concepts. The 2003 ISDA Credit Derivatives Definitions (the "2003 Definitions"[37]) were adopted in February 2003[38].

---

[37] The 1999 Definitions and the 2003 Definitions are referred to together as the "Credit Definitions".

[38] See Coliey, James "New Credit Documentation For A Changing Market" (6 January 2003) Derivatives Week 12–13; (6 March 2003) Fitch Examines Effect of 2003 Credit Derivatives Definitions; Fitch Ratings; New York; Francis, Chris, Kakodkar, Atish and Martin, Barnaby (16 April 2003) Credit Derivative Handbook; Merrill Lynch, London.

7.2 ISDA Standard Confirmation

7.2.1 Key Terms

Credit default swaps are generally documented using the Short Form Confirmation. The key terms and conditions of a Credit Default Swap include:

- Reference entity on which the credit default swap is based.
- Duration/maturity of the transaction; that is, the period for which protection on the reference entity is purchased or sold.
- Types of obligation of the reference entity covered by the credit default swap.
- Credit events in relation to the reference entity that will require payment by the bank selling protection.
- Settlement mechanics of the credit default swap in the case where a credit event occurs.

Exhibit 1.16 sets out an annotated version of the ISDA short form of confirmation.

The key issues in a credit default swap are discussed in the following sections.

Exhibit 1.16   Credit Default Swaps – Confirmation[39]

[Headed paper of Party A]

Date: 15 February 2003

To: [Name and Address or Facsimile Number of Party B]

From: [Party A]

Re: Credit Derivative Transaction

Dear _____ :

The purpose of this [letter] (this "Confirmation") is to confirm the terms and conditions of the Credit Derivative Transaction entered into between us on the Trade

---

[39] The author would like to thank Christopher Whiteley for permission to include material from Whiteley, Christopher "Credit Derivatives: Documentation And Legal Issues" in Das, Satyajit (Editor) (2001) Credit Derivatives & Credit Linked Notes – Second Edition; John Wiley & Sons, Singapore at Chapter 17.

Date specified below (the "Transaction"). This Confirmation constitutes a "Confirmation" as referred to in the ISDA Master Agreement specified below.

The definitions and provisions contained in the 2003 ISDA Credit Derivatives Definitions (the "Credit Derivatives Definitions"), as published by the International Swaps and Derivatives Association, Inc., are incorporated into this Confirmation. In the event of any inconsistency between the Credit Derivatives Definitions and this Confirmation, this Confirmation will govern.

[This Confirmation supplements, forms a part of, and is subject to, the ISDA Master Agreement dated as of [date], as amended and supplemented from time to time (the "Agreement"), between you and us. All provisions contained in the Agreement govern this Confirmation except as expressly modified below.][40]

---

[40]   This wording may be amended to incorporate ISDA Master Agreement terms by reference to the published form if no agreement is signed. If the parties have not yet executed, but intend to execute, an ISDA Master Agreement include, instead of this paragraph, the following: "This Confirmation evidences a complete and binding agreement between you and us as to the terms of the Transaction to which this Confirmation relates. In addition, you and we agree to use all reasonable efforts promptly to negotiate, execute and deliver an agreement in the form of an ISDA Master Agreement, with such modifications as you and we will in good faith agree. Upon the execution by you and us of such an agreement, this Confirmation will supplement, form part of, and be subject to that agreement. All provisions contained in or incorporated by reference in that agreement upon its execution will govern this Confirmation except as expressly modified below. Until we execute and deliver that agreement, this Confirmation, together with all other documents referring to an ISDA Master Agreement (each a "Confirmation") confirming transactions (each a "Transaction") entered into between us (notwithstanding anything to the contrary in a Confirmation), shall supplement, form a part of, and be subject to, an agreement in the form of the 1992 ISDA Master Agreement (Multicurrency – Cross Border) if any Confirmation dated prior to the date of this Confirmation refers to that ISDA Master Agreement and otherwise the 2002 ISDA Master Agreement as if we had executed an agreement in such form (but without any Schedule except for the election of [English Law][the laws of the State of New York] as the governing law and [specify currency] as the Termination Currency) on the Trade Date of the first such Transaction between us. In the event of any inconsistency between the provisions of that agreement and this Confirmation, this Confirmation will prevail for the purpose of this Transaction."

The terms of the Transaction to which this Confirmation relates are as follows:

1. General Terms:

Trade Date:	15th February, 2003
Effective Date:	16th February, 2003[41]
Scheduled Termination Date:[42]	16th February, 2008[43]
Floating Rate Payer:	Party A (the "Seller")[44]
Fixed Rate Payer:	Party B (the "Buyer")[45]
Calculation Agent:[46]	Seller[47]
Calculation Agent City:[48]	London[49]
Business Day:[50]	[ ][51]
Business Day Convention:	Following[52] (which, subject to Sections 1.4 and 1.6 of the Credit Derivatives Definitions, shall apply to any date referred to in this Confirmation that falls on a day that is not a Business Day)

---

[41] The 2003 Definitions assume commencement at 12.01 am Greenwich Mean Time unless otherwise specified.

[42] The Termination Date may be extended to allow for settlement of the Transaction if a Credit Event occurs prior to the Scheduled Termination Date or to provide for a Grace Period to elapse if a Potential Failure to Pay occurs prior to the Scheduled Termination Date or to establish a failure to pay following a repudiation/moratorium.

[43] The 2003 Definitions assume expiry at 11:59 p.m. Greenwich Mean Time unless otherwise specified.

[44] The protection seller.

[45] The protection buyer.

[46] If the Calculation Agent is a third party, the parties may wish to consider any documentation necessary to confirm its undertaking to act in that capacity.

[47] The fallback is that the Seller will be the Calculation Agent.

[48] Calculation Agent City is used to determine the timing of valuations and the effectiveness of any notices following a Credit Event.

[49] The fallback is the city in which the relevant branch of the Calculation Agent is situated.

[50] The Credit Definitions require valuations and payments to be made on a Business Day.

[51] The fallback is to days on which commercial banks and foreign exchange markets are generally open to settle payments in the jurisdiction of the currency of the Floating Rate Payer Calculation Amount.

[52] The fall-back is the Following Business Day Convention. The alternatives are the Modified Following (that is, the following Business Day unless the new date will be in the next calendar month, in which case the preceding Business Day) or Preceding Business Day Conventions.

Reference Entity:	ABC Company Limited
Reference Obligation:[53]	The obligations identified as follows[54]:
	Primary Obligor: ABC Company Finance N.V.
	Guarantor: Reference Entity
	Maturity: 2008
	Coupon: 9%
	CUSIP/ISIN: ●
All Guarantees:	Applicable[55]
Reference Price:[56]	96.50%[57]

---

[53] A Reference Obligation must be specified for Cash Settlement to apply. If a Reference Obligation is specified for Credit Derivative Transactions to which Physical Settlement applies then, subject to the certain conditions, such Reference Obligation is a Deliverable Obligation even though at the time of delivery it does not fall into the Obligation Category or lacks any or all Deliverable Obligation Characteristics.

[54] The Definitions encompass the concept of "substitute reference obligations". In the event that a Reference Obligation is redeemed in whole or the aggregate amounts due under any Reference Obligation have been materially reduced (other than due to any scheduled redemption, amortisation or prepayments), or a guarantee by the Reference Entity of any Reference is no longer valid (other than due to the existence or occurrence of a Credit Event), the Calculation Agent can (after consultation with the parties) identify one or more Obligations to replace such Reference Obligation. The substitute reference obligation must satisfy certain nominated criteria designed to ensure the economic equivalence of the obligations.

[55] Unlike the 1999 Definitions, the 2003 Definitions deal with guarantees separately from other types of obligation. The Obligations of the Reference Entity are deemed to include all Qualifying Affiliate Guarantees. These are effectively "downstream" parent/subsidiary arrangements. In addition, the parties can elect to expand the definition of Qualifying Guarantee to include all guarantees given by the reference entity. This therefore includes any upstream guarantees (where a subsidiary guarantees the obligations of a parent) but also any guarantees of obligations of a third party. Qualifying Guarantees exclude any arrangement structured as a surety bond, financial guarantee insurance policy, letter of credit or equivalent legal arrangement.

[56] The Cash Settlement Amount will be based on the change between the Reference Price and the Final Price of the Reference Obligation.

[57] The fall-back is 100%.

2. Fixed Payments:[58]

Fixed Rate Payer Calculation Amount:	Floating Rate Payer Calculation Amount[59]
Fixed Rate Payer Period End Dates:[60]	16th February, 16th August[61]
Fixed Rate Payer Payment Dates:	16th February, 16th August subject to adjustment in accordance with the Following Business Day Convention
Fixed Rate:	1.50% pa
Fixed Rate Day Count Fraction:[62]	Actual/360[63]

3. Floating Payment:

Floating Rate Payer Calculation Amount:[64]	US$10,000,000
Conditions to Payment:[65]	Credit Event Notice Notifying Party: Buyer or Seller[66] Notice of Physical Settlement[67]

---

[58] The Buyer makes one or more payments of a Fixed Amount during the life of the Transaction. If one payment is made, this is similar to a premium. If regular payments are made, these payments are often based on the yield on the Reference Obligation on the Trade Date. In the latter case, the Buyer may wish to match the calculation of any Fixed Amounts to the terms of the Reference Obligation.

[59] The fall-back is the Floating Rate Payer Calculation Amount.

[60] Period End Dates are used to determine the Calculation Period for which a Fixed Amount is payable.

[61] The fall-back is Fixed Rate Payer Payment Dates. The difference between the two in this Confirmation is the lack of adjustment for days that are not Business Days.

[62] The Day Count Fraction is used to determine the number of days in the Calculation Period for which a Fixed Amount is payable.

[63] The fall-back is Actual/360. The alternatives are Actual/Actual; Actual/365 (fixed); 30/360 (Bond Basis); and 30E/360 (Eurobond Basis).

[64] For an amortising transaction, the amount will be listed in an amortisation schedule.

[65] These requirements must be met before any payment is due from the Seller following a Credit Event. The 2003 Definitions provide a recommended form of Credit Event Notice, Notice of Publicly Available Information (if applicable) and Notice of Physical Settlement.

[66] The fall-back is the Buyer. The alternative is the Buyer or Seller.

[67] If Physical Settlement applies, then the Buyer must give notice of the Deliverable Obligations it will deliver. Failure by the Buyer to deliver as promised will give the Seller the right to buy-in any Bonds or to direct the assignment of (available) Loans to itself or an affiliate.

	Notice of Publicly Available Information Applicable Public Source(s): Standard Public Sources[68] Specified Number: 2[69]
Credit Events:	The following Credit Events shall apply to this Transaction:[70] **Bankruptcy**[71] **Failure to Pay**[72]

Grace Period Extension:[73]	Applicable[74]
Grace Period:	30 calendar days[75]
Payment Requirement:[76]	US$1,000,000[77] or its

equivalent in the relevant Obligation Currency as of
the occurrence of the relevant Failure to Pay
Obligation Default[78]

---

[68] If Notice of Publicly Available Information has been selected by the parties and a Public Source is not specified, the 2003 Definitions provide that the Public Sources will be Bloomberg Service, Dow Jones Telerate Service, Reuters Monitor Money Rates Services, Dow Jones News Wire, Wall Street Journal, New York Times, Nihon Keizai Shimbun, Asahi Shimbun, Yomiuri Shimbun, Financial Times, La Tribune, Les Echos and The Australian Financial Review (and successor publications), the main source(s) of business news in the jurisdiction in which the Reference Entity is organised and any other internationally recognised published or electronically displayed news sources.

[69] The fall-back is two.

[70] The parties must elect which Credit Events apply. Possible Credit Events are Bankruptcy; Failure to Pay; Obligation Default; Obligation Acceleration; Repudiation/Moratorium; Restructuring.

[71] Bankruptcy means bankruptcy of the Reference Entity.

[72] Failure to Pay means a failure to make payments in excess of the Payment Requirement when due under any Obligations.

[73] If Grace Period Extension applies and a Potential Failure to Pay occurs before the Scheduled Termination Date, the party responsible may deliver a Credit Event Notice with respect to a Failure to Pay occurring within the Grace Period.

[74] The fall-back is that the Grace Period Extension doesn't apply.

[75] If the Grace Period Extension applies, the fall-back is that the Grace Period will be no more than 30 calendar days.

[76] Payment Requirement is a threshold amount that applies to the Failure to Pay Credit Event.

[77] The fall-back is US$1,000,000.

[78] Obligation Default means Obligations in excess of the Default Requirement become capable of being declared due and payable as a result of an event of default or similar event. The alternative, Obligation Acceleration, requires that Obligations in excess of the Default Requirement are declared due and payable as a result of an event of default or similar event.

> **Obligation Acceleration**
> **Repudiation/Moratorium**[79]
> **Restructuring**[80]
>   [Restructuring Maturity Limitation[81] and Fully
>   Transferable Obligations[82]: Applicable[83]]
>   [Modified Restructuring Maturity Limitation[84] and
>   Conditional Transferable Obligation[85]:
>   Not Applicable[86]]

[79] Repudiation/moratorium means any repudiation of Obligations in excess of the Default Requirement by the Reference Entity or any government and any government or self-imposed moratorium on payments under Obligations in excess of the Default Requirement.

[80] Restructuring means a unilateral change to certain material terms of any Obligation as a result of a deterioration in creditworthiness.

[81] The Restructuring Maturity Limitation Date is the date that is the earlier of 30 months following the Restructuring Date and the latest final maturity date of any Restructured Bond or Loan (but in no event a date earlier than the Scheduled Termination Date or a date later than 30 months following the Scheduled Termination Date).

[82] Fully Transferable Obligations means a Transferable Bond or any other claim that is transferable without consent.

[83] These provisions narrow the field of Deliverable Obligations following a Restructuring Credit Event because of a potential windfall value in the cheapest-to-deliver option for the Buyer. The parties can only specify that either Restructuring Maturity Limitation and Fully Transferable Obligation *or* Modified Restructuring Maturity Limitation and Conditionally Transferable Obligation apply. Restructuring Maturity Limitation and Fully Transferable Obligation is sometimes known as MR or Mod-R. See discussion later in the Chapter on restructuring provisions.

[84] Modified Restructuring Maturity Limitation Date means the later of (i) 60 months for a Restructured Bond or Loan (and 30 months for other Deliverable Obligations) following the Restructuring Date and (ii) the Scheduled Termination Date.

[85] Conditionally Transferable Obligation includes any claim that is transferable with the consent of the Reference Entity (so long as that consent cannot be unreasonably withheld).

[86] These provisions narrow the field of Deliverable Obligations following a Restructuring Credit Event because of a potential windfall value in the cheapest-to-deliver option for the Buyer. The parties can only specify that either Restructuring Maturity Limitation and Fully Transferable Obligation *or* Modified Restructuring Maturity Limitation and Conditionally Transferable Obligation apply. Modified Restructuring Maturity Limitation and Conditionally Transferable Obligation is sometimes known as MMR or Mod-Mod R. See discussion later in the Chapter on restructuring provisions.

Multiple Holder Obligations[87]: Applicable[88]
Default Requirement:[89] US$10,000,000[90] or its
equivalent in the relevant Obligation Currency as of
the occurrence of the relevant Credit Event

Obligations:[91]

Obligation Category:[92]	*Obligation Characteristics:*[93]
Borrowed Money	Not Subordinated
	Specified Currency[94]

Excluded Obligations: None[95]

4. Settlement Terms:

Settlement Method: [Cash Settlement] [Physical Settlement][96]

Terms Relating to Cash
Settlement:[97]

---

[87] Multiple Holder Obligation means an obligation owed to three or more creditors and which requires the consent of 2/3s of these for any modification to be effective.

[88] The fall-back is that this is applicable.

[89] Default Requirement is a threshold amount that applies to all Credit Events apart from Failure to Pay.

[90] The fall-back is US$10,000,000.

[91] Whether or not a Credit Event has occurred (other than Bankruptcy) will be determined by reference to any Obligations in the category and with the characteristics specified.

[92] The parties should select only one category from Payment; Borrowed Money; Reference Obligations Only; Bond; Loan; or Bond or Loan.

[93] The parties should select any characteristics from Not Subordinated; Specified Currency; Not Sovereign Lender; Not Domestic Currency; Not Domestic Law; Listed; Not Domestic Issuance.

[94] Specified Currency means the lawful currencies of any of Canada, Japan, Switzerland, the United Kingdom and the United States of America and the Euro (and any successor currency to any such currency). If no currency is specified, if the Reference Entity is a Sovereign then the Credit Derivatives Definitions provide that Domestic Currency will be the lawful currency and any successor currency of the relevant Reference Entity. If no currency is specified, if the Reference Entity is not a Sovereign, then the relevant currency is that of the jurisdiction in which the relevant Reference Entity is organised.

[95] The fall-back is none.

[96] The parties need to select between the two options.

[97] This confirmation provides for *both* cash and physical settlement. This is for purposes of illustration only. This would not normally be the case. In practice,

Valuation Dates:[98]	Single Valuation Date[99]: five Business days[100]
	Multiple Valuation Dates: five Business Days[101] and each five Business Days thereafter
	Number of Valuation Dates: Five[102]
Valuation Time:	11.00 a.m. London time[103]
Quotation Method:[104]	Bid[105]
Quotation Amount:[106]	Floating Rate Payer Calculation Amount[107]
Minimum Quotation Amount:[108]	US$1,000,000[109]

---

    one form of settlement would be selected at the time of entry into the transaction.

[98]   Valuation Dates are used to determine the Cash Settlement Amount by calculating a Final Price for Reference Obligation(s). The parties may choose the number of Valuation Dates. The valuation will be based on Quotations from Dealers. If the cash settlement is a fixed or pre-specified amount, this term is not applied.

[99]   The parties select between either a Single Valuation Date or Multiple Valuation Dates.

[100]   The fall-back is five.

[101]   The fall-back is five.

[102]   The fall-back is five.

[103]   The fall-back is 11.00 a.m. in the principal trading market for the Reference Obligation.

[104]   The parties must choose between Bid, Offer and Mid-market.

[105]   The fall-back is Bid.

[106]   Dealers will be asked to give Full Quotations for the Quotation Amount of the Reference Obligation.

[107]   The parties select between an amount in a currency or Representative Amount (defined as an amount that is representative for a single transaction in the relevant market at the relevant time as determined by the Calculation Agent in consultation with the parties). The fall-back is the Floating Rate Payer Calculation Amount.

[108]   If Full Quotations are not available, Dealers will be asked to give quotations for at least the Minimum Quotation Amount of the Reference Obligations. A Market Value calculated using such quotations will be the Weighted Average Quotation. If no Weighted Average Quotation is available, the Market Value will be deemed to be zero.

[109]   The fall-back is the lesser of the Quotation Amount and US$1,000,000.

Dealers:	[4 dealers][110]
Settlement Currency:[111]	US$[112]
Cash Settlement Date:	Three Business Days[113]
Cash Settlement Amount:[114]	The greater of (a) Floating Rate Payer Calculation Amount multiplied by the excess of the Reference Price over the Final Price (if a positive amount) and (b) zero[115]
Quotations:	Exclude Accrued Interest[116]
Valuation Method:	Average Highest[117]

Terms Relating to
Physical Settlement:[118]

Physical Settlement Period:	Five Business Days[119]

---

[110] If no Dealers are specified, they will be selected by the Calculation Agent in consultation with the parties.

[111] The Cash Settlement Amount will be payable in the Settlement Currency.

[112] The fall-back is the currency of the Floating Rate Payer Calculation Amount.

[113] The fall-back is three Business Days following calculation of the Final Price.

[114] If the parties agree at the outset to fix any payments by the Seller following a Credit Event, this should be specified here and the Cash Settlement Date will be three Business Days following satisfaction of all applicable Conditions to Payment.

[115] This is the wording in the 2003 Definitions. The 1999 Definitions refer to the difference between the Reference Price and the Final Price.

[116] If not specified, then the Calculation Agent will determine whether Quotations should include or exclude accrued interest based on current market practice.

[117] Depending on the number of Reference Obligations and Valuation Dates, parties must choose between Market; Highest Average Market; Highest; Average Highest; Blended Market; Blended Highest; Average Blended Market; and Average Blended Highest.

[118] This confirmation provides for *both* cash and physical settlement. This is for purposes of illustration only. This would not normally be the case. In practice, one form of settlement would be selected. Subject to contrary agreement between the parties, the Partial Cash Settlement Terms contained in the Credit Definitions apply automatically in the context of events rendering it impossible or illegal for the Buyer to Deliver or for the Seller to accept Delivery of the Deliverable Obligations on or prior to the Latest Permissible Physical Settlement Date. This should be distinguished from the Partial Cash Settlement of Consent Required Loans, Partial Cash Settlement of Assignable Loans and Partial Cash Settlement of Participations provisions, which are elective. If applicable for any reason, the Partial Cash Settlement Terms will apply in the form prescribed in the Credit Derivatives Definitions unless contrary provision is made by the parties in the Confirmation.

[119] The fall-back is whatever is usual market practice for the Obligations concerned.

Deliverable Obligations:[120]	Exclude Accrued Interest[121]	
Deliverable Obligations:[122]	*Deliverable Obligation Category:*[123]	*Deliverable Obligation Characteristics:*[124]
	Bond or Loan	Not Subordinated Specified Currency[125] Not Contingent[126] Assignable Loan Consent Required Loan Direct Loan Participation[127] Qualifying Participation Seller: any bank rated at least AA or higher[128] Maximum Maturity: 30 years[129]

Excluded Deliverable Obligations: None[130]

---

[120] Following a Credit Event Notice, the Buyer must give the Seller notice of the Deliverable Obligations and amount of Deliverable Obligations it will deliver. The Buyer may give more than one successive Notice of Physical Settlement provided that the cumulative amount to be delivered does not exceed the Notional Amount.

[121] The fall-back is to exclude accrued but unpaid interest.

[122] The Buyer may include in the Portfolio delivered to the Seller any Obligations in the category and with the characteristics specified.

[123] The parties should select only one category from Payment; Borrowed Money; Reference Obligations Only; Bond; Loan; or Bond or Loan.

[124] The parties should select any characteristics from Not Subordinated; Specified Currency; Not Sovereign Lender; Not Domestic Currency; Not Domestic Law; Listed; Not Contingent; Not Domestic Issuance; Assignable Loan; Consent Required Loan; Direct Loan Participation; Transferable; Maximum Maturity; Accelerated or Matured; and Not Bearer.

[125] See discussion above.

[126] Not contingent primarily excludes Obligations where payments are subject to a contingency or determined by reference to a formula or index. However, it expressly does not prevent delivery of convertible or zero-coupon bonds. See discussion later in this Chapter.

[127] A loan participation is a back-to-back arrangement where the lender of record manufactures payments to the participating party equal to receipts on the loan in return for funding or an indemnity.

[128] The Seller will take counterparty credit risk on any Participation Seller.

[129] The maximum period to maturity for any delivered Obligation is calculated from the Physical Settlement Date.

[130] The fall-back is none.

Partial Cash Settlement of Consent Required Loans:[131]   Not applicable
Partial Cash Settlement of Assignable Loans:[132]   Not applicable
Partial Cash Settlement of Participations:[133]   Not applicable
Escrow:[134]   Not Applicable

5. Notice and Account Details

Telephone, Telex and/or: ●
Facsimile Numbers and
Contact Details for Notices:
                              Buyer:
                              Seller:
Account Details
Account Details of Buyer: For A/C of Party B
Account Details of Seller: For A/C of Party A

6. Offices:

Seller:
Buyer:

Closing

Please confirm your agreement to be bound by the terms of the foregoing by executing a copy of this Confirmation and returning it to us [by facsimile].

Yours sincerely,

PARTY A

By: _____

        Name:
        Title:

---

[131] Partial Cash Settlement will apply if Physical Settlement is illegal or impossible but the parties must elect if they also wish Partial Cash Settlement to apply where a Loan cannot be assigned due to lack of any requisite consents.

[132] Partial Cash Settlement will apply if Physical Settlement is illegal or impossible but the parties must elect if they also wish Partial Cash Settlement to apply where a Loan cannot be assigned due to lack of any requisite consents.

[133] Partial Cash Settlement will apply if Physical Settlement is illegal or impossible but the parties must elect if they also wish Partial Cash Settlement to apply where a Participation cannot be effected for any Loan.

[134] Physical Settlement is on a delivery versus payment basis, but either party may require that Physical Settlement takes place using an escrow agent. The Schedule to an ISDA Master Agreement may contain additional provisions relating to the appointment of an escrow agent, but unless otherwise stated these provisions will override in the event of any inconsistency (Section 1(b) of the ISDA Master Agreement).

Confirmed as of the date
   first above written:

PARTY B

By: _____

    Name:
    Title:

7.2.2 Reference Entity

The reference entity is, in effect, the reference obligor underlying the credit default swap. The credit default swap transaction operates to trigger a settlement payment by the seller of protection to the buyer of protection upon the occurrence of a specified credit event affecting the reference entity. In the case of both total return swaps and credit spread transactions, a reference asset is needed. In contrast, in the case of a credit default swap, a reference entity concept is required. The 2003 Definitions cover both sovereign and non-sovereign entities[135]. In the case of a credit default swap on a sovereign entity, the reference entity needs to be identified clearly[136]. This reflects the fact that the sovereign state may act through multiple entities. The 2003 Definitions are primarily designed for use with a single reference entity but can also be used with multiple reference entities.

---

[135] The original Long Form Confirmation was intended mainly for non-sovereign entities.

[136] There is a project initiated by leading dealers to pool data on reference entities; see Cass, Dwight "Goldman Sachs Project Aims To Ease Dispute Over Data" (April 2002) Risk 8–9; Jeffrey, Christopher "Top Dealers Plot Revival Of Project Red" (February 2003) Risk 10.

7.2.3   Reference Obligations

The buyer of protection in a credit default swap purchases an indemnity against a credit event on a reference entity. The extent of protection purchased is defined by the obligations covered.

The 2003 Definitions allow the scope of coverage to be specified as follows:

- Direct obligations of the reference entity[137].
- **Qualifying affiliate guarantees** – this option covers obligations of downstream affiliates guaranteed by the reference entity. Downstream affiliate refers to entities where the reference entity directly or indirectly owns more than 50% of the voting shares (shares or other interests that have the power to elect the Board of Directors).
- **All guarantees** – this option covers obligations *of third parties* guaranteed by the reference entities. One or more of the obligation's characteristics[138] must also be specified. These guarantees are referred to as "qualifying guarantees". The qualifying guarantee must have certain features:
  1. The benefit of the qualifying guarantee must be capable of being delivered together with the delivery of the underlying obligation.
  2. The qualifying guarantee must be capable of assertion against the reference entity.
  3. Qualifying guarantees are deemed to the same deliverable obligation category as the underlying obligation and must satisfy the not subordinated characteristic. In May 2003, ISDA issued a supplement that eliminates the requirement that the qualifying guarantee not be subordinated to any senior Borrowed Money obligation of the obligor. This means that unless "not subordinated" is selected as the obligation characteristic, an obligation guaranteed by the Reference Entity may qualify as an obligation even if subordinated.
  4. Qualifying guarantees and the underlying obligation must satisfy the specified obligation characteristics[139].

---

[137] See discussion below.

[138] These include not subordinated/subordinated; specified currency, not sovereign lender, not domestic currency, not domestic law, listed and not domestic issuance. See discussion below.

[139] These include listed, not contingent, not domestic issues, assignable loan, consent required loan, direct loan participation, transferable, maximum maturity, accelerated or matured and/or not bearer.

Qualifying guarantees do not include:

- Surety bonds, financial guarantee insurance policies and letters of credit.
- Any guarantee that can be discharged as a result of the occurrence of an event other than payment[140].

It is expected that qualifying affiliate guarantees will be standard in the US. This reflects concerns that "upstream" and "sidestream" guarantees may not be legally enforceable. It is likely that other jurisdictions (Europe, Japan, Asia and Australia/New Zealand) will use all guarantees as the market standard[141].

7.2.4   Reference Asset

A specific reference asset (known as a reference obligation) is only strictly required where there is cash settlement (based on the post default price of the specified bond or loan)[142]. In the case of physical settlement, generally *any* security (typically bond or loan) with specified characteristics is eligible for delivery. The reference asset is a specified traded bond or loan asset issued or guaranteed by the reference entity. The initial price of the asset must also be agreed between the parties at the commencement of the transaction, particularly where cash settlement based on the difference

---

[140]   For example, in the Marconi case in 2002, there was a guarantee between Marconi PLC and its subsidiary Marconi Corporation. The guarantee would be discharged once the parent company loans were repaid. In this case, Marconi Corporation bonds etc may not have been deliverable under credit default swaps on Marconi PLC as the guarantee could be discharged by the parent rather than Marconi Corporation's repayment. The approach of market participants was to deliver loans instead of bonds. This was designed to avoid the risk that the guarantee structure may make the bonds undeliverable. See (6 March 2003) Fitch Examines Effect of 2003 Credit Derivatives Definitions; Fitch Ratings; New York at 2; Francis, Chris, Kakodkar, Atish and Martin, Barnaby (16 April 2003) "Credit Derivative Handbook"; Merrill Lynch, London at 69.

[141]   ISDA issued a supplement in May 2003 amending the guarantee provisions in the 2003 Definitions.

[142]   A reference asset may also be needed to determine materiality. If materiality is a pre-condition to payment, then the initial spread to US$ LIBOR on an asset swap basis is also agreed to enable determination of materiality. See discussion later in this Chapter.

between the reference price and the post default price of the security is intended[143].

7.2.5   Transaction Dates

The key transaction dates include:

- **Trade date** – this is the date on which the effective terms of the transaction are agreed between the buyer and seller of protection.
- **Effective date** – this is usually the next business day after the trade date (under previous market practice, the effective date was 3 business days after the trade date). This refers to the date on which the transaction becomes effective. The effective date is important in that credit protection commences on that date. A credit event that occurs prior to that date is not covered.
- **Termination date** – this is the date on which the transaction ends. The credit default swap usually terminates after the agreed period of credit protection or where there is a credit event prior to the scheduled maturity at the time of the credit event.

The confirmation provides for the parties to agree to an extension of the maturity of the transaction in certain circumstances. These circumstances include a potential failure to pay and/or a potential repudiation/moratorium occurring prior to the scheduled Termination Date.

The Grace Period Extension provision is designed to cover the situation where there is a failure to pay on a credit event close to the termination date. It is only applicable where there is a failure to pay. The objective is to cover default on obligations where there is a lengthy grace (or cure period) during which the reference entity can cure a potential event of default from a failure to make a due payment. Where selected, this election has the effect of extending the period of credit protection to the end of the grace period.

The Repudiation/Moratorium Extension Condition works in a similar way where an announcement has been made but none of the other conditions to establish a repudiation/moratorium are satisfied before the

---

[143] A reference obligation is often specified in credit default swaps even if the transaction is to be settled by physical delivery. This may be important if the transaction is a hedge for a particular obligation of the Reference Entity. However, it is probably often force of habit. It may also be useful in the case of restructuring of the reference entity in allowing the establishment of a successor entity.

scheduled termination date. Again, where selected, this election has the effect of extending the period of credit protection.

7.2.6 Payment For Default Protection

The buyer of default protection pays a fee (known in the confirmation as the fixed amount). This fee is usually structured as a per annum amount paid quarterly or semi-annually. The fixed rate in the default swap accrues up to either the scheduled termination date or the date credit protection is triggered, whichever is earlier.

In some transactions, this fee is paid as a lump sum up-front amount. This amount is calculated as the fixed per annum fee discounted back to the effective date at an agreed interest rate. The lump sum up-front amount structure is primarily used to avoid credit exposure for the protection seller to the protection buyer. Where this structure is used, the parties may wish to add an adjustment or "claw back" provision. This requires the protection seller to repay the unamortised amount of the fee in the event of an early termination of the swap.

7.2.7 Credit Events[144]

Types of Credit Events

The occurrence of the credit event triggers the obligation of the seller of protection to make the default payment to the purchaser of default protection. The Credit Definitions allow specification of the following credit events:

1. Bankruptcy.
2. Failure to pay above a nominated de minimus threshold (say in excess of US$1 million) after expiration of a specific grace period (say, 2 to 5 business days).
3. Obligation default or obligation acceleration.
4. Repudiation or moratorium.
5. Restructuring.

There are significant issues in defining the credit events. This reflects the heterogeneous nature of credit obligations (sometimes even for the same borrower).

---

[144] See Brown, Claude "Material PAI'd Up – Defining The Credit Event In Credit Derivatives" (11 December 1996) Financial Products Issue 56 16–18.

In general, items 1, 2 and 5 are commonly used as credit events in credit default swaps for non-sovereign entities[145]. Where the obligor is sovereign, many of the same types of default events are relevant, but there are additional factors that must be considered. For example, the concept of a bankruptcy driven credit event is less applicable. Typical credit events for sovereign entities include items 2, 3, 4 and 5. In the case of sovereign entities, the range of obligations underlying the credit event may also be limited to foreign currency obligations from commercial lenders.

The credit events used are driven by the need for *public information* regarding the credit event, the importance of the event, transparency and lack of ambiguity. There are a number of other possibilities including ratings downgrades below an agreed threshold and credit event upon merger. The ratings downgrade provision and credit event upon merger provision are infrequently used. These are not included in the Credit Definitions.

Bankruptcy

The concept of bankruptcy is comprehensive and covers various types of insolvency proceedings in any jurisdiction. The precise application depends on the jurisdiction of incorporation of the reference entity[146]. Problems with the bankruptcy definition generally arise in emerging markets where comprehensive bankruptcy and insolvency laws may not exist or be immature[147]. The 2003 Definitions revise the provisions in the 1999

---

[145]   Historically, obligation default and obligation acceleration was commonly used.

[146]   The definition was also amended in the 2003 Definitions to exclude certain tests that were felt to be too subjective.

[147]   For example, on 6th October, 1998 the People's Bank of China ("PBOC") gave notice that Guangdong International Trust and Investment Corporation ("GITIC") was unable to pay its debts. PBOC required GITIC to cease business in order to protect creditors. PBOC revoked various regulatory licences. It appointed the Bank of China and Guangfa Securities Co. Ltd. to act as custodians of the assets of the banking and securities businesses of GITIC respectively. GITIC's other business (generally non-financial businesses that were profitable) would continue to operate with the same management. The PBOC also set up a liquidation committee to wind up GITIC under PRC law. There was no precedent for this action under PRC law. It was not clear how these announcements affected credit default swaps on GITIC or whether they constituted an event of bankruptcy. The events, in practice, represented a potential credit event under several different provisions. PBOC's announcement

Definitions to exclude preliminary steps a company might take to try to avoid insolvency[148].

Obligations of the Reference Entity

All credit events other than bankruptcy refer to the obligations of the reference entity. The obligations of the reference entity can be confined to the reference asset or obligation. In practice, the range of obligations used is considerably wider. This is achieved through a concept of obligation categories and characteristics[149]. The categories and characteristics allow the parties to define the range of obligations on which a credit event will trigger payment under the credit default swap.

The categories of obligations include:

- **Reference obligation only** – this includes only the securities/obligations specified to be reference obligations.
- **Bond, loan and bond or loan** – this includes any amounts owed under a certificated debt security (bond), a term or revolving loan (loan) or a combination of the two (bond or loan). The 2003 Definitions make clear that a revolving loan is only included to the extent any advances have been made.

---

that GITIC was unable to pay its debts may have constituted a debt moratorium or repudiation. The winding-up proceedings instituted were less clear. PBOC had acted independently of any judicial authorities. The bankruptcy credit event refers to the appointment of an administrator, provisional liquidator, conservator, receiver, trustee, custodian or similar official over all (or substantially all) the assets of the Reference Entity. However, the provision has different meanings under English or New York law (one of which will be the governing law of the ISDA Master Agreement and/or Confirmation). This created concern about the operation of the credit event provisions in credit default swaps involving GITIC. See Whiteley, Christopher "Credit Derivatives: Documentation And Legal Issues" in Das, Satyajit (Editor) (2001) Credit Derivatives & Credit Linked Notes – Second Edition; John Wiley & Sons, Singapore at Chapter 17 at 700.

[148] For example, in the Marconi case, the company allegedly made statements that could have been interpreted as falling within Clause 4.2(i) of the 1999 definitions ("takes any action in furtherance of, or indicating in, any of the forgoing acts"). This caused some buyers of protection under credit default swaps to consider triggering a credit event.

[149] The same categories and an extended set of characteristics are used to specify the deliverable obligations; see discussion later in this Chapter.

- **Borrowed money** – this includes bonds or loans but is broader. It specifically includes deposits and drawings under a letter of credit. It may also include other forms of finance such as asset backed transactions (leases and title retention security financing).
- **Payment** – this covers any payment obligation including bonds, loans, guarantees, derivative payments, repurchase agreements, collateral payments, trade payables and other payment obligations.

The characteristics of obligations include:

- **Not Subordinated**[150] – this means an obligation that is not subordinated to the most senior reference obligation in priority of payment, or if no reference obligation is specified, then any unsecured and unsubordinated borrowed money obligation of the Reference Entity.
- **Specified Currency** – the obligation currency must be specified. If specified currency applies and no further details are given then it is taken to mean the lawful currencies of any of Canada, Japan, Switzerland, United Kingdom and the United States of America and the Euro (and any successor currency to any such currency) under the 2003 Definitions (Switzerland is excluded under the 1999 Definitions).
- **Listed** – this limits the obligations, if applicable, to bonds listed and/or traded on an exchange.
- **Not sovereign lender/not domestic currency/not domestic law/not domestic issuance** – these provisions are principally directed at sovereign entities. This reflects the desire to limit the credit event to a default in foreign currency debt to commercial lenders. The application of "not sovereign" requires that the obligation must not be owed to a sovereign or supranational organisation (for example, "Paris Club" debt). The "not domestic currency" (excluding the standard specified currencies) and "not domestic law" characteristics refer to the reference entity's own jurisdiction (if sovereign) or jurisdiction of the organisation (if not a sovereign). The "not domestic issuance" refers to the reference entity's domestic market.

---

150 In the 1999 Definitions, the phrase used is *Pari passu ranking*. The requirement is that the obligations must rank equally (pari passu) with the most senior reference obligation or (if none is specified) other unsecured debt of the reference entity.

The categories are mutually exclusive and only one is specified. A number of characteristics are generally selected.

In practice, credit default swaps generally specify the obligations as follows:

- **Category** – "bond or loan", or "borrowed money".
- **Characteristics** – obligation characteristics can be specified but sometimes are not; where specified the common characteristics include "not subordinated" and "specified currency". "Specified currency" is frequently augmented by other currencies relevant to the reference entity.
- **Default requirement** – the obligation must exceed a minimum threshold amount (deemed to be US$10 million unless otherwise agreed and specified).

Failure To Pay

This covers non payment by the reference entity of any amount due and payable under a specified obligation. The amount of the payment is subject to a minimum payment requirement (this is separate from the default requirement on the obligation specified above). The minimum amount is deemed to be US$1 million unless otherwise agreed and specified.

Obligation Default Or Acceleration

These credit events are equivalent to cross-acceleration or cross-default provisions in normal credit documentation. The difference between the two credit events is as follows. Under obligation acceleration, creditors must take action to require immediate payment of amounts owed under the relevant obligation. Under obligation default, creditors must have the right to take action but may or may not have done so. Credit acceleration is factual and reasonably easy to determine. Cross default is more difficult to establish in practice. For all practical purposes, the market ceased to use these credit events by late 2002. Obligation acceleration and default are retained in the 2003 Definitions.

Moratorium or Repudiation

This provision covers the position where the reference entity repudiates or declares a moratorium on its obligations. The provision also covers the position where a government declares a moratorium on the reference entity's obligations. This means that the credit default swap may transfer not just credit risk to the protection seller but also certain legal or political risks. The debt moratorium provisions are primarily relevant to credit default swaps involving sovereign reference entities.

The repudiation/moratorium provisions are substantially different in each of the Long-Form Confirmation, the 1999 Definitions and the 2003 Definitions. The 2003 Definitions set out a two stage test. There must be a declaration of a moratorium or repudiation of obligations by an authorised officer of the reference entity or government authority. This must be followed by a failure to pay within a given period (60 days for obligations other than bonds and, for a bond, 60 days or the first payment date under the bond, whichever is later). The term of the credit default swap is extended to cover any failure to pay following the declaration[151]. This is designed to protect against an unintended triggering of the credit event[152].

The 2003 Definitions provide a recommended form of Repudiation/ Moratorium Extension Notice to be given to trigger the extension of the termination date of the contract.

Restructuring

The original restructuring credit (in the long form confirmation) was based on a material restructuring of the payment obligations under the reference obligation or a forced substitution of new obligations. The question of materiality was difficult in practice, giving rise to disputes. The 1999 Definitions significantly refined the concept of restructuring.

Restructuring was specified as changes in the terms of the reference obligations including[153]:

- The ranking of the debt.
- Change in the currency of payment (other than into certain permitted currencies (G-7 currency or OECD member with a local currency long-term debt rating of either AAA or higher)).
- Reduction in interest or principal payable.

---

[151]   See discussion earlier in this Chapter.
[152]   For example, there was significant debate in the case of Argentina in 2002 as to whether a repudiation/moratorium event had taken place.
[153]   The 1999 Definitions define restructuring to include "obligation exchange" being the mandatory transfer of new assets, securities or obligations in exchange for existing obligations. The 2003 Definitions eliminate the concept of obligation exchange from the definition of restructuring.

- Change in the date of payment or amount of any interest or principal and/or deferral/postponement of either the payment/accrual of interest or principal.

The 1999 Definitions also added a provision that Restructuring is not considered to have occurred where it is not directly or indirectly related to deterioration in the creditworthiness or financial condition of the reference entity.

Restructuring has been among the most controversial credit events. It gave rise to problems in practice which were initially addressed through a number of Supplements. These Supplements have now been incorporated in the 2003 Definitions. The 2003 Definitions provide a choice between several formulations based on different market practice in the United States and in Europe[154].

7.2.8   Credit Event Notice

A credit event triggers the settlement obligations under a credit default swap. The settlement obligation is subject to three conditions to payment. These conditions are a credit event notice, notice of publicly available information (if applicable) and a notice of intended physical settlement (where the transaction is physically settled).

The credit event notice advises the seller of protection that a credit event has occurred, triggering the settlement. The parties can agree that the credit event notice can be given by the protection buyer, or either the protection buyer or seller. The fallback position is the protection buyer. In practice, the protection buyer or seller is generally specified. This creates an interesting timing option. This reflects the fact that a *seller of protection* may want to force settlement on a credit default swap. This will primarily be to limit its potential loss under the transaction. It may also be designed to protect the seller of protection where it has to trigger an offsetting hedge. This is disadvantageous to the buyer of protection who may not be able to replace the contract and may suffer losses in excess of that covered by the triggered credit default swap.

A Credit Event Notice must contain a reasonably detailed description of the facts relevant to the determination that a Credit Event has occurred. The 2003 Definitions set out a recommended form of Credit Event Notice.

---

[154]   See discussion later in this Chapter.

Exhibit 1.17 sets out the forms of the credit event notice and notice of publicly available information. **Exhibit 1.18** sets out the notice of physical settlement.

Exhibit 1.17   Credit Default Swaps – Credit Event Notice

Credit Event Notice

[Date]

[Counterparty Address and Contact Information]
[Non-party Calculation Agent Address and Contact Information]

CREDIT EVENT NOTICE
[AND NOTICE OF PUBLICLY AVAILABLE INFORMATION][155]

Credit Derivative Transaction Details: [Trade Date], [Effective Date], [Reference Entity], [Basket of Credit Derivative Transactions]

Reference is made to the Credit Derivative Transaction between [   ], as Seller, and [   ], as Buyer. Capitalized terms used and not otherwise defined in this letter shall have the meanings given them in the confirmation of the Transaction.

This letter is our Credit Event Notice to you that a [insert type] Credit Event occurred with respect to [insert name] on or about [insert date], when [describe Credit Event].

[This letter also comprises our Notice of Publicly Available Information with respect to this Credit Event. Accordingly, we provide the Publicly Available Information attached hereto.]

Nothing in this letter shall be construed of a waiver of any rights we may have with respect to the Transaction.

Sincerely,

[insert name]

Name:
Title:

ISDA Credit Derivatives Confirmation Copyright © 2003 by INTERNATIONAL SWAPS AND DERIVATIVES ASSOCIATION, INC. 360 Madison Avenue, 16th Floor New York, N.Y. 10017

---

[155]   The bracketed words in the Notice's title and the third paragraph of the Notice need only be included when Notice of Publicly Available Information is specified as Applicable in the related Confirmation.

Exhibit 1.18 Credit Default Swaps – Credit Event Notice/Notice of Physical Settlement

[Date]

[Counterparty Address and Contact Information]

[Non-party Calculation Agent Address and Contact Information]

NOTICE OF PHYSICAL SETTLEMENT

Credit Derivative Transaction Details: [Trade Date], [Effective Date], [Reference Entity], [Basket of Credit Derivative Transactions]

Reference is made to the Credit Derivative Transaction described above (the "Transaction") between [   ], as Seller, and [   ], as Buyer. Reference is also made to the Credit Event Notice [and Notice of Publicly Available Information][156] dated [insert date], previously delivered to you on [insert date].

This letter constitutes a Notice of Physical Settlement. Any capitalized term not otherwise defined in this letter will have the meaning, if any, assigned to such term in the confirmation of the Transaction or, if no meaning is specified therein, in the 2003 ISDA Credit Derivatives Definitions.

We hereby confirm that we will settle the Transaction and require performance by you in accordance with the Physical Settlement Method. Subject to the terms of the Transaction, we will deliver to you on or before the Physical Settlement Date, [[currency/amount]] [outstanding principal balance] [Due and Payable Amount]] of the following Deliverable Obligations:

[describe the Deliverable Obligations to be Delivered, including the outstanding principal balance or Due and Payable Amount for each such Deliverable Obligation] and, if available, the CUSIP or ISIN number (if such identifying number is not available, the rate and tenor of the Deliverable Obligation)].

Yours sincerely,

[insert name]

---

[156] The bracketed language need only be included when Notice of Publicly Available Information is specified as Applicable in the related Confirmation.

7.2.9   Publicly Available Information

The existence of a credit event is usually determined on the basis of publicly available information. This approach is standard to credit default swaps. The standard requirement is for a minimum of two reputable information sources[157]. Information from judicial or equivalent proceedings is also regarded as publicly available information. This provision is required because it is assumed that the seller or buyer of protection does not have a contractual relationship with the reference entity. This means that the parties will only become aware of the occurrence of a credit event from public sources of information.

7.2.10   Settlement After Credit Event[158]

Settlement Mechanisms

Following the occurrence of a credit event, the buyer of protection is compensated by a payment from the seller of protection which is designed to match the erosion of value in the underlying bond or loan arising from the credit event. There are a number of possible types of post default payment, including:

- **Cash settlement** – this can take the following forms:
  1. *Post default price* – this is based on the price of the reference asset following the credit event.
  2. *Fixed payout* – this is based on a pre-agreed fixed percentage of notional principal.
- **Physical Settlement** – this is structured as the payment of an agreed amount by the seller of protection in exchange for delivery of a defaulted credit asset by the buyer of protection.

In practice, physical settlement is the most commonly used settlement mechanism. If cash settlement is used, then the post default price mechanism is preferred[159].

---

[157]   The long form confirmation excluded information from interested parties to ensure that there is no conflict of interest. Under the 2003 Definitions, information will qualify even if a party or its affiliate is cited as the sole source of information, provided that it is acting in the capacity of trustee, fiscal agent, administrative agent, clearing agent or paying agent for an obligation.

[158]   See Brown, Claude "Credit Derivative Payout Mechanisms" (5 March 1997) IFR Financial Products Issue 61 18–22.

[159]   See Cass, Dwight "The Devil's In The Details" (August 2000) Risk 26–28.

Settlement Timing

The timing of settlement varies between the different post default payment structures. Where physical settlement is used, the length of time of the physical settlement period is agreed by the parties and specified (generally 3 to 5 business days). If not specifically agreed, then the physical settlement period is the time, determined by the calculation agent, that it will take to settle all the assets being delivered in accordance with normal market practice. Where the cash settlement option is used, payment is made an agreed number of days after the post default price has been established.

7.2.11 Cash Settlement

The basic concept underlying cash settlement based on post default price is that the seller of protection pays the buyer of protection an amount equal to the erosion in value of the reference asset as a result of the credit event. This is calculated as the notional principal of the credit default swap multiplied by the percentage change in the price of the reference obligation as determined by dealer poll or from price quote services. The process of cash settlement requires the calculation agent to value the reference obligation.

The process has a number of components:

- **Dealers** – a number of dealers are included in the dealer poll method (generally 4 to 6 dealers are used). There is provision to substitute dealers where a specified dealer ceases to exist or to be an active dealer in the relevant obligations.
- **Valuation dates** – the parties select either a single or multiple valuation dates. Multiple valuation dates are frequently used to reduce the risks in establishing a "true" market price. It is usual to include a series of polls (usually 3 to 6 valuation dates) rather than rely on a single valuation date. Where cash settlement is used, the agreed sequence of polls is conducted soon after the credit event (5 to 20 business days) at intervals of 5 to 20 days between valuation dates. This has the effect of extending the amount of time before actual settlement occurs. **Exhibit 1.19** sets out a typical time line of events in establishing a post credit event payment.
- **Calculation** – the calculation requires a valuation using quotations from reference dealers for a specified amount of the relevant reference obligation. The parties must agree whether quotations used should be the highest given or a market value using the average of quotations from several dealers. The parties must agree whether quotations should be based on bid, offer or mid prices (in practice, bid prices are generally

used). The calculation agent calculates the average value over the nominated valuation dates (where multiple valuation dates are used). The settlement amount payable by the protection seller to the protection buyer equals the product of the notional amount of the transaction multiplied by the difference between the reference price agreed at the outset of the transaction and the final price calculated.

- **Quotations** – the valuation process requires dealers to supply quotations to enable the post credit event price to be established. Prices for the bonds can be quoted as including or excluding accrued interest. The form of quotation must be agreed. In practice, accrued interest is generally excluded. On the reference entity's insolvency, claims for interest will normally rank junior to any other claims. If not specified, then the calculation agent will determine whether accrued interest is to be included or excluded based on market practice. Quotations are required to be firm bids by dealers for the reference obligation with a face (due and payable) value equal to or greater than the agreed quotation amount. If no amount is specified, then the Credit Definitions specify that this is the nominal amount of the credit default swap. If it is impossible to obtain quotations for the stated amount, then the Calculation Agent can seek quotations for a lower amount of the reference obligation. The lower amount may be agreed by the parties. If not specified, then the minimum amount is specified to be the lower of the nominal amount of the transaction and US$1,000,000. The level of the minimum amount is important. If no quotations for the minimum amount are available from the dealers, then the value of the relevant reference obligation is deemed to be zero. This triggers a payment by the seller of protection to the buyer of protection equal to the full face value of the transaction. The Credit Definitions include provisions to take into account partial quotations in determining a weighted average quotation.
- **Substitution of reference obligations** – cash settlement is based on the change in value of the reference obligation. The Credit Definitions provide for substitution of the reference obligation where the obligation is redeemed or the amount outstanding is materially reduced by redemption or otherwise (other than scheduled amortisation). Substitution is also permitted where the obligation ceases to be an obligation of or guaranteed by the reference entity.

The establishment of a post credit event value of reference obligations to effect a cash settlement presents problems. The calculation of a post credit event value assumes a liquid distressed debt market and a transparent/ objective polling process. It assumes that the recovery value evident in the valuation process matches the actual recovery rate achieved by the buyer of protection in the credit position being hedged. The conditions specified are not satisfied in all circumstances. In practice, the credit derivatives market favours physical settlement.

Exhibit 1.19   Credit Default Swaps – Determination Of Payout

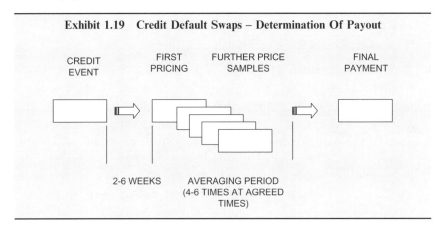

7.2.12   Physical Settlement

Concept

The concept underlying physical delivery is that the buyer of protection delivers a defaulted bond or loan to the seller of protection. The seller of protection must pay the buyer of protection the notional face value of the credit default swap (or a lesser fixed amount if agreed at the time of entry into the transaction).

Physical settlement is designed to realise a gain for the buyer of protection equal to the difference between the face value of the contract and the market value of obligations of the reference entity following the occurrence of a credit event. Physical settlement requires the buyer of protection to deliver a notice of physical settlement.

In the 1999 Definitions, the notice of physical settlement was primarily designed to serve as a notice of intention to deliver specified assets in settlement of the contract. In the 2003 Definitions, the notice of settlement is an express delivery undertaking. If the Buyer does not deliver as promised, the 2003 Definitions give the seller of protection a right to perform its obligations by buying-in bond assets and making payment of the difference between the buy-in price and the reference price to the buyer of protection under the contract. This provision under a credit default swap allows the seller of protection to purchase bonds from a non-affiliated party to settle a contract where the purchaser has failed to deliver within the permitted settlement period. Under the buy-in, the seller of protection deducts the loss of purchasing the bonds from par value and pays the difference to the protection buyer. This is designed to ensure the integrity of the settlement process.

Physical settlement has a number of components:

- **Deliverable obligations** – the buyer of protection may deliver any one of a number of eligible deliverable obligations. Deliverable obligations are specified by a system of nominated categories and characteristics. This is similar to the range of obligations used in calculating credit events. The types of eligible deliverable obligations are discussed in detail below. The ability to deliver any obligation from a range of obligations creates a degree of optionality in the credit default swap. This is referred to as the "cheapest-to-deliver" feature in a credit default swap. In practice, this means that the buyer of protection will generally always deliver the obligation with the lowest market trading price within the range of deliverable obligations. This will be the case irrespective of the specific credit obligation being hedged. It may also affect the pricing of obligations post-default, in that buyers of protection may pay a premium to acquire a deliverable obligation.
- **Face value of bonds to be delivered** – the buyer must deliver obligations equal to the notional value of the credit default swap. In practice, accrued interest is generally excluded. This creates some problems with zero coupon or deeply discounted securities[160].
- **Delivery process** – the delivery process used is specified and designed to ensure that the seller receives good title to the relevant obligations. The delivery process is discussed in detail below.
- **Inability to deliver** – there may be circumstances where settlement by physical delivery is illegal or impossible. Illegality or impossibility is defined as any event occurring that affects the obligations of either the protection seller or buyer. The event is also beyond the control of the parties. Impossibility includes clearing/settlement system failure.

---

[160]   See discussion later in this Chapter.

Illegality expressly includes the effect of any law, regulation or court order. The wording specifically excludes market conditions or a failure to obtain consent to assignment in relation to a loan. In identified situations, the parties may instead choose to deliver through an affiliate. Cash settlement applies where physical settlement cannot be undertaken because of illegality and impossibility. The Credit Definitions also permit the parties to elect that cash settlement will apply in cases where it proves impossible to assign loans or to transfer loans via participation agreements.

Deliverable Obligations

This term is used to specify the range of obligations eligible for delivery by the protection buyer to the protection seller. The deliverable obligations are specified by a similar system of categories and characteristics that is used to specify obligations for the purpose of a credit event. The categories include *reference obligation only, bond, loan, bond or loan, borrowed money* or *payment*. The characteristics of obligations include *not subordinated, specified currency, not contingent, listed and not sovereign lender/not domestic currency/not domestic law/not domestic issuance.*

There are a number of additional potential characteristics for deliverable obligations:

- **Not contingent** – if applicable, this means that any obligation where payment is structured by reference to a formula or index or subject to a contingency is excluded. This is designed to exclude structured notes (where no principal may in fact be payable due to the operation of the formula). In practice, this created problems with convertibles and zero coupon securities[161]. Under the 2003 Definitions, convertible/exchangeable bonds and zero coupon securities are not treated as contingent securities[162].

- **Assignable loan/consent required loan/direct loan participation/transferable** – these provisions relate to physical delivery of a loan obligation. The Credit Definitions specifically encompass the ability to deliver loans only to the extent agreed by the parties. "Assignable loan" refers to loans that are freely transferable. The test of transferability is whether the

---

[161] For a discussion of structured notes, see Das, Satyajit (2004) Swaps/Financial Derivatives – 3rd Edition; John Wiley & Sons, Singapore at Chapter 38.

[162] See discussion later in this Chapter.

obligation can be transferred to institutional investors. "Consent required loan" refers to loans that require the consent of the reference entity or borrower to any assignment. Where a loan cannot be assigned, an interest in the loan can be economically transferred through a loan participation. This is structured as a back-to-back arrangement where receipts under the loan are paid over by the original lender to the loan sub-participant. The structure entails the participant taking credit risk on the borrower and the original lender. The 1999 Definitions distinguish between "direct loan participation" (where payments are received from a person with a direct relationship with the borrower) and an "indirect loan participation" (where payments are received down a chain of persons involving credit risk on each one). Where a loan participation is allowed, the seller of protection will generally place restrictions on the credit quality of any bank through which it takes its participation in order to control its credit risk. The 2003 Definitions only permit direct participations. The 2003 Definitions also include a fallback provision whereby (except in certain circumstances) the buyer of protection can deliver bonds or assignable loans in substitution for consent-required loan assets where the buyer has failed, after reasonable efforts, to obtain any necessary consent. The 2003 Definitions provide a right, subject to certain conditions, for the seller of protection to require such delivery in the same circumstances.

- **Maximum maturity** – the parties may also agree a maximum maturity for any deliverable obligations. It is common for the maximum maturity to be limited to 30 years. The maximum maturity is calculated from the settlement date. This is usually included to avoid any maturity restrictions on the party selling protection. It is also used to avoid delivery of an undated (perpetual) obligation because of uncertainty as to its status as debt or equity.

- **Accelerated or matured** – the parties may also agree that any delivered obligations must be due and payable (whether or not as a result of the relevant credit event). This is generally to allow the seller of protection upon delivery to establish its claim against the obligor in bankruptcy or other legal proceedings. It may also be designed to ensure that the delivered obligation can be traded and cleared in a custodial or settlement system.

- **Not bearer** – the parties may also agree that deliverable obligations may not be in bearer form (that is, payable to bearer and so transferable by a mere transfer of physical possession of the obligation). The restriction on delivery of a bearer security is used where the seller of protection may be prevented from taking delivery of bearer securities (for example, US investors).

The categories are mutually exclusive and only one is specified. A number of characteristics are generally selected. In practice, credit default swaps generally specify the following as deliverable obligations:

- **Category** – bond or loan (including consent required loans) are normally used.
- **Characteristics** – for non-sovereign entities, not subordinated, specified currency, not contingent and maximum maturity is normally used. Listed and/or not bearer may be specified where the seller of protection is restricted as to the types of obligations of which it can take delivery. For sovereign entities, the range of characteristics would be extended to avoid the delivery of official debt or local currency obligations.

Delivery Process

The buyer of protection must provide the seller with a notice of intended physical settlement. The notice must specify reasonable indications of the type and amount of deliverable obligations that the buyer expects to deliver. Physical settlement must take place within an agreed period or a period based on market practice for the obligations being delivered. The protection buyer can decide whether to exercise its rights in relation to the full nominal amount of the transaction or only in part.

If the protection buyer chooses to deliver obligations denominated in currencies other than the agreed base currency, then the value of the obligations will be converted into the base currency at spot exchange rates.

The protection buyer must deliver full title to the delivered obligations. The delivered obligations must be free of any set-off, counterclaim or defence that the reference entity might have against the protection buyer. This excludes counterclaims or defences relating to the legality or validity of the obligation.

It is not uncommon for problems to arise. This has been the case particularly with loans that may not be easily transferable. Physical settlement may also raise particular issues where the relevant credit event is bankruptcy of the reference entity. This is because bankruptcy requires that the rights of all creditors against the insolvent entity are eventually accelerated and valued as of a specified date. This typically will take some time as the court will want to establish details of the debtor's financial position prior to any determination of insolvency. In practice, a credit event will therefore occur and the Buyer's rights exercised prior to the relevant date. However, once a winding-up order is made, this process entails a change in the obligations of the reference entity. After bankruptcy, in the liquidation proceedings each creditor has the same right to prove for payment at the insolvency dividend rate. The value of the proof is defined by reference to whatever previously existed. The legal nature of the proof is a totally new claim with different rights. This may be problematic if the transfer potentially changed rights of set-off or if the proof is not assignable. The problem is jurisdiction specific and needs to be carefully considered.

The 1999 Definitions allowed a 5 business day settlement period. This created a problem whereby a buyer of protection might not be able to take advantage of the contract as a result of the inability to deliver an obligation[163]. The 2003 Definitions provide an alternative delivery process that is complex.

If the Buyer is unable to deliver the specified obligation within the 5 business day period, then the Seller can invoke alternative settlement procedures:

- If the deliverable obligation is a bond, then the Seller can elect to buy-in bonds by delivering a notice to the Buyer with at least 2 business days notice. The provision requires the Seller to seek a minimum of five dealer quotes. The Seller accepts the lowest quote. The Seller settles with the Buyer 3 business days later based on par less the price of the bond (adjusted for brokerage costs).
- If the deliverable obligation is a consent required loan and the Buyer is unable to deliver, having made reasonable efforts to obtain consent, then the Seller can require the Buyer to deliver alternative obligation. This is subject to the condition that the Seller can identify holders who are

---

[163] The case of TXU illustrated the problem. In 2002, TXU Europe filed for bankruptcy. However, many credit default swaps were written on TXU Europe Group. TXU Europe Group did not have any outstanding deliverable obligations. TXU did have an inter-company loan from TXU Acquisitions Ltd (a related company). The loan terms were complex and made it unattractive as a deliverable obligation. Buyers of protection on TXU Europe Group attempted to have the administrator facilitate the sale of TXU Europe's inter-company loans in order to settle credit default swap contracts. [See (6 March 2003) Fitch Examines Effect of 2003 Credit Derivatives Definitions; Fitch Ratings; New York at 8.]

willing to sell the obligation. The Seller must also be able to take delivery without consent of a third party.

The effect of the alternative settlement provisions is to ensure that Buyers do not lose the benefit of the contract if they fail to make delivery[164]. In 2003, ISDA introduced an optional 60 business day cap on settlement that is invoked by the parties by entering into a separate letter agreement.

7.3   Documentation Issues

7.3.1   Overview

The documentation of credit derivatives raises a number of interesting legal issues. The credit default swap documentation framework has also evolved over time. The changes reflect the impact of market events that have highlighted problems or ambiguities within the documentation. This has led to changes/refinements to the documentation. A number of major problem areas have emerged. The documentary issues and specific problems that have emerged in the market are considered in this Section.

7.3.2   Insurance[165]

The structure of a credit derivative contract is similar to an insurance contract. This has created concerns that a credit default swap is an insurance contract. The implications of treatment of a credit default swap as an insurance contract would vary between jurisdictions. These may include:

- The entry into the contract would be illegal unless the seller of protection held appropriate authorisation/licenses as an insurance company. This may result in potential penalties for the seller of protection and render the contract unenforceable at law by one or both parties.
- The buyer of protection (as the insured party) would be subject to the duty to act with utmost good faith (*uberrimae fides*). This would require full disclosure of all risks associated with the reference entity. This would be contrary to market practice where the seller must rely on its own

---

[164]   Under the 1999 Definitions, a failure to deliver could cause the Buyer to lose the benefit of the contract.

[165]   See Whiteley, Christopher "Credit Derivatives: Documentation And Legal Issues" in Das, Satyajit (Editor) (2001) Credit Derivatives & Credit Linked Notes – Second Edition; John Wiley & Sons, Singapore at Chapter 17 at 673–679.

inquiries as to the standing of the reference entity. In the absence of disclosure, the seller of protection (the insurer) may not be liable to make any payment in the case of a credit event.

- The buyer of protection must have an insurable interest in the underlying risk and must be able to identify the specific loss suffered. In practice, this may not be feasible in a credit derivative contract.

The opinion overall appears to be that credit derivatives are not insurance contracts. This reflects the structure of the contract requiring that payment is triggered by an event and not triggered by a proven loss.

7.3.3 Guarantee[166]

The structure of a credit derivative is analogous in certain respects to a guarantee[167]. Classification at law of a credit default swap as a guarantee would also create problems. This is because of the specific treatment of guarantees under the law. These include the doctrine of construing the terms of a guarantee strictly in favour of the guarantor, the proof of loss and the guarantor's right of indemnity against the obligor. The commercial intention of the parties to a credit default swap is significantly different to that of a guarantee. The general legal opinion appears to take the view that credit derivatives are not guarantees.

7.3.4 Confidentiality[168]

The Credit Definitions and the credit default swap confirmation contain representations that make it clear that:

- The parties are free to enter into any private arrangements with the reference entity. This includes the extension of credit or contingent liability transactions such as derivative transactions. These transactions are other than the credit default swap between the parties.

---

[166] See Whiteley, Christopher "Credit Derivatives: Documentation And Legal Issues" in Das, Satyajit (Editor) (2001) Credit Derivatives & Credit Linked Notes – Second Edition; John Wiley & Sons, Singapore at Chapter 17 at 681–685.

[167] The regulatory treatment of credit derivatives is frequently based on this analogy; see discussion later in this Chapter.

[168] See Whiteley, Christopher "Credit Derivatives: Documentation And Legal Issues" in Das, Satyajit (Editor) (2001) Credit Derivatives & Credit Linked Notes – Second Edition; John Wiley & Sons, Singapore at Chapter 17 at 711–713.

• The seller of protection is not relying on financial information or other disclosure regarding the reference entity from the buyer of protection.

This is designed to ensure that the contract does not require disclosure by the protection buyer to the protection seller. It is also designed to ensure that no duty of disclosure should be implied as a term of the transaction.

A bank may owe a duty of confidentiality to the underlying reference entity where it has dealings with the reference entity. These dealings may be the transaction giving rise to the credit exposure that the buyer seeks to hedge. The buyer of protection cannot provide any information to the seller where it would breach confidentiality.

Confidentiality may affect the determination of whether a Credit Event has occurred. A buyer of protection, through its dealings with the reference entity, may have knowledge that a Credit Event has occurred. However, it may be unable to use this because it cannot give the relevant information to the protection seller. In general, the notice of a Credit Event can only be given when information about the relevant event is publicly available. Publicly available information includes official court papers, judicial orders, decrees of any regulatory authority, information made available by a trustee or administrative agent for the relevant obligations or information published by any standard news services. A party cannot rely on any publicly available information where it or an associate is cited as the sole source of the information. The exception is where the information is corroborated or where it was provided by the party acting in a fiduciary capacity (for example, as trustee)[169].

---

[169] In one case which was litigated (Deutsche Bank AG v ANZ Banking Group Ltd), the information about a default by the City of Moscow was placed with a news service at the instigation of Daiwa Europe (a protection Buyer) to trigger a claim against Deutsche Bank AG. Deutsche Bank then (successfully) sought to use this information in making a claim under a back-to-back transaction with ANZ Banking Group Ltd. In effect, it does not matter how the information got into the public domain or whether it clearly reveals every detail. The defences raised by ANZ on these points were dismissed. See later in this Chapter and see Whiteley, Christopher "Credit Derivatives: Documentation And Legal Issues" in Das, Satyajit (Editor) (2001) Credit Derivatives & Credit Linked Notes – Second Edition; John Wiley & Sons, Singapore at Chapter 17 at 713.

7.3.5   Materiality[170]

During the early development phase of the market, the default event was sometimes linked to a concept of materiality to avoid an inadvertent or unintended triggering of a credit event. The concept of materiality was based on a *minimum* change in either the price of the bond or loan or in the spread of the bond or loan relative to a benchmark rate such as US$ LIBOR or US Treasury bonds.

The market practice evolved around the concept of an increase in the asset swap spread (over US$ LIBOR) by a pre-specified amount (say 150 bps). This was calculated by specifying the spread at the time of entry into the credit default swap and then comparing the initial spread to the prevailing market spread *following* a credit event.

This provision was designed to ensure that there has been a *true* credit event triggering the requirement to make the default payment and to avoid the possibility of triggering a credit event when there had not been, in reality, an event of default. Materiality was usually determined simultaneously with the post default price sampling used to determine the settlement payment. It is important to note that where materiality is a requirement, it is not an independent trigger but must coexist with the credit event to trigger the default payment.

The materiality provision was controversial, with considerable debate about its desirability and efficacy between major market practitioners. It is now rarely used in practice. The current short form confirmation does not refer to the concept of materiality in establishing a credit event.

7.3.6   Dispute Resolution[171]

The complexity of certain issues underlying credit default swap documentation dictates that there may be disputes between parties in certain situations. The earlier versions of the credit default swap confirmation and the 1999

---

[170] See Whiteley, Christopher "Credit Derivatives: Documentation And Legal Issues" in Das, Satyajit (Editor) (2001) Credit Derivatives & Credit Linked Notes – Second Edition; John Wiley & Sons, Singapore at Chapter 17 at 715–717.

[171] See Whiteley, Christopher "Credit Derivatives: Documentation And Legal Issues" in Das, Satyajit (Editor) (2001) Credit Derivatives & Credit Linked Notes – Second Edition; John Wiley & Sons, Singapore at Chapter 17 at 713–715.

Definitions suggested separate provisions for dispute resolution might be developed by ISDA. However these were never published and in the 2003 Definitions, all reference to separate dispute resolution provisions is deleted.

7.3.7 Establishing Credit Events

The process of establishing whether credit events have occurred under a credit default swap has been characterised by problems[172] which have been particularly evident in relation to sovereign reference entities. Problems have been encountered in Russia[173], the Asian crisis[174] and Argentina[175]. It is not clear whether the problems are directly related to the credit default swap documentation. They may be related to the process of sovereign defaults and debt restructuring generally[176].

In practice, the problems appear related to the following:

● **Identification of reference entity** – the inadequate specification of the reference entity[177] has been a significant source of problems. This was

---

[172]   See Leib, Barclay T. "What's Default?" (January 2001) Derivatives Strategy 22–27; Morris, Jennifer "The Difficulty Of Defining A Default" (April 2001) Euromoney 134–136.

[173]   See Falloon, William "The Devil In The Documentation" (November 1998) Risk 32–35; Abed, Kamal "Cross Defaults In Moscow" (January 1999) Futures & OTC World 36.

[174]   See Crossman, Alexander "Indonesian Credit Event To Trigger Default Options" (15 August 1998) International Financing Review 89; Roberts, Samantha and Mahrotri, Tarun "Is It Time For A Change?" (April 1999) Asia Risk 12–15.

[175]   See Ferry, John "Argentine Sovereign Debt Sparks Bitter Credit Default Row" (January 2002) Risk 10; Salmon, Felix "Argentina's Messy Debt Exchange" (December 2001) Euromoney 58–62.

[176]   See Salmon, Felix "The Buy Side Starts To Bite Back" (April 2001) Euromoney 46–61.

[177]   In 2000, there was litigation between UBS and Deutsche Bank. The case involved a credit default swap where UBS had bought protection on Armstrong World Industries ("AWI"). Subsequently, AWI was restructured, with AWI's ownership being transferred into a holding company (Armstrong Holding ("AH")). AWI filed for voluntary reorganisation under Chapter 11. UBS sought to claim under the credit default swap on the basis of a bankruptcy credit event. Deutsche Bank refused to pay out under the credit default swap. The matter was subsequently settled. Other parties encountered similar problems with AWI. See Sandiford, Jane "Credit Derivatives Face Uncertainty" (April 2001) FOW 17; Ferry, John "Deutsche Pays Out" (April 2001).

highlighted in the Russian default. Russian debt was issued by a variety of entities; for example, Russian MinFin debt was issued by Vneshekonombank. This created problems in establishing a credit event. In more recent times, there has been greater focus on identification of the precise reference entity in transactions involving sovereigns.

- **Identification of reference obligations** – in credit default swaps involving sovereign entities, the characteristics of the reference obligations may be specified to exclude a range of obligations. This is frequently done to ensure that the credit default swap effectively covers foreign currency debt provided by commercial lenders. In practice, sovereign default or restructuring has affected a variety of obligations. For example, Russia announced a rescheduling of its rouble denominated short term debt (Treasury bills known as GKOs). Where a credit default swap excluded these obligations from the relevant reference obligations (for example, by excluding local currency obligations), there would be no credit event until such time as there was a credit event affecting Russian foreign currency debt (primarily US$ Eurobonds). In the case of Indonesia, there was a failure to make payments on rescheduled Paris Club debt. This would normally be excluded from the range of reference obligations (not sovereign lender). This means that the non payment would not necessarily constitute a credit event.

- **Form of sovereign debt restructuring** – restructuring and rescheduling of sovereign debt takes various forms. The form of the restructuring/ rescheduling dictates whether a credit event is considered to have occurred:

  1. In the Russian default there was litigation between Deutsche Bank and ANZ Banking Group[178]. The English court was asked to consider the terms of two credit derivative transactions where the underlying obligation was a loan by Daiwa Europe to the City of Moscow. The City of Moscow repaid 75% of the loan on 17th August, 1998. It did not repay the remaining balance until the next day. Daiwa used late payment as the basis for a claim against Deutsche Bank under a credit default swap between Daiwa and Deutsche Bank. This claim was made even though Daiwa ultimately

---

Risk 13; Sandiford, Jane "Credit Derivatives Face Successor Hurdle" (30 May– 5 June 2001) Financial Products 1, 6.

[178] See earlier in Chapter.

suffered no loss (other than lost interest arising from the delay). Deutsche Bank claimed a similar payment under a back-to-back transaction with ANZ. ANZ resisted the claim for payment. The court granted Deutsche Bank summary judgment for its claim, enforcing the contract strictly in accordance with its express terms[179].

2. In late 2001, Argentina effectively sought to restructure/reschedule its debt. The precise form of the proposal caused problems under the restructuring provision in the credit default swap documentation. Argentina announced an exchange of its outstanding bonds for new loans. The exchange required local investors to swap US$50 billion of 11% and 12% bonds for new securities yielding 7%. The exchange was voluntary. This created doubts as to whether the exchange offer constituted a credit event under the restructuring provision. At the time of the exchange offer, Argentina was current on all (coupon etc) payments and there was no other credit event. Subsequently, Argentina defaulted on its debt.

In practice, the problem has been one of the *timing* of the credit event rather than the occurrence of the credit event. Given that the credit default swap has a fixed maturity, the timing of the credit event may be crucial.

7.3.8   Restructuring Credit Event[180]

The difficulties with the restructuring credit event have been considerable. The problems were highlighted in the Conseco case.

Conseco was a substantial US insurance/financial services firm. In 2000, Conseco's credit quality deteriorated and the company encountered liquidity problems. The problems led to Conseco entering into discussions with its lenders. The discussions led to a significant restructuring/rescheduling of

---

[179] See Crossman, Alexander "Daiwa In US$50m Default Swap Dispute" (10 October 1998) International Financing Review 88; Whiteley, Christopher "Credit Derivatives: Documentation And Legal Issues" in Das, Satyajit (Editor) (2001) Credit Derivatives & Credit Linked Notes – Second Edition; John Wiley & Sons, Singapore at Chapter 17 at 712–713.

[180] See Watkinson, Lisa and Lee, Young-Sup (5 September 2002) Modified Restructuring – Not The End Of The Story; Morgan Stanley, Fixed Income Research, New York. See also Morris, Jenny "Revisiting The Restructuring Issue" (May 2001) Euromoney 16; Bennett, Oliver "Documentation Dilemmas" (March 2001) Risk – Credit Risk Special Report S6–S7; Douglas-Jones, Jane "Credit Today – Restructuring" (Winter 2001) FOW/ Credit Derivatives 13–15.

certain bank loans. The restructuring agreement included extension of maturity. Other changes included increased interest rates and new covenants (including a commitment to pay down the restructured debt promptly with the proceeds of asset sales). The restructuring constituted a restructuring credit event under credit default swaps on Conseco, triggering payments.

Conseco served to highlight two separate aspects of credit derivatives documentation[181]:

- **Moral hazard issues** – there were credit default swaps outstanding on Conseco. Some of these credit default swaps were alleged to be purchased by lenders to Conseco involved in the restructured facility. It is clear that the lenders had a legitimate financial interest in hedging credit exposure to Conseco. However, the potential influence of these lenders in the restructuring discussions and the form of these arrangements arguably created a conflict of interest. It also created a moral hazard issue. This reflected the fact that the lenders holding purchased protection on Conseco would benefit from the occurrence of a credit event as a result of the restructured/rescheduled debt[182].

- **Impact of the cheapest to deliver option** – Conseco had a variety of outstanding debt ranging in maturity. Following the restructuring, Conseco's short term bonds traded at around 90% of face value. Conseco's longer dated bonds (up to 30 years) traded at prices around

---

[181] There were a number of similar cases. For example, Xerox Corporation entered into a restructuring whereby it agreed to repay US$2.8 billion of an outstanding loan. The bank agreed to extend the maturity of the remaining debt (US$4.2 billion). Xerox agreed to pledge a substantial amount of assets to secure a portion of the remaining debt. Credit default swaps on Xerox were triggered using the restructuring credit event. Buyers of protection delivered structurally subordinated long dated senior bonds trading at prices around 70% of face value. [See (16 October 2002) Standardised Documentation For Credit Derivatives Growth; Fitch Ratings; New York at 5.]

[182] In theory, under the original form of the restructuring provision, a bank with a bilateral credit facility to an entity which it had hedged with a credit default swap, could trigger the swap by restructuring the facility (for example, by extending the maturity). This would be the case where the credit quality of the firm had deteriorated (for example, the firm's publicly traded debt may be trading at 60% of face value). In this case, the bank could trigger the credit default swap by restructuring its bilateral credit facility. The bank could then purchase the publicly traded debt of the firm at 60% of face value and deliver it to settle the credit default swap.

60–70% of face value[183]. Under the 1999 Definitions, the buyers of protection generally had the ability to deliver *any* bond or loan that meets the specified category and characteristics of the deliverable obligations. In this case, the buyers of protection took advantage of the cheapest-to-deliver option and delivered the longer dated bonds in settlement of the credit default swaps. This resulted in the seller of protection being exposed to large losses[184].

The immediate market reaction was negative[185]. Several dealers and market participants refused to sell protection where restructuring was included as a credit event. Other dealers charged a differential premium for transactions where restructuring was included. This fee for including restructuring as a credit event was 10 to 20 bps pa higher than for credit default swaps without the restructuring credit event.

The situation was complicated by an announcement from regulators (the US Federal Reserve and the French Commission Bancaire) that exclusion of the restructuring credit event would result in no regulatory capital relief being available for credit default swaps[186]. This reflected the regulatory view that protection against restructuring was fundamental to transfer of credit risk.

---

[183] The position should be contrasted with other credit events (for example, bankruptcy) that would have had the effect of accelerating all obligations. This would mean that all obligations, irrespective of final maturity, would trade at similar price levels.

[184] This is often described (incorrectly) as structural subordination.

[185] There were a number of cases similar to Conseco. For example, in 2002, Xerox renegotiated its $7 billion revolving credit line. The changes to the loan included (1) to repay $2.8 billion, (2) pledge a substantial amount of assets to secure a portion of the remaining $4.2 billion and (3) extend the maturity from October 2002 by 30 months to April 2005. The maturity extension triggered a credit event. Where there were outstanding credit default swap contracts on Xerox incorporating the standard original restructuring event, buyers of protection were able to trigger the credit default swap and deliver a long-dated maturity bond that was effectively structurally subordinated. The cheapest-to-deliver Xerox bond had a maturity date in 2016 and was trading at 70% of face value. See Hjort, Viktor (19 July 2002) "The Xerox Debt Restructuring – A Moral Hazard Issue?"; Morgan Stanley, Fixed Income Research, New York.

[186] See Rhode, William "Fed Says No To Credit Restructuring" (December 2000) Derivatives Strategy 6.

This forced ISDA to take action to revise the format of the credit default swap documentation. The changes focused on addressing the moral hazard and cheapest to deliver issues. The Restructuring Supplement announced by ISDA allowed the parties to agree to the following[187]:

- **Self dealing provision** – under this provision, the restructuring of bilateral loans cannot trigger the restructuring credit event. The restructuring credit event can only be triggered by the restructuring of a loan where there are at least 4 unaffiliated holders and if a super-majority (2/3) of holders agree to the restructuring. This provision seeks to minimise the moral hazard issues.
- **Restructuring maturity limitation** – in the event that a restructuring credit event occurs, the maturity of deliverable obligations is limited. The buyer of protection can only deliver obligations with a maximum maturity of the earlier of 30 months from the restructuring date or the final maturity of the restructured facility, provided that the deliverable obligation can always have a maturity up to the scheduled termination date of the relevant credit default swap. In addition, deliverable obligations must be fully transferable. The objective of the restructuring maturity limitation is to limit the range of deliverable obligations to shorter dated obligations (not exceeding the duration of the credit default swap itself). This assumes that the price of shorter dated obligations will behave more closely to the restructured facility.

The Modified Restructuring provision has been used in a number of cases[188]. However, the Restructuring Supplement created some

---

[187] See (2001) Restructuring Supplement To The 1999 ISDA Credit Derivatives Definitions; ISDA, New York. See also "Restructuring The Solution" (May 2001) FOW 96; Boughey, Simon "Doubts Over Changes To Default Swap Restructuring Terms" (May 2001) Credit 18–19; Bendernagel, Donald A. and Nasr, Oussama "Legal Documentation And The Restructuring Debate" in (2001) Credit Derivatives 2001 – Issues and Opportunities 21–26.

[188] In 2002, Solutia Inc. restructured $800 million in loans by extending the maturity by 2 years. The restructuring was not bilateral. Under the applicable modified restructuring provision, a restructuring credit event occurred. The owner of protection had the right to deliver to the counterparty a deliverable security maturing in less than two years. The cheapest-to-deliver Solutia security would have been the 7.375% due October 2027 trading at $65. However, because of the restriction under modified restructuring, the cheapest qualifying security for delivery was the 6.5% due October 2002, trading close to

fragmentation in the trading of credit default swaps. Credit default swaps were initially traded on 3 separate bases: R (normal restructuring); MR (modified restructuring) and NR (no restructuring). MR became established as the basic market standard in North America[189]. R was used as the basic standard in European and Asian markets. This reflected the lower level of concern about the issue in these jurisdictions, the problems of covering a greater variety of legal systems and insolvency procedures, and availability of deliverable obligations with the required characteristics. Europe also evolved a modified–modified restructuring approach (MMR; also known as Mod–Mod R).

The 2003 Definitions further altered the position in relation to restructuring. This reflected continued debate between market participants regarding the restructuring issue. The lack of agreement and consensus between market participants resulted in a menu of possible approaches which develop the concepts originally proposed in the Restructuring Supplement. These include:

- **Self dealing provision** – the 2003 Definitions include the concept of a Multiple Holder Obligation. If applicable, the Multiple Holder Obligation excludes restructuring of bilateral loans from constituting a credit event. The basic structure is that used in the Restructuring Supplement.
- **Restructuring maturity limitation** – this provision is intended for physically settled transactions. The 2003 Definitions provide the following choices:
    1. *Restructuring Maturity Limitation and Fully Transferable Obligation* – this was similar to the MR provision embodied in the Restructuring Supplement. It limits the range of obligations deliverable under a credit default swap where the credit event is restructuring. Deliverable obligations are limited to fully transferable obligations (that is,

---

par. As a result, most credit default swaps were not triggered. See Watkinson, Lisa and Lee, Young-Sup (5 September 2002) Modified Restructuring – Not The End Of The Story; Morgan Stanley, Fixed Income Research, New York.
[189] Adherence to the general practice is by no means uniform. For example, JP Morgan announced that it would transact without restructuring for loan book hedges. The underlying regulatory assumption appears to be that the regulators will permit this in limited circumstances (for example, where the hedge term exactly matches the life of the loan).

without any consent requirement) and maturing no later than 30 months following the scheduled termination date of the relevant transaction.

2. *Modified Restructuring Maturity Limitation and Conditionally Transferable Obligation* – this was similar to the MMR approach that had evolved in Europe. It limits the range of obligations deliverable under a credit default swap where the credit event is restructuring. Deliverable obligations include loans where consent is required but cannot be unreasonably withheld or delayed. Deliverable obligations are also subject to a maturity restriction. The maturity limitation is the later of the scheduled termination date of the transaction, (for bonds or loans) 60 months following occurrence of the relevant restructuring, or 30 months following the restructuring date in the case of all other deliverable obligations. Deliverable obligations must be conditionally transferable; that is, consent cannot be unreasonably withheld or delayed. If consent is not received, the seller of protection may designate a third party to take delivery. This designation must occur 5 business days after the physical settlement date or the alternative delivery procedure is used.

The self dealing provision is generally accepted in the market. The US, Europe and Australia/New Zealand commonly incorporate this provision. Japan and Asia have tended not to implement the self dealing provision on the basis that the loan market in these jurisdictions is predominately bilateral in structure.

The position following the introduction of the 2003 Definitions was that there were 4 choices with respect to the restructuring credit events (NR, R, MR or MMR). **Exhibit 1.20** summarises the different restructuring alternatives.

There is a pricing differential between NR, MMR, MR and R credit default swaps. This may be between 5 to 20% of the credit default swap fee[190].

---

[190] For discussion of the valuation of the pricing differential needed to cover additional risk from inclusion of restructuring risk, see Watkinson, Lisa and Lee, Young-Sup (5 September 2002) Modified Restructuring – Not The End Of The Story; Morgan Stanley, Fixed Income Research, New York; O'Kane, Dominic, Pedersen, Claus M. and Turnbull, Stuart M. "The Restructuring

It is not clear that the different versions of the restructuring credit events fully address the identified problems. For example:

- There remains potential ambiguity around the concept of a re-financing of an existing facility and the restructuring of an existing facility[191].
- There is some evidence that there remains considerable value in the delivery option under the MR and MMR[192].

Significant differences remain between market participants. The US market tends to transact on MR. However, increasingly some credit derivatives users are tending towards NR. The trend to NR is driven by the fact that R/MR is regarded as too broad and is seen to discourage participation by some investors. The problem with NR is that it may prevent credit capital relief being obtained. Some banks have begun to trade credit default swaps using NR where they are hedging their own credit portfolios.

European participants favour R or MMR. Europeans are reluctant to adopt MR for a number of reasons, including[193]:

- Europe has not encountered problems with restructuring credit events.

Clause In Credit Default Swap Contracts" in (April 2003) QCR Quarterly vol. 2003-Q1/Q2; Lehman Brothers, Quantitative Credit Research London at 45–59; Reyfman, Alex and Toft, Klaus (13 May 2003) "What Is The Value Of The Restructuring Credit Event?"; Goldman Sachs, Credit Derivatives Research, New York; Reyfman, Alex and Toft, Klaus "What Is The Value Of Modified Restructuring" in Gregory, Jon (Editor) (2003) Credit Derivatives: The Definitive Guide; Risk Publications, London at Chapter 4; Francis, Chris, Kakodkar, Atish and Martin, Barnaby (16 April 2003) Credit Derivative Handbook"; Merrill Lynch, London AT 73–83. See also Douglas-Jones, Jane "Credit Today – Restructuring" (Winter 2001) FOW/Credit Derivatives 13–15.

[191] For example, the renegotiation by Xerox of existing facilities created this problem; see O'Kane, Dominic, Pedersen, Claus M. and Turnbull, Stuart M. "The Restructuring Clause In Credit Default Swap Contracts" in (April 2003) QCR Quarterly vol. 2003-Q1/Q2; Lehman Brothers, Quantitative Credit Research London at 45–59 at 50, 51; Reyfman, Alex and Toft, Klaus "What Is The Value Of Modified Restructuring" in Gregory, Jon (Editor) (2003) Credit Derivatives: The Definitive Guide; Risk Publications, London at Chapter 4.

[192] See O'Kane, Dominic, Pedersen, Claus M. and Turnbull, Stuart M. "The Restructuring Clause In Credit Default Swap Contracts" in (April 2003) QCR Quarterly vol. 2003-Q1/Q2; Lehman Brothers, Quantitative Credit Research London at 45–59.

[193] See (16 October 2002) Standardised Documentation For Credit Derivatives Growth; Fitch Ratings; New York at 5.

- European corporate debt is generally long maturity bonds that may not be capable of delivery under the restructuring maturity limitation provision.
- The European loan market consists largely of consent required loans that would not qualify as fully transferable obligations.
- European banks generally need a close hedge to obtain capital relief.
- MR does not protect sellers of protection adequately.

The Asian market currently favours R. This reflects the fact that the bulk of debt is bilateral loans[194].

The restructuring issue creates problems in trading credit default swaps where the transaction is hedged with a back-to-back credit default swap. This reflects the potential lack of documentary match between different contracts. The restructuring debate has raised concerns that there may be differential ratings of structured credit transactions based on the different restructuring provision used[195].

Basel 2 adds an extra dimension to the restructuring credit event. It requires the restructuring credit event to be included if regulatory capital relief is to be obtained. Restructuring is defined as "restructuring of the underlying obligation involving forgiveness or postponement of principal, interest or fees that results in a credit loss event" (i.e. charge-off, specific provision or other similar debit to the profit and loss account). When restructuring is not specified as a credit event, partial recognition of the credit derivative will be allowed. If the amount of the credit derivative is less than or equal to the amount of the underlying obligation, 60% of the amount of the hedge can be recognised as covered. If the amount of the credit derivative is larger than that of the underlying obligation, then the amount of eligible hedge is capped at 60% of the amount of the underlying obligation. The 60% recognition factor is provided as an interim treatment which the regulators intend to refine prior to implementation[196].

---

[194] For example in Japan, approximately 60% of corporate debts are in the form of loans.

[195] See Merritt, Roger W., Verde, Mariarosa and Grossman, Robert (8 January 2001) "Restructuring: A Defining Event For Synthetic CDOs"; Fitch Structured Finance, New York.

[196] See Basel Committee on Banking Supervision (June 2004) International Convergence of Capital Measurement and Capital Standards: A Revised Framework; Bank for International Settlements, Basel, Switzerland at Paragraphs 191 and 192.

Exhibit 1.20 Credit Events – Restructuring Alternatives

Restructuring Provision	Non Restructuring	Restructuring	Modified Restructuring	Modified Modified Restructuring
Self Dealing				
Multiple holder obligation	Not applicable	Applicable	Applicable	Applicable
Deliverable Obligations				
Maturity	Not applicable	Unrestricted subject to Maximum Maturity selected	30 months from restructuring date or the latest final maturity date of any restructured bond or loan subject to the restriction that it cannot be earlier than the scheduled maturity date of the credit default swap or later than 30 months after such date	60 months from restructuring date for restructured obligations or 30 months from restructuring date for other obligations subject to the restriction that it cannot be earlier than the scheduled maturity date of the credit default swap
Transferability	Not applicable	Unrestricted	Fully transferable	Conditionally transferable

Note: All alternatives are under the 2003 Credit Definitions.

7.3.9   Successor Issue[197]

This focuses on the impact of mergers and other forms of corporate reorganisation on the reference entity. This issue first became prominent when AT & T announced its intention to reorganise itself into 4 separate entities[198]. This would create a problem for credit default swaps in that the original reference entity would cease to exist.

The original form of documentation specified that the credit protection would be transferred to the entity assuming "all or substantially all" of the obligations of the original reference entity. In practice, this test was difficult to apply.

In November 2001, ISDA announced the Successor Supplement that introduced a new test for the determination of successor. The provisions are incorporated in the 2003 Definitions. Where the successor provisions are agreed to by the parties, the new reference entity is specified as:

- Any entity that assumes 75% of the obligations of the original reference entity; or
- If no clear successor exists, then the reference entity is all entities that assume between 25% and 75% of the obligations, with the original credit default swap being split evenly amongst these entities.
- If no entity assumes 25% or more, then the original legal entity will be the successor.
- If no legal entity survives and no entity assumes more than 25% of the obligations, then the entity which assumes the greatest percentage of obligations.

---

[197]   See (2001) Supplement Relating Successor and Credit Events To The 1999 ISDA Credit Derivatives Definitions; ISDA, New York. See also Bennett, Oliver "Splitting Headaches" (July 2001) Risk 36–37; Ferry, John "ISDA Resolves De-merger Successor Problems" (December 2001) Risk 6.

[198]   This problem has been present in other cases. For example, in 2000, National Power in the UK demerged certain assets and subsidiaries. National Power (which changed its name into International Power) transferred assets and debt into a new entity (Innogy). National Power shareholders were given shares in Innogy. This series of transactions raised the issue whether Innogy was a successor to National Power. Under the then used concept of successor this depended upon whether the debt assumed by Innogy amounted to "all or substantially all of the obligations" of National Power.

The new test only uses bonds and loans of the original entity. The successor provision is the generally accepted market standard. The revised successor provision has proved problematic on some occasions[199].

7.3.10   Deliverability of Convertible Securities
And Zero Coupon Securities

Contingent obligations (securities where the principal or interest is indexed to a market variable through a formula) are generally excluded from the specified reference obligations and deliverable obligations under a credit default swap. The deliverability of convertible bonds was not clear under the definition of the *not contingent* characteristic in the 1999 Definitions.

In 2001, the UK government appointed an administrator to manage the affairs of Railtrack Plc. This constituted a credit event under credit default swaps on Railtrack. Buyers of protection (including convertible arbitrage funds) sought to deliver convertible bonds[200] issued by Railtrack in settlement of the credit default swap. Some sellers of protection refused to accept delivery of convertible bonds on the basis that the bonds were contingent securities[201].

---

[199]   In September 2002, the UK hotels/pub group Six Continents ("6C") demerged, becoming Intercontinental Hotels Group ("IHG") and Mitchells & Butlers ("M&B"). The complex transaction resulted in 6C becoming a subsidiary of IHG. The restructure also included a complex rearrangement of the debts of the various entities. After the restructure, 6C had a minimal amount of debt (GBP 18 million). The restructure meant that buyers of credit protection on 6C suffered a loss as the possibility of 6C experiencing a credit event had decreased with the reduction in its debt level. The fee on credit default swaps on 6C fell by 50%. Dealers argued that from an economic perspective IHG had succeeded 6C. The legal position was not clear. The legal opinions concluded that neither IHG nor M&B were a successor company to 6C because the terms of the new loans were different from that of the original 6C debt. The 2003 Definitions did not seem to cover the 6C problem. In June 2003, the position was remedied through the action of lenders to IHG. The lenders requested and obtained cross guarantees between 6C and IHG in order to avoid problems of structural subordination if 6C was used to raise debt [see Brown, Mark "Six Continents Demerger Drives Uncertainty" (July 2003) Euromoney 16–17].

[200]   See discussion of convertible arbitrage in Chapter 7.

[201]   See Hoppe, Stephanie "Convertible To Serve in Credit Swap Settlements" (8–14 August 2001) Financial Products 1,8 ; Patel, Navroz "Railtrack Credit Event: Deliverability Debated" (November 2001) Risk 12.

In November 2001, ISDA announced a Supplement[202] that clarified that convertible bonds were not contingent securities and were deliverable even where the *not contingent* characteristic was selected for deliverable obligations. This was based on the fact the conversion is within the control of the bondholder[203]. The Supplement also clarified the deliverability of zero coupon bonds. The problem arose because the deliverable obligation must bear interest at a fixed or floating interest rate payable on a periodic basis. The Supplement clarified that zero coupon securities (described as accreting securities) were eligible deliverable obligations. This raises the further issue of the *value* of the zero coupon bonds upon delivery. The Supplement specifies that the value of the zero coupon bond is to be calculated as the original price plus the accrued discount calculated using the yield to maturity of the security. The provisions of the Supplement are incorporated in the 2003 Definitions.

7.4 Documentation – Key Trends

The documentation for credit derivatives is inherently complex. It reflects the synthetic nature of credit default swaps and its attempt to replicate the

---

[202] See (2001) Supplement Relating Convertible Exchangeable Or Accreting Obligations To The 1999 ISDA Credit Derivatives Definitions; ISDA, New York.

[203] The status of the ISDA Supplement to the Credit Derivatives Definitions in relation to Convertible securities has proved problematic. In 2002, Nomura commenced legal action against Credit Suisse First Boston ("CSFB") in relation to a credit default swap on Railtrack. The disputed matter was whether convertible bonds constitute "deliverable obligations" under the 1999 Definitions. Nomura had purchased protection under a credit default swap from CSFB on Railtrack. In November 2001, when Railtrack became insolvent, Nomura attempted to settle the credit default swap through delivery of Railtrack convertible bonds. It is alleged that CSFB refused on the basis that the bonds did not meet the "not contingent" deliverable obligation characteristic. ISDA subsequently issued a supplement to its Credit Derivatives definitions stating that bonds convertible at the option of the bondholder (or trustee on behalf of the bondholder) are deliverable obligations. However, CSFB still refused to accept the bonds. Nomura commenced action to enforce its rights under the credit default swap. A central issue to emerge is the fact that ISDA is neither a legal nor a regulatory body and its standard documentation is only a recommendation but does not enjoy any special legal status. In February 2003, the UK courts ruled in favour of deliverability of convertible securities. See Douglas-Jones, Jane "Credit Derivatives Face Legal Challenges" (17–23 July 2002) Financial Products 1–2.

underlying credit exposure indirectly. The documentation has proved generally robust. Despite some problems, the documentation has operated satisfactorily in most transactions. The documentation has survived some severe market tests, including the Russian default, emerging market crises (in Asia and Latin America) and significant corporate defaults (in the US domestic market, UK and Europe). The documentation has also evolved rapidly in response to market concerns and developments.

The ISDA confirmation and definitions have become the accepted market standard used for both trading and structured transactions. The documentation has increasingly become standardised, facilitating trading in credit derivatives. Major areas of standardisation include:

• **Credit events** – there is increasing global standardisation in the credit events used[204]. Market participants (particularly in inter dealer trading) have standardised the credit events as bankruptcy, failure to pay and restructuring. The only major difference between dealers is the form of restructuring credit events. There continues to be differences between North American dealers (who use MR) and European dealers (who prefer R/MMR).

• **Settlement method** – the preferred market settlement method is physical delivery. Deliverable obligations are specified as bonds or loans. The types of deliverable loans include assignable or consent required loans. The adoption of physical delivery reflects the low basis risk in using this form of default settlement. It avoids problems of price discovery in cash settlement. In particular, it avoids the problem of the defaulted bond price being set at zero where prices for the reference bonds in the specified minimum quotation amount cannot be obtained. The use of physical settlement clearly limits the use of the credit default swaps to reference entities where there is a deliverable obligation. In practice, the problem of the potential absence of a deliverable obligation is minimised by specifying a *range* of deliverable obligations. It is also minimised by increasing the range of deliverable obligations to cover loans (assignable/transferable, consent required and participation structures). The use of the basket delivery concept overcomes a problem experienced previously with credit default swaps where the reference asset was the only

---

[204]   See Topping, Mike "CDS Moves To Trans-Atlantic Standardisation" (17–23 April 2002) Financial Products 1,12.

deliverable obligation. A number of situations developed where the volume of credit default swaps outstanding significantly exceeded the outstanding bonds on issue[205]. This led to a number of short squeezes and problems in settlement. The basket delivery feature creates a cheapest-to-deliver option that is difficult to value and may pose risks for the seller of protection.

- **Maturity** – the market trades a standard maturity of 5 years although a range of maturities is available.
- **Standardised quarterly roll dates** – as a matter of market practice, dealers are seeking to implement standardised maturity dates (these are the third Friday in March, June, September and December) with maturity dates being adjusted quarterly.
- **60 Business Day Cap on Settlement** – concern about credit default swaps continuing for extended periods beyond final intended maturity resulted in the ISDA short side letter containing a 60 business day cap on settlement. The side letter agreement provides that if termination has not occurred on or before the 60th business day after the physical settlement date, that date becomes the termination date.

Other key trends in documentation include:

- **Use with insurance contracts** – a number of dealers increasingly use credit insurance policy documentation to hedge ISDA-based credit default swap contracts. This is frequently used where a dealer seeks to transfer credit risk through a credit default swap to an insurance or re-insurance company. Where the insurance/re-insurance company cannot enter a credit default swap, the transaction is repackaged and documented as a

---

[205] For example, during the 1997–1998 monetary crisis in Asia, this problem became evident. Credit default swaps on the Republic of Korea frequently used a Korean Development Bank ("KDB") bond maturing in 2007 as the reference asset and the sole deliverable obligation. The volume of Korean credit default swaps exceeded the outstanding volume of the bonds. This resulted in a short squeeze in the KDB bonds as buyers of protection bid to secure the bonds for delivery into credit default swaps. The KDB bonds actually *rallied* during the Korean fiscal crisis. Similar problems were experienced with credit default swaps on Indonesia referenced to the Indonesian US$400 million sovereign bond maturing in 2006 where the volume of credit default swaps exceeded the outstanding volume on the bonds. See Crossman, Alexander "Indonesian Credit Event To Trigger Default Options" (15 August 1998) International Financing Review 89.

credit insurance policy. The credit insurance policy is structured to replicate the characteristics of the underlying credit default swap that it is hedging[206].

- **Master credit default confirmation**[207] – in order to increase efficiency and speed of documentation, some dealers have developed the concept of a master credit default swap confirmation[208]. This entails the dealers agreeing *in advance* the standard terms of credit default swap transactions to be entered into *between the two dealers*. The terms pre-agreed include credit events, reference obligations, deliverable obligations and settlement mechanism. The terms to be agreed at the time of the trade are limited to the basic economic details[209]. This allows the transaction to be completed efficiently and confirmed with a very simple, short confirmation. The main benefits of the master confirmation approach include eliminating complex negotiations at the time of trading, minimal need for legal intervention at the time of the trade, simple confirmation procedures and reducing the operational constraints in high volume trading. While there are undoubted benefits from standardisation, there are also potential risks. The major risk is that the process may oversimplify the complex nature of some underlying credit risks and increase basis risk/documentation asymmetry in hedges. In 2003, ISDA published its Master Credit Derivatives Confirmation Agreement. The proposed structure would operate as follows:

  1. The parties would enter into a Master Credit Derivatives Confirmation Agreement. This would set out the major pre-agreed terms (known as the General Terms Confirmation).
  2. Each credit default swap transaction would be recorded using a Transaction Supplement that set out the major economic details of the individual transaction.

---

[206] A number of dealers have special insurance vehicles (for example, Deutsche Bank's Global Credit Reinsurance ("GCRe")) to undertake this activity. See Chapter 8.

[207] See "2001: The Year That Tested The Credit Swap Contract" in "Credit Derivatives Update 2002" (March 2002) Euromoney Research Guide 14–16.

[208] The initiative has been driven by JP Morgan which has completed master confirmation with major counterparties.

[209] The major terms to be agreed include: reference entity; reference obligation; trade date; effective date; scheduled termination date; floating rate payer; fixed rate payer; fixed rate payer payment dates; fixed rate; floating rate payer calculation amount and calculation agent city.

Exhibit 1.21 sets out the form of the Master Credit Derivatives Confirmation Agreement and Transaction Supplement for North America and UK/Europe. ISDA also published Master Credit Derivatives Confirmation Agreements for Asia/Japan/Australia and New Zealand. A separate Master Credit Derivatives Confirmation Agreement for sovereign entities was also published. The major differences between the different forms of the Master Credit Derivatives Confirmation Agreements are in relation to Business Day conventions, the All Guarantees Provision, Credit Events (in particular Restructuring) and Deliverable Obligations.

- **Inter dealer settlement format**[210] – as inter dealer trading in credit default swaps has increased, some dealers have increasingly sought to simplify settlement where there is a chain of credit default swaps with the same reference entity and protection buyer/seller. In this case, all contracts are terminated without actually settling (by delivery) the individual transactions. **Exhibit 1.22** sets out this structure.

Exhibit 1.21   Credit Default Swaps – Master Credit Derivatives Confirmation Agreement (North America/Europe/UK)

2003 MASTER CREDIT DERIVATIVES CONFIRMATION AGREEMENT

This 2003 Master Credit Derivatives Confirmation Agreement ("Master Confirmation Agreement") is dated as of [_____] between [_____] ("Party A") and [_____] ("Party B").

The parties wish to facilitate the process of entering into and confirming Credit Derivative Transactions and accordingly agree as follows:

1. *Credit Derivatives Definitions.* This Master Confirmation Agreement hereby incorporates by reference the 2003 ISDA Credit Derivatives Definitions as supplemented by the May 2003 Supplement to the 2003 ISDA Credit Derivatives Definitions (together, the "Credit Derivatives Definitions"). Any capitalized term not otherwise defined herein shall have the meaning assigned to such term in the Credit Derivatives Definitions.
2. *Confirmation Process.* The parties intend to enter into separate Credit Derivative Transactions (each a "Transaction") with respect to each Reference Entity set out in a Transaction Supplement substantially in the form attached as

---

[210]   See "2001: The Year That Tested The Credit Swap Contract" in "Credit Derivatives Update 2002" (March 2002) Euromoney Research Guide 14–16.

Annex 1 (a "Transaction Supplement"). The confirmation applicable to each Transaction, which shall constitute a "Confirmation" for the purposes of, and will supplement, form a part of, and be subject to, the ISDA Master Agreement between Party A and Party B dated as of [], as amended and supplemented from time to time (the "Master Agreement"), shall consist of this Master Confirmation Agreement including the form of General Terms Confirmation attached as Exhibit A (the "General Terms Confirmation"), as supplemented by the trade details applicable to such Transaction as set forth in the Transaction Supplement.[211]

In the event of any inconsistency between (i) this Master Confirmation Agreement, including the form of General Terms Confirmation and a

---

[211] If the parties have not yet executed an ISDA Master Agreement, the following language shall be included: "The confirmation applicable to each Transaction shall consist of this Master Confirmation Agreement including the form of General Terms Confirmation attached as Exhibit A (the "General Terms Confirmation"), as supplemented by the trade details applicable to such Transaction as set forth in the Transaction Supplement and shall constitute a "Confirmation" as referred to in the ISDA Master Agreement specified below. The Confirmation applicable to each Transaction will evidence a complete and binding agreement between the parties as to the terms of the Transaction to which such Confirmation relates. In addition, the parties agree to use all reasonable efforts promptly to negotiate, execute and deliver an agreement in the form of an ISDA Master Agreement, with such modifications as the parties in good faith agree. Upon execution by the parties of such an agreement (the "Master Agreement"), each Confirmation already executed in connection with this Master Confirmation Agreement and all future Confirmations executed in connection with this Master Confirmation Agreement will supplement, form a part of, and be subject to, that Master Agreement. All provisions contained in or incorporated by reference in that Master Agreement upon its execution will govern each Confirmation except as expressly modified below. Until the parties execute and deliver that Master Agreement, each Confirmation confirming a Transaction entered into between the parties in connection with this Master Confirmation Agreement (notwithstanding anything to the contrary in a Confirmation), shall supplement, form a part of, and be subject to, an agreement in the form of the 2002 ISDA Master Agreement as if the parties had executed an agreement in such form (but without any Schedule except for the election of [New York Law] [English Law] as the governing law) on the Trade Date of the first such Transaction between the parties in connection with this Master Confirmation Agreement. In the event of any inconsistency between the provisions of that agreement and a Confirmation, the Confirmation will prevail for purposes of the relevant Transaction."

Transaction Supplement and/or (ii) the Credit Derivatives Definitions and a Transaction Supplement, the Transaction Supplement shall govern for the purpose of the relevant Transaction. The Transaction Supplement shall set forth, at a minimum, all of the information set out in the applicable form of Transaction Supplement attached hereto as Annex 1.

3. *Non-Exclusive.* The parties acknowledge and agree that the execution of this Master Confirmation Agreement does not require them to document Transactions in accordance with this Master Confirmation Agreement.

4. *Preparation of Transaction Supplements.* The preparation of a Transaction Supplement shall be the responsibility of the Seller in respect of the Transaction to which the relevant Transaction Supplement relates.

5. *Miscellaneous.*

   (a) *Entire Agreement.* This Master Confirmation Agreement constitutes the entire agreement and understanding of the parties with respect to its subject matter and supersedes all oral communication and prior writings with respect specifically thereto.

   (b) *Amendments.* An amendment, modification or waiver in respect of this Master Confirmation Agreement will only be effective if in writing (including a writing evidenced by a facsimile transmission) and executed by each of the parties or confirmed by an exchange of telexes or by an exchange of electronic messages on an electronic messaging system.

   (c) *Counterparts.* This Master Confirmation Agreement and each Transaction Supplement documented hereunder may be executed in counterparts, each of which will be deemed an original.

   (d) *Headings.* The headings used in this Master Confirmation Agreement are for convenience of reference only and shall not affect the construction of or be taken into consideration in interpreting this Master Confirmation Agreement.

   (e) *Governing Law.* This Master Confirmation Agreement and each Transaction confirmed by a Confirmation documented hereunder will be governed by and construed in accordance with the law specified in the Master Agreement.

IN WITNESS WHEREOF the parties have executed this document with effect from the date specified on the first page of this document.

[_____]   [_____]

By:_____   By:_____

Name: Name:
Title: Title:
Date: Date:

Re: General Terms Confirmation

Dear Sir or Madam,

The purpose of this General Terms Confirmation (the "General Terms Confirmation") is to confirm certain general terms and conditions of Credit Derivative Transactions entered into between us under the 2003 Master Credit Derivatives Confirmation Agreement between us dated as of [   ] ("Master Confirmation Agreement").

This General Terms Confirmation hereby incorporates by reference the 2003 ISDA Credit Derivatives Definitions as supplemented by the May 2003 Supplement to the 2003 ISDA Credit Derivatives Definitions (together, the "Credit Derivatives Definitions"). In the event of any inconsistency between the Credit Derivatives Definitions and this General Terms Confirmation , this General Terms Confirmation will govern.

All provisions contained in the Master Agreement govern each Confirmation (each as defined in the Master Confirmation Agreement) except as expressly modified below.

The general terms of each Transaction to which this General Terms Confirmation relates are as follows, as supplemented by the Transaction Supplement related to such Transaction:

1. General Terms:

Trade Date:	As shown in the Transaction Supplement
Effective Date:	As shown in the Transaction Supplement
Scheduled Termination Date:	As shown in the Transaction Supplement
Transaction Type:	As shown in the Transaction Supplement
Floating Rate Payer:	As shown in the Transaction Supplement (the "Seller")
Fixed Rate Payer:	As shown in the Transaction Supplement (the "Buyer")
Calculation Agent:	Seller
Calculation Agent City:	If the Transaction Type indicated in the Transaction Supplement is:
	European: London
	North American: New York
Business Day:	If the Floating Rate Payer Calculation Amount indicated in the Transaction Supplement is denominated in:

EUR:	London and TARGET Settlement Day
USD:	London and New York
GBP:	London
CHF:	London and Zurich

Business Day Convention:	Following (which, subject to Sections 1.4 and 1.6 of the Credit Derivatives Definitions, shall apply to any date referred to in this General Terms Confirmation or in the related Transaction Supplement that falls on a day that is not a Business Day)
Reference Entity:	As shown in the Transaction Supplement
Reference Obligation(s):	As shown in the Transaction Supplement
Reference Price:	100%
All Guarantees:	If the Transaction Type indicated in the Transaction Supplement is: European: Applicable North American: Not Applicable

2. Fixed Payments:

Fixed Rate Payer Calculation Amount:	The Floating Rate Payer Calculation Amount
Fixed Rate Payer Payment Dates:	As shown in the Transaction Supplement
Fixed Rate:	As shown in the Transaction Supplement
Fixed Rate Day Count Fraction:	Actual/360

3. Floating Payment:

Floating Rate Payer Calculation Amount:	As shown in the Transaction Supplement
Conditions to Settlement:	• Credit Event Notice
	Notifying Parties: Buyer or Seller
	• Notice of Physical Settlement
	• Notice of Publicly Available Information: Applicable
Credit Event:	The following Credit Events shall apply to this Transaction: Bankruptcy Failure to Pay

| | Grace Period Extension: | Not Applicable |
| | Payment Requirement: | USD 1,000,000 or its equivalent in the relevant Obligation Currency as of the occurrence of the relevant Failure to Pay |

Restructuring: If indicated as applicable in the Transaction Supplement, the following terms shall apply:

Restructuring Maturity Limitation and Fully Transferable Obligation:	If the Transaction Type indicated in the Transaction Supplement is: European: Not Applicable North American: Applicable
Modified Restructuring Maturity Limitation and Conditionally Transferable Obligation:	If the Transaction Type indicated in the Transaction Supplement is: European: Applicable North American: Not Applicable
Default Requirement:	USD 10,000,000 or its equivalent in the relevant Obligation Currency as of the occurrence of the relevant Credit Event

Obligation(s): For the purposes of the table below: **"Yes"** shall mean that the relevant selection is applicable; and **"No"** shall mean that the relevant selection is not applicable.

Obligation Categories: (*Select only one*)		Obligation Characteristics: (*Select all that apply*)	
No	Payment	No	Not Subordinated
Yes	Borrowed Money	No	Specified Currency – Standard Specified Currencies
No	Reference Obligation(s) Only	No	Not Sovereign Lender
No	Bond	No	Not Domestic Currency
No	Loan	No	Not Domestic Law
No	Bond or Loan	No	Listed
		No	Not Domestic Issuance

4. Settlement Terms:

Settlement Method: Physical Settlement
Settlement Currency: The currency of denomination of the
                                            Floating Rate Payer Calculation
                                            Amount

Terms Relating to Physical
Settlement:

Physical Settlement Period: If the Transaction Type indicated in the
                                            Transaction Supplement is:
                                            European: thirty (30) Business Days
                                            North American: as defined in Section 8.6
                                            of the Credit Derivatives Definitions,
                                            but in no event longer than thirty (30)
                                            Business Days
Deliverable Obligations: Exclude Accrued Interest
Deliverable Obligation Category   For the purposes of the table below:
and Characteristics: **"Yes"** shall mean that the relevant
                                            selection is applicable; and
                                            "No" shall mean that the relevant
                                            selection is not applicable.

Deliverable Obligation Categories: *(Select only one)*		Deliverable Obligation Characteristics: *(Select all that apply)*	
No	Payment	Yes	Not Subordinated
No	Borrowed Money	Yes	Specified Currency – Standard Specified Currencies
No	Reference Obligation(s) Only	No	Not Sovereign Lender
No	Bond	No	Not Domestic Currency
No	Loan	No	Not Domestic Law
Yes	Bond or Loan	No	Listed
		Yes	Not Contingent
		No	Not Domestic Issuance

		Yes	Assignable Loan
		Yes	Consent Required Loan
		No	Direct Loan Participation
		Yes	Transferable
		Yes – 30 years	Maximum Maturity
		No	Accelerated or Matured
		Yes	Not Bearer

Partial Cash Settlement of Consent Required Loans: Not Applicable
Partial Cash Settlement of Assignable Loans: Not Applicable
Partial Cash Settlement of Participations: Not Applicable
Escrow: [Applicable] [Not Applicable]

5. Notice and Account Details:

Notice and Account Details for Party A:
Notice and Account Details for Party B:

ANNEX 1

[Buyer Contact Information:]
[Seller Contact Information:]

TRANSACTION SUPPLEMENT
Transaction Type: [European] [North American]

This Transaction Supplement is entered into between the Buyer and Seller listed below on the Trade Date set forth below.

The purpose of this communication is to confirm the terms and conditions of the Credit Derivative Transaction entered into between us on the Trade Date specified below (the "Transaction"). This Transaction Supplement is entered into under the 2003 Master Credit Derivatives Confirmation Agreement dated as of [_____] and, together with the 2003 Master Credit Derivatives Confirmation Agreement and the General Terms Confirmation attached thereto, constitutes a "Confirmation" as referred to in the Master Agreement between the parties, as amended and supplemented from time to time.

The terms of the Transaction to which this Transaction Supplement relates are as follows:

Reference Entity:
[Reference Obligation: [The obligation[s] identified as follows:

Primary Obligor: [   ]
Guarantor: [   ]
Maturity: [   ]
Coupon: [   ]
CUSIP/ISIN: [   ]]]
Trade Date:
Effective Date:
Scheduled Termination Date:
Floating Rate Payer: [   ] (the "Seller")
Fixed Rate Payer: [   ] (the "Buyer")
Fixed Rate Payer Payment Dates:
Fixed Rate: _____%
Floating Rate Payer Calculation Amount: [   ]
Restructuring Credit Event: [Applicable] [Not Applicable]

[Additional Terms: [   ]]

Please confirm your agreement to be bound by the terms of the foregoing by executing a copy of this Transaction Supplement and returning it to us [at the contact information listed above].

[_____] [_____]

By: _____   By: _____
Name: Name:
Title: Title:

ISDA Credit Derivatives Confirmation Copyright © 2003 by INTERNATIONAL SWAPS AND DERIVATIVES ASSOCIATION, INC. 360 Madison Avenue, 16th Floor New York, N.Y. 10017

Exhibit 1.22   Credit Default Swaps – Inter Dealer Settlement

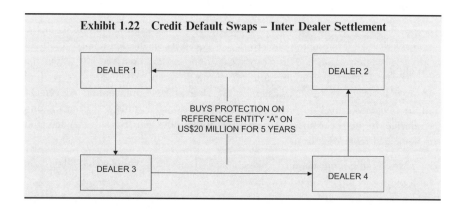

8   Credit Derivatives – Regulatory Treatment[212]

8.1   Overview

Credit derivatives entail the transfer of credit risk. This transfer of risk can be considered at two separate levels:

- **Economic capital relief** – this refers to reduction in economic capital required to be held against a position. This occurs where entry into a credit derivative transaction provides an effective hedge against the risk of loss as a result of credit events (spread changes and/or default).
- **Regulatory capital relief** – this refers to the entry into a credit derivatives transaction which results in a corresponding reduction in regulatory capital required to be held against the credit risk incurred.

Relief from regulatory capital is pivotal to credit derivatives. This reflects the use of these instruments to manage both *economic* and *regulatory capital* held against credit risk. The issues relating to regulatory capital are only relevant to regulated banks subject to supervision by the relevant entity in the jurisdiction[213].

8.2   Credit Derivatives – Regulatory Approach[214]

The emergence of the market in credit derivatives has been greeted by cautious support from regulators. This support is predicated on recognition of the significant potential benefits that credit derivatives offer banks in the management of credit risk[215].

---

[212]   The views expressed here are merely indications of possible methods of treatment and are not intended to be definitive. It is recommended that institutions seeking to enter into credit derivatives obtain appropriate professional advice from their own advisers regarding the required treatment of these transactions for regulatory purposes in the relevant jurisdictions.

[213]   Most major banks will be subject to regulation/capital requirements consistent with BIS recommendations; see Das, Satyajit (2004) Swaps/Financial Derivatives – 3rd Edition; John Wiley & Sons, Singapore at Chapters 33 and 34.

[214]   The regulatory treatment of credit derivatives is discussed in this Chapter. The regulatory treatment of credit linked notes/collateralised debt obligations is discussed in Chapter 3.

[215]   For an overview of some regulatory announcements, see Brown, Claude "Developments In The Legal Documentation and Regulatory Issues for Credit Derivatives " in Storrow, Jamie (Editor) (1999) Credit Derivatives: Key Issues – 2nd Edition; British Bankers' Association, London.

The current bank capital framework is that established by the Basel Accord of July 1988 (Basel 1)[216]. This framework pre-dated credit derivatives. The basic approach taken by the regulators to accommodate credit derivative is to draw analogies with more conventional instruments for which regulatory frameworks already exist. In particular, regulators have used analogies with guarantees/letters of credit (for banking book treatment) and bonds (for trading book treatment) in developing the treatment of credit derivatives for capital adequacy. This framework is due to be ultimately replaced by a revised framework (known as Basel 2)[217].

In reviewing the regulatory framework, it is important to note that regulators of other active participants in capital markets, primarily insurance company regulators, have also begun to review the treatment of credit derivatives.

8.3   Capital Adequacy Guidelines[218]

8.3.1   Basel 1

Credit capital requirements are predicated on regulated banks holding a minimum level of capital (8%) against credit risk. Credit risk is determined in accordance with the conversion of all transactions into risk asset equivalents (based on a system of risk weighting determined by type of transaction and maturity) and the quality (based on broad guidelines) of the counterparty/obligor. The guidelines do not specifically recognise credit derivatives.

The basic regulatory capital position in respect of credit risk under Basel 1 as expressed in the risk weighting calculations is as follows:

- Term loans and the funded component of revolving credit facilities to a corporate counterparty are 100% risk weighted.

---

[216] For discussion of capital adequacy rules applicable to banks, see Das, Satyajit (2004) Swaps/Financial Derivatives – 3rd Edition; John Wiley & Sons, Singapore at Chapters 33 and 34.

[217] See Basel Committee on Banking Supervision (June 2004) International Convergence of Capital Measurement and Capital Standards: A Revised Framework; Bank for International Settlements, Basel, Switzerland.

[218] See Basel Committee on Banking Supervision (1988) Proposals for International Convergence of Capital Measurement and Capital Standards; Bank of International Settlements, Basel

- Unfunded commitments (with a maturity over 1 year) have risk weighting of 50%.

For off-balance-sheet/derivative transactions, the calculation is:

- The mark-to-market on the transactions (if positive) plus an add-on factor calculated as a % of notional principal of the transaction for future exposure (based on volatility of rates/prices).
- The prescribed add-on factors are:

Residual Maturity	Rates	Forex	Equity	Precious Metals	Commodities
Under 1 Year	0.0%	1.0%	6.0%	7.0%	10.0%
1 – 5 Years	0.5%	5.0%	8.0%	7.0%	12.0%
Over 5 Years	1.5%	7.5%	10.0%	8.0%	15.0%

The methodology outlined is used to derive risk asset equivalent that is then weighted within a general framework according to the risk of the counterparty. The counterparty risk weights are as follows[219]:

Risk Weighting	Types of Obligation
0%	Central governments of OECD countries
10%	Public sector entities (other than the central government) located in the same country as the regulated bank
20%	OECD Banks Non-OECD for obligations less than 1 year Public sector entities within OECD outside the bank's home country Multilateral development agencies
50%	Housing finance Foreign exchange and interest rate transaction
100%	All other counterparties and assets.

The counterparty risk weighting system limits the *maximum* risk weighting for a counterparty to a derivative transaction to 50%. This represents a specific exception to the 100% weight applicable to non-bank counterparties.

---

[219] Care is needed in interpreting this matrix as individual regulators have discretion regarding treatment of certain types of obligations.

The basic position under this regime is that banks have to hold the capital (minimum 8%) against the following credit risk:

Type of Transaction	20% Risk Weighted Counterparty (e.g. OECD Bank)	100% Risk Weighted Counterparty (e.g. Corporation)
Fully drawn Loan (> 1 year in maturity)	Face value × 100% × 20%	Face value × 100% × 100%
Unfunded Loan (> 1 year in maturity)	Face value × 50% × 20%	Face value × 50% × 100%
Derivative transaction	[Mark-to-market + (Notional Face value × Variable Add-on Factor)] × 20%	[Mark-to-market + (Notional Face value × Variable Add-on Factor)] × 50%

Parallel to the credit capital regime is the market risk capital guidelines that require the banks to hold 8% capital against the risk of loss from movements in market rates and prices. The market risk is required to be calculated using either standard models prescribed by the BIS or internal models (in effect, Value At Risk ("VAR") models)[220]. Banks are required to hold capital against market risk (in their trading books) from 1 January 1998[221].

8.3.2   Basel 2[222]

Basel 2 changes the basic regulatory capital guidelines. The system is due for introduction around end 2006 with some arrangement to come into effect as at end 2007. Under the proposed scheme, there are two possible frameworks: the standardised approach and the internal rating based ("IRB") approach. The IRB approach is only available with the explicit approval of the regulator.

The standardised approach is similar to Basel 1. It uses a system of credit conversion factors (to generate risk assets) and counterparty credit risk

---

[220]   See Das, Satyajit (2004) Swaps/Financial Derivatives – 3rd Edition; John Wiley & Sons, Singapore at Chapter 18.

[221]   See Basel Committee on Banking Supervision (January 1996) Amendment to the Capital Accord To Incorporate Market Risks; Bank of International Settlements, Basel.

[222]   See Basel Committee on Banking Supervision (June 2004) International Convergence of Capital Measurement and Capital Standards: A Revised Framework; Bank for International Settlements, Basel, Switzerland.

weightings to derive a regulatory capital requirement. Key changes from
Basel 1 include:

- Unfunded commitments (with a maturity under 1 year) have a risk
  weighting of 20%.
- Counterparty risk weightings are based on a combination of type of
  entity and the external credit rating of the counterparty.

The IRB system has two levels – foundation and advanced. It is based on
credit risk modelling techniques[223].

Banks that have received supervisory approval to use the IRB approach
may rely on their own internal estimates of risk components in determining
the capital requirement for a given exposure. The risk components include
the probability of default ("PD"), loss given default ("LGD"), the exposure
at default ("EAD") and maturity (M). Banks are required to use a
supervisory value as opposed to an internal estimate for one or more of the
risk components under certain circumstances.

The IRB approach is based on measures of unexpected losses ("UL") and
expected losses ("EL"). The risk-weight functions produce capital requirements for the UL portion. The risk-weight functions produce capital
requirements for the UL portion. The risk components serve as inputs to
the risk-weight functions that have been developed for separate asset classes.
For example, there is a risk-weight function for corporate exposures and
another one for qualifying revolving retail exposures. The treatment of each
asset class begins with a presentation of the relevant risk-weight function(s)
followed by the risk components and other relevant factors, such as
the treatment of credit risk mitigants. The system is complex and highly
technical.

8.4 Credit Derivatives And Regulatory Capital – Key Issues

A fundamental distinction is necessary in reviewing issues relating to the
treatment of credit derivatives within a regulatory capital framework. This
relates to the difference between:

- **Issuer/counterparty credit risk** – this refers to the credit risk on the issuer
  (in a credit linked note) or the counterparty credit risk (in a credit

---

[223] See Chapter 6.

derivative transaction). This exposure refers to the traditional credit risk inherent in all financial transactions arising from the risk of non performance of the issuer or counterparty.

- **Credit risk on the reference asset or underlying reference entity** –in credit derivatives, this refers to the reference asset or entity, the change in value of which manifests itself in the pay off of the credit derivative.

In credit derivatives, both credit exposures have to be dealt with. This contrasts with traditional financial instruments where only the issuer or counterparty credit risk is relevant.

The major issues in relation to the regulatory requirements of credit derivatives include:

- Inclusion of credit derivatives in either the banking (i.e. credit risk) or the trading books (i.e. market risk) of financial institutions.
- Treatment of the *underlying* reference asset or entity in the books of the entity buying protection or transferring the economic risk of the credit assets.
- Treatment of the *underlying* reference asset or entity in the books of the entity selling protection or acquiring the economic risk of the credit assets.
- Treatment of the counterparty risk on the *credit derivative itself*.
- The degree to which the underlying reference asset in the credit derivative transaction matches any asset held by an institution (which the credit derivative seeks to hedge); in effect, the basis risk on the transaction.

The regulatory treatment problems are different for credit spread products, total return swaps and credit default swaps.

Total return swaps and credit default swaps transfer the credit risk of the underlying credit assets. This means that these transactions impact more directly on the credit risk and therefore on the regulatory capital position. Treatment approaches are considered in the following Sections.

Credit spread products are treated analogous to positions in the underlying assets (a long or short position in a risky asset (bond) and an offsetting position in a risk free security (government bond or swap)). The decomposition allows the market risk of the position to be determined and the regulatory market risk capital requirement to be calculated. The counterparty credit risk is derived by analogy with interest rate products. This would dictate that the counterparty risk be treated as the mark-to-market of the position plus an add-on factor for interest rate products[224].

In examining the potential regulatory treatment of credit derivatives (total return swaps and credit default swaps), there are a number of important preliminary issues, including:

- **Risk transfer** – the difference in risk transfer characteristics revolves around the fact that a total return swap transfers *both the price risk from credit quality changes and the risk of loss upon default.* Any change in credit risk that manifests itself as a change in credit spread that, in turn, results in changes in the market value of the security, is transferred in a total return swap through the final settlement. In contrast, where the change in credit risk is *short of default* (or specified credit event under the credit default swap), there is no corresponding settlement under a credit default swap. A further issue relates to the treatment of *security based* credit derivatives and *loan based* credit derivatives. Most regulators do not differentiate between the two classes of instruments. For example, the Financial Services Authority ("FSA") (previously Securities and Futures Authority ("SFA"))[225] in the UK specifically permits the introduction of loan based credit derivatives in the trading book. Earlier proposals did not allow such inclusion on the basis that it would create an anomaly in respect of credit derivatives that were a synthetic version of the loans themselves. Other regulators have not explicitly recognised this treatment.
- **Basis risk** – the issue of basis risk relates to the degree of correspondence between the asset being hedged and the reference asset/deliverable obligation underlying the credit derivative transaction. Any asymmetry will typically arise from the following sources:
  1. *Size mismatch* – this relates to any mismatch between the face value of the underlying transaction and the notional principal of the credit derivative. The central issue is whether partial protection should be regarded as a hedge, at least up to the face value of the credit derivative transaction.

---

[224] Depending on jurisdictions, the add-on factor may be based on equity or commodity add-on factors; see discussion later in this Chapter.
[225] In the UK, the FSA has been established as a single financial regulator subsuming the responsibilities of the Bank of England and the SFA.

2. *Maturity mismatch* – this relates to the mismatch between the final maturity of the underlying transaction and that of the credit derivative. The problem arises where the maturity of the credit derivative is *shorter* than that of the underlying transaction. This raises the issue whether the hedge is treated as effective given that the risk on the underlying transaction reverts to the original holder at the maturity of the credit derivative.

3. *Reference asset/deliverable obligation mismatch* – this relates to a credit derivative transaction that is referenced to a reference asset or deliverable obligation that is *different* to the underlying transaction being hedged. This creates complexity in determining the extent of the mismatch and the degree to which risk transfer should be recognised.

4. *Currency Mismatch* – this relates to a credit derivative which is denominated in a different currency to that of the underlying obligation being hedged.

5. *Default payment amount and timing mismatch* – this relates to the calculation of the default payment under the credit derivative and the timing of the payment of any amounts due and payable. In cases where cash settlement is used, there is uncertainty as to amount and payment. Similarly, the specification of default may in fact create timing uncertainties – for example, where a materiality test is specified. This creates issues of the degree to which the risk transfer should be recognised.

Importantly, the identified issues are relevant to both issues of *regulatory* and *economic* capital. Economic capital in this context refers to the extent of "true" risk transfer and therefore the level of risk carried by the bank. It focuses on the amount of capital required to be held to manage that risk (separate to any issue regarding the amount of capital to be held against that position under regulatory capital requirements).

In practice, the most important basis risk issues relate to maturity and default payment mismatches. The size mismatch can be dealt with by allowing recognition of the risk transfer only for an amount equal to the notional principal of the credit derivatives. The reference asset mismatch can be dealt with by specifying rules that are designed to determine the extent to which an asset can act as a proxy for the transaction or asset sought to be hedged. Key factors include:

• Correspondence in obligor or effective guarantor between the reference asset and the underlying transaction.

- Equivalent seniority in bankruptcy between the reference asset and the underlying transaction.
- Similar terms and conditions (including default conditions) and cross default provisions between the reference asset and the underlying transaction.

The currency issue is dealt with in practice by recognition of protection and therefore capital to be held against the underlying asset, only to the extent of the daily revaluation of the credit derivative at current market rates.

The maturity mismatch issue is more problematic. In effect, upon maturity of the credit derivative, the party which has used the transaction to hedge its credit exposure effectively re-acquires the credit exposure to the underlying asset (in essence a "rollover" risk). The problem is different between total return swaps and credit default swaps. In the case of a total return swap, the exposure is re-acquired *at the market price at the time the total return swap matures* (this is because the final settlement is based on marking the underlying asset to market even where there has been no default). In contrast, in the case of a credit default swap, the exposure is re-acquired *without any price adjustment* unless there has been a credit event. This means that where there has been deterioration in the credit of the obligor short of default, the party using the swap to hedge re-acquires the exposure at *original price levels*[226].

The issue regarding the default payment relates to certainty of amount and timing. It also relates to the relationship between the loss suffered *on the underlying transaction* and the payout *on the credit derivative*.

In practice, regulators have dealt with these issues by reference to the concept of *virtually complete* credit protection; that is, the protection afforded by a credit derivative will only be recognised where it provides an effective guarantee of the risk of loss on the underlying transaction. Risk transfer short of this level of protection and certainty is disregarded for the purpose of regulatory capital. The specific approach adopted in respect of the mismatches varies between regulators.

---

[226] For an interesting approach to deal with the maturity offset problem, see Hattori, Paul and Varotsis, Paul "The Maturity Offset Problem" (April 1999) Risk 60–61.

8.5   Total Return Swaps – Regulatory Framework

8.5.1   Overview

In the case of a total return swap, the bank providing protection incurs two separate credit exposures against which capital must be held:

- Exposure to the underlying reference asset.
- Exposure to the total return swap counterparty.

The exposure to the underlying is analogous to that under guarantees or standby letters of credit. The exposure on the total return swap itself is analogous to the credit risk on a derivative contract.

The bank seeking protection through a total return swap has exposure on the counterparty in relation to the swap and on the underlying credit asset which continues to be held on the balance sheet of the bank (if the total return swap counterparty defaults). There are two possible approaches to the capital treatment:

- A conservative approach where the bank seeking protection must continue to hold existing capital against the underlying asset and on the counterparty on the total return swap.
- A more reasonable approach where the bank seeking protection is allowed to substitute the risk of the counterparty providing protection against the risk of the underlying reference asset.

In practice, as a general approach, the regulators have adopted the second view where the degree of protection is deemed to be sufficient to effect the transfer of credit risk.

8.5.2   Banking Versus Trading Book Treatment

Total return swaps generally must be treated in the bank's *trading book*. The treatment is conditional on the liquidity of the underlying asset. In order to qualify for trading book treatment, the bank must be able to mark to market the underlying reference asset. Where the liquidity of the underlying asset is not demonstrable, the swap will be included in the banking book. Inclusion in the trading book is conditional upon establishment of a *trading intent* and compliance with the regulated entity's general trading book policy statement agreed with the relevant regulator. In practice, the need to be able to mark the reference asset to market for the purposes of settlement of the total return swap will generally ensure that the transaction is treated in the bank's trading book.

8.5.3 Trading Book Treatment

Basel 1

Inclusion in the trading book means that the capital treatment of the total return swap will conform to the market risk capital requirements[227].

The ability to include transactions in the trading book has significant capital benefits as many (primarily investment grade) traded instruments are risk capital weighted at between 0.25% and 1.6% of the notional value of the transaction compared to 8% if included in the banking book. In the trading book, credit risk is treated as "specific" risk; that is, the risk of price/spread changes related to the individual characteristics of the obligor. The specific risk charge in the trading book may be calculated in the following ways:

- **Internal model based determination of specific risk**[228] – this entails using VAR models incorporating spread volatility to allow estimation of risk exposure from changes in credit risk[229].
- **Basel 1 standardised measurement method**[230] – this entails the use of a standard formula to capture the spread risk. **Exhibit 1.23** sets out the standardised specific risk model.

Where the transaction qualifies for inclusion in the trading book, the total return swap is decomposed into synthetic long or short positions in the underlying asset and an offsetting position in a floating rate note ("FRN") for the interest payments. There is an additional charge for counterparty credit risk on the swap.

---

[227] See Das, Satyajit (2004) Swaps/Financial Derivatives – 3rd Edition; John Wiley & Sons, Singapore at Chapter 34.

[228] See Das, Satyajit (2004) Swaps/Financial Derivatives – 3rd Edition; John Wiley & Sons, Singapore at Chapter 18 and 34. See also Goldman Sachs/SBC Warburg Dillon Read (1998) The Practice of Risk Management: Implementing Processes For Managing Firmwide Market Risk; Euromoney Books, London at 101–107.

[229] VAR based models for specific risk are attractive to banks as they generally reduce the capital required to be held relative to the BIS standardised measurement method. However, the institution's VAR model for specific risk must be specifically approved by its principal regulator. In practice, a limited number of banks have approved specific risk VAR models.

[230] See Basel Committee on Banking Supervision (January 1996) Amendment to the Capital Accord To Incorporate Market Risks; Bank of International Settlements.

The essential issue under this approach is whether the specific risk charge on the synthetic position in the swap can be offset against a position in the asset (that is, the reference asset being hedged). The offset is allowed where the reference asset is identical between the physical holding and the swap. This would be the case only where the underlying asset and the reference asset for the total return swap are the same.

Maturity mismatches (that is, differences between the final maturity of the underlying asset and the maturity of the total return swap) may be allowed. This would allow shorter dated total return swaps to be used to hedge a longer dated physical asset. The regulators are divided on the latter issue. Most regulators accept maturity mismatches on a qualified basis. The approach varies significantly between regulators. The contrasting approaches include partial recognition of protection where the maturity of the credit derivative is less than that of the underlying obligation or no recognition of protection. In the case of partial recognition, some reduction in the specific risk charge would be expected (for example, the higher of the two specific charges may be applied). In the case of no recognition, two specific risk charges would be incurred (one on the position in the asset and an additional charge on the offsetting position in the credit derivative).

Where the reference asset is of the same asset class but not *identical* to the asset being hedged, the position is as follows:

- General risk charges on the two positions are offsetting within the general risk calculations (leaving either zero or a small general market risk charge).
- There is no reduction in the specific risk charge. In fact there could be two full specific risk charges plus the additional counterparty risk charge to be set against the benefit of the reduced general market risk charge. A variety of regulatory approaches have emerged for offsetting positions:
  1. Standard specific risk charges should only apply to the largest leg of the offsetting credit derivative and underlying asset position (that is, standard specific risk charges are not to be applied to each leg separately)[231].
  2. An alternative approach that has been suggested is the allowing of an initial offset between the hedged positions *plus* a residual

---

[231] See Federal Reserve Board (13 June 1997) SR 97–18 (Gen) Application of Market Risk Capital Requirements to Credit Derivatives at 4.

unhedged forward credit exposure after netting as a forward commitment to purchase the reference asset. This approach results in a single specific risk charge remaining (that is, no benefit is recognised in terms of the specific risk charge for a maturity mismatched hedge), but no additional specific risk charge is applied for the hedge[232].

This means in most jurisdictions the specific risk charge is reduced or (in some cases) eliminated in practice.

Exhibit 1.23   Basel 1 Specific Risk Capital Charges

Under the BIS approach, there is a specific risk capital charge to protect against an adverse movement in the price of an individual security deriving from factors related to an individual obligor (as distinguished from market events – general market risk). The specific risk charge is set as follows:

Government	0%
Qualifying	0.25% (< 6 Months)
	1.00% (6 To 24 Months)
	1.60% (> 24 Months)
All Others	8%

The category "government" includes all forms of government paper (including, at national discretion, local and regional governments subject to a zero credit risk weight in the Basel Accord) including bonds, treasury bills and other short-term instruments. National authorities reserve the right to apply a specific risk weight to securities issued by certain foreign governments, especially to securities denominated in a currency other than that of the issuing government.

The category "qualifying" applies to securities issued by public sector entities and multilateral development banks, plus other securities that are:

• Rated investment grade (rated Baa or higher by Moody's and BBB or higher by Standard and Poor's) by at least two credit agencies specified by the relevant supervisor.
• Rated investment grade by one rating agency and not less than investment grade by any other rating agency specified by the supervisor (subject to supervisory oversight).
• Unrated but deemed to be of comparable investment quality by the bank or securities firm and the issuer has securities listed on a recognised stock exchange (subject to supervisory approval).

---

[232] See FSA Board Notice 482 – *Guidance on Credit Derivatives* (July 1998) at paragraph 34–37.

The supervisors would be responsible for monitoring the application of the qualifying criteria, particularly in relation to the last criterion where the initial classification is essentially left to the reporting institutions.

The Basel 2 amendments to the credit capital guidelines propose some changes to the calculation of the specific risk charges[233]. The proposed specific risk charges based on credit ratings are as follows:

External Credit Assessment	Specific Risk Charge
AAA To AA−	0%
A+ To BBB−	0.25% (<6 Months)
	1.00% (6 To 24 Months)
	1.60% (>24 Months)
All Others	8%

Basel 2

Basel 2 amendments to the credit capital guidelines propose some changes to the treatment of total return swaps included in the trading book[234]. The specific risk offset for positions hedged by credit derivatives is as follows:

- **100% offset** – full capital relief (no specific risk capital requirement) will be recognised when the values of two legs (i.e. long and short) always move in the opposite direction and broadly to the same extent. This would be the case where:
  1. The two legs consist of completely identical instruments.
  2. A long cash position is hedged by a total rate of return swap (or vice versa) and there is an exact match between the reference obligation and the underlying exposure (i.e. the cash position).
- **80% offset** – partial capital relief will be recognised when the value of two legs (i.e. long and short) always moves in the opposite direction but not broadly to the same extent. This would be the case when a long cash position is hedged by a credit default swap or a credit linked note. There is a requirement for an exact match in terms, maturity and currency

---

[233] See Basel Committee on Banking Supervision (June 2004) International Convergence of Capital Measurement and Capital Standards: A Revised Framework; Bank for International Settlements, Basel, Switzerland.

[234] See Basel Committee on Banking Supervision (June 2004) International Convergence of Capital Measurement and Capital Standards: A Revised Framework; Bank for International Settlements, Basel, Switzerland.

between the credit derivative and the underlying exposure. In addition, key features of the credit derivative contract (e.g. credit event definitions, settlement mechanisms) should not cause the price movement of the credit derivative to materially deviate from the price movements of the cash position. Where all conditions are met, an 80% specific risk offset will be applied to the side of the transaction with the higher capital charge while the specific risk requirement on the other side will be zero.

- **Partial allowance** – some capital relief will be available when the value of the two legs (i.e. long and short) usually moves in the opposite direction. This would be where the general conditions for capital relief are satisfied except for the following conditions:
  1. There is an asset mismatch between the reference obligation and the underlying exposure.
  2. There is a currency or maturity mismatch between the credit protection and the underlying asset.
  3. There is an asset mismatch between the cash position and the credit derivative although the underlying asset is a deliverable obligation in the credit derivative documentation.

In each of these cases, rather than adding the specific risk capital requirements for each side of the transaction (i.e. the credit protection and the underlying asset), only the higher of the two capital requirements will apply.

In all other cases, a specific risk capital charge will be assessed against both sides of the position.

8.5.4 Banking Book Treatment

Basel 1

Where the total return swap is included in the banking book, the capital treatment is as follows:

- If the swap exactly offsets another position in the same reference asset, then the issuer risk on both positions exactly offset, leaving only counterparty risk on the swap.
- If the swap does not *exactly match* the underlying asset, then whether or not it is recognised as reducing exposure will depend on how closely it matches the underlying asset. There is uncertainty about the treatment under this scenario. The matching process requires satisfaction of the

following criteria:

1. *Reference asset* – the correlation between the asset being hedged and the reference asset underlying the swap (involving consideration of the factors identified above).
2. *Maturity match* – the correspondence between maturities of the positions.
3. *Currency match* – the reference asset in the total return swap and the underlying position are in the same currency.

- If the swap is not hedging an underlying position, then:
  1. If the swap entails a short position, then it is ignored[235].
  2. If the swap entails a long position, then it is treated as a direct credit substitute and the risk weight is that of the reference asset.

The position on maturity mismatches is interesting. There is a wide diversity of approaches:

- No recognition of any reduction in risk.
- One option allows a maturity mismatch subject to the following conditions:
  1. The residual maturity of the credit derivative is at least 1 year.
  2. An additional charge is made for the unhedged forward exposure at maturity of the credit derivative. This is treated as a 50% credit conversion factor against the risk weight of the underlying asset. This is similar to treating the unhedged forward exposure as an unfunded loan commitment.
- Another option is to recognise protection, subject to a 10% deduction of the amount of protection recognised (unless there is a currency mismatch, in which case the deduction is 20%).
- A further option is to allow some recognition of protection based on a linear weighting formula.

The current consensus seems to favour recognition of protection subject to some additional capital requirement for the forward exposure.

Basel 2

The Basel 2 amendments to the credit capital guidelines propose some changes to the treatment of total return swaps included in the banking

---

[235] This reflects the fact that capital in the banking book is only held against assets.

book[236]. In the case of an unhedged long position, the position is similar to that applicable currently, with the bank required to hold capital against the underlying asset at the relevant risk weights.

In the case of a hedged position, the treatment of credit derivatives is under provisions for credit mitigation. The general approach is that capital relief is available subject to capital being held against residual risk. Capital relief is subject to certain minimum standards/criteria including:

- **Types of protection** – only guarantees and credit derivatives (total return swaps and credit default swaps are recognised).
- **Minimum standards** – in general, only direct, explicit, legally enforceable and irrevocable transactions with a maturity of greater than 1 year are recognised for capital relief. For credit derivatives, there are certain additional minimum criteria, including:
  1. *Minimum credit events* – the minimum credit events required are bankruptcy, failure to pay and restructuring[237].
  2. *Settlement* – physical settlement is accepted. Cash settlement is acceptable only if a robust valuation process can be demonstrated.
  3. *Reference asset/obligations* – generally capital relief will require that the reference asset underlying the total return swap is identical to the position being hedged. If there is an asset mismatch, then certain minimum criteria must be met. This includes the same obligor, same seniority/pari passu obligation and similar terms (cross default/acceleration).
- **Eligible providers** – the approach is that only entities with lower risk weighting than the position being hedged are eligible. Entities include sovereigns/public sector entities, banks, corporations and credit linked notes.

As noted above, Basel 2 requires the restructuring credit event to be included if regulatory capital relief is to be obtained. When restructuring is not specified as a credit event, partial recognition of the credit derivative will be allowed. If the amount of the credit derivative is less than or equal to the

---

[236] See Basel Committee on Banking Supervision (June 2004) International Convergence of Capital Measurement and Capital Standards: A Revised Framework; Bank for International Settlements, Basel, Switzerland.

[237] This is subject to ongoing discussion/consultation.

amount of the underlying obligation, 60% of the amount of the hedge can be recognised as covered. If the amount of the credit derivative is larger than that of the underlying obligation, then the amount of eligible hedge is capped at 60% of the amount of the underlying obligation. The 60% recognition factor is provided as an interim treatment which the regulators intend to refine prior to implementation[238].

Full capital relief is proposed where there is an exact match in terms of reference asset, maturity and currency. Under the proposed approach, for guarantees/credit derivatives there is a risk weight adjustment based on the weighted average risk weighting of obligor and protection provider. The adjusted risk weighted asset is:

[(Exposure−Nominal Amount of Protection)
×Risk Weight of Reference Entity]
+[Nominal Amount of Protection
× Risk Weight of Seller of Protection]

Under the proposals, maturity and currency mismatches are permitted subject to capital being held against residual risk as follows:

- For maturity mismatch, the imperfect hedge is recognised. The additional capital requirement is calculated according to the following formula:

$$Pa = P \times (t - 0.25)/(T - 0.25)$$

where:

Pa = value of the credit protection adjusted for maturity mismatch

P = credit protection (e.g. collateral amount, guarantee amount) adjusted for any haircuts

t = min (T, residual maturity of the credit protection arrangement) expressed in years

T = min (5, residual maturity of the exposure) expressed in years

This has the effect of a linear reduction in risk based on the extent of the maturity mismatch.

- Where there is a currency mismatch, the protection amount is reduced by a *haircut* as follows:

$$Ga = G \times (1 - HFX)$$

[238] See Basel Committee on Banking Supervision (June 2004) International Convergence of Capital Measurement and Capital Standards: A Revised Framework; Bank for International Settlements, Basel, Switzerland at Paragraphs 191 and 192.

where:

Ga   = value of credit protection adjusted for currency mismatch
G   = nominal amount of the credit protection
HFX = haircut appropriate for currency mismatch between the credit
       protection and underlying obligation.

If a bank uses the supervisory standards, the appropriate haircut will be 8%. The haircuts must be scaled up using the square root of time formula, depending on the frequency of revaluation of the credit protection. The above treatment is under the Standardised Approach. Banks will also be able to use internal models to establish the appropriate haircut based on a 10-business-day holding period (assuming daily mark-to-market).

In the Internal Rating Based ("IRB") Approach, counterparty risk weights are based on internal assessment of default probability. The treatment of credit derivatives is also different. In the IRB Foundation Approach, the applicable credit mitigation rules are the same as the Standardised Approach. In the IRB Advanced Approach, the applicable credit mitigation rules are more complex and are based on internal models.

8.5.5   Treatment of Counterparty Risk[239]

There is also the issue of the counterparty credit risk against which capital must also be held. The credit capital required is calculated as follows:

Current exposure plus add-on for future exposure.

The replacement cost of the contract is the mark-to-market value of the contract. Under Basel 1, there is uncertainty about the add-on factor for potential future exposure[240].

The regulators appear to favour a variety of approaches, including:

● Interest rate add-ons for qualifying (for specific risk purposes) reference assets and equity product add-ons for non qualifying reference assets[241].

---

[239]   See Das, Satyajit (2004) Swaps/Financial Derivatives – 3rd Edition; John Wiley & Sons, Singapore at Chapter 33. For a discussion of the mechanics of calculating counterparty exposures, see Swaps/Financial Derivatives – 3rd Edition; John Wiley & Sons, Singapore at Chapter 21.

[240]   See Das, Satyajit (2004) Swaps/Financial Derivatives – 3rd Edition; John Wiley & Sons, Singapore at Chapter 33 for the add-on factors.

[241]   See FSA Board Notice 482 – *Guidance on Credit Derivatives* (July 1998) at paragraph 71.

- Equity add-ons for investment grade assets and commodity add-ons for non-investment grade assets.
- Equity add-ons irrespective of asset status.
- An asymmetric approach is feasible. The seller of protection uses interest rate add-ons for qualifying (for specific risk purposes) reference assets and equity product add-ons for non qualifying reference assets. The purchaser of protection uses equity rate add-ons for qualifying reference assets and commodity product add-ons for non-qualifying reference assets

No clear consensus has emerged regarding the add-on factors for potential future exposure.

The Basel 2 amendments to the credit capital guidelines do not propose changes to the calculation of the counterparty risk charges on derivative transactions. However, the following specific add-ons for credit derivatives have been proposed[242]:

	Protection buyer	Protection seller
Total Return Swap		
Qualifying reference obligation	5%	5%
Non-qualifying reference	10%	10%
Credit Default Swap		
Qualifying reference obligation	5%	5%
Non-qualifying reference obligation	10%	10%

8.6 Regulatory Framework – Credit Default Swaps

8.6.1 Overview

The issues in relation to the default swap are similar to those encountered in relation to total return swaps. From the perspective of the bank selling protection, capital must be held against the underlying credit asset. Logically there should be no exposure on the counterparty (the bank seeking protection) as there is no performance obligation on this party under the terms of the transaction. This assumes that the fee for the default swap is payable *in full* at the commencement of the transaction. If the fee is

---

[242] See Basel Committee on Banking Supervision (June 2004) International Convergence of Capital Measurement and Capital Standards: A Revised Framework; Bank for International Settlements, Basel, Switzerland.

payable over the term of the transaction, the bank selling protection has an exposure to the other party equivalent to the receivable of the fee.

The major issue relates to the ability of the bank seeking protection to reduce the risk weighting of the credit asset being hedged to that of the counterparty where the counterparty providing protection has a lower risk weighting. This will be the case in most cases for corporate credit risk where the protection is provided by an OECD bank. This will result in the substitution of a 20% risk weighting versus the 100% risk weighting for the underlying corporate obligation.

The consensus favours the substitution of the counterparty credit risk for the underlying credit risk only where the credit derivative transaction provides "virtually complete credit protection". This should be contrasted with transactions that provide "severely limited or uncertain" protection"[243]. Factors that *may* result in the credit protection being regarded as less than complete would include:

- Term of the hedge being shorter in maturity than the asset or obligation being hedged.
- The reference asset underlying the credit derivative is *not identical* to the hedged asset.
- The payout under the credit derivative may not accurately reflect the actual loss under the asset being hedged as a result of the mechanism for determining payout under the credit derivative being an average of dealer prices or a fixed amount agreed in advance.
- Uncertainty about the timing of the recovery under the credit derivatives because the agreement dictates payment after the pre-determined event or after the occurrence of the event plus satisfaction of additional conditions.

The issue of maturity mismatch is more difficult in the case of a credit default swap. In regard to the maturity mismatch, a potential form of treatment would allow the risk weighting to be reduced, allowing capital relief *for the period of the hedging credit derivative transaction*. The capital requirement and exposure would revert upon the credit derivative expiring. The bank seeking protection would also be required to hold *some additional*

---

[243] See Office of the Comptroller of the Currency, Administrator of National Banks "Guidance for Credit Derivatives" OCC Bulletin 96–43, 12 August 1996.

capital against the implied commitment to repurchase the credit asset after the credit hedge expires.

8.6.2   Banking Versus Trading Book Treatment

For credit default products, the initial regulatory position required inclusion in the banking book. Subsequently, regulators amended the treatment of default products to allow a trading book treatment of credit default swaps[244]. The reason for the change was comments by regulated banks that challenged the regulator's suggestions that credit default swaps lacked clarity in valuation methodology and liquidity. The banks persuaded the central bank that credit default swaps should be eligible for inclusion in the trading book. It should be noted that credit default swaps where the underlying asset is a loan might still be excluded in certain jurisdictions.

Under Basel 2, where a bank conducts an internal hedge using a credit derivative (i.e. hedge the credit risk of an exposure in the banking book with a credit derivative booked in the trading book), in order for the bank to receive any reduction in the capital requirement for the exposure in the banking book, the credit risk in the trading book must be transferred to an outside third party (i.e. an eligible protection provider). The banking book treatment for credit derivatives will be used to calculate the capital requirements for the hedged banking book position.

8.6.3   Trading Book Treatment

The treatment of a credit default swap where it is eligible for inclusion in the trading book follows the logic applicable to total return swaps.

Using this framework, where a credit default swap is referenced to a traded security issued by the relevant issuer, it is treated in the trading book as equivalent to the specific risk of a long or short position in the bond with the maturity of the credit default swap. Where the swap offsets an existing position in the same security (the issuer, seniority, and terms are identical), and where the maturity of the security and the swap is the same, the specific risk charges of the two positions will offset. Where the credit default swap has a shorter maturity, no specific risk offset is allowed and a specific risk charge is applied to either both positions or to the larger of the positions as

---

[244]   See FSA Board Notice 482 – *Guidance on Credit Derivatives* (July 1998) at paragraph 20,71.

specified above. No general interest rate charge is applied to credit default swaps in the trading book.

The proposed treatment under Basel 2 is identical to that for total return swaps. The Basel 2 proposals create special difficulties for credit default swaps. This reflects the fact that credit default swaps do not have a *specific* reference asset. Instead, the transaction references an identified group of obligations that are deliverable in case of a credit event. This means that protection buyers will face a one-sided capital charge where they hedge a credit asset with a credit default swap where the underlying is deliverable.

8.6.4 Banking Book Treatment

Where the credit default swap is included in the banking book, the required treatment is:

- If protection is sold, then the exposure is treated as a direct credit substitute and the risk weight is that of the reference asset.
- If protection is purchased, then the protection conferred will be incorporated in any capital calculation only where certain conditions are met.

The criteria that must be met include:

- The asset match must demonstrate high correlation.
- Protection must cover the full life of the underlying asset.
- The payment structure must have minimal uncertainty. Physical delivery is regarded as a certain payment structure. Cash settlement (based on par less recovery rate) is regarded as an uncertain structure.

Where all three criteria are met, the capital charge will be recognised and based on a full or partial guarantee or letter of credit (depending on the extent of protection conferred) with the risk weight being reduced to that of the counterparty. Where a maturity mismatch exists, the approach adopted is identical to that applicable to total return swaps. Where an uncertain payment structure is used or where a mark to market regime is difficult to implement, an additional charge may be levied to cover the payment uncertainty[245].

---

[245] For example, the FSA appears to take a position that *all* credit derivatives referenced to illiquid underlying assets, including loans, will be subject to an appropriate reserve against valuation uncertainties.

The proposed treatment under Basel 2 is identical to that for total return swaps.

8.7   Treatment of Collateral

Credit derivative transactions are frequently collateralised to enhance the credit risk of the counterparty selling credit protection[246]. The use of collateral affects the capital treatment. The capital impact is central to the use of collateral in credit derivative transactions.

Under Basel 1, only cash and government securities are recognised. Where a transaction is collateralised, the capital held against the position is reduced to the risk weighting of the collateral. This means that the capital held is generally reduced to zero (reflecting the zero risk weighting for cash and OECD sovereigns under Basel 1)[247].

Basel 2 proposes significant changes to the approach to collateral[248]. The basic changes proposed include:

- **Approach** – in order to be eligible for capital relief, a number of minimum conditions must be met. This includes legal certainty, low correlation between the credit risk being hedged and the collateral, and robust risk management. Two systems of recognition of collateral are proposed – comprehensive and simple. In practice, the comprehensive system will be most relevant to derivatives transactions (including credit derivatives).
- **Types of collateral** – the range of securities permitted for use as collateral has increased. The primary types of collateral include cash, gold, sovereign/public sector debt securities [rated BB – or better], bank debt securities [rated BBB– or better] and equities [listed on main index]. Other eligible collateral may include non rated bank paper, equities on listed exchanges and collective investments (units etc).
- **Comprehensive system** – the system is structured as follows:
  1. The system is based on daily margining. In the absence of margining, haircuts are scaled.

---

[246]   For discussion of collateral, see Das, Satyajit (2004) Swaps/Financial Derivatives – 3rd Edition; John Wiley & Sons, Singapore at Chapter 22.

[247]   See Das, Satyajit (2004) Swaps/Financial Derivatives – 3rd Edition; John Wiley & Sons, Singapore at Chapter 33.

[248]   See Basel Committee on Banking Supervision (June 2004) International Convergence of Capital Measurement and Capital Standards: A Revised Framework; Bank for International Settlements, Basel, Switzerland.

2. The proposed system adjusts the underlying exposure by the collateral held. This is undertaken in two ways:
   - *Standard* – under this approach, there is a system of haircuts for exposure, collateral and currency. **Exhibit 1.24** sets out the types of collateral and the applicable haircuts.
   - *Modelling* – this approach will be available to banks with approved market risk models. It entails the bank's own estimate based on VAR type modelling.
3. The adjustment to capital will be subject to a floor disallowance level (15%). The exception is government repos where there will be complete capital relief (0% disallowance) under limited conditions.
4. The relevant eligible collateral amount is the current value of collateral adjusted for the haircut for exposure, collateral and currency risk.
5. The risk weighting of the position is then adjusted subject to any applicable disallowance or minimum capital requirement.

Exhibit 1.24   Basel 2 – Collateral Haircuts

Issue Rating For Debt Securities	Residual Maturity (years)	Sovereign (%)	Other Issuers (%)
AAA to AA−/ A−1	< 1	0.5	1
	1 < ≤ 5	2	4
	> 5	4	8
A+ to BBB−/A−2/A−3/ P−3 and certain other bank securities	< 1	1	2
	1 < ≤5	3	6
	> 5	6	12
BB+ to BB−	All	15	
Main Index Equities (including convertible securities) and Gold	15		
Other Equities (including convertible securities) listed on a recognised securities exchange	25		
UCITS/Mutual Funds	Highest haircut applicable to any security that the fund can invest in		
Cash in the same currency	0		
FX Surcharge	8		

8.8   *Large Exposure Calculations*

Protection sold and purchased is recognised for the purpose of calculating large exposures. For example, under the BOE guidelines, the banks continue to report both the gross and the guaranteed exposures. A bank can choose either the exposure to the protected asset or the exposure to the guarantor to count towards its large exposure limits.

8.9   *Regulatory Position*

The regulatory approach to credit derivative transactions recognises that these transactions create or reduce exposure to counterparty credit risk, general market risk and specific risk (depending on structure). The treatment varies between the trading and the banking book.

In the trading book, the exposure created or transferred depends on the nature and purpose for which the transaction is entered into. Where the transaction is not matched or offsetting (an open transaction), it creates exposure to the relevant risks, functioning as a means to create synthetic credit exposure. Where the transactions are entered into for the purpose of transferring or hedging, the treatment is conditional upon the level of correspondence between the asset being hedged and the credit derivative. The degree of protection conferred depends on whether the transactions are matched (that is, long and short positions in identical assets with the maturity of the underlying transaction and the credit derivatives being exactly the same) or offsetting (where there are mismatches in reference asset or maturity).

In the banking book, the exposure transferred and the capital released is dependent upon the match between the underlying exposure and the credit derivative. Mismatches are generally not encouraged.

The regulatory treatment of credit derivatives highlights several anomalies in the capital adequacy regulations under Basel 1, including:

- Credit derivatives used to replicate traditional loan or bond credit exposures are capable of being treated in the *trading books* as distinct from the banking book[249]. For example, a traditional bank loan/bond to

---

[249]   The authorities have clarified the basis of classification between the banking and the trading book. In order to include a transaction in the trading book, the instrument must be the *subject of an intention to trade and it must be tradeable* (that is, it must be quoted daily in a liquid market or otherwise freely tradeable).

a corporation would traditionally have been booked in the institution's banking book and attract a capital charge of 8%. If the transaction is structured as a total return swap or credit default swap with the same loan/bond as a reference/deliverable obligation, then it could be booked in the bank's trading book and would attract a lower capital charge (1.6%). The advantage of a lower capital charge would be partially offset by the following:

1. The position would have to be marked to market (resulting in greater volatility in earnings).
2. There would be a counterparty risk charge (in the case where the trade was structured as a total return swap).

It is important to note that the same treatment (except for the counterparty risk charge) could be engineered by restructuring the transaction as a tradeable security (a bond). The distortion may impact upon banking practice in determining *how* specific transactions are structured as distinct from the fundamental economics of the transactions.

- The capital treatment in some jurisdictions in some circumstances creates a disincentive to hedge. Credit derivatives may be required to be included in the trading book for capital adequacy purposes. If the credit derivative is being used to hedge an existing credit position in the banking book, then the hedge may be economically efficient but may not provide capital relief. In fact, the overall capital charge may increase. In order to achieve the desired capital relief, it will be necessary to either include the credit derivative in the banking book or transfer the position being hedged into the trading book. This may be difficult or not permitted by the relevant regulator. Where a transaction does not qualify for a risk offset, the proposed treatment may also increase capital requirements. For example, where there is reference asset or maturity mismatch, the hedge (even if it provides an economic reduction in risk) may result in *higher capital charges*. This is because the entity will be required to hold capital potentially against *both* the transaction being hedged and the credit derivative. This clearly creates an incentive *not to hedge*.

See Basel Committee on Banking Supervision (June 2004) International Convergence of Capital Measurement and Capital Standards: A Revised Framework; Bank for International Settlements, Basel, Switzerland.

- There may be differences between the treatment of different types of credit derivatives and different types of instruments which achieve economically similar outcomes. The differences between the treatment of the types of credit derivatives are subtle. It affects such issues as maturity mismatches and default payment mismatches. This may distort the trading in total return swaps as against credit default swaps. The differences between different types of instruments that are used to achieve economically similar results can be illustrated with the example of securitisation. Structures such as Collateralised Debt Obligation ("CDO") transactions[250] can be used in a manner analogous to credit default swaps to hedge the economic credit exposures within portfolios. However, the regulatory capital treatment of the two structures is not always consistent.

The anomalies identified are not derived from the regulatory treatment of credit derivatives but from weaknesses in the treatment of credit risk generally within the regulatory capital framework. Basel 2 seeks to lower the incentives for regulatory arbitrage between the banking and trading books.

9 Summary

Credit derivatives are traditional derivatives re-engineered to a credit orientation. Credit derivatives are principally concerned with the isolation of credit risk as a separately traded market variable. The different products are essentially focused on structuring instruments to allow trading in credit risk in varied forms. The major product in the credit derivatives market is the credit default swap. The documentation of credit derivatives presents significant challenges. Credit derivatives allow hedging or assumption of credit risk by market participants. Credit derivatives can be structured to provide relief against economic and regulatory capital requirements.

---

[250] See Chapter 4.

2
Structured Credit Products

1 Overview

The core of the credit derivatives market involves trading in the key building block products, primarily credit default swaps. However, the product structures within credit derivatives have evolved rapidly. Variations on standard product structures have emerged. Chapter 1 outlined the key credit derivative products. This Chapter covers structured credit products.

The structure of the Chapter is as follows:

- A framework of structured credit products is outlined.
- Individual structured products are then discussed, with the principal focus being on the structure, value dynamics and applications.

2 Structured Credit Products – Framework

Exhibit 2.1 sets out some of the key types of structured credit products[1]. The major drivers for structured credit products include:

- **Additional flexibility** – this focuses on creating additional flexibility for traders and users of credit derivative products.
- **Underlying credit asset** – this covers trading the credit risk of different underlying credit obligations, such as derivative transactions or a credit index.
- **Trading credit risk dimensions** – this entails allowing dealers to trade risks, such as default correlation and recovery rate, and monetise expectations of such risks.

---

[1] For an overview of different forms of structured credit derivatives, see (2003) The Lehman Brothers – Guide To Exotic Credit Derivatives; Lehman Brothers/Risk Waters Group; Perraudin, William (Editor) (2004) Structured Credit Products; Risk Publications.

- **Leverage** – structured credit products frequently enable traders to leverage credit spreads to enhance returns.

The market in structured credit products is driven substantially by their ability to generate incremental yield (by assuming different risks) or hedge specific types of exposures. In practice, the use of structured credit products to generate additional yield or return is the major driver of this market.

The credit derivatives market also covers other types of trading in credit risk. The major example of this form of structured exposure to credit risks is tranched credit structures. This entails the creation of exposure to specific layers or priorities of credit risk. In practice, the bulk of these types of transactions are undertaken in the form of credit linked notes/collateralised debt obligations[2].

Exhibit 2.1 Structured Credit Products – Framework	
Type Of Product	**Structured Credit Products**
Variations on standard credit default swaps	• Portfolio swaps • Swap guarantees • Up-front credit default swaps • Quanto credit default swaps • Credit swaptions
Recovery rate structures	• Recovery rate swaps • Zero recovery credit default swaps
Correlation structures	• First-to-default swaps/ N^{th}-to-default swaps
Credit spread structures	• Asset swaptions/synthetic lending facilities • Structured asset swaps
Constant maturity products	• Constant maturity credit spread products • Constant maturity credit default swaps
Index products	• Credit index products
Capital structure arbitrage/ debt-equity hybrids	• Equity default swaps
Sovereign risk structures	• Currency convertibility products

---

[2] See discussion in Chapters 3 and 4.

3   Portfolio Default Swaps

Standard credit default swaps are based on a single reference entity. Portfolio/basket credit default swaps are similar to conventional credit default swaps. The difference is that the swap is referenced to multiple reference entities (the *portfolio* underlying the swap)[3]. The structure is designed to allow the protection buyer to purchase protection on an entire portfolio of credit risks in a single transaction. The structure allows the seller of protection to obtain exposure to the portfolio in a single transaction.

The key features of the portfolio default swap include:

- The structure is predicated on *proportionate* exposure to the *individual reference entities* for the agreed amount of the nominal amount of exposure. In effect, the transaction is a series of separate credit default swaps documented as a single credit default swap. Losses and payments are based on the performance of the individual credit default swaps. The structure is different to the purchase or sale of credit risk on a portfolio based on the aggregate performance of the portfolio[4].
- The portfolio is either a customised portfolio of reference entities or a pre-determined index of credit risks. Where a predetermined index is used, the reference entities remain static over the term of the swap (generally 5 years). Dealers offer a variety of baskets or indexes based on different sectors/markets. The baskets and indexes are generally updated periodically, with new baskets being offered every 6 months or so[5].

The major benefits of portfolio credit default swaps include:

- **Diversified portfolio** – the structures allows efficient trading in/transfer of a diversified portfolio of credit risks. This is particularly attractive to investors or banks seeking to acquire a diversified portfolio of credit risks. In the case of portfolio default swaps based on an index, the dealer

---

[3]   See Cass, Dwight "Portfolio Default Swaps Move Online" (October 2000) Risk 12.

[4]   See discussion on nth-to-default baskets later in this chapter and collateralised debt obligations ("CDOs") in Chapter 4.

[5]   See discussion later in this Chapter.

may be able to offer a fractionalised exposure where the investor can use a limited amount of capital to acquire a diversified portfolio that would be difficult/impossible to construct directly.

- **Pricing negotiation** – the pricing of a portfolio credit default swap is based on the pricing of the individual credit default swaps. The portfolio credit default swap is generally the nominal face value weighted fees on the constituent reference entities. In practice, it is easier to negotiate the fee for the portfolio than for each of the individual credit default swaps separately. This reflects the fact that the fee paid or received is on the total portfolio.
- **Administration** – documentation and administration of the portfolio credit default swap is inherently more efficient than that for the individual swaps.

4   Swap Guarantees/Market Risk Contingent Credit Default Swaps[6]

Credit default swap structures generally assume that the underlying credit exposure being hedged/assumed is fixed and known. This is the case with credit exposure on bond and loan structures. Where the underlying transaction is a derivative transaction (such as an interest rate swap, cross currency swap etc), the credit exposure is a function of movements in market variables (interest rates, foreign exchange rates, and implied volatility) and the remaining time to maturity[7]. For example, in any swap, forward or option position, the credit exposure between the counterparties is a function of two factors. The first factor is the current mark-to-market value of the transaction (effectively its replacement value at current market rates). The second factor is an estimate of the expected future replacement costs (derived using the expected volatility of the variables affecting the contract value).

The static structure of the conventional credit default swap is not designed to effectively hedge/transfer dynamic credit risk. Swap guarantees

---

[6]   For discussion of the structure and value dynamics of swap guarantee structures, see Chapter 7.
[7]   See Das, Satyajit (2004) Swaps/Financial Derivatives 3rd Edition; John Wiley & Sons, Singapore at Chapter 21.

or market risk contingent credit default swaps evolved around 1995/1996 to allow hedging of this type of credit risk[8].

The swap guarantee is a credit default swap where the notional principal is linked directly to the credit exposure on a swap transaction (that is, the mark-to-market value of the reference transaction). **Exhibit 2.2** sets out the structure of the contract.

The principal features of the structures include:

- In the event of a credit event or default by the reference entity under the swap, the bank providing protection will make a payment to the bank purchasing protection of an amount related directly *to the mark-to-market value of the swap at the time of default.*
- The payment made is based on the expected recovery value estimated from the price of traded bonds of the reference entity.
- The default event may be defined generally or with reference to default on the swap itself.
- The swap guarantee is generally cash settled.
- The credit default swap linked to the value of the swap is capable of being structured in a number of alternative ways:
  1. The default swap may cover *any exposure* under the swap.
  2. The default swap may cover exposure of a pre-agreed amount.
  3. The default swap may cover exposure above a minimum amount.
- The term of the protection can also be varied, with protection available for periods up to the full remaining term of the swap.

The credit default swap linked to the swap value is different from a normal credit swap in that the amount of the default payment is dynamic and linked to the value of the swap (which is a function of *market variables*). The bank buying protection will only suffer a loss if the swap counterparty defaults, there is an amount owing under the swap, and the bank providing protection under the swap also defaults. This multiple contingency structure significantly enhances the credit quality of the exposure that will generally be superior to that of both the swap counterparty and the swap guarantee counterparty.

---

[8] The major portion of these types of transactions relate to swaps (particularly, currency swaps). Consequently, the term swap guarantee is used to designate these types of structures.

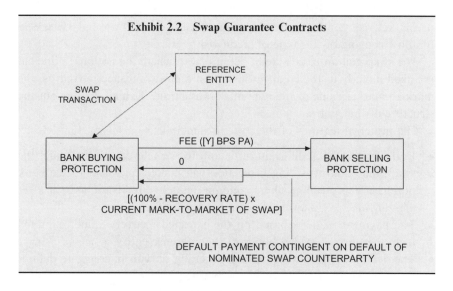

Exhibit 2.2   Swap Guarantee Contracts

5   Up-Front Credit Default Swaps[9]

5.1   *Structure*

Under a conventional credit default swap, the buyer of protection pays the fee required to the seller of protection over the term of the transaction. The fee is paid in arrears (either quarterly or semi-annually) until maturity or a credit event[10]. In an up-front credit default swap, the buyer of protection pays the seller of protection a single payment at the commencement of the contract. In all other respects, the up-front credit default swap is identical to the conventional credit default swap.

Up-front credit default swaps are generally used with distressed credits. Such transactions are usually also only for short maturities (up to one year). This contrasts with conventional credit default swaps that have a standard maturity of five years.

The rationale for up-front credit default swaps includes:

- The structure more closely approximates the direct purchase of a distressed bond in the cash market.

---

[9]   See O'Kane, Dominic and Sen, Saurav "Up-front Credit Default Swaps" (August 2003) Quantitative Credit Research; Lehman Brothers 18–31.

[10]   See Chapter 1.

- The payment of the up-front premium eliminates uncertainty about the receipt or payment of the fee. In particular, it eliminates the credit exposure that the protection seller has to the protection buyer in relation to the fee. The structure also provides an incentive for sellers of protection to assume the risk of distressed credits (as it guarantees the size and timing of the fee payment).
- The structure of the up-front credit default swap creates significantly different risk and payoff profiles to conventional credit default swaps; for example, risk-reward in case of default, valuation and sensitivity to risk factors. This allows buyers and sellers of protection to monetise different views on the underlying credit risk.

5.2 Economics

The payment of the premium up-front alters the performance and dynamics of the credit default swap significantly. This difference is most apparent where the buyer of protection is long the underlying credit risk (in the form of a bond) and purchases protection against default. Where the obligor is distressed and the bond is trading below par, entry into a conventional credit default swap where the holder buys protection against default provides credit protection against principal loss. Where a premium up-front credit default swap is used, the performance of the hedge is dependent upon the occurrence and timing of the credit event. In certain situations, the up-front credit default swap may out-perform the conventional structure.

The only difference between the two structures is the timing of the fee. In an up-front structure, the fee is a known amount that is received at commencement. In a conventional structure, the fee is a series of payments that is uncertain. The uncertainty derives from the risk of default of the buyer of protection and the occurrence and timing of the credit event (if any). This drives significant differences in performance. Where a holder of a distressed bond (trading well below par) hedges with either a conventional or up-front credit default swap, the outcomes are as follows:

- **Reference entity does not experience a credit event** – the position is that the holder experiences a larger initial cash outflow where an up-front credit default swap is used (reflecting the payment of the up-front fee). However, the combined position (long bond plus bought protection under up-front credit default swap) shows a large positive carry (reflecting the absence of periodic fee payments). The position at maturity also reflects a cash outflow (reflecting repayment of the larger initial investment). In contrast, where a conventional credit default swap is used, the transaction will entail a significant negative carry reflecting the high fees paid for protection relative to the income on the bond. On a net present value basis, the differences dictate that a buyer of protection using an up-front credit default swap may achieve superior outcomes where it expects the reference entity not to experience a credit event. The up-front structure enables it to hedge its risk for a known payment.

- **Reference entity experiences credit event** – where the reference entity suffers a credit event triggering termination of the contract, the outcomes depend on the timing of the default. Where a conventional credit default swap is used, the purchaser of protection receives the benefit of protection in return for paying only the fee for the period until default. In contrast, where an up-front credit default swap is used, the fee paid by the buyer of protection is significantly larger. Where a credit event is expected to be imminent, the protection purchaser achieves a superior outcome on a net present value basis where a conventional credit default swap is used. Where the credit event does not occur until late in the maturity of the credit default swap, the position is different. Depending upon the exact timing of the credit event, the up-front credit default swap may give a superior outcome. This is for reasons similar to the factors applicable when the reference entity does not experience a credit event.
- **Reference credit experiences improvement in credit quality** – where the reference entity does not experience a credit event *and* the credit quality improves, the up-front credit default swap may provide a superior outcome. This reflects the fact that the up-front structure has lower sensitivity to changes in spread than a conventional credit default swap. This is because a conventional credit default swap exhibits sensitivity to spread changes on both the fees and the default payment component. In this situation, the purchaser can terminate both transactions. This enables the purchaser to offset the capital gain on the bond against the loss on the credit default swap. The form of protection does not affect the gain on the bond. However, the loss on the up-front credit default swap will usually be less than for a comparable conventional credit default swap.

The analysis indicates that there are differences in the performance of the conventional and up-front credit default swap as a hedge to the underlying bond position. This allows traders to extract value from specific expectations about the probability and timing of default.

The value of an up-front credit default swap is simply the expected payment (notional value less recovery rate where a credit event occurs). In an arbitrage-free world, the pricing of the different structures would reflect market expectations so that traders are indifferent between the conventional and up-front credit default swap structures. In practice, the different pattern of cash flows and the ability to trade expectations of default timing allow traders to alter the dynamics of expected outcomes by using either conventional or up-front structures.

Under normal conditions, up-front credit default swaps are used primarily to trade/hedge distressed credits and also change sensitivity to spread changes.

6   Credit Swaptions

6.1   Structure

Credit swaptions entail an option to buy or sell a credit default swap at a future date at an agreed cost[11]. The structure is similar to swaptions (options to enter into interest rate or currency swaps)[12]. These structures emerged around 2002, reflecting increased volatility in credit markets.

Exhibit 2.3 sets out the economics of a credit swaption. **Exhibit 2.4** sets out a typical confirmation of a credit swaption.

The key features of a credit swaption include:

- **Mechanics** – the basic concept is that the purchaser has the right (but not the obligation) to enter into a credit default swap on a pre-agreed reference credit at an agreed fee. The purchaser has the right to enter into the underlying credit default swap on or by an agreed date. The seller sells these rights to the purchaser. The purchaser pays a fee to the seller of the credit swaption at commencement.
- **Types** – there are two types of credit swaptions:
  1. *Payer* – the purchaser has the right to purchase protection.
  2. *Receiver* – the purchaser has the right to sell protection.
- **Underlying credit default swap** – the underlying of a credit default swap is a conventional credit default swap on the relevant reference entity for a

---

[11]   See Polyn, Gallagher "Credit Volatility Spurs Interest In Credit Default Swaptions Market" (August 2002) Risk 11; Patel, Navroz "Default Swaps: The Next Frontier" (May 2003) Risk 16–17.

[12]   See Das, Satyajit (2004) Swaps/Financial Derivatives 3rd Edition; John Wiley & Sons, Singapore at Chapter 49.

fixed maturity (usually 5 years). The underlying credit default swap has
normal features.

- **Reference entities** – credit swaptions are generally based on either:
  1. *Individual reference entities* – covering individual entities (sovereign,
     financial institutions and non-financial institutions) being nominated
     as the reference entity.
  2. *Credit indexes* – covering the use of customised credit indexes as the
     underlying reference entity for the credit default swap[13].
- **Strike price** – this is the fee for the underlying credit default swap that
  is agreed at the time of entry into the credit swaption. The fee is paid by
  the purchaser to the seller of the credit swaption where the swaption is
  exercised and settled physically.
- **Exercise period** – this is the period during which the purchaser is entitled
  to exercise the credit swaption. Credit swaptions can be structured
  as European (the swaption must be exercised on a fixed date) or
  American (the swaption can be exercised at any time by a fixed date).
  The exercise conventions are consistent with that used in normal
  options. In practice, credit swaptions are generally European (in
  exercise convention) and have relatively short maturity (six to 12
  months). The credit swaption will generally terminate prior to exercise if
  the underlying reference entity experiences a credit event during the
  exercise period.
- **Swaption fee** – this is the fee paid by the purchaser to the seller of the
  credit swaption. It is in fact the option premium.
- **Settlement** – credit swaptions may be settled in the following manner:
  1. *Cash settlement* – this entails the seller paying the purchaser the
     economic value of the contract. For example, in the case of a payer
     credit swaption where fees on the credit default swap increase above
     the strike level, the purchaser would receive the present value of the
     difference between the strike fee and the current market fee (based
     on a dealer poll mechanism).
  2. *Physical settlement* – this entails the purchaser entering into the
     underlying credit default swap with the credit swaption seller. The
     underlying credit default swap, once entered into, operates in an
     identical manner to a normal credit default swap.

---

[13] See discussion later in this Chapter.

Type of Credit Swaption	Payer	Receiver
Structure	Purchaser buys option to buy protection on selected reference entity at agreed strike price (credit default swap spread)	Purchaser buys option to sell protection on selected reference entity at agreed strike price (credit default swap spread)
Payoff	Purchaser exercises if credit default swap spread increases above strike	Purchaser exercises if credit default swap spread decreases below strike
Position of Purchaser	• Purchaser benefits if credit default swap spread increases • Purchaser suffers loss of premium if credit default swap spread decreases	• Purchaser benefits if credit default swap spread decreases • Purchaser suffers loss of premium if credit default swap spread increases
Position of Seller	• Seller benefits by premium if credit default swap spread decreases • Seller suffers loss if credit default swap spread increases	• Seller benefits by premium if credit default swap spread increases • Seller suffers loss if credit default swap spread decreases

Exhibit 2.3   Credit Swaptions

Exhibit 2.4   Credit Swaptions – Confirmation[14]

[Specify Full Legal Name, and Address of Party B]

Our Reference: [   ]

Option on Credit Derivative Transaction

Dear Sir/Madam,

The purpose of this agreement (this "Confirmation") is to confirm the terms and conditions of the Credit Derivative Transaction entered into between [Dealer] ("**Party A**") and [Full legal name of counterparty] ("**Party B**") on the Trade Date specified below (the "Transaction").

---

[14]   The author would like to thank Deutsche Bank for their consent to base the above on the bank's credit swaption confirmation. The author would also like to thank Andrew Baume for his help in arranging the inclusion of the document.

The definitions and provisions contained in the 2003 ISDA Credit Derivatives Definitions, as supplemented by the May 2003 Supplement to the such Definitions (as so supplemented, the "**Credit Derivatives Definitions**") and the 2000 ISDA Definitions (the "**2000 Definitions**"), each as published by the International Swaps and Derivatives Association, Inc. and as modified as set out herein (collectively, the "**Definitions**") are incorporated into this Confirmation. The 2000 Definitions will apply to Section 1 while the Credit Derivative Definitions will apply to Section 2. In the event of any inconsistency between (i) the 2000 Definitions and Sections 1 and 2 of this Confirmation; and/or (ii) the Credit Derivatives Definitions and Section 2 of this Confirmation, this Confirmation will govern.

This Confirmation constitutes a "Confirmation" as referred to in, and supplements, forms a part of and is subject to, the ISDA [Master Agreement/Interest Rate and Currency Exchange Agreement][15] dated as of [date][16], as amended and supplemented from time to time (the "Agreement"), between you and [Dealer]. All provisions contained in the Agreement govern this Confirmation except as expressly modified below. [References herein to a "Transaction" shall be deemed to be references to a "Swap Transaction" for the purposes of the Agreement][17].

This Confirmation evidences a complete and binding agreement between Party A and Party B as to the terms of the Transaction to which this Confirmation relates. In addition Party A and Party B agree to use all reasonable efforts promptly to negotiate, execute and deliver an agreement in the form of the ISDA Master Agreement (Multicurrency-Cross Border) (the "ISDA Form") with such modifications as you and we will in good faith agree. Upon execution by Party A and Party B of such an agreement, this Confirmation will supplement, form a part of, and be subject to that agreement. All provisions contained or incorporated by reference in that agreement upon its execution will govern this Confirmation. Until we execute and deliver that agreement, this Confirmation, together with all other documents referring to the ISDA Form (each a "Confirmation") confirming transactions (each a "Transaction") entered into between us (notwithstanding anything to the contrary in a Confirmation) shall supplement, form a part of, and be subject to an agreement in the form of the ISDA Form as if we had executed an agreement on the Trade Date of the first such Transaction between us in such form with the Schedule thereto (i) specifying only that (a) the governing law is [English law/the law of the State of New York without reference to choice of law doctrine] and (b) the Termination

---

[15] Delete as appropriate.

[16] Insert date of relevant ISDA agreement.

[17] Only include this provision where the Transaction is to be governed by an Interest Rate and Currency Exchange Agreement instead of an ISDA Master Agreement.

Currency is U.S. Dollars, (ii) incorporating the addition to the definition of "Indemnifiable Tax" contained in (page 48 of) the ISDA "Users Guide to the 1992 ISDA Master Agreements" and (iii) incorporating any other modifications to the ISDA form specified below.][18]

1. The Swap Transaction to which this Confirmation relates is a Swaption, the terms of which are as follows:

(a) Swaption Terms:

Trade Date: [   ]
Option Style: European
Seller: [Party A][Party B]
Buyer: [Party A][Party B]
Premium: [USD][EUR] [   ]
Premium Payment Date: [   ]
Exercise Business Day: For non-Euro european currencies:
                                    London and [currency]
                                    For Euro: [London and] TARGET Settlement Day
Calculation Agent: [Seller]

(b) Procedure for Exercise:

Expiration Date: [   ]; *provided, however*, that if a Credit
                                    Event (as defined in the Credit Derivatives
                                    Definitions and further specified below in
                                    paragraph 2(c)) shall have occurred on or before
                                    the Expiration Date (the date of such occurrence,
                                    the "**Credit Event Date**"), then (i) the Buyer shall
                                    not have the right to exercise the Option (or if
                                    it has exercised the Option, such exercise shall be
                                    deemed ineffective), (ii) the Seller shall have the
                                    right to terminate this Transaction as of the
                                    Credit Event Date and (iii) no further payments
                                    will be due from either party under this
                                    Transaction.
Earliest Exercise Time: For non-Euro European ccy: 9:00 a.m.,
                                    [London] time
                                    For Euro: 9:00 a.m., Brussels time
Expiration Time: For non-Euro European ccy: 11:00 a.m.,
                                    [London] time
                                    For Euro: 11:00 a.m., Brussels time
Partial Exercise   Inapplicable
Fallback Exercise: Inapplicable

---

[18]   Delete this paragraph if a Master Agreement is in place between the parties.

(c)   Settlement Terms:

Settlement: Physical

2.   The particular terms of the Underlying Swap Transaction to which the Swaption
     relates are as follows:

Type of Transaction: Credit Derivative Transaction

(a)   General Terms:

Effective Date: [   ]
Scheduled Termination   [   ]
 Date:
Floating Rate Payer: [Party A] [Party B] (the "Seller")
Fixed Rate Payer: [Party A] [Party B] (the "Buyer")
Calculation Agent: [Seller]
Calculation Agent City: [London]
Business Day: London and [New York] [Tokyo] [Sydney]
                                  [TARGET Settlement Day(s)]
Business Day Convention: Following (which subject to Sections
                                  1.4 and 1.6 of the Credit Derivatives
                                  Definitions, shall apply to any date referred
                                  to in this Confirmation that falls on a day
                                  that is not a Business Day).
Reference Entity: [   ]
[Reference Obligation(s):   The obligation(s) identified as follows:
                                  Primary Obligor: [   ]
                                  Guarantor: [   ]
                                  Maturity: [   ]
                                  Coupon: [   ]
                                  [CUSIP] [ISIN]:   [   ]]
All Guarantees: [Applicable[19]/Not Applicable][20]
Reference Price: 100 per cent.

(b)   Fixed Payments:

Fixed Rate Payer   [USD] [EUR] [JPY] [   ]
 Calculation
 Amount:
Fixed Rate Payer   [date] [month] [year] and thereafter each
 Payment   [date] [month], [date] [month], [date]
 Date(s):   [month] and [date] [month]
Fixed Rate: [   ] per cent.
Fixed Rate Day
 Count Fraction:

                                  Actual/360

---

[19]   Use for European
[20]   Use for North American

(c) Floating Payment:

Floating Rate Payer Calculation Amount:	[USD] [EUR] [JPY] [ ]
Conditions to Settlement:	Credit Event Notice

	Notifying Party:	Buyer or Seller [Section 3.9 of the Credit Derivative Definitions shall not apply to this Transaction. "Greenwich Mean Time" in Section 3.3 of the Credit Derivative Definitions shall be replaced by "Tokyo time" for the purposes of this Transaction.][21]
	Notice of Physical Settlement Notice of Publicly Available Information:	Applicable
Credit Events:[22]	The following Credit Events shall apply to this Transaction: [Bankruptcy] [Failure to Pay]	
	[Grace Period Extension: [Payment Requirement:	Applicable/ Not Applicable][23] [USD][EUR] 1,000,000 or its equivalent in the relevant Obligation Currency as of the occurrence of the relevant Failure to Pay [or Potential Failure to Pay, as applicable][24].] [25]
	[Obligation Default] [Obligation Acceleration] [Repudiation/Moratorium] [Restructuring]	

---

[21] Delete if not a Tokyo trade
[22] Delete the Credit Events that are inapplicable
[23] If Failure to Pay is applicable, keep this in, otherwise delete
[24] If Grace Period Extension is not applicable, delete this section
[25] If Failure to Pay is applicable, keep Payment Requirement in, otherwise delete

[Restructuring Maturity   **Applicable]**[26]
Limitation and Fully
Transferable Obligation:

[Modified Restructuring   **Applicable]**[27]
Maturity Limitation
and Conditionally
Transferable Obligation:

Multiple Holder   **Not Applicable/**
Obligation: **Applicable**
                                    [Not Applicable with
                                    respect to Bonds
                                    Applicable with
                                    respect to Loans][28]
Default Requirement: [USD][EUR] 10,000,000
                                    or its equivalent in
                                    the relevant Obligation
                                    Currency as of the
                                    occurrence of the
                                    relevant Credit Event.
Obligation(s):
Obligation
Category:[29]   [Payment]
                                    [Borrowed Money]
                                    [Reference Obligations Only][30]
                                    [Bond]
                                    [Loan]
                                    [Bond or Loan]
Obligation
Characteristics:[31]   [Not Subordinated]
                                    [Specified Currency:
                                        Standard Specified Currencies[; and the lawful
                                        currency of the Commonwealth of Australia
                                        (and any successor to such currency)][32]
                                    [Not Sovereign Lender]
                                    [Not Domestic Currency]

---

[26] Insert if Modified Restructuring – MR (standard fallback for US underlyings)
[27] Insert if Modified Modified Restructuring – MMR (standard fallback for
     European underlyings)
[28] If Obligation Category is Bond or Loan, then select this option
[29] Select one from the list
[30] If Applicable, no Obligation Characteristics should be specified
[31] Delete the Deliverable Obligations that are inapplicable
[32] Include in AUD transactions only.

	[Not Domestic Law]
	[Listed]
	[Not Domestic Issuance]
	[[None Specified]
[Obligation(s)	*Specify any other obligations of a Reference Entity*]
shall include:	
[Excluded Obligations:	[ ]]

(d) Settlement Terms:

Settlement Method: Physical Settlement

Terms relating to Physical
Settlement:

Physical Settlement Period: [Thirty (30) Business Days] / [The longest number
of Business Days for settlement in accordance
with then current market practice of such
Deliverable Obligation, as determined by the
Calculation Agent, after consultation with
the parties.] [,subject to a maximum of thirty
(30) [Business Days][calendar days]]

Deliverable Obligations: [Exclude Accrued Interest]
Deliverable Obligations:
Deliverable Obligation
Category:[33]

[Payment]
[Borrowed Money]
[Reference Obligations Only][34]
[Bond]
[Loan]
[Bond or Loan]

Deliverable Obligation
Characteristics:[35]

[Not Subordinated]
[Specified Currency:
Standard Specified Currencies[; and the lawful
currency of the Commonwealth of Australia
(and any successor to such currency)][36]
[Not Sovereign Lender]
[Not Domestic Currency]
[Not Domestic Law]
[Listed]

---

[33] Select one from the list
[34] If Applicable, no Obligation Characteristics should be specified
[35] Delete the Deliverable Obligation Characteristics that are inapplicable
[36] Include in AUD transactions only.

	[Not Contingent]
	[Not Domestic Issuance]
	[Assignable Loan]
	[Consent Required Loan]
	[Direct Loan Participation]
	[Qualifying Participation Seller:]³⁷
	[Transferable]
	[Maximum Maturity:
	[Thirty (30) years]]
	[Accelerated or Matured]
	[Not Bearer]
	[None Specified]
[Deliverable Obligation(s) shall include:	[Specify any other obligations of a Reference Entity]
[Excluded Deliverable Obligations:	[ ]]
Partial Cash Settlement of Consent Required Loans:	**Applicable/Not Applicable**
Partial Cash Settlement of Assignable Loans:	Applicable/Not Applicable
Partial Cash Settlement of Participations:	Applicable/Not Applicable
Escrow:	Applicable/Not Applicable

[(e)   Additional Terms:

Notwithstanding Section 1.7 or any provisions of Sections 9.9 or 9.10 to the contrary, but without prejudice to Section 9.3 and (where applicable) Sections 9.4, 9.5 and 9.6 if the Termination Date has not occurred on or prior to the date that is 60 Business Days following the Physical Settlement Date, such 60th Business Day shall be deemed to be the Termination Date with respect to this Transaction except in relation to any portion of the Transaction (an "Affected Portion") in respect of which:

(1)   a valid notice of Buy-in Price has been delivered that is effective fewer than three Business Days prior to such 60th Business Day, in which case the Termination Date for that Affected Portion shall be the third Business Day following the date on which such notice is effective; or

(2)   Buyer has purchased but not Delivered Deliverable Obligations validly specified by Seller pursuant to Section 9.10(b), in which case the Termination Date for that Affected Portion shall be the tenth Business Day following the date on which Seller validly specified such Deliverable Obligations to Buyer.]

---

³⁷   Delete if Direct Loan Participation is not applicable.

(f) Notice and Account Details:

Telephone and/or Facsimile Numbers and Contact Details for Notices:	Party A: Party B:

Account Details of Party A:
Account Details of Party B:

(g) Offices:	The Office of Party A for the Transaction is London[; and The Office of Party B for the Transaction is [ ].][38]

3. **Representations:**

Each party will be deemed to represent to the other party on the date on which it enters into this Transaction that (absent a written agreement between the parties that expressly imposes affirmative obligations to the contrary for this Transaction):

(i) **No Actual Loss Required.** The parties agree and acknowledge that the obligation of the Seller exists regardless of whether the Buyer suffers a loss or is exposed to the risk of loss upon the occurrence of a Credit Event, and regardless of whether the Buyer has any legal or beneficial interest in an Obligation of a Reference Entity.

(ii) **Non-Reliance.** It is acting for its own account, and it has made its own independent decisions to enter into this Transaction and as to whether this Transaction is appropriate or proper for it based upon its own judgment and upon advice from such advisers as it has deemed necessary. It is not relying on any communication (written or oral) of the other party as investment advice or as a recommendation to enter into this Transaction; it being understood that information and explanations related to the terms and conditions of this Transaction shall not be considered investment advice or a recommendation to enter into this Transaction. No communication (written or oral) received from the other party shall be deemed to be an assurance or guarantee as to the expected results of this Transaction.

(iii) **Assessment and Understanding.** It is capable of assessing the merits of and understanding (on its own behalf or through independent professional advice), and understands and accepts, the terms, conditions and risks of this

---

[38] Delete if Party B is not a multi-branch party.

Transaction. It is also capable of assuming, and assumes, the risks of this Transaction.

(iv) **Status of Parties.** The other party is not acting as a fiduciary for, or an adviser to it, in respect of this Transaction.

Please confirm your agreement to be bound by the terms of the foregoing by executing a copy of this Confirmation and returning it to us to:

[Dealer] London is acting as principal in this Transaction. The time of transaction will be supplied on request. If applicable, the following will apply: The time of exercise will be supplied on request. Details of arrangements with introducing brokers are available on request.

THIS MESSAGE WILL BE THE ONLY FORM OF CONFIRMATION DESPATCHED BY US. PLEASE EXECUTE AND RETURN IT BY FACSIMILE. IF YOU WISH TO EXCHANGE HARD COPY FORMS OF THIS CONFIRMATION PLEASE CONTACT US.

Yours faithfully,
For and on behalf of

By: _____   By: _____
Name: Name:
Title: Authorised Signatory   Title: Authorised Signatory

Confirmed as of the date first above written:

[FULL LEGAL NAME OF PARTY B]

By: _____   By: _____
Name: Name:
Title: Title:

6.2   *Applications*

Credit swaptions allow traders to take positions on expected migration of credit spreads and fees on credit default swaps reflecting changes in credit quality. The structures allow the creation of asymmetric risk profiles on credit spreads. Credit swaptions have similarities with a range of credit spread driven products such as credit spread options[39], structured (callable/putable) asset swaps and asset swaption structures[40].

---

[39]   See Chapter 1.
[40]   See discussion later in this Chapter.

The major applications of credit swaptions include:

- **Contingent protection** – traders and investors can use credit swaptions to provide contingent protection against changes in credit spread or credit quality. This can be against underlying cash investments or trading inventories. It can also be against positions in asset swaps or credit default swaps.
- **Structured (callable/extendible) credit default swaps** – credit swaptions can be combined with conventional credit default swaps to create structured credit default swaps – callable or extendible credit default swaps[41]. The structure of a callable credit default swap (also referred to as the cancellable credit default swap) illustrates this application of credit swaptions. A callable credit default swap allows the purchaser of protection to cancel the transaction prior to the scheduled maturity. For example, the original maturity of the callable credit may be 5 years, cancellable after 3 years. This is equivalent to the purchase of protection for 5 years under a conventional credit default swap combined with a receiver credit swaption. The receiver credit swaption would allow the purchaser to enter into a position where it sells protection on the reference entity for a period of 2 years, commencing in 3 years time. If triggered (where credit spreads decrease), the receiver credit swaption would entail entry into a 2 year credit default swap that would exactly offset the final 2 years of the conventional credit default swap. This would have the effect of cancelling the credit default swap. The fee paid for the credit swaption would be built into the price of the cancellable credit default swap. This could be by way of a fee payment at commencement or a higher credit spread over the first 3 years. **Exhibit 2.5** sets out an example of a callable default swap.
- **Trading credit spreads** – credit swaptions allow traders to position for expected credit spread changes and credit migration of individual credits/ market sectors. They also allow traders to monetise expectations regarding direction of credit spread changes through sales of naked or

---

[41] This is identical to the use of swaptions in combination with conventional interest rate and currency swaps to create structured swaps; see Das, Satyajit (2004) Swaps/Financial Derivatives 3rd Edition; John Wiley & Sons, Singapore at Chapter 49.

covered credit swaptions to capture the premium. Traders also use credit swaptions to trade the volatility of credit spreads.

The principal use of credit swaptions has been focused on the construction of structured credit default swaps and trading credit spreads. A major application is the construction of callable credit default swaps to hedge the credit risk of convertible bonds in convertible arbitrage transactions[42].

Exhibit 2.5   Callable Credit Default Swap

Assume a dealer purchases protection on ABC Company using a callable credit default swap from an investor. The transaction is for 5 years callable after 1 year. The fee for ABC Company 5 year credit default swaps is 200 bps pa. The callable swap is structured at a fee of 300 bps pa[43].

The callable default swap will operate as follows:

- If in 1 year the market credit default swap spread is higher than 300 bps, then the dealer will not cancel the swap. This means that the dealer will continue to receive protection from credit events for the full 5 years. This protection will be at a cost lower than the market price of protection (as credit spreads on ABC Company have increased). The investor will be exposed to the risk of ABC Company for the full term of the transaction. The investor will have received a higher fee than for an equivalent credit default swap at the commencement of the transaction.
- If in 1 year the market credit default swap spread is lower than 300 bps, then the dealer will cancel the swap and buy protection at a lower cost in the market (if required). The investor will have been exposed to the risk of ABC Company for only 1 year. The investor will have received a return above the equivalent 1 year credit default swap fee for ABC Company.

6.3   Valuation/Hedging

The value of credit swaptions is driven by the volatility of the underlying credit spread (as manifested in the changes in the fee on credit default swaps). This is different to options on bonds. This reflects the fact that the value is based purely on credit spread changes rather than changes in the

---

[42]   See Chapter 7.
[43]   Alternatively, the callable swap could be structured with a fee of 200 bps pa (the market credit default swap spread) plus a premium paid upfront by the dealer to the investor (in return for the right of cancellation).

price of the bond (which include changes in government bonds, swap spreads and issuer credit spreads).

The price of a credit swaption is equivalent to the value of the option on the underlying credit default swap. The underlying in a credit swaption is the forward credit default swap spread as of the option exercise date to the maturity of the underlying credit default swap.

A variety of pricing approaches are currently used including[44]:

- **Adjusted Black-Scholes approaches**[45] – the approach entails the modification of Black's option pricing model on forwards adapted for interest rate swaptions[46]. It is similar to pricing options on credit spreads[47]. The basic model needs to be adjusted for the fact that the swaption effectively terminates if the reference entity experiences a credit event during the exercise period and the swaption has not been exercised. The Black approach has a number of problems. It tends to misprice deep out-of-the-money credit swaptions. In addition, it is not suitable for swaptions where the underlying is a credit index. This is because index swaptions do not terminate if one component of the index experiences a credit event[48].
- **Other approaches** – alternative approaches include:
  1. Using interest rate term structure models[49], specifically using the LIBOR market model adapted for credit risk[50].
  2. Modelling the terminal value of the swaption using the default adjusted forward spread[51].

---

[44] See Pedersen, Claus M. "Valuation Of Portfolio Credit Default Swaptions" (November 2003) Quantitative Credit Research; Lehman Brothers 71–81.

[45] For a discussion of Black-Scholes option pricing models, see Das, Satyajit (2004) Swaps/Financial Derivatives 3rd Edition; John Wiley & Sons, Singapore at Chapter 7.

[46] See Das, Satyajit (2004) Swaps/Financial Derivatives 3rd Edition; John Wiley & Sons, Singapore at Chapter 49.

[47] See Chapter 5.

[48] See Pedersen, Claus M. "Valuation Of Portfolio Credit Default Swaptions" (November 2003) Quantitative Credit Research; Lehman Brothers 71-81.

[49] See Das, Satyajit (2004) Swaps/Financial Derivatives 3rd Edition; John Wiley & Sons, Singapore at Chapter 8.

[50] See Patel, Navroz "Default Swaps: The Next Frontier" (May 2003) Risk 16–17.

[51] See Pedersen, Claus M. "Valuation Of Portfolio Credit Default Swaptions" (November 2003) Quantitative Credit Research; Lehman Brothers 71–81.

Dealers hedge credit swaptions by trading in the underlying credit default swap. This is consistent with the delta hedging approach used in trading options more generally[52]. For example, a dealer long a payer credit swaption would hedge by selling protection on the relevant reference entity in the credit default swap market. The notional amount of the hedge would generally be less than the face value of the credit swaption, reflecting uncertainty of exercise. The delta hedge would be adjusted over time as credit spreads change and the remaining time to maturity of the swaption shortens.

Hedging assumes liquidity in the underlying credit default swap market in the relevant entity. Whilst liquidity has improved, it remains concentrated in selected names. This makes hedging difficult. In addition, volume constraints (both very large and small trade lots) and maturity limitations (the credit default swap is focused on the standard 5 year maturity) also makes accurate hedging difficult. In practice, many dealers hedge credit swaption positions on an integrated basis within their asset swap and credit default swap portfolios. Other dealers may specifically dynamically hedge positions.

7   Quanto Credit Default Swaps

The principal trading currency for credit default swaps is US$. In recent years, a market in credit default swaps denominated in Euro and Yen has also emerged. The predominance of the G-3 currencies creates problems for market participants seeking to hedge or create exposure to a specific reference entity denominated in a different currency.

The problem occurs in the following situations:

- The hedger has a credit exposure to the reference entity denominated in a currency other than US$ (say, Singapore Dollars (S$)) and wishes to hedge. The use of a US$ credit default swap on the reference entity provides an imperfect hedge. It creates potentially significant currency exposures for the hedger.
- The investor wishes to assume credit exposure to the reference entity but denominated in a non US$ currency (say S$). This is, in fact, the case in many parts of the world where the investor is precluded by regulation or

---

[52]   See Das, Satyajit (2004) Swaps/Financial Derivatives 3rd Edition; John Wiley & Sons, Singapore at Chapter 16.

its investment guidelines from investing in foreign currency assets. In Asia, many investors seek credit exposure to international companies for diversification and yield enhancement. This investment is usually in the form of credit linked notes[53]. However, their investment authority prevents the investors from purchasing investment other than in the domestic currency[54].

The problem is generally overcome using quanto credit default swap structures[55].

A quanto credit default swap is identical in structure and design to a conventional credit default swap. The only difference is that the currency of the contract (notional principal, payments and settlement) is set in a currency (say, S$) other than the major traded currencies in the credit default swap market (US$, Euro and Yen). From the perspective of the end-user (irrespective of whether it is a buyer or seller of protection), the contract operates similarly to a normal contract. All cash flows are in the local currency (i.e. S$).

The major difference in a quanto credit default swap is in the dealer's position. This reflects the fact that the dealer will need to hedge the local currency S$ position with an offsetting credit default swap denominated in US$. **Exhibit 2.6** sets out the hedging structure.

The hedge creates a complex currency exposure for the dealer:

- On the fees, the dealer is long S$ against US$.
- In case of a credit event, the dealer is short S$ and long US$.
- The exposures are contingent on the credit event[56]. This reflects the fact that both the fees and the settlement are contingent on whether there is a credit event. If there is no credit event, then the only exposure is on the fees over the full maturity of the transaction. If there is a credit event, then the exposure changes. The fee payments are terminated. The

---

[53] See Chapters 3 and 4.

[54] See Trinephi, Mia "Beyond The Dollar" (October 2002) AsiaRisk – Credit Risk Supplement S8–S9.

[55] The "quanto" refers to the hedging required by the dealer. It has similarities to but is different from general quanto options; see Das, Satyajit (2004) Swaps/ Financial Derivatives 3rd Edition; John Wiley & Sons, Singapore at Chapter 45.

[56] For a discussion of credit contingent currency risk, see O'Kane, Dominic and Schloegl, Lutz "Cross Currency Credit Explained" (14 May 2002) Lehman Brothers Quantitative Credit Research 53–67.

settlement must be effected, giving rise to currency risk on the settlement amount.

The complexity of the hedge derives from the contingent nature of the currency exposure. The likelihood of the occurrence of the credit event or its timing is uncertain. This means a currency hedge using forwards is likely to result in hedging errors. For example, hedging the settlement amount would require estimation of timing, recovery values and the probability of the credit event. In the event that the credit event does not occur, then the dealer is exposed to the risk of (unintended) gain/loss on the hedge. The quanto refers to the dependence of the hedge on the occurrence of a credit event.

In practice, dealers hedge the risk dynamically. This entails the dealer adjusting the face value of the US$ credit default swap (in the example in **Exhibit 2.6**). For example, as the US$ strengthens against the S$, the dealer would reduce the face value of the US$ credit default swap used to hedge. The basic concept is changes in currency values are offset by adjusting the face value of the hedge. The major difficulty with this approach is the practical difficulty in trading in the underlying US$ credit default swap. Problems of liquidity, parcel size and the need to trade in reducing maturity credit default swaps are likely to reduce the efficiency of the dealer's hedge. This is reflected in the pricing and (sometimes) the availability of quanto credit default swaps.

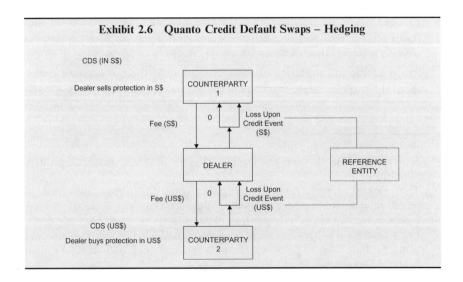

Exhibit 2.6   Quanto Credit Default Swaps – Hedging

8   Recovery Rate Structures

8.1   Recovery Rate Swaps[57]

Recovery rate swaps enable traders and investors to hedge or assume recovery rates risk. The basic structure entails the exchange of the following payments:

- **Fixed recovery rate** – this is a fixed recovery rate (usually 35% to 50%) agreed between the counterparties.
- **Floating recovery rate** – this is the floating or market recovery rate calculated using the traded prices of bonds in the market following a credit event.

The major impetus for recovery rate swaps is risk positions existing in dealer portfolios. A number of CDO structures use binary credit default swaps and fixed recovery rates. This is driven by investor concern at the variability of recovery rates. Structuring binary credit default swaps results in the dealer taking on recovery risk.

Assume the dealer has entered into a binary credit default swap with an investor (through a CDO) where it has fixed the recovery rates at 35%. If market or actual recovery rates are lower (20%) then the dealer suffers a loss. The loss reflects the fact that its loss (80% calculated as 100% minus market recovery rate 20%) is higher than the fixed loss payment (65% calculated as 100% minus fixed recovery rate 35%). If market recovery rates are higher than the fixed recovery rate then the dealer makes a gain. In order to hedge this risk, the dealer can enter into a recovery rate swap where it receives fixed recovery rate (35%) and pays the floating recovery rate. The gain or loss on the recovery rate swap would offset the loss or gain under the binary credit default swap with a fixed recovery rate.

8.2   Zero Recovery Credit Default Swaps

Zero recovery credit default swaps are binary credit default swaps where the payout is equal to the notional principal of the contract.

Under a normal credit default swap, the buyer of protection pays a fee in return for protection against a credit event on an underlying entity or bond.

---

[57]   See Wolcott, Rachel "Recovery Swaps Hit Europe" (August 2004) Risk 12.

If a credit event occurs, then the buyer of protection delivers the issuer's defaulted bonds and receives par from the seller of protection in the credit default swap. Under the zero recovery credit default swaps, where a credit event occurs, the buyer of protection would deliver nothing and receive par from the seller of protection. If the purchaser of protection under the credit default swap owned the issuer's bonds, then it would receive par and would keep the bonds, realising any recovery value following default.

The structure is primarily used to hedge the risk of bank subordinated bonds/capital issues[58]. In a typical structure, the reference asset under the zero recovery credit default swap is a senior bond of the issuer. The senior bond will usually have a cross default clause to subordinated debt. If an issuer defaults on its subordinated debt, then the credit default swap is triggered through the cross default. Where the buyer of protection holds a bank subordinated issue and there is a credit event, the zero recovery credit default swap provides a payout equal to the full notional principal value of the contract. This will effectively protect the holder of subordinated debt, as it is covered against total loss of principal (reflecting the low recovery levels likely on the subordinated issue).

The sellers of protection in a zero recovery credit default swap are generally banks exploiting an anomaly in the regulatory capital treatment of credit default swaps. Banks in some jurisdictions acquire credit exposure to the relevant bank issuer by selling protection under a zero recovery credit default swap. The banks generally treat the risk exposure under the zero recovery credit default swap as a 20% risk-weighted asset. This is based on the fact that the reference bond is senior. This is despite the zero recovery credit default swap being linked (in effect) to a default on bank subordinated paper and the zero recovery value. The arrangement allows banks to get exposure to 20% risk-weighted assets at a higher return than investing in senior bonds.

Zero recovery credit default swaps are also sometimes used to monetise expectations on recovery rates in the event of default[59].

---

[58]   See Ineke, Jackie, Guillard, Olivia and Mareels, Carlo (January 2002) Bank Capital A-Z; Morgan Stanley – Fixed Income Research, London at 148–149.
[59]   See examples in Chapters 3 and 7.

9   First-to-Default/Nth-to-Default Baskets[60]

9.1   First-to-Default Basket – Structure

The first-to-default basket concept is based on credit default based on a *basket* of underlying reference entities. **Exhibit 2.7** sets out an example of a basket linked credit default swap. First-to-default structures can also be structured as credit linked notes[61].

The critical aspect of these transactions is the concept of *first-to-default*. Default payment/settlement under the transaction is triggered by the *first* credit event incurred by *any* of the reference entities included in the basket of credits. If a credit event occurs, then settlement is based on cash settlement or physical delivery based on the defaulted reference credit *for the full notional value of the transaction*. In the case of cash settlement, this would entail payment of an amount related to the decline in value of the defaulted security calculated on the full notional amount of the swap. In the case of physical settlement, the buyer of protection under the first-to-default swap would deliver to the seller of protection defaulted bonds of the relevant reference entity equal to the face value of the transaction in return for payment of the face value.

Under a typical structure, the first-to-default basket is linked to between 3 and 10 underlying reference entities.

The rationale for a first-to-default basket is that the combination of credit risks in the structure creates a lower credit quality than the individual credit standing of the individual reference entities. This reflects the combination of two factors:

- **Default correlation** – the seller of protection is assuming the default correlation risk between the reference entities included in the basket.
- **Leverage** – there is inherent leverage in the structure. In a US$50 million transaction on 4 underlying reference entities, the provider of default

---

[60] See Lucas, Douglas (30 May 2003) "Nth to Default Swap and Notes: All About Default Correlation"; UBS Warburg CDO Insight; O'Kane Dominic, Schloegl, Lutz and Greenburg, Andrei "Leveraging Spread Premia With Correlation Products" (August 2003) Lehman Brothers Quantitative Credit Research 33–44; Lucas, Douglas and Thomas, Alberto "Nth to Default Swap and Notes: All About Default Correlation" in Gregory, Jon (Editor) (2003) Credit Derivatives: The Definitive Guide; Risk Books at Chapter 6; (2003) The Lehman Brothers – Guide To Exotic Credit Derivatives; Lehman Brothers/Risk Waters Group at 8–12.

[61] See Chapters 3 and 7.

Exhibit 2.7	First-To-Default Credit Default Swaps
Buyer of Protection	[Dealer]
Seller of Protection	[Investor]
Notional Principal	US$50 million
Maturity	5 years from Commencement Date
Commencement Date	Next business day
Payments	Dealer pays Enhanced Payments. Investor pays Interest Payments.
Enhanced Payments	3 month LIBOR plus 0.80% pa paid quarterly on an actual/360 basis
Interest Payments	3 month LIBOR paid quarterly on an actual/360 basis
Underlying Reference Entities	Entity A
	Entity B
	Entity C
	Entity D
	[Average Coupon: LIBOR plus [30] bps pa]
Credit Event On Basket	If there is a Credit Event in respect of any one of the Reference Entities (the Defaulted Entity), then the Termination Settlement will occur
Credit Events	Bankruptcy Failure to Pay Modified Restructuring
Termination Settlement	The Buyer of Protection will deliver to the Seller of Protection Deliverable Obligations of the Defaulted Entity with face value equal to the Notional Principal. The Seller of Protection will pay to the Buyer of Protection the Notional Principal.
Deliverable Obligations	Bonds or assignable/consent required loans

protection on a first-to-default basis provides protection *on any of the 4 entities* up to a face value of US$50 million each until the first credit event. The seller of default protection is providing protection on *US$200 million of credit assets*, at least until one of the entities defaults.

First-to-default baskets are similar to a transaction where the protection provider sells protection on *all* the reference entities for an amount equal to the face value of the contract. Where any one reference entity experiences a default/credit event, the credit default swaps on the *other* reference entities are automatically cancelled at no cost to the protection seller. This is equivalent to the protection seller's loss from the transaction being capped at the face value of any one of the credit default swaps. First-to-default baskets are similar in concept and economics to the subordinated tranches in collateralised debt obligations ("CDO's") (specifically, the equity and mezzanine tranches)[62].

9.2   Economics Of First-To-Default Baskets

As noted above, first-to-default baskets are based on default correlation[63]. The performance and the corresponding return to the investor are driven by the likelihood of any of the reference entities defaulting and also the probability of the reference entities *defaulting together*.

The impact of default correlation can be illustrated as follows:

- **Zero correlation** – this assumes that the risk of default of the reference entities is completely independent. This process can be understood using a simple example. Assume a BB rated issuer has a 2% likelihood of defaulting over a 1 year holding period. Assuming zero default correlations, the probability of *any one* of the 4 issuers defaulting can be approximated as the survival probability (1−the cumulative probability of default) of the components of the basket multiplied together. This is calculated (in this example) as $1-(1-.02)^4$ that equates to .08 or 8.00%. **Exhibit 2.8** sets out an example of using this approach assuming zero correlations to quantify the risk of the first-to-default basket.
- **Perfect Correlation (1)** – this assumes that if any reference entity defaults then all other reference entities within the basket will also default *simultaneously*.

Exhibit 2.8   First-To-Default Baskets – Risk/Valuation Issues

1. **AA Credit First-To-Default Basket**

Cumulative Probability of First-To-Default Basket (2 Credits)

		Cumulative Probability of Default			
	Maturity (Years)	1	3	5	10
Issuer	**Rating**				
A	AA	0.02%	0.08%	0.31%	0.89%
B	AA	0.02%	0.08%	0.31%	0.89%
		Survival Probability			
	Maturity (Years)	1	3	5	10
Issuer	**Rating**				
A	AA	99.98%	99.92%	99.69%	99.11%
B	AA	99.98%	99.92%	99.69%	99.11%

---

[62]   See Chapter 4.
[63]   For a discussion of default correlation, see Chapter 6.

Basket					
Maturity (Years)		1	3	5	10
Probability of Survival		99.96%	99.84%	99.38%	98.23%
Probability of Default		0.04%	0.16%	0.62%	1.77%
Times (×) Increase In Default Risk		2.00	2.00	2.00	1.99

Cumulative Probability of First-To-Default Basket (4 Credits)

		Cumulative Probability of Default			
	Maturity (Years)	1	3	5	10
Issuer	**Rating**				
A	AA	0.02%	0.08%	0.31%	0.89%
B	AA	0.02%	0.08%	0.31%	0.89%
C	AA	0.02%	0.08%	0.31%	0.89%
D	AA	0.02%	0.08%	0.31%	0.89%
		Survival Probability			
	Maturity (Years)	1	3	5	10
Issuer	**Rating**				
A	AA	99.98%	99.92%	99.69%	99.11%
B	AA	99.98%	99.92%	99.69%	99.11%
C	AA	99.98%	99.92%	99.69%	99.11%
D	AA	99.98%	99.92%	99.69%	99.11%

Basket					
Maturity (Years)		1	3	5	10
Probability of Survival		99.92%	99.68%	98.77%	96.49%
Probability of Default		0.08%	0.32%	1.23%	3.51%
Times (×) Increase In Default Risk		4.00	4.00	3.98	3.95

2. BB Credit First-To-Default Basket

Cumulative Probability of First-To-Default Basket (2 Credits)

		Cumulative Probability of Default			
	Maturity (Years)	1	3	5	10
Issuer	**Rating**				
A	BB	1.27%	6.20%	11.42%	21.27%
B	BB	1.27%	6.20%	11.42%	21.27%

		Survival Probability			
	Maturity (Years)	1	3	5	10
Issuer	Rating				
A	BB	98.73%	93.80%	88.58%	78.73%
B	BB	98.73%	93.80%	88.58%	78.73%

Basket					
	Maturity (Years)	1	3	5	10
Probability of Survival		97.48%	87.98%	78.46%	61.98%
Probability of Default		2.52%	12.02%	21.54%	38.02%
Times (×) Increase In Default Risk		1.99	1.94	1.89	1.79

Cumulative Probability of First-To-Default Basket (4 Credits)

		Cumulative Probability of Default			
	Maturity (Years)	1	3	5	10
Issuer	Rating				
A	BB	1.27%	6.20%	11.42%	21.27%
B	BB	1.27%	6.20%	11.42%	21.27%
C	BB	1.27%	6.20%	11.42%	21.27%
D	BB	1.27%	6.20%	11.42%	21.27%
		Survival Probability			
	Maturity (Years)	1	3	5	10
Issuer	Rating				
A	BB	98.73%	93.80%	88.58%	78.73%
B	BB	98.73%	93.80%	88.58%	78.73%
C	BB	98.73%	93.80%	88.58%	78.73%
D	BB	98.73%	93.80%	88.58%	78.73%

Basket					
	Maturity (Years)	1	3	5	10
Probability of Survival		95.02%	77.41%	61.57%	38.42%
Probability of Default		4.98%	22.59%	38.43%	61.58%
Times (×) Increase In Default Risk		3.92	3.64	3.37	2.90

If the default correlation within the basket is zero, then the first-to-default transaction is equivalent to selling protection on *all* the reference entities within the basket with a limitation on the maximum loss that can be incurred. This means that the fee to the protection seller should approach the sum of the spreads of the reference entities within the basket. If the default correlation within the basket is one, then the first-to-default basket is equivalent to selling protection on the most risky reference entity within the basket. This means that the fee to the protection seller should approach the spread on the most risky entity within the basket (that is, the highest spread).

In practice, the default correlation is likely to be imperfect. This means that the risk of default on the first-to-default basket is significantly higher than on any individual reference entity. It is possible that a first-to-default basket based on investment grade credit risk could be economically equivalent to a non-investment grade credit risk. The increase in risk is greater where underlying credit risks are non-investment grade. The relative risk of default on the first-to-default basket decreases with increasing default correlations within the basket. For example, if all the entities in the basket are of a similar credit quality (similar default probabilities) and the default correlation between the entities is 1.00, then the risk of the basket is identical to the risk of any one of the individual entities. In effect, there is no increase in risk to the seller of protection. Where the correlation is less than 1.00, the risk to the seller of protection is greater than the risk to any one of the individual entities. **Exhibit 2.9** sets out the relationship between correlation and pricing of a first-to-default basket.

9.3 Pricing/Hedging Of First-To-Default Baskets

The pricing of first-to-default basket structures entails significant challenges. From an intuitive perspective, the pricing of the structure should be bounded by the sum of the default risk premiums on the issuers within the basket (the upper bound) and the risk premium on the weakest credit risk within the basket (the lower bound). The upper bound will clearly overestimate the risk, as the purchaser of protection does not obtain protection on all the components within the basket. The protection is only on the first-to-default and protection on the non-defaulting entities is lost when the first-to-default event occurs. The lower bound is insufficient, as the probability of default on the basket is greater than the probability of default by a single counterparty.

Exhibit 2.9   First-To-Default Baskets – Sensitivity To Default Correlation

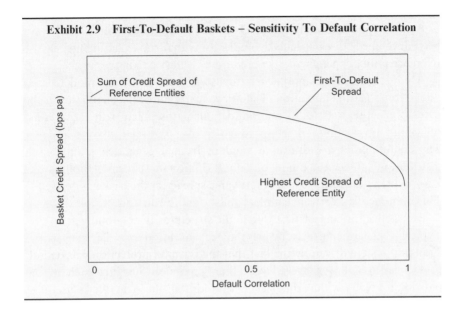

The principal factors determining the value of a first-to-default basket include[64]:

- **Number of reference entities** – as the number of reference entities increases, the risk of a credit event on the basket also increases.
- **Credit quality** – the credit quality of the reference entities impacts upon the risk of credit event on the basket.
- **Recovery rate** – the relevant recovery rate is that on the nth to default reference entity on the basket. The lower the recovery rate, the higher the loss potentially sustained by the seller of protection under the basket.
- **Default correlation** – as noted above, lower default correlation increases the risk on a first-to-default basket. The position with other n^{th} structures is more complex.
- **Maturity** – the effect of maturity is driven by the slope of the credit spread curves for the reference entities.
- **Order of default** – this refers to the exposure of the seller of protection to the order of default. A first-to-default position is more risky than a second or third-to-default position.

---

[64] For a detailed discussion of probability of default, recovery rate and default correlation, see Chapter 6.

A number of quantitative models to price first-to-default baskets have been developed[65]. A particular complexity is that the exact identity of the reference entity experiencing the credit event must be known.

A common pricing approach is to use a times-to-default model based on a Monte Carlo simulation. The approach requires the simulation to be used to generate a series of random default paths. Each path shows a list of default times for each reference entity over the relevant risk horizon. The default times are drawn at random from a generated joint default distribution[66]. Once the timing of default (if any) in each simulation path is known, then the arbitrage free or fair value spread for the basket is derived[67]. This approach is relatively simple, robust, fast to run and flexible.

In practice, pricing of first-to-default structures is not totally scientific. Typically, the pricing drivers are the reasons for doing the transaction. Transactions are driven by the fact that the buyer of protection gets default protection at a lower overall cost than separately hedging each of the individual credits within the basket. In addition, the structure is useful in managing concentration risk within portfolios. The structure provides sellers of protection with additional returns in exchange for assuming the additional risk. The additional return is driven by the default correlation between the reference entities[68]. Where the default correlation is low, the additional spread is higher. Structuring the basket with uncorrelated reference entities of similar credit quality and credit spreads increases the return. Increasing the number of reference entities within the basket also increases the return. In practice, the fee on a first-to-default basket is generally in the range bounded by the sum of the credit default swap fees for all the reference entities and the fee for the highest risk reference entity. Where the default correlation is low, the fee is closer to the sum of the credit default swap fees for all the reference entities. Where the default correlation is high, the fee is closest to the fee for the highest risk reference entity.

---

[65]   See Schmidt, Wolfgang and Ward, Ian "Pricing Default Baskets" (January 2002) Risk 111–114; Mashal Roy and Naldi Marco "Extreme Events And Default Baskets" (June 2002) Risk 119–122; Gregory, Jon and Laurent, Jean-Paul "I Will Survive" (June 2003) Risk 103–107.

[66]   For a common approach of simulating correlated defaults, see Li, David X. "On Default Correlation: A Copula Function Approach" (March 2000) Journal of Fixed Income 43–54.

[67]   For a description of the process used, see (2003) The Lehman Brothers – Guide To Exotic Credit Derivatives; Lehman Brothers/Risk Waters Group at 39–40.

[68]   For discussion of default correlation, see Chapter 6.

The pricing of first-to-default structures is also affected by the hedging of such transactions. This is a factor where there is no natural buyer of protection on a first-to-default basis. It is generally not possible to exactly hedge the first-to-default structure. Where the structure entails buying protection, the dealer will sell protection on *each* of the individual reference entities within the basket. The dealer does not sell protection on each of the reference entities equal to the face value of the first-to-default basket. The amount of protection sold on individual entities is based on the hedge ratio (effectively the credit delta[69]). It will be driven by the trading levels of the individual reference entities in the credit default swap market (in effect, the credit spread)[70] and the default correlation between the reference entities. The hedge ratio will generally be less than 1.00 at commencement of the transaction. The hedge ratios will change over the life of the transaction. The change will be driven by changes in the trading levels of each credit default swap and the default correlation. The dealer will need to adjust the hedges by changing the position it holds in credit default swaps on each reference entity.

The hedge described is difficult to manage. The key problem areas include:

- Estimation of default correlation.
- Changes in credit spread and default correlation over the term of the transaction.
- The transaction costs incurred in trading in the individual credit default swaps as the hedges are re-balanced.

In practice, the hedge of a first-to-default basket will have the following characteristics:

- **Negative carry** – this means that the spread between the fees received (on the credit protection sold) will be less than the fees paid (on the first-to-default basket). For example, in a 4 name basket, the dealer may pay 250 bps in fees to the seller of protection in the first-to-default basket. If the spread on the individual reference entities is 100 bps per annum and

---

[69] See Chapters 5 and 6. For a discussion of deltas and delta hedging in derivatives generally, see Das, Satyajit (2004) Swaps/Financial Derivatives 3rd Edition; John Wiley & Sons, Singapore at Chapters 15 and 16.

[70] This will reflect the expected default probability and recovery rate for the reference entity; see Chapter 6.

the hedge ratio is 55%, then the hedge will earn 220 bps per annum (55% times 100 bps pa times 4). The negative carry is 30 bps per annum (250 bps minus 220 bps).

- **Positive gamma** – this refers to the expected gains on the hedge over the life of the first-to-default basket. The gains on hedge adjustment are the result of the dealer being long gamma. As the hedge ratios change, the required adjustments to the hedge should result in profits for the dealer. For example, as the spread on a particular entity within the basket increases (reflecting credit deterioration), then the dealer will need to sell more protection as the delta will increase. The additional protection will be sold at higher spreads, improving the carry on the trade. If the spread on a particular entity decreases (reflecting credit improvements), then the dealer will need to buy protection to decrease its hedge (falling delta). The dealer will tend to make gains as it is buying protection at better spreads than where it initially sold protection for its hedge.

The hedge is not exact. This reflects the fact that the dealer is basically hedging the spread risk but remains exposed to changes in default correlation. This difficulty in hedging is reflected in the actual pricing of the first-to-default baskets. The exact price frequently reflects dealer demand for gamma and the relative level of negative carry that the dealer is willing to pay in the transaction.

9.4 First-To-Default Baskets – Market

The earliest first-to-default structures entailed high quality underlying credit assets such as Scandinavian sovereign issuers and other large European borrowers[71]. The motivation for the transactions was the need for commercial and investment banks to hedge large credit exposures to these entities. The credit exposures related to capital market activity (interest rate and currency swaps), standby credit facilities and trading limits. The attraction from the perspective of the parties purchasing protection was that these structures enabled reduction of large credit concentrations within their portfolios at an attractive cost.

---

[71] These structures were among the earliest form of structured credit derivatives; see Falloon, William "Freundian Analysis" (December 1997) Risk 60–62.

The providers of protection under the structures were primarily institutional investors seeking higher yields on high quality securities. Far Eastern investors including Japanese institutions, European and Middle Eastern investors were the major providers of these types of credit default protection. The higher yield obtained on the first-to-default baskets was attractive to investors. Some investors did not properly quantify the additional marginal risk of the structure. Investors were also frequently indifferent to the risk of the structure as the underlying credit assets were eligible investments for these investors *on a standalone purchase basis*.

In more recent times, the structure has been used with Japanese banks, emerging markets credits and borrowers from certain industry sectors. The emergence of significant credit problems within the Japanese banking system in the mid-1990s prompted a significant volume of transactions which primarily entailed the sale of default risk on the weaker Japanese financial institutions through the first-to-default credit structures. The driving force was the necessity to reduce the large credit concentration within bank portfolios to this group of obligors. The protection was provided by Asian investors including *better capitalised* Japanese financial institutions, primarily institutional investors, as well as investors in other markets *with low levels of exposure to Japanese bank risk*.

The emerging market transactions involved trading baskets of Latin, South-East Asian and Eastern European risks. The underlying rationale of the transactions was for large international money centre commercial and investment banks active in these markets to diversify or trade out of large risk concentration to particular counterparties. The hedges allowed the banks to continue to transact business with these counterparties. The providers of default protection were again institutional investors and hedge funds willing to take the default risk to these issuers/counterparties.

Other transactions include first-to-default baskets on industry sectors such as telecommunications and media. This was driven by the need for many banks to reduce exposure to these sectors because of large credit concentrations within credit portfolios.

A major driving force of these transactions is that the first-to-default basket format is attractive for the investors assuming the default risk. The structure embedded in notes/securities provides an elegant mechanism for creating the desired exposure while allowing investors to generate incremental *yield*. The additional return provides out-performance relative to the underlying benchmarks against which the performance of the investors is measured. It also creates opportunities to assume certain risks *indirectly* that the investor may not be able to trade *directly*. The disguised leverage of the structures may also be attractive.

In 2004, standardised first-to-default basket structures emerged[72]. The concept is of a standard first-to-default swap on a pre-specified set of reference entities. The structures use established credit indexes to create a number of sector based baskets. In addition, there are diversified baskets with a single name from each sector other than financials or crossover sectors.

The motivations for the standardised first-to-default baskets include:

- Increasing liquidity and encouraging trading in first-to-default structures.
- Increasing price transparency of the structures.
- Developing the first-to-default market as a mechanism for trading and hedging default correlation risk. For example, dealers with default correlation positions from CDO transaction may find the structure useful as a hedging mechanism.

9.5 N^{th}-To-Default Baskets – Variations

9.5.1   Structures

A number of variations on the basic first-to-default structure have developed. These include:

- **Credit Exchange Agreements** – these are first-to-default structures embedded in asset swaps. These structures are discussed in the following Section.
- **Loss limits** – in the case of a credit event, this entails a loss that is limited (for example to 50% of the notional principal). This is similar to selling a binary or digital credit default swap.
- **N^{th}-to-default** – this entails creating exposure to a different order of default. For example, a second-to-default basket allows the protection seller to assume the risk on the second reference entity to default within the basket. This is designed to reduce the risk of loss for the protection seller. The actual risk will depend upon the default correlation within the basket. These structures are discussed in the following Section.

---

[72]   See Ferry, John "Banks Look To Boost First-To-Default Baskets" (August 2004) 10.

- **Adjusted basket structure**[73] – this entails the investor assuming a risk on a basket of credits (say 3 entities) for a period of 5 years. The structure (usually designed as a note) provides the investor with an enhanced return. The structure is adjusted periodically, with the investor assuming the risk on all 3 names only for the first 2 years. At the end of 2 years, the lowest rated entity within the basket is eliminated. The investor has exposure on the remaining 2 names for the next 2 years. At the end of 4 years, the lowest rated entity among the remaining 2 entities in the basket is removed from the basket. The investor has exposure to the remaining entity for the remaining term of the note. The structure is designed to utilise default correlation to enhance the return to the investor. The structure is driven by investors unable to take credit exposure on the lower rated entities within the basket for the full term of the transaction. The investor is able to use short dated credit lines to weaker credit rated entities within a longer dated investment structure. The structure entails the investor taking default correlation risk (including forward default correlation risk) on the entities within the basket[74].

9.5.2 Credit Exchange Agreements

Credit Exchange Agreements are based on the same essential premise as first-to-default baskets. The structure provides the purchaser with the capacity to substitute one credit for another in an asset swap[75]. The transactions are also known as switch asset swaps or asset swap switch options. In return for offering default protection, the writer of the credit exchange option receives a return on the asset swap that is usually higher than the spread on *either* underlying credit on an asset swap basis. The return available is generally closer to the *combined spread* of the two underlying asset swaps.

Exhibit 2.10 sets out the terms of a typical credit exchange transaction. Under the terms of the transaction, the investor combines the credit of a

---

[73] The structure is also known as "wedding cake" (UBS Warburg) or "credit optimiser" (Deutsche Bank).
[74] See Sawyer, Nick "Credit Structures Abound" (September 2002) AsiaRisk 9.
[75] For a description of asset swaps, see Chapter 5. See also Das, Satyajit (2004) Swaps/Financial Derivatives 3rd Edition; John Wiley & Sons, Singapore at Chapter 38.

Exhibit 2.10   Credit/Asset Swap Exchange Swaps

Credit or asset swap exchange agreements allow investors seeking to enhance returns on asset swaps to engineer incremental yield through entry into credit exchange swaps. This type of structure can allow the investor to combine the spreads of two issuers and earn an incremental return that is greater than the spread over LIBOR available for the lower quality issuer.

A typical credit exchange swap is structured as follows:

Asset

Issuer	Issuer (rating A)
Principal Amount	US$20 million
Maturity	5 years
Coupon	7.25% pa annually on a bond basis

Payments

Investor Pays To Dealer	Par value of bonds and Coupons on Asset
Investor Receives From Dealer	3 month LIBOR plus 75 bps reset and payable quarterly on an actual/360 day basis

Credit Event Exchange

Exchange Option	The Dealer, in the event of the occurrence of a Credit Event, may cancel the asset swap. Upon such cancellation, the Dealer will deliver US$20 million of senior debt claims on Issuer B (rating BBB−) in return for the cancellation of the swap and the delivery of the Asset from the Investor.
Credit Event	Any of the following with respect to Issuer B: 1. Bankruptcy 2. Failure to pay 3. Restructuring

---

single A credit with that of a BBB− rated company. The A rated credit would swap into LIBOR plus 20 bps. A similar maturity bond issued by the BBB− rated issuer would swap into LIBOR plus 65 bps. The credit exchange swap allows the investor to receive close to the combined credit spread. Upon occurrence of a default event with respect to the BBB− rated company, the dealer has the right to cancel the swap and deliver the notional amount of (defaulted) senior debt claims on the BBB− company in exchange for delivery of the A rated security.

The economics of the transaction are similar to the first-to-default basket structure. The return enhancement is achieved through taking the risk of the underlying default correlation. The incremental spread generated is dependent upon the individual spreads and on the correlation between the probability of default of the two issuers.

There are variations on the basic concept. A common variation is the credit knockout swap[76]. Under this structure, the investor enters into a normal asset swap. If there is a credit event on the underlying asset (bond), then all future asset swap cash flows are cancelled (knock out). The structure is generally used where high yielding currency flows are swapped into a lower yielding currency. In this case, the credit knockout asset swap will provide the investor with a higher return than a conventional asset swap. The higher return is based on the fact that the forward mark-to-market of the asset swap is generally negative to the swap dealer. The probability of a negative mark-to-market value in the event of a credit event occurring has value to the dealer. This is passed on in the form of a higher return. The structure is priced by stripping the default probabilities on the underlying credit asset and conditioning the swap flows by the cumulative default probability. The correlation between the default risk and the interest rate/currency risk must be incorporated. The structure allows the investor to achieve its desired credit and interest rate exposure without any exposure to the mark-to-market risk of the underlying asset swap (the derivative mark-to-market upon termination). A common variation on the credit knockout structure is to incorporate a final exchange at or about the time of the credit event. The exchange is based on an amount equivalent to the recovery value of the defaulted bonds. This structure is used to eliminate any exposure to currency rates under the asset swap.

9.5.3 N^{th}-To-Default Basket Structures

The concept of first-to-default structures has been extended to allow traders to take sequential default risk positions to any basket of reference entities. These include second-to-default etc structures. The basic rationale of these variations is to increase or decrease credit risk in line with risk preferences. The key driver is the ability to use the implicit default correlation to structure different risk-reward payoffs. **Exhibit 2.11** sets out a comparison of a range of structures including n^{th}-to-default and

---

[76]   See Semonin, Lionel "Structured Hybrid Investments" (September 2002) Asia Risk – Structured Statement.

conventional default structures[77]. The analysis shows the different exposures to default risk, default correlation and loss (recovery rates) that are feasible.

The different structures also create different exposures to default correlation. As noted above, in a first-to-default swap, as default

Exhibit 2.11	N[th]-To-Default Basket Structures – Comparison	
Structure	**Maximum Loss**	**Comments**
4 separate US$25 million credit default swaps on 4 reference entities	US$25 million per credit default swap; maximum loss of US$100 million in total	This is the highest risk structure. Protection seller is exposed to all reference entities for full term and up to a maximum loss of US$100 million.
4 separate US$6.25 million credit default swaps on 4 reference entities	US$6.25 million per credit default swap; maximum loss of US$25 million in total	This is a low risk structure. Protection seller is exposed to all reference entities but up to a maximum loss of US$6.25 million per reference entity and a maximum loss of US$25 million. All the reference entities would need to default and recovery rates would need to be zero for the maximum loss of US$25 million to be reached.
US$25 million first-to-default basket on 4 reference entities	Loss on first-to-default reference entity; maximum loss of US$25 million in total	This structure is more risky than 4 separate US$6.25 million credit default swaps. It is less risky than 4 separate US$25 million credit default swaps. Protection seller is exposed to all reference entities but on the first default, the protection on all other reference entities is extinguished. Maximum loss of US$25 million is incurred if there is a single default and the recovery rate on that entity is zero.

[77] See Lucas, Douglas (30 May 2003) Nth to Default Swap and Notes: All About Default Correlation; UBS Warburg CDO Insight at 5–7.

Structure	Maximum Loss	Comments
US$25 million second-to-default basket on 4 reference entities	Loss on second-to-default reference entity; maximum loss of US$25 million in total	This structure is less risky than a US$25 million first-to-default basket. Protection seller is exposed to all reference entities but the loss on first default is absorbed by the protection buyer. Maximum loss of US$25 million is incurred if there is a second default and the recovery rate on that entity is zero.
US$25 million subordinate basket swap on 4 reference entities (each US$25 million) bearing first US$25 million of losses	Loss on each reference entity up to US$25 million of losses; maximum loss of US$25 million in total	This structure is more risky than a first-to-default basket. Protection seller is exposed to all reference entities in the basket up to the maximum loss of US$25 million.
US$25 million last (fourth)-to-default basket on 4 reference entities	Loss on last-to-default reference entity; maximum loss of US$25 million in total	This structure is relatively low risk. Protection seller is exposed to all reference entities but the loss on the first three defaults is absorbed by the protection buyer. Maximum loss of US$25 million is incurred if all entities in the basket default and the recovery rate on that entity is zero.
US$25 million senior basket swap on 4 reference entities (each US$25 million) bearing last US$25 million of losses	Loss after US$75 million of losses have been incurred; maximum loss of US$25 million in total	This structure is lower risk than the last-to-default structure. Protection seller is only exposed to risk of loss if losses on all defaults are above US$75 million. Maximum loss of US$25 million is incurred if there are a large number of defaults and the losses sustained are very high (low recovery rates).

correlation increases (all reference entities likely to default simultaneously), the risk of the structure (and the credit spread) approaches that on the most risky reference entity. Conversely, as default correlation decreases (reference entities are unlikely to default at the same time), the risk of the structure increases as the protection seller is exposed to all the reference entities. In the latter situation, the credit spread on the basket approaches the sum of all the individual credit spreads. Where the structure is altered, say to a second-to-default structure, the exposure to default correlation also changes. Depending upon structure, the impact of changes in default correlation can be complex. For example, in a second-to-default basket, where the correlation is one, then spread on the structure should be equivalent to that on the second most risky asset in the basket (in effect, the second highest spread). As correlation decreases, the risk of the second-to-default basket will generally fall. For example, if the correlation is zero (the default on the reference entities is independent), then the probability of two reference entities defaulting is low, resulting in a lower spread.

The different sensitivity to default correlation allows traders to trade and monetise different expectations on default correlation.

9.6 N^{th}-To-Default Baskets – Applications

The nth-to-default basket structures are predicated on allowing providers of protection to trade default correlation. As default correlation has historically not been available for trading, the ability to trade and to use this factor to generate incremental income are the major drivers of the structures. The capacity to create leverage is also attractive.

Applications of nth-to-default basket structures have focused upon the following:

- Investors use the structures to generate increased yield on a given notional investment. This entails leveraging the credit spread within the structure. It is particularly attractive as it may allow the investor to implement investment strategies that would be outside its mandate. The ability to customise the size, composition (reference entities), maturity and risk structure is attractive.
- Traders and investors use baskets to hedge credit portfolios. Basket structures are used to hedge particularly the concentration or event risk within large portfolios. The hedging cost is attractive relative to hedging each individual credit within the portfolio.

- The structures allow traders/investors to trade implied and expected default correlation.

N^{th}-to-default structures are increasingly used in sophisticated trading strategies including:

- Creation of synthetic senior positions by taking a long position in a basket of underlying reference entities and buying first-to-default protection on the basket[78].
- Creating a synthetic senior short position by selling first-to-default protection on a basket of underlying reference entities and buying protection on the basket constituents.
- Trading credit convexity by buying or selling first-to-default baskets against offsetting trading in the underlying credit default swaps.

9.7 N^{th}-To-Default Baskets – Ratings[79]

Rating agencies are sometimes asked to rate n^{th}-to-default basket structures. Rating agency models generally focus on the underlying economics of the structures. Moody's uses a Monte Carlo simulation approach similar to that used in rating CDO structures[80]. The basic approach simulates the asset value of the reference entities within the basket over multiple periods. The asset values are adjusted for assumed default correlation. If the asset value falls below a default threshold at any period, then it is assumed to default. The loss upon default is calculated by using recovery rates drawn from a distribution of recovery rates (usually in the form of a beta distribution). The model is calibrated to Moody's historical default statistics. The rating reflects the expected loss of the basket. Standard & Poor's uses a similar approach[81].

---

[78] This is similar to tranched credit structures embedded in notes or collateralised debt obligations ("CDO's"); see Chapter 4.

[79] See (2003) The Lehman Brothers – Guide To Exotic Credit Derivatives; Lehman Brothers/Risk Waters Group at 39–40.

[80] See Chapter 4.

[81] Previously, Standard & Poor's used the "weakest link" approach where the rating of the first-to-default basket was that of the rating of the lowest rated reference entity within the basket.

9.8   First-To-Default Structures – Regulatory Treatment[82]

9.8.1   Basel 1

Under Basel 1, the basic treatment is as follows:

- The buyer of protection is regarded as having purchased protection against only one reference entity. The buyer of protection is generally allowed to choose the single asset recognised as a short position for calculating regulatory capital.
- For the seller of protection, regulatory capital is required to be held against *all the names in the basket*. The capital held should not generally exceed the maximum capital held against the notional principal of the transaction (as the maximum loss is limited to face value of the transaction).

9.8.2   Basel 2

Under Basel 2[83], the banking book treatment of first-to-default baskets is clarified. When obtaining credit protection for the basket, the bank may recognise regulatory capital relief for the asset within the basket with the lowest risk-weighted amount, but only if the notional amount is less than or equal to the notional amount of the credit derivative. Where the bank provides credit protection through such an instrument, the treatment is as follows:

- If the product has an external credit assessment from an eligible credit assessment institution, the risk weight applied to securitisation tranches is applied.
- If the product is not rated by an eligible external credit assessment institution, the risk weights of the assets included in the basket will be aggregated up to a maximum of 1250% and multiplied by the nominal amount of the protection provided by the credit derivative to obtain the risk-weighted asset amount.

---

[82] For example, see FSA Board Notice 482 – *Guidance on Credit Derivatives* (July 1998) at paragraph 26–32,71.

[83] See Basel Committee on Banking Supervision (June 2004) International Convergence of Capital Measurement and Capital Standards: A Revised Framework; Bank for International Settlements, Basel, Switzerland.

In a second-to-default basket, the bank obtaining credit protection through such a product will only be able to recognise any capital relief if first-to-default-protection has also been obtained or when one of the assets within the basket has already defaulted. Where providing credit protection in a second-to-default basket, the capital treatment is similar to a first-to-default basket. The exception is that, in aggregating the risk weights, the asset with the lowest risk weighted amount can be excluded from the calculation.

Where first-to-default and second-to-default baskets are included in the trading book, the basic concepts developed for the banking book will also apply. Banks holding long positions in these products (e.g. buyers of basket credit-linked notes) would be treated as if they were protection sellers and would be required to add the specific risk charges or use the external rating if available. Issuers of these notes would be treated as if they were protection buyers and are therefore allowed to offset specific risk for one of the underlyings, i.e. the asset with the lowest specific risk charge.

10   Synthetic Lending Facilities/Asset Swaptions

The structure is based on allowing institutional investors to derive fee income in return for the provision of a forward commitment to purchase a security. Structurally, the synthetic lending facilities are undertaken as a put option on a revolving bank credit facility, or more typically, an asset swap transaction in relation to an identified reference security. In effect, the transaction entails a participation in an unfunded revolving loan which, at agreed dates, either terminates or converts at the option of the purchaser into a term credit commitment with a predetermined credit spread. The decomposition of the structure reveals embedded credit spread optionality that is sold to generate premium income. The structure is also referred to as an asset swaption or a re-marketing option.

Exhibit 2.12 sets out the terms of a typical synthetic lending facility. **Exhibit 2.13** sets out sample quotations of the structure.

The synthetic lending facility operates as follows:

- The investor receives the up-front fee at the commencement of the transaction.
- The investor also receives the commitment fee until the synthetic funding facility is called upon.

Exhibit 2.12   Synthetic Lending Facility/Asset Swaptions

Issuer

Issuer	ABC Company
Credit Rating	Baa1/BBB+
Reference Bond	7.50% January 2012
Ranking	Senior Unsecured Debt

Structure

Structure	Synthetic Revolving Credit Facility
Notional Principal	US$20 million
Maturity	3 years
Form Of Commitment	Commitment to enter into an asset swap
Settlement Type	Physical or cash
Settlement Date	First business day of each month
Notification Date	5 business days prior to Settlement Date

Pricing

Up-front Fee	30 bps (flat) payable as at Commencement Date
Annual Commitment Fee	25 bps pa payable quarterly
Interest Rate on Asset Swap	3 month LIBOR plus 60 bps payable quarterly in arrears
All-In Spread	Drawn: 71 bps
	Undrawn: 36 bps

Exhibit 2.13   Synthetic Lending Facility/Asset Swaption Quotations

Issuer	Security	Ratings	Maturity (years)	Upfront Fee (bps flat)	Commitment Fee (bps pa)	Spread To LIBOR
A Corporation	8.25% 1 April 2010	A−/Baa1	2	30	25	75
A Corporation	7.90% 1 July 2012	BBB+/Baa1	3	31.5	35	90
B Corporation	0% 15 July 2017	BBB−/Ba1	3	50	40	150
C Corporation	9.25% 15 September 2010	BBB−/Ba1	3	35	30	125
D Corporation	MTN 1 December 2006	A/Baa1	1	10	30	55

- If the facility is exercised, then the reference bond will be sold in an asset swap form to the investor at the agreed margin over the floating interest rate benchmark. The arrangement can be either cash settled or settled by physical delivery.

All terms of the transaction, in particular the structure of the revolving credit, are agreed between the parties. A key element is the specification of the reference bond that can be delivered in asset swap form under the synthetic lending facility. The key terms of the instrument include:

- **Up-front Fee** – this is payable at commencement on the notional amount of the transaction.
- **Commitment Fee** – this is paid (usually quarterly) at the agreed rate until the synthetic lending facility is drawn or expires unexercised.
- **Spread** – this refers to the margin over the nominated floating rate index which is payable on the credit facility or asset swap if the synthetic lending facility is drawn.
- **Settlement Mechanics** – the transaction is usually settled in one of two ways:
  1. If settlement is by delivery, then the reference bonds are delivered to the investors in return for payment of par or a pre-agreed value. The investor enters into an interest swap with the counterparty where it pays the bond coupon and receives the agreed floating rate index plus the agreed spread.
  2. If cash settled, then the asset swap is valued by polling a number of dealers (typically 3 or 4) with the quotes being averaged. The difference in value from par or a pre-agreed value is, if negative (positive), paid by (to) the investor.

The synthetic lending facility structure can include covenant protection which offers the investor additional protection. The format has, on occasion, incorporated increases in the fees or spread in line with any credit rating downgrade.

The structure entails the sale of a structured Bermudan put option on the credit spread on the underlying asset. The option is sold by the investor in the facility.

The primary advantage of the synthetic lending facility is that it is a customised and more liquid form of a traditional bank revolving credit facility. In particular, it offers institutional investors, as distinct from banks/financial institutions, the ability to gain exposure to the loan markets.

The major benefits include:

- Capacity to participate in bank markets without the need to establish the necessary banking infrastructure.

- Ability to customise the terms to a high degree.
- Choice of cash versus physical settlement.
- Enhanced liquidity offered by the capacity to trade the position in the asset swap market (this assumes liquidity of the underlying bond and swap markets).

The synthetic lending facility was originally devised by securities traders seeking to protect inventory positions in bonds or asset swaps as yields fell to historically low levels through the 1990s. The transactions provided protection against losses on inventory in the case of a sudden reversal in the decline of credit spreads. It protected traders against erosion of (often substantial) capital gains that had accrued on some of these positions as a result of the fall in credit spreads. The providers of the facilities included traders and investors seeking exposure to credit spreads. This was in anticipation of decreasing credit spreads. The providers were seeking exposure to credit spreads on an off-balance-sheet basis in order to decrease capital committed to these transactions. A significant issue for traders and investors was that as spreads declined to low levels, the fact that the potential declines became progressively smaller meant that increased degrees of leverage were required to amplify the profit impact of changes in credit spread.

The major participation in synthetic lending facilities is from investors seeking fee earnings from the transactions without the necessity to invest cash in the underlying security. In addition, the fact that the spread implied is usually greater than the spread available on existing revolving credits offers the investor some protection against an increase in the credit spread. The buyers of protection in these structures have included banks with significant asset swap inventory seeking protection against widening of the credit spread. Other parties include investors in high yield assets who combine the purchase of a bond with the simultaneous entry into a synthetic lending transaction/asset swaption. The combination means that the investor receives the higher return on the high yield asset but can limit its loss in the event of a deterioration of credit quality by exercising its rights under the facility and putting the bond on asset swap basis with the seller of protection. This limits its losses to a pre-nominated amount.

A number of structural variations on the basic synthetic lending facility/ asset swaption have evolved. These include callable/putable asset swaps and volume/size options.

11 Structured Asset Swaps

11.1 Callable/Putable Asset Swaps

The callable asset swap is a variation on the standard asset swaption where the dealer placing the asset swap with an investor (asset managers or banks) retains a call option on the asset. The call option entitles the dealer to repurchase the asset swap at a nominated spread over LIBOR at specific dates.

The asset swap is typically callable at the spread at which the asset swap was placed with the investor; that is, at par. The call options are either European or Bermudan structures which are exercisable either at the end of 6 to 12 months or at each interest payment date (quarterly) during a period of a year. If the credit spread on the underlying credit asset decreases, then the call is exercised, enabling the dealer to capture the value from the fall in the spread. The value capture is achieved by the dealer reselling the asset swap package to other investors at the lower credit spread. The transaction basically entails the investor in the asset swap simultaneously selling a call option on the spread to the counterparty.

The investor purchasing the callable asset swap is compensated by a higher spread on the asset swap. The spread is higher than that currently available in the market. In return for the additional spread, the investor sells the call option on the credit spread on the underlying asset. The major attraction for the investor writing the call option is the higher yield received. From the point of view of the dealer, the callable asset swap provides an attractive mechanism for maintaining exposure to decreases in the credit spread on an off-balance-sheet basis. The dealer also has no exposure to an increase in the spread.

The transactions are generally designed to be settled through a physical settlement entailing sale of the asset and an assignment or cancellation of the swap. A variation is the re-couponing or spread reset option. Under this structure, the asset remains with the investor but the spread is reset to the new market level with the swap cash flows being adjusted. The structure may also incorporate an option for the investor to resell the call, but at a lower strike spread level, to enhance returns through the capture of the call premium.

A variation on this structure evolved around 1997 and 1998 during a period of unprecedented volatility in emerging markets. As emerging markets in Asia, Latin America and Eastern Europe collapsed, dealers in emerging markets were increasingly left with large inventories of emerging market debt with large mark-to-market losses[84]. As markets eventually stabilised, at least in relative terms, dealers seeking to divest this "toxic" paper developed special structures to entice investor interest. One such structure was the putable asset swap.

The structure entailed the dealer selling a tranche of emerging market paper to an investor on an asset swap basis. In order to protect the investor against any loss in value, the asset swap would incorporate a provision where the investor would have the right to put the asset swap back to the dealer at a designated spread. The agreed spread was typically the same spread as the asset swap itself or a slightly higher spread. The option was capable of exercise at pre-agreed dates during the life of the asset swap. In effect, the investor was buying and the dealer was selling a put option on the credit spread. The put option premium was usually funded by a reduction in the asset swap spread.

The major attraction of the structure was the ability for dealers to reduce inventory and gain liquidity. The capacity to achieve disposition at prices that were above prices that could be achieved by direct sale was also important. The attraction for investors was the ability to gain exposure to emerging markets at relatively attractive prices (even after the reduction in spread to fund the purchase of the put option) in anticipation of an improvement in values.

11.2   Volume/Size Options

These transactions evolved from the standard asset swaptions/synthetic lending facilities and callable asset swaps. The major driving factor was the decline in credit spreads to historically low levels. Dealers who had either earned significant returns (often unrealised) from contraction in credit spreads or had bond inventory at the lower spread levels became concerned about a potential increase in credit spreads. The volume/size options (also known variously as "double up" options or variable size asset swaps) are designed to hedge this exposure to the risk of credit spreads increasing.

The transaction is structured as an asset swap that is placed with investors (asset managers or banks) at a credit spread above the current market spreads for a comparable standard asset swap. Under the structure, the dealer has the right to place or put an additional volume in face value of

---

[84]   The term "submerging" markets was coined during this time.

the asset swap at the agreed spread to the investor within 6 to 12 months. The exercise structure is similar to that used with callable asset swaps.

The transaction effectively combines the asset swap with the sale by the investor of an asset swaption or synthetic lending facility for a face value equivalent to the additional amount the dealer can put to the buyer of the original asset swap. It is identical to the sale by the investor of a put option on credit spread. The premium received for the sale of the asset swaption/ credit spread put option is used to increase the return on the original asset swap. If the spreads widen, then the additional volume of asset swaps is placed with the investor. If spreads do not increase above the nominated levels, then the asset swap volume remains unaltered.

Investors originally used this structure to enhance the return on assets in a period of narrow credit spreads. The investors were prepared to accept the credit spread risk to receive the premium. They were prepared to purchase the assets at the higher than current market spreads in the event that the option was exercised. During the emerging market crisis of 1997/1998, the structure was used by dealers to reduce inventory of emerging market debt with large mark-to-market losses. The major investors were investors who believed that markets had "overshot" and would ultimately correct to more *normal* levels.

The callable/putable asset swaps and volume/size options are typically documented as asset swap structures.

12 Constant Maturity Credit Products[85]

Constant maturity credit products have also been developed[86]. These structures are designed to allow investors to take customised positions in credit risk. The major products are:

- Constant maturity spread swaps ("CMSS") allow investors to take curve and directional exposure without default risk.
- Constant maturity credit default swaps allow investors to buy or sell protection without credit duration exposure.

In 2003/2004, there was a significant decline in credit spreads. This factor was a key driver in the development of other credit spread products including the CMSS.

---

[85] See Saunderson, Emily "Credit Limits" (April 2004) FOW 18.
[86] For a discussion of constant maturity products, see Das, Satyajit (2004) Swaps/ Financial Derivatives 3rd Edition; John Wiley & Sons, Singapore at Chapter 51.

Exhibit 2.14 sets out an example of a CMSS transaction. The structure of the CMSS is as follows:

- The bank pays a fixed payment in exchange for receiving a floating payment. The floating payment is calculated with reference to the credit spread on a credit default swap on a specific reference entity or a portfolio. Settlements are undertaken quarterly (generally to coincide with the standard credit default swap settlement dates in the market).
- The underlying credit default swap is generally a 5 year maturity standard transaction. This is used as it is the general market benchmark and is the most liquid maturity.
- If a credit event occurs with respect to the reference entity underlying the transaction, then the CMSS contract terminates. This means the CMSS payoffs are confined to credit spread changes, with no payment obligation in the case of a credit event.
- The CMSS transactions generally contain a capped spread (usually set at 800 bps pa).
- Pricing of the CMSS transaction is dependent on the implied forward spreads which is driven by the shape of the credit spread curve for the entity[87].

The basic structure is similar to that of a credit spread swap[88]. The major difference is that the floating spread component is calculated with reference to a constant maturity credit default swap rather than a physical bond.

The development of CMSS reflects both the credit cycle (reduction in credit spreads), the increasing liquidity of the credit default swap market, and increased interest in trading credit spreads. The major applications of CMSS structures include:

- Investors and traders monetising expectations on changes in credit spreads.
- Investors and bank credit portfolio managers hedging credit risk exposure on their credit portfolios.

Constant maturity credit default swaps have also emerged[89]. **Exhibit 2.15** sets out an example of a CMSS transaction.

---

[87] See Chapter 5.
[88] See Chapter 1.
[89] See Patel, Navroz "New Types Of CDS Gets Off The Ground" (April 2004) Risk 12.

Exhibit 2.14   Constant Maturity Spread Swaps – Example

The terms of a typical transaction are as follows:

Reference entity	ABC Company
Notional Principal	US$10 million
Maturity	5 years
Payments	Dealer pays 5 year CMS fixing (capped at 8.00% pa)
	Dealer receives 100 bps pa
CMS Fixing	This is the 5 year credit default swap spread observed for the Reference Entity [3] days before specified payment dates
Payment Dates	Quarterly
Current Spread:	5 years: 60/65 bps pa
	10 years: 80/90 bps pa
Knock Out Event	The transaction will terminate in the event of a credit event (bankruptcy or failure to pay) to the Reference Entity

Exhibit 2.15   Constant Maturity Credit Default Swaps – Example

The terms of a typical transaction are as follows:

Reference entity	ABC Company
Notional Principal	US$10 million
Maturity	5 years
Payments	There are two possible formats:
	Format 1
	Dealer pays CMS Fixing minus 23 bps pa
	Dealer receives contingent payment upon default
	Format 2
	Dealer pays 74% of CMS Fixing
	Dealer receives contingent payment default.
	[Dealer payments are capped at 800 bps pa]
CMS Fixing	This is the 5 year credit default swap spread observed for the Reference Entity [3] days before specified payment dates
Payment Dates	Quarterly
Current Spread:	5 years: 60/65 bps pa
	10 years: 80/90 bps pa

The basic structure is similar to a conventional credit default swap. The major difference is that the maturity is periodically reset and the premium is also adjusted. The underlying credit default swap is standard, using normal credit events and cash or physical settlement.

The product was targeted at bank credit portfolio managers seeking to hedge credit risks. The major advantage of the structure is that the hedge maintains a maturity of 5 years; that is, the most liquid part of the credit default swap curve. However, the uncertainty of hedging cost (effectively the roll cost) and the higher pricing are disadvantages of the structure.

13   Credit Index Products

13.1   Concept

Conventional credit products are generally based on a single identified reference entity. The reference entity is typically a sovereign, financial institution or non-financial organisation. Portfolio default swaps and n^{th}-to-default baskets are also based on the same concept. These products are based on a selected group of identified single reference entities.

In recent years, a number of credit indexes have emerged. These indexes are based on a pre-specified portfolio of reference entities. There is increasing interest in trading credit derivatives and structured credit products *on these credit indexes*. The primary rationale for these credit indexes and the credit products based on the index is investor/trader demand for liquid products on diversified credit portfolios. The investor/trader demand is related to the hedging and assumption of exposure of credit portfolios. Credit index products are examined in this Section.

13.2   Evolution[90]

Credit indexes have their antecedents in bond market indexes[91]. Bond indexes are used extensively as benchmarks for performance measurement and index based investment products[92].

Bond indexes are available on a variety of bonds ranging from sovereign, corporate, high yield and emerging market securities[93]. Non-sovereign bond

---

[90]   For the evolution of the credit index market, see Evans, Nick "Banks Battle For Index-Linked Trade" (April 2002) Euromoney 12; Patel, Navroz "New Dealers, New Products In Credit Investment Market" (May 2002) Risk 6–7; Jeffrey, Christopher "...While Morgan Stanley Adds To Range With Synthetic 'Tracer'" (May 2002) Risk 6–7; Polyn, Gallagher "Credit Portfolio Products Multiply" (December 2002) Risk 19; Dunbar, Nicholas "Accounting Fears Drive Structured Credit Initiative" (June 2003) Risk 9; Patel, Navroz "A Cautious Embrace" (June 2003) Risk Management For Investors – Supplement To Risk S6–S7; Farooqi, Saima "Early Days For Indexes" (September 2003)

indexes inherently have a credit dimension. In the 1990's, increased interest in credit investments and also the weaknesses of traditional corporate bond based indexes drove interest in alternative credit indexes. There were several attempts to implement credit indexes[94]. The most significant innovation was the JP Morgan European Credit Swap Index ("ECSI")[95].

The introduction of the ECSI was significant in that the index tracked the performance of *credit default swaps* on almost 100 European corporations. The ECSI structure was driven by the perceived weaknesses in the structure of corporate bond markets and corresponding corporate bond indexes. These weaknesses included:

• Lack of liquidity in many issues, with liquidity concentrated in a few benchmark large issuers and issues.

Risk Management For Investors – Supplement To AsiaRisk S2–S3; Patel, Navroz "Dow Jones takes Over Trac-x But iBoxx Launch Splits Market" (November 2003) Risk 14.

[91] See Reilly, Frank K. and Wright, David J. "Bond Market Indexes" in Fabozzi, Frank (Editor) (2001) The Handbook Of Fixed Income Securities – Sixth Edition; McGraw-Hill, New York at Chapter 7. Bond market indexes themselves have their origin in equity market indexes. For a discussion about the issues in equity index construction and design; see Das, Satyajit (2004) Swaps/Financial Derivatives 3rd Edition; John Wiley & Sons, Singapore at Chapter 55.

[92] See Efraty, Ravit (March 1995) An Introduction to Index Swaps and Notes; Salomon Brothers US Derivatives Research Fixed Income Derivatives, New York.

[93] A variety of bond price indexes are published by major investment banks, including Salomon Brothers, Lehman Brothers, Goldman Sachs, JP Morgan etc. The indexes are available on a variety of underlying bond universes – for example, investment grade, high yield, emerging market, specific currency markets etc.

[94] Examples include: a corporate loan index (see Lee, Peter "New Index To Boost Loan Trading" (March 1993) Euromoney 10; Lee, Peter "Citi Rates Options On Credit Risk" (June 1993) Euromoney 6; ("Citi Bares Its Soul" (29 October 1994) International Financing Review Number 1054 8), an impaired credit index ("Impaired Loan Index" (1 April 1995) International Financing Review Number 1075 65; "Loan Index Goes With Liquidity Flow" (20 January 1996) International Financing Review Number 1116 76) and a liquid leveraged loan index (Iben, Thomas, Miller, Steven C. and Urban, John E. (September 1993) Introducing The Goldman Sachs/Loan Pricing Corporation Liquid Leveraged Loan Index; Goldman Sachs, New York).

[95] See (11 February 2000) Introducing The Morgan European Credit Swap Index; JP Morgan, London and New York).

- Lack of credit diversity, with a few sectors constituting a large percentage of the exposure.
- Inherent interest rate exposure in fixed rate bonds.
- Lack of flexibility (credit quality, currency, maturity and issue structure) in the cash bond market.
- Lack of well developed repo markets in most corporate bonds that constrain short selling.
- Tax issues relating to coupons on cash bonds as well as legal issues covering distribution and transferability.

These problems led JP Morgan to create an index exclusively based on credit default swaps. The fact that the index created a "pure" credit spread exposure separated from interest rate risk was especially attractive.

The introduction of the ECSI prompted the development of a number of competing credit indexes by other investment banks. This was a period of experimentation as market participants sought to establish the optimal format for a benchmark credit index.

The major areas of difference included:

- **Underlying asset** – the indexes focused on either synthetic credit instruments (credit default swaps)[96] or corporate bonds[97].
- **Trading format** – the development of a credit index does not in itself allow trading in the index. Trading requires the development of index based products. These products can take a variety of formats. Two formats became predominant:
  1. *Exchange-traded fund* ("ETF") – an ETF is an open ended fund that is listed and traded on an established exchange[98]. There were a number of attempts to introduce fixed income ETF's based on credit indexes[99].

---

[96] For example, JPMorgan was a major advocate of credit default swap based indexes.

[97] The major example of a cash bond based credit index was the iBoxx indexes that were supported by a number of major investment banks.

[98] ETF's were originally used in equity markets and have more recently been used with bond markets. For a discussion of ETF's, see Das, Satyajit (2004) Swaps/ Financial Derivatives 3rd Edition; John Wiley & Sons, Singapore at Chapter 55.

[99] Credit portfolio products based on this model included Bank of America/JP Morgan's Core Investment Grade Bond Trust, Goldman Sachs/Barclays Global Investor's iShares GS $ InvesTop Corporate Bond Funds, Morgan Stanley's Tradable Custodial Receipts (Tracers) and Lehman Brothers' Targeted Return Index Securities (Trains); see Patel, Navroz "New Dealers, New Products In

The major advantage claimed was the liquidity and transparency of the ETF structure.

2. *Over-the-counter* (*"OTC"*) – this entailed the use of OTC instruments such as total returns swaps, credit default swaps, credit options and credit-linked notes to trade the credit index. The OTC instruments were traded with the investment bank(s) promoting the index. The advantage claimed was the ability to create unfunded products and also the flexibility of the OTC market.

● **Range of indexes** – there was a proliferation of indexes, with indexes on portfolios of entities segmented by geography, industry, credit quality or market[100].

The rapid development of credit indexes and the proliferation of indexes and structures resulted in problems. The problems included the diffusion of liquidity amongst competing products and the reluctance of participants to commit to specific products as they were wary of the longevity of individual structures. Over time, the market naturally consolidated.

The two major products that gained ascendancy were the Trac-x index (promoted originally by Morgan Stanley and JP Morgan[101] and subsequently taken over by Dow Jones[102]) and the iBoxx index (promoted by a consortium of banks). Both indexes offer a number of indexes covering North America, Europe and Asia. Indexes include broad indexes (based on investment grade or non-investment grade entities) as well as single sector indexes (mainly based on geography). There is some overlap in the underlying entities between the two indexes.

Both indexes are not listed or traded on an exchange. Index products are traded in the OTC markets. Dealers make markets in index total return swaps, options and credit-linked notes based on the index. Trade prices are

---

Credit Investment Market" (May 2002) Risk 6-7; Douglas-Jones, Jane "Credit ETFs And Beyond" (June 2002) FOW 24; Polyn, Gallagher "Credit Portfolio Products Multiply" (December 2002) Risk 19.

[100] For example, see the High Yield Debt Index (HYDI-100) (see "Credit Derivatives – Developing The Market For Credit Risk Transfer" in "Credit Derivatives Update 2002" (March 2002) Euromoney Research Guide 5–13).

[101] The Trac-x subsumed various products promoted previously by the two investment banks.

[102] See Patel, Navroz "Dow Jones Takes Over Trac-x But iBoxx Launch Splits Market" (November 2003) Risk 14.

not public. Quotes are disseminated through multi-dealer electronic trading systems (such as Bloomberg).

There are some differences between the two indexes. Trac-x is based on single name credit default swaps. iBoxx is based, in contrast, on the largest and most liquid benchmark bond issues available in the secondary corporate bond market. The differences in the construction of the indexes mean that they were, to some degree, complementary. For example, some dealers trade both indexes. In late 2003, iBoxx launched iBoxx CDX.NA.IG. This was a 125-entity North American investment grade credit default swap index. This more directly competed with existing Trac-x indexes.

Despite consolidation, the existence of competing credit indexes impeded the development of the market. In 2004, the indexes ultimately merged[103]. This will consolidate liquidity. It will also facilitate dealer and end user participation and product innovation.

13.3   Structure/Mechanics

In this Section, the basic structure of credit indexes based on credit default swaps is outlined[104]. The basic operation of credit indexes based on credit default swaps is as follows[105]:

- Trading in an index based on 100 fixed reference entities for a notional face value of US$100 million entails buying or selling protection on each reference entity (included in the index) for an amount of US$1 million. Most indexes are equally weighted. The currency of the underlying credit default swap is also fixed (usually it is the same as the currency of the index itself).
- The buyer of protection pays the seller a fixed fee in return for the seller assuming the risk on all the underlying reference entities. The buyer of

---

[103]   See "Trac-x and iBoxx Market Indexes Finally Merge" (June 2004) Risk 8; Saunderson, Emily "Index Merger To Boost Credit Market" (June 2004) FOW 18; Trinephi, Mia "A Merging Together" (June 2004) AsiaRisk 22–23.

[104]   There are significant differences between individual indexes and the discussion in this Section is only designed to provide a general overview of the basic methodology. Potential users of any index should seek professional advice upon the detailed structure and characteristics of any credit index.

[105]   For a discussion of traditional bond index construction, see Reilly, Frank K. and Wright, David J. "Bond Market Indexes" in Fabozzi, Frank (Editor) (2001) The Handbook Of Fixed Income Securities – Sixth Edition; McGraw-Hill, New York at Chapter 7.

protection pays the same fee for protection on all the underlying reference entities. Each index contract has a fixed fee that is set at the time of creation of each contract. Differences in individual credit spreads and changes in credit spread over the term of the contract are adjusted for in the trading price of the contract. The fee is paid on the standard credit default swap payment dates (20th March, 20th June, 20th September, and 20th December).

- Each credit index contract is generally based on a fixed maturity. Generally, the index is based on 5 year credit default swaps and has a 5 year maturity. In some cases, the contract is also offered with a 10 year maturity (based on 10 year underlying credit default swaps).

- Each index contract has specified *roll* dates (usually 20th March and 20th September each year during the term of the contract). On each roll date, new contracts are generally created ("on-the-run" contracts). The new contract may be based on reference entities within the previous index. However, it is probable that there will be some differences. The new contract will seek to represent the aggregate market at the relevant time. This will entail changes in reference entities, maturity and the fixed rate. The changes in the index are determined in several ways. A rules-based methodology (determining inclusion or exclusion) can be used to determine the constituents of the index. Alternatively, a dealer poll conducted amongst dealers who act as a market maker of the index can be used to determine the constituents of the index. After the index constituents are established, dealers/market makers submit credit default swap quotes that are used to set the fixed rate for the contract. Importantly, the new contract does *not* have any effect on existing contracts ("off-the-run" contracts). The reference entities, maturity and fixed rate on existing contracts remain unaltered. The existing contracts continue to trade normally.

- The credit events on the underlying reference entities used in credit indexes are bankruptcy, failure to pay and (in some cases) restructuring[106]. Where any reference entity experiences a credit event, the protection buyer settles the contract on a pro-rata notional principal equivalent to weighting of that reference entity in the index. Settlement is

---

[106] The restructuring provision used ranges from "restructuring", "modified restructuring" or "modified modified restructuring"; see Chapter 1.

generally based on physical delivery. The protection buyer delivers a deliverable obligation to the protection seller.

- After settlement where a credit event occurs, the underlying credit default swap is eliminated from the index. For example, in an equally weighted index based on 100 fixed reference entities for a notional face value of US$100 million, the credit event would require the notional to be decreased by 1/100. All other aspects of the original contract would remain unaltered. Reference entities eliminated (as between roll dates) as a result of a credit event are not replaced. In effect, the structure is based on eliminating the underlying credit default swap (on the reference entity that experienced the credit event). This means that the surviving part of the index contract can continue normally.

13.4   Index Products

The major products traded on credit indexes include:

- **Credit default swaps** – these are credit default swaps on the credit index.
- **Total return swaps** – these are total return swaps on the credit index.
- **Options/credit swaptions** – these are options on credit default swaps on the credit index.
- **Credit-linked notes** – these are notes with an embedded credit default swap on the index.
- **Tranched trades** – these are effectively CDO's based on the underlying credit index.

The products are traded by dealers who make markets in the index and on index products. The dealers do not charge for the index itself. Dealers earn fees through the bid-offer spreads in trading the products on the instruments.

13.5   Valuation Issues

The value of the credit index is best illustrated by a credit default swap on a credit index.

The valuation of a credit default swap on the index is driven by the structure of the index. As noted above, the index has a fixed fee that is set at the time of specification. This fixed fee remains unchanged over the full term of the contract. This requires the valuation of the credit default swap to adjust for the current market credit spread.

The basic process is as follows:

- **Intrinsic spread** – this is equivalent to the cost of replicating the index. It will generally be equal to the credit spread on the underlying portfolio of credit default swaps on the relevant reference entities. It should equate to the average credit default swap spread for the underlying reference entities for the specified maturity. This will depend on the market credit default spreads at the relevant time. There may be differences between the *theoretical* intrinsic spread and the actual spread on the index. There are a number of reasons for these differences, including:

  1. *Restructuring credit event* – the credit events in the index may not include restructuring. In practice, market quotes for a credit default swap where (a form of) restructuring is *not* a specified credit event may be difficult to obtain. Dealers tend to adjust market credit default swaps for the exclusion of restructuring events[107]. The theoretical intrinsic spread is therefore calculated by adjusting market credit default swap quotes. This may introduce possible difference.

  2. *Liquidity factors* – at various times, index based credit default swaps have traded at a spread below the implied intrinsic spread. This may reflect the higher liquidity of instruments on the index as well as the administrative convenience of index trades relative to trading in the underlying credit default swaps.

  In practice, the pricing differences are not arbitrageable because of the bid-offer spread in the credit default swap market.

- **Market value** – the market value of the contract is driven by the differences between the fixed fee on the index and the intrinsic spread at the relevant time. The intrinsic spread may be adjusted for market factors. If the intrinsic spread is above the fixed fee, then the contract has value for the protection buyer. The protection buyer must then pay the protection seller an amount at commencement to compensate for the differences in spread. If the intrinsic spread is below the fixed fee, then the contract has value for the protection seller.

- **Quotation convention** – credit default swaps on the index are quoted in the form of a spread. This is then converted into the price that is paid as

---

[107]   No R credit default swaps frequently are quoted at 5% lower spreads than Mod-R quotes. See discussion in Chapter 5.

between the parties. The conversion from spread to price is undertaken using a version of the following formula:

$$Payment = PVO1 \times (MS - FR)$$

Where

   PVO1 = the present value of 1 bps pa on the index payment dates until maturity or default discounted back to the valuation date. The market approach assumes that the PVO1 is calculated using discount factors based on a flat credit default swap curve equal to the index spread, a recovery rate of 35% or 40% and swap rates from the current LIBOR curve.

   MS = current market spread

   FR = fixed fee on the credit index.

The conversion from spread to payment amount entails discounting the difference in credit spread to the transaction date[108].

13.6   Applications

The major users of credit index products include traders/dealers, bank credit portfolio managers and investors. The major applications vary between the different user groups. The principal applications include[109]:

- **Traders/dealers** – credit index products are generally used for the following purposes:
  1. Taking positions (on credit spreads and defaults) on the broad market or specific sectors.
  2. Shorting credit markets.
  3. Hedging trading and inventory positions.
  4. Hedging/trading CDO positions including ramp-up risk on new CDO transactions.
- **Bank credit portfolio managers** – credit index products are generally used for the following purposes:
  1. Hedging credit exposure on loan and bond portfolios.
  2. Hedging CDO positions.

---

[108]   For a discussion of the valuation approach, see Chapter 5.

[109]   The applications of credit index products is similar to applications of equity index products; see Das, Satyajit (2004) Swaps/Financial Derivatives 3rd Edition; John Wiley & Sons, Singapore at Chapter 55.

- **Investors** – this covers asset/fund managers, insurance companies, hedge funds and private banking/retail investors. Credit index products are generally used for the following purposes:

  1. Establishing benchmarks for credit investment and investment performance measurement.
  2. Using funded products linked to credit indexes to create diversified credit portfolios.
  3. Using credit indexes to improve cash management within investment portfolios. This entails hedging exposure on fund inflows pending investment in actual credit assets to minimise adverse impact on fund performance.
  4. Using credit indexes to simulate credit investments for strategic or tactical asset allocation.
  5. Using credit indexes to hedge credit exposures.
  6. Hedge funds use credit indexes to trade credit views, hedge credit risk and also manage CDO investments.
  7. Retail investors have used credit indexes (generally in funded formats) to create diversified credit investments.

Other potential applications of credit index based products have also been identified, including:

- Corporate use of credit index based products to hedge new issuance spread.
- The increased availability of options/volatility products on credit indexes allows increased trading of credit volatility in markets.
- The increase in the range of credit indexes (covering different sectors and sub-sectors) may allow development of correlation trading between different credit markets.

Major advantages of index based products that are claimed include:

- Increased liquidity of the instruments driven by standardisation of the credit portfolios, concentration of liquidity/trading interest, the commitment of dealers/market makers and broad participation.
- The relatively low trading and transaction costs (including tight bid-offer spreads).
- The ability to manage credit portfolios in a flexible manner, including the ability to short sell credit markets.

Disadvantages of index based products include:

- Issues with the construction of credit indexes, including the methodology of altering the constituents of the underlying portfolio.
- Lack of transparency in pricing and trading driven by the OTC nature of the instruments.
- Presence of multiple indexes that segments liquidity and dealer/end-user participation[110].
- Basis risk in using credit indexes to hedge loan and trading portfolios where the constituent credit population varies significantly from the index.

13.7   Product Variations

A number of variations on the basic credit indexes and credit index based instruments have emerged:

- **Futures contract on a credit index** – an exchange-traded futures contract based on a credit index is a logical development. There have been a number of attempts at introducing such a product[111]. The gradual evolution of the market and the emergence of Trac-x and iBoxx have encouraged a number of exchanges to examine the possibility of a futures contract on a benchmark index[112]. A liquid futures contract on a credit index would complement the OTC market in trading on credit indexes. It would also increase the transparency of pricing and facilitate a liquid market in these indexes.
- **Credit spread indexes** – there has been interest in developing index products that transfer "pure" credit spread risk without transferring

---

[110]   As noted above, it seems probable that this problem will recede as the indexes consolidate further.

[111]   The Chicago Mercantile Index introduced a futures contract on a consumer bankruptcy index; see Falloon, William "A Hedge Against Consumer Credit" (May 1998) Risk 16; Arditti, Fred and Curran, John "Futures Contract On The Cards" (November 1998) Credit Risk Special Report – Supplement To Risk 30–32; Payne, Beatrix "Design Faults Stymie QBI" (January 1999) Risk 12.

[112]   See Crabbe, Matthew "Liffe Ponders Credit Swap Contract" (July 1999) Risk 6; Douglas-Jones, Jane and Davey, Emma "Credit Futures In The Pipeline" (June 2002) FOW 10; Trinephi, Mia "SGX Signs MoU With Dow Jones For Trac-x" (February 2004) Risk 12; Trinephi, Mia "Exchanges Look To Futures" (April 2004) Risk Management For Investors – Supplement to AsiaRisk S14–S15.

default risk[113]. A number of credit spread indexes have also been launched[114]. The indices are designed to capture credit spread movements in investment grade and high yield bonds. The indexes were designed to encourage the development of OTC and exchange-traded instruments based on these underlying indexes.

14 Equity Default Swaps

14.1 Evolution

There is an inherent relationship between credit risk and equity prices. This relationship is given by the Merton or structural credit model[115].

The model assumes that the equity in a risky firm is equivalent to a call option on the net asset value of the firm. The net asset value is calculated as the market value of the firm's assets minus the claims on the assets (which include traditional financial claims such as debt and other claims including erosion of asset values) that may result upon default. The position of the bond holder is a combination of the long position in the underlying bond plus the sale of a put option on the company's assets (where the option has a strike price equal to the value of the debt of the entity).

In practice, this relationship is used in credit modelling to provide market based estimates of the risk of default[116]. It is also used in relative value trading strategies seeking to generate returns from mis-pricing of different components of the capital structure of a company (referred to as "capital

---

[113]   See Kalotay, Andrew, Abreo, Leslie and Dorigan, Michael "The Challenge Of Managing Credit Spreads: New Tools On The Horizon" (Fall 1999) Journal Of Applied Corporate Finance 55–61; Choudhry, Moorad and Connelly, Christopher "Trading Credit Spreads" (Autumn 2001) Credit Derivatives – Supplement to FOW 14–15; Choudhry, Moorad "Trading Credit Spreads – The Future" (February 2003) FOW 12–17.

[114]   See Cooper, Lisa "Indexes For The Future" (October 1999) Credit Risk Special Report – Risk 16; Abed, Kamal "S & P Unveils Credit Spread Indices"(18–24 April 2000) Financial Products 5.

[115]   See Merton, R. "On The Option Pricing Of Corporate Debt: The Risk Structure Of Interest Rates" (1974) Journal of Finance vol 29 449–470. The Merton model is discussed in Chapter 6. For a more recent approach using the traditional option pricing framework, see Crouhy, Michel, Galai, Dan, and Mark, Robert "Credit Risk Revisited" (March 1998) Risk – Credit Risk Supplement 40–44.

structure arbitrage")[117]. The equity-credit relationship is increasingly used as the basis of hedging[118]. This entails trading in equities or options on the underlying stock to hedge credit risk or positions in credit default swaps (known as the "E2C" relationship).

In 2003, hybrid products combining elements of credit and equity markets emerged. These products were centred on the equity default swap. Equity default swaps are examined in this Section.

14.2 Structure[119]

An equity default swap transfers the risk of a large decline in the equity price of a reference entity from the protection buyer to the protection seller.

An equity default swap is defined as a contract where the protection buyer transfers the risk that the reference entity will experience an equity default event. The protection buyer pays a fee to the protection seller in return for this protection. The structure of the equity default swap is as follows:

- The reference entity is agreed between the parties. The reference entity is generally referred to as the reference equity.
- The buyer of protection pays a fee to the protection seller.
- An equity default event is agreed between the parties. This is usually if the reference equity trades below 30% of the value of the stock at the time of commencement of the equity default swap contract.
- The settlement of the equity default swap operates as follows:
  1. If there is no equity default event, then the protection buyer receives no payment from the protection seller.
  2. If there is an equity default event, then the contract is triggered and the protection buyer receives a payment from the protection. This payment is usually set at 50% of the value of the reference equity at

---

116   See the detailed discussion of the Merton model in Chapter 6.

117   See detailed discussion in Chapters 5 and 7. See Currie, Anthony and Morris, Jennifer "And Now For Capital Structure Arbitrage" (December 2002) Euromoney 38–43.

118   See discussion in Chapter 5. See also King, Matt (4 September 2001) Using Equities To Price Credit; JP Morgan, London; Naik, Vasant, Trinh, Minh, Balakrishnan, Srivaths and Sen, Saurav "Hedging Debt With Equity" (November 2003) Lehman Brothers Quantitative Credit Research 22–39.

119   See Choudhry, Moorad "An Equitable Life" (July 2004) FOW 57–60.

the time of commencement of the equity default swap contract (this is referred to as the "recovery value").

Exhibit 2.16 sets out a typical term sheet of an equity default swap. **Exhibit 2.17** sets out an example of the operation of an equity default swap. **Exhibit 2.18** sets out the differences between a credit default swap and an equity default swap.

In economic terms, the equity default swap is identical to a digital or binary option on the underlying stock where the strike is set deep out-of-the-

Exhibit 2.16 Equity Default Swaps – Terms	
Reference Equity	[Any stock traded on a recognised stock exchange]
Maturity	[normally up to 5–7 years]
Protection Buyer	[Dealer]
Protection Seller	[Investor]
Notional Amount	[Euro 5 to 20 million]
Reference Equity Price At Inception	Euro 40.00
Equity Default Event	Share price of Reference Equity trades at or below 30% of Reference Equity Price At Inception. The Equity Default Event is based on daily observation based on the closing share price of the Reference Equity.
Recovery Rate	50% of the Notional Amount
Fee	250 bps pa payable quarterly in arrears based on actual/360 year
Obligation of Protection Buyer	Protection Buyer pays the Fee until the earlier of Maturity or Equity Default Event. In the event of an Equity Default Event, the Protection Buyer pays the accrued Fee to the Equity Default Event date 2 business days after the occurrence of an Equity Default Event.
Obligation of the Protection Seller	• If there is no Equity Default Event, then the Protection Seller has no payment obligation. • If there is an Equity Default Event, then the Protection Seller pays the Recovery Rate to the Protection Buyer 2 business days after the occurrence of Equity Default Event.

Exhibit 2.17   Equity Default Swaps – Example

Assume the share price of ABC Company ("ABC") is trading at Euro 40.00. A dealer and investor enter into an equity default swap based on a notional amount of Euro 10 million for 5 years. The Equity Default Event is set at Euro 12.00 (30% of the current share price). The Recovery Rate is set at 50% (Euro 5 million). The Dealer (the protection buyer) pays the Investor (the protection seller) a fee of 250 bps pa (Euro 253,472) payable quarterly.

If there is no equity default event, then the contract runs through till maturity. The Investor has no payment obligation to the Dealer.

If the share price of ABC Company trades below Euro 12.00, then an Equity Default Event has occurred. The Investor pays Euro 5 million to the Dealer.

Exhibit 2.18   Credit Default Swaps Versus Equity Default Swaps – Comparison

Term	Credit Default Swaps	Equity Default Swaps
Reference Entities	Entities traded in the credit default swap market that tend to be confined to large, well known entities.	Majority of large, liquid stocks traded on recognised stock exchanges.
Maturity	Most liquid maturity is 5 years with possible terms of 1 to 10 years	1 to 7 years
Notional Amount	US$10 million to US$25 million with larger sizes feasible in more liquid names	US$5 million to US$10 million
Currency	Primarily US$ with activity in Euro and Yen. Some limited availability in other currencies.	Currency of the underlying stock.
Payment Trigger	Credit events (bankruptcy, failure to pay and (form of) restructuring)	Performance of stock price
Recovery Rate	Generally market based – the trading price of the distressed bonds of the reference entity	Fixed at 50%
Pricing	Driven by credit market; value changes are driven by changes in the market credit spread of the reference entity.	Driven by equity market; value changes driven by changes in stock prices and stock volatility.

money (at 30% of the current value of the shares) and the payout is set at 50% of the contract value[120]. The only difference between an equity default swap and the digital or binary option is the payment of the premium. In an equity default swap, the premium is paid over the life of the transaction on an accrual basis. In an equity option, the premium would generally be paid at commencement.

Equity default swaps are generally documented under the ISDA equity derivative definitions[121]. Key documentary issues include:

- **Adjustment provisions** – the equity definitions confer discretion on the calculation agent to make adjustments where certain events affect the underlying equity securities e.g. market disruptions, dilution etc. The calculation agents must take into account all factors considered relevant in making any adjustment. This includes how the transaction is hedged. This flexibility may be less appropriate in equity default swap transactions.
- **Cancellation events** – the equity definitions allow the parties to the transaction to elect for the transaction to be terminated and valued under certain circumstances. These circumstances include mergers, tender offers, nationalisation, insolvency and de-listing. The cancellation provisions may not be appropriate in equity default swap transactions.
- **Combination of equity default swaps and credit default swaps** – equity default swaps are frequently combined with credit default swaps in CDOs[122]. This creates difficulties because of the conflict between the equity definitions and credit definitions. For example, the merger event and successor events may be incompatible[123].

---

[120] For a discussion of digital options, see Das, Satyajit (2004) Swaps/Financial Derivatives 3rd Edition; John Wiley & Sons, Singapore at Chapter 44.

[121] See Cluley, Paul and Dwyer, Emma "Documenting EDS" (June 2004) AsiaRisk 28–29. There is a choice of the 1996 and 2002 Equity Derivative Definitions. In practice, the 2002 Definitions are commonly used. This reflects the fact that they include mechanics for barrier transactions.

[122] See Chapter 4.

[123] See Cluley, Paul and Dwyer, Emma "Documenting EDS" (June 2004) AsiaRisk 28–29.

14.3 Valuation Issues

The equity default swap can be valued as a digital option on the stock. This presents significant difficulties. The equity options are deep out-of-the money and naturally difficult to value given the exposure to "tail events". Implied volatility and volatility smile estimates for the relevant term are not readily available in the market.

In practice, equity default swap valuation is based on a simulation methodology. Where an equity default swap is valued using a simulation methodology, the likelihood of an equity default event (a share price fall of 70%) is determined by back testing using historical data. This allows a distribution of price changes (over a period equivalent to the term of the relevant equity default swap) to be calculated. This allows the probability, based on past history of the share price change below 30% of commencement value, to be established. The median of the worst case price changes over the relevant period may also be generated. In practice, minimum medians are correlated to equity default swap fee levels. The historical simulation can be complemented/supplemented by Monte Carlo simulations that are used to generate random price paths.

Equity default swaps are hedged either in the underlying equity market or in E2C trades using credit default swaps.

Credit default swaps and equity default swaps are generally closely correlated to implied equity volatility on the relevant entity. Traders focus on the risk of extreme credit/share price events implied by the credit default swap and equity default swap spreads. **Exhibit 2.19** sets out a simple way that traders frequently compare the implied market probability of default.

Exhibit 2.19   Implied Market Probability Of Default

Credit default swap and equity default spread levels imply a market probability of default (credit event or equity default swap trigger event).

The "rule of thumb" calculation is:

Implied probability of trigger $= [(\text{spread} \times \text{maturity})/(100\% - \text{recovery rate})]$

For example, assume:

- 5 year spreads for a reference entity are:
  Credit default swap spread = 80 bps
  Equity default swap spread = 300 bps
- Recovery rate = 50%

The implied probability of trigger event is calculated as follows:

$$\text{Credit default swap} = [(80 \text{ bps} \times 5)/(100 - 50)\%] = 8.00\%$$

$$\text{Equity default swap} = [(300 \text{ bps} \times 5)/(100 - 50)\%] = 30.00\%$$

This is interpreted in the following manner:

- Probability of credit event within 5 years assuming a 50% recovery rate = 8.00%
- Probability of stock price falling 70% within 5 years = 30.00%
- Credit event is 26.7% (8.00%/30.00%) likely as equity default event.

In 2003/2004, when equity default swaps emerged, the spread available on equity default swaps exceeded the spread available on credit default swaps. This led to relative value trading between credit default swaps and equity default swaps. **Exhibit 2.20** sets out an example of this type of trading.

Exhibit 2.20   Credit Default Swaps Versus Equity Default Swaps – Relative Value Trading

Assume that the spread on equity default swaps is higher than the spread on credit default swaps for the same reference entity. The higher spread on the equity default swaps implies that there is higher risk of an equity default event (as implied by stock price volatility).

A trader can take advantage of the negative correlation between credit spreads and equity prices to set up the following relative value trade on a specific reference entity:

Position	Spread (bps pa)
Sell protection under equity default swap	+ 300
Buy protection under credit default swap	−120
Net carry	+180

The positions are for the same notional amount (US$10 million) and same maturity (5 years).

The trader's position is as follows:

- The trader suffers a loss of 50% of notional amount if the share price falls 70% at any time over the 5 years.
- The trader benefits if there is a credit event in relation to the reference entity at any time over the 5 years. The amount of the trader's benefit is not known with certainty as the amount of any gain depends on recovery values implied by market prices of distressed debt following the credit event.

The position accrues net carry in favour of the trader. The position is relatively low risk where the credit event and equity default event occurs simultaneously.

The payoffs of the position are as follows:

1. If the reference entity's credit risk remains the same or improves and the share price does not fall 70%, then the trader earns the net carry on the position.
2. If the reference entity's credit risk deteriorates and the share price falls but there is no credit or equity default event, then the trader earns the net carry on the position.
3. If a credit and equity default event occurs, then the trader earns the net carry on the position until the relevant dates. However, the two positions will only offset each other where the recovery rate on the credit default swap is 50% or lower. This is because in that case, the gain on the credit default swap will be at least equal to the payment required under the equity default swap.
4. If an equity default event take place but no credit event occurs, then the trader incurs the following losses:
   - The trader loses the spread on the equity default swap but has to continue paying the spread on the credit default swap. This means there is negative carry of 120 bps pa on the position.
   - The trader's loss on the equity default swap is not offset by a corresponding gain on the credit default swap.

The risk in 3 above relates to exposure to debt recovery rates. The risk in 4 is more complex, relating to the different trigger events of the two contracts.

In practice, the risk in 4 above may be reduced. This reflects the impact of the negative correlation between credit spreads and equity prices. If the share price does fall significantly to trigger the equity default event (a fall of 70%), then it is likely that the credit quality of the reference entity will also have deteriorated and credit spreads increased. This would allow the trader to terminate the credit default swap in the market to capture value from the change in credit spreads. The gain would offset (in part or full) the loss on the equity default swap. The extent of this offset is difficult to assess as the gain on the credit default swap is affected by the remaining maturity of the transactions.

In practice, the risk of these relative value trades is complex. In some cases, traders leverage the credit default swap position to reduce the risk. For example, in the above example, the trader could purchase protection through credit default swaps on 150% of the notional amount of the equity default swap. This would reduce the carry on the trade to 120 bps. The leverage increases the return on the credit default swap in 3 and 4 above. This leverage can be static or dynamic. In the later case, the trader would adjust positions over time to maintain parity between the position in the equity default swap.

14.4   Product Variations

A number of variations on the basic equity default swap structure have evolved. The variations mainly focus on funded structures including:

- **Equity default swap linked notes** – this is a note where the redemption amount and (sometimes) the coupon are linked to equity default events on a reference equity. The structure is similar to a credit linked note. The major difference is that an equity default swap is embedded rather than a credit default swap[124].
- **Low equity barrier enhanced notes** – this is a variation on the standard equity default swap linked note. The structure entails a capital protected note. The return is linked to equity default swaps on a basket of reference equities (such as an index e.g. Dow Jones Euro Stoxx 50). At each coupon date, the number of equity default events that have occurred to that date are calculated. The coupon depends on the number of equity default events during the life of the note. After an initial threshold (that is, the number of equity default events), the coupon is reduced by a pre-specified amount.
- **Equity collateralised obligations (ECO's)** – this is similar to a conventional synthetic CDO based on an underlying portfolio of credit default swaps[125]. An ECO is a tranched asset backed security based on a portfolio of equity default swaps[126].

14.5   Markets[127]

Equity default swaps were originally promoted by JP Morgan[128]. The product has aroused significant interest but has not been widely adopted or used.

The major drivers of equity default swaps include:

- The Japanese market has been a major driver of equity default swaps. This reflects a combination of factors including very low credit spreads

---

[124]   See Chapter 3.
[125]   See Chapter 4.
[126]   For a discussion of ECO's see Chapter 4.
[127]   See Sawyer, Nick "House Of The Year" (October 2003) AsiaRisk 13; Wolcott, Rachel "Two Of A Kind?" (March 2004) Risk 24–26.
[128]   There are claims that similar products have been traded previously in equity markets.

and a lack of supply of corporate credit/bonds. These factors led to the development of equity default swaps as the product allowed investors to generate additional yield and access corporate credit indirectly from equity markets.

- In 2003/2004, the decrease in credit spreads globally reduced returns to investors. The low spreads meant that investors were assuming risk for insufficient return. In addition, the low credit spreads made it uneconomical to structure CDO transactions. In these circumstances, the higher spreads available on equity default swaps made it possible to achieve investor return expectations.
- There were marked differences in risk valuation as between credit default swap and equity default swap markets. Traders were keen to arbitrage the perceived pricing discrepancies. Equity default swaps, in part, facilitated this trading.

The above factors are primarily secular rather than structural[129]. The long term prospects for equity default swaps are not clear.

15   Currency Inconvertibility Agreements

Structures that deal with specific aspects of sovereign risk in financial transactions have emerged. In the main, the structures are used in emerging markets. This reflects the higher level and central role of sovereign risk in emerging market trading[130].

There are several levels of credit risk in transactions involving emerging markets. They include regulatory risk, market risk (currency, interest rate, and equity price risk), counterparty default risk and sovereign risk.

The sovereign risk element involves a series of risks including the inconvertibility of the currency or non-transferability of the currency. This risk is a central concern of foreign investors in emerging markets (both

---

[129]   Cynics even suggested that equity default swaps were in fact an attempt by equity derivatives desks suffering from the cyclical downturn in equity markets to encroach upon the rapidly growing credit derivatives markets.

[130]   For perspectives on the use of credit derivatives in emerging markets, see Gheerbant, Mark "Managing Country Risk Using Credit Derivatives" in (1998) Credit Derivatives: Applications for Risk Management, Investment and Portfolio Optimisation; Risk Books, London at Chapter 3; Van Der Maas, Paul and Naqui, Nabeel "Credit Derivatives Within An Emerging Market Framework" in Storrow, Jamie (Editor) (1999) Credit Derivatives: Key Issues – 2nd Edition; British Bankers' Association, London at Chapter 6.

direct and portfolio equity investors and purchasers of debt securities). For example, investors in local currency securities may not be able to exchange local currency received from a sale of investments to foreign currency to repatriate capital. This is a significant concern for traders in emerging market securities and financial products. International corporations with local market operations have similar risk in repatriation of earnings.

The aspect of sovereign risk most commonly dealt with in the credit derivatives market is the identified risk of currency inconvertibility or restrictions placed on the free flow of funds. This reflects the fact that this is a central concern of foreign investors. It also reflects the fact that structures linked to default have certain problems in the context of emerging market transactions and sovereign risk generally. In particular, there are a number of events short of actual default that have a material impact on transactions involving emerging market debt. In addition, the actual event of default on sovereign debt is likely to be somewhat remote.

Currency inconvertibility agreements have emerged as a mechanism for dealing with these types of risks. **Exhibit 2.21** sets out an example of one possible transaction structure. **Exhibit 2.22** sets out the structure of an

---

Exhibit 2.21   Currency Inconvertibility Agreements – Example

Assume an investor has local currency investments in an emerging market (in the form of securities issued by non-sovereign issuers located in the relevant jurisdiction). The investor is concerned about the risk of inconvertibility and transfer of funds. The specific exposure under consideration is that the investor may be prevented by government regulations from converting local currency into the foreign currency (say US$) in order to repatriate proceeds from sold investments. The investor decides to hedge the currency conversion risk on its investments.

The currency inconvertibility transaction is structured as follows:

- The agreement is structured to provide protection for a fixed period (1 year) against currency inconvertibility in the relevant jurisdiction on a specified face value amount that is related to the amount of the investor's investment exposure (local currency equivalent of US$25 million). The underlying security or investment does not need to be defined as the protection is not necessarily related to the underlying investment.
- The investor pays a premium to the provider of protection (of say 1.00% pa) based on the face value (US$25 million) equivalent to US$250,000.
- The payoffs under the currency inconvertibility agreement are as follows:
  1. If during the 1 year tenor of the agreement there is no currency inconvertibility event, then the investor receives no benefit and the agreement expires normally.

2. If during the 1 year tenor of the agreement there is a currency inconvertibility event which is continuing at the maturity of the agreement, or alternatively upon the occurrence of the inconvertibility event (usually two business days after exercise), the investor receives the benefit of currency inconvertibility protection as follows:

   - The investor receives the US$ equivalent of local currency face value of the contract from the party providing protection (usually in New York) calculated at the prevailing exchange rate at the time of the payment (the rate determination mechanism is prescribed).
   - In return, the investor pays to the seller of inconvertibility protection the agreed amount of local currency in the emerging market.

The inconvertibility event will generally be defined to include the imposition of regulations (described in broad terms) that have the effect of:

- Preventing or making illegal the conversion of the local currency into foreign currency.
- Preventing or making illegal the payment of the local currency to accounts outside the jurisdiction and/or transferring any funds outside the jurisdiction.
- Prohibiting the receipt of or repatriation outside the jurisdiction of any capital, principal of any security, interest, dividend, capital gain or proceeds of the sale on any assets owned by foreign persons or entities.
- Making the US$ unavailable in any legal exchange market in the jurisdiction in accordance with normal commercial practice.

Additional events that would trigger the inconvertibility event may include:

- A general banking moratorium or suspension of payments by banks or government entities in the jurisdictions.
- A general expropriation, confiscation, nationalisation or other compulsory acquisition or similar action by the government of the jurisdiction that deprives OECD banks of all (or substantially all) of their assets in the jurisdiction.
- Any war, revolution, insurrection or hostile act that has the effect of preventing convertibility of the local currency or transfer of funds to overseas accounts.

The rate at which the conversion is undertaken is usually the exchange rate at the date of settlement. The rate usually used is either the Central Bank published rates or, in the absence of such a rate or where such a rate is manifestly incorrect, a rate determined by a poll of dealers or some other commercially realistic method under the circumstances.

The effect of the transaction protects the investor against restrictions on currency conversion that might prevent repatriation of investments into hard currency or the ability to transfer funds out of the emerging market country through the imposition of currency controls.

Exhibit 2.22   Currency Inconvertibility Agreements – Structure

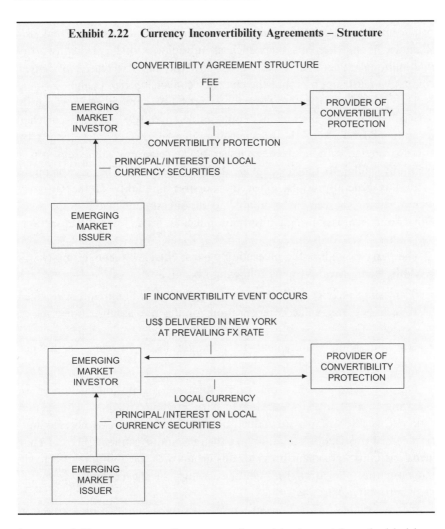

inconvertibility agreement. Structures where this element is embedded in a security are also used[131].

The seller of currency inconvertibility protection effectively assumes the risk of the local currency obligation in relation to currency convertibility. The risk assumed is not significantly different from that in purchasing a foreign currency denominated security issued by an issuer located in an emerging market country. The transaction effectively separates the credit

---

[131]   See Chapter 3.

risk from the currency conversion risk. The separation is important, for example, in the case of issuers such as subsidiaries of large creditworthy multinationals where the credit risk is low (perhaps by reason of parent company credit support), but the currency conversion risk is high.

The pricing of the currency inconvertibility agreement is generally derived from the pricing of comparable maturity foreign currency denominated bonds of the relevant emerging market country (issued by either sovereign or non sovereign issuers). The securities will exhibit a risk premium similar to that evident in these transactions. The risk premium derived is generally adjusted for the possible illiquidity of the currency inconvertibility agreement compared to the investment in the bond itself. Other sources of risk pricing information include trade finance transactions and political risk insurance.

The party providing the protection against currency inconvertibility will generally be motivated by the following objectives:

- The risk of inconvertibility is seen as slight and/or the premium received is seen as a fair value compensation for the risk assumed in terms of expected loss.
- An underlying requirement to purchase local currency to finance planned investments.

The first rationale may motivate a financial institution/insurer or an emerging market investor seeking to earn premium income. The second rationale is relevant for an industrial corporation that has entered into commercial transactions to undertake the relevant investment. The currency inconvertibility agreement provides this group with the ability to effectively monetise this obligation through the capture of the premium from the inconvertibility guarantee.

Inconvertibility protection structures display a number of features in practice:

- The structure is generally more expensive than comparable export credit or officially provided sovereign risk insurance. The difference in cost reflects the non-commercial nature of the insurance provided and the impact of inter-governmental influence.
- Protection may be available for transactions that would traditionally not qualify for protection under other insurance type arrangements.
- The term for which protection is available is relatively short. The market has limited liquidity. The ability to hedge these transactions using emerging market bonds is, despite considerable basis risk, increasingly

allowing the structuring of sophisticated instruments for hedging aspects of sovereign risk.

16 Hybrid Credit Structures

A number of hybrid credit linked structures have emerged[132]. A principal feature is the incorporation of a credit linked element[133] into a standard structured product on interest rate, currency or equity[134]. Typical structures include:

- **Credit linked range accrual notes** – this entails a standard range note where the investor receives an enhanced coupon in exchange for assuming the risk that interest rates, equity/equity index prices or currency rates set within a pre-specified range[135]. The variation entails the investor receiving a credit dependent spread in return for assuming the risk of a loss of coupon and/or (all or part) principal in the event of a credit event on a basket of entities. The investor receives a higher coupon than on a conventional range structure.
- **Credit linked notes with extension option** – this entails a first-to-default credit linked structure where the transaction has a minimum and maximum maturity. Under the structure, the dealer can, at any time before the minimum maturity date, extend the maturity of the transaction to the maximum stated maturity. Where the maturity extension right is exercised, the first-to-default component expires on the minimum maturity date and the structure generally converts into a regular Bermudan callable fixed rate note[136]. The investor receives a

---

[132] See Semonin, Lionel "Structured Hybrid Investments" (September 2002) Asia Risk – Structured Statement; Takagaki, Kazue and Tokukatsu, Reiko "Enhancing Yields" (June 2003) AsiaRisk 24–25.

[133] In these structures, the underlying credit exposure can be to single entities or on a first-to-default on a basket of entities. The first-to-default basket is frequently used because of the additional yield enhancement available.

[134] For a discussion of structured products in interest rates and currencies see Das, Satyajit (2004) Swaps/Financial Derivatives 3rd Edition; John Wiley & Sons, Singapore at Chapter 38, 50, 53, 54 and 58.

[135] See Das, Satyajit (2004) Swaps/Financial Derivatives 3rd Edition; John Wiley & Sons, Singapore at Chapter 53.

[136] See Das, Satyajit (2004) Swaps/Financial Derivatives 3rd Edition; John Wiley & Sons, Singapore at Chapter 50.

higher coupon than on a conventional first-to-default structure. The structure combines credit risk and interest rate risk. The investor's credit risk is limited to the minimum maturity date. The investor assumes interest rate risk from the extension option. The structure eliminates any exposure to the embedded interest rate option unwind costs where there is default on the basket.

- **Credit linked equity notes** – this entails an equity linked note where the investor receives a higher coupon in return for assuming credit risk in addition to the underlying equity risk. In 2004, Bank of China International ("BOCI") issued a 5 year equity and credit linked note (known as Flexibond)[137]. The note was linked to the credit risk on PCCW-HKT (the Hong Kong telephone company). The linkage was in the form of an embedded credit default swap on an unrelated reference entity. If the reference entity experiences a credit event, then the investor is delivered defaulted bonds of the reference entity equal to the face value of the note. The note also entails exposure to HSBC shares. Investors have the option (if there is no credit event on PCCW-HKT) of receiving 109% of the face value at maturity or exchanging the notes for HSBC shares. The conversion into HSBC shares is based on a conversion price of 120% of HSBC's average closing price for the first 3 days following the issue. The notes were callable at any time after the first 3 years. Where called, the investors have the choice of receiving 109% of the face value or the HSBC shares. The credit default swap spread is used to increase the return to the investor.

The structures are investor driven. The primary motivation of the structures is the creation of enhanced return for investors in return for the assumption of specified cross asset correlation risk. It also allows monetisation of specific investor views and limits exposure to undesired risk elements.

Hybrid structures have also emerged for borrowers[138]. The most common is credit contingent cross currency swap. The structure combines a credit default swap with a standard cross currency swap. **Exhibit 2.23** sets out an example of a credit contingent swap. Similar structures have been used with long dated foreign exchange forward contracts.

---

[137] See "Bank Of China International Gets On Board Structured Notes Market" (April 2004) AsiaRisk 31.

[138] See Chapter 7.

Exhibit 2.23   Credit Contingent Cross Currency Swaps[139]

In 2002, Kepco, the South Korean electricity utility, issued a US$650 million bond, swapping the proceeds into Yen. The objective was to refinance an existing yen borrowing.

A credit contingent element was introduced into the currency swap. The swap was referenced to the Republic of Korea. If Korea experiences a credit event, then the currency swap terminates, leaving Kepco with a US$ liability. In the case of a credit event, the defaulted Korean bonds are delivered to Kepco.

The effect of the credit contingent element is to reduce the cost to Kepco. It is equivalent to reinvesting the issue proceeds into a Korean bond that is trading above LIBOR. This is captured by the credit default swap spread that reduces the borrower's costs. Kepco assumes the risk of the sovereign (Korea) defaulting. It also assumes the mark-to-market risk on its underlying US$ liability. It also assumes the inherent correlation risk between the credit risk of Korea and currency rate (specifically the difference between the US$/Won and Yen/Won rate). Given that the Won is likely to depreciate in the case of a sovereign default against all currencies, the major exposure is to changes in the value of the US$/Yen exchange rate.

---

17   Summary

Structured credit derivatives represent a diverse and heterogeneous group of transactions that are principally concerned with the isolation of credit risk as a separately traded market variable. The different products are essentially focused on structuring instruments to allow trading in credit risk in varied forms. The structured credit products are driven by investor demand for specific types of credit exposure. The structures are also driven by the ability to trade non-standard types of credit risk.

---

[139]   See Sawyer, Nick "House Of The Year And Credit Derivatives House Of The Year – JPMorgan" (October 2002) AsiaRisk 10–11; Sawyer, Nick "Dabbling With Credit" (February 2004) Treasury – Supplement To AsiaRisk S28–S29.

3
Credit Linked Notes

1 Overview

Credit linked notes/collateralised debt obligations ("CDOs") are combinations of a fixed income security and an embedded credit derivative. Credit linked notes are designed to allow investors to capture returns on a single underlying bond/loan or a portfolio of bonds/loans. CDOs combine credit linked notes and securitisation techniques to create structured exposure to portfolios of credit risk (generally portfolios of bonds/loans or other credit obligations). This Chapter outlines the rationale, structure and applications of credit linked notes. CDO structures are discussed in Chapter 4.

The structure of the Chapter is as follows:

- The rationale for credit linked notes/CDOs is outlined.
- The different types of credit linked notes structures (credit linked notes and repackaged credit linked notes) are described.
- Examples of credit linked notes are discussed.

2 Credit Linked Notes/CDOs – Rationale[1]

2.1 Overview

Credit linked notes/CDOs entail the combination of a fixed income security and an embedded credit derivative. The credit linked note enables the investor to replicate exposure to a bond or a loan without the necessity of

---

[1] See (1998) Credit Derivatives: Applications For Risk Management; Euromoney Books, London; (1998) Credit Derivatives: Applications for Risk Management, Investment and Portfolio Optimisation; Risk Books, London; Tavakoli, Janet M. (1998) Credit Derivatives: A Guide To Instruments And Applications; John Wiley & Sons, Inc., New York; Francis, Jack Clark, Frost, Joyce A., and

undertaking a direct investment in the underlying credit asset itself. The credit linked note is designed to allow the investor to capture value from movements in the price of an underlying loan asset or bond, credit spreads or default risk.

Whittaker, J. Gregg (Editors) (1999) The Handbook of Credit Derivatives; McGraw-Hill, New York; Nelken, Dr. Israel (1999) Implementing Credit Derivatives; McGraw-Hill, New York; (1999) The JP Morgan Guide To Credit Derivatives; Risk Publications, London; Tavakoli, Janet M. (2001) Credit Derivatives & Synthetic Structures – Second Edition; John Wiley & Sons, Inc., Gregory, Jon (Editor) (2003) Credit Derivatives: The Definitive Guide; Risk Publications, London; Gregory, Jon (Editor) (2003) Credit Derivatives: The Definitive Guide; Risk Publications, London; Tavakoli, Janet M. (2003) Collateralized Debt Obligations And Structured Finance; John Wiley & Sons, Inc., New Jersey. See also Falloon, William "Credit Where Credit's Due" (March 1994) Risk vol 7 no 3 9–11; Reoch, Rob and Masters, Blythe "Credit Swaps: An Innovation In Negotiable Exposure" (1995) Capital Market Strategies 7 3–8; Howard, Kerrin "An Introduction To Credit Derivatives" (Winter 1995) Derivatives Quarterly 28–37; Smithson, Charles with Holappa, Hal "Credit Derivatives" (December 1995) Risk vol 8 no 12 38–39; Whittaker, Greg J. and Kumar, Sumita "Credit Derivatives: A Primer" in Konishi, Atsuo and Dattatreya, Ravi (Ed) (1996) The Handbook of Derivative Instruments; Irwin Publishing, Chicago at 595–614; Masters, Blythe and Reoch, Rob (March 1996) Credit Derivatives: Structures And Applications; JP Morgan, New York and London; Masters, Blythe and Reoch, Rob (March 1996) Credit Derivatives: An Innovation in Negotiable Exposure; JP Morgan, New York and London; Masters, Blythe "A Credit Derivatives Primer" (May 1996) Derivatives Strategy 42–44; Iacono, Frank "Credit Derivatives" in Schwartz, Robert J. and Smith Jr., Clifford W. (Editors) (1997) Derivatives Handbook: Risk Management and Control; John Wiley & Sons, Inc., New York at Chapter 2; Ghose, Ronit (Editor) Credit Derivatives: Key Issues (1997, British Bankers' Association, London); Chase Manhattan Bank "Credit Derivatives: A Primer" (April 1997) Asiamoney Derivatives Guide 2–5; BZW "An Investor's Guide To Credit Derivatives" (June 1997) Derivatives Strategy Credit Derivatives Supplement 1–8; Scott-Quinn, Brian and Walmsley, Julian K. (1998) The Impact Of Credit Derivatives On Securities Markets; International Securities Market Association, Zurich; Citibank/Salomon Smith Barney (2001) Credit Derivatives 2001 – Issues and Opportunities; Risk Publications, London; Finnerty, John D. (1999) Credit Derivatives: An Introduction To The Mechanics; PricewaterhouseCoopers, New York; Storrow, Jamie (Editor) (1999) Credit Derivatives: Key Issues – 2nd Edition; British Bankers' Association, London; Francis, Chris, Kakodkar, Atish and Rooney, Mary (31 January 2002) Credit Default Swap Handbook"; Merrill Lynch, London; "Credit Derivatives Update 2002" (March 2002) Euromoney Research Guide; Francis, Chris, Kakodkar, Atish and Martin, Barnaby (16 April 2003) Credit Derivative Handbook"; Merrill Lynch, London.

The rationale for credit linked notes/CDOs is complex. It is driven by the requirements of both the transferor of credit risk (generally banks/dealers) and the transferee (the investor).

2.2 Credit Linked Notes/CDOs – Rationale

Banks and other financial institutions have traditionally originated and held credit risk[2]. This reflects the central role played by banks/financial institutions in intermediation of capital. However, it has increasingly become evident that acquired credit risk portfolios requires active management. This is driven by rapid changes in credit quality and the requirement to manage concentration risks within banks' credit portfolios. Additional factors driving active management include the fact that returns available on credit risk may not meet risk adjusted return targets and the impact of regulatory capital required to be held against credit risk[3].

The position has been compounded by the illiquidity in credit markets. This has meant that credit risk has traditionally been difficult to trade and transfer.

The general mechanism for transfer/trading of credit risk has been the capital markets, primarily the bond market. While the bond market is an important component of trading in credit risk, it suffers from a number of weaknesses, including:

• The size of the bond markets is relatively small in relation to the universe of credit risks generally. This is despite the development of bond markets over recent years. In North America and (to a lesser extent) Europe, bond markets are a large component of capital markets and funding activities. However, the bond markets' share of *total credit risk* from financial intermediation is modest. In the rest of the developed world, bond markets are a smaller component of credit activities. This means that bank/financial institution based lending is a large part of financial intermediation. In emerging markets, bond markets are generally at early stages of development.

---

[2] For discussion of the changing role of banks in relation to credit risk, see Chapter 68. See also Das, Satyajit "The Credit Revolution" (September 1999) Futures & OTC World 52–61.

[3] See Chapters 4, 6, 7 and 8.

- Where bond markets are available, the major component of the bond market is sovereign/government debt in the form of debt issued by government owned or sponsored issuers. This limits the ability of investors to acquire exposure to corporate credit risk.
- Where corporate bond markets exist, the range of credit risks available is limited. The bond markets are, for the most part, limited to certain large, rated issuers with sizeable funding needs. This is driven by the economics of bond markets. Outside the US high yield market and the European high yield market, there is very limited availability of issues by non-investment grade issuers. The inherent structure of bond markets limits the investible universe available to fixed interest/income investors. This significantly limits the ability to create diversified investment portfolios[4].
- Where appropriate securities are available, the structure of the security (currency, interest rate or maturity) may not be consistent with the investor's requirements. The structures primarily reflect the financing requirements of the issuer. There may also be liquidity concerns about corporate bonds.
- The direct bond market does not provide investors with the ability to create structured exposure to credit risk.

The weaknesses identified have historically limited investor participation in corporate bond markets. In recent years, there has been increasing interest in *credit risk* from investors. This is driven by a number of factors, including:

- In certain countries (for example, UK and Australia), the reduction in government deficits has resulted in a shortage of fixed interest investments. Investors requiring fixed interest securities have been forced to seek alternative forms of investment, including corporate bonds and credit risk.
- Credit risk is increasingly considered a distinct and separate asset class. Analysis of the performance of credit risk indicates that there are

---

[4] For example, in the European Euro denominated corporate bond market, during the period of the late 1990s/early 2000s, investment in *all* available corporate bonds would have resulted in a portfolio dominated by financial services firms (banks and insurance companies), automobile companies and telecommunication/media firms. In the US, during the same period, similar concentration (albeit not to the same degree) would have been evident.

attractive risk adjusted returns available from investing in credit risk. Credit returns also appear to be imperfectly correlated to the returns from other traditional investments (returns from interest rate, equity, property, currency and commodity assets). Investment in credit in a portfolio context appears to enhance return on a risk adjusted basis[5].

- The volatility of credit risk (credit spreads and actual default) provides trading opportunities.

The conditions described create an environment that is favourable to the transfer of or trading in credit risk. Traditional holders of significant credit risk (banks/financial institutions and dealers) are interested in trading credit risk. Fixed income investors are interested in investing in credit risk. This environment has been pivotal in the growth of credit derivatives. Traditional credit derivatives structures (such as credit default swaps) are not ideal for transferring credit risk from banks to investors. These factors have fostered the development of credit linked notes/CDOs.

The issues in transferring credit risk can be illustrated by the example of a bank hedging credit risk on a loan to a reference entity through a credit default swap. The bank buying protection will require the following characteristics of the seller of protection:

- **Acceptable credit quality** – the buyer of protection will seek a protection seller generally with a credit quality superior to that of the reference entity. The buyer will also require that there be low default correlation between the reference entity and the protection seller. The buyer of protection must also, by inference, be able to establish the credit quality of the protection seller.
- **Regulatory capital relief** – the buyer of protection will also require that entering into the credit default swap with the protection seller allows it to obtain a reduction in regulatory capital held against the original exposure to the reference entity. In practice, this dictates that protection can only be purchased from sovereigns (unlikely to sell protection) or OECD banks[6].

---

[5] See Asarnow, Elliot "Corporate Loans As An Asset Class" (Summer 1996) Journal of Portfolio Management; Marker, Jim and Rapoport, Michael R. (1996) Historical Performance of Corporate Loans: An Update Citibank's Corporate Loan Market Review And Outlook – 1st Quarter 1996.

[6] This is the case in the absence of cash/government security collateral being used. Use of collateral raises issues regarding the enforceability of collateral in the

In practice, the required characteristics of the protection seller will limit the capacity to transfer credit risk to investors. The requirement for acceptable and transparent credit quality will limit the scope for trading with investors. The only possibilities would be corporations and insurance companies of acceptable credit quality. In particular, the ability to trade with pension funds, mutual funds/unit trusts, hedge funds and retail investors would be limited[7]. The need for regulatory capital relief will also limit the ability to hedge credit risk with investors. This reflects the fact that investors will generally be 100% risk weighted under the existing Basel 1 regulatory capital framework[8].

In addition, conventional credit derivatives (such as credit default swaps) present significant problems *for fixed income investors*. The issues for investors include:

- **Regulatory/mandate issues** – regulations or restricted investment mandates may prevent the investor from entering into credit derivative transactions directly.
- **Funded investment** – the investor will generally prefer a funded investment. Credit derivative transactions will be off balance sheet and unfunded. The need for a funded investment reflects the fact that the investor will have cash to invest. In addition, the investor may be prevented from borrowing or leveraging the portfolio.
- **Administrative issues** – the investor may find the derivative format administratively difficult. For example, it may not have systems to record and value the derivative transaction. It will also have to enter into a derivative contract (an ISDA agreement). The derivative transaction may also raise complex accounting and tax issues.
- **Listed and rated investment** – the investor may require the transaction to be listed on an exchange and/or rated by major rating agencies. In general, derivatives will not comply with these requirements.

---

relevant jurisdiction. For a discussion of bank regulatory capital, see Das, Satyajit (2004) Swaps/Financial Derivatives – 3rd Edition; John Wiley, Singapore at Chapters 33 and 34.

[7] See Das, Satyajit (2004) Swaps/Financial Derivatives – 3rd Edition; John Wiley, Singapore at Chapter 38.

[8] It may be possible to overcome this through the use of collateral or the trading book treatment.

The identified problems of both banks and investors can be avoided by re-engineering the credit derivative transaction into a credit linked note. The creation of a note, where the credit derivative is embedded within the structure, has the following advantages:

- The investor purchases a security. This potentially avoids problems of regulations/mandates, need for a funded investment and requirement for a listed/rated instrument. It also avoids the administrative issues of a derivative transaction.
- The note structure entails the use of the investment to cash collateralise the embedded credit derivative. This has the benefit of minimising any credit exposure to the protection seller. It also has the benefit of allowing capital relief through the protection buyer's exposure being fully cash collateralised.

In practice, credit linked notes are used to allow the transfer of credit risk from banks to investors in a form that meets the objectives of both parties. The CDO structure has the same advantages. In addition, the CDO allows investors to obtain exposure to a diversified portfolio of credit risk. Credit linked notes/CDOs also allow the creation of highly structured exposure to credit risk for investors. In particular, it allows the creation of credit risk not available directly in the credit markets[9]. Credit linked notes/CDOs are also driven by the capacity to allow investor participation in markets that have traditionally excluded participation from investors (such as the bank loan market).

2.3 *Credit Linked Notes/CDOs – Market*

Credit linked notes/CDOs are primarily driven by investors. The major attraction of this format for credit derivatives is the capacity to create synthetic exposure to the underlying credit. The fact that this can be done using an acceptable and traditional securities format is especially attractive. The advantage of being able to avoid direct investment derives from a number of different sources. In developed capital markets, the advantages

---

[9] The re-engineering of credit derivatives into a structured note format is motivated by the traditional factors that dictate the use of structured notes/synthetic assets generally; see Das, Satyajit (2004) Swaps/Financial Derivatives – 3rd Edition; John Wiley, Singapore at Chapter 38.

derive primarily from the ability to access specific credit risk and the capacity to avoid market frictions (withholding taxes, requirement for custody and foreign exchange transactions). In high yield/non-investment grade and emerging markets, the advantages derive from a wider range of factors, including:

- Regulatory frameworks that may prevent investors directly purchasing the underlying security.
- Presence of often complex and cumbersome procedures to obtain approval in order to make a direct investment.
- Lack of underlying securities of the type (currency, term etc) sought by the investors.
- Difficulties of trading in the underlying market, including lack of liquidity and high transaction costs.
- Lack of development of the infrastructure of investment (particularly for foreign investors), including the absence of well developed settlement, custody and foreign exchange markets.

The difficulties of direct investment coexist with increased demand for investment in the high yield and emerging markets. This demand is driven by a number of factors:

- Search for higher investment returns in an environment of low nominal returns and (during certain periods) low credit spreads.
- Need for diversification of credit risk.
- Increased search for currency diversification within investment portfolios.
- Volatility of asset prices and credit spreads in these markets that provide significant trading opportunities.
- Relative value opportunities in the market segments that may be less efficient and less fully arbitraged than more developed markets.

The combination of increased demand for foreign investment and the presence of these significant barriers to direct investment has encouraged the development of the market for credit linked notes. Credit linked notes are used to allow *economic* investment in the underlying asset without the necessity to make direct investments in these markets. The use of credit linked notes to overcome the absence of suitable cash investments can also be devised. The capacity to create customised and highly structured risk reward profiles within these structures is also attractive.

The identified advantages are particularly important to credit linked structured notes and repackaged credit linked notes. CDOs are driven by additional considerations, including:

- Banks/financial institutions and dealers with large portfolios seek to hedge and restructure credit risk profiles. CDOs enable the issuers to hedge the credit risk of individual counterparties or an entire credit portfolio.
- CDOs allow investors to invest in diversified portfolios of credit risk. Investors in CDOs may find these structures to be more attractive on a relative value basis or offering higher liquidity than comparable securities issued by individual issuers.
- Investors are also attracted by the ability of CDOs to be used in the creation of credit risk structures that may not be directly available in markets.

2.4 Credit Linked Notes/CDOs – Ratings[10]

A feature of credit linked notes is the ability to have the security rated. The key issue in this regard is the basis of the rating.

There are two possible approaches:

- Separation of the performance obligation (the risk on the issuer) and the market risk element (effectively the exposure to the reference entity). This approach would mean that the credit linked note would be rated at the rating level of the security issuer.
- Rating based on the credit risk of *both* the issuer and the reference credit using an *expected loss* approach. This means that the rating of a credit linked note is based on the combined credit risk (probability of

---

[10] For analysis of the rating of credit linked notes, see Andersen, Nels "Rating Implications Of Credit Derivatives" in Das, Satyajit (Editor) (2000) Credit Derivatives And Credit Linked Notes; John Wiley & Sons, Singapore at Chapter 16; Tzani, Rodanthy and Leibholz, Maria "Credit Linked Notes" in Gregory, Jon (Editor) (2003) Credit Derivatives: The Definitive Guide; Risk Publications, London at Chapter 20. See also Pimbley, Joseph "Credit Derivatives And Credit Ratings" (March 1996) Financial Derivatives and Risk; Efrat, Isaac, Gluck, Jeremy and Powar, David (3 July 1997) Moody's Refines Its Approach to Rating Structured Notes; Moody's Investors Service – Global Investors Service, New York Management.

default and loss given default) of the issuer and the embedded reference entity.

The first approach is consistent with the approach used in connection with structured notes with other embedded risk factors (such as interest rate, currency, equity and commodity risk)[11]. The major rating agencies generally favour the second approach on the basis that it more correctly portrays the investment credit risk profile[12].

The expected loss approach seeks to estimate the likelihood of default and the loss given default. In using the expected loss approach to rate credit linked notes, the rating agency seeks to estimate the level of loss that an investor in the note is likely to experience. The process entails an analysis of the following aspects of the transaction[13]:

- The structure of the notes, including transaction cash flows and contingencies affecting payments.
- The credit risk of the transaction including:
  1. The issuer of the note.
  2. The embedded credit risk.
  3. Derivative contract structure including documentary risk (type of credit events; valuation process or delivery risk).
  4. Where a repackaging vehicle is used, risk on collateral, legal and taxation risk of the vehicle and bankruptcy remoteness.
  5. Early termination risk.
  6. Securities law issues.

The modelling entails simulating the effects of credit events on the issuer or collateral and the embedded credit risk. The rating agency will use a variety of techniques (binomial expansion or Monte Carlo simulations)

---

[11] The rating agencies generally denote the additional market risk by the addition of "R" to the overall rating; for example, AAA^R.

[12] The rating agencies were influenced by the fact that some investors used the generic rating of medium term note ("MTN") programs to structure exposure to lower rated obligors (in some cases, to non investment grade credits). This was driven by the investors desire to acquire exposure to credit risk *outside investment guidelines*.

[13] See Tzani, Rodanthy and Leibholz, Maria "Credit Linked Notes" in Gregory, Jon (Editor) (2003) Credit Derivatives: The Definitive Guide; Risk Publications, London at Chapter 20 at 440–447.

to analyse the performance of the note under various scenarios[14]. This approach is used to model the losses on the security. This allows the expected loss to be generated and used as the basis of the rating.

2.5 Credit Linked Notes – Regulatory Treatment

The regulatory treatment of credit linked notes recognises that the issuer's purchased protection against loss through default or specified credit event is fully cash collateralised[15]. The treatment of credit linked transactions is similar to that of a credit default swap. The important difference is that the presence of cash as collateral removes the capital requirement in respect of the credit exposure on the asset sought to be hedged. In effect, there is no capital requirement in respect of the counterparty risk of the seller of default protection. The problems in relation to mismatch of reference asset, maturity and/or default payment mechanism identified above are still relevant.

For the seller of protection, the credit linked note creates exposure to both the issuer and the underlying reference credit. The seller of protection is required to hold capital against the *higher* of the reference obligation and the issuer. The rationale is that the recovery of the principal of the note is most affected by the riskier of the two parties.

3 Credit Linked Notes – Types

There are different types of credit linked note transactions. **Exhibit 3.1** sets out a classification of the types of credit linked notes.
The types of credit linked notes include:

- **Credit Linked Structured Notes** – these are traditional types of structured notes where a fixed income security is combined with a credit derivative (credit default swap, total return swap or credit spread forward/ option)[16]. The structured notes feature a linkage of either coupon or principal to the underlying credit risk component specified by the

---

[14] For a discussion of these approaches, see Chapter 4.
[15] A credit derivative that was fully cash collateralised would presumably be accorded similar treatment.
[16] This structure is similar to structured notes/synthetic assets generally; see Das, Satyajit (2004) Swaps/Financial Derivatives – 3rd Edition; John Wiley, Singapore at Chapter 38.

investor. A high quality issuer (AAA or AA rated) issues the notes. The issuer, in turn, fully hedges the exposure to the embedded credit derivative with a back-to-back credit derivative transaction with a dealer.

- **Repackaged Credit Linked Notes** – this involves a special purpose issuance vehicle ("SPV") or asset repackaging structure to create credit linked structured notes. The repackaging vehicle purchases securities in the secondary market and then re-profiles the cash flows/ credit risk of the underlying securities by entering into credit derivative transactions with a dealer. The repackaged cash flows are then structured as a security and placed with investors. The repackaged credit notes are similar to and complement credit linked structured notes. Synthetic bonds are a form of repackaged credit linked notes. The structure entails the issue of debt out of a special purpose asset repackaging vehicle, where the underlying credit risk exposure is created through a combination of cash securities and credit derivative transactions. The synthetic bond is designed to replicate the characteristics of a fixed interest security issued by the underlying issuer. The major distinctive feature of synthetic bonds is that the notes are designed as *publicly issued and traded securities.* In contrast, credit linked structured notes and repackaged credit linked notes are issued primarily in the form of private placements customised to the requirement of a single investor[17].

- **Credit Portfolio Securitisation/CDOs** – the structure entails repackaging *portfolios* of credit risk (loans/securities and/or counterparty risk on derivatives/off-balance-sheet transactions). This approach uses credit linked note technology and securitisation techniques. The portfolio is usually structured into multiple tranches of securities that are then sold to investors. The issuer of the securities reduces or eliminates the credit risk to existing obligors through the issues.

There is naturally some overlap between the structures. The principles used to construct and hedge the different types of notes are similar.

---

[17] This will generally be the case even where the note is listed and capable of being traded.

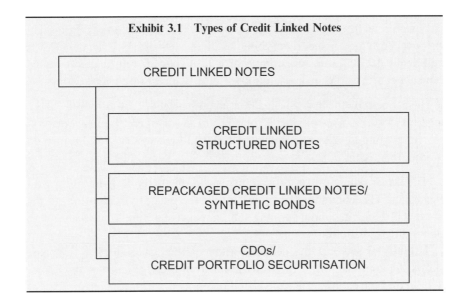

Exhibit 3.1   Types of Credit Linked Notes

CREDIT LINKED NOTES

CREDIT LINKED
STRUCTURED NOTES

REPACKAGED CREDIT LINKED NOTES/
SYNTHETIC BONDS

CDOs/
CREDIT PORTFOLIO SECURITISATION

4   Credit Linked Structured Notes[18]

4.1   Overview

The major types of credit linked structured notes include:

- Total return swap linked notes.
- Credit spread linked notes
- Credit default linked notes.

4.2   Total Return Swap Linked Notes

4.2.1   Structure

The principal object of total return swap linked notes is the simulation of an investment in the underlying asset (generally a bond) or an index (based on a basket of the underlying bonds). The structure allows a separation of the

---

[18]   See Tzani, Rodanthy and Leibholz, Maria "Credit Linked Notes" in Gregory, Jon (Editor) (2003) Credit Derivatives: The Definitive Guide; Risk Publications, London at Chapter 20; Choudhry, Moorad "A Primer On Credit Linked Notes" (April 2004) FOW 45–48.

risk profile, with direct credit risk on the issuer and the underlying market risk exposure to the underlying bonds.

Exhibit 3.2 sets out an example of a total rate of return credit linked note. The structure can be decomposed into two separate transactions:

- Investment by the investor in a floating rate asset (a LIBOR based FRN).
- Entry by the investor into a total return swap where the investor pays the floating interest rate index (LIBOR) and receives the total return on the underlying bond.

The issuer enters into a total return swap on the underlying bond with the dealer. This eliminates any exposure for the issuer to fluctuations in the bond. The issuer generates funding at a known cost of funds (consistent with its funding cost objectives).

Exhibit 3.3 sets out the decomposition of the structure. The first part shows the construction of the transaction from the viewpoint of the issuer. The second part shows the transaction components from the perspective of the investor.

The transaction described is cash settled. It is also feasible to structure the transaction to be settled by delivery. If settled by physical delivery, then the issuer would deliver the underlying bond at maturity of the transaction (1 year or credit event) to the investor in full settlement of the note. The issuer would pay the face value of the note to the dealer (hedging its exposure) in return for delivery of the bond.

The total return swap note can also be structured to effectively short sell the relevant bond market to capture value from a decline in the price of loans from either a deterioration in the credit or increase in credit spreads. Short selling corporate, non-investment grade or emerging market bonds is traditionally difficult. This reflects the difficulty of borrowing non government bonds for the purposes of the short sale. The ability to use the embedded total rate of return loan swap to create the short position is advantageous in this respect. The ability to create this type of transaction depends upon the dealer's ability to enter into or hedge the total return swap.

4.2.2 Product Variations

A number of variations on the basic structure are feasible. The primary variations include the incorporation of leverage and the use of an index rather than an individual bond.

Exhibit 3.2	Total Return Swap Indexed Note
Issuer	AAA or AA rated issuer
Principal Amount	US$20 million
Maturity (years)	The earlier of:
	1. One (1) year from Commencement Date.
	2. The next succeeding payment date following repayment of the full principal and interest due on the Underlying Credit Asset.
	3. Occurrence of a Credit Event on the Underlying Credit Asset.
Underlying Credit Asset	[6.50%] coupon [15 November 2012] final maturity bond issued by [ABC Corporation]
Credit Event	[Bankruptcy or insolvency event], [failure to pay or payment default above a nominated minimum amount which stays uncured for a nominated period] or [restructuring event as defined] affecting the Underlying Credit Asset or [ABC Corporation]
Coupon	3 Month LIBOR plus Margin payable on each Payment Date on an actual/360 day basis
Margin	[250] bps pa
Payment Date	Quarterly
Principal Redemption	The greater of:
	(a) Principal Amount plus Capital Price Adjustment; or
	(b) the Minimum Redemption Level
Minimum Redemption Level	0%
Capital Price Adjustment	Principal Amount times change (either positive or negative) in the Price of the Underlying Credit Asset. The change in the price of the Underlying Credit Asset is calculated as (Current Price − Initial Price)/Initial Price.
Initial Price	94.00
Current Price	The [bid] price of the Underlying Credit Asset as calculated by the Calculation Agent in accordance with the Calculation Method at 11.00 AM (New York time) two business days prior to each Payment Date
Calculation Method	1. By dealer poll under which the Calculation Agent will poll at least 4 and no more than 6 dealers in the loan on agreed dates and use the quoted prices to determine an average price for the Underlying Credit Asset; or
	2. By reference to a screen or quote service.
	[Select one of the above Calculation Methods]
Calculation Agent	[Dealer]

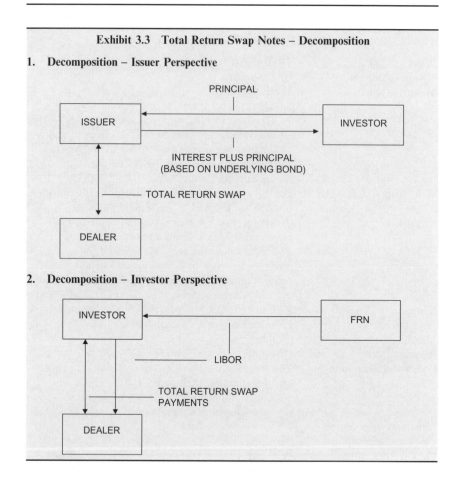

Exhibit 3.3   Total Return Swap Notes – Decomposition

1.   Decomposition – Issuer Perspective

2.   Decomposition – Investor Perspective

The transaction described in **Exhibit 3.2** can be readily restructured to incorporate leverage. This would be achieved by embedding a *higher* face value of total return swaps relative to the face value of the underlying floating rate cash investment in the note structure. **Exhibit 3.4** sets out an example of a structure that features 8 times leverage. **Exhibit 3.5** sets out the construction and hedging of the leveraged note.

The aggressive use of leverage may cause large fluctuations in the value, including the loss of the full investment. The investor's maximum loss is limited by the minimum redemption amount provision to the total value of the investment.

The structure of the transaction introduces some interesting risks for the dealer and investor. The issuer enters into a total return swap (on the required amount) with the dealer to eliminate any exposure to the underlying bond. In the event that the value of the bond underlying the total return swap falls rapidly (in the case of the example described in **Exhibit 3.4**, by 12.5%), the mark-to-market loss on the swap will exceed the face value of the note. The minimum redemption provision means that the value of the note will no longer collateralise the swap. If this event occurs, then the dealer will need to terminate the swap. If the bonds subsequently recover value prior to the maturity of the note, then the dealer will be required to re-establish the swap position. The dealer is therefore faced with a difficult hedging problem.

In order to hedge the leveraged note, the total return swap must be combined with a mechanism to effectively cap the losses at a level which equates to total loss of principal. This is designed to avoid negative redemption values under the note[19]. In practice, this is achieved by altering the terms of the note. In general, if the mark to market value on the swap falls below the level at which the redemption value of the note would be zero, then the note terminates with immediate effect. This is required to allow the dealer to terminate the swaps with no risk of having to reinstate the position before maturity.

The dealer is required by the hedge to trade the underlying bond at the time of terminating the total return swap. This requires the availability of a liquid market in the bonds. The leveraged structure requires the dealer to trade in a larger amount of the bonds. Where the bond price falls suddenly, the dealer must be able to execute the transaction at the relevant time to manage its exposure under the total return swap. The discontinuous behaviour of bond prices may expose the dealer to trading risk in these structures.

Exhibit 3.6 sets out an example of a total return swap linked note where the investor has specific exposure to a high yield index. **Exhibit 3.7** sets out an example of a transaction where the investor has specific exposure to an emerging market index. Total return swaps linked to credit indexes[20] have emerged as an important product.

---

[19] This aspect of construction of leveraged structures is also relevant to leveraged versions of other types of credit linked notes, including credit default linked notes.

[20] See Chapter 2.

The index based structures have the following advantages for the investor:

- Diversified exposure to the sector, allowing reduction of the specific risk of individual bonds.
- Benefits of a liquid and tradeable instrument on the index.
- Avoiding the difficulties that would be associated with directly replicating the index.
- Potential to leverage the exposure in order to generate additional return by embedding a total return swap with a larger notional principal amount. This is optional, depending on the requirements of the investor.
- Ability to short sell the index.

The capacity to effectively short sell assets can be illustrated with the following example. Assume an investor holds an illiquid emerging market or high yield bond. The investor is concerned about the exposure to potential deterioration in the price of the bond. The traditional physical solution to deal with this problem would include:

- Sell the security, giving rise to immediate realisation of a capital gain or loss (with tax and other implications).
- Short sell the security, which may be difficult due to difficulties in borrowing securities.

A potential synthetic solution would be to purchase a total return swap note on an index (the corresponding emerging market or high yield index) that is correlated in its price behaviour to the security held. The note embeds a total return swap where the investor receives the floating rate of interest (LIBOR) and *pays* the total rate of return on the security or index. This effectively provides a hedge for the investor, while potentially overcoming the problems of the transaction costs in the physical market and the practical difficulties of shorting the securities.

Exhibit 3.4   Leveraged Total Return Swap Indexed Note

Issuer	AAA or AA rated issuer
Principal Amount	US$20 million
Maturity (years)	The earlier of:
	1. One (1) year from Commencement Date.
	2. The next succeeding payment date following repayment of the full principal and interest due on the Underlying Credit Asset.

	3. Occurrence of a Credit Event on the Underlying Credit Asset.
Underlying Credit Asset	[6.50%] coupon [15 November 2012] final maturity bond issued by [ABC Corporation]
Credit Event	[Bankruptcy or insolvency event], [failure to pay or payment default above a nominated minimum amount which stays uncured for a nominated period] or [restructuring event as defined] affecting the Underlying Credit Asset or [ABC Corporation]
Coupon	(Leverage Factor times Margin) plus 3 Month LIBOR payable on an actual/360 day basis on each Payment Date
Margin	[250] bps pa
Payment Date	Quarterly
Principal Redemption	The greater of: (a) Principal Amount plus Capital Price Adjustment; or (b) the Minimum Redemption Level
Minimum Redemption Level	0%
Capital Price Adjustment	Leverage Factor times Principal Amount times change (either positive or negative) in the Price of the Underlying Credit Asset. The change in the price of the Underlying Credit Asset is calculated as (Current Price − Initial Price)/ Initial Price.
Leverage Factor	8
Initial Price	94.00
Current Price	The [bid] price of the Underlying Credit Asset as calculated by the Calculation Agent in accordance with the Calculation Method at 11.00 AM (New York time) two business days prior to each Payment Dates
Calculation Method	1. By dealer poll under which the Calculation Agent will poll at least 4 and no more than 6 dealers in the loan on agreed dates and use the quoted prices to determine an average price for the Underlying Credit Asset; or 2. By reference to a screen or quote service. [Select one of the above Calculation Methods]
Calculation Agent	[Dealer]

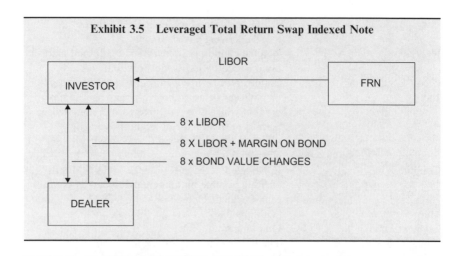

Exhibit 3.5   Leveraged Total Return Swap Indexed Note

Exhibit 3.6   High Yield Indexed Note

Issuer	AAA or AA rated institution
Principal Amount	US$20 million
Maturity	3 years
Coupon	3 Month LIBOR plus 200 bps
Principal Redemption	The greater of:
	(a) Principal Amount plus Leverage Factor × Change In Underlying Credit Asset; or
	(b) The Minimum Redemption Level
Minimum Redemption Level	0%
Leverage Factor	3
Underlying Credit Asset	Nominated High Yield Bond Index
Initial Price	Level of Underlying Credit Asset at the date of issue
Final Price	Level of the Underlying Credit Asset at Maturity
Change In the Underlying Credit Asset	Percentage Change in the Underlying Credit Asset as calculated from the Initial Price and the Final Price

---

Exhibit 3.7   Emerging Market Indexed Note

Issuer	AAA or AA rated issuer
Amount	US$10 million
Maturity	3 years
Issue Price	100.00
Coupon	0.00% pa

Redemption Value	The greater of:
	(a) Redemption amount is based on the following formula:
	Amount × Index/131.8
	(b) Minimum Redemption
Index	JP Morgan Emerging Local Markets Index (in US$) on the Value Date
Minimum Redemption	0.00 %
Value Date	5 business days before maturity

4.3   Credit Spread Notes

4.3.1   Structure

The use of credit spread notes allows the creation of specific structured exposure to *the credit spread*. The transaction does not entail direct credit exposure to the underlying bond or absolute exposure to interest rate risk. The ability to mismatch or vary the duration of the underlying investment and the credit spread to which exposure is sought is also a potential source of additional value.

Exhibit 3.8 sets out an example of a credit spread note. The structure seeks to monetise the investor's expectations on the implied forward credit spread. The investor gains if the spread decreases and loses if the spread increases. The structure entails a fixed income bond and a credit spread forward (where the investor purchases the spread). **Exhibit 3.9** sets out the detailed construction and hedging of the structure.

The notional amount of the credit spread forward can be higher than the face value of the note to create leverage (if required). Additional yield on the note can be engineered by structuring the spread forward at an off-market rate. For example, the transaction can be structured such that the investor can buy the spread forward at a price above the forward price. This creates an intrinsic value that is then present valued and used to enhance the yield on the security.

Exhibit 3.8 Credit Spread Linked Notes – Example 1	
Issuer	AAA or AA rated institution
Principal Amount	US$20 million
Maturity	3 years
Issue Price	100
Coupon	3 Month LIBOR plus 125 bps

Reference Security	[Identified] bond issued by [Sovereign State]
Reference Treasury Benchmark	[Identified US Treasury Bond]
Principal Redemption	Principal Amount plus [Spread Duration Factor × (Initial Credit Spread – Final Credit Spread)]
Credit Spread	Yield of the Reference Security minus Yield of the Reference Treasury Benchmark at Maturity.
Spread Duration	5
Initial Credit Spread	200 bps pa
Final Credit Spread	Credit Spread at Maturity

Exhibit 3.9   Credit Spread Linked Notes – Decomposition

1.   Decomposition – Issuer Perspective

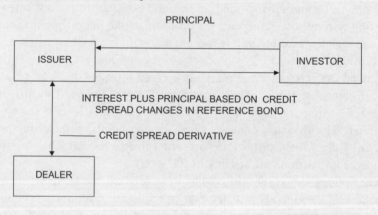

2.   Decomposition – Investor Perspective

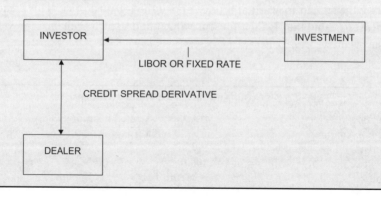

4.3.2   Product Variations

Exhibit 3.10 sets out an example of a credit spread note where the return profile is linked to the performance of the credit spread of a sovereign issue relative to US Treasuries. The rationale of the transaction is that the investor assumes an exposure to the credit spread and seeks to monetise the expectation that the spread will stay within the identified range. The investor benefits if the spread stays within the range. If the credit spread increases or decreases outside the range, then the investor receives a minimum coupon, but clearly suffers a reduction in return[21]. The structure entails the sale by the investor of a digital put and call option on the credit spread. The premium received for the sale of the options is used to enhance the return on the note. The digital payout on the embedded options has the effect of lowering the return to the investor where the spread is outside the nominated range, triggering either the call or put option on the spread. The issuer, in turn, sells the embedded options to the dealer to hedge its own exposure and reduce its cost of funds to its target level[22].

Exhibit 3.11 sets out an example of a credit spread note where the underlying securities are emerging market issues. In this structure, the investor uses the foregone coupon to purchase a call option on a basket of 3 countries that is embedded in the note. The structure links redemption to changes in 3 Brady bonds. The return profile provides for unlimited potential gains but with an assured return of principal. This structure is used in emerging market bonds where the credit spreads can be volatile. Major investors include institutional investors seeking exposure to the emerging market sector without the need to assume direct credit exposure to emerging market issuers. An added advantage is the ability to avoid the risks of trading in emerging market debt.

---

[21]   This structure is focused on the credit spread at maturity. An alternative that is also common entails the coupon being determined *daily* depending on whether the spread is within or outside the nominated range.

[22]   The structure is similar to the range/accrual note structure described in Das, Satyajit (2004) Swaps/Financial Derivatives – 3rd Edition; John Wiley, Singapore at Chapter 53.

Exhibit 3.10   Credit Spread Linked Notes – Example 2

Issuer	AAA or AA rated institution
Principal Amount	US$20 million
Maturity	3 years
Issue Price	100%
Coupon	Zero
Reference Security	[7.25% September 2031] bonds issued by [Sovereign State]
Reference Treasury Benchmark	[Identified US Treasury Bond 6.25% February 2031]
Principal Redemption	1. If Credit Spread at Maturity is between 95 and 140 bps then at 126% of Principal Amount (implied yield to maturity of 8.01% pa).
	2. If Credit Spread at Maturity is below 95 or above 140 bps then at 109% of Principal Amount (implied yield to maturity of 2.91% pa)
Credit Spread	Yield of the Reference Security minus Yield of the Reference Treasury Benchmark at Maturity

---

Exhibit 3.11   Credit Spread Linked Notes – Example 3

In early 1995, following a major selloff in emerging markets, a number of structured notes linked to emerging market securities (usually Brady bonds) were issued. The following note was typical of the securities issued:

Issuer	AAA or AA rated
Maturity	1 year
Coupon	0%
Principal Redemption	The higher of (a) 100 plus (Final Basket Price – Initial Basket Price) or (b) Minimum Redemption
Minimum Redemption	100%
Basket	40% bond of Latin Country A
	30% bond of Latin Country B
	30% bond of Latin Country C
Initial Basket Price	48%

The note combines a zero coupon note with a call option on a basket of three Brady bonds. The call option is engineered through the linking of the redemption value to the price of the Brady bonds. The call option is financed through the forgone interest on the note.

The issue was designed to allow investors to increase exposure on a risk averse basis to emerging market debt following the Mexican crisis – a time when emerging market Brady bond spreads widened by between 100 and 400 bps to their highest levels for many years.

The economics of the transaction were as follows:

- The 1 year yield on AAA or AA rated notes at the time of issue was around 7.00 to 7.25% pa. The breakeven price of the note, to equate the return to that on a conventional note, was around 93.25/93.50%.
- The breakeven price increase on the basket, so that the noteholder would earn the market yield on 1 year securities by the emerging market issuers, was around 14.60/15.10%, implying a final basket price of 55–55.25%.
- The return of principal on the note was guaranteed.

4.4 Credit Default Notes

4.4.1 Structure[23]

Credit default notes entail a combination of a bond and credit default swap. The structure is primarily used to assume or reduce credit default risk on the underlying reference entity. Investors have traditionally used credit default note structures to create synthetic credit exposure to the underlying reference entity.

Exhibit 3.12 sets out an example of a credit default note. **Exhibit 3.13** sets out the construction and hedging of the default note. **Exhibit 3.14** sets out an additional example of credit default linked notes.

The note structure depicted sets out a note linked to a single reference credit. The note combines a fixed interest security (fixed or floating coupon) and a credit default swap where the investor is the seller of default protection on the reference entity. The default payment or recovery rate is engineered into the principal redemption structure. The issuer enters into an offsetting credit default swap with a dealer to hedge its position and generate a known cost of funds. The fee received for the default swap generates the enhanced return on the credit default linked note. If a credit event occurs in respect of the underlying reference credit, then the note transaction terminates. The principal repayment to the investor is adjusted. The principal may be reduced by the amount of the default payment (effectively the cash settlement under the credit default swap calculated

---

[23] See Rutter, James "Credit-linked Comes Of Age" (April 1998) 22; Sandiford, Jane "Noteworthy Credit" (June 1999) Futures & OTC World 45–47.

using the post default price of a reference asset). The transaction may also be physically settled. If a credit event occurs, then physical settlement would entail the issuer delivering defaulted securities to the investor equal to the face value of the note in settlement. The issuer would pay the face value of the note to the dealer (hedging its exposure) in return for delivery of the bond. The calculation mechanics are identical to those applicable to credit default swaps.

The structure has significant credit enhancement aspects. The fact that the credit default swap is embedded in the note means that the credit default swap is *fully cash collateralised*. This results from the fact that in the event of default, the issuer merely adjusts the payment to the investor, reducing the principal repayment by the default payment obligation. The dealer effectively acquires credit protection from the investor (the ultimate seller of protection). The note structure allows substitution of the *credit of the issuer* for the *credit of the investor* as the seller of default protection. This significantly broadens the range of institutions able to provide credit default protection. This is achieved through the separation of the assumption of default risk from the actual counterparty credit risk of the seller of default protection. The concept can be extended using the repackaging/synthetic bond framework. This allows high quality collateral (government or high credit quality bonds (Aa/AA or better) to be used to significantly increase the range of providers of default protection *irrespective of the credit quality of the seller of protection.*

The cash collateralisation is also capital efficient. If the issuer of the credit default note is a sovereign, multilateral development agency or bank issuer, then the dealer may achieve a reduction in credit capital held against the underlying reference entity.

Exhibit 3.15 sets out a variation on the structure of credit default linked notes. In this structure, the bank *directly issues* the credit linked note. The embedded credit default swap is on an obligor to which the bank has a direct credit exposure. This structure can be used to transfer credit risk held by the bank on its own balance sheet. The structure is capital efficient as the credit default swap is fully cash collateralised allowing the counterparty risk to be reduced to zero. This allows significant capital relief in most circumstances where certain criteria in respect of the credit default swap are met[24].

---

[24] See Chapter 1.

Exhibit 3.12   Credit Default Linked Notes – Example 1

Issuer	AAA rated institution
Principal Amount	US$20 million
Maturity	5 years
Issue Price	100%
Coupon	LIBOR plus [150] bps
Reference Entity	[ABC Company]
Reference Obligation	Bonds and loans issued by the Reference Entity
Principal Redemption	1. If no Credit Event has occurred before Maturity, then Principal Amount.
	2. If a Credit Event has occurred before Maturity, then at the date of the Credit Event:
	• Principal Amount minus Default Payment; or
	• Delivery of an amount of the Reference Obligation with face value equal to the Principal Amount.
	[Select one of the above settlement methods.]
Credit Event	Any of the following with respect to Reference Entity
	1. Bankruptcy
	2. Failure to pay
	3. Restructuring
Default Payment	Change in price of the Reference Obligation between the Issue Date and the date which is the specified number of days following the Event Determination Date as determined by a poll of selected dealers in the Reference Obligation.
Event Determination Date	The date specified by the Issuer following the occurrence of a Credit Event

---

Exhibit 3.13   Credit Default Linked Notes – Decomposition[25]

1.   Decomposition – Investor Perspective

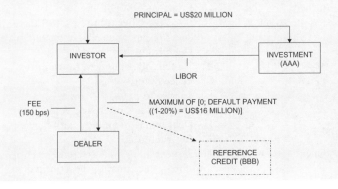

---

[25] The decomposition is based on the AAA/AA rated investment yielding LIBOR flat, the market credit default swap fee being 150 bps pa and the cash settled market recovery rate being 20%.

2. Decomposition – Issuer Perspective

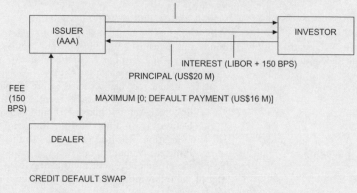

PRINCIPAL CALCULATED AS
(1) IF NO CREDIT EVENT THEN FACE VALUE (US$20 M) OR
(2) IF THERE IS A CREDIT EVENT FACE VALUE MINUS DEFAULT PAYMENT (US$4 M)

ISSUER (AAA)   INVESTOR

INTEREST (LIBOR + 150 BPS)
PRINCIPAL (US$20 M)

FEE (150 BPS)   MAXIMUM [0; DEFAULT PAYMENT (US$16 M)]

DEALER

CREDIT DEFAULT SWAP

Exhibit 3.14   Credit Default Linked Notes – Example 2

Issuer	AAA or AA rated institution
Principal Amount	US$20 million
Maturity	3 months
Issue Price	96.65% of Principal Amount
Coupon	0.00% pa
Reference Security	Republic of Korea 8.75% 15 April 2003
Principal Redemption	1. If no Credit Event in respect of the Reference Security has occurred before Maturity, then Principal Amount. 2. If a Credit Event in respect of the Reference Security has occurred before Maturity, then Default Payment.
Credit Event	Any of the following with respect to Reference Security: 1. Failure to pay 2. Cross default or cross acceleration 3. Debt moratorium/repudiation 4. Restructuring
Default Payment	The Issuer will deliver Reference Securities with face value equal to the Principal Amount to the noteholder

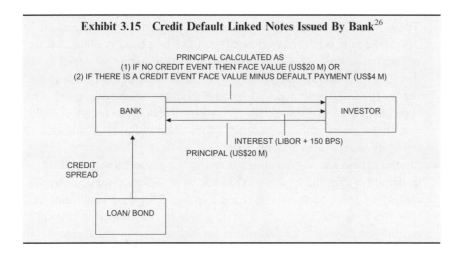

Exhibit 3.15   Credit Default Linked Notes Issued By Bank[26]

4.4.2   Product Variations

There are a number of variations to the basic credit default note structure, including:

- **Callable structures** – the callable credit default note provides the issuer with the ability to call the note prior to maturity. **Exhibit 3.16** sets out the structure of this type of credit default note.
- **Guaranteed principal structures** – these structures are based on ensuring protection of investment principal for the investor. **Exhibit 3.17** sets out an example of a credit default note where the investor is guaranteed return of principal but risks the coupon through linkage to a default event. **Exhibit 3.18** sets out an additional example of this structure. It also introduces the addition of a leverage factor that modulates the exposure in line with the investor's desired risk profile. A similar structure allows risk averse investors to assume credit risk with guaranteed principal returns. This structure entails a note where:
  1. Capital value of the note is returned at maturity.
  2. Investors participate in any upside performance of the underlying credit asset (loan or bond) as captured by the increase in price of the asset above a pre-agreed level.

---

[26] The economics in this example are identical to that in **Exhibit 3.12** and **Exhibit 3.13**.

The note has the return profile of a call option on the underlying credit asset. The note is constructed as either a risk free bond combined with a call on the underlying asset, or purchase of the loan that is hedged by the purchase of a default swap on the asset. In each case, the option is paid for by the forgone or reduced income from the underlying notes. This type of investment is attractive for investors seeking to invest in higher risk transactions within a low risk format. An example of this type of structure is set out in **Exhibit 3.19**.

- **First to default notes** – this entails a credit default note linked to the first-to-default within the basket to enhance yield. For example, an investor seeking to enhance yield within a minimum AA rating constraint may invest in a basket credit default note where the default event is indexed to multiple (say 4) AA rated sovereign issuers. The investor receives an enhanced return relative to the return *on any individual asset*. The higher return compensates the investor for the higher risk, as the default payment can be triggered by default on the *first* of the names to default[27].

- **Emerging market structures** – a variety of structures linked to sovereign credit risk in emerging markets have appeared. **Exhibit 3.20** sets out an example of a credit default note where the reference credit is an emerging market nation, and the return of principal is contingent on performance on external credit obligations and on continuation of currency convertibility. A feature of this type of issue is the shortness of tenor of the issue. **Exhibit 3.21** and **Exhibit 3.22** set out additional examples of this type of structure. Similar structures have emerged in recent years to facilitate synthetic investor exposure to Eastern European domestic markets. Significant regulatory and administrative burdens in making investments and holding domestic securities in these markets have encouraged the use of these types of structures to gain effective economic exposure to the domestic market[28]. **Exhibit 3.23** sets out details of one example of these types of synthetic emerging market structured notes as applied to Eastern Europe. **Exhibit 3.24** sets out details of an additional example as applied in Asia.

---

[27] See discussion in Chapter 2.
[28] See Kim, Theodore "Open All Hours" (April 1997) Euromoney 109–111; Kim, Ted "No KO for GKOs" (August 1997) Futures & Options World 15–17.

Exhibit 3.16   Callable Credit Default Notes

The structure entails a security where the final maturity of the note is 5 years. The redemption of the note is linked to a reference entity and in the event of default, the principal repaid is adjusted by the amount of the agreed default payment. The major differences in the callable versus the non callable structure are the following additional features:

- The note can be called annually or sometimes semi-annually or quarterly (upon provision of appropriate notice) at *the option of the issuer*.
- If the note is not called, then the coupon on the security increases by a preset amount.
- The call and the increase in coupon mechanism are repeated at the specified dates during the life of the note until final maturity, unless the note is called on any of the call dates.

In practice, the issuer uses the structure to purchase default protection to hedge its credit exposure to the reference entity. At each call date, the issuer can elect to maintain protection against default risk of the reference entity *but at an increasing cost*. This increasing cost of protection is embedded in the higher coupons.

Economically, the structure can be used to purchase protection against default over a short term, with the option to extend but at higher cost. The investor, in turn, receives increased returns for assumption of the default risk. If the note is *not* called, then it is probable that the credit risk of the underlying reference entity has increased. The investor receives additional income (the higher yield) to compensate for the increased default risk.

In practice, this structure was used extensively by Japanese banks to purchase protection against credit risk on certain entities. Most of the transactions were not designed to achieve real transfer of risk. They were intended as accounting balance date risk management strategies, with the issuers exercising the call at the earliest opportunity[29].

Exhibit 3.17   Principal Guaranteed Credit Default Linked Notes – Example 1

Issuer	AAA or AA rated institution
Principal Amount	US$20 million
Maturity	5 years or immediately following a Credit Event
Issue Price	100%
Coupon	• If there is no Credit Event, then US$ LIBOR plus 125 bps.
	• If a Credit Event has occurred, then coupon terminates.

---

[29]   For examples, see Mahtani, Arun "Credit Derivatives Bolster Balance Sheets" (21 November 1998) International Financing Review Issue 1260 91.

Reference Entity	[nominated emerging market borrower]
Principal Redemption	Principal Amount.
Credit Event	Any of the following with respect to Reference Entity:
	1. Failure to pay
	2. Cross default or cross acceleration
	3. Restructuring

Exhibit 3.18   Principal Guaranteed Credit Default Linked Notes – Example 2

Issuer	AAA or AA rated institution
Principal Amount	US$20 million
Maturity	3 years
Issue Price	100%
Coupon	(a) 4.50% pa; or
	(b) If a Credit Event has occurred then 0% pa.
Reference Security	[Identified bond of nominated emerging market borrower]
Principal Redemption	Greater of Principal Amount or Principal Amount plus [market value of Reference Security × Factor]
Credit Event	Any of the following with respect to Reference Security
	1. Failure to pay
	2. Cross default or cross acceleration
	3. Restructuring

Exhibit 3.19   Principal Guaranteed Credit Default Linked Notes – Example 3

Issuer	AAA or AA rated institution
Principal Amount	US$20 million
Maturity	5 Years
Issue Price	100%
Coupon	• If there is no Credit Event, then 0.00% pa.
	• If there is a Credit Event, then 5.75% pa (accruing from issue date to the date of the Credit Event).
Redemption Value	• If there is no Credit Event, then 150% of Principal Amount.
	• If there is a Credit Event, then 100% of Principal Amount (payable at Maturity).
Reference Entity	[Nominated emerging market borrower]
Credit Event	Any of the following with respect to Reference Entity
	1. Failure to pay
	2. Cross default or cross acceleration
	3. Restructuring

Exhibit 3.20   Credit Default Linked Notes – Default/Inconvertibility
Structures – Example 1

In 1995, following the financial crisis in Mexico, a special type of short term security was issued. The structure was a credit derivative embedded note. The structure allowed investors to monetise their expectation that Mexico would continue to meet its credit obligations and that the convertibility of the Mexican Peso would continue. The typical structure of the transactions was as follows:

Issuer	A1+/P1 rated issuer
Principal Amount	(up to) US$20 million
Maturity	Between 30 and 90 days
Coupon	Zero
Issue Price	Issued at discount to give investor required yield to maturity
Credit Event	Any default on any Reference Security or inconvertibility of the Mexican Peso into US$.
Reference Entity	Government of Mexico
Reference Security	Cetes, Tesobonos, Bondes, Ajustabones or other securities issued or guaranteed by the Reference Entity.
Principal Redemption	If there is no Credit Event, then Principal Amount. If there is a Credit Event, then the Issuer can satisfy its obligations under the note by local delivery of any of the Reference Securities or its cash equivalent in Mexican Pesos.

The short dated securities were priced to yield the equivalent of LIBOR plus 350 to 450 bps. The investors received significant yield enhancement in return for their willingness to risk the principal investment to the risk of credit default by the Mexican government or the restriction of currency convertibility (between the Mexican Peso and the US$) by the Mexican authorities.

Exhibit 3.21   Credit Default Linked Notes – Default/Inconvertibility
Structures – Example 2

Issuer	AAA or AA rated issuer
Principal Amount	(up to) US$25 million
Maturity	2 years
Coupon	8.00% pa payable semi-annually
Issue Price	100%
Credit Event	• The Government of Brazil restricts the convertibility of the Brazilian Real into US$.

	• Default, rescheduling, moratorium or suspension of payments on Government of Brazil debt.
	• War, civil strife or similar event involving Brazil occurs.
Interest Payments	• If there is no Credit Event, then payment of interest as
And Principal	scheduled and repayment of Principal Amount.
Redemption	• If there is a Credit Event, then the Issuer can defer its payment obligation under the note until 10 days after cessation of such Credit Event, or satisfy its obligations under the note by local delivery of any Real denominated securities issued by the Government of Brazil with face value equal to the Principal Amount.

The investors received significant yield enhancement in return for their willingness to risk deferral of payments on the investment in the event of default by the Brazilian government or the restriction of currency convertibility (between the Real and the US$).

Exhibit 3.22   Credit Default Linked Notes – Default/Inconvertibility Structures – Example 3

Issuer	AAA or AA rated issuer
Principal Amount	(up to) US$20 million
Maturity	1 year
Coupon	0.00% pa
Issue Price	88.00%
Final Redemption	• If there is no Credit Event, then: Principal Amount × (1530/FX) Where FX is the US$/Lebanese Pound Exchange Rate at Maturity
	• If there is a Credit Event, then final redemption will be an amount in Lebanese Pounds equal to Principal Amount × US$ 1/Lebanese Pounds 1530
Credit Event	The Government of Lebanon restricts the convertibility of the Lebanese Pound into US$

The investors received significant yield enhancement (a return of 13.64% pa) and the ability to gain from any appreciation in the Lebanese Pound against the US$. The risk of the investment is that the investor may receive non convertible Lebanese Pounds as payment where restrictions on currency convertibility (between the Lebanese Pound and the US$) are imposed.

Exhibit 3.23   Synthetic Emerging Market Structured Notes – Example 1

An example of this type of structure includes investments in short dated notes linked to Russian GKOs (Russian Treasury Bills). In 1996, the Russian capital markets were deregulated to allow foreign investment in fixed interest securities. This was facilitated by the introduction of the "S" account for foreign fixed income investment. Previous to this initiative, foreign investors were unable to repatriate the proceeds from the GKO and OFZ sovereign debt markets. The establishment of the S account was administratively complex. This encouraged foreign investment indirectly through the use of structured notes where the price performance of the note was linked to the underlying GKO securities.

The transactions were typically structured as follows:

- The investor invested US$ and received an interest rate and principal redemption based on the underlying GKO settled *in US$*. The return received by the investor reflected the interest rate on the GKO as well as the final principal repayment (in the absence of default) converted from roubles into US$ *at the currency rate at maturity*.
- The structure of the transaction transferred the credit risk, interest rate risk and currency risk to the investor. The structure effectively replicated an investment in the GKO itself.
- The seller of the structured note (typically an investment bank with an "S" account) hedged its risk by purchasing the GKO itself and transferring the economic risk and returns through the issue of the notes.

The impact of the transactions can be seen in the following statistics:

- The GKO market increased to approximately US$60 billion by end 1997, with foreign investment representing around 50% of total outstandings.
- GKO interest rates fell from around 40% pa to a pre crisis low of 16.75% pa, in part due to the impact of foreign participation[30].

The structure has also been used in other markets. For example, set out below is a representative structured note that passes Polish government Treasury bill risk through to the investor. The structure is designed (as above) to allow investors, who might not otherwise be able to invest, to participate in the market.

Issuer	Investment bank
Maturity	3 months
Amount	(multiples of) US$5 million equivalent
Redemption	Amount × (1+ Interest Rate) × Currency Adjustment

---

[30]   The default by Russia on its debt in 1998 created significant problems because of the large volume of GKO linked structured notes on issue. See discussion in Chapter 1.

Interest Rate	Polish Zloty 3 month Treasury Bill yield
	(on an actual/360 day basis) minus [margin]
Currency Adjustment	$(0.45 \times US\$1/US\$2) + (0.35 \times DEM\ 1/DEM\ 2)$
	$+ (0.10 \times GBP\ 1/GBP\ 2) + (0.05 \times FFR\ 1/FFR\ 2)$
	$+ (0.05 \times SFR\ 2/SFR\ 2)$

The note is effectively a US$ settled investment that replicates an investment in Polish Zloty Treasury bills. The currency adjustment is designed to embed a basket weighted forward currency position in the note, matching the then current Polish Zloty basket peg in order to reduce the currency risk of the investment.

Exhibit 3.24   Synthetic Emerging Market Structured Notes – Example 2

The structure set out below is a representative structured note that passed Philippines government Treasury bill risk through to the investor. The structure is designed to allow investors, who might not otherwise be able to invest, to participate in the market.

Issuer	Investment bank
Maturity	2 years
Amount	(multiples of) US$5 million
Issue Price	100%
Interest Rate	• If there is no Credit event, then US$ 6 Month LIBOR plus 150 bps.
	• If there is a Credit Event, then 0% pa.
Principal Redemption	• If there is no Credit Event, then Amount in US$.
	• If there is a Credit Event, then Default Payment will apply.
Reference Entity	Bangko Sentral ng Pilipinas ("BSP") (the Central Bank of the Republic of Philippines)
Reference Securities	Treasury Bills issued by BSP equal to the Amount
Credit Event	Any of the following with reference to the Reference Entity:
	1. Failure to pay
	2. Cross default or cross acceleration
	3. Debt moratorium/repudiation
	4. Restructuring BSP restricts the convertibility of the Philippines Peso into US$
Default Payment	Following a Credit Event, the Issuer will not be required to pay any unpaid Interest Rate coupons or Principal Amount. The Issuer will have the option to:
	1. Deliver the Reference Securities to the investor; or
	2. Pay the net proceeds that would result from the sale of the Reference Securities in peso to the investor.

The note is effectively a US$ settled investment which replicates an investment in Treasury Bills issued by the Central bank of the Republic of Philippines.

5 Repackaged Credit Linked Notes

5.1 Concept

Repackaged credit linked notes involve the use of an asset repackaging structure to repackage the credit risk of securities to create credit linked structured notes[31]. The repackaging vehicle purchases securities in the secondary market and then re-profiles the cash flows and the credit risk of the underlying securities by entering into credit derivatives transactions with a dealer. The repackaged cash flows are then bundled up as a security and placed with investors. The concept of repackaged credit linked notes is similar to the general use of asset repackaging vehicles[32].

The motivations underlying repackaged notes and repackaging vehicles are similar to that underlying the market for credit linked notes generally. These include:

- Investor demand for credit risk that is not directly available in the market.
- Relative value considerations where the credit exposure can be created at a more attractive value through structured notes.
- Regulatory and market considerations that favour indirect assumption of the credit exposure relative to direct investment in the security.

The demand for repackaged credit assets relative to *traditional structured notes* is predicated upon the following additional factors:

- **Investor return** – repackaged credit linked notes generally provide superior returns to conventional credit linked structured notes. The additional return derives from:
  1. The issuer of a structured note does not need to be compensated for undertaking the issue.
  2. Relative value considerations, where the repackaging structure can use undervalued securities purchased in the secondary market to collateralise the structure, reducing the cost.
- **Credit selection** – repackaged notes increase the ability of the investor to select the issuer and underlying credit. This allows increased

---

[31] See Hoyland, Jeremy and Bulmer, Sean "Repackage And Prosper" (April 1999) AsiaRisk 25–27.

[32] For discussion of repackaging vehicles, see Das, Satyajit (2004) Swaps/Financial Derivatives – 3rd Edition; John Wiley, Singapore at Chapter 38.

customisation of issuer risk and diversifies the universe of issuers of structured notes.

- **Liquidity** – repackaged notes generally have greater liquidity, as the structure can be reverse engineered to allow the investor to restructure its exposure or sell the note.
- **Flexibility** – repackaged notes allow investments to be structured consistent with investor requirements, without the restriction of needing to satisfy the requirements of the note issuer[33].

These additional factors have contributed to the development of repackaged notes. Repackaged credit notes complement and compete with credit linked structured notes[34].

5.2 Repackaging Vehicles – Structure/Design

5.2.1 Evolution Of Repackaging Technology

The concept of repackaging vehicles evolved out of the asset swap market[35]. The term "asset swap" is a generic term covering repackaging of the cash flows of any security into a required cash flow configuration for an investor. Traditional asset swaps focused on repackaging the interest rate and/or currency risk profile of a security for placement with an investor.

Asset swaps focused on creating synthetic assets for investors. The dominant drivers of this market were: the opportunity to create securities not directly available in the market; generate returns in excess of those available from conventional securities of similar characteristics; and repackaging illiquid assets.

Traditional asset swaps were a combination of the purchase of a security and entry by the investor into a derivative transaction to transform the security's interest rate or currency characteristics. This was problematic for

---

[33] This is relevant despite the fact that the issuer is perfectly insulated from the impact of the embedded derivative and is fully hedged back into LIBOR based funding at an attractive cost.

[34] Dealers operate specialised repackaging vehicles. For example, JP Morgan uses a vehicle called Corsair.

[35] See Chapter 5. For a more detailed discussion of asset swaps, see Das, Satyajit (2004) Swaps/Financial Derivatives – 3rd Edition; John Wiley, Singapore at Chapter 38.

a number of reasons:

- The inability of a number of investors to transact derivatives.
- The credit risk inherent in the derivative transaction.
- The lack of liquidity of the package and the difficulty in trading the synthetic asset except by unbundling it into its components (which could be expensive).
- The administrative complexity of marking to market both the security and the derivative and the complexity of accounting for and establishing the taxation treatment of the transaction.

These problems led investment banks to evolve the concept of securitised asset swaps. Securitised asset swaps were the effective precursors of the repackaging vehicle.

5.2.2   Securitised Asset Swaps

Until September 1985, asset swaps had been traditionally undertaken as private transactions, structured primarily as bilateral transactions or synthetic securities. In September 1985, the concept of the public or securitised asset swap was introduced with two transactions. Hill Samuel led the first transaction. Merrill Lynch Capital Markets arranged the other transaction. **Exhibit 3.25** sets out the structure of the securitised asset swap.

The end result of the repackaging was the creation of a conventional fixed interest security for the investor. The securitised asset swap structure helped the investor avoid any need to either purchase the underlying securities or enter into the swap transaction. The structure met investor requirements in terms of:

- Credit quality.
- Interest rate and currency requirements.
- Capacity to have the security listed, rated, cleared and settled through existing clearing systems.
- Liquidity and ability to be traded.

The structure also subtly changes the risks of the asset swap structure. The dealer has no credit exposure to the investor. This is because the swap is secured over the collateral held by the special purpose vehicle. In contrast, the investor continues to be exposed to the credit risk of both the collateral and the derivative dealer.

The basic structure described continues to be the basis of the design of all repackaging vehicles.

Exhibit 3.25　MECS Securitised Asset Swap Structure

Towards the end of September 1985, the United Kingdom raised US$2.5 billion through the issuance of seven year FRNs due October 1992. The notes were originally priced at 99.70% of face value (net of fees) with a coupon of three month US$ LIBID. The notes were callable after 3 years at the option of the issuer and also putable at the option of the investors (effectively making it a 3 year maturity transaction).

Following the launch of the issue, the sales force of Merrill Lynch noted that there was considerable interest from its investors in *fixed rate* United Kingdom government US$ denominated debt. In particular, the sales force had reported a coupon of approximately 9.375% pa for a 3 year maturity as acceptable to these investors. However, no fixed rate United Kingdom government debt denominated in US$ was available. Consequently, the Merrill Lynch swap and Eurobond syndicate desk set about designing the largest securitised asset swap at that time.

The structure of the transaction was as follows:

- Merrill Lynch bought US$100 million of United Kingdom FRNs.
- The US$100 million of United Kingdom 1992 FRNs were then sold into a special purpose vehicle known as Marketable Eurodollar Collateralised Securities Limited ("MECS").
- Simultaneously, Merrill Lynch arranged an interest rate swap between MECS and Prudential Global Funding Corporation (rated AAA). Under the swap, MECS made payments of US$ LIBID every three months in return for Prudential making payments equivalent to 9.375% pa to MECS. This effectively converted the floating rate US$ cash flow that MECS earned from the United Kingdom FRNs into a fixed rate US$ flow. The swap between Prudential Global Funding and MECS was collateralised by the United Kingdom FRNs held by MECS.
- Merrill Lynch then arranged a Eurodollar bond issue in the name of MECS with a coupon of 9.375% pa and a final maturity of October 1988. The bonds issued by MECS were collateralised with the assets of the trust which was a holding of US$100 million of United Kingdom FRNs and also the contingent liability reflecting the interest rate swap with Prudential. Essentially the package constituted a high quality (AAA) credit risk.

(continued)

5.3　Repackaging Vehicles

5.3.1　Overview

The use of the structure described gradually gained in popularity as a means for repackaging secondary market assets[36]. An important step in the

---

[36]　For a discussion of the evolution of the market, see Das, Satyajit (2004) Swaps/ Financial Derivatives – 3rd Edition; John Wiley, Singapore at Chapter 38.

Exhibit 3.25   Continued

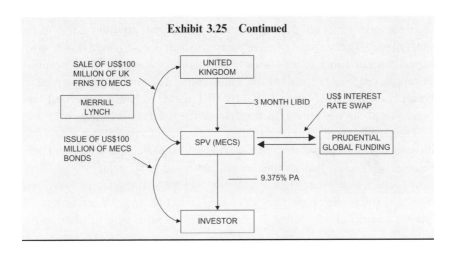

evolution of the repackaging markets was the development of a secondary market in structured notes.

The impetus to secondary market trading in structured notes derived from the market distress period of 1994/1995. Prior to that, secondary market interest had been spasmodic. The activity that had occurred had been related to investors exiting structured investments with the dealer purchasing the note, engineering the reversal of the derivative component(s), and distributing the security as a higher yielding fixed or floating note security to conventional investors in asset swap products. The latter continues to be the basic mechanism for providing any required secondary market liquidity and establishing benchmark secondary market bid prices for these notes.

In late 1994 and early 1995, the volume of structured notes that began to appear for sale increased dramatically as investors exited their investments[37]. The market conditions resulted in dealers rapidly re-positioning

---

[37]   The most notable transaction during this period was the sale of the very large portfolio of structured notes held by Orange County; see Irving, Richard "County In Crisis" (March 1995) Risk 27–32. See also "Earthquake In Southern California" (3 December 1994) International Financing Review Issue 1059 102; "Salomon To Clock Orange County's Work" (10 December 1994) International Financing Review Issue 1060 82; "Orange County Begins Sale Of Portfolio" (17 December 1994) International Financing Review Issue 1061 86; "Banks Suck Up Orange Juice" (24 December 1994) International Financing Review Issue 1062 60.

their secondary market trading in these instruments to allow them to be repackaged. The major buyers of the structured notes were asset swap buyers prepared to purchase structured notes that had been asset swapped to reverse engineer the market risk component. The asset swap was used to typically create a FRN priced off LIBOR targeted to banks, or a fixed rate bond priced off US Treasuries targeted to the fixed income investor.

The development of the secondary market in structured notes saw the introduction of a number of structured note repackaging vehicles. These vehicles were modelled on the securitised asset swap vehicles identified. Such vehicles include Merrill Lynch's STEERS (Structured Enhanced Return Trusts), Salomon Brothers' TIERS (Trust Investment Enhanced Return Securities)[38] as well as similar vehicles operated by other investment banks[39].

The central concept of the trust based structures was their ability to create trust receipts/securities that represented either repackaged structured notes or structured notes specifically created through repackaging which are sold to investors[40]. The trust receipts/securities were rated by one or more of the major rating agencies. The trust receipt/security is tradable to facilitate liquidity. In essence, it is the conversion of asset swaps into public and tradable securities.

5.3.2   Repackaging Vehicles – Structure

The original purpose of the repackaging vehicles was to re-engineer large volumes of structured notes that investors wanted to sell. The notes were converted into conventional fixed income (primarily floating or fixed rate) bonds for re-placement with investors. The structure can be used to *create* structured notes, as distinct from reverse engineer them into conventional

---

[38]   For example, see Klotz, Rick, Dominguez, Nestor, Roy, Sumit, Schwartz, Mike, and Shaffran, Alan (30 March 1995) Trust Investment Enhanced Return Securities (TIERS[SM]); Salomon Brothers US Derivatives Research.

[39]   For examples of other vehicles, see "Laser Shows at Paribas" (21 January 1995) International Financing Review Issue 1065 100; "Laser On Laser" (25 January 1995) IFR Swaps Issue 10 12; "BT TOPS out" (10 February 1996) International Financing Review Issue 1119 54; Rutter, James "Repackaging Of All Kinds Of Credits" (July 1997) Euromoney 29; Nicholls, Mark "TICs Tap Into Swap Spreads" (March 1999) Risk 15; de Teran, Natasha "Warburg Begins Multi-Issue Asset Repackaging Program" (27 June – 3 July 2000) Financial Products 9.

[40]   In non US jurisdictions, as discussed below, a special purpose vehicle is used. The vehicle issues bonds instead of trust receipts.

securities. This led to the emergence of the modern structure of repackaging vehicles. These vehicles currently operate both in the primary and secondary markets.

The structure of a repackaging vehicle is set out in **Exhibit 3.26**. The design of repackaging vehicles is largely standardised. The repackaging vehicle used is either a trust structure (favoured in the US) or a single purpose special company. The vehicles are associated with, but not owned by, dealer or investment banks[41]. The critical issues in structuring the vehicle include:

- The dealer does not own the vehicle. This is to avoid the need to consolidate the assets of the vehicle and maintain regulatory capital against the exposures incurred by the vehicle.
- The vehicle should be bankruptcy remote to the sponsoring entity. This means that the default or bankruptcy of the sponsor does not result in the default or bankruptcy of the special vehicle.

The steps in creating a structured note using a repackaging vehicle are as follows:

- The investor requirements are determined in terms of credit risk, risk profile and exposure required.
- The dealer purchases the required collateral in the secondary market.
- The dealer sells the collateral for value into the repackaging vehicle. The repackaging vehicle generates the liquidity needed to purchase the collateral from the issue of the structured note to the investor.
- The repackaging vehicle enters into derivative transactions with the dealer to:
    1. Convert a conventional security into a structured note with a defined risk profile by embedding the required exposure into the transaction through the derivative transaction.
    2. Convert a structured security into a conventional fixed or floating rate bond by hedging out the derivative elements through the derivative transaction.

The derivative transaction is secured over the assets (the collateral securities) of the repackaging vehicle.
- The repackaging vehicle issues notes (in the case of a company) or trust receipts (in the case of a trust) to the investor in return for value. The

---

[41] The vehicle is often referred to as an "orphan subsidiary".

proceeds of the structured note are used to purchase the collateral securities and if necessary, finance any payment required under the derivative contract. The securities are typically issued under a continuous issuance program such as a MTN program.

- The repackaging vehicle collects the cash flows from the underlying collateral as well as the settlements under the derivative contracts. The net cash flow is paid to the investor over the term of the transaction and at maturity. The structured note is cleared and settled through normal accepted mechanics.
- The investor in the structured notes is generally secured with:
  1. A charge over the collateral. This is usually a second ranking security interest. The dealer/derivatives counterparty will have a first charge securing payments required under the derivative contract.
  2. A charge (first charge) over the derivative contract.
- The investor in the notes is fully exposed to the risk of loss on the collateral securities or the derivative contract. The investor receives any payment received by the repackaging vehicle based on the realisation of the collateral securities adjusted for the benefit/cost of closing out the derivative contracts. The investor's loss is limited to the face value of the note.
- The structured notes issued by the vehicle can (if required) be rated by a rating agency. The rating is dependent upon both the collateral and the credit risk of the derivative counterparty. The typical counterparty to the derivative transaction is a dealer with a high credit rating (minimum A, with a significant number of dealers being AA or better). The issuer selects the credit quality of the underlying security or collateral. The resulting transaction can, at the option of the investor, be issued as a rated or unrated security.

In effect, the repackaging vehicle acts as a conduit to allow the investor to access the underlying security and overlay the specific risk exposure required through the derivative contract. The repackaging vehicle funds itself through the issue of the structured notes. The risk and return profile of the structured note is attributable to the underlying collateral and the derivative contract.

There are a number of repackaging vehicles active in the market. These include the vehicles mentioned above, as well as other vehicles such as those associated with major investment banks. Examples include: JP Morgan (CRAVE – Custom Repackaged Asset Vehicle Trust), Barclays

(ALTS – Asset Linked Trust Securities), Deutsche Bank (CROWNs, EARLs etc), ING (SNAP – Structured Note Asset Packages), UBS (SPARC – Special Purpose Asset Repackaging Company) etc.

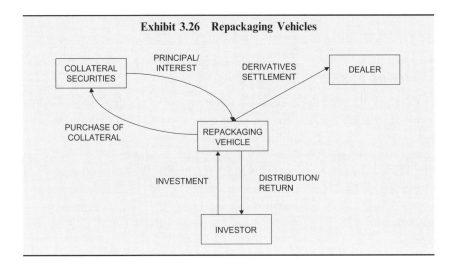

Exhibit 3.26 Repackaging Vehicles

5.3.3 Types of Vehicle

The types of vehicles used are:

- **Single purpose standalone issuers** – where a separate entity is established *for each issue* of structured notes.
- **Multiple issuance structures** – where a broad flexible structure is in place that allows the same entity to undertake different issues of structured notes.

The selection between the types of vehicles is dictated by the desire to maximise administrative flexibility and speed of execution, and minimise the costs of establishing the repackaging vehicles.

Multiple issuance structures have grown in popularity. Their popularity derives from:

- Lower cost of such structures, reflecting the capacity to amortise the set up and ongoing costs over a larger volume of issues.
- Speed of execution; as the structure is *permanently in place*, transactions can be completed in a relatively short time scale.

- Benefits of administration of fewer vehicles.
- Opportunity for individual investment banks to brand their repackaged products. The brand awareness has significant benefits in terms of achieving the status of an established issuer, facilitating ready acceptance by investors.

Two types of multiple issuance vehicles are commonly used:

- Program Issuers.
- Multiple Issuer or "Umbrella" Programs.

Program issuers are designed as single legal entities that issue multiple series of structured notes. Each note is specifically secured over the specific assets and derivatives used to create the note. This is achieved by a combination of specific charges and limited recourse agreements that limit the recourse of the investor (as creditor) to specified assets and derivative transactions. Each series of notes is isolated from other assets and the contract held by or entered into by the issuer through the non-recourse mechanism – often referred to as a "firewall". **Exhibit 3.27** sets out the structure.

The program issuer format is attractive because of its low cost, lower administrative requirements and speed and flexibility in use.

The critical issue is in relation to the effective segregation of assets. This is important both from a legal and ratings perspective, as well as from the point of view of investors. In the event that assets underlying one issue were in default and the required separation had not been achieved, then the investors could potentially seek recourse to *all assets and contracts of the vehicle*. This phenomenon (referred to as "tainting") would have far reaching effects. The issuer itself could be in default, compromising *all issues*, not just the one in default. This may lead to litigation *against the issuer* and could prevent the operation of the vehicle.

This means that the program issuance format is not used in all jurisdictions. It is only used in jurisdictions where an appropriate level of

---

42 Legislation in Guernsey (part of the UK Channel Islands) recently established the protected cell company ("PCC"). The structure allows the statutory segregation of the assets of each cell from the liabilities of other cells. The availability of PCCs was initially limited to funds and insurance entities. There are plans to extend the PCC concept to SPVs. See Mercer, Vincent "Why So Special?" (March 2004) FOW 40–43.

legal comfort on the firewalls can be established[42]. In practice, two other provisions can be used to manage this risk:

- Program issuance structures are not used where the underlying assets being securitised vary significantly in terms of credit quality from one issue of structured notes to another.
- The structure incorporates substitution rights, enabling assets to be removed from the structure in order to protect the rating of the vehicle[43].

The alternative is the multiple issuers or umbrella structure, where a separate vehicle is used for each issue, but a master documentary framework governing the individual issuers is established. **Exhibit 3.28** sets out the structure.

This type of structure has the following characteristics:

- The problems of tainting are avoided.
- Individual companies must still be established and administered over the transaction term.
- The process is facilitated by the common master documentation, with speed being increased by advance creation of a number of issuance vehicles.
- Cost is higher and the threshold size of the transaction and/or its profitability must be larger to support the higher cost.

The multiple issuer structure is generally favoured where the underlying assets are of higher risk, the underlying assets are of significantly *different* credit risk, or the legal risk of "tainting" is high.

The vehicles are generally based in favourable tax and regulatory environments such as Holland, Netherlands Antilles, Channel Islands (such as Jersey or Guernsey), Cayman Islands, or British Virgin Islands. The major factors driving selection between the jurisdictions include:

- Tax regimes.
- Legal framework; particularly in terms of contract law, segregation, and bankruptcy remoteness.
- A benign regulatory framework.
- Political stability.
- Cost factors.

---

[43] Following the emerging market collapse in 1997/8, this provision was used to remove Korean assets from some vehicles. This reflected the sharp deterioration in Korea's credit rating during this period.

- Availability of services such as legal firms, accounting firms, and management companies.
- Physical location in terms of distance from major financial centres.
- Time zones that allow trading overlap with normal trading hours in key trading jurisdictions.

The vehicles are generally rated by the major rating agencies[44]. The rating is based on the individual issue and key factors driving ratings such as:

- Credit quality of the collateral.
- Credit quality of the derivative counterparty.
- Market risks such as currency, interest rate risk and term to maturity.
- Structure of the transaction, including legal and taxation risks.

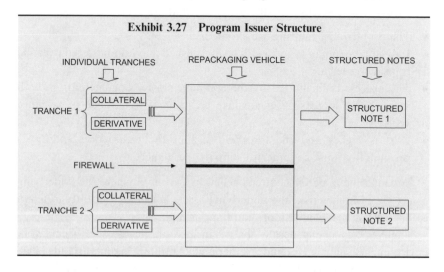

Exhibit 3.27   Program Issuer Structure

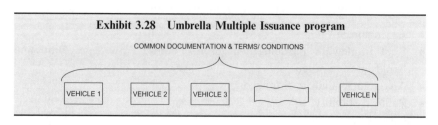

Exhibit 3.28   Umbrella Multiple Issuance program

---

[44]   See Das, Satyajit (2001) Structured Notes & Hybrid Securities – Second Edition; John Wiley & Sons, Singapore at Chapter 17.

5.4   Repackaged Credit Linked Notes – Structures

In general, there are two types of repackaged credit linked note transactions:

- **Creation of exposure to a selected credit risk (synthetic credit assets)** – this entails purchasing high quality collateral assets that are converted through a credit derivative to provide exposure to a selected credit risk nominated by the investor. The repackaged security, in this case, provides the investor with indirect exposure to the selected reference entity/asset. The structure is created to provide the investor with exposure to the underlying credit risk. The structure may allow the investor to circumvent regulatory and legal constraints on the investment and to structure the exposure consistent with its objectives.
- **Creation of exposure to high quality credit risk (asset credit swaps)** – this entails buying an asset in the secondary market and entering into a credit derivative transaction to *reduce* the risk to the obligor/issuer of the underlying security. The repackaged security enables the investor to acquire exposure to the derivative dealer (via the credit derivative). The repackaged security generates a return that is lower than that on the underlying security, but higher than the normal return that would be available on an equivalent security for *the higher rated* credit (the derivatives dealer). This type of transaction may be motivated by relative value considerations where the asset swap is used to arbitrage the valuation of different credits in the capital market.

The mechanics of the construction of a synthetic credit asset are as follows:

- The repackaging vehicle purchases high quality securities in the market.
- The repackaging vehicle enters into a credit derivative transaction with a dealer. This can be a total return swap or a credit default swap.
- The repackaging vehicle issues securities that pay a return to the investor that equates to the return on the reference credit/asset.
- At maturity or following a credit event, the security issued by the repackaging vehicle repays the investment principal value or an amount based on the value of the underlying reference asset.

The cash flow structure of the synthetic credit asset is dependent on the type of credit derivative embedded as follows:

- Where a total return swap is used, the return on the underlying high quality securities is paid to the dealer. In return, the dealer pays the return on the reference asset. This corresponds to the return received by the investor on the note. At maturity, the dealer effects a cash settlement with the repackaging vehicle based on the change in value of the reference asset. If the reference security increases in value, then the dealer pays a net settlement amount to the repackaging vehicle to increase the value paid out to the investor. If the reference security falls in value, then the dealer receives a net settlement amount from the repackaging vehicle. The repackaging vehicle funds this payment from the proceeds of the high quality collateral securities held by the vehicle. This reduces the payment to the investor. In the case where there is a credit event, the transaction terminates immediately. There is a cash settlement between the repackaging vehicle and the dealer. The settlement is based on the decline in value in the reference asset. The repackaging vehicle funds the payment from the proceeds of the sale of the high quality collateral securities held by the vehicle. If the total return swap is physically settled, then the repackaging vehicle pays the face value in return for accepting delivery of the defaulted reference asset. The repackaging vehicle sells the defaulted asset in the market. The proceeds received are used to repay the note. Where there is a credit event, the payment to the investor is therefore reduced.

- Where a credit default swap is used, the dealer pays a periodic fee in return for the repackaging vehicle agreeing to make a default payment in the event of a default by the reference entity. This fee, combined with the return on the high quality underlying collateral securities, makes up the return to the investor. At maturity, if there has been no default on the reference entity, then the investor receives the repayment of the principal investment financed by the maturing high quality collateral securities. If there is a credit event in relation to the reference entity, then there is a cash settlement by the repackaging vehicle to the dealer. This is based on the decline in value in a reference asset. The repackaging vehicle funds this payment from the high quality collateral securities held by the vehicle. If the credit default swap is physically settled, then the repackaging vehicle pays the face value in return for accepting delivery of defaulted assets. The repackaging vehicle sells the defaulted asset in the market. The proceeds received are used to repay the note. Where there is a credit event, the payment to the investor is therefore reduced.

The mechanics of the synthetic credit asset structures ensure that the investor has a direct exposure to the reference entity/asset. **Exhibit 3.29** sets out an example of a transaction creating a repackaged credit linked note using a credit default swap.

The mechanics of an asset credit swap are as follows:

- The repackaging vehicle purchases the underlying securities issued by the reference credit.
- The vehicle enters into a total return swap with the dealer. Under the swap, the dealer receives the return on the underlying securities and pays LIBOR plus a margin to the repackaging vehicle.
- At maturity, the dealer pays the face value of the note to the vehicle, unless it is in default. The dealer receives delivery of the underlying securities. In the case of a credit event on the underlying asset, the note terminates immediately and the settlement described is also effected.

The repackaging structure is designed to immunise the investor from any credit exposure to the underlying asset. The repackaging structure creates an exposure to the underlying securities *and* the derivative dealer. In this structure, to avoid any exposure to the underlying securities, the obligation of the derivative dealer to pay is *absolute*, irrespective of the performance of the reference asset. In effect, the dealer's obligation to pay the LIBOR plus margin is unconditional. The dealer has an entitlement to receive the return on the underlying securities (both interest and principal). In this way, the only exposure assumed by the investor is to the higher rated derivative dealer.

In practice, synthetic credit assets are the more commonly used structure. This reflects the fact that the credit asset swap is effectively an arbitrage on the funding cost of the dealer. Dealers will generally not allow the structure to be used to arbitrage against their market funding rates.

Any repackaged structure entails additional risks[45]. The repackaging structure entails the investor assuming the credit risk of the collateral and the reference entity/asset. The investor also assumes market risk.

Where the transaction terminates at maturity, the underlying collateral matures at face value (equal to the original investment in the note). This reflects the fact that the maturity of the collateral is matched to the term of the note. In the case where there is a credit event on the reference entity/asset, the transaction terminates. Upon termination, the collateral must be

---

[45] See discussion in Das, Satyajit (2004) Swaps/Financial Derivatives – 3rd Edition; John Wiley, Singapore at Chapter 38.

sold to realise the proceeds required to make settlements under the credit derivative and to repay principal. The sale of the collateral may not realise the face value of the collateral. This reflects the impact of market risk. The lower sale proceeds may reflect changes in interest rates or credit spreads. It may also reflect the effect of a negative migration in the credit quality of the collateral. The risk of the lower proceeds is borne by the investor. This is because the dealer generally has a prior claim on the proceeds to meet the settlement under the derivative contract. The residual proceeds (after the derivative settlement) are received by the investor.

In certain circumstances, the market risk may affect the dealer. If the value of the collateral falls sharply, then the derivative settlement may exceed the collateral proceeds. In this case, the dealer bears the loss. This is because the investor's loss is limited to the face value of the note/investment.

The market risk identified is only present in repackaged notes. Where a conventional credit linked structured note is issued, the market risk of any prepayment is assumed by the issuer. This reflects the fact that the issuer agrees to terminate the transaction where there is a credit event. The termination is at face value. The termination proceeds are then used to undertake settlement of the derivative and any residual value is paid to the investor.

Exhibit 3.29   Repackaged Credit Linked Notes – Example

Assume that the investor requires a credit default note identical to that described in **Exhibit 3.12**. The note is to be issued by an asset repackaging vehicle.
   The structure is constructed as follows:

- The investor purchases a 5 year note issued by the repackaging vehicle for US$20 million.
- The repackaging vehicle purchases US$20 million of AAA rated collateral with a maturity of 5 years.
- The repackaging vehicle sells credit protection on ABC Company to the dealer for 5 years. The credit default swap is for US$20 million.

The cash flows of the repackaged credit linked note are as follows:

- At commencement, the repackaging vehicle received US$20 million. The cash is used to purchase the AAA collateral securities.
- If there is no credit event in respect of ABC Company (the reference entity):
  1. At each interest payment date, the repackaging vehicle receives interest on the AAA rated collateral (say at US$ LIBOR plus 30 bps) and the fee on the credit default swap from the dealer (say 150 bps pa). The repackaging pays out a coupon on the credit linked note of US$ LIBOR plus 180 bps.

2. At maturity, the repackaging vehicle receives US$20 million from the maturing principal of the AAA rated collateral. There is no settlement under the credit default swap. The repackaging vehicle repays US$20 million to the investor.

- If there is a credit event in respect of ABC Company:
1. Interest payments cease and the note terminates.
2. The settlement of the notes takes place as follows:
- Where the credit default swap is cash settled, the repackaging vehicle is required to pay the dealer the cash settlement amount. The cash settlement amount is calculated under the credit default swap as the change in market price of the reference asset between the time of entry into the swap and an agreed period after the credit event. Assume the price change in this case is 80% (recovery rate of 20%). The repackaging vehicle would need to pay US$16 million to the dealer. The repackaging vehicle sells the AAA collateral securities. Assume it receives US$20 million from the sale. The repackaging vehicle pays US$16 million to the dealer in settlement of the credit default swap. The repackaging vehicle pays the residual amount of US$4 million to the investor.
- Where the credit default swap is physically settled, the repackaging vehicle pays US$20 million to the dealer in return for delivery of US$20 million face value of defaulted ABC Company bonds (an asset that meets the category/characteristics of defined deliverable obligations). The US$20 million payment is funded from the sale of the AAA collateral. The repackaging vehicle settles with the investor in one of the following ways. The repackaging vehicle can immediately sell the defaulted securities in the market. Assume that the bonds are trading at 20% of face value (US$4 million). The sale proceeds are paid to the investor in settlement of the note. Alternatively, the repackaging vehicle can deliver the defaulted bonds to the investor in settlement of the note.

The following aspects of the structure should be noted:

- The investor will nominate the credit quality of the collateral and select the underlying credit risk (ABC Company).
- The security arrangements will be as follows:
1. The dealer will take a first charge/security interest over the collateral.
2. The investor will receive a second charge/security interest over the collateral and a first charge over the payments or deliveries by the dealer under the credit default swap.

The security structure will mean that the settlement under the credit default swap will have priority over any claims by the investor to the collateral proceeds.

The additional value in the structure is generated through the ability to use high yielding collateral within the prescribed credit quality range required by the investor. In practice, this means the use of asset backed and/or structured securities.

The structure is set out in the following diagram:

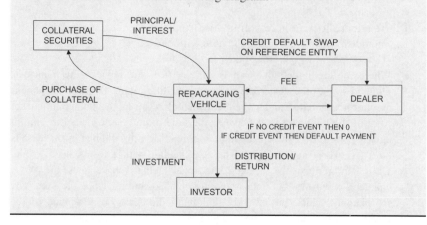

5.5   Repackaged Credit Linked Notes – Examples

There are a wide variety of repackaged note structures[46]. In this Section, some examples of repackaged credit assets are set out. The principal focus is on synthetic credit assets. The asset credit swaps are more straightforward transactions that are designed to pay a floating rate return on a high quality underlying credit, and are targeted in general to money market investors looking for a yield pick-up.

Common repackaged credit note structures include[47]:

- **Maturity transformation structures** – this entails the repackaging of longer term securities for investors seeking short term exposure. **Exhibit 3.30** sets out an example of a transaction to create short term exposure to underlying assets that have longer maturities.
- **Diversified credit portfolio structures** – this entails the creation of exposure to a diversified portfolio of credit risk (on a leveraged or

---

[46]   For an indication of the size of the market in these types of notes, see Mahtani, Arun "Synthetic Structures Facilitate Leveraged Loan Boom: (28 November 1998) International Financing Review Issue 1261 85.

[47]   The examples described here are in addition to the more traditional structures of credit linked structured notes described above. These types of credit linked notes can and are structured using repackaging vehicles in addition to the more traditional direct issuance structures.

unleveraged basis). **Exhibit 3.31** sets out an example of using a repackaging vehicle to create diversified exposure to a portfolio of bonds. **Exhibit 3.32** sets out an example of a transaction where the repackaging vehicle creates exposure to one or more credits *on a leveraged basis.*

- **Structured credit risk** – this entails creating structured exposure to credit risk, including exposure to default correlations or recovery rates. **Exhibit 3.33** sets out an example of using a repackaging vehicle to create a first-to-default security[48]. **Exhibit 3.34** sets out an example of transactions involving recovery rate expectations, using a repackaging vehicle to structure it as a note.

Exhibit 3.30 Repackaged Credit Assets – Example 1

A common form of repackaging is the restructuring of the cash flows of assets with a longer maturity into a structured note where the investor has exposure to the asset for a shorter term. Generally these transactions have been structured as follows:

- The repackaging vehicle purchases the longer dated security.
- The repackaging vehicle enters into a credit spread swap with a dealer for a period of say, 1 year. The maturity corresponds to the maturity of the structured note issued by the repackaging vehicle. Under the terms of the swap (equivalent to a forward on the credit spread on the security) at maturity:
  1. The dealer pays a settlement amount equal to the amount of any depreciation in the value of the security in the event that the credit spread increases.
  2. The dealer receives a settlement amount equal to the amount of any appreciation in the value of the security in the event that the credit spread decreases.
- The repackaging vehicle issues a structured note for a maturity that is identical to that of the credit spread swap. The structured note is collateralised by the underlying longer dated security and the credit spread swap.
- The structured note pays a return to the investor equivalent to US$ LIBOR plus a spread generated off the coupon on the security and the credit spread swap.
- At maturity, the structured note pays out at par. This is achieved as follows:
  1. The underlying securities are liquidated in the market.
  2. The credit spread swap is settled with the dealer, with the repackaging vehicle paying (receiving) cash in the event of an increase (decline) in the value of the underlying security. Where the repackaging vehicle has to make the payment,

---

[48] See Chapter 2.

the payment is financed by the excess of liquidation value of the underlying security over the amount required to redeem the structured note at par.

3. The combination of the liquidation amount and the credit spread swap settlement equates to the total cash available for payment to the investor.

• The repackaging vehicle may also enter into additional derivative transactions (usually an interest or currency swap) with the dealer to re-profile the cash flow of the underlying security into the desired framework (generally US$ floating rate LIBOR).

The investor's risk in this transaction is on the underlying asset and the dealer. The transaction enables the investor to complete the maturity spectrum of investments. The investor uses the credit spread swap to hedge the market risk on the sale of the underlying longer dated asset at maturity of the structured note.

The overall structure is set out below:

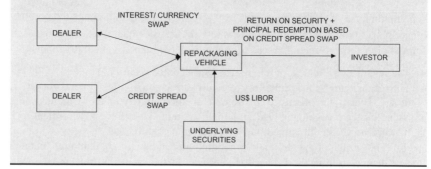

Exhibit 3.31   Repackaged Credit Assets – Example 2

The structure creates an investment where the investor has exposure to a diversified portfolio of securities. The transaction is structured as follows:

• The repackaging vehicle issues a structured note to the investor.
• The cash proceeds of the note are used to make an investment in high quality bonds.
• The repackaging vehicle enters into a series of total return swaps with a derivative dealer to gain exposure to a variety of bonds. The total return swaps have a total notional principal equivalent to the value of the investments in the high quality bonds that are used to fully collateralise the swaps[49].

---

49   See discussion earlier in this Chapter in relation to the hedging of such structures by the dealer.

- The structured note return to the investor is (usually) a floating rate return calculated as LIBOR plus a margin. The return is equivalent to the payments received under the total return swaps. The return from the underlying high quality bond investments is used to fund the floating rate payments under the total return swaps.
- At maturity, the structured note pays out the value of the securities underlying the total return swaps. An appreciation in value adds to the pool of funds generated from the liquidation of the high quality collateral pool and is available for distribution to the investor. Any depreciation in the value of the securities underlying the total return swaps is funded by the collateral pool and reduces the payment to the investor in the structured note.

The structure is designed to allow an investor, through the investment in the structured note issued by the repackaging vehicle, to obtain economic exposure to the diversified portfolio of securities. The major benefits include the higher level of diversification that is obtained and the elimination of administration costs of managing a portfolio of securities.

The overall structure is set out below:

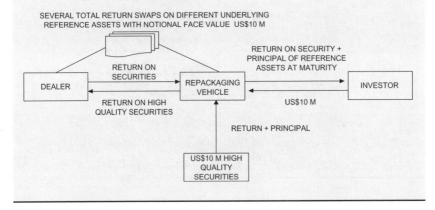

Exhibit 3.32 Repackaged Credit Assets – Example 3

The structure creates leveraged exposure to a portfolio of bonds. The essential transaction dynamics are exactly the same as that identified in **Exhibit 3.33**. The only additional element is that the total return swap entered into is for a notional principal *greater than* the face value of the collateral[50].

---

[50] See discussion earlier in this Chapter in relation to the hedging of such structures by the dealer.

The structure will operate as follows:

- The repackaging vehicle uses the proceeds of the issue of structured notes to purchase high quality securities that are then used to collateralise the total return swaps.
- The collateral will represent approximately 10 to 20% of the notional principal of the total return swaps entered.
- The structured note redeems at maturity, as in the previous example. However, the investor can only lose the principal face value of the structured note, not the notional value of the total return swaps entered into.

The rationale for the structure is the high returns an investor can generate from the leverage embedded in the transactions. Unlike traditional forms of leverage (such as purchasing the underlying securities on margin), the loss that can be suffered by the investor is constrained to the face value of the structured notes (effectively the collateral amount).

The overall structure is as follows:

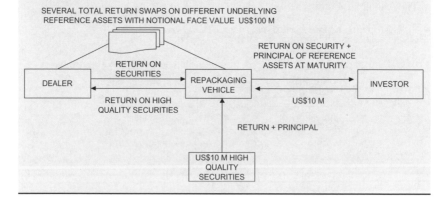

Exhibit 3.33   Repackaged Assets – Example 4

The structure creates a higher yielding structured note through leveraged exposure to multiple credit risks through a first-to-default basket.

The structure will operate as follows:

- The repackaging vehicle issues a structured note for face value of US$10 million.
- The proceeds of the note are invested in high quality securities.
- The repackaging vehicle enters into a credit default swap on a first-to-default basis with a dealer. The first-to-default swap operates as follows:
    1. The repackaging vehicle receives a fee in return for assuming the credit risk on a portfolio of securities (US$40 million, made up of 4 securities of US$10 million).

2. In the case of a credit event on *any* of the securities, the first-to-default swap is triggered and the *defaulted security* is delivered to the repackaging vehicle.

3. The repackaging vehicle uses the proceeds from the sale of the high quality securities to purchase the defaulted securities.

- The investor in the structured note receives the return on the portfolio of high quality collateral together with the fee under the credit default swap.

- At maturity, where there has been no credit event, the settlement under the structured note is at par from the proceeds of the maturing high quality collateral. In the case of a credit event, the investor can elect that the issuer physically settle (by receiving delivery of the defaulted bonds) or cash settle (the repackaging vehicle selling the defaulted bonds at the post default price in the market).

A number of variations are feasible. For example, the credit default swap may be structured on the basis of a pre-agreed default loss amount (an assumed recovery rate). This would mean that instead of physical delivery of the defaulted security, the repackaging vehicle would make a pre-agreed payment (the loss or par minus the recovery rate assumed) to the dealer. This structure has the advantage for the investor of a known loss in the event of default.

The rationale for the structure is that the investor provides first loss protection on a first-to-default basis on a portfolio of securities, allowing the monetisation of default correlation[51]. The structure enables the value to be released to the investor by way of enhanced return on the note. An additional driver for these transactions has been the ability to use these structures to create securities that may not be available in the market. For example, assume the investor is seeking a B rated investment that is unavailable. The investor can synthesise the B credit rating exposure by purchasing a first-to-default note where the first-to-default portfolio consists of, say 4 BB rated securities. The combined risk of the portfolio on a first-to-default basis is higher than the risk of default on any individual security. This higher risk equates to a single B type exposure[52]. This allows the creation of specific types of credit exposure unavailable directly in the market.

Exhibit 3.34   Repackaged Credit Assets – Example 5

The structure is designed to create a higher yielding investment by monetising expectations on recovery rates[53]. The structure operates as follows:

- The repackaging vehicle issues a structured note to the investor. The return on the note is linked to the price performance on a specified reference security.

- The repackaging vehicle pays an enhanced return to the investor while there is no event of default on the underlying securities.

---

[51] See Chapter 2.
[52] For discussion of pricing issues on first-to-default baskets, see Chapter 2.
[53] The structure is similar to zero recovery credit default swaps, see Chapter 2.

- In the event of default, the investor suffers a loss equal to the full face value of the note. The investor has no right to take physical delivery of the underlying reference security. The investor does not have any recourse against the issuer of the structured note or the repackaging vehicle on any recovery value on the defaulted securities.

In effect, the structure provides the investor in the note an enhanced return predicated on the investor giving up *any recovery value on the underlying security*.

The repackaging vehicle generates the enhanced return by using the structured note proceeds to purchase the reference security. Simultaneously, the repackaging vehicle enters into a transaction with a dealer who agrees to purchase the asset at nominal value (US$0.01 per US$1 million face value of bonds) in the event of default. The dealer pays a periodic fee for that right which is passed on to the investor in the structured note.

The dealer purchasing the right to buy the asset at nominal value in the case of default creates exposure to recovery rates in the case of a credit event. This structure may be attractive to distressed debt traders expecting a credit event and wanting exposure to recovery rates. The structure can also be used to create leveraged exposure to different expected recovery rates.

6   Synthetic Bonds

6.1   Structure

Synthetic bonds are an extension of repackaged credit linked notes. The transactions are similar transactions involving the use of asset repackaging vehicles. The major difference is that the credit linked note issued to investors is designed as a *public* security. The security is rated by one or more of the major rating agencies and is tradeable in order to facilitate liquidity.

The distinguishing characteristics of the synthetic bond transactions from typical repackaged credit linked notes include:

- Transactions are frequently driven by the dealer (usually a bank/ financial institution) to reduce risk to the relevant reference entity. This contrasts with typical credit linked structured note/repackaged credit linked note transactions that are driven by investors seeking exposure to a particular underlying reference entity or to create the structured exposure to credit risk.
- The size of the transactions of synthetic bonds is generally significantly larger than the size of repackaged credit linked notes. Typical synthetic bond transactions have been large (US$400 million plus). In contrast,

typical credit linked structured notes/repackaged credit linked notes are in the range of US$10 to 20 million (on average).

- The synthetic bond is designed as a public or quasi-public[54] issue. The issue is expected to trade in the secondary market. In contrast, credit linked structured notes/repackaged credit linked notes are generally structured as private placements that are held to maturity. In the event that the investor needs liquidity, in the case of typical credit linked structured notes/repackaged credit linked notes, this is achieved by restructuring the security into a format (a US$ LIBOR based FRN) by reverse engineering the derivative components.

6.2 Synthetic Bonds – Example

There have been a number of examples of synthetic bonds. The most notable examples of these transactions involve JP Morgan who issued two synthetic bonds[55]. The deals include a $594 million transaction where the underlying credit exposure is to Wal-Mart, the US retailing corporation, and a US$460 million transaction where the underlying exposure is to Walt Disney, the US entertainment company[56]. **Exhibit 3.35** sets out the structure, including the construction and hedging, of the Wal Mart synthetic bond.

Exhibit 3.35   Synthetic Bonds – Example

1.   Transaction

In late 1996, JP Morgan arranged an issue of a synthetic bond where the underlying credit was Wal-Mart. The unique feature of the transaction was that the transaction was completed *independent* of Wal-Mart. Wal-Mart did not issue the bonds nor guarantee the payment of interest and/or principal.

The transaction details were as follows:

Issuer	A special purpose trust
Underlying Credit Risk	Wal-Mart
Amount	US$594 million (issued as US$576 million in notes and US$18 million in subordinated certificates)

---

54   For example, a Rule 144a issue in the US domestic market.
55   See Irving, Richard "Credit Notes In Record Deals" (January 1997) Risk 9.
56   The second transaction for Walt Disney was originally unconfirmed, although it is mentioned in press reporting, see "More Credit To JP Morgan" (5 February 1997) IFR Financial Products 16–17.

Maturity	10 year final (early amortisation giving an average life of 5.8 years)
Yield	Treasury plus 65 bps
Market	Rule 144 A issue

The transaction operates as follows:

- The investor purchases the note for value.
- The investor receives repayment of interest and principal provided Wal-Mart is not in default.
- In the event of default by Wal-Mart, the investor receives repayment of principal equivalent to the recovery value of Wal-Mart debt.

The relevant default event under the terms of this transaction is the default of Wal-Mart under a referenced credit obligation. The specific terms of default of Wal-Mart were as follows:

- Payment default or event of bankruptcy or insolvency (as established by publicly available information); *and*
- The satisfaction of a materiality test whereby the definition of default required that any event of default would be deemed not to have occurred unless the spread on Wal-Mart public debt increased by a pre-specified amount (believed to be 150 bps pa). This was designed to ensure that there was no frivolous triggering of the default[57].

A specified process is used to establish the recovery value of Wal-Mart debt if a default occurs and is established. It is linked to the traded market value of existing Wal-Mart bonds. The process requires a dealer poll of 5 market makers in the reference obligations. The poll is to be conducted every two weeks for 3 months following default. The investor has the option of requiring either early redemption based on the dealer poll (conducted as soon as possible after default), or redemption based on actual recovery values within an 18 month period. In the event that the 18 month period proves insufficient to derive actual recovery values, the recovery value is calculated using a further dealer poll mechanism at the end of 18 months. This process was designed to replicate (as closely as possible) the *actual payoffs* where the investor held physical bonds issued by Wal-Mart.

2. Structure

The Wal-Mart synthetic bond is believed to have been structured as follows:

- The repackaging vehicle uses the proceeds of the issue to purchase collateral securities.
- The repackaging vehicle enters into a credit default swap with a dealer (presumably JP Morgan).

---

[57] For discussion of materiality, see Chapter 1.

The cash flows of the repackaged credit linked note are as follows:

- At commencement, the repackaging vehicle received the issue proceeds. The cash is used to purchase the collateral securities.
- If there is no credit event in respect of Wal-Mart:
  1. At each interest payment date, the repackaging vehicle receives interest on the collateral and the fee on the credit default swap from the dealer. The repackaging pays out a coupon on the notes based on these receipts.
  2. At maturity, the repackaging vehicle received the maturing principal of the collateral. There is no settlement under the credit default swap. The repackaging vehicle repays the face value of the notes to the investor.
- If there is a credit event in respect of Wal-Mart:
  1. Interest payments cease and the note terminates.
  2. The settlement of the notes takes place. The repackaging vehicle is required to pay the dealer the cash settlement amount. The cash settlement amount is calculated under the credit default swap as the change in market price of the reference asset between the time of entry into the swap and an agreed period after the credit event. The repackaging vehicle sells the collateral securities. The repackaging vehicle pays the dealer the settlement amount under the credit default swap. The repackaging vehicle pays the residual amount to the investor.

The Wal-Mart structure is believed to have had an extra component. The dealer entered into a total return swap with the repackaging vehicle to reduce the credit risk of the structure (see below).

3. Synthetic Bonds – Risks

The structure of synthetic bonds (consistent with repackaged credit linked notes involving asset repackaging vehicles) entails three levels of risk:

- Risk to the reference credit.
- Risk to the underlying collateral.
- Risk to the dealer.

The primary objective of structuring is to create exposure only to the reference credit. This is particularly important in a synthetic bond transaction. This is because only the investor in a normal bond would be exposed to this risk.

The risk to the underlying collateral and to the dealer is minimised through the structure. This is achieved in a number of ways:

- Using high quality collateral such as US Treasury securities or AAA rated securities.
- The risk to the dealer is similarly managed by transacting with AAA or AA rated counterparties. Credit enhancement (cash collateralisation of the derivative exposure) is used to manage the credit risk on the derivative. Another approach is the concept of a contingent dealer that steps into the position of the dealer in

the event of default to perform the originally contracted obligations under the derivative contracts.

In the Wal-Mart transaction, the risk to the underlying collateral is reduced by the structure. The dealer entered into a total return swap with the repackaging vehicle. This was in relation to the collateral held by the repackaging vehicle. The structure of the total return swap was that the repackaging vehicle paid the cash flows on the collateral to the dealer in return for a series of payments. The total return swap was structured so that the payment by the dealer was not contingent upon receipt of payment from the repackaging vehicle. This was designed to convert the credit risk of the collateral to the counterparty risk of the dealer. The risk to the dealer is low because of the high credit quality of JP Morgan (AAA[58]). The risk to the dealer was further reduced by the use of a contingent dealer to perform the obligations of JP Morgan in case of default.

The Wal-Mart synthetic bonds were rated at the same credit quality level as the direct obligations of Wal-Mart itself.

6.3   Implications of Synthetic Bonds

The issue of synthetic bonds raises a number of issues for the underlying reference entities and for intermediaries.

The underlying reference entity effectively suffers a diminution in its control of the market in *its own debt securities*. For example, the Wal-Mart transaction was priced at a yield spread to Treasuries of 65 bps (at issue). This compares favourably to publicly traded Wal-Mart debt that was trading at the relevant time at an approximately 40/45 bps spread to Treasuries. This discrepancy is partially attributable to the inherent additional risks of the synthetic bond structure. It may create pricing pressures as well as constraining the issuer's direct access to the underlying credit market.

The implication for dealers is relatively less complicated. The synthetic debt issues highlighted the ability to synthetically repackage non-traded credit risk into a bond format. This allowed distribution of the risk to investors in public markets. Synthetic bonds provide the capacity to transfer large amounts of credit risk into the capital market in a liquid and tradeable form. The familiarity of the investment format allows the credit risk to be sold to a wide range of investors.

---

[58]   The rating is at the time of issue.

7 Summary

Credit linked notes represent an adaptation of the structured note concept to credit markets. The embedded cash collateral feature implicit in credit linked structured notes greatly broadens the range of counterparties able to sell or provide credit protection in financial markets. The concept of structured notes has evolved rapidly in response to bank demands for instruments to manage credit risk and capital (both economic and regulatory). Investor demand for credit risk and structured exposure to credit risk has become an important component of the market.

4

Collateralised Debt Obligations[1]

1 Overview

Credit linked notes/collateralised debt obligations ("CDOs") are combinations of a fixed income security with an embedded credit derivative. Credit linked notes are designed to allow investors to capture returns on (generally) a single reference entity (underlying bond/loan) or (occasionally) multiple reference entities (a portfolio of bonds/loans). CDOs entail the use of

---

[1] See (1998) Credit Derivatives: Applications For Risk Management; Euromoney Books, London; (1998) Credit Derivatives: Applications for Risk Management, Investment and Portfolio Optimisation; Risk Books, London; Tavakoli, Janet M. (1998) Credit Derivatives: A Guide To Instruments And Applications; John Wiley & Sons, Inc., New York; Francis, Jack Clark, Frost, Joyce A., and Whittaker, J. Gregg (Editors) (1999) The Handbook of Credit Derivatives; McGraw-Hill, New York; Nelken, Dr. Israel (1999) Implementing Credit Derivatives; McGraw-Hill, New York; (1999) The JP Morgan Guide To Credit Derivatives; Risk Publications, London; Tavakoli, Janet M. (2001) Credit Derivatives & Synthetic Structures – Second Edition; John Wiley & Sons, Inc.; Gregory, Jon (Editor) (2003) Credit Derivatives: The Definitive Guide; Risk Publications, London; Tavakoli, Janet M. (2003) Collateralized Debt Obligations And Structured Finance; John Wiley & Sons, Inc., New Jersey; Ali, Paul and de Vries Robbe, Jan Job (2003) Synthetic Insurance and Hedge Fund Securitisations; Thompson Legal & Regulatory Limited, Australia; Choudhry, Moorad (2004) Structured Credit Products; John Wiley, Singapore; Perraudin, William (Editor) Structured Credit Products; Risk Books, London. See also Falloon, William "Credit Where Credit's Due" (March 1994) Risk vol 7 no 3 9–11; Reoch, Rob and Masters, Blythe "Credit Swaps: An Innovation In Negotiable Exposure" (1995) Capital Market Strategies 7 3–8; Howard, Kerrin "An Introduction To Credit Derivatives" (Winter 1995) Derivatives Quarterly 28–37;

securitisation techniques to create structured exposure to portfolios of multiple reference entities (portfolios of bonds/loans or other credit obligations). Chapter 3 covered credit linked notes. This Chapter deals with CDO structures.

The structure of the Chapter is as follows:

- The structure of CDOs is outlined.
- The applications of CDOs are discussed
- The rating methodology used with CDOs is examined.
- The evolution of CDO structures is described. This includes the different underlying credit assets used in CDOs and structures such as single tranche CDOs.
- The risk return dynamics of CDO investments are analysed.
- The regulatory capital treatment of CDOs is outlined.

Smithson, Charles with Holappa, Hal "Credit Derivatives" (December 1995) Risk vol 8 no 12 38–39; Whittaker, Greg J. and Kumar, Sumita "Credit Derivatives: A Primer" in Konishi, Atsuo and Dattatreya, Ravi (Ed) (1996) The Handbook of Derivative Instruments; Irwin Publishing, Chicago at 595–614; Masters, Blythe and Reoch, Rob (March 1996) Credit Derivatives: Structures And Applications; JP Morgan, New York and London; Masters, Blythe and Reoch, Rob (March 1996) Credit Derivatives: An Innovation in Negotiable Exposure; JP Morgan, New York and London; Masters, Blythe "A Credit Derivatives Primer" (May 1996) Derivatives Strategy 42–44; Iacono, Frank "Credit Derivatives" in Schwartz, Robert J. and Smith Jr., Clifford W.(Editors) (1997) Derivatives Handbook: Risk Management and Control; John Wiley & Sons, Inc., New York at Chapter 2; Ghose, Ronit (Editor) Credit Derivatives: Key Issues (1997, British Bankers' Association, London); Chase Manhattan Bank "Credit Derivatives: A Primer" (April 1997) Asiamoney Derivatives Guide 2–5; BZW "An Investor's Guide To Credit Derivatives" (June 1997) Derivatives Strategy Credit Derivatives Supplement 1–8; Scott-Quinn, Brian and Walmsley, Julian K. (1998) The Impact Of Credit Derivatives On Securities Markets; International Securities Market Association, Zurich; Citibank/Salomon Smith Barney (2001) Credit Derivatives 2001 – Issues and Opportunities; Risk Publications, London; Finnerty, John D. (1999) Credit Derivatives: An Introduction To The Mechanics; PricewaterhouseCoopers, New York; Storrow, Jamie (Editor) (1999) Credit Derivatives: Key Issues – 2nd Edition; British Bankers' Association, London; Francis, Chris, Kakodkar, Atish and Rooney, Mary (31 January 2002) Credit Default Swap Handbook"; Merrill Lynch, London; "Credit Derivatives Update 2002" (March 2002) Euromoney Research Guide; Francis, Chris, Kakodkar, Atish and Martin, Barnaby (16 April 2003) Credit Derivative Handbook"; Merrill Lynch, London.

2 CDOs/Credit Portfolio Securitisation Structures

2.1 Overview

Credit linked notes entail the combination of a fixed income security with an embedded credit derivative. The credit linked note enables the investor to replicate exposure to a reference entity or reference asset (traded bond or loan). The transaction eliminates the necessity of undertaking a direct investment in the security itself or entering into the underlying credit derivative transaction directly. The credit linked note is designed to allow the investor to capture the return on the underlying credit risk. Credit linked structured notes and repackaged credit linked notes are designed to achieve these objectives.

CDOs are the generic term used for credit portfolio securitisation. It entails repackaging *portfolios* of credit risk (loans/bonds and/or derivatives/ off-balance-sheet transactions) for sale to investors. CDOs repackage credit risk into multiple tranches of securities that are then distributed to investors. The issue of the securities is designed to reduce or eliminate the credit risk to existing obligors. CDOs/credit portfolio securitisation structures are characterised by a number of distinctive features:

- The transaction encompasses a *portfolio* of credit risks rather than an individual credit risk.
- The transaction may be:
  1. *Issuer driven* – the transaction is primarily motivated to transfer credit risk or access funding.
  2. *Investor driven* – the transaction is primarily motivated to provide structured exposure to credit risk in a form required by investors.
  3. *Arbitrage driven* – the transaction is dealer driven to provide profits from differences between the market price of the underlying assets and the price at which the securitised risk can be sold in structured form.
  In practice, a combination of factors drives individual transactions.
- The credit portfolio securitisation structures are predicated upon credit derivatives techniques (in particular, credit default swaps and credit linked note technology), asset repackaging structures and securitisation technology (particularly the techniques used in collateralised bond obligations ("CBOs") and collateralised loan obligations ("CLOs") transactions).
- The use of tranching techniques to create highly structured types of credit risk profiles.

From the perspective of banks with credit portfolios, the key driving forces underlying the development of CDO structures include:

- **Capital management** – the reduction of the regulatory capital committed to support credit portfolios, particularly low yielding loans to highly rated corporations.
- **Balance sheet management** – the ability to shift assets off balance sheet and enhance return on equity through these structures.
- **Funding** – for lower rated banks, these structures have been an effective mechanism for raising funding[2].
- **Credit risk management** – the structure transfers the credit risk of the underlying assets to investors to reduce risk.
- **Management of client relationships** – the structure allows banks and financial institutions to separate the management of credit risk from the management of client relationships. The banks/financial institutions continue to maintain relationships with clients even where that relationship would normally create concentration of credit risk. This is because the CDO allows the bank to shed or separately manage its exposure.

From the perspective of investment banks/dealers, the key driving factors driving development of CDO structures include:

- **Arbitrage profits** – dealers generate earnings from differences between the market price of the underlying assets and the price at which the securitised risk can be sold in structured CDO form.
- **Credit trading** – CDO structures create trading flow in the underlying credit assets (bonds) and credit derivatives (credit default swaps) that generate additional sources of earnings for dealers.

From the perspective of investors, the key driving forces underlying the development of CDO structures include:

- **Access to assets/risks** – the structure allows investors to access diversified portfolios of credit risk in a simple format. The transactions also create structured assets available for investment.

---

[2] For example, the structure has been used by Japanese banks suffering from the effect of the Japanese funding premium. See Paul-Choudhury, Sumit "Fables of Reconstructions" (March 1998) Credit Risk Supplement to Risk 20–24; Rutter, James "Selling The Securitisation Story" (May 1998) Euromoney 8–10.

- **Investment assets** – CDOs provide investment managers with the potential to increase assets under management on a leveraged basis, allowing the generation of additional fund management fees.
- **Returns** – the credit spreads available on CDOs are attractive compared with those of equivalent credit risk. This provides relative value investors with significant yield enhancement opportunities.
- **Structured exposure** – the transaction can be engineered to provide investors with access to investments not directly available in the market or to provide structured exposure to credit risk. Credit assets with different credit quality are generally created. The credit quality ranges from high quality (AAA for senior tranches), intermediate (A to B for mezzanine tranches) and unrated (equity). This allows investors to match investment requirements to available assets. It may also have other advantages for investors. The number of AAA rated entities is limited. Structured assets created through CDO technology may allow investors to diversify high credit quality investment portfolios by increasing the range of available assets.
- **Performance history** – the risk adjusted return and default history of asset backed structures is favourable. This has encouraged institutional investor participation in the market[3].
- **Liquidity** – the CDO market has developed secondary market trading and liquidity. This offers an investment alternative to the (often) less liquid corporate bond market.

For banks, CDOs represent an evolution of the application of credit derivatives to credit risk management. It represents a shift in focus to *portfolio level* and *strategic* applications. These include:

- Management of portfolio credit risk, including concentration risk.
- Transferring credit risk by using synthetic sales and securitisation techniques without undertaking loan sales, assignments or participations.
- Management of regulatory capital.

For investors, CDOs allow participation in credit markets and the creation of highly structured credit risk profiles.

---

[3] See discussion later in this Chapter.

2.2 CBO/CLO Structures

2.2.1 Market Evolution

The basic technology of the CDO market is derived from the CBO/CLO market. CBO structures were originally developed around 1987. The market did not show significant volume until the 1990s when the segment emerged as one of the fastest growing areas of the bond market and asset backed securities.

The original driver for the market was the repackaging of high yield bonds for placement with investors. A major factor underlying the development of the market was activity by insurance companies. Insurance companies with significant holdings of high yield bonds were driven to CBO structures by the lack of liquidity of the securities. An additional factor was the application of the National Association of Insurance Commissioners' ("NAIC") risk weighted reserve requirements in the USA. The reserve requirement made these securities expensive to hold. In response to these pressures, the insurance companies repackaged the high yield assets into CBOs, enabling the riskier tranches to be transferred to their holding companies (which were not subject to the reserve requirements). The insurance companies continued to hold the repackaged higher credit quality securitised debt that was subject to lower capital requirements[4].

In a precursor to the more recent activity in the market, CLO structures also emerged and were focused on banks with problem loans seeking to securitise these loans using asset backed structures. There was only limited interest in these structures. In the 1990s, the factors identified above became more important, encouraging rapid development of the market.

2.2.2 Concept[5]

CBOs and CLOs represent an application of traditional concepts of securitisation and asset backed securities ("ABS") to bonds and commercial loans[6].

---

[4] The reserve requirements are as follows: NAIC 1 – 1%; NAIC 2 – 2%; NAIC 3 – 5%; NAIC 4 – 10%.

[5] For an overview, see Feinne, Linda, Papa, Albert, Craighead, Bradford and Arsenault, Brian (19 September 1997) CBOs/CLOs: An Expanding Securitisation Product; JP Morgan Securities Inc; Lawrence Richter Quinn "Slicing Up Bank Loans" (22 December 1997) Investment Dealers' Digest; (18 December 1997) Bank Collateralised Loan Obligations: An Overview; Fitch Research Structured

CBO/CLO structures are similar to ABS structures as follows:

- A stand–alone special purpose issuing vehicle ("SPV") is established. The vehicle is bankruptcy remote to the loan originator.
- The SPV purchases a portfolio of assets (bonds or loans) from the originator(s).
- The SPV funds the purchase through an issue of several tranches of securities and a residual equity portion.
- The securities issued are rated on the basis of the credit quality of the asset pool and the credit is enhanced through the use of credit enhancement techniques.
- The investors rely on the cash flow from the underlying asset pool to receive interest and principal payments.

Exhibit 4.1 sets out the structure of a CBO and CLO respectively.
The differences between the CBO and CLO structures include:

- **CBOs** – the SPV issues a mix of investment grade and non-investment grade debt against a purchased collateral pool consisting of typically US$ high yield/non investment grade securities and more recently, non investment grade emerging market debt.
- **CLOs** – while structurally similar to the CBO, the underlying collateral consists of bank loans, typically investment grade, but some non investment grade loans may be included.

The nature of the underlying collateral pool also dictates the structure to some degree. For instance, the ability to transfer bonds into the SPV is relatively straightforward. The transfer of loan assets (particularly bilateral loans) is more problematic. It requires assignment of/participation in the loans to the SPV. This may require the consent and agreement of the obligor.

Finance Asset-Backed Special Report; (4 November 1996) CLOs Meet Investor Appetite For Loans; Fitch Research Structured Finance Special Report.

[6] For an overview of securitisation, see Rosenthal, James A. and Ocampo, Juan M. (1988) Securitization Of Credit; John Wiley & Sons, New York. See also Zweig, Philip L. (1989) The Asset Securitization Handbook; Dow Jones-Irwin, Home-wood, Illinois; Fabozzi, Frank J. (Editor) (2001) The Handbook Of Fixed Income Securities – 6th Edition; McGraw-Hill, New York at Chapters 24–32.

1. CBO Structure

Exhibit 4.1   CBO/CLO Structure

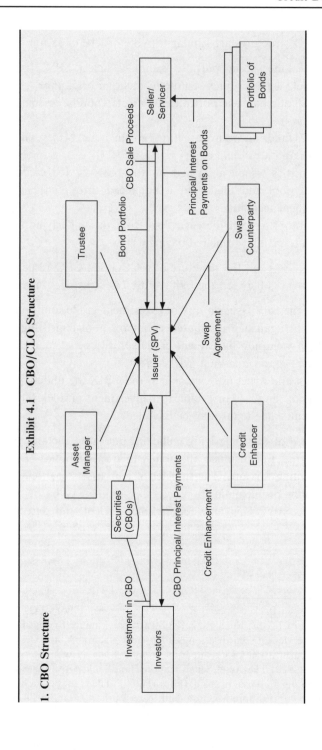

2. CLO Structure

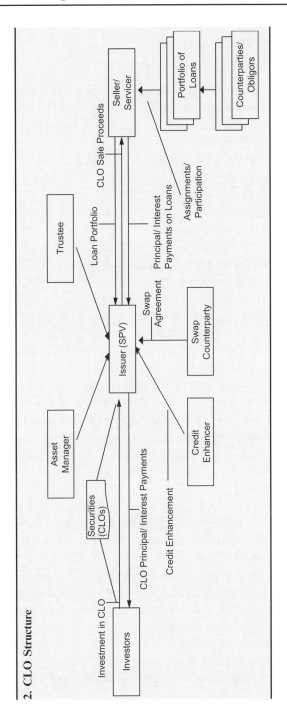

2.2.3   Structural Dynamics

There are several structural issues including:

- **Single versus master trust structure** – traditional CBO/CLO structures use a single purpose vehicle. Some CLO transactions have been structured using a master trust structure that permits the issue of multiple series of notes out of a single vehicle.
- **Revolving structure** – some CBO/CLO transactions include:
  1. *Ramp-up period* – this refers to a period during which the initial collateral is purchased by the SPV.
  2. *Revolving period* – during which the collections on the underlying asset pool are reinvested in *new* assets, followed by a period in which the bond principal is repaid. This is known as the "replenishment" model.
- **Management of asset pool** – there are two types of structure: static and dynamic (often referred to as managed). In a static structure, the underlying assets are not traded. The investor acquires an interest in the asset pool that remains in place until repayment or default. The only trading in a static structure will derive from requirements during the ramp-up or revolving period. In a dynamic structure, the underlying assets within the pool are actively managed. In a dynamic structure, it is necessary to nominate a manager to actively manage the asset pool. In the case of CBOs, this is an asset manager with expertise in the underlying assets. In the case of CLOs, this is the originator of the assets or an asset manager with credit trading expertise.
- **Cash flow versus market value structures** – this is driven by the static or dynamic nature of the structure. There are basically two types of CBO/CLO structures:
  1. *Cash flow structures* – where all payments to the investors in the securities are met from and secured over the cash flows from the underlying collateral asset pool. This is generally the structure used in static transactions.
  2. *Market value structures* – where reliance is placed on periodic (daily or weekly) mark-to-market values of the collateral portfolio. If the market value of collateral assets declines below threshold levels, some portion of the collateral is sold and some notes retired to allow the over collateralisation level to be preserved. This is generally the structure used in dynamic structures.

Cash flow structures are used for both CBOs and CLOs. In contrast, market value structures have historically been used generally with CBOs.

Market value structures are generally designed to allow inclusion of certain assets that are currently non income producing, such as distressed bonds, but which are attractive from a return perspective. The structures also require different levels of trading. The cash flow structures require only limited trading by the manager of the asset pool within prescribed investment guidelines. The market value structure requires more active trading.

Many of the above features of the CBO/CLO market are relevant to the current CDO markets.

In the 1990's, the CBO/CLO market was characterised by spasmodic activity. The major focus was transactions based on high yield/non-investment bonds and loans, and emerging market bonds. In the late 1990's, the modern CDO market emerged.

3   Modern CDO Structures

3.1   Concept

The term CDO is used to cover all forms of credit risk securitisation. In practice, there are two primary structures: a classical CLO transaction and synthetic securitisation structures. Each of the structures is considered in detail below. Examples of actual transactions are used to outline the structures.

3.2   CLO Transactions – Structure

One of the first major CLO transactions completed was by National Westminster Bank Plc ("NatWest") of the UK. The transaction – Repeat Offering Securitisation Entity Funding ("R.O.S.E.") – represented the securitisation of a US$5 billion portfolio of corporate loans from NatWest's balance sheet[7]. **Exhibit 4.2** sets out the structure of the transaction.

Subsequently, a number of similar transactions have also been completed. These include transactions for US banks (Nations Bank, Citibank), European banks (ABN-Amro), and Japanese banks (IBJ, Tokyo Mitsubishi, DKB, and Sumitomo Bank). The transactions are all similar, although individual transactions are characterised by (often significant) structural differences.

---

[7]   See Caplen, Brian "Will NatWest's Deal Backfire?" (October 1996) Euromoney 38–40; Hagger, Euan and Ball, Matthew "How Sweet is NatWest's ROSE?" (November 1998) Corporate Finance 22–26.

The classical CLO type transactions assist the sponsor banks in achieving the following objectives:

- The sponsor bank reduces exposures to selected clients and reduces concentration risks through the CLO. The overall exposure is reduced to the amount of the tranches (usually only the equity component of the transaction) retained by the sponsor bank. However, as the risk retained is the subordinated element (usually the first loss), the sponsor bank will bear significant risk[8]. This may be similar to the actual economic risk on the underlying portfolio. In practice, this means that the risk reduction may not be significant. The major benefit is the limitation on the *maximum* credit loss achieved. Where the sponsor bank retains the equity component and all other parts of the capital structure are placed with investors, the maximum loss is limited to the amount of its investment.
- The sponsor bank may achieve reduction of regulatory capital levels as a result of the transaction. The sponsor will have to hold capital against the tranches retained rather than capital against the underlying portfolio. This reflects the fact that the risk on the underlying risk is transferred in the CLO structure to the holders of the securities issued against the pool of credit assets. In practice, this means that the amount of regulatory capital required to be held by the sponsor may change. Any reduction will depend upon the initial capital requirement on the underlying assets and the amount/type of subordinated tranches retained by the sponsor. In a typical transaction involving investment grade assets, some reduction of regulatory capital should be achieved.
- The sponsor banks may obtain balance sheet management benefits. This is achieved by transferring the assets off balance sheet into the securitisation vehicle. This means that the assets are off balance sheet to the sponsor bank (other than the retained equity or subordinated components). The form of transfer may be important in achieving balance sheet benefits. An assignment/novation or other sale of the asset by the sponsor to the vehicle is likely to ensure balance sheet benefits. Where a sub-participation structure is used, the accounting treatment is more complex and will vary between jurisdictions. The transfer of the

---

[8] The first loss piece is generally referred to as "hurt money" or "the skin in the game". This refers to the fact that the participation of the sponsor bank as an equity (first loss or subordinated) investor is designed to avoid moral hazard or agency problems.

assets off balance sheet may also assist in improving certain accounting/ performance ratios.

- The sponsor bank achieves an increased level of diversification of funding sources. The transaction allows the sponsor to gain capital market access in the form of funding through the ABS market. The CLO transaction effectively separates the credit quality of the *sponsor bank* from the funding (which relies on the quality of the *collateral assets*). Where the underlying assets are of high credit quality relative to the sponsor bank, the transaction may generate lower cost funding for the sponsor.

The CLO structure has significant disadvantages from the viewpoint of banks, including:

- The bank's asset portfolio may be unsuitable for securitisation. This will be the case where there is a predominance of non-funded types of exposures such as revolving credits, unfunded commitments and counterparty risk on derivatives.
- Transfer of the credit obligations without advising the borrower or the cooperation of the borrower may be difficult in some jurisdictions. The potential for damage to the client relationship may limit the utility of the structure. Where sub-participations are used to transfer the loans without the consent of the borrower, the investors in the CLO issue are exposed to the credit risk of the sponsor bank holding the original loans. In effect, there is performance risk on the seller. This will generally limit the rating of the highest rated tranche of CLO securities to that of the sponsor bank[9]. This dictates that the CLO structure using sub-participation to transfer the loans is restricted to sponsor banks with a strong issuer credit rating.
- Economic and regulatory capital requirements may be unchanged where the sponsor bank retains the major component of the credit risk in the form of the equity tranche in a typical transaction. Under regulatory guidelines, there is an advantage in minimising the equity or first loss component of the transaction in order to allow the bank to benefit from the low level recourse rules[10]. This means that in practice there is a tendency to focus on *investment grade* loan commitments. This is because the capital treatment encourages banks to securitise high credit quality

---

[9] See discussion later in the Chapter.
[10] See discussion later in the Chapter.

assets, thereby potentially lowering the overall asset quality of the institution[11]. This lowers the value of these types of transactions to banks.

- The actual cost of funding achieved through these transactions may be unattractive for banks with a low cost of funds. The comparative cost of funds is evident from the Table below[12]:

Type	Rating	Spread (bps to 3 Month LIBOR)	Rating	Spread (bps to 3 Month LIBOR)
Corporate	AA	0–5	BBB	50–70
Asset Backed Securities				
Collateralised Mortgage Backed Securities	AA	25–30	BBB	80–90
Credit Card Asset Backed Securities	AA	10–15	BBB	100–120
Collateralised Loan Obligations	AA	18–23	BBB	110–160
Collateralised Bond Obligations	AA	35–45	BBB	130–180

Other issues may include:

- The cost and length of time needed to complete a CLO.
- The need to change bank loan administration operations to accommodate the CLO operation.

From the viewpoint of the investor, the structure provides the following advantages:

- **Access** – the investor obtains access to a large well diversified portfolio of risk in a relatively simple format for investment. An important aspect of the structure is that the minimum investment may be modest (US$1 million). It would be impossible to construct a similarly diversified credit portfolio with such a small investment.

---

[11] This is an issue affecting any form of securitisation generally.
[12] See Feinne, Linda, Papa, Albert, Craighead, Bradford and Arsenault, Brian (19 September 1997) CBOs/CLOs: An Expanding Securitisation Product; JP Morgan Securities Inc at p 5.

- **Structured exposure** – the investor is provided with the ability to invest in different tranches of securities, enabling it to assume its preferred level of credit risk.
- **Liquidity** – the structure uses listed and rated bonds that are capable of being traded by the investor. This provides the investor with liquidity where there are dealers prepared to make markets in the securities.
- **Return** – the issue provides the investor with the ability to assume credit risk and generate returns from this risk. The return provided is generally attractive on a relative value basis (based on the spreads on comparably rated issues).

Exhibit 4.2   CLO Structures – R.O.S.E. Transaction[13]

1. Overview

R.O.S.E. Funding was a securitisation collateralised by a portfolio of US$5 billion of NatWest's corporate loans. The transaction was completed in November 1996 and was for a period of 5 years. The transaction appears to have been designed to free capital by selling down a portion of the bank's low yielding corporate loan portfolio.

2. Structure

The overall structure is set out in the diagram below.

R.O.S.E. Structure

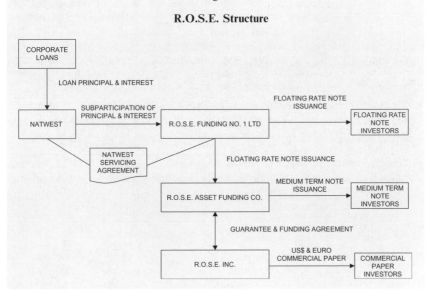

---

[13] The description of the structure is based on (27 January 1997) R.O.S.E. Funding; Fitch Research Structured Finance New Issue.

Source: (27 January 1997) R.O.S.E. Funding; Fitch Research Structured Finance New Issue.

The basic structure was as follows:

1. R.O.S.E. purchased a portfolio of US$ and £ loans from NatWest (see details of asset portfolio below).
2. R.O.S.E. financed this purchase through the issue of multiple tranches of securities:

Tranche	Rating	US$ million	£ million	Pricing (Margin over US$ or £ LIBOR)
Senior Class A1	AA	750	600	8 bps
Senior Class A2	AA	750	600	18 bps
Senior Class A3	AA	500	600	22 bps
Mezzanine A4	A	25	16	40 bps
Mezzanine A5	BBB	27	18	65 bps
Class	Unrated	100		

Several structural aspects of the transaction should be noted:

- R.O.S.E. purchased sub-participations in drawn and undrawn loan commitments entered into by NatWest. Under the sub-participations, R.O.S.E. paid to NatWest the total US$ and £ amounts of the loans sub-participated and received from NatWest all amounts received by NatWest under the loans. The sub-participations do not represent a purchase of the loans themselves and the legal title to the loans remains with NatWest. R.O.S.E. does not have recourse to NatWest for payment defaults under the loans. The identities of the underlying loan obligors were not disclosed to the investors in R.O.S.E[14].
- The loan portfolio includes revolving credit facilities. R.O.S.E. is structured so that repayments under revolving facilities are maintained in a cash pool from which further advances under revolving facilities can be made as required.
- During an initial period of 18 months (the substitution period), R.O.S.E. may use funds from redemptions to purchase substitute sub-participations if the relevant loan meets all eligibility criteria.

---

[14]   Note that the use of sub-participation agreements to transfer the risk means that the highest tranche rating is limited to NatWest's rating of AA.

- After the completion of the substitution period, the notes will be subject to mandatory redemption in accordance with the following priorities:

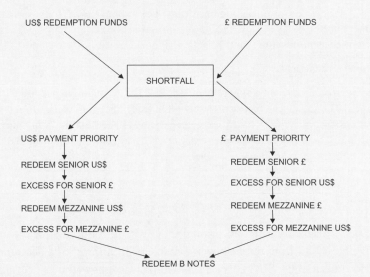

Source: (27 January 1997) R.O.S.E. Funding; Fitch Research Structured Finance New Issue.

3. Asset Portfolio

The asset portfolio consisted of some 201 loans with a value of US$4.97 billion entered into by NatWest. The characteristics of the loans were as follows:

- **Types** – numerous structures including revolving facilities, term loans etc.
- **Maturity** – all loans had a maturity of 5 years or less.

The rating of the asset portfolio was predicated on the following:

- **Obligor credit quality** – this was based on an analysis of the NatWest internal credit scoring system by comparing internal ratings with rating agency categories and actual default experience with external studies.
- **Diversification** – the portfolio was geographically diversified (13 countries including UK (60%), US (27%) and other investment grade countries (13%)). The industry exposure was also well diversified, with the largest exposure to any one industry totaling 7.79% (food industry). The portfolio was also well diversified in terms of individual obligors, with the largest single exposure to an obligor being £75 million.
- **Market risk profile** – this consists of basis risk (mismatches between the interest rates received and the interest rate obligations on the CLOs in terms of interest rate benchmarks) and currency risk (multi-currency options). The basis risk was managed through a swap with NatWest that fully hedged any mismatch. The

currency risk was managed by NatWest and through conversion of any drawing other than in US$ or £ into one of those two currencies.

NatWest operated as loan administrator. The rating agencies conducted due diligence on NatWest's capabilities in administering the transaction. This was an important element in rating the transaction.

4. Credit Enhancement

The major form of credit enhancement was the use of subordinated tranches of securities. The credit enhancement levels (effectively the sizes of the lower rated tranches of securities) were based on stress tests conducted by the rating agencies. The stress test focused on default probabilities, recovery rates and timing and obligor concentration levels within the portfolio.

3.3   Credit Linked Note CLO Transaction

In 1997, a variation on the traditional CLO was introduced with the credit linked note CLO transaction. Swiss Bank Corporation ("SBC") launched the first transaction – SBC Glacier Limited. It was followed by a transaction for Credit Suisse launched by CSFB – Triangle[15]. A number of transactions have subsequently been completed based on the template developed. **Exhibit 4.3** describes the structure of the SBC Glacier transaction[16].

The concept underlying the transactions is the use of credit linked notes to transfer the credit exposure from the sponsor bank to the SPV. The credit linked notes form the collateral for the issue of securities by the SPV. The credit linked note is structured normally. It is issued by the CLO sponsor and references the payment obligations of an individual obligor under a loan or other transaction. The defining element is the use of the credit linked note to transfer the credit risk and hedge the sponsor bank's credit exposure *without the transfer of the actual loan or contract*.

The use of credit linked notes in CLO transactions represents an interesting combination of securitisation and credit derivative technology. The major benefits of the structure are similar to those described

---

[15]   See Ainger, Will "CSFB To Top Largest Credit Derivatives Deal With USD 5 Billion Synthetic CLO" (29 September 1997) Derivatives Week 1, 9, 10.

[16]   See Lee, Peter "SBC Taps Its Credit Pool For Cash" (October 1997) Euromoney 16; Chow, Robert "A New Leaf for the ROSE" (January 1998) Institutional Investor 74–75.

above in relation to traditional CLO structures. There are differences including:

- The structure avoids issues in respect of perfecting the asset transfer, including avoiding any need for an assignment. This has numerous aspects, including avoiding any impediment to the client relationship, the maintenance of confidentiality in respect of the client, and also simplification of the legal issues in terms of perfection of the security (which is now focused on the credit linked note).
- The structure allows the sponsor bank to hedge and manage credit risk through the credit linked note. This should achieve reductions for the bank in terms of both economic capital and regulatory capital. The regulatory capital relief will be achieved if the criteria in respect of normal credit default swaps are satisfied.

Some of the disadvantages in respect of the CLO structure identified above persist, including:

- The actual cost of funding achieved through these transactions may be unattractive for banks with low cost of funds. This will depend on the implicit rate on the credit linked note after stripping out the embedded credit default swap transaction and the rate demanded by investors on the securities issues collateralised by the credit linked notes. In particular, the potential funding disadvantage will be governed by the extent to which these notes are treated as different from ABS transactions.
- The balance sheet benefits of the classical CLO structure are not achieved. The underlying transactions continue to remain on the balance sheet of the sponsor bank. This is despite the fact that the credit linked note effectively transfers the credit risk to the SPV and thence to the investors.

The credit linked note CLO structure also introduces new issues including:

- The transaction is fundamentally dependent on the credit standing *of the issuer of the credit linked notes* (the sponsor bank). This is because there is no effective separation of the underlying credit obligation in the portfolio of the selling bank. In effect, there is full performance risk on the seller. This dictates that this structure is inevitably restricted to sponsor banks with a strong issuer credit rating. This is necessary because the rating agencies will treat the credit linked notes as a primary debt obligation of the sponsor bank, which is contractually obligated to pass through the underlying reference obligations payments of each credit linked note to the CLO SPV. This effectively limits the rating of the highest rating tranche of CLO securities to that of the sponsor bank.

• The ability to create the required credit linked notes themselves may be subject to practical limitations. The necessity to link loss estimates to reference securities means that the universe of obligors to which this technique can be applied is restricted primarily to those with some outstanding traded/deliverable securities. The use of fixed recovery amount notes can overcome this problem to some degree.

The advantages for investors are identical to those for the classical CLO structure.

In historical terms, the credit linked CLO represents a link between traditional structures (CLO) and modern structures (synthetic securitisation).

Exhibit 4.3   Credit Linked Note CLO Transactions – SBC Glacier Transaction[17]

1. Overview

SBC completed the Glacier transaction in September 1997. The transaction for a total of approximately US$1.7 billion was successful, with the issue of bonds being oversubscribed. The transaction was predicated on transferring the risk on a portfolio of corporate loans so the bank could reduce the capital held against the loans in order to improve its return on risk capital. The interesting aspect of the transaction is its combination of CLO and credit derivative technology.

2. Structure

SBC Glacier Finance Limited ("Glacier") is a Cayman Island incorporated limited liability company that acts as the issuer of the CLO securities. It is a SPV which is bankruptcy remote to SBC. The issuer was structured under a Master Trust Facility enabling Glacier to undertake further CLO issues for SBC.

---

[17] The description of the structure is based on "SBC Glacier Finance Ltd" (November 1997) Standard & Poor's Structured Finance.

The overall structure of the transaction is set out in the diagram below.

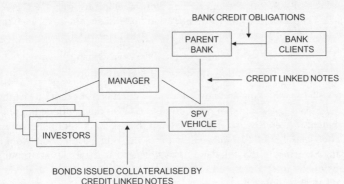

The transaction operates as follows:

- Glacier issued two series of notes each totaling US$870 million of floating rate and zero coupon notes. The notes are expected to mature in 5 and 7 years from the date of issue. The notes were issued in the following tranches:

Type	Series 1997 – 1	Series 1997 – 2
Class A	US$798.225 million floating rate notes	US$798.225 million floating rate notes
Class B	US$36.105 million floating rate notes	US$29.58 million floating rate notes
Class C	US$20.88 million floating rate notes	US$10.44 million floating rate notes
Class D	US$10.875 million floating rate notes	US$26.1 million floating rate notes
Class E	US$3.915 million zero coupon notes	US$5.655 million zero coupon notes

- The proceeds of the notes were used to purchase credit linked notes issued under a MTN program guaranteed by SBC (acting through its New York Branch). As described in more detail below, the credit linked notes are linked to the credit risk of SBC's corporate customers. The credit linked notes constitute the collateral for the notes issued by Glacier.
- The notes issued by Glacier were direct and limited recourse obligations payable solely from the collateral consisting of the credit linked notes.
- The investors in the Glacier notes received repayments of interest and principal derived from the corporate loans/transactions underlying the credit linked notes. SBC acts as administrator of the loan facilities to collect and pass through payments.
- In the event of losses on the underlying loan obligations, investors in the Glacier notes bear the losses. The losses are calculated as the face value of the credit linked notes less the post credit event redemption amounts paid upon the

defaulted obligations. This is calculated as the post default market value of the reference security nominated under the credit linked notes or a fixed percentage (51%). The allocated principal and interest are paid sequentially on each payment date within a series in accordance with a specified priority structure to protect the highest ranking Class A notes.

The structure also incorporated a number of special features:

- **Asset transfer** – the loans and commitments undertaken by SBC which underlie the credit linked notes were not transferred to Glacier but continued to remain on SBC's balance sheet. SBC receives cash from the sale of credit linked notes which could effectively be used to finance the loans (retiring existing borrowing).
- **Revolving Structure** – the collateral asset portfolio is dynamic in structure. The proceeds of the issue were used to purchase the initial portfolio of credit linked notes. The credit linked notes are redeemable at par on every quarterly interest payment date. Where credit linked notes are redeemed or mature, Glacier can purchase additional credit linked notes within the specified collateral guidelines (see below). This dynamic feature is available during the revolving period that continues until an amortisation event or expected maturity, whichever is earlier. This feature is designed to allow SBC to adjust its credit hedge. Where the underlying loan has been repaid or the exposure on a derivative contract has changed due to market price movements, the existing credit linked note may not match SBC's credit exposure. SBC can then repay the relevant credit linked note and issue a new credit linked note that matches the current exposure profile.

3. Asset Portfolio

The underlying asset portfolio consisted of credit linked notes issued by SBC and referencing underlying corporate loans that have been entered into by SBC. The characteristics of the credit linked notes include:

- The notes are a US$ denominated senior unsecured debt obligation of SBC acting through its New York Branch issued under its medium term note program.
- Each credit linked note references a specified individual borrower or dealer. SBC established the face value of the credit linked note based on its estimate of credit exposure to the underlying obligor under either a loan or a derivative transaction.
- Each credit linked note pays a floating rate of interest based on 3 month LIBOR plus a designated spread. The credit linked notes all have a bullet maturity.
- Each credit linked note has both an optional redemption (at par on any quarterly interest payment date) and a mandatory redemption date which is triggered by a credit event occurring on the underlying reference obligation.
- Credit event, in respect of the notes and a reference obligor, is defined as payment default, bankruptcy, insolvency, debt restructuring or a similar event.
- In the event of default, the recovery amount is calculated in one of two ways:
  1. *Reference security note* – this is calculated as the average bid price on the basis of quotations from five dealers on the specified senior unsecured security of

the reference obligor payable on a redemption date 25 business days after the credit event.

2. *Fixed percentage notes* – this is specified as 51% of the face value of the notes (effectively a pre-estimate of the recovery rate) payable on a redemption date 5 business days after the credit event.

The rating agencies placed stringent guidelines on the composition of the credit quality of the underlying asset portfolio of credit linked notes. These criteria were required to be satisfied both initially when the initial collateral is purchased, and also in the event of further purchases of credit linked notes.

The guidelines are as follows:

- Minimum SBC internal rating of C9 (around a B) on reference obligor at the time of credit linked note purchase.
- Maximum concentration limits:
  1. 8% for any single industry.
  2. 5% aggregate exposure to countries with a sovereign rating of less than AA−.
  3. 2% to any single obligor.
  4. 50% for aggregate exposures to obligors with SBC internal rating of C5 to C9 (effectively below BBB−; that is, non investment grade).
- Maturity limit of:
  1. Weighted average credit linked maturity of no more than 4.25 years.
  2. Maturity date of each credit linked note at the time of acquisition must not exceed the expected maturity date of the last maturing series.
- Minimum of 25% in fixed percentage notes.
- Credit linked portfolio must total 106% of the principal outstanding of all but the last maturing series.

The rating of the asset portfolio of credit linked notes was predicated on the following:

- **Credit rating of SBC** – this was the rating of SBC (AA+) as obligor under the credit linked notes.
- **Obligor credit quality** – this was based on an analysis of SBC's internal credit scoring system by comparing internal ratings with rating agency categories and actual default experience with external studies. The guidelines also restricted the types of underlying obligor risks that could be purchased through the credit linked notes.
- **Diversification and maturity profile** – the portfolio was structured to maintain a high degree of diversification and limit maturity through the portfolio collateral guidelines.
- **Interest rate risk profile** – at closing, Glacier entered into an interest rate swap with SBC designed to cover the risk of narrowing spreads between performing credit linked note assets and note liabilities. This was structured as a basis

swap where:

1. SBC paid Glacier a quarterly amount equal to the positive difference between the weighted average rate on Glacier's notes and the weighted average rate on the performing (non defaulted) credit linked notes, based on the notional amount equal to the weighted average principal amount of performing credit linked note collateral.

2. Where the weighted average rate on the performing credit linked notes exceeded the weighted average rate on Glacier issued notes, Glacier paid SBC an amount equal to any excess spread over 0.25% on the notional amount.

SBC operated as administrator of the credit linked note collateral portfolio and ensured that the portfolio was managed in accordance with the collateral guidelines. The rating agency (Standard & Poor's) maintained continuous surveillance based on a monitoring process.

4. Credit Enhancement

The credit enhancement embedded in the CLO structure included:

- **Subordination** – approximately 8.25% of each series of notes was subordinated to provide credit enhancement to the more highly rated tranches.
- **Early amortisation provisions** – both series had early amortisation triggers based on adverse changes in portfolio credit quality (as evidenced by charge offs exceeding 2% of the initial principal balance) and accompanying negative carry from post default cash recoveries. These are designed to protect investors.

4 Synthetic Securitisation[18]

4.1 Structure

In December 1997, JP Morgan completed an innovative synthetic transaction that highlighted the potential for synthetic portfolio securitisation using credit default swaps. The transaction – Broad Index Secured Trust Offering ("BISTRO") – was effectively a large capital market securitisation of a US$9.722 billion credit default swap executed by JP Morgan against its underlying corporate credit exposures. The transaction

---

[18] See Watzinger, Herman "Cheap And Easy" (March 2000) Risk – Credit Risk Special Report S10–S13: Specht, Birgit "Synthetic Securitisation Enters New Generation" in (2001) The Guide To Opportunities In Global Fixed Income 2001".

was designed to hedge the bank's credit risk to these obligors[19]. **Exhibit 4.4** sets out the structure and details of the BISTRO transaction.

The synthetic securitisation significantly changed the CDO market. It quickly became the major accepted technique for structuring and transferring credit portfolios.

The synthetic securitisation structure is significantly different to the more traditional CLO structures. The major differences include:

- **Balance sheet management** – traditional structures entail the effective sale of the credit asset and its transfer off-balance-sheet to the sponsoring entity. Unlike traditional arrangements, the synthetic securitisation structure does not have any balance sheet management implications. This is because the structure shifts only the credit risk of the underlying transaction through the credit default swap, but the assets continue to remain on the sponsor bank's balance sheet.
- **Credit risk transfer** – traditional structures transfer the risk primarily through sale of the asset. The risk transfer in a synthetic securitisation is effected through a credit default swap. This is similar to the mechanism used in a credit linked note CLO transaction. The credit risk transfer is also different in terms of the risk that is retained. As described above, in a typical CDO the credit risk is fully tranched and sold to third party investors. In practice, the sponsor or transferor will generally have to retain some risk. The risk retained is generally the equity risk tranche. In a synthetic securitisation, the sponsor retains the equity tranche but also may retain the highest (least risky) tranche of risk. This is the super senior tranche. In some cases, the super senior tranche is transferred to investors or banks. The super senior tranche is effectively a re-tranching of the senior (usually AAA) tranche. As noted below, it is designed primarily to reduce the funding cost of the transaction for the sponsor[20].
- **Funding** – traditional structures create funding for the sponsor. In a CLO, this takes the form of the sale proceeds of the assets. In a credit linked note CLO, the funding is the principal investment received on the sale of notes. The synthetic securitisation, unlike traditional structures, does

---

[19]   See Paul-Choudhury, Sumit "BISTRO Opens For Business" (January 1998) Risk 8–9.
[20]   See later in the Chapter for a discussion of the nature of super senior tranche.

not generate funding. The underlying asset/transaction is not transferred or credit linked notes are not issued. Therefore, no financing is created. This means the synthetic securitisation does not allow access to new sources of funding. For highly rated banks, it means that the traditional CLO disadvantage of a higher funding cost (relative to the sponsor bank's own cost of funds) is minimised. **Exhibit 4.5** sets out the cost difference between a conventional CLO and a synthetic securitisation transaction.

- **Use of funds** – in traditional structures, the proceeds of the CDO issues are used to acquire the underlying credit portfolio directly (CLO) or indirectly (credit linked note CLO). In a synthetic securitisation, the transfer of risk is unfunded, taking the form of a credit default swap on the underlying credit assets. The issue proceeds are used to acquire high credit quality assets (government or near government). These assets are used to partially collateralise the credit default swap. The use of collateral is designed to guarantee performance and assist in obtaining regulatory capital relief.
- **Volume of securities sold** – a significant benefit of the synthetic securitisation structure is that it significantly reduces the amount of securities required to be placed with capital market investors. This is because the transaction does not necessitate the total collateral portfolio being purchased or financed. The amount of securities sold is dependent on the level of capital needed to collateralise the underlying credit default swap. In the BISTRO transaction described in **Exhibit 4.4**, this was only US$697 million (US$729 million inclusive of the reserve account) on a portfolio of US$9.722 billion. This equates to around 7.50% of the total notional amount of the underlying credit risk portfolio. This is achieved through the creation of the super senior tranche which is generally unfunded and structured as a credit default swap.
- **Economic and regulatory capital** – traditional structures are designed to achieve both economic and regulatory capital release by reducing risk. The regulatory capital reduction is contingent on certain conditions being met. The synthetic securitisation structures seek to achieve *economic* risk reduction. This is achieved despite the fact that the entire risk may not be transferred. The sponsor can retain both the equity and super senior tranches. In effect, the sponsor remains exposed to the highest and lowest layers of credit risk. Economic risk reduction is achieved by transferring the substantial risk of the portfolio (other than the equity) to the investors in the externally

issued notes. This is effected by pledging the high credit quality assets purchased with the proceeds of the issue as collateral in support of the credit default swap. The retained risk of loss (the super senior tranche) is regarded as relatively low. The structure of synthetic securitisation complicates regulatory capital relief. This is because the structure is not fully funded or collateralised. Where the sponsor retains the super senior tranche, regulatory capital relief is complicated by the fact that the risk transfer is not complete. In practice, regulatory capital may be available if certain conditions are met. Where the super senior risk is hedged with a third party, regulatory capital relief is available based on the identity of the party entering into the super senior credit default swap[21].

The basic structure of synthetic securitisation is relatively homogenous. There are differences between jurisdictions driven primarily by the regulatory capital treatment. The differences focus on the super senior tranche. In the BISTRO structure described in **Exhibit 4.4**, the sponsor bank retains the super senior risk. This is generally not the case in many jurisdictions such as Europe[22]. In order to qualify for regulatory capital relief, the super senior tranche must be transferred to a third party. In practice, the super senior risk is transferred using an unfunded credit default swap. It is usually transferred to an OECD bank or re-insurance company in order to obtain capital relief for the sponsor. **Exhibit 4.6** sets out the structure generally used for European transactions[23].

---

[21] See discussion on regulatory capital treatment later in this Chapter. See also Das, Satyajit (2004) Swaps/Financial Derivatives – 3rd Edition; John Wiley, Singapore at Chapters 33 and 34.

[22] See Parolai, Richard and Lewis, Jonathan "The Mechanics of European Synthetic CLOs" (3–9 August 1999) Financial Products 8–9; Saunderson, Emily "New Deal for Europe" (October 1999) Risk – Credit Risk Special Report 20; Burke, Jeanne "The Synthetic Solution" (January 2001) Institutional Investor 33–35.

[23] For a sample of other transactions, see "Warburg Launches Eisberg" (10 October 1998) International Financing Review Issue 1254 39; Abed, Kamal "BNP To Complete Synthetic Securitisation" (27 July–2 August 1999) Financial Products 3 Abed, Kamal "KBC Bank Plans First Synthetic CLO Securitisation" (10–16 August 1999) Financial Products 1–2; Abed, Kamal "BCI To Complete Synthetic Securitisation" (27 July – 2 August 1999) Financial Products 1–11.

Exhibit 4.4   Synthetic Securitisation – BISTRO Transaction[24]

1.   Overview

In December 1997, JP Morgan launched a US$697 million issue of credit linked notes through BISTRO, a SPV. In effect, BISTRO issued bonds to finance a collateral pool of US$ Treasury securities that were used to collateralise a credit default swap entered into by BISTRO with JP Morgan. Under the terms of the swap, JP Morgan hedged US$9.722 billion of credit exposure to its corporate customers. The innovative structure differs from the classical CLO or credit linked note CLO in that it transfers the *pure* credit risk of the underlying credit exposures without providing any financing for JP Morgan and has no balance sheet impact.

2.   Structure

The structure of the BISTRO transaction is as follows:

- BISTRO issued US$697 million of 5 year notes in two tranches:

Type	Senior Notes	Subordinated Notes
Amount (US$ million)	460	237
Rating	AAA	Ba2
Yield (Spread bps over US$ Treasuries)	60	375

- The issue proceeds are used by BISTRO to purchase 5 year US Treasury notes.
- BISTRO entered into a 5 year credit default swap on a portfolio of credit exposure with a total notional face value of US$9.722 billion with JP Morgan. JP Morgan pays a fee to BISTRO. In return, BISTRO assumes the default risk on this portfolio. The

---

[24] See Efrat, Isaac (21 August 1998) BISTRO Trust 1997–1000; Moody's Investors Service Structured Finance New Issue Report. See also Feinne, Linda, Papa, Albert, Brown and Lecoq, Sophie (8 September 1998) Value in Bistro; JP Morgan Securities, New York.

- portfolio is static and consists of identified reference entities. BISTRO's obligations under the credit default swap are collateralised by a pledge of the US Treasury Notes.
- BISTRO also holds a US$32 million reserve account funded for 5 years. This represents the equivalent of the equity component of the transaction. It is refundable to JP Morgan in the event it is not required.
- During the term of the transaction, BISTRO pays the coupons on the issued debt out of the coupon received from the US Treasuries and the fee on the credit default swap received from JP Morgan.
- At maturity, if there are no credit events on the reference entities, then the investors in BISTRO receive the return of principal based on the maturing US Treasury notes.
- In the event of a credit event on any of the underlying reference entities, any loss suffered (net of any recovery) will be met in the following order:
  1. Reserve account.
  2. The Treasury bond collateral pool.

  Where losses exceed the reserve account, the drawings on the Treasury bond collateral pool reduce the amount available to meet repayment of the notes issued. The holders of the subordinated debt meet any loss first. The senior debt holders incur losses only after losses exceed the subordinated debt amount. To the extent that losses exceed the reserve account and the Treasury bond collateral pool, there are no funds available in BISTRO to meet losses. These losses are met by JP Morgan.

- The loss amount on the underlying reference credits is calculated as either:
  1. Average work-out recovery value.
  2. Physical delivery of senior unsecured claims against individual reference credits.

- Any default payment is made at maturity; that is, after 5 years.

The structure is set out in the diagram below.

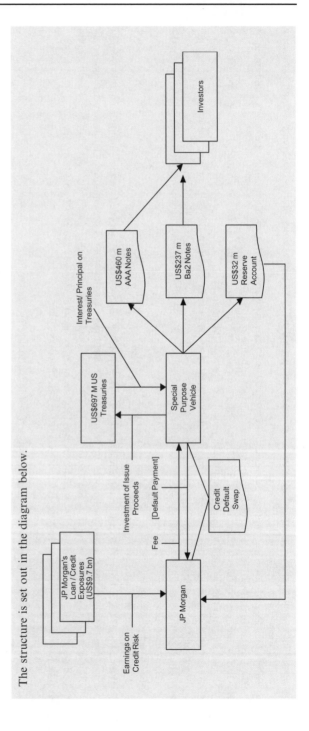

3. Risk Profile

The risk profile of the credit portfolio after the BISTRO transaction is set out below:

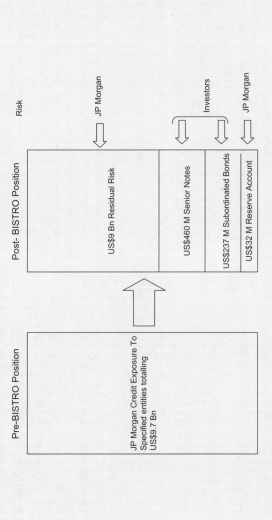

Risk Re-Adjustment Through Synthetic Securitisation

Under the structure, JP Morgan retains the following risk on its underlying credit portfolio:

- First loss piece of US$32 million (0.33%).
- Final loss piece of US$8,993 million (92.5%). This risk is referred to as the "super senior" exposure.

The first loss component is equivalent to the expected loss on the credit portfolio. The next US$697 million (7.17%) is borne by the BISTRO subordinated and senior noteholders, in that order. The final loss piece represents losses exceeding US$729 million. This is borne by JP Morgan. However, based on the fact that the senior notes are rated AAA, the risk of this loss is obviously low.

4. Asset Portfolio

The credit portfolio on which JP Morgan purchased protection has the following characteristics:

- **Obligor credit quality** – the portfolio is of relatively high credit quality obligors. The weighted average credit quality is A2/A. The lowest credit quality is A3/BBB+. As a proportion of the overall portfolio, A3 obligors represent 22.7% of the portfolio and BBB+ obligors represent 4.4% of the portfolio.

- **Portfolio diversification** – the portfolio is well diversified in terms of geography (80.4% US; 2.3% Canada; 17.3% Europe); industry (29 industries); and individual obligors (307).

The asset portfolio is characterised by some interesting features:

- All 307 obligors are identified in the prospectus, both by name and amount of exposure (not exceeding a maximum of US$37 million).

- The asset portfolio includes obligors to whom JP Morgan had no exposure. This effectively created a short credit position for JP Morgan which either enabled the bank to undertake transactions with that obligor in the future on a fully credit hedged basis or to profit from changes in the pricing of the obligor's credit risk.

- The asset portfolio is static and cannot be altered during the life of the transaction.

- The credit exposure can be derived from any type of transaction ranging from drawn loans, unfunded standby loan commitments and exposures on derivatives.

5. Credit Enhancement

The credit enhancement within the structure is primarily based on the following:

- First loss retention by JP Morgan.
- The subordinated tranche structure of the issue.

Exhibit 4.5   CDO Costs – CLO Versus Synthetic Securitisation

The following analysis compares the cost of transferring/hedging credit risk through a CDO structured as a fully funded CLO or a synthetic securitisation[25].

The cost of the CLO will be as follows:

Tranche	Size (%)	Market Cost (% pa over LIBOR)
AAA	95.00	0.30
A2	1.50	0.80
Baa2	1.50	1.50
Equity	2.00	
Total	100.00	0.32

The total cost is calculated as the weighted average cost of the individual tranches. No cost is attributed to equity as it is assumed to be taken up by the sponsor and treated as a residual claimant.

The cost of the synthetic securitisation will be as follows:

Tranche	Size (%)	Market Cost (% pa over LIBOR)
Super senior	92.00	0.00
AAA	3.00	0.30
A2	1.50	0.80
Baa2	1.50	1.50
Equity	2.00	
Total	100.00	0.04

The cost reduction is driven by the reduction in AAA securities issued.

In certain jurisdictions, the super senior exposure must be hedged to obtain regulatory capital relief. This would have the effect of increasing the cost as follows:

Tranche	Size (%)	Market Cost (% pa over LIBOR)
Super senior	92.00	0.10
AAA	3.00	0.30
A2	1.50	0.80
Baa2	1.50	1.50
Equity	2.00	
Total	100.00	0.14

---

[25]   The capital structure and pricing used is purely hypothetical and is used to illustrate the process.

The introduction of the super senior tranche is the basis for the significant cost reduction in the cost of a synthetic securitisation relative to a conventional CLO structure. The super senior piece is traditionally transferred to reinsurance companies or monoline insurance companies. The pricing difference between the super senior market and the conventional AAA asset backed security market drives the economics. The option of a super senior piece is only available in a synthetic structure as it is not fully funded.

The cost difference between the two structures has significant impact upon the return to equity investors in these structures. The synthetic structure generates significantly enhanced returns for equity investors of a given level of credit spread on the underlying portfolio. Equity investors generally require returns in the range of 15 to 20% pa. These returns are easier to achieve using a synthetic structure.

Exhibit 4.6   Synthetic Securitisation – C*Star Transaction[26]

1.   Overview

In June 1999, Citibank/Salomon Smith Barney launched a synthetic securitisation – C*Strategic Asset Redeployment Program 1999-1 Limited ("C*Star"). The transaction represented the first public synthetic securitisation of a European credit portfolio. The transaction was repeated in November 1999 with C*Star 1999-2 Corp and also in a transaction for a credit portfolio involving Banca Commercial Italiana (SCALA 1 Limited). Similar transactions have been used by a number of other European banks.

2.   Structure

The basic structure of C*Star is similar to the BISTRO transaction described in **Exhibit 4.4**. There are a number of differences, driven primarily by regulatory considerations.

The basic structure is as follows:

- Citibank assembled a portfolio of Euro 4 billion of corporate credit risk.
- Citibank hedged its risk on this portfolio through a series of separate transactions:
  1. Citibank retained the first loss portion of Euro 40 million (1% of the portfolio).

---

[26]   See Murra, Francesca "C*Star Points The Way Forward" (September 1999) International Securitisation Review Issue 40; The author wishes to acknowledge the assistance of Herman Watzinger for providing information on the above transaction.

2. Citibank entered into a credit default swap with C*Star, a SPV domiciled in Jersey, covering Euro 280 million of credit risk (7% of the portfolio). This swap was collateralised with German government bonds.
3. Citibank entered into credit default swaps with OECD banks covering Euro 3,680 million (92% of the portfolio).
- C*Star issued the following tranches of 10 year notes:
  1. Euro 100 million Class A notes (rated AAA/Aaa) bearing interest at Euribor + 21 bps (2.5% of the portfolio).
  2. Euro 128 million Class B notes (rated A/A2) bearing interest at Euribor + 48 bps (3.2% of the portfolio).
  3. Euro 52 million Class C notes (rated BB/Ba2) bearing interest at Euribor + 300 bps (1.3% of the portfolio).

The Euro 280 million proceeds of the Note issue were invested in German government bonds to collateralise the credit default swap with Citibank.

The risk transfer within the structure is set out below:

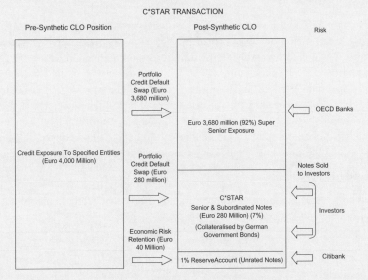

C*STAR TRANSACTION

Under the transaction structure, Citibank bears the first 1% of losses. The investors in the C*STAR notes bear the next 7% of credit losses. The remaining 92% of losses (the super senior tranche) are borne by the OECD bank counterparties to the credit default swap.

The C*STAR structure is similar to the BISTRO structure and has similar advantages, including:

- **Credit risk transfer** – Citibank sheds credit exposure to the underlying counterparties.

- **Cost effective risk transfer** – the fact that Citibank retains the underlying transactions and only the risk is hedged means that the higher funding spread on the transaction is only paid on about 7% of the total portfolio. Given that the coupon on the AAA/Aaa tranche is around 21 bps, and assuming a funding cost for a highly rated bank of around LIBOR minus 15 bps, this translates into a cost saving of around 36 bps pa.
- **Separation of underlying transactions from credit hedge** – this enables a wide variety of transactions to be hedged.

The differences between BISTRO and C*STAR relate primarily to the super senior tranche. In BISTRO, this is retained by the sponsor bank (although it could then be separately hedged). In C*STAR, this risk was hedged through a credit default swap with OECD banks. The primary motivation of this structure was BIS credit capital relief. The C*STAR structure enables a reduction in risk capital to 20% from 100% for the underlying portfolio. The credit default swap on the super AAA tranche is usually attractively priced, reflecting the low risk on this tranche.

3. Asset Portfolio

The underlying portfolio of Euro 4 billion consisted of 164 transactions to 152 obligors. The transactions were primarily loans of which 67% were then currently undrawn. The obligors were primarily from Europe (excluding Greece), Norway and Switzerland.

Individual obligors were not specifically identified. The structure is rated, with the ratings being based on a mixture of external ratings and Citibank's internal credit ratings (mapped to rating agency external ratings). Approximately 40% of the portfolio must be externally rated at all times; the other 60% has mapped ratings. The portfolio is subject to limits on industry and individual obligor concentration limits.

4. Credit Enhancement

The structure uses the sponsor retained first loss provision and the tranched notes to enhance the credit structure of the portfolio.

4.2 Synthetic Securitisation – Assessment[27]

The first issue of BISTRO securities was successfully placed under difficult market conditions in December 1997. Since its introduction, the synthetic securitisation has gained acceptance and has gained ascendancy to become the primary method of transferring and investing in credit portfolios.

---

[27] See Paul-Choudhury, Sumit "BISTRO Opens For Business" (January 1998) Risk 8–9.

From the viewpoint of a bank seeking to transfer credit risk, the synthetic securitisation structure has similar advantages to more traditional CDO structures. The synthetic securitisation structure has a number of additional advantages, including:

- It is focused on the reduction of economic risk rather than the sale of assets. This reflects the unfunded structure and the creation of the super senior tranche (which the sponsor may retain).
- It is significantly lower in cost to the traditional structures. This reflects the reduction in AAA rated securities that must be sold and the substitution of this component of the capital structure with the super senior tranche.

The synthetic securitisation structure offers investors similar advantages to other CDO structures. This includes access to a well diversified portfolio, return from credit risk, relative value and liquidity. The synthetic securitisation also offers some additional features, including:

- **Risk Leverage** – this entails the ability to use the tranching mechanism to manufacture highly structured credit risk profiles. This is examined in the following Section.
- **Prepayment risk** – the synthetic securitisation structure generally does not have prepayment risk and/or extension risk, unlike comparable ABS transactions. This reflects the fact that the underlying risk is in the form of a credit default swap with a fixed maturity.

An interesting aspect of the investor analysis of the BISTRO securities is the disclosure of the underlying obligors and the static nature of the portfolio. This contrasts with the aggregate disclosure in terms of broad portfolio characteristics and the revolving and dynamic nature of some conventional CLO structures. This allows the investor to base the investment decision on both the ratings analysis and its own analysis of the underlying asset portfolio. This is not specifically an advantage of the structure as similar disclosure is feasible under other CDO formats.

4.3   Risk Leverage

The synthetic securitisation transaction explicitly introduces the concept of risk leverage in the process of trading portfolios of credit risk. The ability to structure specific credit risk profiles is inherent in CDO technology. The original BISTRO structure specifically used this as a central element of the transaction.

Traditional CDO structures take underlying credit portfolios and tranche them into investible securities for investors. The primary focus is on medium to high credit risk assets. The tranching is designed to enhance the credit quality of the underlying credit portfolio and create high quality (AAA or AA) securities. This is designed to enhance the investor base in these assets and also lower the explicit cost of funding these assets. It also re-distributes the credit risk of the portfolio by segmentation. For example, the equity and mezzanine investors take higher default risk in return for higher returns. In contrast, super senior and senior investors trade off return for lower risk.

The synthetic securitisation structures have traditionally used this risk leverage in a different manner. The most significant feature of the original BISTRO transaction is that the inherent risk on the underlying portfolio is to a high grade universe of obligors. The structure entails using tranching technology to increase risk in the mezzanine or subordinated tranche (rated BB). In effect, the mezzanine investor is taking a leveraged exposure to a high grade obligor universe to generate extra yield from the consequent lower rating.

The synthetic **BB** or high risk exposure is created through risk leverage. Risk leverage entails re-apportioning the risk through tranching (creation of loss layers). The *total* amount of the equity and mezzanine tranches (the subordinated elements) determines the credit quality of the senior tranche (AAA). Within the subordinated components, changes in the amount of equity can be used to engineer the desired risk of the mezzanine tranche.

In the original BISTRO transaction (see **Exhibit 4.4**), the investor in the subordinated BB notes is effectively selling protection on the second loss on the total portfolio (US$237 million or 2.44% of the portfolio or 2.45% if the JP Morgan first loss piece is deducted). The leverage arises because the underlying portfolio is larger (US$9,722 million) than the notional amount the investor risks. The leverage also arises because the level of equity (US$32 million or 0.33%) is deliberately reduced to increase the risk of the mezzanine tranche. If a credit event occurs, then the second loss piece will take a disproportionately large loss. This is because it must absorb the entire second loss across the entire portfolio. For example, only 7 to 8 obligors in the entire portfolio (2.3 to 2.6% of the obligors in the portfolio) would have to default for the entire BB tranche to be lost. This is based on average individual exposure and assumes zero recovery rates.

In effect, the additional risk and return is largely created through the use of leverage. In terms of risk, this may compare favourably with taking *direct exposure* to lower rated corporate credits. This may be so particularly at the end of the credit cycle where the subordinated notes in the original transactions were considered to offer more attractive returns and lower risk than comparable conventional corporate bonds of equivalent rating.

The availability of risk leverage allows investors to structure specific credit risk profiles consistent with their expectations of credit market performance. As discussed below, the risk of such structures is also different to traditional credit risk, entailing exposure to default correlation and idiosyncratic credit risk.

5 CDO Structures – Comparison

The evolution of the structures has created competitive alternatives for the transfer of risk. It has created different methods for banks seeking to manage the risk of, and capital committed to, credit exposure assumed in servicing their corporate relationships. It has also created different structures for investors to acquire exposure to credit risks.

The structures have a number of common elements including:

- The use of the bankruptcy remote special purpose entity to acquire a portfolio of credit risk.
- The credit risk may be transferred through the sale of assets or synthetically (using a credit default swap).
- The portfolio is then tranched to create investible securities that are placed with investors. The investors in the securities receive the return on the underlying credit portfolio and bear the risk of loss from credit events.

The economics of the CDO format are driven by

- The ability to transfer credit risk to unregulated (by banking regulators) entities where an economic capital structure is used to fund the assets. This facilitates potential regulatory arbitrage between the bank regulatory capital regime and economic risk of the assets[28].
- The use of tranching/loss layering techniques to create differentiated credit risks that are placed with investors. The creation of specific risk allows holders of risk or investment banks structuring CDOs to

---

[28] See later in this Chapter. See also Das, Satyajit (2004) Swaps/Financial Derivatives 3rd Edition; John Wiley, Singapore at Chapter 33.

specifically transfer the risk to investors willing to assume the identified risk at the most cost effective price.

There are a number of competing structural models. **Exhibit 4.**7 sets out the comparative features of the competing structures. **Exhibit 4.8** sets out the impact of the CDO structures on regulatory capital and returns for the sponsor bank

As noted above, the synthetic securitisation structure now dominates. The dominant position reflects the combination of lower funding cost, simplicity, execution speed and flexibility. It is driven by the relative standardisation and homogeneity of credit default swaps. It is also driven by the increasing liquidity of the credit default swap market.

Exhibit 4.7   CLO, Credit Linked Note CLO and Synthetic Securitisation – Comparison

Feature	CLO	Credit Linked Note CLO	Synthetic Securitisation
Asset Transfer Mechanism	Assignment or participation	Credit linked note	Credit default swap
Economic Capital	Risk is reduced by the amount of assets transferred less the first loss position retained	Risk is reduced to the extent that the credit linked note hedges the underlying credit exposure, less any equity piece in the CLO retained	Risk is reduced to the extent that the credit exposure is transferred less the first loss position assumed (which is less than that needed for a CLO), and to the extent that losses exceed the protection purchased, triggering the final loss position where this is retained by the sponsor bank
Regulatory Capital	Relief available dependent on quantum of first loss position	Relief available dependent on the credit linked notes providing virtually complete protection	Limited relief available prima facie but may be able to be achieved if certain conditions are met

Feature	CLO	Credit Linked Note CLO	Synthetic Securitisation
Balance Sheet Impact	Assets are transferred off balance sheet	Assets remain on balance sheet	Assets remain on balance sheet
Funding	Funding generated as a result of the sale	Funding generated as a result of sale of credit linked notes	No funding generated
Client Relationship	Clients may need to be advised where an assignment is required. Client particulars are not usually disclosed in the offering document	Clients do not need to be advised. Client particulars are not usually disclosed in the offering document	Clients do not need to be advised and disclosure of client particulars is optional in the offering document
Credit Rating of Selling Bank	Important in rating where participation structure is used; not important where assignment structure is used	Important in rating	Not relevant
Amount of Securities	Equal to approximately face value of loans sold	Equal to approximately face value of loans sold	Equal to the level required to shed economic risk but will generally be significantly lower than face value of assets hedged

Exhibit 4.8   CDO Transactions – Impact on Sponsor Bank

1. **Assumptions**

Assume a portfolio of 5 year loans/credit default swaps totalling US$1,000 million. Assume the portfolio currently earns 0.75% pa in net interest income. The sponsor bank decides to transfer the credit risk of the assets using a CDO transaction.

All the loans are to 100% risk weighted corporations. Assume the sponsor bank must hold 8.00% regulatory capital against the portfolio. The sponsor bank's cost of capital is 15% pa.

2. CDO Transactions

Two possible CDO transactions are considered:

- A traditional fully funded cash flow CLO.
- A synthetic securitisation.

The capital structures and costs of the two structures are summarised below[29]:

Structure	Fully Funded CLO		Synthetic Securitisation[30]	
Tranche	Size	Market Cost	Size	Market Cost
Super senior			92.00%	0.10%
AAA	95.00%	0.30%	3.00%	0.30%
A2	1.50%	0.80%	1.50%	0.80%
Baa2	1.50%	1.50%	1.50%	1.50%
Equity	2.00%		2.00%	
Total	100.00%	0.32%	100.00%	0.14%

3. Capital And Earning Impact

The capital impact of the CDO transactions is calculated as follows[31]:

- 8.00% capital is held against the original underlying portfolio.
- In the case of the fully funded cash flow CLO transaction, the sponsor is assumed to hold capital against the equity tranche. It is assumed that the rest of the capital structure is placed with investors. The sponsor bank is required to hold 100% capital (deduction from capital) against the equity.
- In the case of the synthetic securitisation transaction, the sponsor is assumed to hold capital against the equity tranche. It is assumed that the rest of the capital structure is placed with investors. It is also assumed that the super senior tranche is hedged with a 20% risk weighted counterparty. The sponsor bank is required to hold 100% capital (deduction from capital) against the equity. It is also required to hold capital against the super senior tranche based on the 20% risk weighting.

The capital position before and after the transaction is summarised below.

The position before the CDO transactions is[32]:

Portfolio (million)	$1,000
Capital	8.00%
Initial Capital (million)	$80

---

[29] The capital structure and pricing used is purely hypothetical and is used to illustrate the process.

[30] The structure assumes that the super senior tranche is hedged rather than retained by the sponsor bank.

[31] See discussion later in this Chapter.

[32] All amounts are rounded to the nearest million.

The position after the fully funded cash flow CLO transaction is:

First Loss (million)	$20	
Total (million)	$20	2.00%

The position after the synthetic securitisation is:

First Loss (million)	$20	
Super Senior (million)	$15	
Total (million)	$35	3.47%

The capital savings are as follows:

	After CLO		After Synthetic Securitisation	
Initial Capital (million)	$ 80.0	8.00%	$ 80.0	8.00%
After Transaction (million)	$ 35.0	3.47%	$ 20.0	6.00%
Saving (million)	$ 45.0	4.53%	$ 60.0	2.00%

The benefit of the capital (per annum) released is summarised below:

	CLO	Synthetic Securitisation
Capital Released (million)	$ 60.00	$ 45.0
Cost of Capital	15%	15%
Capital Benefit (million)	$9.00	$ 6.79
Cost of CDO (million)	$3.20	$ 1.36
Net Benefit (million)	$5.81	$ 5.44

The analysis of the benefit assumes:
- The capital released can be redeployed (either in other businesses, investments or repurchasing capital) to generate at least the sponsor bank's cost of capital.
- The cost of the CDO cost is calculated using the CDO funding cost derived above.

The impact on the reported earnings and return on regulatory capital is summarised below:

	CLO			Synthetic Securitisation		
	%	$ Million	Return On Capital	%	$ Million	Return On Capital
Earning Pre CDO	0.75	$7.50	9.38%	0.75%	$7.50	9.38%
CDO Cost	0.32	$3.20		0.14%	$1.36	
Net Earnings	0.43	$4.31	21.53%	0.61%	$6.15	17.70%

6   CDO Ratings

6.1   Overview

CDO ratings are not fundamentally different to the rating of conventional securities. It is generally a credit opinion that allows investors to compare the relative credit quality of instruments within a consistent evaluation framework. Importantly, ratings are investment recommendations and do not provide a guarantee against loss.

Typically, CDO transactions will be rated by one or more of the major international rating agencies – Moody's Investors Service ("Moody's"), Standard & Poor's ("S&P") and Fitch Rating ("Fitch"). Each rating agency has its own methodology for rating transactions. There are similarities in the approaches used. There are also a number of differences.

6.2   CDO Rating – Approach

The rating of CDO transactions is based on the techniques used to evaluate other structured transactions such as ABS transactions[33]. The generic approach by the rating agencies is based on the following criteria:

- **Asset quality** – this examines the credit quality of the collateral assets in terms of repayment ability, diversification of the portfolio (default quality) and asset maturity. The assessment of credit quality is similar irrespective of whether the underlying credit assets are bonds, loans, credit linked notes or credit default swaps. The credit quality is based on existing ratings (by the rating agency rating the CDO), rating by another rating agency[34] or internal rating by the originator or sponsor. Where internal ratings are used as the basis of CDO rating, the rating agency will need to undertake a review of the internal rating model and map

---

[33]   See Falcone, Yvonne Fu and Gluck, Jeremy (3 April 1998) Moody's Approach To Rating Market Value CDOs; Moody's Investors Service Global Credit Research; (17 March 1997) CBO/CLO Rating Criteria; Fitch Research Structured Finance Asset-Backed Special Report; (February 1998) CBO/CLO Criteria Update: Market Innovations: Standard & Poor's Structured Finance Ratings Asset Backed Securities; Yoshizawa, Yuri (28 July 2003) Moody's Approach To Rating Synthetic CDOs; Moody's Investors Service; (1 August 2003) Global Rating Criteria For Collateralised Debt Obligations; Fitch Rating; (September 2003) Criteria For Rating Synthetic CDO Transactions; Standard & Poor's.

[34]   Where a rating by another rating agency is used, the rating level may be adjusted – a practice known as "down notching". For the approach of one rating agency see (18 July 2002) New Approach For Structured Finance CDO Collateral Review; Fitch Rating.

internal ratings to the agency's own rating model. The process is designed to assess the credit quality of the underlying credit portfolio (often referred to as the "collateral pool"). Key characteristics established through this process are portfolio credit quality (default probability, loss given default (recovery rates) and diversity). The weighted average life and coupon are also established.

- **Transaction structure** – this process is focused on analysing the transaction structure including:
  1. *Capital Structure* – this covers the amount of notes to be issued, interest rate payable and (target) rating of individual tranches.
  2. *Cash flow analysis* – this focuses on timing of cash flows, any mismatch between cash inflows and outflows, and the impact of reduced cash flows from default on any portfolio asset. Key areas of focus are priority of payments, level of overcollateralisation and interest coverage
  3. *Market risk* – this examines any interest rate or currency mismatch between the cash flow from the asset pool and the required payments on the securities to be issued and the derivative transactions in place to manage these risks. This analysis will include evaluation of the credit quality of the dealer acting as counterparty in any derivative transaction.
- **Asset manager** – this analyses the ability of the asset manager to perform the ongoing management of the asset portfolio and the credit quality of the asset manager[35].
- **Legal risks** – this includes review of the legal structure to ensure bankruptcy remoteness of the SPV, the effectiveness of transfer of title to the collateral, legal enforceability of the contracts, and other legal issues associated with the structure.
- **Transaction monitoring** – the exact role of transaction monitoring varies between structures e.g. static, replenishment or dynamic management. In all cases, the rating agency will re-analyse expected losses based on portfolio performance and changes. This will drive upgrades or downgrades of individual CDO tranches. In replenishment and dynamically managed structures, the rating agency will focus on compliance with pre-specified tests and coverage ratios.

---

[35] See the analysis in (8 December 1997) Management of CBOs/CLOs; Fitch Research Structured Finance Special Report.

The rating will depend on the evaluation of the following:

- **Expected credit losses** – a major component of the risk of CDO securities is the level of expected credit losses for the assets in the portfolio. This is a function of:
  1. *Expected default rate* – each obligor is assigned a rating to establish a default probability that is based on historical default rates and maturity.
  2. *Timing of defaults* – the timing of defaults and the impact of differences in default timing are considered.
  3. *Recovery rates or default severity* – this focuses on the level of recovery following default and the timing of any such recovery. This is estimated based on historical data of defaults and recoveries.
- **Stress testing** – the rating process emphasises stressing the asset portfolio in terms of default rates, default timing, recovery rates and recovery timing with a view to analysing the ability of the asset portfolio to meet the obligations issued by the SPV.
- **Credit enhancement** – the structure will incorporate one or more types of credit enhancement. The level and type of credit enhancement will be determined by the rating desired on the securities issued by the SPV. Typical types of credit enhancement include:
  1. *Subordination/over collateralisation* – over collateralisation entails creating an excess of assets (collateral) over liabilities (the highly rated debt tranches). This is achieved through tranching the debt – that is, issuing different series of debt with different payment priorities, in particular, the issue of subordinated debt and equity tranches. The tranching ensures that there is over collateralisation of the more highly rated tranches. The lower rated subordinated debt bears a higher risk of loss that is compensated for by the higher return received.
  2. *Payment structure* – the allocation of cash flow from the asset pool to repayment of the issued securities is also used to engineer the credit risk. Common techniques include[36]:
     - *Sequential pay* – this requires repayment of senior debt in full before payment of more junior tranches of debt.
     - *Fast pay/slow pay* – this requires a more rapid paydown of senior debt than that on more junior debt.

---

[36] In practice, this is referred to as the "waterfall".

3. *Excess spread* – there is usually a surplus of cash flow from assets over the level that is required to service the securities on issue. This excess spread can be maintained within the SPV to build up reserves against future credit losses and liquidity risks to provide additional protection for bondholders.

4. *Cash reserves* – a cash reserve account (held in the form of highly rated securities) can be created by over funding the structure to enhance the credit quality of the structure.

5. *Financial guarantees* – this involves a third party financial guarantee or insurance policy, typically provided by a monoline insurer (known as the insurance "wrap"). This transfers the risk of the assets to a guarantor. The typically highly rated (AAA) insurance company guarantees timely payment of principal and interest.

6. *Other* – this would include variations on the above as well as guarantees of collateral or note holder payments, liquidity puts on bond payment dates, or credit default swaps.

6.3 Credit Portfolio Characteristics

Within the rating framework, the rating agency will typically require certain specified tests to be satisfied initially. Where the structure allows the asset manager the ability to trade in the underlying assets and add new assets to the portfolio (either a replenishment or dynamically managed structure), the test must also be met periodically over the term, usually quarterly or semi-annually. Irrespective of the degree of management of the underlying portfolio permitted by the structure, in the event of breach, early amortisation of the notes may be required.

The primary tests include:

- **Collateral quality tests** – this ensures that the asset portfolio complies with the following criteria:
  1. *Weighted average rating factor* ("WARF") – a minimum weighted average credit rating for the asset portfolio is specified.
  2. *Diversity test* – a minimum level of diversity (issuer, industry and country) must be maintained. This can be specified in different ways. For example, Moody's may use the concept of a diversity score[37]. Other measures may include limits on exposure to an individual entity, industry or country.

---

[37] See discussion below.

3. *Maximum maturity profile* – a minimum amount of principal must be available for amortisation of the bonds on each payment date. This may be specified as a weighted average life ("WAL") test.

- **Coverage tests** – these tests are designed to ensure that specified levels of over collateralisation are maintained for notes. The tests include:

  1. *Collateral balance tests* – the principal outstanding on the asset portfolio must exceed or equal the level of outstanding bonds. This can be specified in terms of either par value (traditionally used for non-market value CDOs) or market value (traditionally used for market value CDOs).

  2. *Interest coverage ratio* – the interest due to the bondholders will be payable from the interest or income to be received from the asset portfolio during the collection period. The interest payments are required to be covered to specified levels by the cash flow received from the collateral assets. Other tests may include weighted average coupon ("WAC") or weighted average spread ("WAS"). These are used primarily to determine interest proceeds of a CDO.

6.4 Credit Portfolio – Treatment Of Loans/Credit Default Swaps

There are a number of specific issues with regard to the rating of CDOs where the underlying assets are loans or credit default swaps.

In the case of loans, the issues relate to the following factors:

- The documentation of loans is less standardised than for bonds and can be more complex.
- Loan terms can vary in terms of principal repayments, interest payment dates, interest rates payable etc. In addition, loan terms can be renegotiated or restructured by mutual agreement between the lender and borrower.
- The secondary market for loans is less liquid than the bond market.
- The mechanism for transfer of the lender's rights in the loan to the SPV is more problematic.

In practice, it is the last issue that creates the greatest problems in a CLO transaction. In CDOs involving bonds, the transfer of the interest in the bonds can be made relatively simply (by delivery in the case of a bearer bond or registration of a transfer of the interest in the case of a registered bond).

In CLOs, there are a number of means for transferring the seller's interest in a loan. These include:

- **Assignment** – this represents the full legal assignment of the rights of the seller in the loan. This requires notification and (in some cases) approval of the borrower. This allows a direct contractual nexus to be established between the SPV (as buyer) and the borrower.
- **Participation** – this represents a right to receive the cash flows of the referenced loan. If the sale is undertaken without the knowledge and agreement of the borrower, the participation creates a contractual relationship only between the seller (the original lender) and the SPV (as buyer). This means that if the seller becomes insolvent, the SPV may be an unsecured creditor in bankruptcy *of the selling lender,* without direct recourse to the borrower. This will generally have a rating impact on the structure and will create a rating linkage between the rating *of the seller* and the rating of the notes[38]. For US banks, an additional complication is the right of set off. Under law, the Federal Deposit Insurance Corporation may, in the event of insolvency of a bank, reduce the amount of any outstanding loan by the amount of any deposit held by the institution. In addition, the bank may have other rights of set off, including contractual rights agreed by the borrower. Any set off would have the effect of diminishing the cash flows due to the SPV. This risk can be managed by contractual waivers of rights to set off, or by tracking set off exposure.

Non-disclosure and the absence of a requirement to seek the consent of the borrower dictate that sponsors prefer participation agreements.

---

[38] There is a notable exception to this general rule. The NationsBank Commercial Loan Master Trust had a rating of AAA for its highest rated tranche. This is higher than that of NationsBank, the sponsor bank, which was rated AA−. Fitch IBCA based this rating on a review of the security interest in each eligible loan, the legal documentation and the enforceability of the security interest in the event of the insolvency of the sponsor banks. It concluded that the default risk of the relevant securities was substantially independent of the seller's insolvency. The position for US federally regulated banks appeared to be that where the asset transfer is structured as a participation with a back up of a perfected first security interest, the rights of the purchaser under the participation will be protected in the event of an insolvency of the selling bank under the FIRREA regulations.

The legal problems with participation structures favour assignments. Some hybrid structures have also developed:

- **Contingent assignments** – where the selling bank would only be obligated to assign in the event of a decline in *its credit rating* below an agreed threshold.
- **Credit derivatives/credit linked notes** – where the risk on the loan is synthetically transferred using credit derivative technology.

In the case of credit default swaps, the issues are similar. The major factors are the different documentation, the specific credit events used and the settlement methodology used. In practice, the rating agencies focus upon the following:

- The documentation used is expected to be the standard market ISDA format.
- The credit events (bankruptcy, failure to pay and (types of) restructuring) used are examined[39]. In practice, the major issues relate to the definition of restructuring used.
- The settlement method (physical or cash) is also considered. The robustness and certainty of the process and the impact on assumed recovery rate are key considerations.

These issues are important in establishing the risk of a trigger event and resulting loss sustained by investors.

6.5   CDO Rating – Tranche Modelling & Rating[40]

6.5.1   Concept

The key role of rating agencies is the rating of individual CDO tranches. This is a major factor in determining investor willingness to invest in, and pricing of, each of the classes of securities.

The process of CDO rating requires the analysis of the risk of the underlying credit risks, transaction structure and asset manager. This analysis must then be translated into the risk on specific tranches of debt securities.

---

[39]   In practice, the definition of default under a credit default swap is generally wider than that used by rating agencies. Rating agencies generally define default as bankruptcy, failure to pay and distress exchange of securities.

[40]   For an overview, see Hawkins, Paul "Synthetic Securitisation And Structured Portfolio Credit Derivatives" in Gregory, Jon (Editor) (2003) Credit Derivatives: The Definitive Guide; Risk Publications, London at Chapter 10.

The risk of the portfolio affects the risk of individual tranches differently. This reflects the fact that the risk of loss on the *entire* portfolio is assigned to each tranche *in a specific order of loss*. Equity investors absorb the first losses on the entire portfolio. Holders of mezzanine and senior tranches only incur losses where the losses on the entire portfolio increase above a pre-specified threshold. It is only when the total amount of equity is written down to zero that mezzanine investors suffer loss. Senior investors incur losses only when both equity and mezzanine securities have been written down to zero.

There are differences between different CDO structures including:

- In a cash or fully funded structure (CBO or CLO), the risk is allocated to individual tranches by the payment priority specified in the waterfall. Cash flow (principal or interest) from the underlying portfolio are first used to meet the obligation on senior debt securities. If these obligations are fully met, then proceeds are paid to the subordinated tranches.
- In a synthetic securitisation structure, the settlement under the credit default swap is funded by the assets held by the SPV. The settlements offset against the individual tranches in a specified order. Settlements are offset against the equity tranche, mezzanine tranche and finally senior debt.

The basic methodology used models the loss distribution of the underlying credit portfolio[41]. The portfolio distribution is usually skewed. A given level of losses is expected. This is consistent with the overall credit quality of the portfolio. For typical investment grade portfolios used in CDOs, the distribution will indicate a small amount of losses. The distribution will indicate that zero losses or very high losses are low probability events. The loss distribution on an individual tranche will depend upon some additional factors. It will depend upon the specific order of loss bearing. It will depend upon specific loss thresholds i.e. the part of the loss distribution below and above the relevant tranche. **Exhibit 4.9** sets out the conceptual structure of a portfolio loss distribution and the tranching process.

For a given portfolio, there are a number of tranching possibilities. For each transaction, a portfolio loss distribution is derived. This distribution then forms the basis of establishing the loss profile of each tranche (based on the specified loss threshold). The rating of each tranche can then be derived.

---

[41] For a detailed discussion of the process of credit modelling of a portfolio, see Chapter 6.

The key choices include: the number of tranches; level of subordination; and rating of individual tranches. In practice, the sponsor or arranger will seek the tranche structure that provides the lowest cost of funding. This will require minimisation of the expensive subordinated tranches. In contrast, the investor will seek a tranche structure that provides the highest level of return for a given risk level. This will require reasonable subordination and adequate compensation levels. This tension must be resolved in each CDO transaction. This means that no unique tranching solution generally exists.

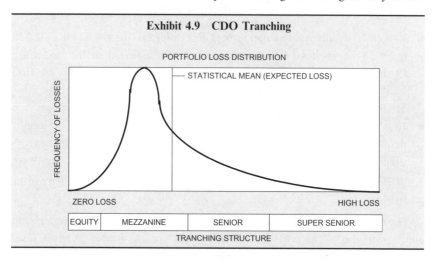

Exhibit 4.9   CDO Tranching

6.5.2   *Rating Agency Modelling*[42]

The approach described is the generic methodology adopted in establishing the rating of CDO securities. There are differences of emphasis between different rating agencies in relation to their analysis. The major differences are in the following areas:

- Rating measure.
- Modelling approach.

---

[42]   The discussion in the Section is designed to provide a brief overview of the rating methodologies used by the major rating agencies. It is not designed to be a comprehensive analysis of their rating approach. Readers should also note that the rating approaches are constantly reviewed and amended. Readers should contact the individual rating agencies for details of the current rating methodologies in general or for a specific transaction.

The rating measure varies between the different agencies. Moody's ratings are based on an assessment of the expected loss of the securities. This entails taking into account the probability of default and the recovery rate (the loss given default). S & P and Fitch ratings are based on an assessment of the probability of default of the securities. This entails only the default probability. This means that where recovery rates vary, Moody's ratings reflect the expected loss. In contrast, S & P and Fitch ratings only reflect default probability and are unaffected by differences in recovery rates.

The different rating measures affect the rating of individual CDO tranches. This reflects the fact that an individual tranche's economic performance is complex. A tranche will only be affected by credit events if losses reach a specified threshold[43]. The threshold is equal to the amount of subordinated securities that must absorb losses before the relevant tranche is affected. The size and subordination of the subordinated tranches therefore determine the economic performance of the specific tranche.

Where the default probability is the primary measure of economic performance (S & P and Fitch), the probability of default on an individual tranche is given by the probability that losses exceed the threshold. This means that the level of subordination is the primary determinant of the default probability and therefore the rating of the securities.

Where expected loss is the primary measure of economic performance (Moody's), both the level of subordination *and the size of the subordinated tranche* are relevant in determining the rating of the securities. For example, if the level of subordination below the tranche being rated is small in size, then the likelihood of losses exceeding the subordinated tranche size is high. This translates into a higher expected loss in case of default on the tranche being rated. If the subordinated tranche is large, then the probability of default may not be different but the chance of losses exceeding the threshold are lower. This translates into a lower expected loss in case of default on the tranche being rated. This means that the level of subordination as well as the size of the subordinated tranches affect the rating of securities.

The individual rating agencies also use different modelling approaches in rating CDO transactions. Some of the key differences in approach are discussed below.

Moody's methodology is based on the concept of the diversity score and the binomial expansion model. The model assumes that any diverse

---

[43] This is also referred to as the "attachment point".

portfolio populated by multiple obligors of different size, maturity and risk can be compared to an equivalent portfolio populated by obligors of equal size, same maturity and risk. The two portfolios have equivalent loss characteristics. This allows the expected loss of any portfolio and tranche to be calculated explicitly.

This approach uses the concept of the diversity score. The diversity score is used to account for default correlation within the portfolio. The diversity score model translates a given portfolio (of different sizes and correlation) into an equivalent portfolio that is uncorrelated. It represents a number of independent bonds that replicates portfolio return. The diversity reflects the distribution of par amounts and default correlation. This process is necessary because if the non-homogenous portfolio has large risk concentrations then the expected loss of subordinated tranches in a CDO (equity and mezzanine) will increase. **Exhibit 4.10** sets out the process of determining the diversity score.

The homogenous equivalent portfolio is defined under the diversity score model. It is an equivalent portfolio of equally sized, equal default probability and uncorrelated obligations. The expected loss of any tranche is then calculated using probability of a nominated number of obligors defaulting. This is done using the binomial expansion technique[44]. The binomial technique is relatively robust and easy to implement. Stress testing is used to supplement the basic methodology. For example, the diversity score deals with intra-industry correlation. Inter-industry correlation is accounted for by stressing default probability rates. Moody's applies

---

[44] The basic binomial model is as follows:
- The probability of default is given by:

$$P_j = \frac{D!}{j!(D-j)!} p^j (1-p)^{D-j}$$

where P_j = probability of having j defaults
D = # of Diversity Bonds in a portfolio
P = weighted average default probability of the pool
- The expected loss is calculated as follows:

$$E(L) = \sum_{j=1}^{D} P_j L_j$$

where L_j represents the loss for the notes under scenario j

recovery rates based on the underlying portfolio to establish loss given default. In some cases, a distribution of recovery rates may also be used.

Moody's also uses a variety of other approaches. Moody's have developed double and multi-binomial models. The basic approach is to divide the portfolio into a series of homogenous smaller portfolios. A diversity score for each of these portfolios is calculated. The binomial expansion method is used to generate the expected losses for the sub-portfolio. The loss distributions of the sub-portfolios are then combined to generate the loss distribution of the entire portfolio. This approach is used primarily for portfolios that are unique or non-homogenous. For example, this approach is used for portfolios that display "credit barbells" – a portfolio that has a high rated and a low rated component. It may also be used

---

Exhibit 4.10   Moody's Diversity Score

The diversity score is calculated using the following steps:

- Each obligation issued by the separate obligors is identified. This entails aggregating the exposures of each obligor into a single obligation with combined size, maturity, weighted average default probability and loss given default.
- The portfolio is then transformed into an equivalent correlated portfolio with equal exposure sizes.
- The obligors are mapped to identified industries. Moody's has approximately 34 industry codes.
- The equivalent number of uncorrelated assets is established by mapping each industry score based on the following table:

Diversity Score for Number of Obligors in the Same Industry

Number of Firms In Same Industry	Diversity Score
1	1.00
2	1.50
3	2.00
4	2.33
5	2.67
6	3.00
7	3.25
8	3.50
9	3.75
10	4.00
> 10	Individually Determined

- The mapped scores are summed to give the diversity score for the portfolio.

where the equity in the capital structure is small. Moody's use Monte Carlo simulations for modelling more complex portfolios (structured finance CDOs or asset based loans on aircraft or ships).

S & P and Fitch do not use the diversity score approach. S & P use Monte Carlo simulations to model the portfolio[45]. The model uses pair-wise correlations[46]. The Monte Carlo simulation uses individual ratings (as a proxy for default probabilities), correlations and recovery rate assumptions to generate the portfolio loss distribution. This allows the generation of loss percentiles on the portfolio. This in turn allows the probability of losses exceeding a given threshold being established. If the stressed default probability is lower than the level for a given rating level, then the tranche is rated at that level. Fitch uses a similar approach based on a Monte Carlo simulation[47]. There are some differences. For example, the Fitch model uses a multiple step simulation. In addition, Fitch uses recovery assumptions that are related to rating category. Both S & P and Fitch use variations on the standard approach for modelling more complex portfolios.

7   CDO Market

7.1   Overview[48]

The CDO market developed in the late 1980s in the form of CBOs. The basic concept that has driven the market since inception is the use of securitisation techniques to repackage bonds or loans into rated asset backed securities for investors. The market has developed rapidly since the

---

[45]   The model is named "CDO Evaluator".

[46]   Historically, S & P captured correlation by stressing default probabilities. For example, higher stress tests were applied to industries that have a higher correlation.

[47]   The model is named 'VECTOR". Prior to the introduction of this model, Fitch used a different approach. It rated CDO tranches based on the minimum level of subordination needed to cover loss. This required analysis of the weighted average portfolio default probability and recovery rate. Correlation was covered by explicit analysis of the largest concentration risks in the portfolio. There were specific concentration limits (by industry, combination of industry and obligor). Fitch required each tranche to be capable of absorbing a certain number of defaults by large obligors.

[48]   See Merritt, Roger, Gerity, Michael, Irving, Alyssa and Lench, Mitchell (6 February 2001) Synthetic CDOs: A Growing Market For Credit Derivatives";

mid 1990s as the CDO market has become integrated with credit derivatives activity generally. The development of synthetic securitisation methodologies has increased the range of risk available in the CDO market. In this Section, the market structure for CDOs is reviewed.

7.2 CDO Transactions – Classification

There are a number of methods for classification of CDO transactions[49]. **Exhibit 4.11** sets out a possible classification scheme.

The CDO market may be classified using the following dimensions:

- **Balance sheet versus arbitrage structure** – the focus is on the motivation/ objectives of the sponsor. The key features of each structure are summarised below:
  1. *Balance sheet structures* – these are transactions that are driven by the desire of the holder of credit risk (generally a bank) to transfer credit

---

Fitch Ratings – Structured Finance, New York. See also Petersen, Michael "Squeezing The Bank Balance Sheet From Both Sides" (September 2000) Euromoney 339–341; Cass, Dwight "CDO Market Looks To New Structures" (December 2000) Risk – Alternative Risk Strategies S23–24; Sandiford, Jane "Building A Structured Credit Solution" (April 2001) FOW 38–48; Petersen, Michael "Master Chefs Of The Credit Market" (June 2001) Euromoney 54–66; Gibson, Lang "Synthetic Multi Sector CBOs" (Winter 2001) FOW/Credit Derivatives 16–23; Handling, Erica "Indebted To Securitisation" in (2001) Finance 2001: Legalease Special Report 59–61; Polyn, Gallagher "Credit Portfolio Products Proliferate" (February 2002) Risk 22–23; Douglas-Jones, Jane "Repackaging Using Credit Derivatives" (February 2002) FOW 41–43; BNP-Paribas "A New Generation Of Credit Derivatives" in (March 2002) Risk – Credit Risk Supplement; Murphy, Eileen "Overview of the CDO Market" in Gregory, Jon (Editor) (2003) Credit Derivatives: The Definitive Guide; Risk Publications, London at Chapter 9; Hawkins, Paul "Synthetic Securitisation And Structured Portfolio Credit Derivatives" in Gregory, Jon (Editor) (2003) Credit Derivatives: The Definitive Guide; Risk Publications, London at Chapter 10; Choudhry, Moorad "Integrating Credit Derivatives And Securitisation Technology: The Collateralised Synthetic Obligation" in Gregory, Jon (Editor) (2003) Credit Derivatives: The Definitive Guide; Risk Publications, London at Chapter 11; Tavakoli, Janet M. (2003) Collateralized Debt Obligations And Structured Finance; John Wiley & Sons, Inc., New Jersey.

[49] For example, see Merritt, Roger, Gerity, Michael, Irving, Alyssa and Lench, Mitchell (6 February 2001) Synthetic CDOs: A Growing Market For Credit Derivatives"; Fitch Ratings – Structured Finance, New York.

risk. The bank seeks regulatory capital relief, credit risk reduction, access to funding and/or reduction in balance sheet size. The underlying assets are typically bank loans (primarily investment grade). In these transactions, the sponsor bank generally holds the first loss or equity component of the structure. This has forced the sponsor bank to focus on investment grade loans. This is in order to reduce the size of the equity component required to ensure favourable regulatory capital treatment. Historically, the structures also attracted insurance companies who used CBO techniques to re-tranche existing assets to obtain capital relief in terms of reserves to be held against assets.

2. *Arbitrage structures* – these are generally secondary market transactions initiated by an investment bank/asset manager designed to take advantage of relative value opportunities in the market. Undervalued assets are purchased and repackaged to lock in a value differential. This value is realised by the sponsor as the spread between the cash flow from the asset portfolio and the servicing requirements on the bonds issued to finance the purchase. Historically, the primary assets used were typically high yield bonds and emerging market bonds. Recent structures have focused on investment grade loans and high yield/leveraged bank loans. Recent structures also use credit default swaps to acquire the underlying credit risk. The senior higher rated tranches are sold to normal asset investors while the subordinated junior tranches are targeted at investors seeking higher returns and/or a leveraged exposure to a pool of credit assets.

- **Funded versus synthetic structure** – this focuses on the methodology used to transfer risk. The key features of each include:
  1. *Funded* – this is a cash funded structure. It is typically structured as a securitisation (such as CLO). The assets are transferred to a SPV. The assets are fully cash funded with the debt issued by the securitisation vehicle. Repayment is directly tied to the cash flow of the assets.
  2. *Synthetic* – this structure uses a credit derivative (generally a credit default swap) to transfer the credit risk to a special purpose vehicle. The synthetic CDO structure simulates the risk behaviour of a cash funded CDO. This is done without a transfer of legal title. The proceeds of the issue by the securitisation vehicle are invested in high grade securities to collateralise the credit default swap.

In practice, synthetic CDOs have emerged as the predominant structure. This reflects the superior economics of the structure.

- **Static versus dynamic (managed) structure** – this focuses on the underlying portfolio of credit risk. It relates to whether the portfolio of credit risk is assembled and maintained without change for the life of the transaction or is actively traded to optimise value. The key features of each approach are as follows:

  1. *Static* – under this structure, the identified portfolio of credit risk is assembled and held to maturity. There is generally no management of the portfolio.

  2. *Dynamic (managed)*[50] – under this structure, the portfolio of credit risk is actively managed by the appointed manager. The use of the manager is designed to optimise the return on the portfolio by trading in the underlying assets. The interest of the manager is sought to be aligned to that of the investors by ensuring that the manager is an equity investor in the transaction. The level of management varies. In most dynamic structures, there are several controls on the level of trading/active management by the manager.

  In practice, there are hybrid structures. These are generally static transactions where there is a ramp-up period to allow assets to be acquired or where prepayments can be replaced/substituted (known as replenishment or substitution structures). This feature is used to deal with prepayment risk or the structure of loan transactions.

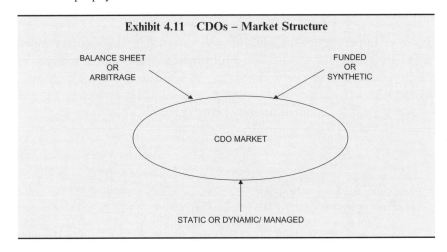

Exhibit 4.11   CDOs – Market Structure

BALANCE SHEET OR ARBITRAGE

FUNDED OR SYNTHETIC

CDO MARKET

STATIC OR DYNAMIC/ MANAGED

---

[50] The basic model has evolved from the market value CDO structure (see discussion above).

7.3 CDO Structures – Market Evolution[51]

The types of CDO structures that are undertaken reflect the motivations of the originators of credit risk (primarily banks) and investors (fixed income fund managers). The original driver for the market was the repackaging of high yield bonds for placement with investors. This was complemented by the demand from investors for high yielding investments based on repackaged high yield or emerging market securities. In the late 1990s, the market was driven by demand from banks to transfer credit risk and obtain regulatory capital relief. Subsequently, the market has been driven by demand from investors for credit based investments.

The initial driver in the recent period of market activity was bank requirements to transfer credit risk. This was motivated primarily by capital management and credit risk management requirements. This meant that balance sheet CDOs were a major part of market activity. Activity focused on static, synthetic balance sheet CDOs originated by banks.

As the market developed, the structure of the market changed. There was a shift to arbitrage CDOs. This reflected increased demand from investors for structured credit exposure. It also reflected the fact that the balance sheet CDO market was rapidly saturated. Increasingly, banks were unwilling to transfer credit risk to investors. This reflected the fact that such transfers reduced earnings and there was limited scope for utilisation of any capital released.

The arbitrage CDO market is largely investor driven. It also provides attractive opportunities for banks/dealers to generate incremental earning from structuring skills, origination/distribution skills and investment in the structures. This market is dominated by synthetic, arbitrage structures. **Exhibit 4.12** sets out a typical structure designed to provide investors with leveraged exposure to an underlying loan portfolio[52].

---

[51] See Gibson, Lang "Synthetic Multi-Sector CBOs" (Winter 2001) Credit Derivatives Supplement – FOW 16–23; Ferry, John "CDO Evolution Gathers Pace" (January 2004) Credit Risk Supplement – Risk S2–S3; Nasser, Tarek and Tierney, John F. (29 April 2003) Synthetic CDOs: Recent Market Developments; Deutsche Bank.

[52] The major banks/dealers established arbitrage CDO programs to service investor requirements. For example, the CSLT program (Chase Manhattan), SEQUILS/MINCs (JP Morgan), SERVES (Bank of America) and ECLIPSE (Citibank).

Over time, the CDO market has become more complex. This reflects both the type of activity (for example, balance sheet or arbitrage) and the structures used. In the next Section, the different structures that have proliferated are examined.

Exhibit 4.12   Repackaged Credit Assets – SEQUILS/MINCS Structure

In April 1999, JP Morgan launched the SEQUILS/MINCS transactions[53]. The objective of the transaction was to allow investors to invest in leveraged loans.

The structure operates as follows:

- SEQUILS and MINCS are special purpose vehicles.
- SEQUILS issued US$712.5 million in AA rated senior notes. The proceeds were used to purchase leveraged loans from the primary market, the secondary market and from JP Morgan's own portfolio.
- SEQUILs entered into a credit default swap on US$114 million (16% of the total portfolio) with JP Morgan. SEQUILS pays a fee out of the interest income received from the underlying portfolio of leveraged loans. The credit enhancement provided through the credit default swap enables the portfolio to achieve the high investment grade ratings on the notes issued out of the SEQUILS vehicle.
- JP Morgan, in turn, entered into a transaction with MINCS to reduce the credit risk assumed under its credit default swap with SEQUILS. This was done through the issue of credit linked notes by JP Morgan to MINCS. The payments on the credit linked notes are linked to the credit performance of the underlying leveraged loan portfolio in SEQUILS. MINCS finances the purchase of the credit linked notes through the issue of US$114 million of BBB rated notes to investors.
- The transaction operates as follows:
  1. In the event there is no default on the underlying loans, SEQUILS receives the interest on the loans which is used to make payments to investors in the notes and JP Morgan under the credit default swap. JP Morgan uses the fee received to make payment to MINCS, that in turn uses the receipts to finance payments to noteholders. At maturity, the cash flow from maturing loans is used to make principal repayments to SEQUILS noteholders. At maturity, JP Morgan repays the principal of the credit linked notes to MINC that in turns repays the noteholders in MINCS.
  2. In the event of default on the underlying loans, SEQUILS claims under the credit default swap with JP Morgan (to a maximum of US$114 million). JP Morgan covers any default payment to SEQUILS by reducing the principal repaid to MINCS under the credit linked notes. MINCS, in turn, reduces the principal paid on the notes issued to investors by MINCS.

---

[53]   See Mahtani, Arun "JPM Launches Next Generation Credit Vehicle" (17 April 1999) International Financing Review Issue 1279 99.

The structure of the notes issued is as follows:

- All notes issued by SEQUILS and MINCS are floating rate notes with a legal final maturity of 12 years.
- Notes issued by SEQUILS were offered as a standard structured AA rated issue to investors at a small yield premium to comparable issues.
- Notes issued by MINCS were offered to investors at an expected return of LIBOR plus 400 bps. The expected coupon was LIBOR plus 150 bps and a potential return of LIBOR plus 550/600 bps.

The SEQUILS/MINCS vehicle structures were cash flow based. This contrasts with market value based structures. The cash flow based structures rely on expected cash flows generated from the underlying asset pool. In contrast, market value structures rely on changes in market values of the underlying assets. Cash flow based structures are more stable in high stress scenarios where market values may move in a very volatile manner[54].

The objective of the structure was to provide investors access to a diversified portfolio of leveraged loans. The structure also effectively bifurcates the returns – SEQUILS investors obtain exposure to the lower risk component while MINCS investors obtain exposure to the higher risk elements through assuming the first loss position[55].

8   CDO Structures – Variations

8.1   Overview

As noted above, the CDO market has come to be dominated by synthetic securitisation transactions. The other CDO structures continue to be used in certain circumstances.

The synthetic securitisation structure has proved attractive and popular. It has rapidly become the accepted format for the transfer of credit risk. This reflects the significant advantages of synthetic securitisation in structuring and transferring credit risk. Its dominance is based on its superior economics and the availability of participants willing to assume the super senior risk tranche at attractive pricing.

The market volumes have been impressive. For example, JP Morgan is estimated to have issued approximately US$2 billion in synthetic CLO BISTRO offerings, covering the credit risk of portfolios totalling in excess of

---

[54]   See discussion in relation to CBOs/CLOs below.
[55]   MINCS investors are approximately 6 times leveraged to the performance of the portfolio. This is similar to the logic of all tranched CDO transactions.

US$20 billion during 1998[56]. Other banks/dealers and investment banks launched similar structures. Synthetic securitisation transactions have been undertaken in Europe[57], Asia-Pacific[58], Australia[59] and South Africa[60]. Investors throughout the global financial markets are now active investors in CDO investments.

As the market has developed, a wide range of product structures has emerged. The major structural variations within the CDO market focus upon the following areas:

- Differences in the type of risk that is being transferred. This is at two different levels:
  1. Different types of underlying credit assets have been used as the basis for CDO transactions including mortgage loans, loans to small and medium enterprises ("SME"), asset backed loans and credit risk on derivative transactions. This is in addition to more traditional credit assets such as corporate loans and bonds.
  2. CDOs of structured assets including asset backed securities, CDOs, credit indexes and managed funds.
- Differences in the actual structure of the transaction itself, in particular, different forms of synthetic securitisation transactions. This included synthetic securitisations undertaken without a SPV. It also includes single tranche CDOs. This is where the investment banks do not place the

---

[56] See Booth, Tamzin "The Good, The Bad And The Ugly" (January 1999) Institutional Investor 65–66 at 66; "Credit Derivatives: House Of The Year" (March 2001) Risk 14.

[57] For perspectives on European synthetic CLOs, see Parolai, Richard and Lewis, Jonathan "The Mechanics of European Synthetic CLOs" (3–9 August 1999) Financial Products 8–9. See also (27 July–2 August 1999) Financial Products 3; (10–16 August 1999) Financial Products 1–2; "Warburg Launches Tip of Eisberg" (10 October 1998) International Financing Review Issue 1254 39; "European Credit Risk Hedge" (March 1999) Global Finance at 27.

[58] See discussion of Asian potential for synthetic securitisation in "Asian Banks Get Taste For Synthetic CLOs" (9 October 1999) International Financing Review Issue 1304 97; Sawyer, Nick "A New Twist To ABS" (February 2002) Asia Risk 27–29.

[59] See Wood, Duncan "CBA Secures First For Credit Risk Exposure" (August 1999) Asia Risk 8; see transaction called Medallion Trust 5 July 1999.

[60] See (May 2002) "Fresco 2002"; Fitch Rating – Structured Finance, Pre-Sale Report; Bolin, Lynn "South Africa Sees First Synthetic Vehicle Securitisation" (19–25 June 2002) Financial Products 4.

complete structure initially but hedge the underlying risk in the credit default swap market.

Each of these variations is considered in this Section.

There have also been variations in the types of CDO securities issued. Traditional CDO structures use fixed or floating rate securities. Inflation index linked CDO securities have also been issued[61]. These structures have been driven by demand from pension funds and insurance companies[62].

8.2 CDO Variations – Non Standard Assets

Traditional CDO structures are based on underlying portfolios of corporate (investment grade and high yield) or emerging market bonds and loans. In recent years the CDO framework has been used to transfer the risk of a variety of other assets. This entails the use of synthetic securitisation to transfer credit risk on different types of underlying portfolios.

Transactions have included:

- Portfolios of mortgages (both residential and commercial).
- Loans to SME's
- Asset backed financing transactions.
- Credit exposures on derivatives transactions.

Portfolios of mortgages (both residential and commercial) are traditionally securitised using a fully funded/cash structure. In recent years, synthetic securitisation of mortgage portfolios has been completed.

This entails the use of a credit default swap to transfer the credit risk of commercial or residential mortgages into a SPV for the purpose of securitisation. Where the underlying asset is commercial mortgages, the reference obligation in the credit default swap is specified as a corporate loan secured by real property. This enables the seller of protection (the SPV and ultimately the investor) to obtain access to the underlying collateral for the loan. A similar process can be applied to residential mortgages.

The use of synthetic securitisation structures is driven by the significant advantages of the credit default swap as the basis for risk transfer. It avoids the need to transfer the underlying assets. This is especially attractive in

---

[61]   For a discussion of inflation linked bonds and derivatives, see Das, Satyajit (2004) Swaps/Financial Derivatives 3rd Edition; John Wiley, Singapore at Chapter 69.

[62]   See Wolcott, Rachel "New CDO Adds Variety To Linker Market" (August 2004) Risk 14.

Europe where complex regulations and tax issues made traditional asset sales difficult.

The market commenced in late 1998 when JP Morgan and Commerzbank completed synthetic securitisation transactions on mortgage portfolios. The transactions used credit default swaps to transfer the default risk on mortgages to institutional investors. The JP Morgan transaction (reported to be around US$1.5 billion) was undertaken on behalf of a German bank. The Commerzbank transaction (reported to be around US$1.0 billion) was in respect of its own portfolio. The transactions were similar in structure to the basic synthetic securitisation format described and were driven by the desire to achieve regulatory capital relief[63]. A significant number of these types of transactions have been successfully completed.

Traditional CDO structures have used credit assets where the obligors are large well known, (frequently) rated corporations and sovereign entities. Synthetic securitisation structures have been used to transfer risk on SME loans[64].

SME loans present special difficulties, including:

- The underlying obligations are unlikely to be rated. This necessitates reliance on internal rating of the originating institution or sponsor.
- There is generally a wide variety of transactions including fully drawn loans, revolving credit facilities, receivables, asset backed loans/leases and guarantees. The facilities may be secured or unsecured. Where secured, the collateral is varied including real estate, plant/equipment, receivables and personal guarantees. The documentation of these transactions is also frequently non-standardised.
- There are issues about geographic concentration and default correlation. The SME portfolios are generally geographically specific, being confined to a country. This is similar to mortgage portfolios. However, unlike residential mortgage portfolios, SME loans are insufficiently granular to allow reliance on actuarial analysis of historical loss performance.
- SME loans present special challenges under credit default swap documentation in establishing credit events and recovery levels/loss given default.

---

[63] See "First Synthetic Securitisations Surface" (25 January 1999) Derivatives Week vol VIII no 4 1,14.

[64] There is no consistent definition of SME loans. For example, in Europe, loans to usually private corporations with annual sales of say, Euro 50 million or less, are generally classified as SME loans.

CDOs based on SME loans have been cash or synthetic structures. As in the broader CDO market, synthetic structures have emerged as the preferred format. Transactions completed include:

- A number of CDOs have been undertaken with the sponsorship of governments/supra-nationals. **Exhibit 4.13** sets out an example of this type of transaction undertaken by Germany's Kreditanstalt fur Wiederaufbau ("Kf W")[65].
- Individual banks have completed SME loan CDOs. **Exhibit 4.14** sets out an example of a transaction undertaken by UBS[66]. A number of similar transactions have been completed[67].
- Transactions linked to a SME default index have also been completed. Gerling Credit Insurance (an affiliate of insurance company Gerling Konzern AG) hedged the credit risk on small to medium sized company exposures through an issue arranged by Goldman Sachs[68]. The Euro denominated transaction entailed the issue of a series of 3 year credit linked FRNs. There were three classes of notes rated Aa2, A2 and Baa2. The payoffs on the FRNs were linked to a reference portfolio of over 90,000 obligors in Europe. The investor's returns were contingent on annual insolvency rates remaining below nominated levels. If annual insolvency rates exceed 2.1%, 2.6% or 3.3%, then the principal and coupons in each of the three classes of notes decline according to the extent of any excess in accordance with a formula. In addition, if the cumulative losses exceed 5.4%, 5.9% or 6.6%, then the principal and coupons in each of the three classes of notes also decline according to the

---

[65]   The European Investment Fund and a number of state sponsored entities have facilitated SME CDOs. The support has included guaranteeing tranches of CDOs.

[66]   See Abed, Kamal "UBS Structures First Swiss Synthetic CLO" (4–10 July 2000) Financial Products 3.

[67]   For example, Deutsche Bank has undertaken a number of SME loan based CDOs – CORE and CAST. CORE was structured as a cash securitisation. CAST was structured as a credit linked note CLO. See Abed, Kamal "Deutsche Switches To Synthetic Securitisation of Mittelstand Loans" (16-2 November 1999) Financial Products 1,16; Crabbe, Matthew "Deutsche Bank's Cast Of Thousands" (December 1999) Risk 10. The major transactions were undertaken in Europe. The structure is increasingly used in other markets. In 2003, the Commonwealth Bank of Australia undertook a synthetic securitisation of A$2.5 billion of SME loans; see Williams, Marion "The Rise Of Securitisation" (February 2004) CFO-Board Briefing 4–7.

[68]   See Rhode, William "Credit, The Final Frontier" (May 1999) Risk 7.

extent of any excess in accordance with a formula. The solvency index is compiled by Dun and Bradstreet. The major driver for these transactions is the ability to hedge the credit exposure on a large diverse unrated universe of obligors on a cost effective basis[69].

Synthetic securitisation transactions have also been used to transfer the credit risk on asset backed financing. The major types of loans used in synthetic securitisation transactions are secured over transportation assets (aircraft or ships). **Exhibit 4.15** sets out a description of a transaction (Leonardo) undertaken by the Italian bank BCI to transfer risk on a portfolio of aircraft loans. A synthetic securitisation of a portfolio of shipping loans has also been completed[70].

Transactions involving asset backed loans require the credit default swap to be highly structured to address the specific underlying credit asset. The rating of the synthetic securitisation structure on asset backed loans is also more complex. This reflects the fact that there is significant reliance on the future value of the underlying asset. If an obligor defaults then the loss (if any) suffered depends on the value of the asset pledged as collateral. The portfolio correlation is also more complex. This reflects the fact that the obligors will tend to be from the same industry (e.g. airlines). This means that there will be significant default correlation and also correlation between defaults and re-sale value of the assets. This means the modelling task is more involved. In practice, the rating agencies use specialised models based on Monte Carlo simulation to rate these transactions.

Traditional CDO structures are based on the credit risk from simple credit assets such as loans or bonds. An increasing amount of credit risk is in the form of counterparty risk; primarily, credit exposures on derivatives.

The underlying credit risk in a derivative transaction is complex[71]. The major issues are that it is stochastic and can take positive or negative (no credit exposure) form. In addition, the exposure is not known with certainty at the time the transaction is entered into. In effect, derivative credit exposure is a complex combination of credit risk *and market risk*. For complete risk transfer, both risks need to be simultaneously transferred. In practice, this has

---

[69] The transaction is similar to credit index based CDOs discussed later in the Chapter.

[70] See Hoppe, Stephanie "Shipping Industry Sees Its First Synthetic Loan Securitisation" (29 August–3 September 2002) Financial Products 3.

[71] See Das, Satyajit (2004) Swaps/Financial Derivatives 3rd Edition; John Wiley, Singapore at Chapters 21 and 22.

proved difficult. Swap guarantees can be used to transfer the entire credit risk of a derivative transaction[72]. These transactions are difficult to arrange.

Synthetic securitisation structures have been used to hedge the credit risk on counterparties in derivative transactions. **Exhibit 4.16** sets out an example of a CDO securitising derivative counterparty credit exposures. The structures used do not generally seek to deal with the variability of the derivative exposure fully. In practice, synthetic securitisations of derivative credit exposure have been used to shift risk up to a given amount. The sponsor has retained the market risk element of the credit risk above the specified amount.

These transactions have been used to free up inter-bank trading lines and enhance additional trading capacity[73]. The structures have been attractive with investors primarily because of the high credit quality of the bank counterparties included in the reference portfolio. The structures are also attractive as they allow banks to hedge the credit risk at a lower cost than that achievable through the credit default swap market. The market in derivatives counterparty risk securitisation is gradually developing[74].

8.3 CDO Variations – Structured Assets

8.3.1 Overview

The range of assets used in CDOs has changed dramatically in recent years. In the previous Section, the focus was on credit risk from transactions other

---

Exhibit 4.13   CDO – SME Loans: Example 1

Kreditanstalt fur Wiederaufbau ("KfW") is a development finance institution in Germany. The Federal Republic of Germany guarantees KfW's obligations. KfW have the following CDO programs designed to securitise the credit risk of SME loans:

- **PROMISE (Program for Mittelstand Loan Securitisation)** – this program is used for SME loans.
- **PROVIDE** – this program is used for non-Pfandbriefe eligible residential mortgages.

---

[72] See Chapter 2.

[73] UBS (Alpine transactions) and Deutsche Bank (Eirles transactions) have undertaken these types of transactions. However, transactions designed to achieve regulatory capital relief have also been undertaken (ABN-Amro's Amstel transaction). See Thind, Sarfraz "Derivatives Securitisation Takes Off" (June 2004) Risk 58–60.

[74] See Thind, Sarfraz "Derivatives Securitisation Takes Off" (June 2004) Risk 58–60.

The basic structure is set out below:

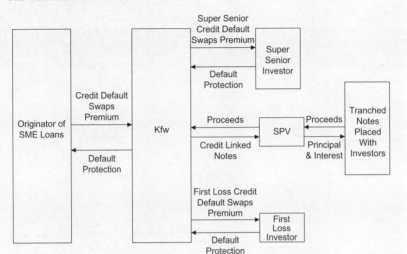

The key elements of the structure are as follows:

- KfW (either alone or working with arrangers) consolidates SME loans from a number of originators.
- KfW acquires the risk of the underlying portfolio through a credit default swap where KfW sells protection on the underlying portfolio to the originator bank. KfW is 0% risk weighted under Basel 1 capital rules because of its government guarantee. This makes it economic for KfW to act as the counterparty to the credit default swap.
- KfW then transfers the risk to third parties in tranched form:
  1. The first loss and super senior risk is transferred through credit default swaps.
  2. The intermediate risk is transferred by KfW issuing credit linked notes to a SPV[75]. The notes are linked to the underlying SME loans.
  3. The SPV then issues tranched notes to the ultimate investors.
  4. Investor return is based on the performance of the underlying SME portfolio.

KfW also uses an alternative structure that is a pure synthetic securitisation. In this structure, the intermediate risk is also transferred using an unfunded credit default swap. The SPV used the proceeds of the tranched notes to purchase high quality securities[76] to collateralise the credit default SPV under which it sells protection to KfW.

---

[75] This structure is identical to the credit linked note CLO described earlier in the Chapter.

[76] This can take the form of KfW medium term notes or bonds which are guaranteed by the German government and rated AAA.

Exhibit 4.14   CDO – SME Loans: Example 2

In 2000, UBS AG ("UBS") used a structure (HAT (Helvetic Asset Trust) AG ("HAT") to transfer the risk on a Swiss Franc ("CHF") 2,500 million reference portfolio of SME loans. The structure appeared to be driven primarily by the desire to reduce the concentration risk of its loan portfolio to this segment.

The basic structure was as follows:

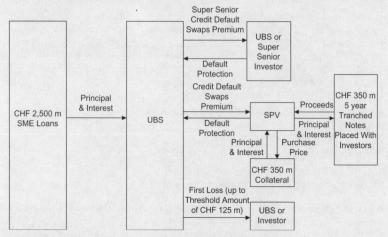

The key elements of the structure were as follows:

- UBS used a portion (CHF 2.5 billion) of its underlying Swiss SME portfolio as the basis for the transaction.
- UBS transferred its credit risk using a synthetic securitisation structure as follows:
  1. UBS retained the equity of the structure of CHF 125 million (5%). It is not known whether UBS retained this risk initially or for the term of the transaction.
  2. UBS entered into a credit default swap with a SPV (HAT) for CHF 350 million (14%). This was designed to hedge its exposure on the underlying portfolio to losses above CHF 125 million up to a maximum of CHF 350 million.
  3. UBS either retained or hedged the super-senior exposure (CHF 2.025 billion or 19%) on the portfolio.
- HAT issued 5 year tranched notes in the market to investors. HAT issued CHF 250 million of senior notes and CHF 100 million of subordinated notes.
- HAT invested the issue proceeds in CHF 350 million of AAA rated bonds issued by Oesterreichische Kontrollbank, guaranteed by the Republic of Austria. The bonds were used to collateralise the performance of HAT under the credit default swap with UBS.
- Investors in the bonds issued by HAT relied on the cash flows from the collateral and credit default swap to make principal and interest payments to investors. In effect, the investors assumed the risk of the collateral and the underlying reference portfolios (for losses above the threshold amount).

The structure of the transaction provides an insight into the complexity of securitising SME portfolios:

- The structures used UBS's internal rating system to evaluate and communicate the credit quality of the SME obligors.
- Obligors are not identified individually.
- The portfolio was subject to diversity requirements (using Moody's industry diversity score measure). This included maximum industry concentration limits, maximum individual exposure limits and geographical diversification requirements.
- The structure of the credit default swap was not standard and included the following provisions:
  1. Credit events were limited to bankruptcy and failure to pay.
  2. Default payment was based on a cash settlement based on a fixed 50% recovery rate.

Exhibit 4.15   CDO – Asset Backed Loans[77]

1. Overview

In 2001, BCI (an Italian bank) undertook the first synthetic securitisation of an asset backed portfolio. The portfolio consisted of aircraft financing and aviation industry loans. The transaction was done in conjunction with Merrill Lynch International ("Merrill Lynch"). The transaction undertaken through Leonardo Synthetic Plc ("Leonardo") was structured to obtain capital relief and free up credit lines. The transaction was designed to allow investors to obtain access to a credit portfolio consisting of airlines in Europe, US and Asia.

2. Structure

The transaction structure was similar to that used in C*STAR and other European synthetic securitisation transactions[78].

The basic structure was as follows:

- BCI assembled a portfolio of US$1 billion of aircraft related credit risk.
- BCI hedged its risk on this portfolio through a credit default swap with Merrill Lynch on 100% of the portfolio.
- Merrill Lynch purchased protection on 19.0% of the portfolio from Leonardo. The funded portion of the credit transfer was 15.5%.

---

[77] The author wishes to thank Stepania Allegra, Fedele Cova and Valentina Cicerone (of IntesaBCI) for providing information on the above transaction.

[78] See **Exhibit 4.6** above.

- Leonardo issued the following tranches of notes:
  1. Euro 56 million Class A notes (rated AAA/Aaa/AAA) bearing interest at Euribor + 45 bps (5.0% of the portfolio).
  2. Euro 84 million Class B notes (rated AA/Aa2/AA) bearing interest at Euribor + 70 bps (7.5% of the portfolio).
  3. Euro 33.6 million Class C notes (rated A/A2/A) bearing interest at Euribor + 115 bps (3.0% of the portfolio).

  The Class A, B and C notes were publicly placed. The credit default swap of Euro 35.3 million (rated BBB/Baa2/BBB) representing 3.5% of the portfolio was privately placed.
- The notes were in descending order of seniority. The payment of principal and interest on the notes is linked to the credit performance on the underlying portfolio. Losses on the portfolio are allocated sequentially to the notes in reverse order of seniority.
- The proceeds of the note issues were invested in Italian government bonds and a cash deposit with BCI. The Class A and B notes are secured over Italian government bonds. The Class C notes are secured over the BCI deposit. The collateral is pledged in favour of BCI under the credit default swap with Merrill Lynch.
- There was a super senior unfunded portion that was hedged by Merrill Lynch with a third party.

The risk transfer within the structure is set out below.

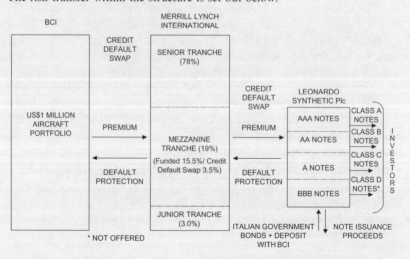

The transaction structure features a number of non-standard features reflecting the nature of the underlying obligations, including:

- The reference obligations included loans and secured letters of credit. The major part of the portfolio was secured over aircraft.

- The notes have a final legal maturity of 2019 but the expected average lives are significantly shorter.
- BCI and Leonardo have the ability to call the notes unconditionally after 5 and 12 years. BCI and Leonardo have the right to call the notes after year 3 in case of regulatory change and at any time if the amount of reference obligations falls below 10% of the initial notional principal.
- Up until December 2005, BCI has the right to replenish the portfolio if there are prepayments or substitute 10% of the obligations consistent with rating guidelines.
- The definition of credit events differs from standard ISDA credit default swap confirmation language. The primary credit events are failure to pay and bankruptcy. The investor is only exposed to a failure to pay by the airline. Investors have no exposure to a failure to pay of any special purpose entity used in the financing[79].
- Default payments (credit losses) are calculated as follows:

1. For secured obligations, the difference between the value of the reference obligation and BCI's share of the aircraft value. If BCI cannot recover the aircraft and realise value within 12 months, then the payment is calculated using the appraisal value of the aircraft. This was designed to limit the period of exposure to repossession for the investors.

2. For unsecured obligations, the difference between the value of the reference obligation and the market value of a reference obligation 60 days after the credit event.

3. Asset Portfolio

The initial portfolio consisted of 31 obligors from 20 countries. 7 reference entities were each more than 3% of the portfolio. 3 obligors contributed over 40% of the total portfolio. The longest obligation in the portfolio was 14 years with an average life of 5 years. There were a total of 153 aircraft from 8 manufacturers represented in the portfolio. The average loan to value ratio was below 70% and fell quite rapidly. Unsecured obligations were only 3% of the portfolio. Unsecured obligations can only be replaced/substituted with secured obligations.

4. Credit Enhancement

The structure uses the first loss provision, the privately placed credit default swap and the tranched notes to enhance the credit structure of the portfolio. BCI obtains credit risk protection and capital relief directly through the credit default swap with Merrill Lynch.

---

[79] The underlying aircraft financing structures (Japanese leveraged and operating leases, US leveraged leases, ownership or commission foreign sales corporation arrangements) frequently use special purpose vehicles.

Exhibit 4.16   CDO – Derivative Credit Risk

In 2000, UBS used a structure – Alpine Partners ("Alpine") – to transfer the credit risk under derivative transactions[80]. The objective was for UBS to hedge its credit exposure to a number of counterparties.

The structure was as follows:

- UBS entered into a credit default swap covering UBS London Branch's credit exposure to its counterparties to Alpine. The reference pool consisted of 1,075 transactions with 59 counterparties.
- Alpine issued 4 tranches of amortising floating rate notes ("FRN") totalling US$750 million. The rating of the notes ranged from AAA/AA (for the senior tranche) and BBB+/BB (for the 2 mezzanine tranches). The equity tranche was unrated. The notes had a final maturity of between 9 and 10 years.
- It is understood the equity tranche was taken by UBS[81].
- Alpine paid the issue proceeds to UBS against a promise to make payments to service the FRN issues.
- In case of default, UBS's obligation to pay the FRN investors was reduced. This effectively transferred the counterparty credit risk to the investors.

The structure of the transaction provides an insight into the complexity of securitising credit exposure under derivative transactions:

- Obligors are not identified individually. The initial portfolio was subject to minimum and average credit rating and diversity requirements. This included maximum industry concentration limits, maximum individual exposure limits and geographical diversification requirements.
- There was a maximum exposure limit for each counterparty. The aggregate exposure limit for all reference entities was equal to the face value of notes issued as of the transaction commencement date.
- The covered transactions were interest rate and currency derivative transactions. It was a requirement that covered transactions be documented under the market standard ISDA Master Agreement[82].
- The counterparty pool can be altered by UBS subject to controls and compliance with pre-specified exposure and credit quality tests. The ability to modify the pool

---

[80]   See Cass, Dwight "UBS Securitises Swap Portfolio Via New SPV" (November 2000) Risk 6–7; Sandiford, Jane "New Synthetic From UBS" (16–22 January 2001) Financial Products 2.

[81]   See Jeffrey, Christopher "UBS Structures Second Alpine Risk Capacity 'Enhancer'" (May 2003) Risk 9.

[82]   See Das, Satyajit (2004) Swaps/Financial Derivatives 3rd Edition; John Wiley, Singapore at Chapter 30.

is presumably useful in managing the market risk component of counter-party credit risk. For example, if market price changes convert the credit exposure with a specific counterparty to a negative amount (UBS has no credit exposure) then the bank may want to substitute that counterparty within the reference pool.

- The structure of the credit default swap was not standard and included the following provisions:
  1. Credit events were bankruptcy, repudiation/moratorium and failure to pay on a covered transaction or other obligation.
  2. Default payment was based on a cash settlement mechanism. If a credit event occurred then the UBS obligation to pay Alpine (and ultimately the investors) was reduced by an amount. This amount was equal to the replacement value of all transactions (after netting) under the relevant ISDA master. If the replacement value was negative (that is, UBS was obligated to pay the defaulted counterparty), then the replacement value was set to zero. The payment amount was capped by the pre-specified exposure level for that counterparty[83].
  3. Recovery rates were based on actual recoveries made. In the case of a credit event, the payment obligation was reduced by the full amount of the loss (up to the maximum amount). The investor was entitled to receive any payment received by UBS from the defaulted counterparty. This was structured as a participation agreement whereby the investor participated in any recovery.

In 2003, UBS undertook a further transaction – Alpine II[84]. This entailed a 7 year amortising Euro 1.5 billion transaction based on counterparty credit risk on derivatives. The reference pool was 75 counterparties. The structure was similar but there were the following differences:

- A Euro 1.25 billion super senior credit default swap was used to lower the cost of the risk transfer.
- The structure allowed the inclusion of counterparty credit risk originating from equity and commodity (energy) derivatives.

---

[83] This effectively means that UBS only transfers the credit risk up to the maximum amount. If changes in market risk dictate that the UBS exposure is larger than this amount, it is unhedged.

[84] See Jeffrey, Christopher "UBS Structures Second Alpine Risk Capacity 'Enhancer'" (May 2003) Risk 9.

than conventional loans or bonds. In recent years, a range of structured assets has also been used for CDOs.

This change has been most marked in arbitrage CDOs. The underlying assets used in arbitrage CDOs traditionally include high yield bonds/loans and emerging market bonds. In recent years, the focus has been substantially on investment grade bonds and bank loans (including leveraged loans[85]). The range of credit risk available in these underlying markets is finite. This has led to experimentation with a range of structured assets[86]. Assets used in recent years as the underlying assets for arbitrage CDOs include[87]:

- Asset backed securities.
- CDOs
- Credit index linked CDOs
- Private equity/hedge funds
- Equity default swaps.

The key drivers underlying this shift are interesting. Some of the factors are secular while others are structural in nature.

Secular factors include the range of credit risk available in the corporate bond and credit default swap market. The limited range of underlying obligors proved a significant limitation on CDO market development. In addition, the high levels of default, specifically in the US credit markets around 2001/2002, made investors wary of CDOs based on corporate bonds and loans. This drove the move to CDOs of more structured assets. Some of the activity was also driven by market conditions. For example, the high risk premium (often well above likely loss expectations) and liquidity premium on structured assets (in particular, CDO tranches) allowed the structuring of certain transactions. Similarly the need for liquidity in certain industries (private equity) promoted the application of CDO technology.

Structural factors include:

- The default and recovery rate experience of ABS securities that make them especially attractive for use in CDOs.

---

[85]   Traditionally, in the US domestic market, loans with an interest rate of at least 150 bps over LIBOR are referred to as leveraged loans.

[86]   See BNP-Paribas "A New Generation Of Credit Derivatives" in (March 2002) Risk – Credit Risk Supplement.

[87]   Other assets suggested include pooled loans; see Wilkinson, Barrie and Kuritzes, Andrew "Can Loan Pooling Rescue CLOs?" (February 2002) Risk 36–37.

- The migration risk on ABS securities is different to that of corporate risk.
- The low default correlation between ABS and other credit risk is also useful.

The impact of some secular factors has already started to decline. Rapid compression in the credit spreads on ABS (in part driven by the demand from originators of structured finance CDOs) forced pricing convergence with CDOs of traditional assets.

8.3.2 Structured Finance/ABS CDOs[88]

Concept

Structured finance transactions are CDOs of ABS/structured finance issues[89]. The structure of structured finance CDOs is similar to that used with conventional CDOs. Originally, the structured finance CDOs were designed as funded transactions. As discussed below, synthetic structured finance CDOs have also been undertaken.

The boundaries between traditional CDOs and structured finance CDOs have become less clearly defined. Conventional CDOs based on corporate credit risk often included a "bucket" or limit for ABS.

Structure

The key elements of structured finance CDOs include:

- **Underlying assets** – the primary assets used are ABS. The major types of ABS used in structured finance include:
  1. Residential mortgage backed securities.
  2. Commercial mortgage backed securities.
  3. Consumer ABS (e.g. credit card backed securities, automobile loans).
  4. Commercial ABS (e.g. equipment backed securities).
  5. CDO securities[90].

---

[88] See Ganapati, Sumita and Tejwani, Gaurav (3 July 2002) Structured Credit Strategies: The Case For Structured Finance CDOs; Lehman Brothers – Structured Credit Research, New York; (11 March 2003) A Guide To Structured Finance CDOs; Credit Suisse First Boston, New York. See also Gibson, Lang "Synthetic Multi-Sector CBOs" (Winter 2001) FOW/Credit Derivatives 16–23.

[89] The market is often referred to as the re-securitisation market.

[90] This is a separate market referred to as the CDO of CDO or CDO^2 market; see discussion late in this Chapter.

In practice, structured finance CDOs have focused on ABS CDOs (using diversified portfolios of asset backed securities) and CMBS CDOs (using primarily real estate portfolios such as collateralised mortgage backed securities and real estate investment trusts). ABS CDO transactions have been based on ABS mezzanine and subordinate tranches.

- **Portfolio structure** – the precise composition of a structured finance CDO varies. Key factors include the market pricing of different ABS, requirements of CDO investors and the asset manager's specific skill set. In practice, structured finance CDOs specify a range of ABS that can be included in the portfolio. There are limits on individual types of ABS that may be included in the portfolio. Key portfolio structure guidelines are specified by the rating agency rating the individual transaction. Key guidelines include:
    1. *Portfolio credit quality* – this is designed to ensure that the average credit quality of the portfolio remains at or above a specified level. It is specified in terms of WARF limits and minimum rating requirements.
    2. *Portfolio diversity* – this is designed to restrict sector concentration and ensure adequate diversification of the portfolio. It is specified in terms of measures such as diversity scores as well as maximum single issue, industry concentration and specific limits on particular types of securities.
    3. *Single servicer concentration limits* – this reflects specific issues with the structure of ABS transactions. In ABS transactions, the issuer as servicer is responsible for loan payments and management of delinquent payments. Financial distress of the servicer may affect the servicing quality and ultimately the loss performance on the underlying assets. In practice, this risk is managed by placing a limitation on exposure to a specific servicer based on the credit quality of the entity.
    4. *Cash flow characteristics* – this is designed to ensure that the asset portfolio generates sufficient income to service the liability structure of the transaction. It is generally specified in terms of minimum weighted average coupon/spread on assets. There are usually also limits on fixed/floating composition of the portfolio, maximum average life and maximum discretionary trading.
- **Transaction structure** – structured finance CDOs are typically designed as funded cash flow structures. The underlying portfolio is floating rate.

Fixed rate ABS are hedged using interest rate swaps or caps. The capital structure consists of floating rate notes. Multiple tranches range from senior (rated around AAA/AA), mezzanine (rated around BBB) and equity. Typical structured finance CDOs have higher leverage (lower levels of equity) than conventional CDOs. This reflects the fact that the underlying portfolio credit quality is usually investment grade. Credit enhancement is provided by a senior/subordinated structure with a ·repayment waterfall. Additional credit support is provided by coverage tests (over collateralisation and interest coverage). There are minimum ratios for each tranche. These ratios are evaluated periodically to determine payment priority. If tests are not met then cash flow is diverted at the failure level to amortise the senior securities. If the coverage test is subsequently met, then the payments may resume to the relevant tranche.

- **Operation** – structured finance CDOs generally have the following timelines:
  1. *Ramp up* – this is usually a period of up to 6 months during which the asset manager assembles the portfolio. In general, the asset manager will have a significant portion of the portfolio assembled at closing of the CDO. In effect, the manager "warehouses" the ABS portfolio.
  2. *Reinvestment* – this is a period of 3 to 5 years during which the principal cash flows (amortisation, calls and prepayments) from the portfolio assets are reinvested in new ABS within the portfolio guidelines.
  3. *Paydown period* – this is the period after the reinvestment period through to final legal maturity. Principal cash flows are used to amortise the most senior notes. In general, structured finance CDOs generally amortise at a higher rate reflecting the risk of prepayment on the underlying assets.
  4. *Call option* – there is generally a non-call period, usually until the end of the reinvestment period. The transaction is then callable by equity. In general, the amortisation of senior debt after the reinvestment period will reduce the leverage in the structure. This reduction in leverage in practice makes it attractive to call the transaction prior to legal maturity.
- **Maturity** – the legal final maturity of a structured finance CDO is generally longer than for conventional CDOs. CDOs based on loans or bonds have a maturity of 5 to 12 years. The legal final maturity of structured finance CDOs is longer; up to 35 years. This reflects the term

of the ABS. In practice, the actual life is likely to be shorter. This reflects the fact that likely rapid de-leveraging of the structure will lead equity to call well performed transactions. A number of innovations are also used to reduce the weighted average life of structured finance CDOs:

1. *Step up coupon* – this entails the mezzanine coupon stepping up by a large margin (say, 500 bps) after 12 years. The increased cost is likely to provide equity holders with an incentive to call the transaction. This is likely to work satisfactorily in a well performed transaction. The call may not be attractive to equity holders if higher than expected losses are incurred on the portfolio.

2. *Turbo mezzanine* – this entails excess interest (in excess of a pre-determined capped equity return) being used to amortise the mezzanine tranche during the reinvestment phase of the transaction. This has the effect of reducing the amount of high cost mezzanine debt. It may also reduce the cost of the mezzanine debt as it reduces its average life and its risk. Senior investors are not significantly affected as there is a straight substitution of mezzanine by over collateralisation.

3. *Auction call* – this entails the CDO trustee conducting a regular auction after 10 years whereby bids are sought from the market for the underlying portfolio. In a well performed portfolio, the auction call is likely to be in-the-money. This reflects the performance of the underlying portfolio. With the passage of time, the ABS assets generally would have stabilised with respect to defaults, prepayments etc. The shorter remaining life would also generally reduce the applicable spread. It also reflects the reduction in the CDO liabilities. Auction call redemptions are used to repay CDO liabilities. In a poorly performed portfolio, the auction call would not be in-the-money and hence less likely to be triggered.

Modelling/Rating

The modelling and rating of structured finance CDOs is complex[91]. The overall modelling process used by the different rating agencies is conventional. It is based on binomial expansion or a variation (Moody's)

---

[91]   See Cuccovillo, Francesco and Hermann, Markus "Structured Finance CDOs: An Analytical Framework – Part 2 (8 December 2003) Derivatives Week 8–9.

or Monte Carlo simulation (S & P or Fitch). The complexity relates to assets underlying the ABS. Key issues relate to modelling key parameters. The major problems relate to correlation within the portfolio and recovery rates. The position is complicated by the limited amount of historical data available.

ABS default rates are modelled in various ways. Moody's assumes the same loss rate for an equivalent rated corporate security. S & P and Fitch assume lower default rates, reflecting the evidence of greater rating stability and lower downgrade risk. The lower default rates reflect the structure, including credit enhancement, for ABS. It also reflects the use of bankruptcy remote vehicles allowing isolation of the asset pool from the originator.

ABS are based on well diversified pools of assets where credit mitigants are deployed to enhance credit quality. This means that ABS portfolios have a lower exposure to event risk. The lower level of event risk implies a higher degree of default correlation of the asset class. This means that an understanding of the default correlation is critical to modelling and rating structured finance CDO transactions.

Incorporating default correlation in structured finance CDOs entails a series of issues. The first entails the level of aggregation (e.g. by transaction, master trust, guarantors or servicers). The second entails the methodology for determining correlation between asset classes. In the case of corporate debt, there is a straightforward binary relationship. In ABS transactions, there is a web of dependencies. Finally, the level of concentration within a portfolio must be checked through different filters (e.g. specific asset class, sponsor, servicer, and transaction vintage).

The individual rating agencies use different methodologies to analyse the correlation risk. Moody's uses a diversity score. Moody's assigns a lower diversity score for structured finance securities. Default correlation is assumed to be high (up to 30%) within some sectors. Multiple debt tranches of the same ABS transaction, tranches originated by the same entity or wrapped by the same insurer are usually considered highly correlated. S & P use an asset correlation model across different industries and asset classes. A 30% correlation is used within an ABS sector and 10% between ABS sectors. Fitch uses a sector scoring model and also adjusts the default stress multiple.

Recovery rates for ABS depend upon a number of factors:

- **Type of asset** – the recovery rate generally increases if the underlying pool of the ABS is composed of diversified and unrelated assets.

- **Initial rating** – a higher initial rating will typically translate into a higher recovery rate.
- **Size of tranche** – in general, small tranches display binary behaviour implying low recovery rates.
- **Workout horizon** – in general, complexity of structures reduces market value. This means a longer time horizon is required to determine and realise the real value of ABS.

In practice, all rating agencies use some or all of the above factors to determine recovery rates. The assumed recovery rates are generally higher than for corporate bonds.

The difficulty in estimating parameters introduces a model risk component in analysing and rating structured finance CDOs. It is unclear whether this risk is either significant or fully compensated for in the pricing of structured finance CDO tranches.

Key Drivers

The primary drivers of CDOs of ABS are the following factors:

- **Pricing of ABS** – structured finance issues (particularly, the mezzanine and subordinate tranches) exhibit significant liquidity and risk premiums relative to equivalent rated securities. The additional spread appears to be larger than that driven by pure credit and structural factors. The major factors driving this spread differential include complexity of structure, small issue sizes (for mezzanine and subordinate tranches) and a limited investor universe. The higher credit spread on ABS can be used to create higher yielding CDOs[92].
- **Credit quality of ABS** – historical data indicates that the credit risk on ABS may be lower then for comparable corporates. The default experience of ABS compares favorably to equivalent corporate bonds[93]. An additional feature of ABS that make them attractive for CDOs is that structured finance securities have generally performed better than similarly rated corporations in terms of historical rating migration. ABS are also characterised by lower exposure to event risk than

---

[92]   See Sawyer, Nick "Squeezing More Juice" (June 2004) AsiaRisk 26–27.
[93]   For discussion of the credit quality of ABS, see Howard, David R., Carosielli, Brian R., Mezzanotte, Claire, Lans, Diane M., Higgins, Kenneth and Scatassa, Joanne (8 January 2001) Structured Finance Default Study; Fitch Ratings, New York.

comparable corporate bonds. High quality ABS tranches are frequently combined with corporate credit risk. The inclusion of high quality ABS generally increases the average credit quality of the underlying credit portfolio. ABS also generally display low default correlation with the corporate credit risk, enhancing portfolio diversification. ABS also display a back ended default profile that is valuable in structuring CDOs. The credit quality of ABS is valuable in structuring CDOs. It allows higher levels of leverage. This may allow enhanced returns on equity investments.

- **Distribution of structured finance securities** – the CDO structure increases the range of potential investors in structured finance securities. This is driven by the fact that it is possible, through tranching techniques, to create highly rated securities from the underlying portfolio of assets. It also may enhance liquidity, at least in the higher rated credit classes.

Structured finance CDOs also present significant challenges:

- The structural complexity creates additional modelling risk. All ABS have some level of model risk. In a structured finance CDO, this risk is compounded. Estimates of default rates, default correlation and recovery rates are inherently more uncertain. This is compounded by the lack of historical data of ABS performance.
- Structured finance CDOs introduce exposure to:
  1. *Prepayment rates* – structured finance CDOs are more likely to receive prepayments. Prepayment creates exposure to reinvestment risk. The prepayments also affect the amortisation and risk profile of individual tranches. This means that investors are inherently exposed to prepayment risk indirectly.
  2. *Servicer risk* – investors are exposed to servicer risk. The financial distress of any individual servicer can affect the performance of underlying assets. The correlation impact of concentration amongst servicers creates a type of event risk. This is managed by concentration limits. In practice, additional comfort is gained from the fact that back-up servicers will generally be available to take over in case of default by a servicer.
  3. *Correlation risk* – the correlation between different ABS is difficult to model. This means that investors are exposed to the risk that actual default correlation varies significantly from those assumed. In practice, the default correlation assumed by rating agencies in

modelling structured finance CDOs is relatively conservative. However, the lack of historical experience makes it difficult to quantify this risk. The level of correlation used has a significant impact on the expected return of structured finance CDOs. Where actual default correlations are higher than assumed, there is a significant increase in the risk of debt and a resulting transfer of value from debt holders to equity.

Structured Finance CDOs – Variations[94]

Since 1999, structured finance CDOs have emerged as a significant component of the CDO market. The emergence of structured finance CDOs reflects the higher spreads available and investor concern about event risk in corporate bonds/loans. Over time, the excess spread has been arbitraged away and structured finance CDO returns are closer to those available on conventional CDOs. A major factor in the structured finance CDO market has been the reduction in credit spreads on ABS since 2003.

The market has adapted to the altered conditions. A number of variations to the standard structured finance CDO have emerged including:

- **Synthetic structured finance CDOs**[95] – synthetic structures have been employed to reduce the funding cost. Other advantages include avoiding/ reducing the ramp-up period and the use of fixed recovery rates. Synthetic structures require the credit default swap to be adjusted to the ABS structure, including amending the definition of credit event and also the settlement mechanism[96].
- **Alternative liability arrangements for structured finance CDOs** – a variety of structures designed to optimise the funding cost of structured finance CDOs have been employed, including:
  1. Use of a dynamic funding mechanism (variable funding notes or delayed drawdown of funds) to reduce the negative carry in the vehicle during the ramp-up phase of the transaction.

---

[94] See Wolcott, Rachel "Collateral Managers Get Creative" (April 2004) Risk 68–69.

[95] See (17 February 2004) Synthetic Structured Finance CDOs; Fitch Ratings, New York.

[96] For example, credit events are generally specified as failure to pay ABS principal and/or interest. An event such as bankruptcy or restructuring is not relevant to the structure.

2. Some structured finance CDOs have incorporated commercial paper ("CP") funding to reduce funding costs. The use of CP requires a provision whereby the issuer must have a liquidity facility to finance the structure to fund if the notes cannot be placed.
3. Some structured finance CDOs incorporate repo[97] programs, enabling the funding of ABS purchases to reduce funding costs.

8.3.3 CDOs Of CDOs[98]

A CDO *of a CDO* (known as a CDO^2) is a variation on the concept of structured finance CDOs. The major differentiating factor is that a CDO^2 is based on a portfolio of CDO tranches. Transactions have generally focused on portfolios of mezzanine tranches of CDOs backed by corporate assets. The dynamics of CDO^2 are similar to that of structured finance CDOs generally.

The CDO^2 market developed in the late 1990's[99]. To date, a modest number of transactions have been completed. The market developed in a period of deterioration in credit markets. During this period, CDO tranches were downgraded and values fell/yields rose. Liquidity of CDO securities was impaired sharply. In addition, investor demand for new CDO securities (in particular subordinated or mezzanine tranches) diminished.

The principal drivers of CDO^2 transactions included:

• High yields were available on CDO tranches. This was a result of investors selling CDO tranches for well below economic value. The selling was driven by rating downgrades (sometimes below investor thresholds) and concern about the CDO market generally. This allowed a number of boutique structuring houses and investment banks (with superior modelling technology and capital) to purchase distressed CDO tranches and re-securitise them through the CDO^2 structure.

---

[97] For a discussion of the repo market, see Das, Satyajit (2004) Swaps/Financial Derivatives 3rd Edition; John Wiley, Singapore at Chapter 6.

[98] See Smith, Darren "CDOs Of CDOs: Art Eating Itself?" in Gregory, Jon (Editor) (2003) Credit Derivatives: The Definitive Guide; Risk Publications, London at Chapter 13; (2 February 2004) CDO Squared: A Closer Look At Collateral; Fitch Ratings, New York.

[99] See Currie, Antony "UBS Brings Transparency To Murky CDOs" (January 2002) Euromoney 28; Sawyer, Nick "Adding Complexity" (December 2003) Credit Risk Supplement – AsiaRisk S12–S13.

- The ability to create a market for "new" mezzanine CDO securities. The CDO^2 structure effectively uses the same underlying credit risks but increases aggregate diversification as the exposure to individual credits is reduced. High quality CDO securities should also display low correlation with corporate/ABS/private equity credit risk.
- Arrangers of CDO transactions use CDO^2 to repackage residual positions from previous transactions or inventory for placement with investors. This allowed CDO arrangers to make prices for CDO tranches and trade in the secondary markets.

The value available in secondary and primary CDO tranches allowed a number of economically attractive transactions to be structured for investors.

The modelling and analysis of CDO^2 transactions is demanding. The analysis is focused on establishing the relative value of a tranche and then its value in the context of a re-securitisation. The analysis has to be done by the arranger in assembling and then repackaging the assets. It must also be undertaken by the rating agency seeking to establish the rating of the CDO^2 tranches.

There are no generic standard models to establish the price or value of secondary CDO^2 tranches. A major problem is the lack of transparency regarding CDO transactions. In general, traders active in CDO^2 structures use their own internal models to value CDO securities. It is arguable that this lack of transparency and absence of standard models has facilitated the "arbitrage" that underlies CDO^2 transactions.

The analysis focuses on the known and projected cash flows of the tranche being priced. Key areas of focus are:

- Quantitative factors such as portfolio losses, expected loss and variance in expected loss.
- Qualitative factors such as manager, structure (including substitution and trading rights/guidelines) and legal issues.

There are two primary approaches to modelling value of CDO tranches:

- **Re-rating** – this involves evaluating a secondary market CDO tranche by re-rating the transaction using the current asset portfolio, interest rates and capital structure. This requires detailed information on the portfolio structure. In practice, the structure may be re-rated to the portfolio constraints with adjustments reflecting any changes in portfolio credit quality. The major issue relates to distressed assets.

- **Simulation** – this involves simulating the portfolio and the individual tranche loss performance using a Monte Carlo approach. The simulations use a default model (such as Merton's structural model[100]) within a single, period-by-period or correlated times to default framework. Each of these approaches uses the credit risk of the individual asset and default correlations to analyse the loss performance on the portfolio. The attachment point on each tranche is then used to analyse the performance of individual tranches.

The approach outlined allows the value of any individual CDO tranche to be determined. This forms the basis of the arranger or trader acquiring the asset for the purpose of re-securitisation through a CDO^2 transaction.

The tranches of a CDO^2 are rated normally. The rating problems are similar to those for structured finance CDOs.

There is limited default rate data on CDO securities. It is usually derived from equivalent corporate debt. There are a number of problems, including the recognition of default. This reflects the fact that mezzanine CDO tranches (such as those used in CDO^2 transactions) are designed to absorb credit losses in a number of ways (e.g. deferring and capitalising interest payments). This means that a failure to pay interest on a CDO mezzanine tranche does not necessarily constitute a default event for the tranche. This means that default may not be recognised until maturity. This is generally addressed by a reduction to tranche ratings or by assuming that two or some number of missed payments is equivalent to default.

The issue of default correlation is also problematic. The sector approach used in ABS has some problems when applied to CDO tranches. This reflects the fact that individual exposures are larger than those that exist in certain types of ABS (residential mortgage and consumer finance assets). In a CDO^2 transaction, the likely presence of overlapping entities between tranches creates problems. The use of conservative diversity scores or correlations is used to counter this risk.

The recovery values on ABS are generally assumed to be higher than for comparable corporate debt. This is applicable to ABS portfolios where the underlying assets are a large number of small loans. In CDO portfolios, the larger individual exposures and the mezzanine tranches are designed to absorb losses that will generally result in lower recoveries.

---

[100] See Chapter 6.

The economic value in CDO^2 transactions is driven by a number of factors. The high spreads available on CDO mezzanine tranches are a major factor. The loss structure of CDOs is also a key factor. In a CDO, equity investors take the first loss position in return for potentially high returns (15 to 25% pa) based on their highly leveraged position. The return to equity is reduced as defaults occur in the underlying asset portfolio. In contrast, investors in CDO^2 transactions benefit from the credit enhancement in the *original* CDO transaction. For example, an equity investor in a CDO^2 transaction has a de facto second loss position. Initial defaults on the original CDO are borne by the equity investor in the transaction. The equity position in a CDO^2 transaction is protected to a degree on the underlying assets. Similarly, mezzanine and senior investors receive the benefit of this "double subordination". This increases the stability of returns for CDO^2 investors. This means that CDO^2 transactions are attractive on a risk reward basis.

The CDO^2 market is a small component of the CDO market. This reflects the fact that the complexity of the structure and the modelling challenges have deterred significant investor participation[101].

8.3.4 Credit Index CDOs

Credit products based on standardised credit indexes[102] have gained in popularity[103]. Credit index linked CDOs entail a CDO where the underlying is an index rather than an actual specified credit portfolio. CDO transactions based on the key benchmark indexes such as DJ Trac-X and iBoxx have emerged[104]. This allows the trading of very large diversified portfolios of credit risk within a CDO format.

The basic structure is straightforward. The standard tranching technique used in CDO transactions is applied to the reference asset portfolio underlying the index. The credit index CDO divides the credit risk of the underlying index into different tranches based on specified attachment

---

[101] See Sawyer, Nick "Squeezing More Juice" (June 2004) AsiaRisk 26–27.
[102] See Chapter 2.
[103] See Patel, Navroz "Index Linked Synthetic CDO Debuts" (March 2002) Risk 8.
[104] The original attempts include transactions based on an index that is based on Moody's annualised default index (made up of more than 2,000 underlying reference entities).

points. A full range of tranches including equity, mezzanine, senior and super senior can be created.

The use of a standard tranching structure on a pre-specified fixed portfolio is designed to facilitate the creation of a liquid instrument. The structure seeks to capitalise on the increasing liquidity, efficiency (low transaction costs) and transparency of trading in the credit index itself.

The major features of credit index CDOs include:

- Credit index CDOs exhibit higher liquidity than similar conventional CDO securities. This reflects the benefits of the standard portfolio, liquidity of trading in the index and standardised tranching. In addition, the commitment of a number of dealers to provide a market-making facility assists in liquidity.
- Credit index CDOs are transparent in pricing and trade at lower transaction costs than conventional CDO securities.
- Credit index CDOs offer traders and investors structural flexibility. This includes the ability to create both long and short positions in a CDO tranche. This is a significant advantage as traditionally it is difficult to short CDO tranches. Credit index CDO products can be created in a variety of formats including funded/unfunded, fixed/floating rate and in any currency.

Credit index CDOs are attractive to traditional CDO investors. The major advantage is the lower transaction cost, pricing transparency and enhanced liquidity.

Credit index CDOs are also attractive to traders and investors who can use it for the following applications:

- Credit index CDOs can be used to hedge CDO residual, inventory or trading positions. Traditionally, hedging requires trading in individual single name credit default swaps. This is expensive and incurs high transaction costs. Standardised credit index CDO tranches that can be bought or sold allow increased efficiency if hedging. The indexes are relatively diverse and an aggregate, geographic or industry index can be used to manage the relevant risk. The indexes should capture broad market changes in value. The trader is left with the basis risk between the portfolio being hedged and the credit index. This risk may be lower than the market risk hedged by the credit index transaction. The basis risk must be managed separately by the trader.

- Credit index CDO tranches can be used to trade default correlation. Each tranche in a CDO has specific exposure to default correlation[105]. Investors in subordinated tranches (equity and mezzanine) are generally short correlation. These investors gain as correlation increases. In contrast, senior tranche investors are generally long correlation. These investors lose as correlation increases. This reflects the increased risk of loss on senior tranches. Each tier in the capital structure of a CDO represents a position on credit risk and default correlation. Traditionally, it has been difficult to trade default correlation because of the difficulty in shorting CDO tranches. The emergence of credit index CDOs and the relative liquidity and low transaction costs of trading in tranches allows some level of correlation trading. For example, an investor sells protection on the equity tranche and purchases protection on a more senior tranche. The trade on the senior tranche will be larger in face value terms (say 2 to 3 times). The transaction would generally be spread neutral, insensitive to changes in spread but would provide the trader with protection from a large systemic rise in defaults. This reflects the fact that the trader is long default correlation risk.

8.3.5   Collateralised Fund Obligations[106]

Collateralised Fund Obligations ("CFOs") are CDO structures where the underlying assets are a portfolio of managed funds. Typical assets of CFOs include hedge funds, private equity and mezzanine funds. CFOs are designed with the objective of allowing investors to gain exposure to a diverse portfolio of funds, typically using a fund-of-funds manager.

Exhibit 4.17 sets out the basic features of hedge funds and fund-of-funds of hedge funds. Private equity funds focus on venture capital, start up funding or capital (equity, mezzanine or senior debt) for leveraged and management buy-outs or other leveraged transactions.

Exhibit 4.18 sets out the principal features of CFO structures. The basic structure of a CFO is as follows:

- CFO transactions are generally structured as arbitrage, market value, managed CDOs.

---

[105]   See discussion later in this Chapter.

[106]   See Mahadevan, Sivan and Schwartz, David (January 2002) CDO Insights: Hedge Fund Collateralised Fund Obligations; Morgan Stanley – Fixed Income Research, Global – Structured Credit, New York.

- The underlying portfolio will consist of a fund-of-funds that invests in hedge funds. The underlying portfolio will be circumscribed by guidelines designed to ensure the diversification of the hedge fund investments. This will usually take the form of investment limits based on fund, fund manager and investment strategy. In addition, where the underlying is private equity investments, there are generally industry and vintage concentration limits.
- The manager seeks to manage the underlying portfolio within the established guidelines. The manager seeks to maximise return while limiting volatility.
- The ramp-up period for CFOs is more variable than for a normal CDO. It is a function of the asset (ramp up periods for hedge funds are faster than for private equity funds), market condition, manager and size of transaction.
- The capital/funding structure of a CFO is similar to a standard CDO. A range of rated debt securities (senior and mezzanine) and equity is issued to investors.
- The securities issued are serviced from the income and realised capital gains generated by the manager from the underlying assets. A significant proportion of cash flows from the underlying portfolio is in the form of sales proceeds/market value gains as investments are realised. Liquidity facilities may also be used to provide interim cash flows. These liquidity facilities take the form of surplus/reserve cash accounts, unused funds or revolving credit facilities.
- Equity investors receive the residual income and capital gains (in effect, the outperformance of the CFO manager relative to the borrowing cost of the CFO embedded in the issues of debt).
- Debt investors receive agreed interest payments. Debt holders benefit from credit protection measures such as market value collateralisation and minimum net worth of equity tests. If minimum levels are not met, then the manager must bring the structure back into compliance through changes in portfolio composition or by liquidating positions. Generally, the cure periods in CFOs are longer than for conventional CDO structures. This reflects the lower liquidity of the underlying investments.

The debt tranches of CFOs are generally rated. The rating agencies use an approach commonly applicable to market value CDOs. Ratings are based on advance rates rather than on stressed default rates and tranche expected losses. Advance rates focus on how much of the asset can be used as collateral to raise rated debt funding. Advance rates are determined by the credit quality and price volatility of the asset.

Advance rates for hedge funds are based on the volatility and liquidity of the fund using historical performance data. The determination of advance rates for private equity funds is similar. In both cases, rating agencies will focus on redemption terms. The focus will be on permitted redemption timing and required notice. Most funds only allow redemptions at specified intervals (monthly, quarterly or annually) and require notice periods of between 7 and 180 days. Limited redemption dates and longer notice periods generally translate into lower advance rates.

Rating agencies will generally undertake a thorough due diligence process focusing on the investment policies, surveillance procedures employed and the operational aspects of the fund. Rating agencies will base their quantitative analysis on the historical performance of individual funds and the fund-of-funds. Key performance measures include maximum drawdowns (worst case cash outflows), peak-trough performance and correlation performance (at the fund-of-funds level). Rating agencies will generally stress test the portfolio. Simulations may be used for portfolios where historical information is not readily available (e.g. in some private equity funds).

Rating agencies focus on surveillance procedures. A particular focus is "style drift". This is where the fund manager changes its investment strategy outside its stated objectives. Style drift tends to occur when the hedge fund performs poorly, has large unrealised profits or when investment opportunities are scarce.

In practice, CFO structures have sometimes been wrapped by monoline insurers to meet the requirements of debt investors. Under the approach, the insurer agrees to guarantee the performance of the debt in return for payment of a fee. The rating of the insurer attaches to the debt tranches. Monoline insurers have been interested in CFO structures, seeing it as an extension of their CDO business and allowing access to hedge fund risk that they have limited exposure to.

CFOs allow investors to access investments that are traditionally difficult to access. Investors benefit from the risk tranching feature of CFOs. The manager focuses on maximisation of the total return of the underlying portfolio within specified risk (volatility) constraints. This allows adjustment of the risk profile of the investment.

Debt investors in a CFO have a rated debt investment where the underlying assets are a fund-of-funds on hedge funds. CFOs will also generally display low default correlation with the corporate/ABS credit risks enhancing portfolio diversification. The rating of the CFO debt tranches also allows investors prevented by mandate/investment regulations from investing in hedge funds to access this market segment. Equity investors gain leveraged exposure to a diversified portfolio of hedge funds. It enables the hedge fund to obtain attractively priced debt to finance its hedge fund investments. An issue with CFO structures is the relative lack of liquidity of CFO investments. Additional issues include the administrative cost of the CFO structure.

The CFO market commenced in 2001[107]. The market remains a modest component of the total CDO market. The early structures entailed CFOs based on private equity investments. The early transactions used CFOs to liquefy private equity investments. This was attractive in an environment when the initial public offering market was effectively closed. It also allowed private equity managers to obtain debt funding at attractive rates. A number of CFOs based on hedge fund portfolios have also been completed. CFOs have been completed both as private placement and public transactions. Investors in CFOs have received higher spreads than for comparable conventional CDOs. The complexity of the structure has limited the growth of the CFO market.

Exhibit 4.17   Hedge Funds[108]

1. Hedge Funds

Hedge funds are private investment vehicles (generally structured as private partnerships). The principal characteristics of hedge funds include:

- Focus on absolute or total returns rather than relative return benchmarked against a market index.
- Return benchmarked against cash returns.
- Ability to short sell and use (sometimes high) levels of leverage.

---

[107] See Schenk, Carola "Private Equity CDOs Trigger Rush To Derivatives" (July 2001) Risk 6; Dwyer, Rob "Private Equity And Hedge Fund Deals In The Pipeline" (May 2002) Credit Risk" Securitisation Supplement – Risk S8–S9; Leander, Ellen "Private Equity Firms Launch CLOs" (May 2002) Credit Risk" Securitisation Supplement – Risk S3; Patel, Navroz "Dashed Hopes" (July 2003) Credit Risk Supplement – Risk S7; Wolcott, Rachel "CFOs Come Out In Private" (April 2004) Risk 65–66.

[108] See Mahadevan, Sivan and Schwartz, David (January 2002) CDO Insights: Hedge Fund Collateralised Fund Obligations; Morgan Stanley – Fixed Income Research, Global – Structured Credit, New York at 5–13.

The following Table sets out the basic types of hedge funds that are commonly available

Type Of Fund	Strategy
Directional/Event Driven 1. Macro trading 2. Systems trading 3. Discretionary or event driven	The primary characteristic of these funds is leveraged speculation on market direction based on macro-economic views, events or momentum. Strategies are based on fundamental analysis or models.
Relative Value 1. Statistical arbitrage 2. Convergence arbitrage 3. Multi-strategy	The primary characteristic of these funds is based on capturing spread from pricing relationships between different securities with similar qualities or pricing components of a security package. Strategies entail low/minimal market risk but assume basis/correlation risk. Strategies are based on fundamental or statistical analysis.
Equity Trading 1. Variable bias 2. Long/short or pairs trading 3. Convertible arbitrage 4. Merger arbitrage 5. Capital structure arbitrage	The primary characteristics of these funds are combinations of equity securities or debt and equity securities. Strategies entail low market risk and assume basis/correlation risk. Strategies are based on fundamental analysis.
Credit Trading 1. Distressed securities 2. Complex securities	The primary characteristics of these funds are based on assuming credit risk. Strategies entail low interest rate risk but assume credit risk (default and credit migration) and basis/correlation risk. Strategies are based on fundamental analysis.

The economics of hedge funds are characterised by the following:

- High returns relative to risk although this is not uniform across all types of hedge funds or all time periods.
- A wide range of return volatility.
- Low correlation of hedge fund returns with other assets (e.g. equity markets).
- Low correlation of returns between different types of hedge fund strategies.

The economics of hedge fund performance should generally be interpreted with care. This reflects the impact of sustainability of returns, survivorship bias and the return variance (i.e. fat tails).

The economics of hedge funds (particularly the low correlation to other asset classes and between hedge fund strategies) are attractive to investors. This has led to most investors allocating a part of their portfolios to hedge fund investments (usually labelled alternative investment strategies ("AIS")).

2. Fund-Of-Hedge-Funds

A common investment approach for hedge funds is to invest in a portfolio of hedge funds. This reflects the use of diversification to manage the risk and smooth the volatility of hedge fund returns.

In practice, a portfolio of hedge funds can be constructed in the following manner:

- **Direct investment** – this entails fund selection, investment and monitoring by the investors
- **Fund-of-funds** – this entails investment in a fund-of-funds where the manager undertakes the selection of the funds and performance monitoring in return for payment of a management fee.

Many investors favour the fund-of-fund approach. This reflects the new nature of the asset class and the large number of hedge funds. It also reflects the economics of a fund-of-fund manager undertaking the time-consuming and complex process of analysis, review and due diligence of individual hedge funds.

The primary features of a fund-of-hedge-funds include:

- **Fund selection** – under direct investment, investors must identify, review, select and monitor hedge fund investments. In a fund-of-funds approach, the investor employs the fund-of-fund manager in this role. The manager will generally have a competitive advantage in identifying funds, performing reviews, undertaking due diligence and also monitoring performance. Moreover, the fund-of-funds manager is likely to perform these tasks in a consistent and systematic manner. The fund-of-fund approach also has some disadvantages. The search process is not perfect, the screening process may not be exactly matched to the investor's requirement and the monitoring process may not provide precise information relevant to the investor. In addition, the fund-of-fund manager will generally not structure the investment in a form that is most favourable to specific investor requirements.
- **Investment issues** – this is concerned with risk and return issues. Under a fund-of-funds structure, risks are generally averaged through the inherent process of diversification across investment styles, funds and managers. This equates to lower risk and averaged performance. The major advantage is the instant diversification through a single investment. The disadvantage of the fund-of-funds approach is that it naturally dilutes the returns of better performing funds. In addition, the investor has no control over allocation of investments to funds or investment styles.
- **Cost** – under direct investment, the investor only incurs fees for the individual hedge funds themselves. In a fund-of-funds approach, the investor incurs two fees: a fee charged by the fund-of-funds manager as well as the individual hedge fund fee. The fund-of-funds manager may however be able to negotiate lower fees for the fund than the investor.
- **Administrative issues** – under a direct investment approach, the investor bears the accounting and cash flow management responsibilities. Under a fund-of-funds approach, the manager will consolidate information and undertake a significant portion of the administrative tasks.

In recent years, hedge fund indexes have also emerged, consolidating the fund-of-funds investment approach.

Exhibit 4.18 Collateralised Fund Obligations ("CFOs") – Structural Features

Structural Feature	Typical Cash Flow CDO	Typical Market Value CDO	Hedge Fund CFO	Private Equity CFO
Manager Focus	Maximise cash flow to investors, minimise defaults	Maximise total return, restrain volatility	Maximise fund of funds performance	Maximise fund of funds performance
Ramp Up Time	1 week to 3 months	3 to 6 months	3 months	6 months to 3 years
Estimated Percentage of Commitments Invested	100%	95–100%	95–100%	85–95%
Source of Income (Coupon Payments)	Coupon cash flows from collateral	Market value gains (proceeds primarily from sale of assets) and liquidity facilities	Liquidity facility; amounts not drawn down and market value gains	Liquidity facility
Leverage	5–25×	5–10×	4–8×	3–5×
Liquidity Facility	None or small eligible investments pool in collateral balance	Asset side – reserve accounts; Liability side – revolvers	Asset side – reserve accounts and unused proceeds; Liability side – revolvers	Asset side – reserve accounts and unused proceeds; Liability side – revolvers
Coverage Tests	Par coverage ratio; Interest coverage ratio	Market value over collateralisation ("OC"); minimum net worth of equity	Market value over collateralisation; minimum net worth of equity	Market value over collateralisation; minimum net worth of equity
Credit Protection	Diversion of cash flow from mezzanine and equity to senior	Liquidation to pay down senior classes to bring OC levels back	Liquidation into cash or to pay down senior classes	Liquidation into cash but with long cure period
Cure Periods	None	2 weeks	30–180 days	Longer

Structural Feature	Typical Cash Flow CDO	Typical Market Value CDO	Hedge Fund CFO	Private Equity CFO
Diversity	Diversity score concept	Diversity score concept	Fund diversification along several dimensions including strategy, sub-strategy, fund and fund manager	Similar to hedge fund CDOs
Diversity Restrictions	Failure of diversity score threshold imposes trading restrictions	Failure of diversity score threshold does not impose trading restrictions but impacts coverage test calculations	Reallocations that resulted in diversity restrictions would not be permitted	Similar to hedge fund CDOs
Ratings Basis	Stressed default rates	Advance rates – price volatility basis	Advance rates – price volatility and liquidity basis along with due diligence process	Advance rates – simulation along with due diligence process

Source: Morgan Stanley; see Mahadevan, Sivan and Schwartz, David (January 2002) CDO Insights: Hedge Fund Collateralised Fund Obligations; Morgan Stanley – Fixed Income Research, Global – Structured Credit, New York at 15.

8.3.6   Equity Collateralised Obligations

There is increasing convergence between the credit and equity markets. This has created interest in using equity to hedge credit derivatives (known as E2C trades)[109]. It has also created structured products such as equity default swaps[110]. An equity default swap is economically a deep out-of-the-money (strike is 30% of current share price) digital equity put option (fixed payout is 50% of initial share price). Equity collateralised obligations ("ECOs") are a tranched asset backed security based on a portfolio of equity default swaps.

The basic structure of an ECO transaction is similar to a CDO. The key features include:

- The asset portfolio consists of equity default swaps. In practice, portfolios consisting of a combination of credit default swaps and equity default swaps have been used.
- The portfolio is tranched normally. Equity, mezzanine and senior debt tranches are generally issued.
- Investors in the equity tranche assume the first losses (payouts) on the underlying portfolio. Mezzanine investors are protected against the first losses. Where losses exceed the amount of the equity tranche, the mezzanine investors bear additional losses. Senior investors will only suffer losses if the losses on the underlying portfolio exceed the combined total of the equity and mezzanine tranches.
- Payoff triggers and settlement mechanisms on the underlying equity default swaps are conventional.

ECO structures allow tranched investments in a portfolio of stocks via the equity default swap. The advantages claimed for ECOs are similar to those applicable to equity default swaps generally. These include greater transparency, ease of establishing payout event and known payout. The ECO structure is designed to allow investors access to equity default swaps on a tranched and rated basis.

ECOs present significant rating challenges[111]. The risk and price behaviour of equity default swaps is different to that of credit default swaps.

---

[109]   See Chapter 5.
[110]   See Chapter 2.
[111]   See Kappor, Vivek, Cheung, Lily and Howley, Christopher (October 2003) Equity Securitisation: Risk And Value; Standard & Poor's, New York. See also Sawyer, Nick "Rating Equity" (April 2004) AsiaRisk 32–33.

Rating agencies generally model the underlying portfolio to evaluate the chance of each reference equity trading below the trigger level (30% of the initial share price). The historical simulation is adjusted for different market regimes. The regimes generally examine the portfolio under normal, stress (market falling by say 20–30%) and crash conditions (market falling by say 50%). In each regime, the volatility and portfolio correlation is adjusted. The portfolio correlation is adjusted to high positive levels (say 0.8 or 80%) under stress and crash conditions. The tranching is then derived from the generated loss distribution. This approach has generally resulted in high levels of subordination in ECO transactions. Other modelling approaches (stochastic processes and jump processes) are also being considered.

The ECO market has only recently emerged[112]. The majority of transactions have been in Japan. This reflects the lack of availability of corporate credit assets and the low credit spreads in Japan. Equity default swaps and ECOs seek to generate incremental yield under these conditions. In practice, many ECO transactions use a portfolio that combines credit default swaps and equity default swaps[113]. The additional yield from equity default swaps increases the available return on CDOs to investors. The inclusion of a small (around 10%) portion of equity default swaps in the asset portfolio also limits the increase in subordination levels to a modest degree. Some CDOs of a portfolio of equity default swaps have also been completed[114].

8.4 Synthetic Securitisation – Structural Variations

8.4.1 Synthetic Securitisation Without Special Purpose Vehicles

In a conventional synthetic securitisation transaction, a SPV is generally used to issue debt and fund the collateral securing the credit default swap used to transfer credit risk. Synthetic securitisation structures can be undertaken without the interposition of a vehicle.

Exhibit 4.19 sets out the structure used. The structure is based on using a series of credit default swaps on different layers of risk. The credit default

---

[112] See Wolcott, Rachel "Two Of A Kind" (March 2004) Risk 24–26; Sawyer, Nick "Rating Equity" (April 2004) AsiaRisk 32–33.

[113] This creates specific documentary risks; see Cluley, Paul and Dwyer, Emma "Documenting EDS" (June 2004) AsiaRisk 28–29.

[114] See Cluley, Paul and Dwyer, Emma "Documenting EDS" (June 2004) AsiaRisk 28–29.

swaps are executed with OECD banks or cash collateralised to ensure capital relief.

The structures are generally private transactions. The primary motivations for such transactions include capital management (reducing capital requirements or improving return on capital) and/or credit risk management (including reduction in concentration risk). The assets generally used include balance sheet credit assets (loans, asset backed leases etc) and off-balance-sheet credit exposures (derivatives).

Arbitrage based transactions are also feasible (usually using the trading book). In arbitrage transactions, the bank sells protection in the credit default swap market to acquire the risk that is then tranched and placed with investors.

The typical terms are around 5 years. A right to break after 2 years, usually for regulatory reasons, may be incorporated. The transactions generally incorporate the right to substitute credit assets. The substitution rights are subject to restrictions based on rating criteria (such as geography/sector diversity, size of exposure, concentration limit and minimum credit rating (generally investment grade)). The transactions feature disclosure of reference entities (except in mid-market credits). There is no disclosure of facility terms.

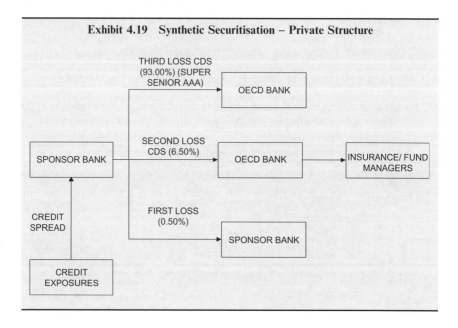

Exhibit 4.19 Synthetic Securitisation – Private Structure

8.4.2 Single Tranche CDOs

Structure[115]

As the CDO market developed, the CDO structure itself has evolved. A number of dealers developed flexible managed structures designed to accommodate individual investors. The flexibly managed structure is known as the single tranche CDO. The flexible structures entail a more actively managed capital structure of the CDO.

In a normal CDO, the complete tranched capital structure (equity, mezzanine, senior and super senior) is simultaneously placed with investors. The key differentiating feature of a single tranche CDO is that the dealer will initially place only a single component of the capital structure. The dealer will retain and hedge the remaining elements of the capital structure. The structure of a single tranche CDO is set out in **Exhibit 4.20.**

Most of the elements of these transactions are similar to conventional synthetic CDOs. A typical single tranche CDO transaction would operate as follows:

- The investor nominates the type of investment sought (say, AAA rated senior).
- The investor, the dealer and manager work together to select and structure a portfolio of a specified number of obligors (around 100).
- The dealer uses a special purpose vehicle to enter into the required credit default swaps to assemble the portfolio. The dealer creates the various layers of risk using normal tranching technology.
- The dealer enters into a funded credit transfer transaction with the investor. This takes the form of an issue of funded notes by the vehicle to the investor. It may also entail a credit default swap with a second repackaging vehicle that issues the notes to the investor. The proceeds of the notes are invested in high quality securities to collateralise the credit default swaps.
- The single tranche CDO operates in a manner consistent with a normal CDO.

---

[115] See Choudhry, Moorad "Cleared For Take-Off" (December 2003) FOW 44–46; Bernard, Alex and Pormokhtar, Farzin "New Challenges In The Correlation Market" (December 2003) Risk – Sponsor's Statement; (2004) Bank Of America Guide To Advanced Correlation Products; Bank of America/Risk Publications – Supplement to (July 2004) Risk.

Rationale

The structure was driven by a number of factors. One factor was difficulties in structuring and executing a CDO transaction. A normal CDO where the complete capital structure is placed is complex to execute. Multi tranche structures require time to market and execute. The dealer usually hedges riskier tranches first. This means that junior tranche holders have greater influence on the leverage and selection of underlying assets. This makes it difficult to reconcile different investor requirements (that is, the needs of super senior, senior, mezzanine and equity). This means that in many transactions the capital structure provides greater rewards for the more junior tranches by optimizing the more senior tranches' size and spread. There were also problems in simultaneously securing all classes of investors in a CDO transaction.

The value dynamics in a single tranche CDO are different. The transaction is structured around a *single investor*. This means that the investor controls the entire structure. This includes selection of underlying assets, maturity, currency, leverage and rating. Single tranche transactions are also faster to execute. The dealer will generally execute the transaction off its trading desk, executing the required credit default swaps to hedge the transaction. As these hedges are lower in nominal amount than the size of the underlying portfolio, the hedges are easier and quicker to execute.

The design and structure of single tranche CDOs makes them easier and flexible to manage. This was evidenced in 2004 when the Italian company Parmalat experienced financial difficulties[116]. Parmalat was a reference entity in a number of single tranche CDO transactions. Following the credit event, a number of tranches in such transactions were downgraded by rating agencies. Dealers restructured some transactions at the request of investors. This required substituting reference entities or altering the capital structure. This type of restructuring is easier in a single tranche CDO transaction than in a conventional CDO.

The development of single tranche CDO structures was facilitated by the development of large trading books in credit risk that included the ability to model and trade default correlation risk. The development of these trading books allowed dealers to hedge the credit risk on the retained tranches, enabling single tranche structures to be created.

---

[116] See Wolcott, Rachel "Single-Tranche CDOs Ride Spreading Parmalat Down-grades" (February 2004) Risk 8.

Credit correlation books developed in response to a number of factors, including:

- There was an increasing requirement for dealers to trade/make markets in CDO tranches. This was evident in 2001/2002. In the aftermath of the sharp rise in global corporate default rates, many CDO tranches suffered losses. Senior and mezzanine CDO tranches were frequently downgraded and traded below par value. Many investors were forced to sell their CDO holdings. These investors required dealers to make them market prices in these CDO tranches. As there was little investor demand except at uneconomic prices, dealers were forced to hold these securities in inventory and hedge the risk. The hedges entailed buying protection in the credit default swap market on some of the reference entities in the underlying portfolio. This required development of credit correlation trading capabilities. Some investors used similar techniques to hedge the risk of investments in CDO tranches[117].
- Increase in trading liquidity in credit default swaps allowed dealers to actively trade and manage credit risk. As credit default swaps become a commoditised trading product, dealer focus shifts to creating more volume for their "flow" desks. The creation of credit correlation books drives natural trading positions and increases trading volumes to supplement client flows. This enabled the trading desks to develop and increase in size.
- Improvements in credit modelling were also a catalyst in development of credit trading books. Increased understanding of credit risk, both individual and within a portfolio, allowed traders to develop hedging and trading technology that facilitated running credit books.
- As the credit derivatives market became increasingly liquid, profit margins fell. Maintenance of profitability increasingly required greater structuring skills or assumption of trading risk. The development of trading books allows major dealers to use capital to enhance profit margins in transactions.

Some temporary factors also influenced the emergence of credit trading books. This included reduced credit spreads in the market. This meant that

---

[117] See Berd, Arthur M. and Tejwani, Gaurav "Managing Risk Exposures In CDO Tranches" (14 May 2002) Lehman Brothers Quantitative Credit Research Quarterly 22–41.

a standard fully placed CDO structure was difficult to execute at a satisfactory profit level. The ability to structure and place individual tranches in response to specific demand allowed the execution of transactions that would otherwise be impossible. An additional factor was the inability to attract subordinated investors in CDO structures in 2001/2002 as default rates increased. The ability to hedge the default risk internally allowed dealers to execute CDOs despite the absence of subordinated investors.

Single Tranche CDOs – Variations

The basic format of a single tranche CDO entails a 5 year transaction based on a static portfolio of usually investment grade corporate credits that are actively traded in the credit default swap market.

There are a number of variations on the standard single tranche structure including:

- **Other credit risk** – this entails adding different types of credit risk to the underlying portfolio. Common additions have included a high yield bucket allowing a part of the portfolio to include non investment grade credit names and asset backed securities (including CDO tranches).
- **Managed single tranche structure** – in static single tranche CDOs, the underlying portfolio is pre-specified and cannot be altered. In a managed single tranche CDO, an appointed manager can alter portfolio structure by substituting credits in the portfolio to mitigate potential losses. The ability to actively manage the portfolio alters the value dynamics. Trading losses can reduce coupon or subordination. The reverse holds for trading gains. Portfolio composition is controlled by conventional tests designed to ensure credit quality and diversity.
- **Loss limited structures** – structures where the loss to the investor is limited have also developed. These include structures where trading gains and excess cash flows are used to build reserves that reduce the impact of default losses. Alternative structures have reduced risk of loss using different structuring approaches. Some dealers have structured single tranche notes where the principal of the single tranche is rated AAA but the interest on the notes is lower rated (say A or BBB+). This allows the investor to earn higher returns but limit losses in case of defaults to the coupon amount.

Risk Management[118]

The major difference between this structure and traditional CDOs is that the dealer still retains the risk of the underlying portfolio *other than the component transferred under the single tranche CDO* (the AAA rated senior tranche in **Exhibit 4.20**). In a normal structure, the dealer would have placed the equity (or part thereof), senior and super senior parts of the structure. The dealer must manage the retained risk.

The dealer generally manages the residual risk using the following techniques:

- **Risk transfer** – this entails finding investors in super senior, senior and equity components of the structure. In effect, the dealer transfers the risk to these investors. This is the traditional approach used in CDOs.
- **Risk management** – this uses portfolio credit trading techniques to manage the portfolio risk. This entails modelling the credit risk and default correlation of the portfolio and then using this to manage the portfolio[119]. This is referred to as "credit delta/gamma trading".

In practice, dealers combine the risk transfer and portfolio risk management techniques to manage the structure.

Credit hedging in a single tranche CDO entails managing the underlying asset portfolio by varying the amount of protection sold on individual obligors. **Exhibit 4.21** sets out the basic hedging process.

In a traditional CDO transaction, the dealer would enter into credit default swaps on each of the reference entities for the full notional principal of the transaction. This means the dealer has sold protection on the entire portfolio. The CDO provides a 100% hedge for the dealer with 100% of gains or losses being experienced by the CDO investors.

In contrast, in a single tranche CDO, the dealer will effectively hedge the risk on *some* of the original names in the portfolio by entering into credit default swaps. In practice, this is done by selling protection in varying amounts on the names in the portfolio. The dealers will generally hedge by selling protection on the reference entities around the actual single tranche

---

[118] See (2004) Bank Of America Guide To Advanced Correlation Products; Bank of America/Risk Publications – Supplement to (July 2004) Risk.

[119] See Hatstadt, Philippe "New Greeks For Synthetic CDOs: Correlation Trading In Full Swing" (January 2004) Risk – Sponsor's Statement. See also Patel, Navroz "The Right Tools" (July 2003) Credit Risk Supplement – Risk S2–S3.

CDO note that has been placed. For example, if the single tranche CDO note is highly rated (AAA) then the dealer will need to sell protection on the less risky names in the portfolio. This reflects the fact that the dealer retains the risk on more risky (likely to default) reference entities. If the single tranche CDO note is equivalent to equity or mezzanine, then the dealer will sell protection on the more risky names in the portfolio. This reflects the fact that the single tranche CDO note provides the dealer with protection against the earlier losses in the portfolio.

The dealer uses models to calculate the likelihood of each underlying credit defaulting. The credit models use a default function for each entity, assumption of loss given default, and a dependence structure of default (default correlation) to generate a complete loss distribution for the portfolio and then for the individual tranches based on their attachment points[120]. The model is used to derive hedge parameters for the structure for each tranche. This is credit delta of the portfolio[121]. Generally, the credit delta for each reference entity will initially be less than the full notional amount of the exposure within the portfolio. The delta will reflect the likelihood of each reference entity defaulting based on the market spread (implied default risk and loss given default) and default correlation.

The dealer must manage the hedge dynamically. The hedge changes will be driven by changes in market credit spreads, changes in default correlation and actual defaults within the portfolio. The dealer seeks to generate excess returns between the income on the portfolio adjusted for credit losses (if any) and the payments to the investor.

The dynamic management of the hedge is often difficult in practice. Large changes in market credit spreads will generally result in net hedging gains or losses to the dealer. This is a function of gamma risk (effectively the convexity of the tranche value with regard to credit spreads). For example, if the dealer has purchased protection in a single tranche CDO on a senior tranche, then as credit spreads increase uniformly, the value of the protection increases. In effect, the purchased protection is closer

---

[120] For a discussion of credit models, see Chapter 6. For a discussion of modelling CDO tranches, see discussion earlier in the Chapter.

[121] For a discussion of deltas and delta hedging in derivatives generally, see Das, Satyajit (2004) Swaps/ Financial Derivatives 3rd Edition; John Wiley & Sons, Singapore at Chapters 15 and 16.

to being at-the-money. This means the deltas will increase. The dealer will need to sell more protection. This protection can be sold at higher credit spreads, resulting in trading profits to the dealer. In effect, the dealer has a long gamma position. However, if the dealer has purchased protection on the equity tranche, then the position will be different. An increase in credit spreads will result in a fall in deltas. This is because the position of equity is not as sensitive to credit spreads. This reflects the position in the capital structure and the risk of loss. This will mean that the dealer will be required to reduce its hedge by purchasing protection. This protection will be purchased at higher cost, triggering trading losses. In effect, the dealer is short gamma.

Additional problems exist in dynamic hedging. For example, if the likelihood of default is high, then the primary focus of the dealer is not credit spread but recovery rates. This will require the dealer to manage the risk of recovery rates changing. This will typically be done by trading bonds of the distressed firm to match the first order sensitivity of the tranche to changes in recovery rates. A further problem is that of "the jump to default". For example, a low risk/low credit spread firm may default suddenly as a result of an unexpected exogenous event. In this case, the rapid change in delta may be difficult (if not impossible) to manage.

The dealer is exposed to a number of risks in using credit delta hedges. There is significant model risk. The credit models used are based on a variety of assumptions that may not be realised in practice. In addition, parameter estimates such as credit spreads and particularly default correlation must be determined. Market credit spreads are generally available for standard credit default swap maturities (5 years). Market prices for other maturities may be less reliable. Default correlation estimates are more problematic. There is no direct trading in default correlation. This makes it necessary to derive model based estimates. Increasingly, the implied correlation of credit index tranched CDO trades is used to calibrate default correlation estimates[122]. The dealer is also exposed to execution risks in hedging the credit delta hedges. Changes in market liquidity affect the

---

[122] For a discussion of some of the issues in using implied correlation, see Mashal, Roy, Naldi, Marco and Tejwani, Gaurav "The Implications Of Implied Correlation" (July 2004) Risk 66–68.

ability of the dealer to manage the hedges and also the cost of hedging. The risk is exacerbated by the fact that it is difficult, in practice, to hedge default correlation risk with other dealers. This means a risk, once assumed, must be held and managed through to maturity.

Dynamic credit trading, as described, requires significant commitment in terms of quantitative/modelling resources and risk assumption. A few major dealers have invested significantly in developing these capabilities.

Exhibit 4.20   Single Tranche CDO

A conventional CDO where the entire capital structure is placed with investors is structured as follows:

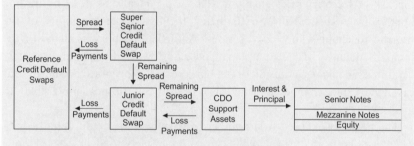

A single tranche CDO structure would be as follows:

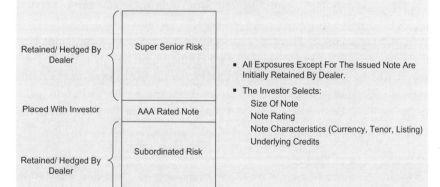

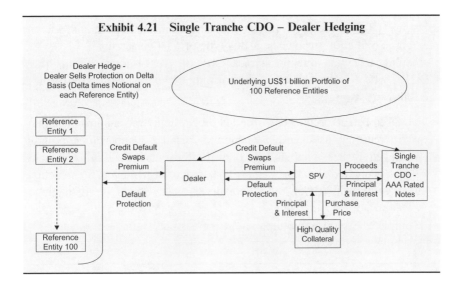

Exhibit 4.21   Single Tranche CDO – Dealer Hedging

9   CDO Investments – Economics and Performance

9.1   *Structure*

In previous Sections, the focus has been on the structure of CDOs. In this Section, the focus is on CDO investments from the perspective of investors.

Investor demand for credit investment products is a key driver of CDO structures. The major features of CDOs that have proved attractive to investors include:

- Ability to invest in a diversified portfolio of credit risk that would not normally be available for investment.
- Capacity to invest in structured credit exposure, specifically risks that are not available directly in the cash market. This includes:
  1. *Different risks* – through the creation of different tranches of securities by loss layering.
  2. *Leverage* – the ability to use the CDO structure to leverage exposure to the underlying credit risk.
  3. *Management expertise* – access to specialised credit management skills to enhance the return on the portfolio. This is considered particularly important in inefficient and illiquid markets such as leveraged bank debt.

The ability to create structured credit exposure has been increasingly important for investors. This has driven the demand for synthetic managed arbitrage CDO structures. It has also driven investor demand for the mezzanine and equity tranches in this type of CDO structure.

Exhibit 4.22 sets out the typical structure of a managed arbitrage CDO[123]. The CDO market has increasingly become standardised around the following format:

- CDOs are structured as cash/funded or synthetic transactions. The market increasingly uses synthetic structures because of superior economics.
- Managed rather than static structures have increased in popularity. This has created some problems[124]. A variety of management structures have evolved in response to the experience of investors with managed CDO structures.
- Complete capital structures and (increasingly) single tranche CDO structures are used.

Exhibit 4.22   Arbitrage CDOs – Structure

1. Cash/Funded CDOs

Structure

The general structure of a managed arbitrage cash/funded CDO will be as follows:
- An investment bank/dealer arranges the CDO.
- The CDO is established as a special purpose vehicle ("SPV"). The SPV will contain the assets and liabilities and will be managed by an appointed manager.
- The CDO will be based on a portfolio of credit risk (generally high yield bonds, emerging market bonds, bank loans (including leveraged loans) or other securities).
- The credit risk is transferred into the vehicle. This will be through the SPV purchasing securities.
- The capital structure of the CDO will consist of a series of securities (equity, mezzanine and senior). A typical capital structure is outlined below[125]:

Class	% of Portfolio	Rating	Spread (bps to LIBOR)	Over Collateralisation (% of Portfolio Subordinated)
Senior	94.0	AAA	40	6.38
Mezzanine	4.0	BBB/BB	250–500	2.04
Equity	2.0	Not rated		

---

[123] See Nassar, Tarek and Tierney, John F. (29 April 2003) "Synthetic CDOs" Recent Market Developments; Deutsche Bank, London.

[124] The equity structure set out is the simplest structure used. There are a variety of other equity structures that are used; see elsewhere in Chapter.

[125] The structure will vary significantly depending on the credit quality of underlying securities/risks.

- The securities are placed with investors. Investors seeking leveraged exposure to the portfolio will invest in the equity and mezzanine tranches. The manager will generally co-invest in the equity tranche.
- The capital raised from the issue of debt and equity is used to fund the purchase of securities.

Operations

The operation of the typical cash/funded CDO will be as follows:

- The CDO will generally have a life of 12 years. There is a ramp-up period during which the portfolio is assembled. There is a 5 year re-investment period during which the collateral is actively managed. This is followed by a 7 year unwind period during which the liabilities are repaid using the cash flow/proceeds of the portfolio.
- The equity holders generally have a call option (after a non call period of 5 years) to terminate the transaction.
- The cash flows within the structure during normal operation will be as follows:
  1. *Reinvestment period* – all cash flows received are used to service the debt in order of seniority. The excess interest is distributed to the equity investors. The manager reinvests all excess principal in new assets within pre-specified portfolio guidelines.
  2. *Repayment period* – during this period, excess interest payments decrease. Principal surplus is used to repay the debt securities in order of seniority. If all debt is repaid, then all cash flows accrue to the equity investors.
- Where there are credit losses on the reference portfolio, the value of the assets will be impaired.
- Where there are credit losses on the portfolio, the investors suffer losses in the following way. The value of assets relative to liabilities is reduced, decreasing over-collateralisation levels for senior investors in the capital structure. In addition, interest coverage of liabilities is impaired. Where losses are incurred and the value of the credit portfolio falls below specified levels, distributions to equity investors are suspended. This can also occur if interest coverage levels fall below specified levels. The excess cash flow is then directed to repay debt securities in accordance with a specified seniority. If collateralisation and interest coverage are restored to satisfactory levels, then the distributions to equity resume. If losses increase or interest coverage declines, than payments on mezzanine debt securities may also be suspended, with cash flows being used to repay senior liabilities.

Role Of CDO Manager

The CDO manager is generally an asset manager (insurance company or investment manager) or a specialised credit manager/hedge fund. The CDO manager should ideally have expertise, experience and a sound history of success in management of credit portfolios. The selection of the CDO manager is based on a thorough evaluation and due diligence of its capabilities. Specialist asset managers use the CDO structure to access investment funds and lock in long term management contracts.

The CDO manager is responsible for the management of the portfolio. The manager, in conjunction with the trustee, is responsible for ensuring compliance with the structural requirements of the CDO. The use of a specialist manager is designed to allow the investors (particularly the equity and mezzanine investors) to benefit from the trading skills of the manager. This skill will generally lock in trading profits and minimise losses on distressed securities. This is through security selection and tactical purchases or sales from the underlying portfolio.

The CDO manager is compensated by payment of fees that are structured as a base component and a performance-based incentive component. A non-monetary benefit of the structure is that a CDO manager obtains access to a larger pool of investors and also increases the size of its assets under management.

2. Synthetic CDOs

Structure

The general structure of an arbitrage CDO will be as follows:

- An investment bank/dealer will arrange the CDO.
- The CDO will be established as a special purpose vehicle ("SPV"). The SPV will contain the assets and liabilities. The SPV will be managed by an appointed manager (if it is a managed structure).
- The CDO will be based on a portfolio of credit risk (generally investment grade bank loans and bank loans (including leveraged loans) or other securities). The asset will generally not be physical or cash assets (such as loans or bonds). It will consist of single name credit default swaps.
- The credit risk will be transferred into the vehicle. This will generally use credit default swaps (in a synthetic structure).
- The capital structure of the CDO will consist of a series of securities (equity, mezzanine, senior and super senior). A typical capital structure will be as follows:

Class	% of Portfolio	Rating	Spread (bps to LIBOR)	Over Collateralisation (% of Portfolio Subordinated)
Super	90.0	Not Rated	10	11.11
Senior	4.0	AAA	40	6.38
Mezzanine	4.0	BBB/BB	250–500	2.04
Equity	2.0	Not rated		

- The senior and mezzanine securities are placed with investors. Investors seeking leveraged exposure to the portfolio will invest in the equity and mezzanine tranches. The manager will generally co-invest in the equity tranche.
- The proceeds of the securities placed are invested in high quality securities to collateralise the credit default swaps.
- The dealer may retain the super senior risk. It can also be transferred to a third party. This would be done using an unfunded credit default swap.

Operations

The operation of the synthetic CDO over its term will be as follows:

- The CDO will generally have a life of 5 years. This will conform to the maturity of liquid credit default swaps of 5 years.
- The fees received from the portfolio of credit default swaps together with the interest on the collateral is used to service the super senior swap (if applicable), the senior debt and the mezzanine debt. Any excess spread is paid to the equity investors.
- Where there are credit losses on the reference portfolio in a synthetic structure, there will be payments due under the credit default swap. This is met by liquidating collateral to cover payments under the credit default swaps. This will reduce the principal amount of high grade securities available to repay the CDO investors. At the end of the transaction, the remaining collateral is repaid to investors in order of seniority.
- Synthetic structures are significantly simpler than cash/funded structures and do not generally require a cash flow waterfall structure or over collateralisation or interest coverage tests.

Role Of CDO Manager

Early synthetic CDOs were static. The static format structure is relatively transparent and simple. It was also driven by the large arbitrage margins available. Investors focused on analysing the initial portfolio of credit risk.

The adverse credit cycle of 2000 to 2002 exposed the problems of static structures. Unexpected deterioration in credit quality and default correlation resulted in losses to investors. This led to the evolution of the managed synthetic CDO structure. Under this arrangement, investors appointed a manager to trade the reference credit portfolio to avoid losses and also to monetise gains (from spread tightening). The underlying theory was that the manager would be able to identify poorly performing credits and thereby effectively improve the performance of the portfolio.

This is similar to the structure used in funded structures, in particular high yield CDOs. There were important differences. The role of the manager was frequently circumscribed with controls (this is known as "lightly managed") including:

- The investor generally selected the initial portfolio but also nominated an additional universe of obligors that the manager could trade.
- The investment manager was permitted under the terms of the investment management agreement to replace a fixed amount (around 5%) of outstanding notional amount each year.
- The use of automatic substitution rules if an obligor's credit spread increased by a fixed level (usually nominated as a multiple of its initial spread) or its rating deteriorated (usually by a fixed amount from its initial rating).

The management structure may include the establishment of an initial cash pool (sometimes referred to as a "margin trading account") to cover substitution costs.

3. Comparison Of Funded Versus Synthetic Structures

The basic features of the two structures are set out below:

Feature	Funded CDO	Synthetic CDO
Underlying Assets	Corporate, high yield or emerging market bonds	Investment grade credit default swaps
Size of Portfolio	40 to 60 bonds	100 to 150 obligors
Term	6–12 years	5 years
Capital Structure	Senior, mezzanine and equity	Super senior, senior, mezzanine and equity
Funding	Fully funded	Partially funded
Performance Triggers	Overcollateralisation and interest coverage triggers to protect senior classes	Typically minimal to none
Managed	Managed	Static or Managed (generally within pre-specified boundaries)

9.2 CDO Investments – Economics/Risk Analysis[126]

9.2.1 Overview

Investments in a CDO structure are complex securities. There are generally two sources of risk – the credit risk of the asset and the CDO structure.

The economics of CDO investments are driven by the credit risk of the underlying portfolio. The risk and return of the investment is directly related to the underlying portfolio of credit risk. This means that losses as a result of default are a major risk of the structure. An additional engineered risk is the structure of priorities that governs the order of claims on the cash flows/ value of the underlying assets. This means that risk is either reduced or increased depending on the position in the capital structure. Risk increases where the securities are structurally subordinated such as for the mezzanine

---

[126] See Duffie, Darrell and Garleanu, Nicolae "Risk And Valuation Of Collateralised Debt Obligations" (January/February 2001) Financial Analysts Journal 41–59; Li, David and Skarabot, Jure "Valuation And Risk Analysis Of Synthetic Collateralised Debt Obligations: A Copula Function Approach" in Gregory, Jon (Editor) (2003) Credit Derivatives: The Definitive Guide; Risk Publications, London at Chapter 14; Nassar, Tarek and Tierney, John F. (29 April 2003) Synthetic CDOs" Recent Market Developments; Deutsche Bank, London; During, Alexander and Nassar, Tarek (15 May 2003) Valuing Synthetic CDOs; Deutsche Bank, London; Smithson Charles "Hedging A Portfolio Of Structured Credit Assets" (October 2004) Risk 66–69.

and equity investors. The equity and mezzanine investors must absorb the first and second losses on the credit portfolio, thereby increasing the risk.

Effectively there are two separate types of risk in CDO investments:

- **Risk of realised loss** – this covers actual credit events/defaults that result in realised losses that reduce the cash payments to CDO security holders.
- **Risk of mark-to-market losses** – this covers changes in the underlying asset portfolio short of actual credit event/default. This covers changes in credit quality/credit spreads and changes in default correlation. These changes may affect the expected losses on one or more CDO tranches. This generally translates into changes in the required spread on the tranche, resulting in the security trading away from par value. If there are no actual credit events/defaults and the CDO securities are held to maturity, then the investor does not suffer a cash loss. However, the change in value of the CDO security results in mark-to-market value changes. These changes will result in realised losses if the relevant tranches are sold.

In practice, investors in CDO securities are exposed to both risks. Subordinated tranches (equity and mezzanine) are exposed to both risks. Senior tranches are generally more exposed to mark-to-market risk. This reflects the fact that risk of actual loss is low in senior tranches, reflecting the credit enhancement embedded within the structures.

9.2.2   Valuation/Pricing of CDO Tranches

The valuation and risk analysis of CDO tranches is based on the standard modelling techniques used with CDO transactions. It is similar to the approach used by major rating agencies to derive the credit rating of CDO securities[127].

The fundamental approach entails the following steps:

- The loss distribution for individual reference entities is established from estimates of default probability and loss given default.
- The loss distribution for the portfolio is derived from the individual loss distributions and some measure of co-dependence of defaults using some form of default correlation.

The valuation of individual CDO tranches requires an additional step. This relates to the fact that portfolio losses are not borne proportionately.

---

[127]   See discussion earlier in the Chapter. For a detailed discussion of credit modelling, see Chapter 6.

Individual tranches have different exposure to default risk based on subordination and structural protection. The performance of each tranche is dependent on the timing of default and the loss given default relative to the size of loss bearing tranches subordinated to the securities being assessed.

The pricing of credit risk in a risk neutral framework is relatively straightforward. For an individual credit, the pricing (that is, the present value of credit spread received) must equal the expected value of the losses (that is, the present value of expected payments in case of credit event/default).

A similar approach is used for credit portfolios and CDO tranches. For a loss bearing tranche, the breakeven pricing equates to the credit spread required to equal the expected aggregated losses attributable *to that tranche*. This requires derivation of the distribution of cumulative losses from the start of the transaction to maturity of the transaction. Losses are allocated to individual tranches in order of seniority and consistent with the structural rules applicable to the CDO. This allows derivation of the cumulative loss distribution *for each tranche*. The tranche losses will vary depending upon seniority. The pricing of each CDO tranche (required credit spread) equates to the expected losses for each tranche.

In practice, the modelling is complex. This reflects difficulties in establishing parameter estimates (default probabilities, recovery rates and default correlation). It also reflects the needs to simulate the losses over time as individual tranche performance is sensitive to the *timing of default* as well as *number and loss severity of defaults*. Differences in models and parameter estimates mean that market pricing of CDO tranches does not conform to model breakeven levels.

9.2.3 CDO Tranche Risk Measures

Overview

The modelling approach used allows derivation of risk measures for each tranche[128]. These sensitivities to key parameters provide the ability to measure and hedge/manage the risk of individual tranches[129].

---

[128] See Schloegl, Lutz and Greeberg, Andrei "Understanding Deltas Of Synthetic CDO Tranches" (November 2003) Lehman Brothers Quantitative Credit Research 45–54; Hatstadt, Philippe "New Greeks For Synthetic CDOs: Correlation Trading In Full Swing" (January 2004) Risk – Sponsor's Statement; Leo, Peck-Chao "The Impact of Correlation On Synthetic CDOs" (April 2004) Asia Risk – Sponsor's Statement.

[129] These risk measures are similar to the Greek letters used to denote option

The risk measures are useful for the following market participants:

- **Traders** – the risk measures allow traders to manage the risk of CDO transactions. This risk management covers trading in CDO tranches, managing inventory/residual position and (most importantly) single tranche CDOs.
- **Investors** – the risk measures allow investors to measure the risk of individual CDO tranches. This is important in two contexts:
  1. It allows estimation of exposures to individual reference entities for the purpose of recording and reporting exposures to individual credits. In a CDO, irrespective of tranche, investors do not have proportionate exposure to each reference entity. The exposure depends upon the position in the capital structure, the order of default and the loss severity. This creates problems in managing traditional investment portfolios within specific credit limits and restrictions. Credit risk measures (such as credit delta) can be used to allocate specific exposure to the relevant counterparty[130].
  2. It allows risk management of CDO investments by enabling investors to specifically hedge risk in CDO tranches using the risk measures. For example, an investor may buy protection in the credit default swap market on one or more reference entities against a position in a CDO tranche to reduce risk or capture relative value from market pricing anomalies. Instruments used to hedge individual name exposures in a CDO portfolio include: cash bond positions, put options on bonds, credit default swaps/total return swaps on individual entities, credit default swaps/total return swaps on credit indexes, n[th]-to-default baskets, cash equity positions and equity put options.

Credit Risk Measures

The principal risk measures include[131]:

- **Credit spread sensitivity (Delta)** – this measures the change in the value of a CDO tranche for a given change in the credit spread (1 bps)

---

risk and manage option portfolios. See Das, Satyajit (2004) Swaps/Financial Derivatives 3rd Edition; John Wiley & Sons, Singapore at Chapters 15 and 16.

[130] Dealers increasingly provide this information to investors for limit compliance and risk management.

[131] The risk measures are not standardised at this point in time. Different analysts use similar but different risk measures.

applicable to an individual reference entity. The credit delta is generally calculated assuming a parallel shift in credit spread. A portfolio will have multiple deltas corresponding to the number of reference entities in the portfolio. An alternative credit delta can be calculated to measure the sensitivity of the CDO tranche value for a parallel shift in credit spread for all reference entities within the portfolio (i.e. systemic rather than individual credit spread changes). Credit deltas are increasingly important. They measure the quantum of exposure within the portfolio to individual reference entities. This allows a trader or investor to proxy the risk to an individual reference entity and then combine and record credit exposure across all their activities against limits. The credit delta also measures the hedge required by a dealer where it is long or short an individual CDO tranche. This is especially important in single tranche CDOs. For example, to hedge the risk of a short position in a CDO tranche (dealer has purchased protection from the investor), the dealer will need to sell protection on each of the reference entities in the specified portfolio based on its credit delta. The credit delta has a separate application in single tranche CDOs with substitution rights. In these transactions, the credit delta is used to proxy the gain or loss from individual reference entity substitutions within the portfolio.

- **Credit spread convexity (gamma)** – this measures the change in credit delta for a given change in the credit spread (1 bps) for an individual reference entity. Gamma measures the degree of hedging risk. Gamma equates to the change in value of a CDO tranche net of changes in value of an offsetting delta hedge to a change in credit spreads. There are, in practice, two gammas:
  1. *Portfolio gamma* – this refers to the impact of a parallel spread change for all reference entities within the portfolio. This will generally reflect the market wide movements in credit spreads. In practice, in the absence of company specific information, credit spreads generally move in line with market or industry movement. This is reinforced by the practice employed by most dealers where the dealers adjust credit spreads (consistent with general market changes) in the absence of a specific credit spread change in a specific reference entity.
  2. *Individual gamma* – this refers to the impact of an idiosyncratic change in the credit spread in an individual reference entity. This will

inevitably reflect the release of company specific information. Individual gamma will rarely follow the normal convex behaviour experienced with portfolio gamma. Individual gamma will affect individual CDO tranches differently. For example, a large rise in credit spreads on a reference entity will indicate a higher risk of default. This will translate into an increased risk of loss on the CDO equity. This is equivalent to a loss driven by differences in realised credit spread and default correlation relative to model assumptions.

- **Default sensitivity** – this measures the sensitivity of the value of a CDO tranche to the default of an individual credit in the underlying portfolio. It measures the impact of a credit event and loss severity on the relevant tranche. Default sensitivity will vary significantly depending on position in the capital structure. It will also depend upon timing of the default and the history of defaults within the portfolio.
- **Correlation sensitivity (Rho)** – this measures sensitivity of the value of a CDO tranche to given changes in default correlation (usually 0.01 or 1%). Depending upon the factor model used, the correlation sensitivity is calculated in relation to each reference entity. The impact of correlation varies between CDO tranches. Equity tranches have a long correlation position. Senior tranches are short correlation. The correlation position of mezzanine tranches is more complex. It depends upon the attachment point. It also depends upon the size of the equity tranche, timing of default and experienced default history (erosion or increase in subordination).
- **Time decay (theta)** – this measures sensitivity of the value of a CDO tranche to given changes in remaining time to maturity (1 day). Decreases in remaining maturity have different effects depending upon the specific CDO tranche. Senior tranches increase in value with reduction in time to maturity. Subordinated tranches (equity and mezzanine tranches) generally experience decreases in value with reduction in time to maturity.

The risk measures described are generally calculated on the assumption that all other parameters remain unchanged. In practice, this is unlikely to occur. This gives rise to complex inter-relationships e.g. sensitivity to simultaneous changes in credit spread and default correlation. In addition, there are cross gammas e.g. the impact of changes in correlation on individual credit deltas. This complicates risk measurement and risk management.

CDO Tranche Behaviour[132]

CDO tranche behaviour is driven by two primary factors:

- Changes in market credit spread (in effect, changes in default probability and loss given default)
- Changes in default correlation.

The impact on individual tranches varies significantly. The major factor is the seniority and precise priority structure[133].

All tranches are affected by changes in credit spread. If credit spreads increase on all reference entities, then the expected loss on the portfolio increases. This increases the theoretical price of each tranche.

The notional amount or face value of the securities caps the loss on each tranche. This means that as spreads increase, the risk of loss moves from the subordinated tranches (equity and mezzanine) to the senior tranches. As spreads widen, the initial increase in risk is absorbed by the subordinated tranches. As expected losses increase further, the credit enhancement becomes fully utilised, and the senior tranche becomes increasingly exposed to the risk of loss. This means that credit spreads on senior tranches are more sensitive to changes in credit spread. This is particularly the case where credit spreads move up sharply.

Senior CDO tranches exhibit negative price convexity with reference to credit spread movements. In contrast, the convexity of mezzanine tranches can shift. Spread increases imply higher expected losses. At very high losses around the size of the mezzanine tranche, additional spread increases would not affect the mezzanine tranche. A similar behaviour is apparent in CDO equity.

---

[132] See Li, David and Skarabot, Jure "Valuation And Risk Analysis Of Synthetic Collateralised Debt Obligations: A Copula Function Approach" in Gregory, Jon (Editor) (2003) Credit Derivatives: The Definitive Guide; Risk Publications, London at Chapter 14; During, Alexander and Nassar, Tarek (15 May 2003) Valuing Synthetic CDOs; Deutsche Bank, London; Hatstadt, Philippe "New Greeks For Synthetic CDOs: Correlation Trading In Full Swing" (January 2004) Risk – Sponsor's Statement.

[133] In this Section, the typical behaviour of individual tranches is discussed. The discussion is general. The actual behaviour of tranches in a specific transaction is affected by the exact structure and the precise circumstances. In some circumstances, the tranche behaviour could vary significantly from that normally observed.

The position is different where credit spreads increase on a specific or a few reference entities. This reflects the fact that the subordinated tranches are exposed to firm specific risk; that is, idiosyncratic or event risk. This means that equity and mezzanine tranches are sensitive to these changes. This behaviour reflects the impact of default correlation changes. The increase in the credit spread of one reference entity reflects the fact that correlation within the portfolio has decreased, exposing equity and mezzanine tranche holders to additional risk.

CDO tranche behaviour is significantly affected by default correlation. Correlation affects the shape of the portfolio loss distribution. Zero correlation creates a portfolio loss distribution where extreme outcomes (no or large losses) have relatively low probabilities. Higher correlation (moving towards 1.00) changes the shape of the distribution so that extreme outcomes have higher probabilities. As correlation increases, the tails of the distribution become fatter. As correlation increases, the mean of the loss distribution remains unaltered but the variance of losses increases.

The changes in default correlation affect the individual CDO tranches. This reflects the fact that the loss layering structure means that investors in each tranche have exposure to different default events. For example, equity and mezzanine investors, in reality, are exposed to a few of the reference entities in the portfolio. This is because the subordinated investors suffer losses from the first and second losses in the portfolio. It also reflects the fact the investor's loss is capped by the size of the tranche. This means that changes in default correlation and the shape of the loss distribution change the risk of loss for all tranches.

Equity investors are long correlation. In contrast, senior investors are short correlation. Mezzanine investors are generally less sensitive to correlation. Mezzanine tranches are generally either slightly short or long correlation depending upon the structure.

As correlation increases, the risk of defaults on the portfolio increases[134]. This would mean that there is greater risk of loss on the equity tranche. The risk of loss on senior tranches also increases. This reflects the fact that the chance of extreme losses *exceeding* the size of equity and mezzanine tranches also increases. At high correlation levels, senior investors are more exposed

---

[134]   For example, if the correlation is 1.00 (100%), the portfolio would be equivalent to the investment in a single asset with the characteristics of the portfolio. This would mean that the subordinated tranches (equity and mezzanine) would be as risky as the equivalent asset.

to the risk of loss. In contrast, a decrease in correlation transfers the risk of loss into the equity tranche and improves the position of the senior tranche.

The sensitivity of the mezzanine tranche to changes in default correlation is more complex. The mezzanine tranche has the credit enhancement provided by the equity tranche. This means that the mezzanine tranche is less sensitive to correlation changes[135]. However, correlation shifts still affect the performance of the mezzanine tranche. Initial increases in correlation increase the expected loss on the mezzanine tranche. After a certain point, further increases in correlation have less impact. This reflects the size of mezzanine tranches. At higher correlation levels, the risk of loss is transferred to senior tranches. The impact of correlation also depends on other factors. Higher absolute spreads translate into a higher level of correlation at which the sensitivity of the mezzanine tranche changes from positive to negative. This is consistent with the shift of risk to tranches that are higher in the capital structure where correlation increases.

In 2003/2003, the CDO market exhibited a correlation skew[136]. The skew meant that implied default correlation in CDOs on equity and senior tranches was significantly higher than for mezzanine tranches. For example, implied correlation was around 15–25% for equity, 0–10% for mezzanine (rated BBB) and 20–30% for senior/super senior tranches (rated AAA). There is no consensus as to the factors underlying the skew. The most probable explanation is the segmentation of markets (that is, inefficient markets) or mis-specification of models[137].

An alternative way of understanding the behaviour of CDO tranches is in terms of option theory[138]. Under this approach, the equity investor has purchased a call option on the cash flows from the portfolio. The option has a strike equal to the attachment point of the equity tranche in the

---

[135]   In practice, some investors frequently seek mezzanine investments that are relatively immune to correlation shifts.

[136]   For a discussion of volatility skews, see Das, Satyajit (2004) Swaps/Financial Derivatives 3rd Edition; John Wiley & Sons, Singapore at Chapter 9.

[137]   See (2004) Bank Of America Guide To Advanced Correlation Products; Bank of America/Risk Publications – Supplement to (July 2004) Risk at 10.

[138]   See Li, David and Skarabot, Jure "Valuation And Risk Analysis Of Synthetic Collateralised Debt Obligations: A Copula Function Approach" in Gregory, Jon (Editor) (2003) Credit Derivatives: The Definitive Guide; Risk Publications, London at Chapter 14; During, Alexander and Nassar, Tarek (15 May 2003) Valuing Synthetic CDOs; Deutsche Bank, London.

transaction. If the correlation level increases, then the variance of the portfolio credit loss distribution increases. The increase in dispersion of the loss distribution increases the value of the call option. This equates to a lowered credit spread for the CDO equity investors.

Senior investors have sold a put option on the cash flows from the portfolio. The option has a strike price equal to the attachment point of the mezzanine tranche. An increase in the dispersion of the portfolio adversely affects the performance of the put option. This translates into a higher required credit spread for the CDO senior investors.

Mezzanine investors have a spread position. CDO mezzanine tranche investors are long a call option on the cash flows from the portfolio with a strike equal to the attachment point of the mezzanine tranche. CDO mezzanine tranche investors are short a put struck at the attachment point of the equity tranche. Increases in correlation and corresponding increases in the variance of the credit loss distribution result in increases in the value of the purchased call option. It also results in a decrease in the value of the sold put option. The sensitivity of the CDO mezzanine to correlation shifts represents the offsetting effect of the two option value changes.

The sensitivity of the different tranches highlights the differences between systemic (a general market-wide change) and idiosyncratic or event risk (specific changes affecting individual reference entities). Equity investors are exposed to idiosyncratic or event risk. This reflects the fact that any default affects the performance of the equity tranche. In contrast, senior tranches are more exposed to systemic risk; that is, a deterioration in overall credit quality of the portfolio. Mezzanine tranche behaviour is somewhere in the middle.

The different tranches also exhibit different sensitivity to timing of default. Default timing is implied, to a degree, by the credit spreads. Low credit spreads generally mean better credit quality. This is consistent with these reference entities tending to default later in time. This means that exposure to the better quality reference entities is concentrated in the senior tranches.

The inter-relationship of credit deltas and default correlation is interesting. For a given reference entity, the default correlation is a critical element in its credit delta in a tranched portfolio. For example, a reference entity with low default correlation to the rest of the portfolio will have a large delta for the equity tranche. It will have lower deltas for the other tranches. Low default correlation is consistent with high idiosyncratic or event risk. If the default correlation increases, then the equity credit delta declines. In contrast, the delta for higher tranches increases.

The inter-relationship between credit deltas and remaining time to maturity is also interesting. For a given reference portfolio, the low credit spread reference entities (low default risk) are more likely to default later. This means that the credit delta for these names is higher for senior tranches. If default occurs later, it is likely that the subordinated tranches will have experienced losses by that time and therefore will provide less credit enhancement. This means that the sensitivity of the equity and mezzanine tranches to correlation increases is less for those reference entities. This reduces the credit delta.

CDO Tranche Hedging/Trading

The tranche risk measures are used for hedging by traders. This is frequently used in single tranche CDOs. It is also used to manage risk more widely e.g. inventory or residual positions.

The absolute credit spread is hedged by using the credit deltas. This entails the trader offsetting the credit deltas of a tranche. For example, where the trader has structured a single tranche CDO for an investor (effectively purchased protection on a part of a portfolio), it would need to sell protection based on the credit delta on each of the reference entities. This hedge would then need to be dynamically managed as the credit deltas change in response to market credit spread changes, default correlation shifts and actual defaults. In efficient capital markets, the income generated from the credit default swaps where the trader has sold protection should exactly equate the credit spread paid on the single tranche CDO before any dealer profit.

In practice, this hedging is difficult[139]. The major issues include:

- Difficulties in optimally hedging both the credit spread and default risk exactly.
- Transaction costs incurred in trading credit default swaps to rebalance the hedge.
- Market constraints such as lack of liquidity (in particular, for distressed credits) and lack of availability of credit default swaps with a maturity matching the remaining term of the CDO (the credit default swap market focuses on a standard 5 year maturity).

---

[139]   See Boughey, Simon "The Correlation Conundrum" (April 2004) Risk – Credit Risk Supplement S11–S12.

• The hedge is highly model and input dependent. *Realised* changes in credit spread and default correlation may vary significantly from model assumptions, leading to hedging losses. Similarly, hedge changes lag changes in credit spreads and default correlation changes, leading to hedge slippage.

These difficulties dictate that traders use a range of hedging approaches. For example, CDO equity tranches are frequently hedged using a simple static hedge. The trader will sell (buy) protection on a few names within the portfolio against a short (long) single tranche CDO equity position. The protection is on the riskiest reference entities within the portfolio; that is, the credit most likely to default. Traders sometimes enter into credit default swap hedges on a notional principal larger than the CDO equity tranche being hedged. A constraint on the hedge is the net carry on the combined position. For example, where a short CDO equity position is hedged by selling protection, the trader will need to earn sufficient income from the sold protection to cover the payment to the note holder and its profit margin. The hedge also entails significant hedging risk. If a reference entity unexpectedly defaults as a result of idiosyncratic or event risk, then the trader will be exposed to a mismatch on the hedge.

Similar approaches can be used for mezzanine or senior CDO tranches. A hedge for the mezzanine tranche consists of buying or selling protection for the relevant reference entities that, in terms of default probability, correspond to the position of the mezzanine tranche in the capital structure. Senior tranches can be hedged using a similar approach. These hedges have the same issues as those identified with the hedge of the CDO equity tranche. In practice, traders may choose not to hedge the senior tranches on the assumption that the credit enhancement reduces the risk of actual losses. The credit spread risk must still be managed.

Hedging default correlation risk presents additional challenges. There is no outright trading in default correlation risk. Traders can only trade correlation risk indirectly in the form of structured products (such as n^{th}-to-default baskets)[140] or trading in CDO tranches. These hedges are difficult and illiquid. This has prompted traders to use a variety of approaches to the management of default correlation risk.

---

[140]   See Chapter 2.

One approach has focused on using available instruments to hedge correlation risk. This includes n^{th}-to-default baskets and (increasingly) tranched credit index products. Traders frequently use *implied correlation* backed out of market prices of these instruments. The structure of these products (multiple reference entities) means that pairwise correlation cannot be directly calculated. This means that only constant pair-wise correlation can be derived.

The increased popularity of CDOs based on standardised credit indexes has led dealers to increasingly use constant market implied default correlation. The implied correlation is derived from market prices/spreads on traded tranches of credit index CDOs.

The use of CDOs based on standardised credit indexes raises a number of issues:

- **Index Composition** – in practice, the composition of the index and the reference entities underlying the CDO will frequently not coincide. This means that the dealer using the tranched credit index to hedge faces basis risk that must be managed.
- **Implied Correlation** – the implied correlation is referred to as the *compound* implied correlation. This entails using a specified model (typically a Gaussian copula model[141]) to derive a required spread on a CDO tranche given a single asset correlation and individual credit default swap spreads. Given a tranche spread and individual credit default swap spreads, a single asset correlation can be calculated. The problem with compound correlation is that for a given transaction, more than one correlation can be derived. This is problematic as the differences between the different compound correlations can sometimes be significant. Given that compound correlation is frequently used to market and rank tranches in relative value terms creates problems. This problem is most marked in the case of mezzanine tranches. Some market practitioners favour *base* correlation. Base correlation uses an approach predicated on treating each tranche as options on portfolio cash flows. The mathematics underlying base correlation allows the derivation of a single solution. This reflects the fact that the mezzanine tranche is treated as a long and short position in two equity tranches (with different attachments points). This means that the equity spread is a simple function of correlation. However, base correlation has a number of

---

[141]   See Chapter 6.

weaknesses. It relies on a large pool of underlying credits and uses the average credit spread. This means that the case of a single reference entity's credit spread widening does not affect based correlation significantly. However, actual tranche prices changes can be significant in these circumstances. Base correlation calculations are also subject to various problems, specifically in relation to the degree of precision. At this stage, there is no market consensus as to the appropriate method for calculating implied correlation[142].

- **Single versus pairwise correlation** – irrespective of the methodology used, the implied correlation approach does not provide pairwise correlation between the underlying reference entities. In practice, junior tranches in a CDO are sensitive to changes in the pairwise correlation. The modelling does not fully capture the risk or facilitate hedging.

Other potential methods of hedging include the use of equity correlation swaps[143]. Equity correlation swaps are structured on a basket of between 10 and 20 equity stocks and payout the difference between realised or actual correlation and the agreed level based on a fixed $ value per correlation point. There is increasing interest from reinsurance companies and hedge funds in assuming the correlation risk.

Other approaches focus on trading default correlation. This entails the trader trading expectations of *actual* correlation against *implied* correlation used to price transactions[144]. In practice, this involves either purchasing or selling specific tranches (primarily CDO equity and mezzanine tranches) or combination trades. The transactions entail different positions on net credit delta, spread convexity or default risk.

One strategy is to structure mezzanine pieces that have limited sensitivity to correlation shifts. The position is then delta hedged using individual credit default swaps.

Another strategy is to purchase CDO equity and short CDO mezzanine. The structure is designed to give the trader a leveraged credit exposure to the

---

[142] See Patel, Navroz "Cracking The Correlation Conundrum" (August 2004) Risk 40–42.

[143] The structure is similar to a volatility or variance swap; see Das, Satyajit (2004) Swaps/Financial Derivatives 3rd Edition; John Wiley & Sons, Singapore at Chapter 46.

[144] This is similar to trading strategies in options; see Das, Satyajit (2004) Swaps/ Financial Derivatives 3rd Edition; John Wiley & Sons, Singapore at Chapters 15 and 16.

underlying portfolio. The short mezzanine position is designed to protect the investor. The cost of the protection is the credit spread paid away on the mezzanine debt. The position will generally have positive carry unless default rates are significant. The default correlation position entails the trader being long correlation (in the equity tranche) and short correlation (mezzanine tranche).

The long CDO equity/short mezzanine position entails significant risks[145]. The combined position only provides a hedge if losses on the portfolio exceed the attachment point of the mezzanine tranche. This means that both the equity and mezzanine positions are entirely wiped out. In this situation, the hedge functions as intended. If losses are less than this amount, then it is likely that the loss on the equity tranche (first losses) will be larger than the value of the short mezzanine position. The combined position will also experience problems on a mark-to-market basis. An increase in credit spreads will not affect the equity and mezzanine tranches identically. It is likely that the equity tranche will lose more value than the gain on the short mezzanine position. This reflects the fact that the increase required in equity return will be larger than the change in return required on the mezzanine tranche.

The combined position is also sensitive to the timing of defaults. If there are no defaults in the early part of the transaction, the high excess cash flow to equity may generate sufficient return to offset a change in value of the mezzanine debt. This reflects the highly leveraged nature of the equity position.

9.3 CDO Tranches – Investment Analysis

9.3.1 Overview

The economics and sensitivity of individual CDO tranches are complex. The complexity derives from the behaviour of the underlying credit portfolio and the tranching of payments and losses. The structure creates interesting risk/return profiles for investors. The investment characteristics vary significantly between the senior/super senior, mezzanine and the equity tranches in CDOs.

Senior and super-senior investors have exposure to a large diversified portfolio of credit risk. They have low risk as a result of the credit

---

[145]   See Tavakoli, Janet M. (2003) Collateralized Debt Obligations And Structured Finance; John Wiley & Sons, Inc., New Jersey at 261–265.

enhancement embedded within the CDO structure. The investor in the equity and mezzanine tranches in a CDO is compensated for the additional risk through higher returns. Equity investors are residual claimants receiving the excess cash flow after servicing the senior and mezzanine securities. Equity investors have a highly leveraged exposure to the credit risk of the portfolio. The mezzanine investors receive returns that are consistent with the credit rating of the securities. Mezzanine investors also take some concentration risk, reflecting their position in the capital structure.

The high potential returns have encouraged investors to invest in the subordinated tranches in CDO transactions. Investment interest has been based on the argument that these investments (in particular, CDO equity) are an alternative investment class that has the potential to add value to the portfolio of long term investors. This is based on the returns available, the volatility of returns and the low correlation between CDO equity and other investment classes.

9.3.2 CDO Equity Investments[146]

CDO equity investors have a highly leveraged exposure to a diversified credit portfolio. CDO investors have a high risk-return position.

The equity investors are residual claimants receiving the excess cash flow (excess spread) of the transaction[147]. Depending on the transaction, the excess payments can range between 1.50 to 3.00% pa where the underlying portfolio is continuing to perform. This equates to a return of 15 to 20% pa.

Generally, the equity investor's return is front ended. Return of initial investment will usually occur by approximately 4 to 5 years into the term of the transaction for a funded CDO with a 12 year maturity. The equity investor will receive minimal distributions during the repayment period. The equity investors receive the distribution of the remaining collateral principal at maturity.

In a well performing transaction, the investor will use the call option to retire the transaction after around 7 to 8 years of its original term.

---

[146] See Reyfman, Alex and Toft, Klaus "Asset Management CDO Equity – A Growing Alternative Investment Asset Class" (April 2001) Risk – Sponsored Article; Flanagan, Christopher and Milton, Timothy (14 January 2002) CDO Equity: Credit Hedging And Relative Value.

[147] The equity structure set out is the simplest structure used. There are a variety of other equity structures that are used; see elsewhere in this chapter.

This reflects the rapid de-leveraging of the structure. The embedded call option can have significant value, in particular for transactions involving high yield bonds. This reflects the possibility of capital appreciation from spread compression. The value of the call option is lower where the underlying credit assets are floating rate (bank and leveraged loans). This reflects the fact that the borrowers can prepay and re-finance floating rate loans relatively easily.

The performance of equity in a synthetic securitisation CDO structure is similar. The major difference is that there is generally no call option (reflecting the shorter 5 year life).

In recent years, the return to CDO equity investors has frequently been capped. Payments above a pre-specified level are diverted to more senior investors or maintained in the form of a reserve against future losses.

The high return is provided in return for the equity investor assuming a high risk of loss. This derives from the fact that the CDO equity investor bears the first losses on the entire portfolio. Several factors drive the returns from the investment, including the excess spread, the credit losses, the value of the call option (if applicable) and the performance of the manager.

The equity investor is assuming the risk of first credit losses on the portfolio. The losses affect the equity investor in several ways. If the losses reach a specified level/the value of the collateral falls or interest coverage decreases below certain levels, then excess interest is diverted from equity investors. It is used to pay down debt to de-leverage the CDO. In addition, credit losses reduce the amount of assets and the corresponding interest payments, reducing the return to the investor.

The CDO equity investor has a substantial exposure to cumulative default rates, default correlation and default timing. The performance of CDO equity is adversely affected by increasing default rates, lower default correlation (higher idiosyncratic or event risk) and concentration of defaults in the early part of the life of the structure.

The risk to the equity investor is exacerbated by the leverage within the CDO structure. The size of the first loss layer and the nature of the underlying portfolio drive the degree of leverage. A small first loss piece will concentrate the credit risk of the portfolio. The characteristics of the portfolio, in particular the diversity of the portfolio and the default risk, will also drive leverage. Increases in diversity of the portfolio will increase leverage. This is because increased diversity will reduce the probability of zero default, thereby increasing the probability of losses on the equity.

9.3.3 CDO Mezzanine Tranches[148]

Mezzanine notes are the second loss tranche in a CDO transaction. Mezzanine tranches rank above equity and are subordinated to senior debt. Mezzanine notes in CDOs generally have credit ratings in the range A to B. The notes have the profile of a normal subordinated debt instrument. Mezzanine tranches are used in CDOs to allow equity to be more leveraged. It is also used to achieve a higher rating for senior tranches.

The return on mezzanine tranches is predictable as the coupon is pre-determined. Returns on CDO mezzanine securities generally offer superior returns to equivalent rated corporate bonds and mezzanine pieces in other ABS transactions. Unlike equity, there is no ability to participate in excess returns (captured by equity).

Several factors drive the returns from CDO mezzanine investments, including the level of the coupon, the credit losses, the CDO structure and the performance of the manager (if the CDO is dynamically managed). The risk to the investor is increased by leverage.

The mezzanine investor is exposed to losses in the underlying portfolio once the first loss protection of the equity tranche is used. The degree of risk leverage is driven by the size of the first loss/equity securities. If the equity portion is small (for example, in a balance sheet synthetic CDO of a high quality portfolio), then the mezzanine investment is leveraged. There is a high concentration of risk and significant exposure to low default correlation (idiosyncratic or event risk)[149].

---

[148] See Ganapati, Sunita and Tejwani, Gaurav "Language Diversity and Risk In Portfolio Default Swaps" (September 2000) Credit Risk Management – Supplement to Institutional Investor; Mahadevan, Sivan and Schwartz, David (June 2002) CDO Insights: Understanding Mezzanine Notes – Sensitivity Measures And Structural Innovation; Morgan Stanley – Fixed Income Research, Global – Structured Credit, New York; Reyfman, Alex and Toft, Klaus (30 May 2001) Mezzanine Classes Of Investment Grade Synthetic CDOs – An Investor's Guide; Goldman Sachs, New York; Reyfman, Alex and Toft, Klaus "Space Age Synthetic" (Summer 2001) Credit Derivatives 28–32.

[149] For example, consider the example of the transaction set out in **Exhibit 4.4**. The structure of the BB rated US$237 million mezzanine tranche is engineered using risk leverage. The underlying portfolio is high quality. This would normally translate into mezzanine debt that was investment grade. In order to reduce the mezzanine tranche rating to BB to comply with investor requirements, the equity tranche is reduced in size (to US$32 million or 0.33%). The impact of the structure can be seen when the impact of defaults is considered. The total

The size of the first loss/equity security and the diversity of the portfolio interact in determining the exact level of risk leverage. Where the collateral pool experiences higher than expected defaults, the equity component of the portfolio can be rapidly reduced. Under these conditions, the mezzanine debt becomes the *de facto equity* in the structure, without the ability to participate in any upside performance. Where there is significant impairment of the collateral pool, interest payments to the mezzanine debt holders can be deferred and compounded.

This means the mezzanine debt is highly sensitive to the performance of the assets. It is particularly exposed to the diversity and default correlations within the portfolio. In particular, for smaller CDO portfolios, there may be significant portfolio sampling risk.

In recent years, there has been increased concern that mezzanine investors are not adequately compensated for the investment risks. This has led to a number of structural innovations designed to protect mezzanine investors from some of the risks. The structural features are also designed to enhance the return for mezzanine investors. The enhancements focus on using cash flow diversion to protect mezzanine debt, additional return features and increasing alignment of equity/debt interests. **Exhibit 4.23** sets out a number of structural enhancements used in practice.

9.3.4 CDO Senior/Super Senior Tranches

Senior CDO Tranches

Senior CDO tranche investors have highly rated investments. The senior investment is on a diversified portfolio of credit risk and benefits from the structural credit enhancement.

In general, the risk of actual cash loss on the senior tranches is low. However, the senior tranches have significant mark-to-market risk. Where default rates on the portfolio increase, the realised losses reduce the equity

---

portfolio consists of 307 names and has a total notional value of US$9,722 million. This equates to an average exposure of US$31.67 million. Assuming a 35% recovery rate, the average loss in case of a credit event is equal to US$20.58 million. This means that the equity tranche bears the first 1 to 2 defaults (0.33% to 0.65% of the reference entities). The mezzanine tranche bears the next defaults – between 3 and 13 (0.98% to 4.23% of the reference entities). In effect, the mezzanine investors have a high level of exposure to idiosyncratic or event risk in the portfolio.

Exhibit 4.23   CDO Mezzanine Notes – Structural Enhancement

Structural Enhancement	Description/Analysis
Protection through cash flow diversion	
Capped equity payment	This entails capping the equity payments. The residual cash flow is diverted to pay down debt (mezzanine or pro rata) or reinvested in the portfolio. Where used to pay down debt, the capped equity payment reduces the financing cost, reduces leverage and reduces risk for the mezzanine or all debt holders. Where reinvested in the portfolio, the capped equity payment builds par and avoids early amortisation of the structure. The capped equity payment reduces equity returns and front loaded equity returns. It also reduces leverage for equity investors.
Direct pay trigger	This entails a trigger below second priority test. If triggered, then it requires either pay down cost (mezzanine or pro rata). This has similar advantages to the capped equity payment. Equity investors are generally not diluted where the structure performs well. The direct pay trigger has similar disadvantages to the capped equity payment. The disadvantages are particularly severe where the CDO performs poorly.
Ratings migration trigger	This entails diversion of cash flows where the weighted average rating factor ("WARF") compliance test is not met. Cash flows are diverted to pay down debt (mezzanine or pro rata) or reinvested in the portfolio. The rating migration trigger reduces mezzanine risk where the quality of the portfolio deteriorates. It also allows the manager to restore the value of the portfolio. The rating migration trigger has similar disadvantages to the capped equity payments and direct pay triggers.
Tighter coverage test	This entails increasing the trigger levels, with failure requiring pay down of debt. This has the effect of an early trigger of over collateralisation test. This has the disadvantage of restricting the manager's trading flexibility.

Structural Enhancement	Description/Analysis
Risk adjusted coverage test	This generally entails incorporating a haircut Caa basket. If the test is not met, the cash flows are diverted to pay down debt (mezzanine or pro rata). This reduces the risk to mezzanine debt holders where the portfolio quality deteriorates. The effect of the test is to reduce the manager's trading flexibility. The risk adjusted coverage test places reliance on ratings as an indicator of defaults.
De-lever with interest proceeds	This entails paying down with interest proceeds first. This has the effect of increasing excess spread on future interest payments. The major disadvantage is the deferral of front loaded payment to equity investors.
De-lever pro rata	This entails paying down pro rata. The structure reduces mezzanine risk but has negative implications for the rating of senior debt.
Minimum hard coupon	This entails nominating partial pay-in-kind ("PIK") coupon. This has the advantage of ensuring a minimum level of current coupon. The major disadvantage is the negative implications for the rating of senior debt.
Market value test	This entails forcing maintenance of loan to value ("LTV") ratio. This forces the manager to adjust the structure to asset price changes. The market value test is difficult to implement as managers may be forced to liquidate during periods of stress. There may also be trading liquidity issues.
Subordination	
Lower leverage	This entails reducing leverage by increasing the size of the equity in the CDO. This reduces mezzanine risk but also reduces the equity investor's returns and leverage.
Return enhancement	
Additional spread	This entails a higher spread on mezzanine notes. This would entail the mezzanine investor receiving higher returns when the value of the investment is not impaired (that is, the CDO performs well). The additional spread to mezzanine investors dilutes equity returns and may negatively impact upon the rating of senior notes.

Structural Enhancement	Description/Analysis
Step up coupon	This entails the coupon on the mezzanine notes increasing by a pre-specified amount where the credit quality of the portfolio deteriorates (for example, based on WARF measures). This has the advantage of providing additional return when the risk increases. This assumes that the higher coupon can and is paid. The step up coupon affects the CDO structure adversely, as interest costs increase as the portfolio deteriorates. This may have negative implications for the rating of senior notes.
Equity participation	This allows the mezzanine investors to receive a share in the equity upside. This can be structured in several ways, including equity warrants or a participation arrangement (investor receives capped equity coupon under certain conditions). The equity participation increases return to the mezzanine investors. The equity participation does not affect the risk of the mezzanine note holders. The structure also dilutes equity returns.
Interest Alignment	
Equity and debt ownership	This entails requiring CDO managers to subscribe debt and equity[150]. This is designed to align the interests of debt and equity holders and reduce the risk arising from moral hazard. The disadvantage is that CDO managers may not be able or willing to commit capital in this way.
Performance fees	This entails subordination of CDO manager's fees to mezzanine debt payments. This has the effect of placing the manager's fees at risk. The structure does not require a capital commitment from the CDO manager or increase the manager's risk.

Source: The above is adapted from Mahadevan, Sivan and Schwartz, David (June 2002) CDO Insights: Understanding Mezzanine Notes – Sensitivity Measures And Structural Innovation; Morgan Stanley – Fixed Income Research, Global – Structured Credit, New York at 20.

---

[150] This is analogous to "strip" investing (that is, investors taking every type of security pro rata) in a leveraged buyout transaction.

and mezzanine tranches, in turn impairing the level of credit enhancement within the structure. This was apparent during 2000 to 2002 as senior tranches in a number of CDOs were downgraded.

Senior CDO investors receive attractive returns relative to equivalent rated corporate securities. This is in addition to the benefits of diversification. The excess returns reflect the following factors:

- CDO investments are treated as structured finance/ABS securities and attract a premium relative to equivalent corporate credits.
- Credit markets historically appear to overestimate default risk. Implied default probabilities (backed out of traded market instrument prices such as credit default swap spreads) are generally significantly higher than actually experienced default rates. In addition, credit markets exhibit higher spreads due to trading anomalies[151]. These excess spreads can be used to generate senior investments with attractive risk profiles using CDO technologies.
- CDO investments may benefit from "ratings arbitrage"[152]. In rating a specific CDO tranche, rating agencies determine the level of subordination to reduce the default probability or expected loss to the level required for the target rating. Rating agencies use their own specified historical probabilities of default. These default probabilities are generally lower than that implied by market credit spreads. This means that the size of the senior tranches is larger than that implied by market spreads. The return on the senior tranches is based on current market spreads (higher than that implied by historical default probabilities). This produces excess returns to CDO senior investors. The default analysis ignores the impact of default correlation. The excess return is in part compensation for the correlation risk assumed.

Super Senior CDO Tranches

The high cost of AAA rated senior debt has driven the shift to synthetic structures. The economics of the super senior tranche are interesting[153].

---

[151] See Amato, Jeffrey D. and Remolana, Eli M. "The Credit Spread Puzzle" (December 2003) BIS Quarterly Review 51–63.

[152] See During, Alexander and Nassar, Tarek (15 May 2003) Valuing Synthetic CDOs; Deutsche Bank, London at 18–19.

[153] See Tavakoli, Janet M. (2003) Collateralized Debt Obligations And Structured Finance; John Wiley & Sons, Inc., New Jersey at Chapter 9.

The super senior tranche represents a further loss allocation within the senior tranche. The super senior investor assumes the risk of loss on the underlying credit portfolio where losses exceed the subordinated tranches (equity and mezzanine). The super senior risk is either retained by the dealer or sponsor or placed with third party investors.

The principal investors in super senior risk are re-insurers and monoline insurers. The super senior risk is structured as an unfunded credit default swap. The super senior pricing has hovered around 10 bps pa. It has moved in the range of 8 bps pa to 15 bps pa depending on market conditions. The demand for super senior risk is driven by a number of factors:

- Re-insurers have acquired credit risk to diversify their risk portfolios. The relatively low correlation between the high quality (super senior) credit risk and traditional reinsurance risk (catastrophe etc risk) has been attractive.
- The market pricing of credit (including the super senior tranche) is well above the implied spread based on historical default experience[154]. The super senior investors are frequently compensated for other risk (such as liquidity risk) through the spread. Super senior investors are generally more prepared to assume the liquidity risk because of the nature of their business.
- The demand for super senior investments and pricing is affected by the applicable regulatory regime. Super senior investors such as reinsurance companies are not subject to arbitrary regulatory capital regimes for credit risk. This means that they can align capital and reserves to the economic risk of the super senior tranche. This allows such investors to price super senior risk at more aggressive levels than regulated banks who would have to hold high levels of credit capital against such exposures.

The use of super senior technology raises complex issues, including:

- The actual credit quality of the super senior tranches is unclear. The super senior tranche is not rated by rating agencies. Dealers often claim that the super senior tranche is of superior credit quality to AAA rated securities[155].

---

[154] Model estimates of the breakeven credit spread on super senior tranches are often around 1 bps; that is well below the market pricing of the risk.

[155] It is referred to as AAAA.

- There is little discussion of the attachment point of the super senior tranche. As it is not rated, there is no formal requirement to set the attachment point in consultation with rating agencies[156]. This makes it difficult to benchmark different super senior tranches. In practice, the attachment point is negotiated with the super senior investors[157].

- The impact on the senior tranche of creating a super senior tranche is rarely considered. The attachment point for the senior tranche does not alter if a super senior tranche is introduced. This reflects the fact that the super senior tranche is simply a sub-tranching of the AAA senior tranche. There may be risk differences in the AAA tranche between the two structures. Assume a funded structure that has 94% AAA senior debt and 6% subordination (4% mezzanine and 2% equity). A synthetic structure on the same portfolio would entail a structure that is 90% super senior, 4% AAA senior and 6% subordination. The AAA senior is assumed to be the same in both structures. In the synthetic structure, the 4% senior tranche supports the super senior tranche. It is, in effect, a *first loss* element of the total AAA senior tranche. This means it bears more risk than the super senior tranche. This risk is most likely to be in the form of mark-to-market risk. This is because the risk of default is low. If the underlying portfolio experiences losses that impair the amount of equity/mezzanine available, the AAA tranche has greater downgrade risk within a synthetic structure with a super senior tranche. This reflects the loss tiering and the smaller size of the senior tranche. It is not clear if the market pricing captures this potential risk difference.

---

[156] In any case, any such discussion would be redundant as the rating agencies do not formally acknowledge the super senior tranche and the highest rating category is AAA.

[157] In practice, the senior and subordinated (equity and mezzanine) tranches total around 8.00% of the notional face value of the portfolio. This is particularly the case where the transaction is a balance sheet regulatory capital transaction. This facilitates getting regulatory approval for capital relief. In effect, the argument is that under Basel 1, the bank would be required to hold 8% capital against the position. If the synthetic securitisation structure entails an 8% capital structure (equity, mezzanine and senior) then the total amount of capital against the underlying risk has not changed. In effect, the argument is that the sponsor bank has *never* held capital against the *implicit* super senior risk.

9.4 CDO Investment Performance

The advantages of CDOs have attracted significant investment from investors. This investment was driven by a number of factors, including the relatively high returns available[158]. It was affected by the fact that ABS historically have lower default rates/ratings transitions than comparable corporate debt[159].

In the period around 2000/2001, a number of significant problems with CDOs emerged[160]. A number of investors suffered large losses on CDO equity investments. **Exhibit 4.24** sets out an example of the problems experienced by American Express[161].

The deterioration in the CDO investments was reflected in losses on equity investments. It was also reflected in losses on mezzanine and senior securities driven by a sharp decline in market value as the relevant tranches were downgraded. This reflected the decline in the value of the underlying assets as credit quality decreased.

The credit losses highlight a number of issues with CDO structures including:

- **Credit cycle** – the losses in this period were largely driven by the credit cycle. Default rates increased sharply due to the economic recession in the USA. In addition, a number of event risk factors (such as the accounting frauds in the USA and Europe) affected default rates. Given that the CDO investments ultimately are based on a portfolio of credit assets, a systemic deterioration in credit risk is likely to affect

---

[158] See Cass, Dwight "CDOs Outperform High-Yield Bonds" (September 2001) Risk 11.

[159] For example, see Howard, David R., Carosielli, Brian R., Mezzanotte, Claire, Lans, Diane M., Higgins, Kenneth and Scatassa, Joanne (8 January 2001) Structured Finance Default Study; Fitch Ratings, New York. See also Hay, Jon "Afloat On The Credit Markets" (November/December 2001) Structured Finance International 12–19.

[160] See Spinner, Karen "CDOs Under Fire" (November 1998) Derivatives Strategy 18–25; Bennett, Oliver "The Trouble With CDOs" (April 2001) Risk 60–62; Sandiford, Jane "CDOs Show Potential" (June 2001) FOW 21; Schenk, Carola "Tackling CDO Risk" (September 2001) Risk – Risk Management For Investors S6–8; Hay, Jon "Afloat On The Credit Markets" (November/December 2001) Structured Finance International 12–19; "New Solutions" (May 2002) Credit 32–37.

[161] A number of other investors were also affected; for example, see Marshall, Julian "Abbey Cleans Out The Cupboard" (August 2002) Euromoney 10–12.

performance of CDOs. The impact of the credit downturn was exacerbated by the use of leverage and the implicit correlation positions for CDO equity and mezzanine investments.

- **Performance of balance sheet CDOs** – a number of regulatory capital driven balance sheet synthetic CDOs had senior and mezzanine tranches downgraded, in some cases significantly[162]. The majority of portfolios in these transactions were investment grade and often of high quality. The major causes of deterioration in credit quality included specific event risk factors that affected some large diverse portfolios. This included a number of high profile defaults/problems (Xerox, Eastman Kodak, Enron and K-Mart), problems related to asbestos liability and Californian electricity utilities. The specific events combined with the relatively small size of the equity component rapidly affected the mezzanine securities[163].

- **Performance of arbitrage CDOs** – the deterioration in credit quality of the arbitrage CDOs was driven by the following factors:
  1. In the case of arbitrage CDOs based on high yield bonds, the rapid slowdown in the US economy and the end of the telecommunications/media/internet bubble affected performance. The fact that the issuers from the telecommunications/media sector had dominated activity in the high yield market exacerbated the impact.
  2. In the case of arbitrage CDOs based on emerging market bonds, the crises in Asia, Eastern Europe and Latin America in 1997 to 2002 were the major factors affecting performance. A key element of this was the rapid contagion effect, whereby the high correlation in performance between different sectors in emerging markets exacerbated losses.

- **Credit investment analysis** – the experience highlighted a number of weaknesses in the process of analysis of the CDO structures and portfolios:
  1. The lower rated securities in a CDO structure proved extremely vulnerable to early default/deterioration in credit quality. This is

---

[162] See Sandiford, Jane "CDOs Show Potential" (June 2001) FOW 21; Hay, Jon "Afloat On The Credit Markets" (November/December 2001) Structured Finance International 12–19.

[163] See Hay, Jon "Afloat On The Credit Markets" (November/December 2001) Structured Finance International 12–19 at 15.

because the distributions, particularly to equity, are front loaded. The clustering of defaults in the period 1999 to 2002 highlighted the weaknesses of analysis that tended to assume a static default rate per annum.

2. The impact of default correlations and low recovery rates highlighted modelling problems. The performance of CDOs reflected the impact of adverse default correlation shifts. The holders of equity and mezzanine tranches in a CDO structure are significantly exposed to default correlation changes/idiosyncratic default or event risk. This risk led to significant losses and downgrades in CDO tranches.

3. The impact of a period of sustained stress on the portfolio also appears to have been underestimated in the modelling/credit assessment. The absence of a standard market modelling approach was also problematic[164].

4. The basic logic of an arbitrage CDO exploits the fact that market credit spreads are significantly higher than indicated by actual historical default data. This reflects the fact that other factors may drive the market credit spread (capital market inefficiency (liquidity, regulatory, accounting and tax) and practical constraints in diversification of credit risk). CDO structures seek to profit from the spread difference between the (lower quality) assets paying high credit spreads and the (higher quality) liabilities paying lower credit spreads. The CDO structure transforms the low quality assets by using over collateralisation to cover default losses. The economics of the transaction are driven by the gap in spreads between the assets and liabilities being wider than the difference in expected credit losses. The strategy relies on the ability to create highly diversified portfolios of credit risk. In practice, this is not feasible to the degree needed. This means that the high spreads available reflect the undiversified credit risk assumed by CDO investors[165]. Where credit losses are experienced, the subordinated tranches bear this risk. This appeared to be the case in the relevant period. The CDO managers

---

[164] See Schenk, Carola "Tackling CDO Risk" (September 2001) Risk – Risk Management For Investors S6–8; Hay, Jon "Afloat On The Credit Markets" (November/December 2001) Structured Finance International 12–19.

[165] See Amato, Jeffrey D. and Remolana, Eli M. "The Credit Spread Puzzle" (December 2003) BIS Quarterly Review 51–63.

were unable to fully diversify, exposing the subordinated investors to significant losses.

- **Performance of managers** – the constraints on the ability to trade to preserve the value of the credit portfolio have also been problematic. Key constraints have included the unavailability of investments of the required type, limited liquidity and the restrictive nature of the CDO structure. The factors have increased the difficulty for managers in protecting the value of CDO transactions. Other issues include the impact of lack of transparency/information on some underlying risks and the conflicts of interest/moral hazard issues in CDO structures[166]. The relative inexperience of managers in these structures has also been problematic. A major concern has been the adverse incentives within traditional CDO structures. This includes the fact that all excess spread earned through trading the underlying portfolio

---

Exhibit 4.24   CDO Investments – American Express Case Study[167]

In 2001, American Express ("Amex") wrote off in excess of US$1 billion on its CDO and high yield investments. Amex took a write down of US$182 million in the first quarter of 2001, and a further write down of US$826 million in August 2001.

The losses related to investments in high yield bonds and CDOs. The losses were primarily related to Amex's Financial Advisors unit. The unit was under pressure to increase returns (to allegedly around 20% pa on equity). The unit sought to increase return by increasing exposure to the junk bond market (from 8% to 12% of its portfolio). In addition, the firm started to use CDOs to leverage its returns. Amex had investments in approximately 60 CDOs.

Amex estimated that its CDO/high yield portfolio was worth US$1.4 billion at the end of the first quarter of 2001. The portfolio declined in value to US$370 million by the end of the second quarter of 2001. The losses included the costs of reducing investment to the CDO/high yield sector.

The losses appeared to be driven by the slowing in the US economy and the rise in bond default rates. The losses exceeded anticipated losses. The volatility of bond prices as default rates increased also contributed to the losses.

---

[166] There are currently a number of initiatives to improve disclosure regarding CDOs, including one from Goldman Sachs; see Currie, Antony "The Magic Mix Is Now Revealed" (June 2002) Euromoney 16.

[167] See "American Express CDO Case" (February 2002) FOW 50.

accrues to the equity investor (which generally will include the manager). This creates an incentive to maximise yield on the portfolio, perhaps at the expense of increasing the risk of the underlying portfolio.

The experience over the period 1999 to 2002 served to highlight problems in the CDO market. The problems do not derogate from the basic benefits and advantages of the structure. The experience during this period did not result in a total withdrawal by investors from the CDO markets. While some investors did reassess their participation, the market has continued to grow subsequently.

The problems highlight issues that need to be considered in structuring and investing in CDOs. The CDO market has sought to address some of these problems in a number of ways:

- The credit modelling approach has evolved to seek to overcome deficiencies. The major move has been to stress scenarios. There is also increased focus on recovery rate and default correlation behaviour.
- The risk of structures has been reduced. This has been through using higher quality underlying credit risk and reducing leverage (increasing the equity tranche).
- There is now increased investment in credit research and obtaining skills/ expertise required to evaluate CDO investments.
- There is increased scrutiny of a manager's credentials and performance. The assessment and due diligence has been strengthened. This has included the use of self managed CDOs where the *investor* controls the underlying portfolio and has the option to modify the constitution of the credit risks. This is usually structured as a substitution right subject to a set of controls, including maintaining the rating of the various elements of the capital structure and the availability of cash to meet the substitution costs.
- Increased efforts to reduce moral hazard issues and align the interest of manager, investor and investment bank/dealer. This includes subordination of the equity investment of the manager. It also includes changes in the fee structure (reduction in fees if credit losses rise/interest coverage falls), deferral of (a portion of) the fees till maturity and commitment to support transactions by injecting capital under certain circumstances. The fee structure can be related to different performance measures such as the amount of equity outstanding at the end of the transaction.

9.5 Managed CDO Structures

The original CDO structures were entirely static. This meant that investors were exposed to the risk of the specified entities for the entire life of the transaction. The advantage of the static structure is that the investor can fully evaluate the risk of the underlying reference entities. The risk of the static structure is that change in credit quality results in losses. In effect, a static CDO operates as a position on overall credit markets and their expected performance. Any hedging or risk management must be done outside the CDO structure.

Many static CDOs experienced losses (equity and mezzanine tranches) and downgrades (mezzanine and senior tranches). Managed CDOs emerged in response to the problems of static CDOs[168]. The managed CDO entailed appointing a manager to trade the underlying reference entity to reduce the risk of loss (on deteriorating entities) and capturing gains (from improving entities). The manager was required to manage the composition of the portfolio within credit quality and diversification constraints. The manager was also required to stay in compliance with the conditions of the transaction at all times.

The managed model proved problematic. Key problems that emerged with the fully or unconstrained management model included:

- A key problem was the lack of experience of CDO managers and the absence of a pool of credit portfolio managers.
- Managers experienced difficulties in managing positions within the complex structure. Key problems included the unavailability of investments of the required type, limited liquidity and the restrictive nature of the CDO structure.
- The trading costs (losses incurred in managing the risk of the portfolio) affected returns to equity and mezzanine investors.
- Conflicts of interest and moral hazard issues were evident. These affected the management of the portfolio.

---

[168] See Nassar, Tarek and Tierney, John F. (29 April 2003) "Synthetic CDOs" Recent Market Developments; Deutsche Bank, London; Polyn, Gallagher "Bespoke Panacea?" (May 2003) Risk – Credit Risk Supplement S4–S6; "Synthetic CDOs – Manage Your Own CDO" (May 2003) Risk – Sponsor's Statement.

These factors increased the difficulty for managers in protecting the value of CDO transactions. In fact, many managed CDO results were adversely affected by the active management.

The problems resulted in a refinement of the managed structure. Key changes included:

- **Portfolio selection** – in managed transactions, it is now most common for the investors to work with the dealer to select the underlying portfolio. A secondary list of reference entities may also be agreed in advance. The manager can only add names from the specified list to the original portfolio. This is designed to avoid the investor being exposed to the manager's choice of reference entity within generic portfolio guidelines.
- **Management strategy** – restrictive guidelines are used to limit the manager's discretion and management strategies used. Key guidelines include:
  1. The portfolio can only be "lightly' managed. This is usually defined by limiting discretion to replacing up to 5% of the portfolio in any given year.
  2. Automatic trading rules may be used, including the requirement to reduce exposure to any credit where the market spread increases by a fixed amount (say, 150 bps pa) or where the entity is downgraded below a specified threshold.
  3. Substitution rights may be included whereby the investor can request a change in the underlying reference portfolio. The substitution may result in a net gain or cost to the investors. This reflects the trading cost. In the case of a single tranche CDO, this will reflect the value change in the investor's position and the dealer's re-hedging cost.
  4. Some CDOs also include the ability to take short positions to hedge the reference portfolio within the structure itself.
- **Trading costs** – a reserve fund may be established to absorb the trading cost of substituting a deterioration credit within the portfolio. The reserve may be initially funded. Alternatively, excess cash flows/spreads above certain specified hurdle equity returns are diverted to the reserve fund to finance trading costs. Similarly, trading gains may be transferred to reserves to meet future trading losses. Trading or rebalancing costs may also be absorbed by changes in the subordination of the tranche.
- **Compliance tests** – limits and tests to assess the portfolio's quality were also tightened. For example, the market value of securities purchased (rather than face value) is used to assess over collateralisation levels.

The hope continues to be that a sound asset manager will add value to the CDO transaction's performance.

The impact of moral hazard issues and potential conflicts of interest in CDO transactions has also attracted close scrutiny. These conflicts exist at multiple levels. There are potential conflicts between the dealer and the investors. There are potential conflicts between the different classes of investors. There are also potential conflicts between investors and the manager.

The inherent conflicts relate to the different exposures of individual participants. This can be illustrated with an example. In any CDO, if the transaction performs poorly (higher defaults than expected), then the equity tranches are generally seriously eroded. Under these circumstances, the manager (who is usually an equity co-investor) has an incentive to increase the risk of the portfolio to the maximum degree within portfolio guidelines. This reflects the fact that the equity investor captures all the benefits of outperformance on the portfolio. Any additional losses will affect the mezzanine and senior tranches.

Interestingly, the same position exists where the transaction performs well in the early years. The high returns to equity mean that the CDO equity investor has achieved its target return. Under these circumstances, the equity investor can use the leverage in the structure to increase the risk. It will benefit from any outperformance with little or no risk, having already received return of its original investment.

These problems have caused problems in the management of CDO structures. Many of the changes to the terms of mezzanine debt and equity are driven in part by a desire to improve the alignment of interests.

10   CDOs – Regulatory Capital Treatment[169]

10.1   Approach

A significant driving factor behind CDOs (particularly balance sheet CDOs) is the regulatory capital relief on the credit risk hedged through the

---

[169]   See Andrews, David, Heberlein, Helene, Olson, Kim, Moss, Jim and Olert, John S. (4 February 2004) Securitization And Banks: A Reiteration Of Fitch's View Of Securitisation's Effect On Bank Rating In The New Context Of Regulatory Capital And Accounting Reform; Fitch Ratings.

structure. This is consistent with the general use of securitisation and risk transfer techniques used by banks to manage regulatory capital[170].

CDOs are treated as securitisation transactions for capital adequacy. The treatment of securitisation transactions is complex[171]. The treatment for conventional CLOs and synthetic securitisation transactions is different. The capital treatment described below relates to credit risk in the banking book[172]. This reflects the fact that the majority of credit risk is held in the banking book. Credit securitisation transactions can be undertaken out of the trading book. In this case, the treatment would be consistent with the treatment of credit derivatives in the trading book[173].

10.2   Basel 1

Conventional securitisation transactions such as the CLO structures described are an effective means for reducing risk. In order to achieve favourable regulatory capital treatment, the retained first loss position must be less than 8%[174]. For example, US regulators (the Federal Reserve Board, FDIC and OCC) apply low level recourse rules. Retention of a first loss

---

[170] For discussion of the regulatory capital, see Das, Satyajit (2004) Swaps/ Financial Derivatives 3rd Edition; John Wiley & Sons, Singapore at Chapters 33 and 34.

[171] Basel 1 did not deal with securitisation. Subsequently, different central banks and bank regulators have implemented different regulations.

[172] The views expressed here are merely indications of possible methods of treatment and are not intended to be definitive. It is recommended that institutions seeking to enter into credit derivatives obtain appropriate professional advice from their own advisers regarding the required treatment of these transactions for regulatory purposes in the relevant jurisdictions.

[173] For discussion of capital adequacy regulations as they affect credit derivatives transactions, see Chapter 1.

[174] This can typically only be achieved where the underlying portfolio is investment grade. In a typical CLO transaction, the size of the unrated first loss piece for an investment grade portfolio would be in the region of 2 to 3% where the mezzanine tranche of debt to be issued against the asset pool is sought to be rated investment grade (BBB). This means that CLO transactions are difficult to justify economically because of the high funding cost for banks with access to low cost funding, except as a mechanism for creating regulatory relief. It has the perverse aspect of allowing banks to shed lower risk assets and create higher levels of credit risk on their retained assets. In effect, this is a form of credit capital arbitrage which forces the existing credit capital guidelines to reflect lower risk weighting for investment grade risk.

position of more than 8% is treated as a financing rather than a sale. This results in the requirement to hold capital equal to 8% of the underlying pool.

Retention of a first loss position of less than 8% allows capital to be reduced proportionally to the face value of the retained position. Under this approach, in bank securitisation transactions, capital must be held against the retained first loss position. The capital held is generally 100% of the exposure (referred to as a reduction to/deduction from capital).

The treatment of synthetic securitisation transactions is more complex[175]. There is a divergence between regulators in the approach adopted.

Synthetic securitisation structures do not necessarily achieve prima facie regulatory capital relief. This is despite the fact that it may act as an economic hedge of the credit risk on the underlying transaction. This is because, based on the current risk-based capital rules, the mismatch in collateral underlying the credit default swap dictates that the reduction in risk weighting to 0% is only available *on the notional amount of the cash or government collateral*.

The current regulatory position for synthetic securitisation transactions (referred to as synthetic CLOs in the regulatory guidelines) is not settled. The US Federal Reserve and OCC issued guidelines in November 1999[176]. The approach taken covers the treatment of sponsor banks and investors in notes issued under these structures. The guidelines apply to banking book transactions.

The treatment of investors in notes issued under synthetic securitisation transactions is relatively straightforward. Investors in notes must assign risk weights appropriate to the risk weighted assets underlying the notes.

The regulatory position for synthetic securitisation is based on classification into 3 separate types of transactions:

- **Transaction 1** – this entails a banking organisation hedging the *whole* notional amount of the reference asset portfolio through a synthetic CLO. The proposed regulatory treatment requires that the cash proceeds

---

[175] See Watzinger, Herman "Cheap And Easy" (March 2000) Risk – Credit Risk Special Report S10–S13.

[176] See Pelham, Mark "US Regulators Address Synthetic CLOs" (23–29 November 1999) Financial Products 1,11; Cass, Dwight "Fed Issues CLO Guidelines" (December 1999) Risk 11.

are treated as collateral and the capital required is reduced to the collateral risk weighting.

- **Transaction 2** – this covers a banking organisation hedging *part* of the notional amount of the reference asset portfolio through a synthetic CLO. The bank retains a high quality risk position (that is, it absorbs any loss in excess of the junior loss position). The proposed treatment is that there will be a reduction in capital on the part hedged with the synthetic CLO (to collateral risk weighting). There is a requirement that capital be held against the high quality (super senior) position.

- **Transaction 3** – this covers a banking organisation hedging *part* of the notional amount of the reference asset portfolio through a synthetic CLO. The bank retains first loss risk position. The proposed treatment is for capital to be the higher of:
  1. *Approach 1*: hold $ for $ capital against loss retained but no capital against additional risk.
  2. *Approach 2*: hold 8% against loss retained with second loss position being viewed as completely collateralised (at collateral risk weight).

Under the proposed approach, the US regulators provide the possibility of the sponsoring bank obtaining regulatory capital relief on the super senior tranche (effectively the risk retained by the sponsor bank after the first loss and external cash collateralised component has been exhausted). The capital relief would be available *without the need to enter into a credit default swap* with an OECD bank. This capital relief is contingent on the sponsor bank being able to satisfy the following requirements:

- The sponsor bank must demonstrate that it has transferred virtually all the risk on the underlying credit risk portfolio through the synthetic securitisation. Indicators of virtual total protection will include:
  1. The issuance of notes rated by a major rating agency.
  2. The most senior tranche based must be rated AAA/Aaa.
  3. The structure must include a first loss provision that is retained by the sponsor bank. This first loss position must be equal to (certainly no greater than) a reasonable estimate of the expected loss on the reference portfolio. This first loss provision must be deducted from the capital of the sponsor bank.

- The sponsor bank must be able to demonstrate that it can evaluate the remaining banking book risk exposures and also demonstrate adequate capital resources to support these exposures. This may take the form of an internal rating system and credit modelling process. Any such system must be based on credible and verifiable capital assessment methodology, including stress testing.

- The sponsor bank must also ensure adequate public disclosure of the risk profile and capital adequacy consequences of synthetic securitisation transactions. This would include economic, regulatory and accounting consequences of the transaction.

If the bank meets the requirements, then the regulators may assign the unhedged senior position to the 20% risk weighting category.

Exhibit 4.25 sets out the impact of a CDO transaction (funded or synthetic securitisation) on the capital held against a portfolio under the current treatment.

The US regulators assess individual transaction structures separately on a case-by-case approach. It is possible that, based on the structure of

---

Exhibit 4.25   Synthetic Securitisation – Capital Treatment

Assume a US$1 billion portfolio of 100% risk weighted fully drawn loans. The portfolio would require the bank to hold regulatory capital equal to US$80 million (8%) against the portfolio.

Assume the bank transfers the risk on the portfolio through a funded securitisation or synthetic securitisation transaction. Assume the transactions entail the following structure:

Tranche	Funded/Cash Securitisation	Synthetic Securitisation
Equity	1%	1%
Mezzanine/Senior	93%	7% (invested in government securities)
Super senior		92%

Under the funded/cash securitisation structure, the capital requirement would be as follows:

$$[(1.00\% \text{ (equity)} \times 100\%) + (93\% \text{ (mezzanine/senior)} \times 0\%)$$
$$= 1\% \text{ or US\$10 million}$$

Under the synthetic securitisation, assuming the super senior tranche qualifies for 20% risk weighting, the capital requirement for the portfolio would be as follows:

$$[(1.00\% \text{ (equity)} \times 100\%) + (7\% \text{ (mezzanine/senior)} \times 0\%)$$
$$+ (92\% \text{ (super senior)} \times 1.6\%)] = 2.47\% \text{ or US\$24.7 million.}$$

The transaction has the effect of freeing up approximately between US$55.3 million (5.53%) and US$70 million (7%) in capital, depending on the structure used.

individual transactions, the capital treatment may be varied or adjusted from transaction to transaction.

European regulators require the super senior tranche to be hedged with an OECD bank to obtain capital relief.

In practice, capital relief may be possible through the trading book. This would require structuring the transaction as an internal credit default swap between the banking book and the trading book *within the sponsor bank*. Under this structure, the banking book achieves a reduction in the risk weighting. In the trading book, the credit default swap is subject to mark-to-market and the risk capital rules. If the transaction has been structured economically and efficiently, this may enable the desired regulatory capital relief to be achieved. This is because the retained risk in many transactions would be minimal in terms of economic risk models. It is far from clear whether this strategy is one that would be accepted by regulators.

10.3 Basel 2[177]

Under Basel 2, there is a specified framework treatment for securitisation transactions. The proposals are predicated on the following principles:

- Securitisation can serve as an efficient way to redistribute credit risk.
- The Committee regards securitisation as a potential arbitrage technique that is employed to avoid maintaining capital commensurate with the risk exposure of a given financial entity.
- There is a need to align regulatory capital charges with the economic risk.

The treatment of securitisation under the new proposed regulations will depend on the model adopted by individual banks (standardised model or IRB model). The capital requirement covers where the bank is investing in securitised ABS structures and where the bank originates and transfers the risk. In the second case, the treatment is driven by whether the originating bank retains exposure to its own securitised risk. CDO transactions are treated as a form of securitisation.

The treatment of banks investing in ABS securities (including CDO tranches) entails the bank holding credit capital against the tranches based

---

[177] See Basel Committee on Banking Supervision (June 2004) International Convergence of Capital Measurement and Capital Standards: A Revised Framework; Bank for International Settlements, Basel, Switzerland.

on risk. The primary proposal is that securitisation tranches should be weighted in accordance with a specified risk weighting categorisation. The standardised approach is reliant on rating. The most important change is that holdings of securitisation tranches rated below BB− (B+ or below) and all unrated tranches will be deducted in full from capital. Banks using IRB models will be required to hold capital based on the supervisory formula approach or rating based approach. Originating banks must deduct all retained securitisation exposures rated below investment grade (i.e. BBB−).

Banks using securitisation (including CDOs) to transfer risk will be able to obtain capital relief. Reduction in capital is driven by the tranches (risks) retained and any explicit or implicit credit support provided by the originating bank. Basel 2 uses the approach of the "clean break" and penalises support by the originating bank.

An originating bank may exclude securitised exposures from the calculation of risk weighted assets only if certain conditions are met. Originating banks must hold regulatory capital against any securitisation exposures they retain. The specific conditions for a traditional securitisation (a fully funded cash flow CDO) include:

- Significant credit risk associated with the securitised exposures has been transferred to third parties.
- The securities issued cannot be obligations of the transferor. Investors must only be able to claim against the underlying pool of exposures.
- The transferor must not maintain effective or indirect control over the transferred exposures. The assets must be legally isolated (e.g. through the sale of assets or through subparticipation) so that the exposures are beyond the reach of the transferor and its creditors, even in bankruptcy or receivership. The transferor is deemed to have maintained effective control over the transferred credit risk exposures if it is able to repurchase from the transferee the previously transferred exposures in order to realise their benefits or is obligated to retain the risk of the transferred exposures. The transferor's retention of servicing rights to the exposures will not necessarily constitute indirect control of the exposures.
- The securitisation cannot include terms that require the originating bank to alter or improve the underlying exposures, allow increases in a retained first loss position or credit enhancement provided by the originating bank, or increase the yield payable to investors and

third-party providers of credit enhancements in response to a deterioration in the credit quality of the underlying pool.

For a synthetic securitisation transaction, the originating bank must comply with the conditions applicable to a traditional securitisation. There are a number of additional requirements. Where a synthetic securitisation structure is used, the approach relies on the credit risk mitigant regime. The hedge of the underlying exposure may be recognised for risk-based capital purposes only if the following additional conditions are satisfied:

- Credit risk mitigants must comply with the requirements affecting the credit derivatives used under the credit risk mitigation framework[178].
- Eligible collateral and guarantors must comply with general Basel 2 rules. Eligible collateral pledged by a special purpose entity is recognised.
- The instrument used to transfer credit risk may not contain terms or conditions that limit the amount of credit risk transferred. This includes clauses that materially limit the credit protection or credit risk transference (e.g. significant materiality thresholds below which credit protection is deemed not to be triggered even if a credit event occurs, or those that allow for the termination of the protection due to deterioration in the credit quality of the underlying exposures).

For synthetic securitisations, there is a further issue regarding the treatment of the super senior tranche where this is retained by the originating bank. This is covered as the "treatment of unrated most senior securitisation exposures". If the most senior exposure in a securitisation is unrated, a bank that holds or guarantees such an exposure may determine the risk weight by applying the "look-through" treatment, provided the composition of the underlying pool is known at all times. In the look-through treatment, the unrated most senior position receives the average risk weight of the underlying exposures subject to supervisory review. Where the bank is unable to determine the risk weights assigned to the underlying credit risk exposures, the unrated position must be deducted.

Under the Basel 2 rules, CDO transactions to obtain capital relief will still be feasible. The position for funded securitisations is similar to that currently in operation in most jurisdictions. The position relating to synthetic securitisation structures is more complex. The current proposal

---

[178] See Chapter 1.

is to treat the super senior position as a senior tranche provided all the conditions for inferring a rating from a lower transfer are fulfilled.

A broader issue under Basel 2 relates to the alignment of regulatory and economic credit risk capital. This may reduce incentives for CDO type risk transfer. This will certainly be the case where the primary motivation for the transaction is to arbitrage the difference between regulatory and economic credit risk capital.

11 Summary

CDOs represent an adaptation of the securitisation concept to credit markets. CDO structures have evolved rapidly in response to bank demands for instruments to manage credit risk and capital (both economic and regulatory) and investor demand for credit risk and structured exposure to credit risk. The market has evolved a variety of financial structures to transfer credit exposure and create structured credit exposures. The structures are often hybrids employing concepts from securitisation, credit derivatives and structured note markets. CDO technology has become an important part of capital markets facilitating transfer and investment in credit risk portfolios.

5
Credit Derivatives Pricing and Valuation

1 Overview

The pricing of credit derivatives entails the following different processes:

- **Credit derivatives pricing** – this is focused on the pricing and valuation of instruments such as credit default swaps. The pricing is based on a replication/arbitrage-free pricing approach. The pricing of credit derivatives is driven off the pricing of debt securities in capital markets. The observed market pricing of debt securities and credit risk is generally used in this process. This reflects the necessity of hedging, valuation and price discovery in the spot market.
- **Credit modelling/credit portfolio management** – this activity is focused on the pricing of credit risk generally within a portfolio context. It is focused on establishing the expected and unexpected credit losses on a portfolio and the amount of capital that must be held against that risk. It is also focused on the return required to compensate for the assumed risk. This is based on credit and default risk modelling.

This Chapter focuses on the pricing of credit derivatives in the market. Chapter 6 focuses on the issue of credit modelling.

The structure of the Chapter is as follows:

- The approach to pricing of credit derivatives is described.
- The process of pricing credit default swaps in an arbitrage-free framework is outlined.
- The basis between the cash market and the credit default swap market is examined.
- Alternative pricing and valuation approaches (using hazard models) are described.

- The use of equity markets to hedge credit default swaps (E2C (equity to credit) model) is examined.
- The pricing of total return swaps and credit spread products is also analysed.

2 Credit Default Swaps – Pricing Approach[1]

2.1 Overview

The pricing of credit default swaps is not significantly different from the pricing of derivatives generally[2]. The pricing of credit in general terms is evident from the traded prices of securities in financial markets. The available prices must be put into a tractable framework for the pricing, valuation and hedging of credit default swaps. The approach used is to replicate/hedge credit derivatives from available market instruments to establish a risk free hedge. The pricing of the derivative contract reflects the cost of the hedge.

Exhibit 5.1 sets out the relationship between cash instruments and credit derivatives[3]. The fundamental relationship between credit derivatives and

---

[1] See Brooks, Robert and Yan, David Yong "Pricing Credit Default Swaps And The Implied Default Probability" (Winter 1998) Derivatives Quarterly 34–41; Duffie, Darrell "Credit Swap Valuation" (January/February 1999) Financial Analysts Journal 73–87; Blacher, Guillaume "Guidelines For Pricing And Risk Managing Credit Derivatives" (28–29 November 1999) Financial Products 8–9; Hull, John C. and White, Alan "Valuing Credit Default Swaps I: No Counterparty Default Risk" (Fall 2000) Journal of Derivatives 29–40; Hull, John C. and White, Alan "Valuing Credit Default Swaps II: Modelling Default Correlation" (Spring 2001) Journal of Derivatives 12–21; Francis, Chris, Kakodkar, Atish and Martin, Barnaby (16 April 2003) Credit Derivative Handbook"; Merrill Lynch, London at 13–28; O'Kane, Dominic and Turnbull, Stuart "Valuation Of Credit Default Swaps" (April 2003) Lehman Brothers Quantitative Credit Research 28–44.

[2] See Das, Satyajit (2004) Swaps/Financial Derivatives 3rd Edition; John Wiley, Singapore at Chapter 4.

[3] The model assumes that the credit spread is entirely compensation for credit or default risk. In practice, there is a liquidity premium. Fundamental pricing models frequently fall short of fully accounting for the entire credit spread. Asset swap pricing models (which take an arbitrage-free relationship to other market instruments) do not separate any potential liquidity premium and the default risk component.

cash instruments is as follows:

- The pricing of *any risky security* must reflect the return on a risk free asset plus a risk margin. The risk margin must compensate the investor for the risk assumed which, in this instance, is the risk of default[4].
- Credit derivative transactions merely strip out and isolate the default risk in order to facilitate the separate trading of aspects of credit risk.

The inherent relationship implies the ability to price, value and hedge credit derivatives. This requires taking offsetting positions in the cash instruments (a risky bond and a risk free bond) to replicate the payout on the credit derivative contract.

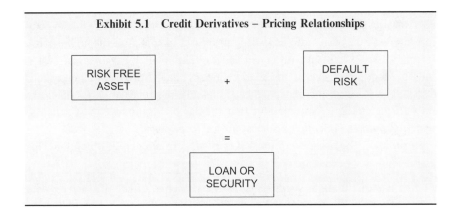

Exhibit 5.1   Credit Derivatives – Pricing Relationships

2.2   Credit Default Swaps/Cash Instruments – Pricing Relationship To Asset Swaps

The approach outlined would entail the use of a corporate bond and a risk free (government) bond to replicate credit default swaps. In practice, the cash market prices used are not the spread to the risk free rate but the asset

---

[4]   In this context, credit pricing represents an extension of the Capital Asset Pricing Model for the pricing of *all risky assets*, in that the holder of a risky bond must receive a return in a risk neutral world whereby the excess return (the spread) compensates the holder for the additional risk (default of losses from changes in credit quality).

swap price[5]. This is equivalent to the spread to US$ LIBOR[6] under an asset swap. **Exhibit 5.2** sets out the structure and valuation of asset swaps[7].

The asset swap approach used in practice reflects the structure of a credit default swap. A credit default swap is analogous to a floating rate note issued by the reference entity that is funded at LIBOR. Alternatively, a credit default swap is similar to a fixed rate bond issue by the reference entity that has been asset swapped into a floating rate asset that is then funded in the repo market. This means that the credit default swap trades at a level that is benchmarked to the asset swap market rather than the spread to a risk free (government) bond.

The importance of the asset swap spread reflects the fact that *all* credit assets are increasingly traded on a spread to US$ LIBOR basis. This reflects the increased availability and liquidity of global swap/derivative markets. This allows the ready transformation of assets, irrespective of currency and interest rate basis, into a floating rate asset in US$ and through a cross currency basis swap into other currencies. The availability of asset swaps and the depth and size of the market means that it provides a ready and reasonably transparent means for establishing the relative value of credit assets. This characteristic dictates that the asset swap market serves as the principal *market information source for credit pricing*.

In practice, the asset swap market is used in pricing credit default swaps for the following reasons:

- The use of the asset swap removes the principal effects of interest rate exposure on the fixed rate bond. This isolates the impact of the credit spread changes[8]. The asset swap is the spread to LIBOR. This approximates the issuer specific component of the credit spread[9]. The use of

---

[5]   For a discussion of different measures of credit spreads, see O'Kane, Dominic and Sen, Saurav (March 2004) Credit Spreads Explained; Lehman Brothers Fixed Income Quantitative Credit Research, London.

[6]   LIBOR equates to the rate at which prime (approximately AA rated) banks fund each other in the inter-bank market.

[7]   For discussion of asset swaps, see Das, Satyajit (2004) Swaps/Financial Derivatives 3rd Edition; John Wiley, Singapore at Chapter 38.

[8]   In practice, this does not absolutely remove all exposure to interest rates since credit spreads are frequently a function of the steepness of the yield curve.

[9]   See Das, Satyajit (2004) Swaps/Financial Derivatives 3rd Edition; John Wiley, Singapore at Chapter 11.

a par asset swap structure also minimises the impact of the bond trading above or below face value and yield curve shape.

- The asset swap market provides benchmark prices for a wide range of credit risks. It is a traded benchmark price that is relatively transparent and available.
- It provides the ability to value and mark-to-market existing positions.
- It also provides a mechanism for the traders to hedge transactions.

Exhibit 5.2   Asset Swaps[10]

1. Concept

Asset swaps involve extending the underlying concept of liability swaps to the creation of synthetic assets. "Asset swap" is a generic term for the repackaging of a security, usually a debt security. It entails altering the features of the underlying asset in terms of either interest rate (fixed or floating rate) or currency. For example, an asset swap may entail altering the interest rate of a debt security paying fixed interest rates into floating interest rates or from floating rate into fixed rate. It may also alter the cash flows of a debt instrument with interest and principal payments in one currency (yen) into interest and principal payments in another currency (US$).

The market for assets swaps (consistent with other synthetic assets) exists primarily for the following reasons:

- Existence of an arbitrage (similar to a liability arbitrage) enabling the creation of a higher yielding investment than an equivalent asset directly available in the market.
- Lack of availability of a particular investment with the desired credit, interest rate or currency characteristics in conventional form that creates the opportunity to generate a synthetic investment using the asset swap.

Asset swaps are predicated on the fact that investors often require a set of cash flows that is unavailable directly in capital markets. In order to create the desired

---

[10] See Partridge-Hicks, Stephen, and Hartland-Swann, Piers (1988) Synthetic Securities; Euromoney Publications, London, England. See also Krishnan, Suresh E. "Asset Based Interest Rate Swaps" in Beideleman, Carl R. (1991) Interest Rate Swaps; Business One Irwin, Homewood, Illinois at Chapter 8; Efraty, Ravit (2 October 1995) An Introduction To Asset Swaps; Salomon Brothers, New York; Arbitrage Research and Trading "Two Become One" (June 2000) FOW 74–78.

cash flows, the investor combines an existing cash market instrument and a swap to create the synthetic asset.

2. Asset Swap Structures

The basic mechanics of an asset swap are similar to that of a liability swap. The asset swap will usually entail a series of linked steps:

- The underlying physical security is purchased for cash.
- Cash flows (both interest and principal (in the case of a cross-currency asset swap)) are linked to either an interest rate or a currency swap to change the interest rate or currency denomination of the investment into the desired form.
- The overall package is held by the investor or, if assembled by a dealer, is sold to an ultimate investor as an asset in its synthetic form.

Table 1 sets out the basic structure of an asset swap involving an interest rate swap. **Table 2** sets out the basic structure of an asset swap involving a currency swap.

Table 1
Asset Swap Involving Interest Rate Swap

Assume the underlying transaction in this case is the purchase of a US$10 million fixed rate US$ bond with a maturity of three years and a coupon of 8.00% pa payable semi-annually. The fixed rate US$ bond is swapped into a floating interest rate asset (synthetic FRN) yielding LIBOR plus 75 bps through an interest rate swap.

The structure of the transaction is set out below:

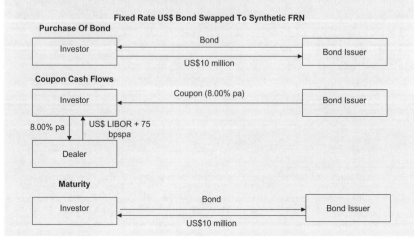

The detailed cash flows (from the viewpoint of the investor) are set out below:

Year	Bond Cash Flows ($)	Swap Payments ($)	Swap Receipts ($)	Net Cash Flows ($)
Spot	− 10,000,000			−10,000,000
0.5	+ 400,000	−400,000	+ 6 month LIBOR + 75 bps	+ 6 month LIBOR + 75 bps
1.0	+ 400,000	−400,000	+ 6 month LIBOR + 75 bps	+ 6 month LIBOR + 75 bps
1.5	+ 400,000	−400,000	+ 6 month LIBOR + 75 bps	+ 6 month LIBOR + 75 bps
2.0	+ 400,000	−400,000	+ 6 month LIBOR + 75 bps	+ 6 month LIBOR + 75 bps
2.5	+ 400,000	−400,000	+ 6 month LIBOR + 75 bps	+ 6 month LIBOR + 75 bps
3.0	+ 400,000 +10,000,000	−400,000	+ 6 month LIBOR + 75 bps	+ 6 month LIBOR + 75 bps +10,000,000

The combination of the purchase of the bond and the entry into the interest rate swap enables the investor to create a synthetic FRN investment. The investor has no exposure to fixed rates under the structure. The investor's exposure under the asset swap includes:

- Exposure to the credit risk of the issuer of the bond.
- Exposure to the credit risk of the swap counterparty.
- Market risk on the floating interest rate.

Table 2
Asset Swap Involving Currency Swap

Assume the underlying transaction in this case is the purchase of an A$10 million fixed rate A$ bond with a maturity of three years and a coupon of 8.00% pa payable semi-annually. The fixed rate A$ bond is swapped into a floating interest rate US$ asset (synthetic US$ FRN) yielding US$ LIBOR plus 125 bps through a currency swap.

The structure of the transaction is set out below:

Fixed Rate A$ Bond Swapped Into Synthetic US$ FRN

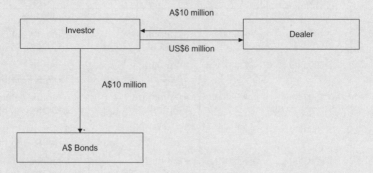

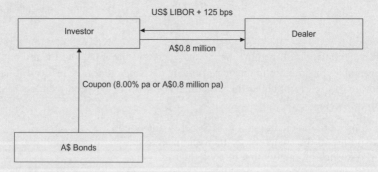

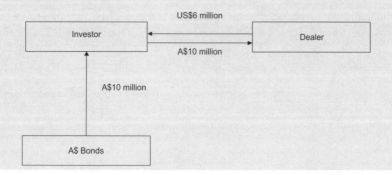

The detailed cash flows (from the viewpoint of the investor) are set out below:

Year	Bond Cash Flows (A$)	Swap Payments (A$)	Swap Receipts (US$)	Net Cash Flows (US$)
Spot	−10,000,000	−10,000,000	−6,000,000	−6,000,000
0.5	+400,000	+400,000	+6 month LIBOR + 125 bps	+6 month LIBOR + 125 bps
1.0	+400,000	+400,000	+6 month LIBOR + 125 bps	+6 month LIBOR + 125 bps
1.5	+400,000	+400,000	+6 month LIBOR + 125 bps	+6 month LIBOR + 125 bps
2.0	+400,000	+400,000	+6 month LIBOR + 125 bps	+6 month LIBOR + 125 bps
2.5	+400,000	+400,000	+6 month LIBOR + 125 bps	+6 month LIBOR + 125 bps
3.0	+400,000 +10,000,000	+400,000 +10,000,000	+6 month LIBOR + 125 bps +6,000,000	+6 month LIBOR + 125 bps +6,000,000

The combination of the purchase of the bond and the entry into the currency swap enables the investor to create a synthetic US$ FRN investment. The investor has no exposure to A$ in currency or A$ fixed rates under the structure. The investor's exposure under the asset swap includes:

- Exposure to the credit risk of the issuer of the bond.
- Exposure to the credit risk of the swap counterparty.
- Market risk on the US$ floating interest rate and US$.

3. Pricing/Valuation[11]

In practice, the structuring of an asset swap is more complex. Investors in synthetic assets will generally prefer an investment at par with the fixed or floating coupons equal to the purchase yield of the synthetic asset. This process is referred to as a "par" asset swap. This is driven by a variety of reasons including tax treatment, accounting issues and administrative convenience[12].

---

[11] See Francis, Chris, Kakodkar, Atish and Martin, Barnaby (16 April 2003) "Credit Derivative Handbook"; Merrill Lynch, London at 29–34.

[12] A structure where the bond is purchased at market price is also feasible. This is known as the "market price structure" asset swap.

Structural problems are created by factors such as accrued interest on the underlying security and/or any discount or premium on the purchase of the debt security (reflecting differences between the coupon of the security and the current market yield for the asset). This requires significant adjustments to the asset swap to convert the cash flows of the security to the desired pattern[13]. The cash flows are adjusted using an "off-market" interest or currency swap.

Table 3 sets out an example of structuring an asset swap, including the required adjustments. Under a par structure, the investor in the asset swap purchases the package at the notional face value of the bonds underlying the transaction. This will be the case regardless of the market price of the bond (above or below par). The difference from face value of the bonds is accommodated by adjusting the cash flows under the swap. The off market swap changes the counterparty risk under the swap.

Table 3
Asset Swap – Detailed Structure

Assume the following asset swap is structured on 23 March 2001.
The market conditions are as follows:

- A US$ bond is trading in the secondary market on the following terms:

Amount:	US$10 million face value
Maturity:	21 August 2006
Coupon:	7.50% pa (Annual 30/360 day basis)
Yield:	9.85% pa
Settlement:	30 March 2001
Price:	90.43436 or US$9,043,436
Accrued interest:	4.56250 or US$456,250

- The US$ swap market is trading at 8.23/8.30% pa (annual bond basis) versus six month US$ LIBOR for a final maturity of 21 August 2006.

The investor decides to purchase the bonds and create a synthetic US$ FRN as follows:

- On 30 March 2001, the investor pays US$9,499,686 to purchase the bonds.
- To convert the investment into the desired synthetic US$ FRN at an investment value of US$10 million or the par value of the bond, the following off market

---

[13]   The adjustments required in structuring an asset swap are similar to those required in relation to structuring non generic swaps; see Das, Satyajit (2004) Swaps/Financial Derivatives 3rd Edition; John Wiley, Singapore at Chapters 10 and 38.

interest rate swap is also transacted:

1. Investor pays swap counterparty an additional US$500,314 on 30 March 2001 to bring its investment to US$10 million.
2. Investor pays swap counterparty US$750,000 every 21 August commencing 21 August 2001 and ending 21 August 2006. Note that the first payment reflects the full annual coupon rather than the accrual from settlement.
3. Investor receives from swap counterparty a margin over 3 month LIBOR based on a principal amount of US$10 million. The first payment is on 21 May 2001 (for a broken or stub period) and then quarterly thereafter on 21 August, 21 November, 21 February and 21 May with the final payment on 21 August 2006.

The margin relative to three month LIBOR is calculated as follows:

	(% pa)
Bond Coupon	+7.50
Swap Fixed Rate	−8.30
Adjustments	
1. Additional initial payment	+1.15
2. Full first coupon	+1.02
Margin	+1.37

Notes:
1. All rates on an annual basis.
2. Calculated as US$456,250 discounted back to 30 March 2001 from the coupon payment date of 21 August 2001 and then amortised over each coupon date at swap rate (8.30% pa).
3. Amortisation of US$500,314 over each coupon date at swap rate (8.30% pa).

The margin of 1.37% pa is on an annual bond basis and must be converted to quarterly money market basis. The margin on a quarterly money market basis to the investor would be 1.27% pa (127 bps)[14].

The investor receives US$ 3 month LIBOR plus 127 bps quarterly on its initial investment of US$10 million.

The combination of the purchase of the bond and the entry into the interest rate swap enables the investor to create a synthetic FRN investment. The investor has

---

[14] This is calculated as the swap rate (8.30% pa annual) plus the spread (137 bps annual) de-compounded into quarterly equivalent (9.34% pa) to derive the quarterly spread (bps) by deducting the quarterly swap rate (8.05% pa) which is then converted to a LIBOR/money market basis to provide the final spread of 127 bps (129 bps × 360/365).

no exposure to fixed rates under the structure. The investor's exposure under the asset swap includes:

- Exposure to the credit risk of the issuer of the bond.
- Exposure to the credit risk of the swap counterparty. The exposure under the swap is greater than for a normal interest rate swap. This is because the investor makes two additional payments (the initial payment and the full coupon payment) that are recovered over the term of the transaction.
- Market risk on the floating interest rate.

The use of the par structure is problematic from a pricing/valuation perspective. This is because the asset swap spread tends to be *bond specific*. This means two bonds with similar maturity and trading at similar yields to maturity, but with different coupons and market prices, could provide different asset swap spreads. This reflects the valuation and pricing adjustments required under the off market swap.

Traders frequently use an alternative measure of value for asset swaps. This is used, in particular, to determine the relative pricing of asset swaps and credit default swaps. This measure is the zero volatility spread (known as the Z spread).

The conventional bond spread is simply the difference between the yield to maturity of the bond and a benchmark of the same or similar maturity (risk free bond or swap). This spread measure does take into account the term structure of the benchmark. This means that the spread will not be the same across all maturities. This is referred to as the spread being volatile. The Z spread corrects for this volatility. This is achieved by measuring the spread over the full term structure benchmark curve.

The process by which the Z spread is derived is as follows:

- Each individual cash flow of the bond is valued using the swap curve[15]. Discount factors for each maturity are used to value the bond cash flows. This will generally result in an implied bond price. This may vary from the value of the bond in the cash market using standard yield to maturity measures.
- The Z spread equates the implied price and the cash price of the bond. In effect, the Z spread is the constant spread across all maturity points that, when applied to the term structure of swap rates, equates the implied price and the cash price of the bond. The Z spread is calculated by iteration.

The Z spread should provide a more accurate spread of a bond. This will generally be the case where the yield is steep.

---

[15] For a discussion of the swap curve and its derivation, see Das, Satyajit (2004) Swaps/Financial Derivatives 3rd Edition; John Wiley, Singapore at Chapter 5.

3 Credit Default Swaps – Hedging/Pricing

The pricing of credit default swaps is based on the fundamental arbitrage relationships to *actual traded market instruments*. As noted above, the underlying market instrument used is an asset swap.

Exhibit 5.3 sets out the process by which the trader can use underlying assets to establish hedges against the position in the credit default swap[16].

The mechanics of the static hedge where the term of the asset and the credit default swap are exactly matched are as follows:

- **Short asset/sold default protection** – this is referred to as the short basis trade. The trader borrows and sells the underlying bond. The trader invests the proceeds of the short position. The net effect is that the trader loses the net spread on the asset. The trader sells protection on the reference entity (the issuer of the bond) and receives a fee for this protection from the protection buyer. The fee should equate to the spread accruing against the trader on the underlying asset. If there is no credit event, then the bond matures. The maturing investment proceeds are used to repurchase the bond and replace the borrowed bond. If there is a credit event, then the trader must settle under the credit default swap. The trader receives delivery of a bond (an eligible deliverable obligation) and pays the face value of the credit default swap. The payment is financed from the investment of the short sale proceeds. The bond received is used to close out the bond borrowing position.

- **Long asset/purchased default protection** – this is referred to as the long basis trade. The trader purchases the underlying bond and finances the position (either by a repo[17] or money market borrowings). The net effect is that the trader accrues the net spread on the asset. The trader purchases protection on the reference entity (the issuer of the bond) and pays a fee for this protection to the protection seller. The fee should equate to the spread accruing to the trader on the underlying asset. If there is no credit event, then the bond matures. The maturing proceeds are used to repay the borrowing used to fund the bond. If there is a credit event, then the trader settles under the credit default swap. The trader delivers the bond (assuming it is an eligible deliverable obligation) and

---

[16] This approach is also referred to as the funding arbitrage model.

[17] See Das, Satyajit (2004) Swaps/Financial Derivatives 3rd Edition; John Wiley, Singapore at Chapter 6.

receives the face value of the credit default swap. The payment received is used to repay the borrowing.

The static hedge implies that the fee on the credit default swap closely approximates the spread on the underlying asset adjusted for costs of the hedge. This follows the arbitrage-free pricing approach.

In practice, this means that the fee or spread on the credit default swap will approximate the spread on the asset swap. Any spread difference will be arbitraged. For example, if the credit default swap spread is below the asset swap spread, the trader could lock in a positive margin by purchasing the asset swap and hedging with a credit default swap. If the credit default swap spread is above the asset swap spread, the trader could lock in a positive margin by selling protection under a credit default swap and hedging by shorting an asset swap. This assumes that the hedges can be established and freely traded.

The relationship means that the value of the credit default swap will be related to the credit spread. This will be particularly true where the maturity of the credit default swap and the bond, whose credit spread is used, are of exactly the same maturity.

In practice, the static hedge is not perfect. The efficiency of the hedge is dependent upon the following factors:

- **Asset trading/repo markets** – the static hedge assumes the ability to trade in the underlying asset. Asset swap prices are typically only quoted on larger (and better rated) companies. It also assumes the ability to finance the position. It assumes the ability to borrow the underlying bond for the purpose of short selling. In practice, the ability to borrow the bond for the term of the credit default swap at a fixed cost is difficult to achieve.
- **Hedge basis risks** – the static hedge entails a number of basis risks:
  1. *Non par asset*[18] – this relates to the fact that the credit default swap is a par asset. In contrast, the underlying bond may be trading at a premium or discount. This means that the credit default swap only hedges the difference from par in the case of a credit event. In practice, this is adjusted by undertaking a par asset swap in order

---

[18]   See O'Kane, Dominic and McAdie, Robert "Trading The Default Swap Basis" (October 2001) Risk (sponsored statement).

to re-profile the cash flows of the asset[19]. However, this does not eliminate the problem. If there is a credit event on the underlying asset, then the trader is left with an off-market interest rate swap that must be terminated. The interest rate swap creates exposure to absolute interest rates and yield curve shape for the trader. The risk will depend on whether the asset is trading at a discount or premium. If the asset is at a premium, then the swap mark-to-market will initially be negative to the dealer (in case of default, the dealer would owe money under the swap). If the asset is at a discount, then the swap mark-to-market will initially be positive (in case of default, the dealer would be owed money under the swap). In both cases, the asset will gradually converge to par. This means that the trader has a potential gain or loss on the hedge conditional upon the credit event (both occurrence and timing)[20].

2. *Deliverable obligation* – the seller of protection is effectively a seller of a cheapest to deliver option. This arises because the buyer has the right to deliver any of the qualifying deliverable obligations. In practice, the buyer will deliver the cheapest asset[21]. This creates a problem for a trader selling protection. This reflects the fact that it needs to short the asset that is likely to be delivered in case of a credit event. In practice, the cheapest to deliver obligation will be difficult to identify in advance. This creates a basis risk equal to the price difference between the defaulted asset that the trader is short and the cheapest to deliver defaulted bond.

- **Maturity matches** – the static hedge will only be efficient where the maturity of the credit default swap and the underlying asset is exactly matched. This is because the credit default swap does not protect against deterioration of the credit short of default (that is, increase in credit spreads resulting in a fall in asset value). Traders will be most affected in a long basis hedge where the credit default swap is for a maturity shorter

---

[19] For discussion of how this is done, see earlier in the Chapter. See also Das, Satyajit (2004) Swaps/Financial Derivatives 3rd Edition; John Wiley, Singapore at Chapters 10 and 38.

[20] This is an example of a credit contingent market risk exposure, see O'Kane, Dominic and Schloegl, Lutz "Cross Currency Credit Explained" (14 May 2002) Lehman Brothers Quantitative Credit Research 53–67.

[21] See discussion in Chapter 1.

than the underlying reference asset. This is because the change in value of the hedge is not offset by a corresponding cash payout on the credit default swap itself. In practice, it will be difficult to hedge with an asset with an identical maturity due to market constraints.

- **Market frictions** – in practice, the pure arbitrage price is affected by market inefficiency. This is the result of market frictions, including funding costs that deviate from LIBOR, counterparty credit risk and regulatory capital treatment of the transactions.

The imperfections of the static hedging process result in the credit default swap trading at a positive or negative margin to the market credit spread. This is referred to as the credit default swap basis.

The imperfections of the static hedging process have a number of implications for trading credit default swaps. Credit default swaps are difficult to hedge efficiently in practice. This is not uncommon in derivative trading[22]. This dictates that the static hedge is used only as an approximate hedge and for a short period of time. This reflects the understanding that the only accurate hedge for any credit default swap position is an equal but opposite trade.

The difficulty in hedging credit default swap positions has led a number of dealers to merge *all forms of trading of credit risk into a single group*. This would cover all credit risk/credit spread exposure to the reference entity covering loans, bonds, convertible bonds and credit derivatives. This integration is to maximise the capacity to net exposure to credit spread changes for the same entity or similar entities (for example, same industry). The integration also allows maximum efficiency in hedging with net exposure being hedged in the most efficient market available at a given time[23].

There are several models for trading credit default swaps which have emerged:

- **Bond trading model** – this approach treats credit default swaps as analogous to long or short positions in corporate bonds. Exposures are managed within specified market risk limit structures covering exposure to change in credit spreads. Exposures and positions are managed in

---

[22]   For example, see Das, Satyajit (2004) Swaps/Financial Derivatives 3rd Edition; John Wiley, Singapore at Chapters 12 to 16.

[23]   See "Credit Derivatives – Developing The Market For Credit Risk Transfer" in "Credit Derivatives Update 2002" (March 2002) Euromoney Research Guide 5–13 at 11–12.

conjunction with trading in corporate bonds and other credit assets. Investment banks/dealers favour the bond trading model.

- **Banking model** – this approach treats credit default swaps as analogous to loan trading. The sale of default protection is treated as making a loan/financial guarantee. The purchase of protection is treated as selling a loan or asset. Exposures are managed within traditional banking credit limits. The trader will buy protection where it has an existing credit exposure to the reference entity and is willing to sell this exposure. The trader will sell protection where it has existing credit limits and is willing to extend credit on the terms of the credit default swap. The banking model is generally used by commercial banks.

Exhibit 5.3   Credit Default Swaps – Hedging

1.   Trader Sells Credit Protection

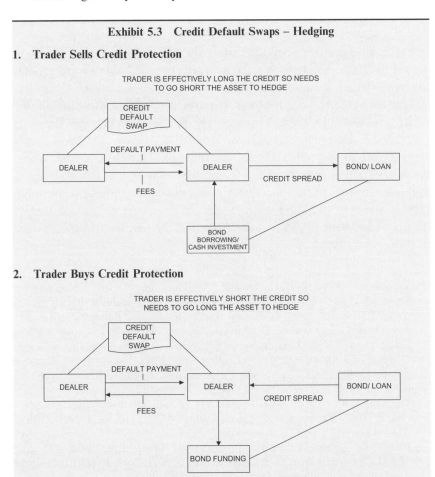

4   Credit Default Swaps – Basis[24]

4.1   Concept

The synthetic (credit default swap) market and cash (bonds and asset swap) markets are similar. The markets all represent different means of trading credit risk. In practice, the pricing in the two markets trade closely. There may be some divergence in pricing in the two markets reflecting structural differences and trading flows. The difference in market pricing between cash instruments and credit default swap prices is referred to as the "basis".

The cash-synthetic basis is defined as:

Credit default swap fee minus credit spread on cash asset

The basis is positive when the cash credit spread is lower than the credit default swap fee. The basis is negative when the cash credit spread exceeds the credit default swap fee.

The measurement of the basis requires careful consideration of the underlying measures used. The arbitrage relationship between the asset swap spread and credit default swap is based on a fixed rate bond that is trading close to face value. In practice, this will not always be true. Where bonds are trading away from face value (for example, due to credit migration or changes in overall market spreads), the basic arbitrage relationship between the asset swap and the credit default swap is more problematic. As the bond trades significantly away from par, the par asset swap structure

---

[24]   See Warren, Doug, McHugh, Joe and Nasr, Oussama "Relative Value Between The Cash And Synthetic Market" in Citibank/Salomon Smith Barney (2001) Credit Derivatives 2001 – Issues and Opportunities; Risk Publications, London at 9–11; O'Kane, Dominic and McAdie, Robert (May 2001) "Explaining The Basis: Cash Versus Default Swaps"; Lehman Brothers, London; O'Kane, Dominic and McAdie, Robert "Trading The Default Swap Basis" (October 2001) Risk (sponsored statement); Reyjman, Alex and Toft, Klaus "Evolution Of A Standard" (Autumn 2001) FOW 20–23; "Credit Derivatives – Developing The Market For Credit Risk Transfer" in "Credit Derivatives Update 2002" (March 2002) Euromoney Research Guide 5–13 at 10–13; Francis, Chris, Kakodkar, Atish and Martin, Barnaby (16 April 2003) Credit Derivative Handbook"; Merrill Lynch, London at 35–43; Hjort, Victor "What's Driving The Default Swap Basis?" in Gregory, Jon (Editor) (2003) Credit Derivatives: The Definitive Guide; Risk Books, London at Chapter 3.

may affect the asset swap spread. This may provide an inaccurate estimate of the true risk of the bond. This means that in practice, traders are careful to ensure that the correct measurement of the basis is being used to assess relative value and trading opportunities[25].

4.2 Basis – Key Determinants

The basis is driven by a number of technical and market factors including:

- Difference between the cash instrument and credit default swaps.
- Trading between the cash market and credit default swap markets[26].
- Market factors.
- Event factors.

There are a number of significant structural differences between the cash market and the credit default swap market, including[27]:

- **Cheapest-to-deliver option** – the buyer of protection is effectively the owner of a cheapest-to-deliver option in the case of a credit event. This allows the buyer to maximise the payout under the credit default swap. This would tend to drive the basis positive, reflecting the premium on the option.
- **Credit events** – there are subtle differences in the default events in credit default swaps and the underlying cash markets; for example, the restructuring credit event. This means that credit default swaps may potentially be triggered by events that may not trigger default on the corresponding physical credit asset. This would tend to dictate a positive basis. This reflects the additional compensation sought by the protection seller for this additional risk.
- **Bond versus credit default swap terms** – there are several aspects, including:
  1. In recent years, bonds featuring step-up coupons that are linked to rating changes have been issued. The adjustment of the coupon affects the bond but not the credit default swap. This means that where a deliverable obligation has step-up coupons, the credit

---

[25] See Francis, Chris, Kakodkar, Atish and Martin, Barnaby (16 April 2003) "Credit Derivative Handbook"; Merrill Lynch, London at 33–34.

[26] See Warren, Doug, McHugh, Joe and Nasr, Oussama "Relative Value Between The Cash And Synthetic Market" in Citibank/Salomon Smith Barney (2001) Credit Derivatives 2001 – Issues and Opportunities; Risk Publications, London at 9–11.

[27] Many of the differences are driven by documentary issues, see Chapter 1.

default swap should trade below the corresponding bond (negative basis).

2. The risk on a cash instrument is on the price paid (capital value plus accrued interest). In contrast, the risk on a credit default swap is based on the face value of the contract. Where a cash instrument trades above or below face value, the exposure to the investor varies relative to that of a seller of protection under a credit default swap. This would dictate that the basis is positive (negative) where the issuer's deliverable obligations are trading below (above) face value[28].

3. Under a credit default swap, the purchaser of protection is required to pay the fee up until the date of the credit event. In contrast, under a cash instrument, the investor generally does not receive any accrued interest in the case of a credit event. This may result in the basis being negative.

- **Regulatory capital treatment** – the treatment of traditional credit assets and credit default swaps is significantly different. These differences are specific to each jurisdiction and also to organisations. For example, the ability to book credit default swaps in the trading book may allow the purchaser of credit risk to lower regulatory capital requirements in some cases[29]. This may generate both a positive or negative basis.

- **Additional counterparty risk** – under a credit default swap, the buyer of protection assumes credit risk on the seller of protection[30]. In effect, it has an implicit default correlation position in case of a credit event on the reference entity. The buyer of protection may also need to hold regulatory capital against this risk. This would tend to generate a negative basis. This reflects the additional risk to the buyer of protection.

- **Liquidity/availability** – the relative liquidity of the cash and credit default swap markets may drive the basis. In practice, liquidity in credit default swaps is focused on 5 year maturity transactions. Liquidity is more variable at different maturities although it is increasing. In the cash market, liquidity is also complex. For example, trading is only possible

---

[28] Where the bond is trading well below face value as a result of financial distress, the additional risk is adjusted for using the upfront fee structure, see Chapter 2.

[29] See discussion in Chapter 1, 3 and 4.

[30] The risk may be mitigated by credit enhancement techniques such as collateralisation; see Das, Satyajit (2004) Swaps/Financial Derivatives 3rd Edition; John Wiley, Singapore at Chapter 22.

in available cash instruments. This may create gaps in the term structure of risk that may be filled by credit default swaps. The impact of liquidity and availability will vary between different entities. In the bond market, investors generally prefer large benchmark liquid issues. This means that corporations with smaller size issues often trade at a lower spread (negative basis) in the credit default swap market. The basis may also be driven by demand for bonds by a specific issuer. For example, issuers with strong retail investor followings often trade at spreads in the bond market below the spread in the credit default swap market (negative basis). This may also happen to tightly held issues. The basis may also be driven by factors driving demand in the credit default swap market. For example, some names are required frequently in structured portfolio transactions/CDO's to provide diversity. These names frequently trade at a spread in the credit default swap market below that in the bond market (negative basis). Liquidity/availability factors may have a positive or negative impact on the basis.

- **Shorting/repo market** – this factor has several implications for the basis:
  1. Buying protection using a credit default swap is equivalent to short selling the underlying credit asset. In practice, constraints in short selling corporate assets mean that credit default swaps represent an attractive mechanism for creating a short position. This tends to generate a positive basis as the credit default swap spread widens relative to the cash market spread. This factor is especially important where traders/investors form a negative credit view on a firm or sector[31].
  2. There is an element of optionality in the repo market that can also affect the basis. A bond investor can finance a bond either by balance sheet borrowings or in the repo market. The investor will generally select the lowest cost option. In the repo market, where there is demand for borrowing the bond for the purpose of short selling, the bond is said to go on "special". In effect, it becomes cheaper to fund the bond in the repo market (often at very low funding costs). This means that a bond investor is always long the repo option. This option

---

[31] For example, in 2002, the basis on France Telecom widened to 300 bps as concerns about the telecommunications sector and the issuer (liquidity and leverage) became evident. Similarly, in late 2002, concerns about the German banking system saw the basis on several German banks, including Commerzbank, increase sharply.

does not exist where the investor synthetically acquires the exposure through the credit default swap. This tends to generate a positive basis as the credit default swap spread widens relative to the cash market spread.

- **Funding** – credit default swaps are unfunded transactions. The credit default swaps are also off balance sheet. In contrast, cash transactions require funding and are on balance sheet. This means that the funding cost of the seller of protection is relevant to the basis. In addition, the requirement of the seller of protection for off-balance-sheet treatment and leverage is also important. For participants that fund above LIBOR/ inter-bank rates, the credit default swap is an attractive alternative method for acquiring exposure. As most participants fund above inter-bank rates, the basis may tend to be negative.

- **Positive credit default swap fees** – the credit default swap fee is priced off the asset swap spread. The asset swap spread is the implied margin relative to LIBOR. This creates some distortion in the market. Market participants with funding costs above LIBOR will generally prefer to acquire credit exposure synthetically through a credit default swap. This reflects the fact that for these participants, the implied spread to LIBOR enhances their return relative to physical purchase of the asset. Some highly rated entities trade below LIBOR. However, the credit default swap fee is positive. This means that it is generally attractive for participants to sell protection on these entities to generate enhanced returns. These factors tend to generate a positive basis.

- **Trading risk** – there are several trading risk differences between the cash and credit default swap markets. These relate to the termination of the transactions. In the case of a bond, a sale terminates all exposure. In the case of a credit default swap, termination may require an opposite position. This will entail maintaining the two positions to maturity. This will defer realisation of any gain or loss and create additional credit exposure. This will tend to generate a positive basis. In an asset swap, the investor is exposed to the risk of loss on the swap in the event of default. This will tend to generate a negative basis.

Trading activity in the cash and credit default swap market also drives the basis. This focuses on:

- **Basis trading/arbitrage** – traders frequently take positions on the basis. If the basis is significantly positive or negative, then traders will seek to arbitrage the cash-credit default swap basis. If the basis is negative, then traders will purchase the asset and buy default protection to lock in a positive spread. If the basis is positive, then the trader will sell protection and short the asset. Traders will also take positions on the basis. One common strategy seeks to take advantage of the increasing positive basis where an entity's credit risk deteriorates. This reflects the interest in shorting the entity's credit assets. Traders commonly buy the bond and buy protection on the issuer. The transaction will generate profits where the entity's credit deteriorates as anticipated and the credit default swap fee increases more than the spread on the bond[32]. Traders may also seek long basis trades to benefit from the embedded options in the credit default swap. These options are the cheapest to deliver option and the repo option (the trader is long the bond that can be lent out in the repo market to enhance earnings on the position). This type of trading activity will tend to ensure that the basis does not become significantly positive or negative.

- **Curve trading** – traders actively trade the term structure of credit spread in the credit default swap market. Traders will sell long dated protection and buy short dated protection in a carry trade. The trader is credit

---

[32] For example in April 1999, traders could have entered the following transaction – purchase JC Penney bonds at LIBOR + 70 bps and purchase protection at 65 bps. Both transactions were for 5 years. In 1 year, the credit quality of JC Penney deteriorated. The bonds were trading at LIBOR + 355 bps. The credit default swap was trading at 400 bps. The transaction would have resulted in the trader earning a positive carry of 5 bps for 1 year and a profit of 50 bps pa for 4 years on the basis shifting from −5 to + 45 bps. [See Warren, Doug, McHugh, Joe and Nasr, Oussama "Relative Value Between The Cash And Synthetic Market" in Citibank/Salomon Smith Barney (2001) Credit Derivatives 2001 – Issues and Opportunities; Risk Publications, London at 9–11 at 10]. In 2001, Ericsson 5 year credit default swaps were trading 5–10 bps lower than the bonds. This was interesting as the bonds contained a rating driven step up in the bond coupon. Traders could have bought the bonds and hedged the credit risk through a matching credit default swap. The credit risk deteriorated and the basis moved from negative to positive (from −5/10 bps to +70/100 bps). This allowed traders to lock in around 300 bps in capital profit in the position. [See "Credit Derivatives – Developing The Market For Credit Risk Transfer" in "Credit Derivatives Update 2002" (March 2002) Euromoney Research Guide 5–13 at 13]. In both cases, the trader assumed no outright exposure to the credit risk of the underlying entity.

neutral during the term of the shorter credit default swap. The trader will generally earn a positive spread between the price of the longer dated and shorter dated credit default swaps, and should also benefit from the declining term to maturity of both trades. This is because the term structure of credit spreads is generally upward sloping. If there is no default during the term of the shorter dated credit default swaps, then the trader has a sold protection position for the remaining term. The trader is exposed to a widening on the spread on the underlying credit. The trader's exposure is to the spread widening beyond the implied forward credit spread at the time of entry into the transaction. The forward spread will generally be higher than the spot spreads[33]. This type of trading activity will affect the size of the basis and the term structure of the basis.

- **Capital structure trading** – where the issuer has several types of debt as part of a complex capital structure (generally in leveraged transactions such as leveraged buyouts), traders may trade the different layers of debt. The difference between the different layers of debt is seniority and priority/ranking in bankruptcy. This will result in differences in recovery rates. The pricing of the credit default swaps should reflect the different losses given default[34]. Where the pricing does not reflect the anticipated differences in recovery rate, traders may buy protection at one priority level and sell protection on a different priority level. The trades will be for different nominal amounts to equalise the expected recoveries. This type of activity has an impact on trading volume and pricing and affects the basis. The impact may be both positive and negative.

A number of market factors also affect the basis. Some of the market factors are structural. Others are related to short term trade flows arising out of market events and transactions.

---

[33] See discussion later in the Chapter.

[34] For example, a crude way of estimating this is to combine the credit default swap prices and expected default probability. For example, assume an entity has a 5% probability of default. Assume the credit default swap on senior debt trades at 250 bps and the credit default swap on subordinated debt is trading at 500 bps. If the assumed recovery rate on senior debt is 50%, then the implied recovery rate on subordinated debt is 0%.

The basis is affected by the segmentation of the credit markets. Different participants only trade specific segments. This has the impact of allowing the two market segments (the cash market and the default swap market) to clear at different price levels.

For example, in the late 1990s, the reinsurance companies entered the credit risk market. The reinsurers were only able to acquire credit risk synthetically using the credit derivatives market. The demand for synthetic credit assets resulted in the basis becoming negative for a sustained period as a result of the mismatch in supply and demand in the market segment. Traders took on long basis spreads to supply credit risk to the investors. The traders were only willing to do so at a positive margin (the negative basis). Similarly, large structured credit trades (synthetic portfolio trades and CDOs) frequently create large temporary increases in the supply of protection. Traders must then purchase bonds or sell protection to acquire offsetting risk. In theory, market factors could potentially make the basis positive or negative. In practice, it has generally generated a negative basis from an excess of available sellers of protection.

Short term events also significantly affect the basis. The two major factors are:

- **Mergers and acquisitions/corporate restructuring** – large funding transactions associated with large mergers/acquisitions and corporate restructuring transactions affect the basis. This reflects the activity of lenders in hedging credit exposure to comply with internal and prudential requirements[35]. This has the effect of generating a positive basis.
- **Convertible arbitrage** – this entails the purchase of convertible bonds that are then separated into the equity and debt component. The credit risk on the bond is frequently hedged using a credit default swap[36]. Issuance

---

[35] For example, in 2000, France Telecom arranged a large debt facility in conjunction with the planned IPO of its mobile/cellular phone subsidiary Orange. Lenders to the facility assumed a large exposure to France Telecom. Most lenders sought to hedge this risk in the credit default swap market. This had the effect of increasing the credit default swap prices for short maturities (around 1 year) to almost the same level as for 10 years. The basis became sharply positive. The basis decreased and the credit spread curve steepened once the hedging was completed.

[36] For a discussion of convertible arbitrage, see Chapter 7. See also Das, Satyajit (2004) Swaps/Financial Derivatives 3rd Edition; John Wiley, Singapore at Chapter 56.

of convertible bonds has an immediate impact on credit default swap spreads. Announcement of convertible bond issues generally leads to a widening of the credit basis as the market anticipates hedging demand associated with convertible arbitrage transactions[37]. Convertible arbitrage also affects the term structure of credit default swap spreads. The credit risk on convertible bonds is generally hedged in the credit default swaps market to the put date. This has the effect of creating an uneven shape of "kink" in the term structure of credit default swap spreads around the put date.

4.3   Basis Behaviour

The determinants of the basis identified interact in a complex manner. A number of them dictate a positive basis while others favour a negative basis. **Exhibit 5.4** sets out the typical impact of the different factors. **Exhibit 5.5** sets out the actual cash-credit default swap basis for a number of actively traded corporate reference entities.

In practice, the behaviour of the basis appears to follow some patterns. In general, the market displays the basis smile[38]. High (AA or better) and low rated (BBB or lower) bonds frequently exhibit a significant positive basis. Bonds in the middle of the credit rating spectrum exhibit relatively low levels of basis. **Exhibit 5.6** sets out the general shape of the cash-credit default swap basis.

The positive basis on high rated bonds reflects the fact that credit default swaps trade at a positive spread. In contrast, many AA or AAA issuers trade below LIBOR in the bond market. The positive basis in lower rated bonds reflects the ability to short sell through the credit default swap market. This is important where the credit is deteriorating and the demand for protection exceeds supply. In general, positive basis is

---

[37]   In late 2002, Fiat announced a US$2.2 billion exchangeable bond. The basis on Fiat increased by around 50 bps following the announcement of the issue.

[38]   See "Credit Derivatives – Developing The Market For Credit Risk Transfer" in "Credit Derivatives Update 2002" (March 2002) Euromoney Research Guide 5–13 at 12–13; See Francis, Chris, Kakodkar, Atish and Martin, Barnaby (16 April 2003) Credit Derivative Handbook"; Merrill Lynch, London at 41–42.

frequently associated with higher rated names, issuers with good retail name recognition (physical bonds trade at premium), event factors and distressed or lower rated names. Negative basis is associated with market segmentation, creating an excess of supply of protection. Opportunities to trade/arbitrage the basis generally restrict the basis from becoming too large.

The basis also impacts increasingly on the primary bond market. This is because the net position in the credit default swap market has implications for the bond market. For example, where traders have a large accumulated short position (bought protection), the position may allow the dealer to bid for new issues. The bond purchased in the primary market provides a hedge for the underlying credit default swap position[39]. This increasingly influences the size and pricing of new issues.

As noted above, large positive and negative basis can be theoretically arbitraged. If the basis becomes negative, then traders can buy the asset swap and hedge the credit risk using credit default swaps. This allows the trader to lock in the positive carry. The arbitrage will tend to force the basis back into equilibrium levels. This means that in practice, a negative basis of over 20/25 bps pa is relatively rare.

If the basis becomes positive, then traders would need to short the asset swap and sell protection under credit default swaps. In practice, this is difficult as there may be constraints to shorting the bonds. This means high positive basis may persist in certain situations.

---

[39] In 2001, traders had large short positions (bought protection) on Alcatel. This was based on the anticipated deterioration of the credit quality of the company. In late 2001, Alcatel credit default swaps were trading with a positive basis of 60 bps (credit default swaps exceeded bond credit spreads). Alcatel brought a new issue to market. The new issue was priced at close to the credit default swap levels. The "price talk" issue was around LIBOR + 275 (the mid market price for 5 year credit default swaps). The issue was priced at LIBOR + 260 bps. The bond issue was oversubscribed. There was significant demand from credit derivatives traders who purchased the new bonds to close out the synthetic short positions on Alcatel. See "Credit Derivatives – Developing The Market For Credit Risk Transfer" in "Credit Derivatives Update 2002" (March 2002) Euromoney Research Guide 5–13 at 11–12.

| Exhibit 5.4 | Cash-Credit Default Swap Basis – Behaviour[40] | | |

Factors	Positive Basis	Positive or Negative Basis	Negative Basis
Structural	• Cheapest-to-deliver Option • Credit events • Shorting/repo market • Positive credit default swap fee	• Bond versus credit default swap terms • Regulatory capital treatment • Liquidity/ availability	• Credit default swap counter-party risk • Funding • Trading risk
Trading		• Basis trading/ arbitrage • Curve trading • Capital structure trading	
Market	• Mergers & acquisitions/ corporate restructuring • Convertible arbitrage	• Segmentation	

| Exhibit 5.5 | Cash-Credit Default Swap Basis – Examples | | | | |

2002

Reference Entity	Credit Default Swap (mid price in bps pa)	Theoretical Asset Swap Spread (bps pa)	Basis (bps pa)	Currency	Maturity (years)
European					5
British American Tobacco	62.5	72.3	−9.8	Euro	5
British Telecom	95.5	106.4	−10.9	Euro	5
Commerzbank	68	50.8	17.2	Euro	5
DaimlerChrysler	117.5	87.9	29.6	US$	5
Ericsson	630	498.4	131.6	US$	5
KPN	255	215.3	39.7	Euro	5
Renault	82	74.2	7.8	Euro	5
Telia	65	48.5	16.5	Euro	5
Suez Lyonnaise	49	46.6	2.4	Euro	5
Volvo	62.5	74.8	−12.3	Euro	5

---

[40] The Table is based on but not identical to Francis, Chris, Kakodkar, Atish and Martin, Barnaby (16 April 2003) "Credit Derivative Handbook"; Merrill Lynch, London at 35.

Exhibit 5.5 Continued					
Reference Entity	Credit Default Swap (mid price in bps pa)	Theoretical Asset Swap Spread (bps pa)	Basis (bps pa)	Currency	Maturity (years)
America					
AOL Time Warner	250	213.4	36.6	US$	5
Bank Of America Corp	37	28.6	8.4	US$	5
Caterpillar Inc.	38	45	−7	US$	5
Delphi Auto Systems	90	91.6	−1.6	US$	5
Ford Motor Credit Systems	187.5	156	31.5	US$	5
GMAC	122.5	128.3	−5.8	US$	5
Household Finance	140	100.4	39.6	US$	5
Merrill Lynch	78	68.1	9.9	US$	5
Motorola	320	249.4	70.6	US$	5
TRW Inc.	145	130.3	14.7	US$	5

Source: CreditTrade as published in (July 2002) FOW49.

2004[41]

Reference Entity	5 year (September 2009 Maturity) Credit Default (bp pa)	Reference Obligation	Theoretical Asset Swap Spread (bp pa)	Basis (bp pa)
European				
Accor	80	5.75% Jul-06	33	47
AXA	28	6% Jun-13	29	−1
Bayer AG	44	6% Apr-12	57	−13
Compagnie St Gobain	33	4.75% Jul-09	32	1
DaimlerChrysler AG	83	7.75% Jan-11	93	−10
Enel SpA	29	5.875% Dec-05	1	28
GUS PLC	44	6.375% Jul-09	36.5	7.5
ING BANK NV	14	6% Mar-10	14	0
MM02 PLC	55	6.375% Jan-07	33	22
Telecom Italia SpA	65	7.25% Apr-12	74	−9

---

[41] I would like to thank CreditTrade (Mike Bardrick, Chris Fry and Adam Goern) for supplying the 2004 data.

Reference Entity	5 year (September 2009 Maturity) Credit Default (bp pa)	Reference Obligation	Theoretical Asset Swap Spread (bp pa)	Basis (bp pa)
American				
Altria Group Inc	160	7.75% Jan-27	180	−20
AT&T Corp	305	7.3% Nov-11	245	60
The Boeing Company	32	8.75% Aug-21	86	−54
Carnival Corporation	52	6.15% Apr-08	48	4
Countrywide Home Loans Inc	52	5.625% Jul-09	26	26
Eastman Kodak Company	180	3.625% May-08	80	100
Ford Motor Credit Company	175	7.25% Oct-11	184	−9
News America Inc	62	6.625% Jan-08	20	42
Sun Microsystems Inc	131	7.65% Aug-09	154	−23
The Walt Disney Company	51	6.375% Mar-12	45	6

Source: **CREDIT**TRADE   T: +44 (0) 20 7098 1600
F: +44 (0) 20 7098 1699

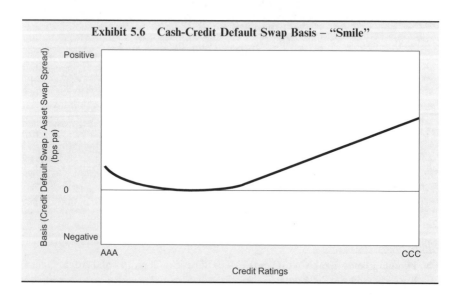

Exhibit 5.6   Cash-Credit Default Swap Basis – "Smile"

5   Hazard/Default Probability Pricing Models[42]

The asset swap based pricing/hedging model is the primary model used in practice to price credit default swaps. However, the price of a credit default swap should implicitly reflect the following factors:

- Default probability of the reference entity.
- Expected loss given default (that is, the recovery rate on the reference asset or deliverable obligations).
- Counterparty risk on the credit default swap (that is, default probability of the seller of protection and the joint default probability (default correlation) of the reference entity and the seller of protection).

The identified factors can be incorporated into a hazard or default probability pricing model to generate an arbitrage free credit spread.

The default probability pricing model is predicated on the basic approach used in all swap valuation[43]. Under this approach, the credit default swap is separated into its two sets of cash flows. It is assumed that at commencement of the transaction, the net present value ("NPV") of the two sets of cash flows is zero. **Exhibit 5.7** sets out the basic model. **Exhibit 5.8** sets out an example of applying the model.

The key inputs required are default (survival) probabilities and recovery rates. These can be derived using a variety of methods used in normal credit modelling[44]. Alternatively, the inputs can be derived from the asset market (bonds/asset swaps and/or credit default swaps)[45].

The default probability pricing approach is a technical model that is closely related to the asset swap pricing approach. In practice, this is the

---

[42] See Duffie, Darrell "Credit Swap Valuation" (January/February 1999) Financial Analysts Journal 73–87; Hull, John C. and White, Alan "Valuing Credit Default Swaps I: No Counterparty Default Risk" (Fall 2000) Journal of Derivatives 29–40; Francis, Chris, Kakodkar, Atish and Martin, Barnaby (16 April 2003) "Credit Derivative Handbook"; Merrill Lynch, London at 13–34; O'Kane, Dominic and Turnbull, Stuart M. "Valuation Of Credit Default Swap Contracts" in (April 2003) QCR Quarterly vol 2003-Q1/Q2; Lehman Brothers, Quantitative Credit Research London at 28–44.

[43] See Das, Satyajit (2004) Swaps/Financial Derivatives 3rd Edition; John Wiley, Singapore at Chapter 10.

[44] See Chapter 6.

[45] This approach can also be used to back out default probabilities from credit spreads; see Chapter 6.

result of the fact that survival probabilities and recovery rates can be derived from the asset market that is used to hedge the credit default swap. In theory and under efficient market assumptions, the default probability pricing model should provide identical pricing to the asset swap based pricing. In practice, this is unlikely to be the case.

The two models will result in identical credit spreads only where the cash market is used to derive the default (survival) probabilities and recovery rates that are used in the model. If historical default probabilities of default are used, then there may be significant differences. This is the result of the fact that market credit spreads are higher than theoretical credit spreads implied by historical default probabilities. This may reflect the market overestimating the risk of default. It may also reflect the impact of other factors on the observable market spread. These factors include liquidity, regulatory, accounting and tax issues. It may also reflect the inefficiency of the capital market. The high credit spread may also reflect difficulty in diversification of credit risk. The distribution of returns on corporate credit risk is highly skewed. This would require very large portfolios to fully diversify the unexpected losses on a portfolio. This may not be possible in practice. This may mean that the credit spread incorporates a component for undiversified credit risk[46].

In practice, credit default swaps are priced relative to the cash market (asset swaps). As discussed below, the default probability model is used primarily for the valuation of existing credit default swaps. This includes valuation for the purpose of profit and loss determination, risk (market and credit risk) determination and for unwinding/trading existing positions. The model is also used for valuing off-market credit default swaps (including unwinding positions) or non-standard structures.

Exhibit 5.7   Credit Default Swaps – Valuation Model

The credit default swap is analysed as the following cash flows:

- **Fixed leg** – this is the series of fees paid by the buyer of protection. The present value ("PV") of these cash flows is determined by discounting the cash flows back to the valuation date as follows:

$$PV \text{ (Fixed Leg)} = \sum_{t=1}^{n} DF_t \times CDSS \times AF_t \times SP_t$$

---

[46] See Amato, Jeffrey D. and Remolana, Eli M. "The Credit Spread Puzzle" (December 2003) BIS Quarterly Review 51–63.

Where:

DF_t = discount factor for t_0 to t_1 (theoretically, this should be the risk free
discount factor but in practice the swap discount factor may be used)

CDSS = fee (spread) on credit default swap (bps per annum)

AF_t = accrual factor for t_{n-1} to t_n

SP_t = survival probability of reference entity for t_0 to t_1

- **Floating leg** – this is the contingent cash flow payable by the seller of protection
seller in case of a credit event. The PV of these cash flows is as follows:

$$PV \text{ (Floating Leg)} = \sum_{t=1}^{n} DF_t \times (SP_{n-1} - SP_n) \times (1 - RR)$$

Where:

DF_t = discount factor for t_0 to t_1 (theoretically, this should be the risk free discount factor but in practice the swap discount factor may be used)

SP_t = marginal survival probability of reference entity from t_{n-1} to t_n

RR = recovery rate of delivered obligation.

The survival probability is defined as 100% minus the default probability for the
reference entity for the relevant period.

Exhibit 5.8   Credit Default Swap Valuation – Example

In the example below, the risk neutral credit spread for a bond is derived. The spread
on a credit default swap equates to the bond credit spread by arbitrage arguments.
The model is structured as follows:

- The cash flows of the bond are identified.
- The default probabilities for the issuer and the recovery rate for the type of
obligation are identified.
- The survival probability (1 minus the default probability) is calculated.
- The recovery adjusted default payment is calculated from the default probability
and the recovery rate assumed.
- The original bond cash flows are then adjusted for the risk of default by
calculating the expected cash flows assuming the risk of default.
- The adjusted bond cash flows are then discounted (using the risk free rate) to
solve for the credit spread that equates the internal rate of return on the adjusted
cash flows of the bond to the risk free rate.

Assume a 1 year bond where the issuer is estimated to have a 1 year default
probability of 0.50%. Assume the recovery rate is 35% (that is, loss given default is
65%). Assume 1 year risk free (government bond rates) are 5.00% pa.

Based on the above information, a risk neutral credit spread of 34 bps can be calculated as follows:

Years	0	1
Cash Flows ($)	(100.00)	105.34
Default Probability (%)		0.50
Recovery Rate (%)		35.00
Survival Probability (%)		99.50
Recovery Adjusted Default Payment (%)		0.175
Adjusted Cash Flows	(100.00)	105.00
Discount Factor (at risk free rate)		0.9524
Discounted Cash Flows ($)		100.00
Present Value of Bond ($)	100.00	

The approach outlined can be extended to derive risk neutral spreads (assuming knowledge of a default probability and recovery rate) for longer maturities. For longer maturities, more complex simulations using conditional probabilities are required.

6   Credit Default Swaps – Trading/Valuation

6.1   Credit Default Swaps – Termination

In this Section, the trading and valuation of credit default swaps is considered. Trading refers to establishing and then terminating the transaction prior to scheduled maturity or a credit event. Where a credit default swap is traded before maturity, the value of the transaction has to be established. Valuation refers to establishing the mark-to-market value of a credit default swap prior to scheduled maturity. The mark-to-market will generally be required to determine profit and loss on the transaction. The mark-to-market will also be required to calculate risk on the transaction. This will include market risk (value at risk[47]) and counterparty credit risk[48] on the transaction.

---

[47]   See Das, Satyajit (2004) Swaps/Financial Derivatives 3rd Edition; John Wiley, Singapore at Chapter 17, 18, 19, 20 and 34.

[48]   See Das, Satyajit (2004) Swaps/Financial Derivatives 3rd Edition; John Wiley, Singapore at Chapter 21, 22 and 33.

The approach to valuation for trading and mark-to-market purposes is similar. This reflects the fact that the mark-to-market should align closely to the actual market price at which the transaction could be traded or terminated.

Trading in credit default swaps is generally driven by the following reasons:

- Termination of the underlying business rationale (for example, the credit risk being hedged) to which the credit default swap transaction is related.
- Realisation of profit/minimisation of losses from the credit default swap transaction.

In the cash market, trading entails purchasing or selling a bond or equivalent. The transaction offsets an existing position. There are no residual positions or risks. Trading a credit default swap is similar. However, the structure of the credit default swap as an over-the-counter contract with mutual obligations creates structural complexity[49]. In order to terminate a credit default swap, the counterparty enters into an economically equal but opposite position for the remaining life of the original transaction. This can be undertaken in several ways:

- **Reverse transaction** – this would require the counterparty to enter into an equal but opposite transaction (an offsetting credit default swap) *with a counterparty other than the original dealer*. This offsetting credit default swap would, when combined with the original transaction, result in the counterparty having no exposure under the original credit default swap. No payment between the parties is required where the offsetting credit default swap is transacted at the rates prevailing at the time of the termination. The economic value (if any) on the original transactions is reflected in the cash flows between the two transactions over the remaining life of the two transactions. **Exhibit 5.9** sets out the structure of a reverse credit default swap.
- **Swap sale or assignment** – this would entail the counterparty assigning or novating its position in the existing credit default swap to a new third party. The fair market value (cash payment) of the swap is paid to (by)

---

[49] This is identical to the termination structure in any OTC derivative contract, see Das, Satyajit (2004) Swaps/Financial Derivatives 3rd Edition; John Wiley, Singapore at Chapter 10.

the counterparty by (to) the dealer assuming the swap position. **Exhibit 5.10** sets out the structure of a credit default swap assignment[50].

- **Swap Cancellation** – this would require the counterparty to enter into an equal but opposite credit default swap with the *original* counterparty. The swap reversing the original transaction is entered into on the *original swap terms* (dates and rates). This second swap will, when revalued at the *rates prevailing on the termination date*, have positive or negative value. This value will be paid between the two counterparties to equate the values and will equal the termination payment. Upon cancellation, all future cash flows and obligations are removed. **Exhibit 5.11** sets out the structure of a swap cancellation.

In economic terms, there should be no difference in valuation between the three alternatives. This is particularly the case where no counterparty credit risk is assumed to exist. In practice, the transactions have significant differences in cash flow, accounting/taxation treatment and counterparty risk implications. These differences may drive valuation differences.

The key differences between the techniques include:

- **Income recognition** – under a reverse transaction, the counterparty will recognise and realise its profit or loss over the remaining term of the mirror contracts[51]. In contrast, under an assignment or cancellation, this profit or loss will be recognised and realised immediately.
- **Cash flow** – under a reversal, there is no immediate cash flow, with any gains or losses being received or paid over the life of the swap. In contrast, there is an immediate cash receipt or payment triggered under an assignment or cancellation.
- **Credit risk** – the use of an offsetting credit default swap results in two credit exposures (under the original and the second swap). In the case of an assignment, the existing credit exposure continues to exist, but to the dealer assuming the transaction. In the case of a cancellation, all credit exposure is eliminated. This impacts upon credit risk in terms of use of credit limits and regulatory credit capital requirements.

---

[50] The ISDA 2003 Credit Definitions incorporate provisions (including a novation agreement and confirmation) to facilitate assignments of credit default swaps.

[51] This assumes that the transactions are not treated on a mark-to-market basis. Where the transactions are treated on a mark-to-market basis, the (unrealised) gain or loss would be recognised immediately.

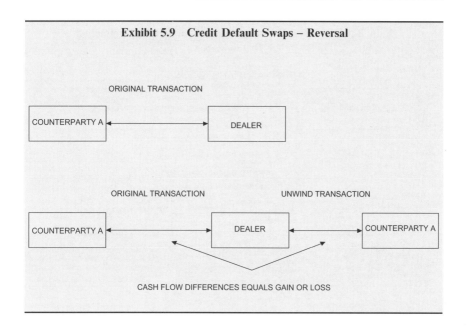

Exhibit 5.9   Credit Default Swaps – Reversal

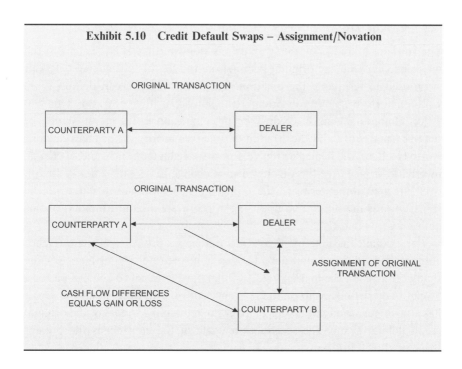

Exhibit 5.10   Credit Default Swaps – Assignment/Novation

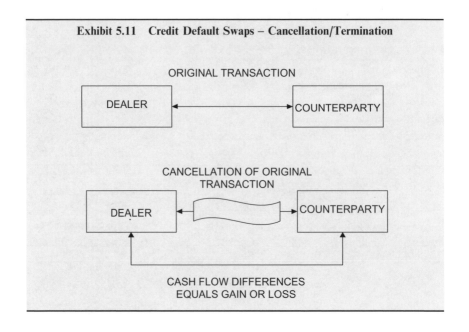

Exhibit 5.11   Credit Default Swaps – Cancellation/Termination

6.2   Credit Default Swaps – Valuation Of A Termination

The value of a credit default swap at any point in time is equivalent to the difference between the original transaction and the offsetting credit default swap used to terminate the position. The value of the credit default swap will derive from changes in pricing (the spread on the contract). This will reflect changes in market credit spreads, migration in the credit quality of the reference entity and the remaining time to maturity of the credit default swap. In effect, the dealer will have a positive (gain from favourable change in spread) or negative (loss from adverse change in spread) annuity stream over the remaining term of the contract. The termination value of the transaction is the present value (using appropriate discount factors) of this annuity.

For example, assume the dealer has purchased protection on a reference entity under a 5 year credit default swap at a spread of 100 bps pa. Assume that after 2 years, the market credit spread has increased to 150 bps pa for a 3 year credit default swap on the reference entity. This means that the dealer has a positive annuity of 50 bps pa over the remaining 3 years of the original credit default swap. The termination value of the contract is the present value of the 50 bps pa over the 3 years.

The methodology outlined assumes the annuity stream is risk free. In practice, this is not the case. If there is a credit event under the credit default swap, then the payments would cease. In order to incorporate the risk of default, the present value of the cash flows is adjusted. Each of the annuity cash flows is weighted by the estimated survival probabilities of the reference entity of the credit default swap. **Exhibit 5.12** sets out the steps in determining risk adjusted discount factors and the termination or mark-to-market value of a credit default swap.

In practice, the use of methodology outlined creates some differences relative to conventional mark-to-market of cash instruments (bonds or asset swaps). Default/survival probability adjusted discount factors will reduce the mark-to-market of the credit default swap. This means that a credit default swap will sometimes exhibit a lower mark-to-market gain or loss than a comparable cash position. The credit default swap will also exhibit lower risk (as measured by risk measures such as duration[52]) than a comparable cash position.

Exhibit 5.12   Credit Default Swaps – Termination Value/Mark-To-Market Methodology

1.   Derivation Of Risk Adjusted Discount Factors

The key element of this methodology is to derive risk adjusted discount factors that incorporate the survival probabilities of the reference entity. This is done within the framework of the hazard or default probability pricing model.

In theory this can be done from historical default probabilities and recovery rates. In practice, it is bootstrapped from available market credit spreads. This entails the following steps:

- The first step is to identify the observed credit spread for the reference entity for the specified maturity. In practice, for a termination this will inevitably be the interpolated credit spread. The market credit spread will be derived from asset swaps or (increasingly) credit default swaps.
- Once a credit spread is established, the hazard or default probability pricing model is used to derive implied loss given default[53]. For an assumed recovery rate,

---

[52]   See Das, Satyajit (2004) Swaps/Financial Derivatives 3rd Edition; John Wiley, Singapore at Chapter 5 and 15.

[53]   For details on the bootstrapping of default/survival probabilities from market spreads, see Chapter 6.

the default probability and (by inference) the survival probabilities across maturities are calculated[54].

• The default risk adjusted discount factors at each relevant maturity point are then calculated as follows:

Discount Factors (generally discount factors of the swap curve[55])
times the Survival Probability

2.   Calculation Of Termination Value/Mark-To-Market Of Credit Default Swap

When the risk adjusted discount factors are known, the termination value of the credit default swap can be established as follows:

• The first step is to determine the annuity payments that are receivable or payable. This entails taking the contracted spread on the credit default swap and the current market spread to the maturity of the original transaction.
• The present value of 1 bps ("PVO1") or dollar value of the 1 bps ("DVO1") of the annuity stream is calculated as follows:

$$PVO1/DVO1 = (\text{Notional Value of Transaction}/10{,}000)$$
$$\times \sum(\text{Swap Discount Factors} \times \text{Survival Probabilities})$$

• The termination value of the credit default swap will then be stated as:

$$\text{Termination Value} = \text{Annuity} \times PVO1/DVO1$$

6.3   Credit Default Swaps – Revaluation

The credit default swaps are revalued in order to establish the mark-to-market valuation of the transaction. It is also used to determine the market and credit risk of the transaction. It can also determine the liquidation value of the swap in case of default by one of the parties to the credit default swap.

---

[54]   The assumed recovery rate can significantly impact upon the implied default/ survival probabilities; see Chapter 6.

[55]   This is not strictly risk free (as noted early in the Chapter) but will generally represent the market cost of borrowing or investment for dealers; see Das, Satyajit (2004) Swaps/Financial Derivatives 3rd Edition; John Wiley, Singapore at Chapter 5.

The valuation methodology for establishing the current value of a credit default swap for termination and mark-to-market purposes is similar. This reflects the fact that the mark-to-market should align closely to the actual market price at which the transaction could be traded or terminated. There are a number of subtle differences, including:

- Termination values use actual tradable prices to value the transaction. In contrast, mark-to-market value frequently uses the mid-point of market price. In other words, the bid-offer spread is commonly not incorporated.
- Credit spreads for each reference entity for all maturities are not always available. This means the specific credit spread curves used to revalue specific transactions must be generated from incomplete data sets. In practice, this means using proxies to adjust historically observed spreads. For example, spread changes in the broad market or industry can be used to adjust known historical spreads where an actual market sample was not available. Frequently, complete term structures are not available and interpolated spread or a flat term structure of spreads is used.

The general practice followed by dealers is as follows:

- Credit default swaps are revalued against *actual* observed market prices or spreads where available. Mid-point spreads are commonly used.
- Where market prices/spreads are unavailable, model based values are used. The basic methodology followed is that used to establish termination values.
- Dealers maintain reserves against model and other risks in the valuation process[56].
- Dealers and risk managers perform regular tests of the valuations, models and process to ensure the integrity of the process[57].

---

[56] See Das, Satyajit (2004) Swaps/Financial Derivatives 3rd Edition; John Wiley, Singapore at Chapter 20.

[57] See Das, Satyajit (2004) Swaps/Financial Derivatives 3rd Edition; John Wiley, Singapore at Chapter 20.

7 Credit Default Swaps – Other Pricing Factors

7.1 Impact Of Restructuring Credit Events[58]

The framework for valuation of credit default swaps described does not incorporate the potential impact of differences in credit events specified in the contract. The major contractual provision likely to impact upon valuation is the restructuring credit event. There are potentially four separate forms of restructuring that could be specified: NR (no restructuring); R (restructuring or old restructuring); Mod R or MR (modified restructuring); or Mod Mod R or MMR (modified modified restructuring)[59]. The different restructuring provisions affect the potential payout of the contract and consequently the pricing/valuation of the credit default swap. This value impact is primarily by restricting the range of deliverable obligations; in effect, altering the value of the cheapest-to-deliver option embedded in a credit default swap.

The value of the restructuring event is based on the following factors:

- The likelihood of the credit event (if any) taking the form of a restructuring.
- The expected recovery rate following a restructuring credit event.

The likelihood of a restructuring credit event is influenced by the capital structure of the reference entity and the type and structure of its liabilities.

---

[58] For discussion of the valuation of the pricing differential needed to cover additional risk from inclusion of restructuring risk, see Watkinson, Lisa and Lee, Young-Sup (5 September 2002) Modified Restructuring – Not The End Of The Story; Morgan Stanley, Fixed Income Research, New York; O'Kane, Dominic, Pedersen, Claus M. and Turnbull, Stuart M. "The Restructuring Clause In Credit Default Swap Contracts" in (April 2003) QCR Quarterly vol. 2003-Q1/Q2; Lehman Brothers, Quantitative Credit Research London at 45–59; Reyfman, Alex and Toft, Klaus (13 May 2003) "What Is The Value Of The Restructuring Credit Event?"; Goldman Sachs, Credit Derivatives Research, New York; Reyfman, Alex and Toft, Klaus "What Is The Value Of Modified Restructuring" in Gregory, Jon (Editor) (2003) Credit Derivatives: The Definitive Guide; Risk Publications, London at Chapter 4; Francis, Chris, Kakodkar, Atish and Martin, Barnaby (16 April 2003) "Credit Derivative Handbook"; Merrill Lynch, London AT 73–83. See also Douglas-Jones, Jane "Credit Today – Restructuring" (Winter 2001) FOW/Credit Derivatives 13–15.

[59] See Chapter 1.

The expected recovery rate is driven by a number of factors:

- The type of restructuring event in the contract that specifies the range of deliverable obligations.
- The outstanding liabilities of the reference entity *at the time of the restructuring credit event* including remaining term to maturity and structures/contractual terms. For example, the value of the restructuring option is higher where the reference entity has liabilities with long maturities or trading at low prices.

In practice, the relevant parameters are difficult to estimate. There is limited historical information. In addition, it is not clear that the empirical data will be helpful given that each default may have unique or specific characteristics.

The parameters may also not be independent. In the credit default swap market, banks are frequently buyers of protection. Banks use the credit default swap to hedge the credit risk on loans to and other transactions with the reference entity. Where the reference entity experiences financial distress, the bank faces conflicts of interest in minimising the loss of its transactions and maximisation of the profit on the credit default swap[60]. Where restructuring is not included, it is conceivable that bankers may alter their behaviour to institute bankruptcy to protect their position. This in turn may have an impact of recovery rates. This means that the type of credit events included in a credit default swap, the probability of specific credit event and recovery rates are related.

A number of models designed to quantify the value of a restructuring event have emerged[61]. The models generally use the probability of a

---

[60] See discussion on Conseco and other cases in Chapter 1.
[61] See Watkinson, Lisa and Lee, Young-Sup (5 September 2002) Modified Restructuring – Not The End Of The Story; Morgan Stanley, Fixed Income Research, New York; O'Kane, Dominic, Pedersen, Claus M. and Turnbull, Stuart M. "The Restructuring Clause In Credit Default Swap Contracts" in (April 2003) QCR Quarterly vol. 2003-Q1/Q2; Lehman Brothers, Quantitative Credit Research London at 45–59; Reyfman, Alex and Toft, Klaus (13 May 2003) "What Is The Value Of The Restructuring Credit Event?"; Goldman Sachs, Credit Derivatives Research, New York; Reyfman, Alex and Toft, Klaus "What Is The Value Of Modified Restructuring" in Gregory, Jon (Editor) (2003) Credit Derivatives: The Definitive Guide; Risk Publications, London at Chapter 4; Francis, Chris, Kakodkar, Atish and Martin, Barnaby (16 April 2003) "Credit Derivative Handbook"; Merrill Lynch, London at 73–83.

restructuring credit event and the payoff of the cheapest-to-deliver option in case of a restructuring credit event to derive a value of the restructuring. In effect, the credit default swap contract is analysed as providing three outcomes: no credit event; "hard" credit event (bankruptcy or failure to pay); and "soft" credit event (restructuring). Each outcome has a different payoff; that is, different recovery rates. The recovery rates are modelled by computing the value of the cheapest-to-deliver bond calculated as the expected discounted value of all outstanding bonds available for delivery. The model outcomes are highly sensitive to the assumed likelihood of a restructuring credit event (relative to other credit events) and the recovery rate differences. These assumptions are difficult to verify or calibrate.

In practice, Mod R places the greatest restrictions on the range of deliverable obligations. In contrast, R places the least restrictions on the range of deliverable obligations. Mod Mod R is somewhere in between Mod R and R in the restrictions on the range of deliverable obligations. This means that the value of the restructuring is highest (higher credit spread) in R contracts. Mod Mod R is next highest (lower credit spread) followed by Mod R contracts (lowest credit spread). Generally, Mod R credit default swaps trade approximately 1–5%[62] above the credit spread for a NR transaction. Mod Mod R credit default swaps trade slightly above Mod R spread (approximately 1 to 7% above the credit spread for a NR transaction). NR transaction trade at the highest spreads (approximately 5 to 20% above the credit spread for a NR transaction[63].

7.2 Counterparty Risk On Credit Default Swap[64]

The valuation methodology outlined assumes the absence of counterparty risk on the parties to the credit default swap. In practice, the bilateral and over-the-counter structure of the credit default swap introduces counter-party credit risk[65].

---

[62] The 1 to 5% refers to the percentage of the credit spread.

[63] The information is based on market conditions at the time of writing and is subject to significant change and volatility.

[64] See O'Kane, Dominic and Schloegl, Lutz "A Counterparty Risk Framework For Protection Buyers" (14 May 2002) Lehman Brothers Quantitative Credit Research 42–51.

[65] For a discussion of counterparty risk in derivative contracts, see Das, Satyajit (2004) Swaps/Financial Derivatives 3rd Edition; John Wiley, Singapore at Chapter 21.

The counterparty risk on the credit default swap is asymmetric. The seller of protection under a credit default swap has low credit exposure to the purchaser of protection. This reflects the fact the protection buyer's obligation is limited to payments of the credit spread or fee on the credit default swap. If the protection buyer stops paying the required payments, then the protection seller terminates the contract.

The protection seller is exposed to mark-to-market changes in the credit spread on the credit default swap. The protection seller suffers a loss where the credit spread on the reference entity decreases. In effect, the protection seller loses the mark-to-market gain on the contract.

The quantum and risk of loss is relatively low. This is because the size of the mark-to-market gain is limited to a zero credit spread. Credit default swaps do not trade at negative spreads. The correlation between credit spread changes and default correlation may also limit loss. If the credit spread on the reference entity increases and the protection buyer defaults, then the protection seller will not suffer a loss. It is only where the credit spread decreases and the protection buyer defaults that the protection seller suffers a loss.

The purchaser of protection is exposed to the protection seller. The exposure is significant. In the case of a credit event on the underlying reference entity, the protection buyer's exposure to the seller may equal the full face value of the contract. The protection buyer is also exposed where there is a significant deterioration in the credit quality of the reference entity short of a credit event (for the purpose of the credit default swap contract). The exposure is to the loss of mark-to-market gains where the protection seller defaults and the contract terminates.

A number of pricing models for credit default swaps incorporating counterparty risk have been suggested[66]. The model combines the following risks to derive the value of the contract:

- **Default risk** – this refers to the probability of default of the reference entity and the protection seller.
- **Recovery rate** – this refers to the recovery rate of the reference entity and the protection seller.

---

[66] See O'Kane, Dominic and Schloegl, Lutz "A Counterparty Risk Framework For Protection Buyers" (14 May 2002) Lehman Brothers Quantitative Credit Research 42–51.

• **Default correlation** – this refers to the default correlation between the reference entity and the protection seller and specifically the *order* of default. The joint default frequency generally does not measure the likelihood of one entity default before another. In counterparty risk, the order of default is critical. This is because the protection buyer will generally suffer a loss where the protection seller defaults *before* the reference entity. In practice, this requires measurement of all joint defaults within the time horizon where the protection seller defaults before the reference entity. This is generally estimated from the equity markets[67].

In practice, the impact of counterparty credit risk on the pricing of credit default swaps is limited. This reflects market practice. The majority of credit default swap trading is between highly rated dealers. Where there is concern about counterparty credit risk on either party, the transaction will be collateralised[68]. One or both parties will be required to collateralise any mark-to-market exposure on the transaction. Acceptable collateral will include cash and government securities. The structure of collateral agreements varies but will entail a combination of any initial deposit and daily collateral to cover mark-to-market changes in value. This will reduce the counterparty risk of the transaction.

8 E2C (Equity To Credit) Hedging

8.1 Concept

The basic hedge of credit default swaps entails trading in the underlying credit asset (typically using asset swaps) to replicate the risk assumed. There has been increasing interest in using equities to price and hedge credit default swaps[69]. This approach is based on the inherent relationship

---

[67] See Chapter 6.

[68] See Das, Satyajit (2004) Swaps/Financial Derivatives 3rd Edition; John Wiley, Singapore at Chapter 22.

[69] See King, Matt (4 September 2001) Using Equities To Price Credit; JP Morgan, London; Keenan, Sean C., Sobehart, Jorge R. and Benzschawel, Terry L. "The Debt And Equity Linkage And The Valuation Of Credit Derivatives" in Gregory, Jon (Editor) (2003) Credit Derivatives: The Definitive Guide; Risk Publications, London at Chapter 5.

between credit risk and equity prices. The relationship is commonly based on the Merton or structural credit model[70].

The model assumes that the equity in a risky firm is equivalent to a call option on the net asset value of the firm. The net asset value is calculated as market value of the firm's assets minus the claims on the assets (which include mainly traditional financial claims such as debt) that may result upon default. The position of the bond holder is a combination of the long position in an underlying bond plus the sale of a put option on the company's assets (where the option has a strike price equal to the value of the debt of the entity).

In practice, this relationship can be applied in several ways. It is used in credit modelling to provide market based estimates of the risk of default[71]. It is also used in relative value trading strategies seeking to generate returns from mis-pricing of different components of the capital structure of a company (referred to as "capital structure arbitrage")[72]. The equity-credit relationship is increasingly used as the basis of hedging[73]. This entails trading in equities or options on the underlying stock to hedge credit risk or positions in credit default swaps (known as the "E2C" relationship).

8.2 E2C Model Issues

The basic Merton model provides an elegant theoretical linkage between equity and debt markets. The practical use of the model to implement hedging and trading strategies is challenging.

---

[70] For a discussion of the Merton model, see Chapter 6. See Merton, R. "On The Option Pricing Of Corporate Debt: The Risk Structure Of Interest Rates" (1974) Journal of Finance vol 29 449–470. For a more recent approach using the traditional option pricing framework, see Crouhy, Michel, Galai, Dan, and Mark, Robert "Credit Risk Revisited" (March 1998) Risk – Credit Risk Supplement 40–44.

[71] See discussion of the Merton model in Chapter 6.

[72] See discussion in Chapters 2 and 7. See Currie, Antony and Morris, Jennifer "And Now For Capital Structure Arbitrage" (December 2002) Euromoney 38–43.

[73] See also King, Matt (4 September 2001) Using Equities To Price Credit; JP Morgan, London; Naik, Vasant, Trinh, Minh, Balakrishnan, Srivaths and Sen, Saurav "Hedging Debt With Equity" (November 2003) Lehman Brothers Quantitative Credit Research 22–39.

The Merton model enables debt credit spreads to be derived from information about equity market prices, the risk free rate and the structure of debt contract. In practice, the derived spreads are not consistent with spreads observed in the market. The model requires asset volatility to be set to unrealistic levels to reconcile market observations and model credit spreads. The values of the firm's assets and volatility implied from equity and debt prices are also not consistent[74].

The performance of the model has significant implications for its use in hedging credit risk. For example, one study tested an empirical hedging methodology that used a regression analysis of bond excess returns against equity returns. The model implied low hedge ratios (2–4% for A–/BBB rated entities and 12–20% for non-investment-grade entities). Where the entity's equity was used to hedge debt issues, the reduction of volatility (the effectiveness of the hedge) was low (7–15% for A–/BBB rated entities and 15–22% for non-investment-grade entities). There was a large residual related to the performance of the *credit market as a whole*. This implies that credit positions hedged using the equity of the entity may still have significant exposure to changes in the overall credit market. Hedges using both the equity and credit market were more effective for investment grade (50–71% A–/BBB rated entities). There was no significant improvement in the performance of the hedge for non-investment-grade entities. The study concluded that hedging credit with equity was imperfect. It required an understanding of systematic market behaviour and should be complemented by scenario analysis[75].

The discrepancies between observed spreads and model outcomes appear to be driven by the fact that market conditions do not satisfy the restrictive assumptions of the Merton model.

---

[74] See King, Matt (4 September 2001) Using Equities To Price Credit; JP Morgan, London; Keenan, Sean C., Sobehart, Jorge R. and Benzschawel, Terry L. "The Debt And Equity Linkage And The Valuation Of Credit Derivatives" in Gregory, Jon (Editor) (2003) Credit Derivatives: The Definitive Guide; Risk Publications, London at Chapter 5; Naik, Vasant, Trinh, Minh, Balakrishnan, Srivaths and Sen, Saurav "Hedging Debt With Equity" (November 2003) Lehman Brothers Quantitative Credit Research 22–39.

[75] See Naik, Vasant, Trinh, Minh, Balakrishnan, Srivaths and Sen, Saurav "Hedging Debt With Equity" (November 2003) Lehman Brothers Quantitative Credit Research 22–39.

Key assumptions not satisfied include the no arbitrage assumption. The model assumes debt and equity trading will eliminate arbitrage opportunities. Market imperfections (such as limitations on short selling) and large transaction/hedge re-balancing costs means that the no arbitrage conditions may not hold. The failure may be more marked in the case of loan and bond markets. There may be additional problems in the construction of the hedge portfolio. The debt and equity markets appear to be segmented, with only limited interest and capital available to arbitrage pricing discrepancies between debt and equity securities. This means that the Merton model outputs (pricing and default predictions) may contain significant biases[76].

The weaknesses in the Merton model have created interest in extensions of the model[77]. Some of these models are more complex mathematically. The models are also unable to completely eliminate differences between market observed spreads and model implied spreads.

In practice, the use of E2C models requires understanding that the Merton approach and its extensions do not appear to fully capture the relationship between equity and debt market prices. The use of potentially mis-specified models will generally provide imperfect equity hedges for credit positions. The advent of E2C trading may actually create arbitrage opportunities between bond, equity and credit default swap markets[78].

8.3 Equity Based Hedging

In practice, dealers in credit default swaps use equities to hedge credit positions. The hedge is predicated on a Merton type structural model.

---

[76] See Keenan, Sean C., Sobehart, Jorge R. and Benzschawel, Terry L. "The Debt And Equity Linkage And The Valuation Of Credit Derivatives" in Gregory, Jon (Editor) (2003) Credit Derivatives: The Definitive Guide; Risk Publications, London at Chapter 5.

[77] See Sobehart, Jorge R. and Keenan, Sean C. "The Need For Hybrid Models" (February 2002) Risk 46–52. See examples in Keenan, Sean C., Sobehart, Jorge R. and Benzschawel, Terry L. "The Debt And Equity Linkage And The Valuation Of Credit Derivatives" in Gregory, Jon (Editor) (2003) Credit Derivatives: The Definitive Guide; Risk Publications, London at Chapter 5.

[78] See examples in Keenan, Sean C., Sobehart, Jorge R. and Benzschawel, Terry L. "The Debt And Equity Linkage And The Valuation Of Credit Derivatives" in Gregory, Jon (Editor) (2003) Credit Derivatives: The Definitive Guide; Risk Publications, London at Chapter 5 at 87–88.

The bond investor is selling the shareholder a put on the company's assets (in effect, the right to default). The position may be hedged as follows:

- Purchase the bond (or sell protection under a credit default swap).
- Short the stock of the issuer.

The behaviour of the hedge will be as follows:

- If the asset value falls, then the stock price falls by more than the bond price. This reflects the position in the capital structure of the securities and the corresponding recovery rates.
- The gains on the short stock position will offset the erosion of the bond value.

Alternatives or variations to the above strategy include:

- The use of put *options* as an alternative to the short stock positions.
- The use of basis hedges using beta adjusted positions in the market equity index to enhance hedge liquidity.

The major problem with this dynamic hedge is the risk of decoupling of the performance of the two securities (basis risk). This can be illustrated with the example of a takeover announcement. Under these circumstances, the stock price rises, creating losses on the short stock position. Matching gains on the bond price may not offset the losses. This reflects the fact that the credit position of the bond holders may not be affected by the takeover to the same degree as that of the equity holders. This risk favours the use of equity put options as the hedging vehicle.

There has been increased interest in using out-of-the-money equity put options to hedge credit default swap positions[79]. The use of equity options as credit hedges has been driven primarily by convertible arbitrage funds. The funds have sought to use out-of-the-money equity put options to hedge stripped convertible bond positions[80]. A principal driving factor was the decline in equity volatility levels in 2002. The implied volatility levels on the out-of-the-money equity puts meant that the puts offered value relative

---

[79] See Kassam, Altaf and Grebnev, Alex "Using Equity Options For Credit Protection" in (15 May 2002) European Equity Derivatives – Weekly Volatility Analyst Issue 8; Goldman Sachs Derivatives & Trading Research 2–4.

[80] For discussion of convertible arbitrage, see Chapter 7.

to using credit default swaps to hedge the credit risk[81]. The strategy could be used in two ways. The out-of-the-money equity put could be used as a substitute for purchasing protection using a credit default swap. The relationship can also be used to trade. This would entail selling protection under a credit default swap and hedging the risk by purchasing an out-of-the-money equity put option.

Where out-of-the-money equity puts are used, the face value of the positions may need to be adjusted to reflect the performance of the credit default swap and the option. If there is a credit event, then it is likely that the value of the firm's shares will decline to close to zero. This means that the equity put will be equivalent to the strike price of the option. If there is a credit event, then the value of the firm's debt will decline to the expected recovery rate (this will generally be above zero). The difference in price change in the credit position and the equity option must be accounted for in the hedge.

Traders generally use a simple equity-to-credit formula such as that embedded in CreditGrades^{TM} [82] to undertake the hedge. The model derives a risk-neutral probability of default that includes a market risk premium designed to cover for default rate volatility/uncertainty[83]. CreditGrades^{TM} provides a calculation of risk neutral probabilities and an implied 5 year credit default swap spread using this methodology for 11,000 companies[84].

In practice, the hedging model is not precise. The hedge may function adequately on a cash or payout basis. This means that where there is a default on the credit or the bond survives to maturity, the hedge will generally operate reasonably. However, the equity hedge generally provides unsatisfactory protection against mark-to-market changes in the value of bond or credit default swaps. Discrepancies in day to day changes in the mark-to-market values of the bond/credit default swap and the short equity/long equity put hedge are common. This reflects the low precision of the

---

[81]   See Kassam, Altaf and Grebnev, Alex "Using Equity Options For Credit Protection" in (15 May 2002) European Equity Derivatives – Weekly Volatility Analyst Issue 8; Goldman Sachs Derivatives & Trading Research 2–4.

[82]   See Finger, Christopher C. (Editor) (2002) CreditGrades^{TM} – Technical Document; RiskMetrics Group, New York.

[83]   Models such as KMV (see Chapter 6) do not generally include this risk premium.

[84]   See Evans, Nick "Peering Through Murky Waters" (June 2002) Euromoney 18–19.

model, input errors and trading difficulties. In practice, traders must use significant judgment in managing the hedge to ensure its efficacy.

8.4   E2C Hedging – In Practice

E2C models and their application to credit hedging and trading are at an early stage of evolution. They are typically used for the following applications:

- Traders, credit portfolio managers and investors use E2C models to provide information on credit migration and assessment of credit quality.
- Traders compare equity volatility to cash-credit default swap basis to develop trading strategies[85].
- Traders use equity positions to hedge credit default swap positions and bond positions (in particular non investment grade bonds) to manage income volatility.
- Traders and hedge funds trade discrepancies between debt and equity markets by entering into relative value trades between equity and debt markets[86] (often referred to as capital structure arbitrage[87]).

The increased use of the E2C model and the commitment of capital to trade pricing differences between debt and equity markets may have the impact of increasing the pricing consistency between the markets. However, there is significant model risk in this activity.

9   Alternative Hedging Strategies

Future prospects for structuring dynamic hedges include the introduction of loan value or credit indexes and the supply of credit risk adjusted securities. The emergence of credit indexes[88] and the possible introduction of traded futures and options on these indexes would allow the structuring of hedges of bond and credit default swap positions.

---

[85]   See Francis, Chris, Kakodkar, Atish and Martin, Barnaby (16 April 2003) "Credit Derivative Handbook"; Merrill Lynch, London at 42–43.

[86]   See examples in Chapter 2 and 7.

[87]   See Currie, Antony and Morris, Jennifer "And Now For Capital Structure Arbitrage" (December 2002) Euromoney 28–43.

[88]   See Chapter 2.

A number of securities where the behaviour of the security is linked to credit factors have emerged[89]. These include:

- Loans where the credit spreads are a predetermined function of rating.
- Bonds where the interest paid is a function of rating.
- Spread is a function of a periodic auction process that presumably reflects alterations in perceived default risk (issued by Merrill Lynch as Spread Adjusted Notes ("SPANs")).
- Bonds with a pre-determined put to the issuer in the event that the issuer's credit quality deteriorates. For example, the ill fated Korean Development Bank bond issue with an investor put at par in the event that the issuer was downgraded below A−[90].
- Auction-rate preferred stock where the dividend rate is reset by a Dutch auction, typically every 49 days, but with no maturity. These transactions are treated as Tier II regulatory capital for commercial banks and "equity" by the U.S. Internal Revenue Service. The dividend rate is a high frequency barometer of issuer credit quality[91].

The securities may allow traders to hedge credit risk through trading in the credit sensitive notes to offset exposure to credit derivative positions.

10   Total Return Swaps – Hedging/Pricing

Total return swaps are priced/hedged using the underlying asset (generally a bond) on which the total return swap is based. The dealer can generally hedge in the following ways:

- **Counterparty transactions** – this is predicated on a bank or investor with an offsetting position in the underlying bond entering into the opposite transaction to the original total return swap.
- **Trading in the reference asset** – this entails the purchase or short sale by the dealer of the reference bond to hedge its position in the total return swap. **Exhibit 5.13** sets out the structure of the hedge for a total return swap where the dealer is the total return payer.

---

[89]   See Gregory-Costello, Miles "Credit Limits" (July 2000) Risk 24–29.
[90]   See Irvine, Steven "Credit Where Credit's Due For KDB" (July 1997) Euromoney 16.
[91]   In 1991, Citicorp went through a financial distress period where their ARPS dividend rate soared to about 500 bps from a prior average of around 50 bps.

The valuation basis for counterparties is based on the market price of the underlying bond. This will be the current secondary market price for the actual bond. Supply and demand for specific classes of exposures (in terms of country, industry and borrower) would be the principal driving force for the price of the underlying bond.

In addition, the pricing of the transaction would reflect the cost of the synthetic hedge, including:

- Balance sheet or capital utilisation (both economic and regulatory).
- Counterparty risk exposure.
- Transaction costs.
- Adjustments for the position of the parties relative to access to the asset and funding cost.

The pricing of total return swaps will reflect the following factors:

- Cost of the asset, including the cost of borrowing the asset for the short sale.
- Funding cost of the dealer.
- Balance sheet costs and regulatory capital charges for the dealer.

An alternative methodology is to hedge using a surrogate or proxy instrument. This usually entails a combination of credit/bond indexes and/or financial market indicators (principally interest rates or equity prices). The approach relies on the correlation between the return on proxy instruments and the reference asset being hedged. This approach is only applicable in limited circumstances.

The use of proxy hedges developed in the US high yield markets. It treats a corporate debt obligation as a combination of an investment in a risk free asset (a government bond) and an investment in the *equity* of the issuer. The empirical research[92] indicates that the correlation between the returns on corporate debt and US Treasury yields decreases as the credit quality (measured by rating parameters) decreases. This decrease in correlation to risk free debt returns is paralleled by an *increase* in the correlation between the bonds and the equity of the issuer as the credit quality declines.

---

[92] See Bookstaber, Richard and Jacob, David P. "The Composite Hedge: Controlling The Credit Risk Of High Yield Bonds") (March April 1986) Financial Analysts Journal 25–36; Grieves, Robin "Hedging Corporate Bond Portfolios" (Summer 1986) The Journal of Portfolio Management 23–25; Ramaswani, Murali "Hedging The Equity Risk Of High Yield Bonds" (September–October 1991) Financial Analysts Journal 41–50.

Exhibit 5.14 sets out this type of relationship[93]. The evidence suggests the possibility of a proxy hedge combining positions in government bonds (or government bond futures) and positions in the individual stock (or the equity index). There is evidence that a dynamically managed composite hedge significantly outperforms a conventional interest rate hedge.

This logic can be extended to use a mixture of government securities/ futures on government securities and positions in equity stocks/equity indexes to replicate high yield bond indexes. The technology may be potentially applicable to total return swaps. The underlying instruments can be used to hedge and price *index based* total return swaps. This hedging approach avoids the inefficiencies and high transaction costs of replication or hedging using physical assets. The basis risk is very significant. In practice, few (if any) practitioners use this approach to hedging total return swaps (on a single reference asset or an index).

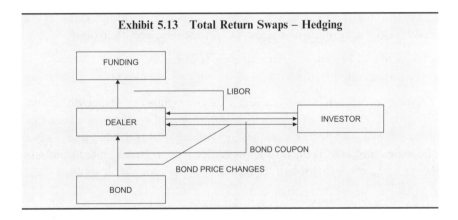

Exhibit 5.13   Total Return Swaps – Hedging

---

[93]   The underlying logic of this relationship is based on the Merton structural model that specifies that all corporate securities are claims on the value of the firm. Equity is characterised as a residual claim akin to a call option on the net asset value of the firm (ie assets net of liabilities). Using put call parity, this means that corporate debt equates to the security combined with the sale of a put option structure on the assets of the firm. This analysis is fundamental to the derivation of default risk discussed in detail below. For discussion of this approach, see Black, F., and Scholes, M. "The Pricing of Options and Corporate Liabilities" (1973) Journal of Political Economy vol 81 637–754; Merton, R. "On The Option Pricing Of Corporate Debt: The Risk Structure Of Interest Rates" (1974) Journal of Finance vol 29 449–470; Geske, R. "The Valuation Of Corporate Liabilities As Compound Options" (1977) Journal of Financial and Quantitative Analysis 541–552.

Rating Level	Correlation With Treasury Bonds	Correlation With Equity
Aaa – A	0.86	0.09
Baa – Ba	0.77	0.25
B – Caa	0.51	0.28

Source: Bookstaber, Richard and Jacob, David P. "The Composite Hedge: Controlling The Credit Risk Of High Yield Bonds" (March April 1986) Financial Analysts Journal 25–36 at 26

11 Credit Spread Forwards & Options – Hedging/Pricing

11.1 Approach

The credit spread is the compensation received by the investor for credit risk assumed. There are a number of specific aspects to the pricing of credit spread products. The major element is the determination of the credit spread. This, in turn, can be separated into several specific issues:

- Nature and behaviour of credit spreads generally.
- Pricing credit spread derivatives.

Credit spread derivatives are forwards and options on the credit spread. The pricing/valuation and trading of credit spread products are based on normal derivative pricing techniques for deriving forward and option pricing. The underlying asset is the credit spread. Hedging is based on replication of the specific exposure through trading in the underlying cash securities[94].

11.2 Credit Spreads – Term Structure

The theory of term structure of interest rates is relatively well developed[95]. The term structure of credit risk is relatively less well understood, although it has begun to attract increased attention[96].

---

[94] For discussion of pricing of forward and option contracts, see Das, Satyajit (2004) Swaps/Financial Derivatives 3rd Edition; John Wiley, Singapore at Chapters 6 and 7.

[95] See Das, Satyajit (2004) Swaps/Financial Derivatives 3rd Edition; John Wiley, Singapore at Chapter 5.

[96] See Litterman, R. and Iben, T. (1988) Corporate Bond Valuation And The Term Structure Of Credit Spreads": Goldman Sachs Financial Strategies Group; New York; Jerome, S. "Using Default Rates To Model The Term Structure Of Credit Risk" (September–October 1994) Financial Analysts Journal 25–32.

The credit spread generally increases in line with increasing default risk and maturity. The observed behaviour of credit spreads is set out in **Exhibit 5.15**. In practice, the credit spread seems to increase with maturity for higher credit quality bonds. The term structure of credit spreads for lower credit quality bonds is often flat or (for low credit quality issuers) inverse.

The behaviour of credit spreads for lower credit quality firms reflects the impact of the following factors[97]:

- The concept of "crisis at maturity", predicated on the risk generated by liquidity pressures created by the need to re-finance near term maturing debt (which is often confronted by lower credit quality and highly leveraged firms).
- The pattern of default risk for lower credit quality firms whereby default risk is higher in absolute terms but the marginal default risk for lower rated firms decreases with maturity. In contrast, the marginal default risk of higher rated firms increases with maturity[98].

The pattern of marginal default risk for lower credit quality firms is consistent with the following:

- Life cycle of ratings outlook whereby lower rated firms face higher short term risk which is resolved by survival or default.
- Mean reversion processes in ratings outlook whereby lower rated issuers improve, middle rated issuers stay the same, and higher rated firms tend to decline on average.

A complete term structure of credit spreads is required to allow the pricing of credit derivatives[99].

---

[97] See Jerome, S. "Using Default Rates To Model The Term Structure Of Credit Risk" (September–October 1994) Financial Analysts Journal 25–32; Zheng, C.K. "Understanding The Default-Implied Volatility For Credit Spreads" (Summer 2000) Journal Of Derivatives 67–77.

[98] See Chapter 6.

[99] For an overview of how credit curves are constructed in practice, see Li, David "Constructing A Credit Curve" (November 1998) Risk – Credit Risk Special Report 40–44.

Exhibit 5.15   Credit Spreads – Term Structure

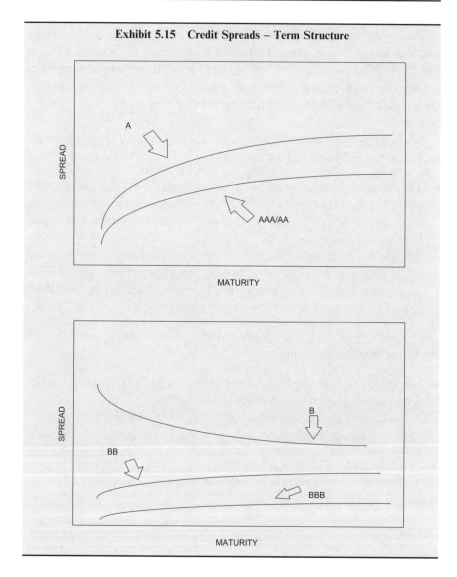

11.3   Credit Spreads – Pricing Forwards

The calculation of the forward on the credit spread follows traditional forward pricing principles[100]. The forward credit spread is calculated as the

---

[100]   See Das, Satyajit (2004) Swaps/Financial Derivatives 3rd Edition; John Wiley, Singapore at Chapter 6.

difference between the forward yield on the relevant bond/security minus the forward risk free/swap rate. **Exhibit 5.16** sets out an example of the calculation of forward spreads. **Exhibit 5.17** sets out an analysis of forward credit spreads. Forward credit default spreads are calculated using an identical methodology[101].

The mathematics of forward spread calculations indicates that in the case of a positively (negatively) sloped yield curve, the forward credit spreads increase (decrease). In practice, the term structure of *spot* credit spread creates potentially significant richness in the pattern of forward credit spreads. Forward credit spreads appear to be poor indicators of future spot spreads. Forward credit spreads also appear to be more volatile than the underlying securities.

The calculation of forward credit spreads may, under certain circumstances, require adjustment for convexity. This reflects the fact that a forward interest rate will not always correspond to the yield on the corresponding forward bond because the relationship between the bond price and bond yield is non linear. This may require a convexity adjustment to be incorporated[102].

Exhibit 5.16   Forward Credit Spread Calculations

In the example set out below, the forward credit spread is calculated as the difference between the forward yield for the underlying swap rates and the yield applicable on the issuer security (issuer in this context is used to merely signify a non risk free issuer).

The forward swap and issuer security rates are calculated as follows[103]:

$$(1 + R_{t1})^{t1} 1 * (1 + R_{t1 \times 2})^{t2-t1} = (1 + R_{t2})^{t2}$$

Where

R_{t1} = the par interest rate to time t1
R_{t2} = the par interest rate to time t2
$R_{t1 \times 2}$ = the forward interest rate between time t1 and t2
t1, t2 = the time to maturity in days from the present divided by 365

---

[101] See Berd, Arthur M. "Forward CDS Spreads" (November 2003) Lehman Brothers Quantitative Credit Research 40–44.

[102] For discussion of convexity issues, see Das, Satyajit (2004) Swaps/Financial Derivatives 3rd Edition; John Wiley, Singapore at Chapters 6 and 48.

[103] All rates are expressed in consistent time units, usually annual effective rates.

Rearranging to solve for the forward interest rate: $R_{t1 \times 2} = [(1 + R_{t2})^{t2}/(1 + R_{t1})^{t1}]^{1/(t2-t1)} - 1$

Date	1 July 2002	
Forward Date	1 July 2003	
Final Maturity	1 July 2012	
Security Type	Swap	Company X
Yields		
To Forward Date (% pa)	3.00	4.05
To Final Maturity (% pa)	5.00	7.45
Credit Spreads		
To Forward Date (% pa)	1.05	
To Final Maturity (% pa)	2.45	
Forward Credit Spread		
Forward Yields (% pa)	5.22	7.83
Forward Credit Spread (% pa)	2.61	
Difference Between Current And Implied Spreads (bps)	15.98	
Difference Between Current And Implied Spreads (%)	6.52	

The principal point to observe is the difference between the spot spread and the *implied forward spread*. The difference, in strict terms, should be carefully considered as the spot spread is for the securities to the *final maturity date*. In contrast, the implied forward spread is for a slightly *shorter* maturity out of the forward date.

Exhibit 5.17   Forward Credit Spreads – Patterns

In the following case, the term structure of implied forward credit spreads is estimated. The term structure is calculated from an assumed swap curve and an assumed corporate (non-government issuer) yield curve. The forward credit spreads are calculated for a number of separate forward dates – 1 year forward, 3 years forward, and 5 years forward – as well as the spot (current) date. The credit spreads calculated as of these dates are for all maturities up to 5 years at 6 month intervals. The results are set out as a series of graphs showing the spot credit spread and the implied forward credit spread across the yield curve at each of the forward dates compared to the spot spread. The principal objective of the analysis is to highlight the pattern of implied forward credit spreads relative to the current spot spreads.

Assume the following yield curve and credit spreads:

Maturity (Years)	Swap Rate (% pa)	Bond Rate (% pa)	Credit Spread (% pa)
0.5	5.40	5.55	0.15
1	5.20	5.43	0.23
3	5.35	5.77	0.42
5	5.70	6.17	0.47
7	5.75	6.60	0.85
10	5.85	6.95	1.10

The spot and forward spreads are as follows:

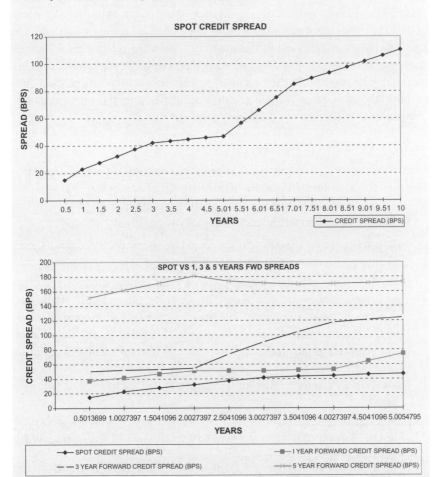

11.4   Credit Spread Options – Pricing

11.4.1   Approach

The valuation of credit spread options is identical to valuation of spread options generally[104]. The credit spread option structure is effectively an option on the forward credit spread between the nominated securities. The key determinants of value in credit spread options are the forward spread and the volatility of this parameter.

Economically, the forward spread is the differential between the forward rates of the two securities at the option expiration date. The forward rates are usually estimated using the current spot yield for the security and the financing rate (repo, LIBOR etc rate) to the option maturity. As noted above, the forward rate estimated using this technique is not exactly equal to the security's forward yield at the theoretical forward price. This is because the security displays convexity. For short dated options, the difference is not material. The price of the credit spread option prior to expiration is sensitive to both the spot rates for the relevant securities and the interest rate to expiration that determines the forward spread.

11.4.2   Volatility Estimation[105]

Under the historical or empirical approach, volatility estimates are calculated as the standard deviation of logarithms of the price changes of a sample time series of historical data for the asset price.

The calculation procedure entails the following steps:

- The time series of historical data is specified. This will usually be the series of daily, weekly or monthly price observations for the relevant asset. For debt securities, either price or yield can be used.
- The price changes are calculated to measure the periodic (daily etc) return on the asset. In practice, the price relatives are utilised; that is, one plus the return or the observation at time t1 divided by the observation at the previous point in the time series t0. While the standard deviation can be calculated for either the returns or the price relatives, the first leads to inaccuracies, reflecting the nature of the log normal distribution

---

[104] See Das, Satyajit (2004) Swaps/Financial Derivatives 3rd Edition; John Wiley, Singapore at Chapter 45.

[105] For a discussion of volatility estimation see Das, Satyajit (2004) Swaps/ Financial Derivatives 3rd Edition; John Wiley, Singapore at Chapter 9.

based on the effect of compounding. This means that the calculation using the price relatives is preferred. The difference is not significant for calculations involving relatively short data series, but becomes increasingly significant as the data series increases in size.

● The standard deviation of the price relatives is then calculated.

The interpretation of the standard deviation is as follows:

● The standard deviation computed equates to the volatility over the relevant time interval (for example, daily).
● The periodic observation is then scaled to give the annualised volatility of the asset price returns. This is done using the following relationship:

$$\sigma_{annual} = \sigma_{daily} \times \sqrt{\text{number of days}}$$

where the number of days would be set at either 250 or 260 days[106].

The volatility of the forward spread is complex. It reflects the volatility of the underlying securities and the correlation between yield movements between the two securities. There are a number of ways to model the volatility of the forward spread, including:

● Historical volatility of the spread between the *actual* two securities.
● Historical volatility of the spread between two securities *having constant maturities* equivalent to the actual underlying securities (say, 2 year constant maturity bond against 10 year constant maturity security[107]).
● Estimated yield spread volatility based on the average yield of each security, the historical yield volatility of each security and the historical correlation between the two.
● Estimated expected future yield spread based on the actual yields on the securities at transaction date, the implied volatility of options on each security, and an estimate of the future correlation coefficient.

In practice, the forward credit spreads appear to be relatively more volatile than the underlying securities. This higher spread volatility reflects

---

[106]   Note that the daily volatility is scaled using the square root of the time interval. This reflects the fact that the assumed uncertainty about the asset price does not increase linearly.

[107]   For a discussion of the concept of constant maturity securities, see Das, Satyajit (2004) Swaps/Financial Derivatives 3rd Edition; John Wiley, Singapore at Chapter 51.

the following:

- Lower absolute level of spread (a 1 bps change in credit spread results in a larger *percentage change* than an equivalent change in the absolute yield level on the security).
- Imperfect correlation between the security and risk free rate.

Exhibit 5.18 sets out an example of the calculation of the volatility of the credit spread as well as the yield volatility of the underlying security.

The alternative method for estimating volatility is implied volatility. The implied volatility approach calculates volatility as implied by the current market value of options. This is undertaken by specifying the option price and calculating the volatility that would be needed in a mathematical option pricing formula to derive the specified market price as a fair value of the option. The calculation of implied volatility is usually done using an iterative procedure.

Exhibit 5.18　Historical Spread Volatility – Calculation

Assume the following rates and spreads:

Period	Risk Free Interest Rate (% pa)	Spread (% pa)
0	6.030	0.450
1	6.010	0.460
2	5.990	0.430
3	5.990	0.430
4	6.000	0.410
5	6.040	0.440
6	6.010	0.450
7	6.020	0.430
8	6.050	0.430
9	6.040	0.410
10	5.980	0.420
11	5.950	0.440
12	5.960	0.430
13	5.960	0.410
14	5.930	0.450
15	5.950	0.420
16	5.980	0.440

Period	Risk Free Interest Rate (% pa)	Spread (% pa)
17	5.970	0.410
18	6.010	0.410
19	6.040	0.420
20	6.020	0.400

The rates and spreads are depicted in the graphs below:

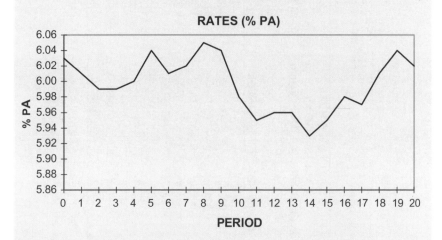

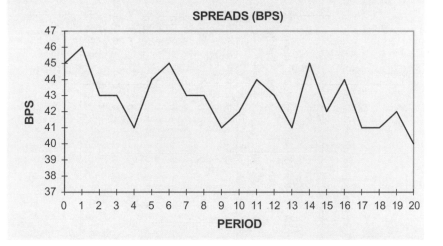

The rate and spread volatility is calculated in the Table below:

Period	Risk Free Interest Rate (% pa)	Spread (% pa)	Interest Rate (% pa)	YIELD VOLATILITY CALCULATIONS		SPREAD VOLATILITY CALCULATIONS	
				Spread Relative $(S_t/(S_{t-1}))$	Daily Return $U_i = \ln(S_t/(S_{t-1}))$	Yield Relative $(S_t/(S_{t-1}))$	Daily Return $U_i = \ln(S_t/(S_{t-1}))$
0	6.030	0.450	6.480				
1	6.010	0.460	6.470	1.02222	0.02198	0.99846	(0.00154)
2	5.990	0.430	6.420	0.93478	(0.06744)	0.99227	(0.00776)
3	5.990	0.430	6.420	1.00000	0.00000	1.00000	0.00000
4	6.000	0.410	6.410	0.95349	(0.04763)	0.99844	(0.00156)
5	6.040	0.440	6.480	1.07317	0.07062	1.01092	0.01086
6	6.010	0.450	6.460	1.02273	0.02247	0.99691	(0.00309)
7	6.020	0.430	6.450	0.95556	(0.04546)	0.99845	(0.00155)
8	6.050	0.430	6.480	1.00000	0.00000	1.00465	0.00464
9	6.040	0.410	6.450	0.95349	(0.04763)	0.99537	(0.00464)
10	5.980	0.420	6.400	1.02439	0.02410	0.99225	(0.00778)

Period	Risk Free Interest Rate (% pa)	Spread (% pa)	Interest Rate (% pa)	YIELD VOLATILITY CALCULATIONS		SPREAD VOLATILITY CALCULATIONS	
				Spread Relative (St/(St−1))	Daily Return Ui = ln(St/(St−1))	Yield Relative (St/(St−1))	Daily Return Ui = ln(St/(St−1))
11	5.950	0.440	6.390	1.04762	0.04652	0.99844	(0.00156)
12	5.960	0.430	6.390	0.97727	(0.02299)	1.00000	0.00000
13	5.960	0.410	6.370	0.95349	(0.04763)	0.99687	(0.00313)
14	5.930	0.450	6.380	1.09756	0.09309	1.00157	0.00157
15	5.950	0.420	6.370	0.93333	(0.06899)	0.99843	(0.00157)
16	5.980	0.440	6.420	1.04762	0.04652	1.00785	0.00782
17	5.970	0.410	6.380	0.93182	(0.07062)	0.99377	(0.00625)
18	6.010	0.410	6.420	1.00000	0.00000	1.00627	0.00625
19	6.040	0.420	6.460	1.02439	0.02410	1.00623	0.00621
20	6.020	0.400	6.420	0.95238	(0.04879)	0.99381	(0.00621)
Standard Deviation (Per Period)					4.894%		0.527%
Annualised Volatility (Days)	250.				79.386%		9.334%

The relative volatility is as follows:

Rate volatility: 9.33% pa
Spread volatility: 79.39% pa

11.4.3   Valuation Models

Spread options can be priced using a variety of models. Spread options can be equated to and valued as exchange options in certain circumstances[108]. Two separate approaches exist for the valuation of spread options. These include:

- **Modelling the spread as an underlying asset** – this approach will generally allow analytical solutions based on the Black-Scholes-Merton[109] model to be derived[110]. The advantage of this approach is its relative simplicity. The approach creates significant problems. It assumes that the spread will never become negative. This may be a reasonably tractable assumption where the spread is likely to be positive (yield on a risky security is compared to the yield on a risk free security). This is clearly inconsistent where the spread is between two assets where negative spreads are feasible. This problem is introduced by the implicit assumption of the log normal distribution of the spread as an asset price. In addition, the log normal assumption suggests that spread fluctuation size would increase for large spreads and decrease for small ones (the proportionality impact), which is not supported by evidence. One possible means of coping with the difficulties posed by the assumption of log normality (particularly in respect of the spread price being negative) is to assume a normal (as opposed to log normal) distribution where volatility is calculated on the *absolute price change* annualised standard deviation.

---

[108]   For an adoption of the Margrabe approach, see Bhansali, Vineer (1998) Pricing and Managing Exotic and Hybrid Options; McGraw-Hill, New York at 69–79.

[109]   See Das, Satyajit (2004) Swaps/Financial Derivatives 3rd Edition; John Wiley, Singapore at Chapter 7. The version used is Black's commodity forward/futures pricing model; see Black, Fischer "The Pricing of Commodity Contracts" (March 1976) Journal of Financial Economics 3 167–179.

[110]   See Garman, Mark "Spread the Load" (December 1992) Risk 68–84; McDermott, Scott "A Survey of Spread Options For Fixed Income Investors" in Klein, Robert A. and Lederman, Jess (Editors) (1993) The Handbook of Derivatives & Synthetics; Probus Publishing: Chicago, Illinois at Chapter 4 at 102–111. See also Heenk, B.A., Kemna, A.G.Z. and Vorst, A.C.F. "Asian Options on Oil Spreads" (1990) Review of Oil Spreads" 511–528; Bhansali, Vineer (1998) Pricing and Managing Exotic and Hybrid Options; McGraw-Hill, New York at 29–33.

- **Using multi (two) factor options models** – this approach is generally implemented using a numerical approach[111]. It is assumed that each security has a log normal distribution. A binomial distribution or Monte Carlo simulation is used to find the expected value of the option at expiry. This is then discounted back to the valuation date to derive the present value of the option. This approach incorporates the separate volatility of the underlying assets and the correlation between the two assets to derive the spread option value. This approach is preferable in that it does not suffer the same restrictions as the first approach.

Exhibit 5.19 sets out an example of an analytical option pricing model for spread options. **Exhibit 5.20** sets out an example of pricing a spread option.

Exhibit 5.19   Spread Options – Analytical Pricing Model[112]

The pricing of a call option is:

$$C_t = e^{-rt}[(S_t - K)N(h) + \sigma\sqrt{t}N'(h)]$$

where

$$h = (1/\sigma\sqrt{t})(S_t - K)$$

where

K = strike yield spread
S_t = forward yield spread at time t

---

[111] See Garman, Mark "Spread the Load" (December 1992) Risk 68–84; Ravindran, K. "Low Fat Spreads" (October 1993) Risk 66–67; Ravindran, K. "Exotic Options" in Dattatreya, Ravi E. and Hotta, Kensuke (1994) Advanced Interest Rate and Currency Swaps: State-of-the Art Products, Strategies & Risk Management Applications; Probus Publishing: Chicago, Illinois; Pearson, Neil D. "An Efficient Approach For Pricing Spread Options" (Fall 1995) Journal of Derivatives 76–91; Ravindran, K. (1998) Customised Derivatives: A Step-by-Step Guide to Using Exotic Options, Swaps and Other Customised Derivatives; McGraw-Hill, New York at 274–278, 331–332.

[112] The version set out here is from McDermott, Scott "A Survey of Spread Options For Fixed Income Investors" in Klein, Robert A. and Lederman, Jess (editors) (1993) The Handbook of Derivatives & Synthetics; Probus Publishing: Chicago, Illinois at Chapter 4 at 109–110.

$\sigma =$ volatility (standard deviation of yield spread)
r = risk free rate
t = time to option maturity
N(h) = standard normal distribution

The equivalent pricing for a put option is:

$$P_t = e^{-rt}[(K - S_t)(1 - N(h)) + \sigma \sqrt{t} N'(h)]$$

where

$$h = (1/\sigma \sqrt{t})(S_t - K)$$

Exhibit 5.20   Spread Options – Valuation Example

Assume an option on the spread between two bonds. The example assumes the following parameters:

Bond 1 Current Yield (% pa)	6.70
Bond 2 Current Yield (% pa)	6.30
Current Spread (% pa)	0.40
Strike Spread (% pa)	0.40
Maturity	3 months
Volatility – Bond 1 (% pa)	14.00
Volatility – Bond 2 (% pa)	19.00
Interest Rates (% pa)	5.50
Correlation	0.80

The spread option premium is 0.14%[113].

11.5   Credit Spread Products – Trading/Hedging

In practice, credit spread derivatives are hedged through trading in the underlying cash instruments. This entails trading physical long and short positions in the underlying credit assets and the management of these positions over the life of the transaction. **Exhibit 5.21** sets out the structure for hedging both long and short forward positions in credit spreads.

---

[113]   The option is priced using a binomial model.

The hedge is not exact for the following reasons[114]:

- **Convexity** – the hedge, as structured, does not incorporate any adjustment for convexity (the non linearity in the relationship between prices and yields). In practice, the hedge would need to be dynamically managed to adjust for the convexity changes as the yields on the underlying instruments changed. The dealer will tend to be long or short convexity, as the convexity and volatility of the underlying bond will generally be different from that of the risk free security. This risk is difficult for the trader to hedge perfectly in practice.
- **Market structure** – difficulties in shorting the relevant bonds (that is, the absence of an effective bond borrowing mechanism) may create significant difficulties in hedging.
- **Cost issues** – some of the hedge costs (the repo rate and the bond borrowing cost) may be difficult to estimate at the time of establishing the hedge. For example, where the trader is long the risky bond, its receipt of the coupon is dependent upon the absence of default. In the event of default, the coupon flows are lost. This exposure is difficult to hedge in practice and must be covered by a pricing adjustment.

Key issues in hedging include:

- Utilisation of balance sheet and/or capital to support the positions.
- Liquidity of underlying asset.
- Availability of mechanisms for short selling securities.
- Transaction costs, including uncertainty regarding costs such as that of shorting securities.

The use of futures contracts on the relevant government bond and interest rate swaps overcomes some of the problems of replicating credit spread forwards using physical securities.

Credit spread options are usually hedged dynamically through trading in the underlying assets. Credit spread options cannot usually be efficiently replicated by trading in options on the underlying bonds. The portfolio of options is generally more expensive, reflecting the separate payoff which

---

[114] For discussion of hedging issues, see Iacono, Frank "Credit Derivatives" in Schwartz, Robert J. and Smith, Jr., Clifford W. (editors) (1997) Derivatives Handbook: Risk Management and Control; John Wiley & Sons, Inc., New York at Chapter 2.

allows each option to be separately exercised to maximise the value of individual options. This reflects the fact that the spread option is insensitive to absolute rate levels, while the option portfolio is generally sensitive to the overall absolute level of rates[115].

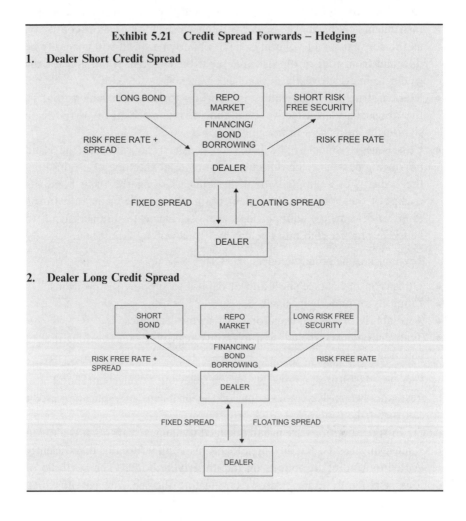

Exhibit 5.21   Credit Spread Forwards – Hedging

1. Dealer Short Credit Spread

2. Dealer Long Credit Spread

---

[115]   This is often expressed as the fact that the $ duration of the option portfolio is not zero while the $ duration of the yield spread option is zero.

12 Summary

Credit derivatives pricing is based on a replication/arbitrage free pricing approach. In practice, the pricing of credit derivatives is driven off the pricing of debt securities in capital markets (generally the asset swap market). This reflects the necessity of hedging, valuation and price discovery in the spot market. Implementation of hedges is generally constrained by limitations in the underlying bond and credit markets. This leads to pricing differences between the cash and credit default swap markets (known as the basis). An alternative pricing approach uses a hazard or probability of default to derive a credit default swap spread. There is increasing interest in using equity prices to price and hedge credit positions (known as E2C). Other credit derivatives (total return swaps and credit spread forwards/ options) are priced using replication techniques.

6

Credit Modelling/Credit Portfolio Management[1]

1 Overview

The pricing of credit derivatives is based on a replication/arbitrage free pricing approach driven off the pricing of debt securities in capital markets. This reflects the necessity of hedging, valuation and price discovery in the spot market. The market pricing of debt securities and credit risk is generally taken as a given. Credit modelling is focused on the pricing of credit risk generally within a portfolio context. It is focused on establishing the expected and unexpected credit losses on a portfolio and the amount of capital that must be held against that risk. It is also focused on the return required to compensate for the assumed risk. This is based on credit and default risk modelling. Credit derivatives activity reflects in part the interaction between the two approaches to credit risk pricing.

Chapter 5 outlined the pricing and valuation of credit derivatives. This Chapter focuses on credit modelling and credit portfolio management. The structure of the Chapter is as follows:

- The nature and behaviour of default risk is considered.
- The approach to modelling credit risk is outlined.
- The estimation of different parameters used to quantify credit risk, including credit exposure at default, recovery rates, default probabilities, default rate volatility and default correlation, is outlined.
- The concept of expected and unexpected credit losses is discussed.

---

[1] The author would like to thank Greg Gupton for his comments on an earlier draft of this Chapter. The author would especially like to thank Greg Gupton for his updating the example of the application of the CreditMetrics[TM] approach for inclusion in this Chapter.

- The derivation of credit spreads designed to compensate for credit losses is outlined.
- The modelling of credit risk within a portfolio context is analysed.
- The interaction between credit modelling and market pricing of credit derivatives is considered.

2 Nature/Behaviour of Credit Risk[2]

2.1 Overview

Credit modelling focuses on the pricing of credit risk within a portfolio context. Credit modelling uses a number of approaches to establish the

---

[2] There is now a significant body of literature on credit risk modelling. For a review of the literature, see Kao, Duen-Li "Estimating And Pricing Credit Risk: An Overview" (July/August 2000) Financial Analysts Journal 50–66. The references listed here are the ones that the author finds most useful in practice. The list is not comprehensive. See Gupton, G.M., C.C. Finger and M. Bhatia (2 April 1997) CreditMetrics[TM] – Technical Document ; JP Morgan Inc, New York; Caouette, John B., Altman, Edward I. and Narayanan, Paul (1998) Managing Credit Risk; John Wiley & Sons, Inc., New York; Cossin, Didier and Pirotte, Hugues (2001) Advanced Credit Analysis; John Wiley & Sons, Chichester; Arvantis, Angelo and Gregory, Jon (2001) Credit: The Complete Guide To Pricing Hedging And Risk Management; Risk Books, London; Crouhy, Michel, Galai, Dan, and Mark, Robert (2001) Risk Management; McGraw-Hill, New York at Chapters 7 to 11. See also Skora, Richard "Rational Modelling of Credit Risk and Credit Derivatives" in (1998) Credit Derivatives: Applications for Risk Management, Investment and Portfolio Optimisation; Risk Books, London at Chapter 10; Jarrow, Robert "Current Advances In The Modelling Of Credit Risk" (May/June 1998) Derivatives 196–202; Locke, Jane "Credit Check" (September 1998) Risk 40–44; Keating, Con "Credit Derivatives" (October 1998) Futures & OTC World 32–33; "Round Table Discussion – Credit Risk" (November 1998) FOW/Middle Office III-XV; Arvantis, Angelo, Browne, Christopher, Gregory, Jon and Martin, Richard "A Credit Risk Toolbox" (December 1998) Risk 50–55; James, Jessica "Pricing and Other Risks of Credit Derivatives" in Storrow, Jamie (1999) Credit Derivatives: Key Issues – 2nd Edition; British Bankers' Association, London at Chapter 7; Keating, Con "Opening Credit" (March 1999) Futures & OTC World 40–46; Keating, Con "If And When" (April 1999) Futures & OTC World 40–44; Keating, Con "Bond Experiences" (May 1999) Futures & OTC World 26–34; Keating, Con "Construction Time Again" (June 1999) Futures & OTC World 37–44; Keating, Con "Fuzzy Bearings" (July 1999) Futures & OTC World 66–71; JPMorgan "The Price Of Credit" (December 1999) Risk 68–71; Hayt, Greg "How To Price Credit Risk" (January 2000) Risk 87–88; Hayt, Gregory "How To Price A Credit Derivative" (February 2000) Risk 60–61; Young, Greg and

expected and unexpected credit loss on a portfolio and the amount of capital that must be held against that risk. The capital required to be held is used to generate the return required to compensate for the assumed risk. Credit derivative pricing, in contrast, is based on replication from cash instruments.

Credit modelling focuses on the following elements:

- Evaluating credit risk of a reference entity on individual transactions or in a portfolio context.
- Establishing the characteristics of and managing credit portfolios.

Credit modelling encompasses a variety of issues:

- Analysis of default risk and loss given default.
- Quantification of credit risk on an individual and aggregate basis.
- Development of pricing models for both valuations of individual credits and portfolios.

Credit risk modelling underlies valuation of certain types of credit derivatives based on portfolios of credit risk, such as certain structured credit products (for example, n^{th}-to-default and collateralised debt obligations).

2.2   Default Risk – Behaviour

Default risk refers to the inability of an entity to service its financial obligations or perform its financial obligations. Default occurs relatively infrequently. The typical firm has a default probability of around 2.00% in any year[3]. There are significant differences in the risk of default between entities. A key characteristic of default is that in the event of default, the loss suffered on average is generally significant (around 50% or more of the exposure).

Bhagat, Chetan "Credit Risk's Softer Side" (April 2000) Asia Risk 30–32; Keenan, Sean and Sobehart, Jorge "A Credit Risk Catwalk" (July 2000) Risk 84–88; Belmont, David, Yeo, Angeline and Chong, Paul "Constructing A Credit Risk Model" (December 2000) Asia Risk 3539; O'Kane, Dominic and Schlogl, Lutz (February 2001) Modelling Credit: Theory And Practice; Lehman Brothers, London.

[3]   See Crosbie, Peter J. "Modelling Default Risk" in Das, Satyajit (Editor) (2001) Credit Derivatives And Credit Linked Notes – Second Edition; John Wiley & Sons, Singapore at Chapter 9 at 369.

The risk of default may be characterised as the sale by the lender in a risky bond of deep out-of-the-money puts on the net asset value of the firm[4]. However, the quantification of credit risk and market risk is different. The empirical research[5] on the nature of default risk highlights a number of key difficulties that both distinguish it from credit risk and also increase the problems associated with measuring this risk accurately. The key issues include:

- **Variability of credit risk** – the risk of loss arising from the default by an obligor can be separated into two specific components: the expected loss and the unexpected loss (uncertainty/volatility of loss). Expected losses are derived from the size of exposure, the probability of default and loss given default. The risk of credit loss derives primarily from the volatility of the expected loss. This is particularly important for the following reasons:
  1. The variability of default risk within a portfolio is substantial. The largest default probability may be significantly larger (say, 100 times) than the smallest default probability.
  2. The default risk itself is dynamic and subject to large fluctuations.
  3. Within a well diversified portfolio, the loss behaviour is charac- terised by lower than expected default credit losses for much of the time. There is a high probability of very large losses that are incurred infrequently.
  4. The portfolio loss distribution exhibits a skewed pattern (reflecting the impact of default correlation).
- **Distribution of credit losses** – the credit loss distribution is typically highly skewed. **Exhibit 6.1** sets out a comparison of market risk and credit risk loss distributions. The credit loss distribution shows the highly skewed distribution of credit losses. The distribution highlights the significant risk of large losses in a credit portfolio. The diagram illustrates the fundamental differences in loss distributions between traditional financial assets (debt, equity, currency and commodity) and credit. Market returns are relatively symmetrical and can be approximated by

---

[4]   This framework was first suggested by Merton, R. "On The Option Pricing Of Corporate Debt: The Risk Structure Of Interest Rates" (1974) Journal of Finance vol 29 449–470. See discussion of the Merton model later in the Chapter.

[5]   See (1995) Derivative Credit Risk: Advances in Measurement and Management; Risk Publications: London at Chapter 3, 4, 5, and 6.

normal/log normal distributions, although the distribution may be fat tailed. In contrast, credit returns are asymmetric, highly skewed and are not well approximated by normal/log normal distributions. The distribution reflects the basic structure of credit risk or risky debt returns. This trades off a small excess return (the credit spread received) against the risk of losses (zero or small if there is no default versus very large in case of default). The full distribution of credit losses is significantly more difficult to generate than a corresponding market risk distribution. It requires more information beyond simple summary statistics such as a mean and standard deviation. Typically, generation of the full distribution of a credit risk portfolio will require every possible combination of credit states and value changes contingent upon the credit states being generated. This usually is done through simulation methodology.

- **Correlation between default risks** – the *correlation* between default events also significantly affects the nature of credit risk. In practice, default correlation is generally low. For example, an equity portfolio will typically exhibit correlation between returns on the individual components of the portfolio of around 0.3 to 0.6 (30% to 60%). In contrast, a portfolio of credit risk will typically exhibit correlation between defaults of around 0.1 to 0.3 (10% to 30%) or lower. The low level of default correlation means that the *systematic risk* of a portfolio is small relative to the *unsystematic risk* of the portfolio (that is, the individual contribution of risks to the portfolio is greater). The higher level of non systematic risk dictates that the benefits of diversification are greater. In effect, a high degree of diversification is essential as an inadequately diversified portfolio may result in a significantly lower return on risk than would have been the case had the level of non systematic risk been lower. This points to a significant problem in credit risk management in that a large portfolio of obligors will typically be less diversified than say, an equivalent portfolio of equities. In effect, it requires a significantly higher number of names to fully diversify a credit portfolio than an equivalent portfolio of equities. One researcher has argued that it requires 350 names to achieve an equivalent level of diversification in a debt portfolio as 30 names in an equity portfolio[6]. This highlights the

---

[6]   See Levin, Ron (1997) Challenges of Managing Credit Portfolios; JP Morgan Securities Inc. See also Amato, Jeffrey D and Remolana, Eli M "The Credit Spread Puzzle" (December 2003) BIS Quarterly Review 51–63. The authors

fact that diversification in a credit portfolio is focused primarily on reduction of loss given default. Diversification achieves this by reducing the size of individual exposures. This has the effect of reducing the loss given default in any individual default. The other effect that diversifies an equity portfolio is the upward and downward movement of stock prices. In contrast, the movement in a credit portfolio has a downward bias when defaults occur. This means that many more names are needed to diversify a credit portfolio than a comparable equity portfolio.

- **Requirement for active management** – default risks can be effectively managed through diversification. It also requires active management, reflecting the dynamic nature of risk. Credit risk approximates the risk of the sale of deep out-of-the-money put options on the value of the obligor firm's net assets. This approach dictates that as the quality of an individual credit or portfolio declines, the portfolio becomes more leveraged[7]. This increase in risk is exacerbated by the fact of serial dependence in changes in credit quality changes (the historical tendency of a downgrade in credit rating to be followed by subsequent downgrades). This is in contrast to independent daily changes/returns in other financial market assets (in effect, the efficient market hypothesis of random returns). The serial dependence can increase the volatility of a credit portfolio and accelerate portfolio risk. This means that portfolio re-balancing is necessary as a means of materially reducing this effect. In practice, the illiquidity of credit markets may impede this adjustment process. This means that the consequences of lack of liquidity may be significantly greater for a credit portfolio compared to a market risk portfolio.

---

provide an interesting example of the difficulty of diversifying credit risk. They consider two $3 million notional portfolios divided equally between 100 and 300 reference entities with identical default probabilities (.50%), loss given default (50%) and independent default times. The expected loss of both portfolios is calculated as $7,500 (0.25%). There is a greater than 1% probability of unexpected losses on the 100 reference entity portfolio of $45,000 (1.50%). There is a greater than 1% probability of unexpected losses on the 300 reference entity portfolio of $25,000 (0.83%). The example illustrates the benefits of diversification. However, a 300% increase in the number of reference entities only reduces the unexpected loss by 45%. The diversification has limited impact on unexpected losses that remain 333% of the expected losses. The authors argue that credit spreads in the market reflect the difficulty of diversifying credit portfolios.

[7]   In effect, the delta of the options is increasing.

The significant differences between credit risk and market risk imply:

- Market risk exhibits higher correlation between risks (both within asset classes and across asset classes) which allows hedging as well as positioning/trading whereby outright price risk is traded for basis risk.
- Credit risk exhibits lower correlation, creating difficulties in hedging and trading, and forcing reliance on portfolio diversification mechanisms.

These factors which tend to differentiate credit risk from types of risk such as market risk (see discussion below) dominate both the quantification and pricing of credit risk.

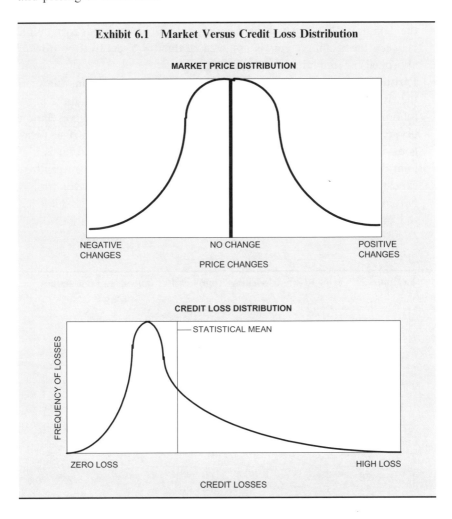

Exhibit 6.1 Market Versus Credit Loss Distribution

3   Credit Modelling Approach

Credit modelling focuses on estimation of losses in assuming the relevant risk. The pricing is based on recovery of the projected losses. Pricing/valuation of credit risk focuses on estimating the expected and unexpected credit losses arising from default risk.

Credit risk is modelled as a function of the credit exposure under the transaction at default, the default probability of the reference credit, and the expected recovery rate. Two pricing approaches are required:

- **Individual transactions** – this covers the modelling of *single transactions* on a standalone basis. The pricing components include the loss exposure, the default probability and the recovery rate. In practice, no correlation between these components is assumed. **Exhibit 6.2** sets out the pricing approach for individual credit derivatives.
- **Portfolios** – this requires capture of the pricing interactions between the risk on individual transactions. The pricing components for a portfolio include the exposure on individual transactions and the correlation between defaults by reference entities within the portfolio. The focus is on the correlation between defaults within the portfolio (that is, the joint default probability). In practice, potential correlation between loss exposure and recovery rate or probability of default and recovery rate is not considered. The latter correlation is difficult to model. **Exhibit 6.3** sets out the pricing approach for a portfolio of credit derivatives.

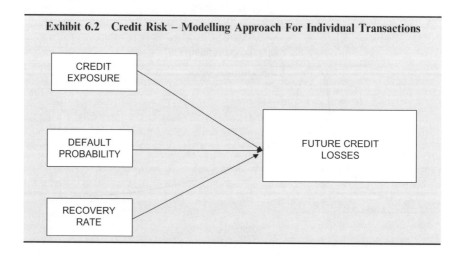

Exhibit 6.2   Credit Risk – Modelling Approach For Individual Transactions

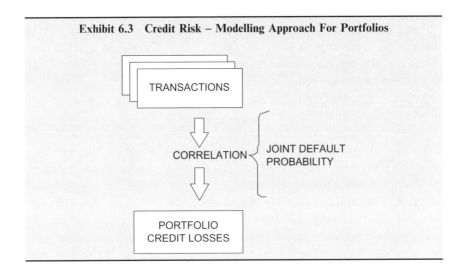

Exhibit 6.3   Credit Risk – Modelling Approach For Portfolios

4 Modelling Credit (Loss) Exposure

Credit or loss exposure refers to the amounts exposed to risk of loss at the time of default. In effect, this is the amount at risk in the event of default prior to adjustment for recovery. It is also referred to as exposure at default ("EAD").

Loss exposure can be classified into two categories:

- **Static** – this encompasses loan or bond type exposures. The exposure is inherently stable and *independent* of changes in market variables. The typical methodology for measurement of loss exposure is based on the face value of the loan or bond (adjusted for accrued interest).
- **Non-static** – this encompasses loss exposures that are *dynamic* in nature. The exposure is usually a function of a stochastic market variable, generally a market price for an asset. Typical examples include derivative products. The loss exposure is measured using the replacement cost based on the mark-to-market value of the transaction. For these instruments, the credit or loss exposure, at least, at any point of time, can be equated to the *market risk* of the transaction[8].

---

[8] For a discussion of credit risk in derivative transactions, see Das, Satyajit (2004) Swaps/Financial Derivatives 3rd Edition; John Wiley, Singapore at Chapter 21.

Loan and bond type exposures are driven by the face value of the transaction. This approach masks the fact that changes in market rates (both absolute and credit spreads) have the ability to affect the value of the transaction and the credit risk to the investor. In this regard, the true exposure is not the face value but the *present value* of the remaining cash flows over the nominated risk horizon. This would be calculated using zero coupon rates derived from the current yield curve (incorporating the credit risk of the obligation) to discount the remaining cash flows. The zero rates used will need to be the *forward* zero curve at the nominated risk horizon.

Undrawn commitments present different problems. The exposure is a function of the amount currently drawn under the facility, expected changes in the level of drawings and the spreads/fees needed to revalue the drawn and undrawn portions of the facility. The amount drawn under the commitment is related to credit quality. As obligor credit quality deteriorates, the drawings under the facility will typically increase. Similarly, as obligor credit quality improves, drawings tend to be repaid. The evolution of exposure is complicated by the fact that drawings are influenced by covenants required to be satisfied *prior to drawings* and pricing structures. The covenants tend to reduce volatility. The covenants are designed to allow the lenders to be released from their obligation to fund where the obligor credit quality declines beyond certain pre-nominated levels.

Various models can be used to capture this pattern on exposure. Some modelling approaches seek to capture commitment behaviour by assuming that drawings increase upon downgrade and decrease with an upgrade in credit quality[9]. Other models often simply assume that the lender's exposure is to the full face value of the facility.

Financial guarantees (including letters of credit) are simpler in that they will be called in the case of default. Consequently, they are equated to loans.

The face value of market risk instruments is usually a notional amount. The notional amount is only used to calculate the payments and is itself not usually paid-out or at-risk. The exposure under dynamic market risk instruments is taken as the replacement value of the transaction plus an additional factor for future exposure. The replacement value is driven by

---

[9] See Gupton, G.M., C.C. Finger and M. Bhatia (2 April 1997) CreditMetrics[TM] – Technical Document; JP Morgan Inc, New York at 43–46; Gupton, Greg "CreditMetrics[TM] – Assessing The Marginal Risk Contribution Of Credit" in Das, Satyajit (Editor) (2001) Credit Derivatives And Credit Linked Notes – Second Edition; John Wiley & Sons, Singapore at Chapter 13 at 565.

the market factors used to price the instrument, and is based on the expected average exposure assuming certain levels of volatility. The future exposure is designed to cover changes (often rapid) in the level of exposure and is calculated with reference to the volatility of the relevant market factors.

The exposure under non static transactions exhibits two characteristics: the stochastic nature of the exposure and the possibility of zero or negative exposures. The key point to note is that exposure on a non static transaction will alter with changes in the underlying market risk factor (which dictates exposure) and the time to maturity. In the case of interest rate derivatives, the exposure increases then decreases over time as the remaining term to maturity becomes shorter. In the case of currency derivatives, the exposure increases but does not decrease, reflecting the exposure on the principal amount of the transaction. Depending on the changes in the market risk variable, it is possible that the transaction will result in zero or negative exposure. This means that in the event of default the non defaulting party will not have any amount owing as the result of the default, but will in fact owe the counterparty a termination sum. In this case, there is obviously no credit risk on the counterparty, although it is not possible to predict this in advance. Similar considerations are applicable to equity and commodity derivatives. The exposure under derivative contracts is therefore not predictable with certainty but will usually be less than the face value of the transaction[10].

In measuring the loss exposure on non static instruments, it is useful to differentiate between the expected and unexpected credit exposure. The expected credit exposure is usually calculated as the loss exposure at the relevant points in time, and the average expected credit exposure is calculated as the average of the expected credit exposures over a given period of time (generally, the life of the transaction). The unexpected credit loss is the worst case loss exposure calculated as the maximum exposure at a point in time. The average unexpected loss is the average worst case exposure

---

[10] In the Asian monetary crisis during 1997 and 1998, the mark-to-market credit exposure on derivative transactions involving affected currencies (Korean Won, Thai Baht, Indonesian Rupiah etc) exceeded (in some cases) the face value of the transactions, reflecting the very large movements in currency values, interest rates and equity prices.

calculated as the average of the worst case exposures over a given period of time[11].

5 Modelling Recovery Rates[12]

The concept of recovery rate focuses on the amount of any loss exposure likely to be recovered from a counterparty following default. The recovery rate is crucial in establishing loss given default. The loss suffered is equal to (1−Recovery Rate).

In most defaults, investors in the securities recover some portion of their investment. The recovery is often after a significant period. The recovery may take a number of forms including cash, securities (debt or equity) and occasionally assets of the business. The recovery rate may be defined as the percentage of par value of the security recovered by the investor.

There are two separate elements to the recovery rate: the recovery rate itself (net of the cost of recoveries including legal, staff etc costs) and the adjustment for time value, reflecting the discounting of the recovery rate from the eventual date of recovery to the date of default. The potential for delay arises from the time taken to complete the legal process required to facilitate the recovery of amounts owed, as well as the time taken to realise the value of the counterparty's assets (if relevant).

There are two general approaches to modelling recovery rates:

- Using recovery experience on public and/or rated securities collated by the major rating agencies. **Exhibit 6.4** sets out the mean recovery rates on defaulted instruments published by Moody's Investors Service.
- Information internal to the organisation based on its experience in the case of default.

---

[11] For discussion of approaches to dealing with market driven exposures, see Rowe, David M. and Reoch, Robert D. "Aggregating Market Driven Credit Exposures: A Parameterised Monte Carlo Approach and Implications for the Use of Credit Derivatives" in (1998) Credit Derivatives: Applications for Risk Management, Investment and Portfolio Optimisation; Risk Books, London at Chapter 4.

[12] See Hamilton, David T., and Varma, Praveen (January 2004) Default And Recovery Rates of Corporate Bond Issues; Moody's Investors Service, New York. See also Altman, Edward I., and Kishore, Vellore M. "Almost Everything You Wanted To Know About Recoveries On Defaulted Bonds" (November/ December 1996) Financial Analysts Journal 57–64.

- Application of emerging statistical models designed to forecast recoveries conditioned on such things as debt/seniority type, industry, leverage and capital structure of the issuer and the state of the economy[13].

Market derived recovery rates are generally based on the *trading price* of the defaulted instrument. This price is used as a proxy of the present value of the expected ultimate recovery. The market price is obtained by sampling dealers approximately 1 month after default. The approach is based on the fact that it provides an *immediate* measure of recovery and it corresponds to a traded market estimate of the anticipated recovery rate. It assumes that investors can effectively liquidate any position in the securities. The loss would equate to the recovery level equivalent to the spot traded price of the defaulted bonds.

This approach has significant advantages. Other approaches would require tracking *actual* recoveries over the progress of the bankruptcy. Actual recoveries would then need to be discounted back to estimate the recovery rate. This would require tracking payments on defaulted bonds for a potentially long period and then discounting these payments back to generate a recovery rate. It would also require valuation of securities issued in exchange for the original obligation. Valuation may prove problematic given that the securities are issued by a defaulted or restructured issuer. In practice, this forces the use of market prices of defaulted bonds.

Increasingly, loan workout date based recovery rates are being sought. This would entail cash flows tagged by date post accrual to be measured. A number of rating agencies are undertaking work to obtain this data especially for middle market loans.

The recovery rates appear to be affected by the following factors:

- **Type of instrument and seniority** – the recovery rate is related to the financial instrument, the seniority of the obligation and its place in the issuer's capital structure. **Exhibit 6.4** sets out a comparison of recovery

---

[13] There are at least two separate efforts that have each generated predictive models; see Altman E. I., A. Resti and A. Sironi (December 2001) "Analyzing and Explaining Default Recovery Rates", (Report Submitted to ISDA) (see: http://www.isda.org/whatsnew/index.html); Gupton, G.M. and R. M. Stein (February 2002) "LossCalc[TM]: Moody's Model for Predicting Loss Given Default (LGD)" (Moody's Special Comment) (see: http://riskcalc.moodysrms.com/us/research/lied/losscalc.asp).

rates for different instruments by capital priority. There are some differences in the recovery rates between securities markets and bank loans[14].

- **Industry** – the issuer's industry affects recovery rates. **Exhibit 6.5** sets out average recovery rates by industry category. This may be driven by the nature of the assets within the issuer, including the capacity to redeploy the assets.

- **Jurisdiction** – the jurisdiction or geography of the issuer appears to affect recovery rates. The key driver is differences in bankruptcy law and practice that influence the loss given default.

- **Ratings** – ratings seek to rank order securities with respect to relative expected loss rates. This is the product of the expected default rate and the expected loss severity in the event of default. A number of studies have examined the extent ratings affect relative recovery rates – in particular, on defaulted senior unsecured bonds. This entails the analysis of the relationship between recovery rates and issuers' ratings at some time prior to default. The studies tend to show that issuers rated investment grade within 5-years prior to default have higher recovery rates regardless of when the rating was investment grade. As issuers move closer to default, the separations between recovery rates for speculative grade and investment grade become wider. The studies also show that as default becomes more and more likely, issuer ratings more explicitly differentiate between recovery rates for different issuers. For example, in the year prior to default, there is a monotonic relationship between realized recovery rates. Issuers rated Aa one year prior to default have the highest recovery rates followed by issuers rated A and so on[15].

The recovery rates display significant variability as follows:

- **Volatility of recovery rates** – the recovery rates exhibit significant variability. **Exhibit 6.6** sets out some data on the variability of recovery rates. Recovery rates range widely. The distribution of recovery rates does

---

[14]   See Carty, Lea V. and Lieberman, Dana "Defaulted Bank Recoveries" (November 1996) Moody's Investors Service Global Credit Research; Grossman, Robert J , Brennan, William T. and Vento, Jennifer (22 October 1997) Syndicated Bank Loan Recovery Study; Fitch Research – Structured Finance, Credit Facilities, Special Report.

[15]   See Hamilton, David T., and Varma, Praveen (January 2004) Default And Recovery Rates of Corporate Bond Issues; Moody's Investors Service, New York at 15.

not appear to be normal. The distribution is asymmetric and skewed. There is significant dispersion around the mean. There are also large differences between the first and third quartile[16].

- **Variability over time** – the recovery rates vary significantly over time. The recovery rates appear to be linked to overall economic conditions[17]. During periods of growth, recovery rates are near or above average. During periods of recession, recovery rates are below (often significantly 15–21%) average[18]. Speculative grade recovery rates tend to follow a mean reversion process with long-term average recovery rates of roughly 40%. Recovery rates tend to be higher during economic boom times and lower when the economic cycle is in a downturn. Over a twenty-one year period of 1982–2003, recovery rates have ranged between approximately 50% in 1986 and approximately 20% in 2001. The recovery rates tend to fluctuate within this range, around a long-term mean of 40%[19].

- **Correlation between recovery rates and default rates** – recovery rates and default rates are generally negatively correlated. This means that higher than average default rates tend to coincide with lower than average recovery rates; the converse is also true. A simple regression model shows that much of the annual variation in recovery rates (R^2 of 60%) can be explained by the aggregate default rates[20].

---

[16] See Hamilton, David T., Cantor, Richard and Ou, Sharon (February 2002) Default And Recovery Rates of Corporate Bond Issues; Moody's Investors Service, New York at 16.

[17] There is mounting evidence that the stage in the economic cycle strongly influences recoveries. This effect is most pronounced for unsecured debt, which doesn't have the buffer of a specific asset. See Gupton. G.M. and R.M. Stein (February 2002) LossCalc[TM]: Moody's Model for Predicting Loss Given Default (LGD); Moody's Investors Service, New York.

[18] See Hamilton, David T., Cantor, Richard and Ou, Sharon (February 2002) Default And Recovery Rates of Corporate Bond Issues; Moody's Investors Service, New York at 17.

[19] See Hamilton, David T., Cantor, Richard and Ou, Sharon (February 2002) Default And Recovery Rates of Corporate Bond Issues; Moody's Investors Service, New York at 14–15.

[20] See Hamilton, David T., Cantor, Richard and Ou, Sharon (February 2002) Default And Recovery Rates of Corporate Bond Issues; Moody's Investors Service, New York at 14–15.

Exhibit 6.4	Recovery Rates					
	Value Weighted			Issuer Weighted		
	2003	2002	1982–2003	2003	2002	1982–2003
Defaulted Instrument						
Bank Debt						
Senior Secured	76.0%	63.1%	59.3%	64.6%	65.9%	65.1%
Senior Unsecured	80.0%	99.1%	41.3%	80.0%	99.0%	44.7%
All Bonds	39.7%	31.7%	33.8%	40.2%	36.7%	35.4%
Equipment Trust	NA	36.7%	61.0%	NA	32.5%	62.1%
Senior Secured	54.1%	56.8%	50.3%	60.3%	49.8%	51.6%
Senior Unsecured	44.4%	30.9%	32.9%	41.2%	31.9%	36.1%
Senior Subordinated	29.2%	20.7%	29.0%	36.6%	25.3%	32.5%
Subordinated	12.0%	29.0%	27.1%	12.3%	27.9%	31.1%
Junior Subordinated	39.7%	NA	22.9%	40.4%	NA	24.5%
Preferred Stock	1.1%	31.7%	6.5%	1.1%	9.0%	15.3%
All Instruments	39.8%	31.7%	31.8%	39.4%	35.0%	33.9%

Source: Hamilton, David T., and Varma, Praveen (January 2004) Default And Recovery Rates of Corporate Bond Issues; Moody's Investors Service, New York at 13.

Exhibit 6.5	Average Recovery Rates By Industry Category		
	Issuer Weighted Mean Recovery Rate		
	2003	2002	1982–2003
Utility – Gas	48.00%	54.60%	51.50%
Oil and Oil Services	NA	44.10%	44.50%
Hospitality	64.50%	60.00%	42.50%
Utility – Electric	5.30%	39.80%	41.40%
Transport – Ocean	76.80%	31.00%	38.80%
Media Broadcasting and Cable	57.50%	39.50%	38.20%
Transport – Surface	NA	37.90%	36.60%
Finance and Banking	18.80%	25.60%	36.30%
Industrial	33.40%	34.30%	35.40%
Retail	57.90%	58.20%	34.40%
Transport – Air	22.60%	24.90%	34.30%
Automotive	39.00%	39.50%	33.40%
Healthcare	52.20%	47.00%	32.70%
Consumer Goods	54.00%	22.80%	32.50%
Construction	22.50%	23.00%	31.90%
Technology	9.40%	36.70%	29.50%
Real Estate	NA	5.00%	28.80%
Steel	31.80%	28.50%	27.40%
Telecommunications	45.90%	21.40%	23.20%
Miscellaneous	69.50%	46.50%	39.50%

Source: Hamilton, David T., and Varma, Praveen (January 2004) Default And Recovery Rates of Corporate Bond Issues; Moody's Investors Service, New York at 14.

Exhibit 6.6   Recovery Rates – Variability

2003

Defaulted Instrument	Value Weighted Mean	Issuer Weighted					
		Mean	Median	Minimum	Maximum	Standard Deviation	Number of Observations
Bank Debt							
Senior Secured	76.0%	64.6%	82.9%	11.9%	100.8%	33.5%	21
Senior Unsecured	80.0%	80.0%	80.0%	80.0%	80.0%	NA	1
All Bonds	39.7%	40.4%	0.1%	0.1%	100.5%	26.0%	65
Senior Secured	54.1%	60.3%	1.3%	1.3%	100.5%	32.9%	9
Senior Unsecured	44.4%	41.2%	0.1%	0.1%	99.5%	24.7%	34
Senior Subordinated	29.2%	36.6%	0.8%	0.8%	94.5%	20.2%	17
Junior Subordinated	12.0%	12.3%	3.0%	3.0%	25.1%	8.1%	5
Preferred Stock	1.1%	1.1%	NA	NA	NA	NA	1

Source: Hamilton, David T., and Varma, Praveen (January 2004) Default And Recovery Rates of Corporate Bond Issues; Moody's Investors Service, New York at 13.

1970–2000

Class Of Debt	1970–2000 Average Recovery Rate	Median (%)	Standard Deviation (%)	Minimum	Maximum	1st Quartile	3rd Quartile
Senior Secured Bank Debt	64.0%	72.0%	24.4%	5.0%	98.0%	45.3%	85.0%
Senior Unsecured Bank Loans	49.0%	45.0%	28.4%	5.0%	88.0%	25.0%	75.8%
Senior Secured Bonds	52.6%	53.8%	24.6%	1.6%	103.0%	34.8%	68.6%
Senior Unsecured Bonds	46.9%	44.0%	28.0%	0.5%	122.6%	25.0%	66.8%
Senior Subordinated Bonds	34.7%	29.0%	24.6%	0.5%	123.0%	15.1%	50.0%
Subordinated Bonds	31.6%	28.5%	21.2%	0.5%	102.5%	15.0%	44.1%
Junior Subordinated Bonds	22.5%	15.1%	18.7%	1.5%	74.0%	11.3%	33.0%
Preferred Stock	18.1%	11.1%	17.2%	0.1%	86.0%	6.4%	24.9%

Source: Hamilton, David T, Gupton, Greg and Berthault, Alexandra (February 2001) Defaults And Recovery Rates of Bonds 2000: Moody's Investors Service, New York at 44.

6   Modelling Default Probability

6.1   Overview

The probability of default refers to the risk that an entity is unable to service its obligations. There are several different approaches to modelling default. The principal approaches include:

- **Rating models** – this uses ratings agency data to establish the probability of default. It also uses ratings migration data to capture value changes in a security arising from changes in credit risk.
- **Statistical models** – this typically uses linear discriminant or logit analysis of financial ratios, but may also use a wide range of techniques such as neural networks.
- **Equity price/structural (contingent claim or Merton) models** – this uses equity volatility to see how close the firm is to the market leverage is to zero (that is, the number of standard deviations from default).
- **Credit spread models** – this uses bond credit spreads to derive the default probability consistent with the risk adjusted return on the bond.

The equity price and credit spread models are frequently described as market models, reflecting their foundation in available market price information.

6.2   Modelling Default Probability – Ratings Agency Based Models

Ratings agency default models can be used to identify the risk of default for a firm with a known *current* rating. The basic methodology is as follows[21]:

- **Definition of default** – default is generally defined for a bond as a missed or delayed disbursement of interest and/or principal. It also covers bankruptcy (or equivalent) or a distressed debt exchange (where the investors are offered new securities that amount to a diminished financial obligation or the exchange is driven by the issuer seeking to avoid default)[22].

---

[21] The basic methodology described is that used by Moody's Investors Service. Other ratings agencies use similar approaches. See Hamilton, David T., and Varma, Praveen (January 2004) Default And Recovery Rates of Corporate Bond Issues; Moody's Investors Service, New York.

[22] A concept that is paramount here is that the definition of default used must be the same for the default rate calculation as it is for recovery rate calculation.

- **Calculation methodology** – the basic approach is based on individual issuers. Issuers are arranged into annual cohort groups. Default rates for a given time horizon are calculated as the number of defaulting issuers divided by the number of issuers that could have defaulted. The denominator is adjusted for withdrawn ratings.

The model is based on historical default experience. It also incorporates the impact of macro-economic cycles. Default risk is specified as a function of two primary factors – current rating and time to maturity of the obligation. There are two types of default risk:

- **Cumulative risk of default** – measures the total default probability of a firm over the term of the obligation.
- **Marginal risk of default** – measures the *change* in default probability of a firm over a sequence of time periods.

Exhibit 6.7 sets out the cumulative and marginal default probabilities calculated by Moody's. The marginal default probabilities in these Tables are taken as the simple arithmetical differences between the cumulative default probabilities at each year. The analysis shows that cumulative default probabilities increase with a decline in ratings levels, but that marginal default risks *decrease* in the lower rating categories. The pattern of marginal default probabilities is consistent with the behaviour of credit spreads discussed previously.

Ratings models can also be used to estimate the probability of a change in value of the security. This is calculated as the result of changes in value from changes in credit spread as a result of changes in rating (ratings migration) or default[23].

Where a firm or entity is not rated, it is still possible to use ratings agency default models and statistics. This will usually entail the following process:

- Use the firm's financial data to calculate key accounting ratios. The accounting ratios usually used are those utilised by the rating agencies themselves.
- The accounting performance (as captured by the ratios) is compared to the comparable median for *rated* firms in both the industry and the universe of rated entities. The comparison is designed to allow a rating equivalent to be determined.

---

[23] See discussion of the CreditMetrics[TM] methodology later in the Chapter.

- Based on the *theoretical rating*, the default probabilities appropriate for that particular rating category are then used.

The ratings based approach raises a number of issues:

- The default probabilities are sample specific. The sample is the universe of rated obligations. Any bias in the sample will naturally affect the results.
- Pricing is based on aggregate statistics and issuer level information is lost. The approach used relies on a single factor – the issuer's current ratings. All relevant information is assumed to be incorporated in the rating. This is especially problematic for migration statistics.

Exhibit 6.7   Default Probabilities

The following Table sets out the cumulative default probabilities (%) as calculated by Moody's Investors Service (for the period 1970–2003):

Years	1	2	3	4	5	6	7	8	9	10
Aaa	0.00	0.00	0.00	0.04	0.12	0.20	0.29	0.39	0.50	0.62
Aa	0.02	0.03	0.06	0.15	0.24	0.34	0.43	0.53	0.60	0.68
A	0.02	0.09	0.23	0.38	0.54	0.72	0.91	1.12	1.35	1.59
Baa	0.20	0.57	1.03	1.62	2.16	2.69	3.24	3.80	4.42	5.10
Ba	1.26	3.48	6.00	8.59	11.17	13.53	15.44	17.37	19.22	21.01
B	6.21	13.76	20.65	26.66	31.99	36.56	40.79	44.21	47.19	50.02
Caa-C	23.65	37.20	48.02	55.56	60.83	65.53	69.36	73.65	75.94	77.91
Investment Grade	0.08	0.23	0.44	0.70	0.96	1.23	1.50	1.78	2.09	2.42
Speculative Grade	5.02	10.15	14.84	18.90	22.45	25.51	28.06	30.35	32.37	34.27
All Corporate	1.60	3.23	4.71	5.99	7.07	7.99	8.76	9.46	10.10	10.73

Years	11	12	13	14	15	16	17	18	19	20
Aaa	0.74	0.88	1.03	1.12	1.21	1.31	1.43	1.55	1.55	1.55
Aa	0.77	0.93	1.12	1.37	1.51	1.67	1.91	2.12	2.43	2.70
A	1.86	2.10	2.37	2.61	2.94	3.35	3.78	4.23	4.74	5.24
Baa	5.83	6.63	7.44	8.27	9.12	9.91	10.71	11.45	12.09	12.59
Ba	23.01	25.16	27.24	29.16	30.88	32.81	34.53	36.13	37.38	38.56
B	52.24	54.09	55.95	57.77	59.21	60.37	60.73	60.73	60.73	60.73
Caa-C	80.23	80.23	80.23	80.23	80.23	80.23	80.23	80.23	80.23	80.23
Investment Grade	2.78	3.16	3.57	3.97	4.41	4.86	5.34	5.80	6.27	6.69
Speculative Grade	36.17	38.04	39.86	41.55	43.03	44.61	45.92	47.09	48.02	48.90
All Corporate	11.36	12.00	12.65	13.26	13.86	14.48	15.08	15.65	16.17	16.65

The following Table sets out the marginal default probabilities (%) calculated from Moody's Investors Service cumulative default probabilities:

Years	1	2	3	4	5	6	7	8	9	10
Aaa	0.00	0.00	0.00	0.04	0.08	0.08	0.09	0.10	0.11	0.12
Aa	0.02	0.01	0.03	0.09	0.09	0.10	0.09	0.10	0.07	0.08
A	0.02	0.07	0.14	0.15	0.16	0.18	0.19	0.21	0.23	0.24
Baa	0.20	0.37	0.46	0.59	0.54	0.53	0.55	0.56	0.62	0.68
Ba	1.26	2.22	2.52	2.59	2.58	2.36	1.91	1.93	1.85	1.79
B	6.21	7.55	6.89	6.01	5.33	4.57	4.23	3.42	2.98	2.83
Caa-C	23.65	13.55	10.82	7.54	5.27	4.70	3.83	4.29	2.29	1.97
Investment Grade	0.08	0.15	0.21	0.26	0.26	0.27	0.27	0.28	0.31	0.33
Speculative Grade	5.02	5.13	4.69	4.06	3.55	3.06	2.55	2.29	2.02	1.90
All Corporate	1.60	1.63	1.48	1.28	1.08	0.92	0.77	0.70	0.64	0.63

Years	11	12	13	14	15	16	17	18	19	20
Aaa	0.12	0.14	0.15	0.09	0.09	0.10	0.12	0.12	0.00	0.00
Aa	0.09	0.16	0.19	0.25	0.14	0.16	0.24	0.21	0.31	0.27
A	0.27	0.24	0.27	0.24	0.33	0.41	0.43	0.45	0.51	0.50
Baa	0.73	0.80	0.81	0.83	0.85	0.79	0.80	0.74	0.64	0.50
Ba	2.00	2.15	2.08	1.92	1.72	1.93	1.72	1.60	1.25	1.18
B	2.22	1.85	1.86	1.82	1.44	1.16	0.36	0.00	0.00	0.00
Caa-C	2.32	0.00	0.00	0.00	0.00	0.00	0.00	0.00	0.00	0.00
Investment Grade	0.36	0.38	0.41	0.40	0.44	0.45	0.48	0.46	0.47	0.42
Speculative Grade	1.90	1.87	1.82	1.69	1.48	1.58	1.31	1.17	0.93	0.88
All Corporate	0.63	0.64	0.65	0.61	0.60	0.62	0.60	0.57	0.52	0.48

Source: Hamilton, David T., and Varma, Praveen (January 2004) Default And Recovery Rates of Corporate Bond Issues; Moody's Investors Service, New York at 25.

6.3 *Modelling Default Probability – Credit Spreads*[24]

Credit spreads represent the margin relative to the risk free rate designed to compensate the investor for the risk of default on the underlying security. In essence, it is the *market price of default risk*. It is particularly important

---

[24] In this Section, available market credit spreads are used to derive implied default probabilities. The reverse is also possible; that is, for given default probabilities (implied survival probabilities) and recovery rates, it is possible to solve for the arbitrage free credit spread. This approach is frequently used to implement the pricing/valuation of credit default swaps. See discussion in Chapter 5.

in that it is the market's estimate of the issuer's *specific* credit risk. Default probabilities can be derived directly from credit spreads[25].

The credit spread is calculated as:

Credit Spread = Bond Yield minus Risk Free/Swap Yield.

The model is based on the concept of the risk neutral credit spread. The risk neutral credit spread is the credit spread that compensates the investor for the default risk assumed. The underlying logic is that the risk neutral credit spread, in an efficient capital market, makes an investor *indifferent* between a risky bond and a risk free security. The risk neutral spread calculation typically assumes par bonds, a holding period equal to maturity or default (whichever occurs first), risk neutrality and arbitrage free capital markets. Within this framework, the risk neutral spread can be defined as:

$$C = Y - Rf$$

Where

 C = Risk neutral credit spread
 Y = Yield of risky bond
 Rf = Yield on risk free bond

C is a function of the default risk of the risky bond. It is feasible to use marginal default risk and recovery rate estimates to approximate C. Given Rf and C, it is feasible to solve for Y which, using weighted average cash flows, *equates to* Rf. This requires weighting each cash flow of the risky bond by the probability of default and the recovery rate to calculate the default risk adjusted risky bond cash flows. The approach outlined allows the derivation of a credit spread given a term structure of risk free rates, default probabilities and recovery rates. Alternatively, given credit spreads, it can be used to recover one of the other three variables, provided two of these are known. The approach does not incorporate the variability in (or distribution of) default probabilities or recovery rates. **Exhibit 6.8** sets out an example of the derivation of a risk neutral credit spread and default.

The availability of a complete term structure of risk from limited observations allows, in theory, the calibration of default rates from market data.

---

[25]   See Jerome, S. "Using Default Rates To Model The Term Structure Of Credit Risk" (September–October 1994) Financial Analysts Journal 25–32; Li, David "Constructing A Credit Curve" (November 1998) Risk – Credit Risk Special Report 40–44.

Credit spread models are based on the default probability being derived from the term structure of credit spreads of a particular issuer observable in the market. The major advantage of this methodology is that it is issuer specific. Additional advantages include that it is market based. The credit spread approach also raises a number of difficult issues:

- There are a number of mutually dependent unknowns (credit spread, default probability and recovery rate). Consequently, assumptions must be made about either the default probability or the recovery rate in order to solve for the unknown variable given a credit spread.
- A complete term structure of credit spreads may not be available for an issuer. This problem is analogous to modelling the yield curve generally. This may reflect the lack of issuance across the whole maturity spectrum by particular issuers. This would require estimation of the relevant credit spreads.
- The credit spread may incorporate the impact of non credit factors such as liquidity, tax and regulations. These factors may affect the credit spread. This would require the *pure* credit spread to be derived by adjusting the market credit spread[26].

Exhibit 6.8 Modelling Default Probabilities From Credit Spreads

In the example below, the risk neutral credit spread for a bond is derived. In the second part of the example, a default probability is derived from a market credit spread.
  The model is structured as follows:

- The cash flows of the bond are identified.
- The default probabilities for the issuer and the recovery rate for the type of obligation are identified.
- The survival probability (1 minus the default probability) is calculated.
- The recovery adjusted default payment is calculated from the default probability and the recovery rate assumed.
- The original bond cash flows are then adjusted for the risk of default by calculating the expected cash flows assuming the risk of default.
- The adjusted bond cash flows are then discounted (using the risk free rate) to solve for the credit spread that equates the internal rate of return on the adjusted cash flows of the bond to the risk free rate.

---

[26] Market credit spreads are higher than theoretical credit spreads implied by historical default probabilities reflecting factors such as liquidity, regulatory, accounting/tax and the difficulty in diversification of credit risk; see Amato, Jeffrey D and Remolana, Eli M "The Credit Spread Puzzle" (December 2003) BIS Quarterly Review 51–63.

Assume a 1 year bond where the issuer is estimated to have a 1 year default probability of 0.50%. Assume the recovery rate is 35% (that is, loss given default is 65%). Assume 1 year risk free (government bond rates) are 5.00% pa.

Based on the above information, a risk neutral credit spread of 34 bps can be calculated as follows:

Years	0	1
Cash Flows ($)	(100.00)	105.34
Default Probability (%)		0.50
Recovery Rate (%)		35.00
Survival Probability (%)		99.50
Recovery Adjusted Default Payment (%)		0.175
Adjusted Cash Flows	(100.00)	105.00
Discount Factor (at risk free rate)		0.9524
Discounted Cash Flows ($)		100.00
Present Value of Bond ($)	100.00	

Assume the market credit spread is 65 bps pa for 1 year for the relevant firm. The 1 year default probability can be derived from the spread information. The 1 year default probability is estimated as 0.95% as follows:

Years	0	1
Cash Flows ($)	(100.00)	105.65
Default Probability (%)		0.95
Recovery Rate (%)		35.00
Survival Probability (%)		99.05
Recovery Adjusted Default Payment (%)		0.3313
Adjusted Cash Flows	(100.00)	105.00
Discount Factor (at risk free rate)		0.9524
Discounted Cash Flows ($)		100.00
Present Value of Bond ($)	100.00	

The approach outlined can be extended for longer maturities to derive risk neutral spreads (assuming knowledge of a default probability and recovery rate) or default probabilities (assuming a known credit spread and recovery rate). For longer maturities, more complex simulations using conditional probabilities are required.

6.4 Modelling Default Probability – Equity Prices

6.4.1 Concept

Default prediction models based on equity prices derive from the original thesis by Fischer Black, Myron Scholes and Robert Merton (it is referred to as the Merton Model)[27]. The best known application of the model is the Expected Default Frequency ("EDF") model developed by KMV Corporation (now known as Moody'sKMV[28]). The EDF model is used by a number of commercial banks and other entities to measure default risk[29]

6.4.2 The Merton Model – Overview

The approach assumes that the equity in a risky firm is equivalent to a call option on the net asset value of the firm. The net asset value is calculated as market value of the firm's assets minus the claims on the assets (which include traditional financial claims such as debt and other claims including erosion of asset values) that may result upon default. The position of the bond holder is a combination of the long position in the underlying bond plus the sale of a put option on the company's assets (where the option has a strike price equal to the value of the debt of the entity). **Exhibit 6.9** sets out the basic concepts underlying the approach.

Example 6.9   Equity As Call Option – Merton Model

Assume a company with the following market value balance sheet:

Assets	$	Liabilities	$
Assets	100	Equity/shareholders' funds	60
		Debt	40
Total	**100**	**Total**	**100**

The market value of assets is derived from the market value of liabilities. The market value of liabilities is based on the market value of the equity (number of shares times share price) and the value of debt.

---

[27] See Black, Fischer and Scholes, Myron "The Pricing Of Options And Corporate Liabilities" (May–June 1973) Journal of Political Economy 81 637–659; Merton, R. "On The Option Pricing Of Corporate Debt: The Risk Structure Of Interest Rates" (1974) Journal of Finance vol 29 449–470; for a more recent approach using the traditional option pricing framework, see Crouhy, Michel, Galai, Dan, and Mark, Robert "Credit Risk Revisited" (March 1998) Risk – Credit Risk Supplement 40–44.

[28] In 2002, Moody's Investors Service bought KMV Corporation; see Cass, Dwight "KMV Acquisition Throws Up Rating Industry Questions" (March 2002) Risk 7.

[29] See Brady, Simon "The Cutting Edge of Credit" (November 1998) Euromoney 76–79.

Assume the asset value of the firm evolves over time. The corresponding values for debt and equity are then derived.

	Asset Value (\$)	Equity (\$)	Debt (\$)
Example 1	300	260	40
Example 2	20	0	20

The contractual features of each instrument drive the values for equity and debt. Debt has priority in its claims on cash flow. Debt claims are capped at the face value of debt. Equity claims are subordinated but have full participation in any increase in the asset value of the company above the value of debt. The structure of equity payoffs is summarised below:

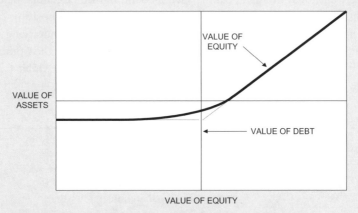

The analysis highlights the behaviour of debt and equity:

- Equity shareholders participate fully in the increased value of the value of the firm (the increase in the market value of assets). Any loss is limited to the price paid for the shares. The payoff corresponds to that of a call option where the underlying is the net asset value of the firm.
- Debt holders have sold a put option on the net asset value of the firm. If the asset value of the firm falls below the value of debt, then the equity investors abandon the implied call option. In effect, the equity shareholders exercise the put option with a strike price equal to the value of the debt.

6.4.3 EDF^{TM} Model[30]

Moody'sKMV calculates a measure of default probability based on the Merton model. Moody'sKMV Corporation markets the Credit Monitor[TM]

[30] The discussion of Moody'sKMV's approach is based on publicly available information. See Crosbie, Peter J. "Modelling Default Risk" in Das, Satyajit (Editor) (2001) Credit Derivatives And Credit Linked Notes – Second Edition;

which uses equity prices and financial information to derive the EDF^{TM} (the default probability over a period of 1 to 5 years).

The EDF^{TM} model adapts the Merton model as follows:

- Default probability is specified as being driven by 3 factors:
  1. Market value of the assets of the firm.
  2. Riskiness of the firm's assets measured as the uncertainty/risk of asset value.
  3. Firm's contractual liabilities such as debt.
- The dynamics of asset behaviour determine the risk of default. Asset values evolve over time as a function of volatility of the asset values. If asset values are less than the claims on the asset value, then the firm defaults, which is to say the call option held by the shareholders is abandoned, or the shareholders exercise the put option written by the debt providers.
- The default risk of the firm is the risk that the market value of assets falls below the book value of liabilities. The risk of default of the firm increases as the value of the assets falls to the book value of liabilities. Default occurs when the market value of assets is insufficient to repay the liabilities. The firm's net market value can be defined as:

Market value of asset − liabilities (default point)

A firm is likely to default when its net market value reaches zero. In practice, the relevant liabilities are not the total book value of liabilities. This is because long term liabilities are not immediately due and payable. The default point lies somewhere between the firm's current/short term liabilities and total liabilities. The risk of default is driven by the asset volatility. Asset value, asset volatility (risk) and leverage are combined into a measure of default risk (referred to as distance-to-default) as follows:

Distance to default = [market value of asset−default point]/
                      [market value of assets times asset volatility]

John Wiley & Sons, Singapore at Chapter 9; Crosbie, Peter J. and Bohn, Jeffrey R. (14 January 2002) "Modelling Default Risk"; KMV Corporation, San Francisco. The approach described here seeks to explain in general terms the theoretical approaches underpinning proprietary prediction models of default risk such as EDF^{TM}. It is not designed to be a complete or comprehensive description of these complex models. Persons wishing to learn more about the models are advised to contact MoodysKMV directly.

The model allows derivation of the default probability as the probability that asset values will be lower than the value of the claims on the asset. **Exhibit 6.10** sets out the approach underlying the option based model.

The EDF^{TM} model calculates the default probability of the firm as follows:

- Estimate asset value and volatility.
- Estimate the distance to default from the asset value, asset volatility and the book value of liabilities.
- Calculate the default probability from the distance to default and the default rate for given levels of distance to default.

The implementation of this type of model requires determination of the following parameters:

- Asset values.
- Asset value volatility.
- Liabilities (default point).

The estimation of the required parameters is subject to some difficulties:

- The market value of real assets is difficult to determine because of the absence of liquid secondary markets, the difficulty in valuing intangible assets, and the conventions and assumptions underlying the measurement and presentation of accounting based financial information.
- The volatility of asset values is similarly difficult to measure. This reflects the absence of traded markets and the requisite levels of price transparency in the real underlying assets.
- The measurement of liabilities is complicated by the fact that the claims may have different maturities and are governed by different credit conditions.

In order to overcome the identified problems, Moody'sKMV estimates the asset value and asset volatility from market value and volatility of traded equity. The asset volatility can be estimated using the option pricing approach developed by Black, Scholes and Merton which captures the relationship between asset value, asset volatility, equity value and equity volatility. Using this approach, the available equity value and equity volatility can be used to solve for the market value of asset and asset volatility. This requires the simultaneous solution of the following two relationships:

Equity value = Option function ([asset value], [asset volatility],
[capital structure], [interest rate])

Equity volatility = Option function ([asset value], [asset volatility],
[capital structure], [interest rate])

The two equations are solved to determine the asset value and asset volatility implied by current market equity values, volatility and capital structure.

Market equity volatility incorporates the effect of asset volatility and degree of firm leverage. This means that the market equity volatility must be adjusted for leverage. The relationship between equity and asset volatility is as follows:

$$\sigma_e = V_a / V_e \Delta \sigma_a$$

Where

σ_e = volatility of firm equity
σ_a = volatility of firm assets
V_a = market value of firm assets
V_e = market value of firm equity
Δ = the hedge ratio

In practice, the derivation of asset volatility is more complex. This is because the relationship only holds instantaneously. Changes in market leverage as equity prices change bias the results. Moody'sKMV use a complex iterative procedure to solve the asset volatility. The procedure commences with an initial estimate of volatility to estimate the asset value and to de-lever the equity return. The resulting asset volatility is then used in an iteration that generates new asset values and new asset returns until there is convergence. The asset volatility derived from the iteration is then combined with country, industry and size averages to produce a better estimate of the asset volatility. This is done using Bayesian statistics.

The cumulative liabilities are the debt due to mature in the relevant risk horizon.

The asset value, asset volatility, and the cumulative liabilities allow the default risk of the firm to be calculated. The measure is calculated by determining the distance in volatility measures (standard deviations) between the asset value and the point at which the asset value will fall below the liabilities. The default probability is then determined based on the distance to default.

The distance to default is specified as:

Distance to default = [market value of asset − default point]/
[market value of assets times asset volatility]

The default probability is established using historical information of historical defaults and bankruptcies. Moody'sKMV use large databases of companies to determine historical default frequencies. The default probability is calculated as the historical likelihood of default for a given distance to default. For example, if a firm is 6 standard deviations from default, the default probability is based on the proportion of firms 6 standard deviations away from default that defaulted over the relevant risk horizon. The default probabilities captured through this measure are then used as an indicator of future default rates (EDF^{TM} in the Moody'sKMV model).

Several aspects of the modelling should be noted:

- The default point is defined as the firm's cumulative liabilities and amortisation schedule. This is assumed to be fixed. In practice, firms may adjust their liabilities. It is difficult to specify the behaviour of liabilities. Moody'sKMV incorporates this uncertainty in the mapping of the distance to default.
- It is unlikely that the normal distribution is a good representation of the underlying asset value distribution. This is because the default point, as discussed above, is itself variable. The resulting empirical distribution used has much fatter tails than a normal distribution.
- EDF^{TM} is normally calculated for 1 year. EDF^{TM} measures are available for up to 5 years. The model used is largely identical. The cumulative liabilities (default point) incorporate all maturing debt during the period. This assumes that all maturing debt is refinanced short term (a conservative assumption that may overstate default probabilities). Asset values and asset volatility are also scaled to the longer time horizon. The distance to default is calculated using the asset value, asset volatility and default point for the risk horizon. The default probability is then inferred using the historical default information.

Exhibit 6.11 sets out a sample calculation of EDF^{TM}. **Exhibit 6.12** sets out a comparison of EDF^{TM} and rating default probabilities.

The major issues with this type of model include:

- The model is generally forward looking and dynamic. This reflects the fact that it uses equity prices. To the extent that equity prices impound information about future cash flows, the default measure will be forward looking. The measure adjusts automatically as equity prices and volatility changes.

- The model is relatively robust. It can be adjusted to deal with off-balance-sheet liabilities. The model appears to be transportable and capable of being adapted to different markets. It also appears to work reasonably well with thinly traded and closely traded firms.
- The performance of the model appears robust. However, there has been criticism that the model does not function as intended[31].

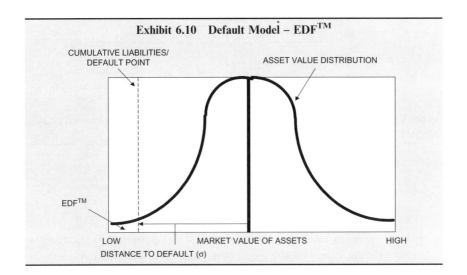

Exhibit 6.10   Default Model – EDF™

Exhibit 6.11   Default Model – EDF™ – Example

Variable	Value	Notes
Market value of equity	US$22.6 billion	Share price × shares outstanding
Book liabilities	US$49.1 billion	Balance sheet
Market value of assets	US$71.7 billion	Option pricing model
Asset volatility	10%	Option pricing model
Default point	US$36.9 billion	Liabilities payable within 1 year
Distance to default	4.8	Ratio: $[72-37]/[72 \text{ times } 10\%]$[32]
EDF™ (1 year)	21 bps	Empirical mapping between distance to default and default frequency.

Source: Crosbie, Peter J. "Modelling Default Risk" in Das, Satyajit (Editor) Credit Derivatives And Credit Linked Notes – Second Edition; John Wiley & Sons, Singapore Chapter 9 at 382.

---

[31] See Topping, Mike "Research Reveals Flaws In Popular Credit Model" (1–7 May 2002) Financial Products 3.

[32] Any growth in the asset value between the time of calculation and 1 year is ignored.

Exhibit 6.12   Default Model – EDF^{TM} Versus Ratings Agency Default Measures

The following Table sets out default probabilities (bps) and the corresponding risk rating levels:

EDF^{TM}	S & P	Moody's
2 to 4	AA or better	AA2 or better
4 to 10	AA/A	A1
10 to 19	A/BBB+	Baa1
19 to 40	BBB+/BBB−	Baa3
40 to 72	BBB−/BB	Ba1
72 to 101	BB/BB−	Ba3
101 to 143	BB−/B+	B1
143 to 202	B+/B	B2
202 to 345	B/B−	B3

Source: Crouhy, Michel, Galai, Dan, and Mark, Robert (2001) Risk Management; McGraw-Hill, New York Chapter 9 at 379

6.4.4   EDF^{TM} Model – Variations/Extensions

There are a number of variations on the basic model, including:

- **Private company models** – a difficulty with this approach is the requirement that the equity of the firm whose default risk is being modelled is publicly traded. In practice, the absence of traded equity can be overcome. This is achieved through the use of various proprietary models[33]. The basic approach is predicated on the basis that the fundamental process of default and default drivers is the same between private companies and companies whose equity securities are traded publicly. The key default drivers (market value of assets, volatility of asset values, level of external liabilities) must be determined in the absence of equity prices. Typical private company models (such as those used by firms such as Moody'sKMV) estimate the firm's equity value and volatility of asset values from accounting data. This is then transformed into

---

[33]   See Nyberg, Michael, Sellars, Martha and Zhang, Jing (17 October 2001) "Private Firm Model®: Introduction To The Modelling Methodology"; KMV Corporation, San Francisco. See McQuown, J.A. "Market Versus Accounting Based Measures Of Default Risk" in Nelken, Israel (Editor) (1997) Option Embedded Bonds: Price Analysis, Credit Risk And Investment Strategies"; Irwin Professional Publishing, Chicago at Chapter 5.

asset values and volatility and combined with data on liabilities (obtained directly) to generate default risk estimates. The approach works best when applied to a private firm that has a close comparable public firm[34].

- **Hybrid models** – a number of hybrid models combining the Merton approach with other forms of credit modelling have emerged. These models combine a structural model based on Merton's approach and a statistical model based on empirical analysis of historical data[35]. Key inputs into the hybrid model include ratings (if available), financial statement information, equity market information and macro economic variables[36].

7 Modelling Expected Versus Unexpected Losses

7.1 *Expected Versus Unexpected Credit Losses*

The identified factors (loss exposure, recovery rate and default probability) are combined to determine the expected and unexpected credit loss. Expected loss is defined as the average expected credit loss. It is analogous to a credit loss provision. In contrast, unexpected credit loss is the *worst case* credit loss. It is equivalent to the economic risk capital required to be held against the risk of this unexpected loss.

Expected loss for an individual credit risk is calculated as follows:

$$\text{Expected loss} = \text{Loss Exposure} \times \text{Default Probability} \times (1 - \text{Recovery Rate})$$

---

[34] For example, modelling the EDF of Mars that has a close comparable public firm (for example, Hershey).

[35] See Sobehart, J.R. and Stein R.M. (2000) Moody's Public Firm Risk Model: A Hybrid Approach to Modelling Short Term Default Risk; Moody's Investors Service, New York.

[36] The hybrid models are controversial and have caused significant debate; for example, see Sobehart, Jorge and Keenan, Sean "The Need For Hybrid Models" (February 2002) Risk 73–77; Kealhofer, Stephen and Kurbat, Matthew "Predictive Merton Models" (February 2002) 67–72. The merits of the hybrid models relative to the pure Merton model are currently not resolved.

This assumes statistical independence and no correlation between the factors. A more complex approach would entail incorporating the statistical dependence and correlation between the factors.

Expected loss for a portfolio is calculated as follows:

$$\text{Expected loss} = \text{Loss Exposure} \times \text{Default Probability} \times (1 - \text{Recovery Rate})$$
$$\times \text{Probability Function Incorporating Default Correlation}$$

Unexpected loss is calculated as the worst case loss exposure based on the worst case probability of default. This is calculated as the expected loss plus the variance of the expected loss based on a nominated level of confidence (say, 99 or 99.9% confidence).

Exhibit 6.13 sets out the pattern of expected and unexpected loss exposure. **Exhibit 6.14** sets out the relationship between the expected loss and the unexpected loss.

The major significance of these concepts is that the pricing of the credit risk must reflect the following:

- The expected loss must be charged and recovered in full.
- The unexpected loss must be covered by capital committed against that exposure and the required return on the credit derivative transaction must recover the cost of risk capital committed.

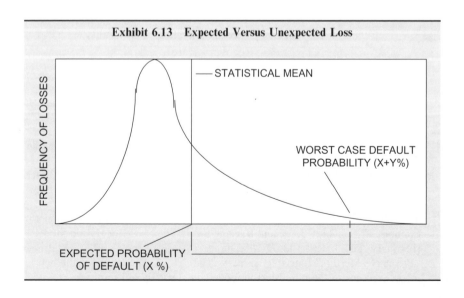

Exhibit 6.13 Expected Versus Unexpected Loss

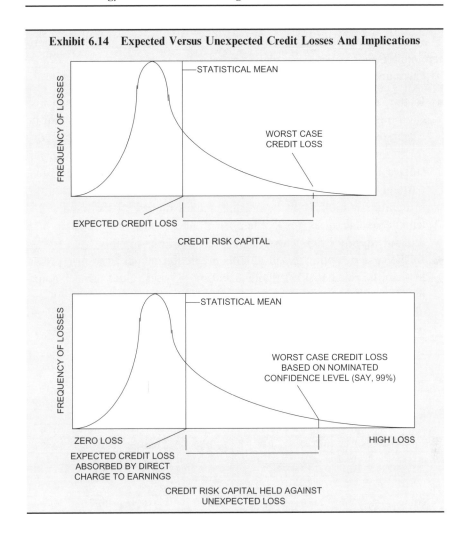

Exhibit 6.14 Expected Versus Unexpected Credit Losses And Implications

7.2 Default Volatility

The expected loss is equivalent to the average default probability for the relevant maturity for the relevant entity adjusted for the recovery rate. The unexpected losses incorporate the volatility of default rates and the default rate distribution.

The volatility of default rates reflects the degree to which default rates vary from one period to the next. This variation can be substantial. The volatility of default rates displays characteristic patterns. Lower rated firms display both a higher default probability and higher default rate volatility.

The default rate volatility is driven by various factors including macro economic trends/cycles.

There are several ways of measuring default volatility, including:

- In the case of ratings agency type default models, the unexpected loss can be modelled as the *distribution of default probabilities*. This can be calculated as the range of defaults for a particular credit rating category for a specific maturity. This data is available from the cohort group studies done by ratings agencies. The often low number of defaults, particularly at the higher rating levels, and the fact that the distribution of defaults is unlikely to be normal, makes the use of this data problematic as the basis for prediction of unexpected loss. **Exhibit 6.15** sets out Moody's estimates of 1 year default rate volatility[37].
- In the case of option based default prediction models, the unexpected loss can be calculated off the distribution of asset values using a nominated confidence level. This approach also needs to make assumptions about the nature of the underlying distribution that may prove too difficult to predict in practice.

Exhibit 6.15 Default Rate Volatility (%)							
Rating	Mean	Median	Standard Deviation	Minimum	Maximum	1st Quartile	3rd Quartile
Aaa	0.00	0.00	0.00	0.00	0.00	0.00	0.00
Aa	0.02	0.00	0.12	0.00	0.69	0.00	0.00
A	0.01	0.00	0.06	0.00	0.27	0.00	0.00
Baa	0.15	0.00	0.28	0.00	1.36	0.00	0.28
Ba	1.21	0.89	1.33	0.00	5.43	0.30	1.39
B	6.53	5.87	4.66	0.00	22.78	3.93	7.41
Caa−	24.73	21.79	21.79	0.00	100.00	10.37	34.21
Investment Grade	0.06	0.00	0.10	0.00	0.33	0.00	0.10
Speculative Grade	3.77	3.42	2.87	0.42	10.47	1.68	5.12
All Corporate	1.24	1.01	1.07	0.09	3.77	0.09	1.65

Source: Hamilton, David T., Cantor, Richard and Ou, Sharon (February 2002) Default And Recovery Rates of Corporate Bond Issues; Moody's Investors Service, New York.

---

[37] See also Keenan, Sean C., Hamilton, David T., and Carty, Lea V. "Historical Defaults and Recoveries For Corporate Bonds" in Das, Satyajit (Editor) (2001) Credit Derivatives And Credit Linked Notes – Second Edition; John Wiley & Sons, Singapore at Chapter 10.

8   Credit Modelling – Individual Positions

Credit models combine loss exposure, recovery rates, default rates and default rate volatility into a quantification of the risk of a transaction. This allows the derivation of the pricing required to compensate for that risk. In the case of credit portfolios, the correlation between the individual components (most significantly, the default correlation) must be incorporated.

For individual exposures, two types of models are feasible:

- **Default risk model** – this approach focuses on losses contingent on *default only*. Changes in mark-to-market value of the position as a result of changes in spreads are not incorporated. It is associated with hold to maturity exposures. The default risk model is applicable to *all* credit risk. **Exhibit 6.16** sets out a simple default risk model for a static (loan exposure) and a non static exposure (an interest rate and a currency transaction).

- **Credit spread model** – this approach encompasses changes in the value of the instrument resulting from changes in credit quality short of default. Changes in value of the instrument as a result of changes in credit spread are incorporated. The model is relevant for trading/mark-to-market portfolios. Credit risk is captured as a form of market risk (value at risk). The credit spread model is particularly suitable for bonds and tradable instruments. **Exhibit 6.17** sets out an example of this approach using the CreditMetrics^{TM} rating transition model[38].

Exhibit 6.16   Credit Models – Default Risk Model[39]

1.   Approach

The default risk model is used to establish the expected and unexpected loss on a BBB rated firm. The analysis is for 5 years.

---

[38]   For a detailed description of the CreditMetrics^{TM} Approach; Gupton, G.M., C.C. Finger and M. Bhatia (2 April 1997) CreditMetrics^{TM} – Technical Document; JP Morgan Inc, New York; Gupton, Greg "CreditMetrics – Assessing The Marginal Risk Contribution Of Credit" in Das, Satyajit (Editor) (2001) Credit Derivatives And Credit Linked Notes – Second Edition; John Wiley & Sons, Singapore at Chapter 13.

[39]   Please note that the pricing example set out is merely intended as an example. The assumed unexpected losses etc are merely hypothetical and are in no way intended to provide an indication of suggested pricing levels for default risk.

The model operates as follows:

1. The credit exposure for loans is assumed to be the face value of the transaction, while for derivatives it is assumed to be percentages of face value (a lower percentage for average expected exposure and a higher percentage for expected worst case exposure).
2. In the case of derivatives, the probability for positive exposures to the bank is set at 50%. This implies that 50% of the time there will be no exposure under the transaction, as market price fluctuations will result in the bank owing a termination payment to the counterparty in the case of default.
3. The expected loss is calculated based on the expected default probabilities for the relevant maturity for the particular credit rating.
4. The unexpected loss is calculated from the default volatility exhibited for the rating using the cohort analysis.
5. The recovery rate assumed is that for unsecured obligations (36.2%). In the unexpected loss case, recovery rates are assumed to be zero.
6. The cost of capital is assumed to be 15% pa pre-tax and the interest rate for amortisation purposes is set at the swap rate for the relevant maturity (5.00% pa).

The model is used to derive an arbitrage free or risk neutral capital charge for the assumption of the credit risk. This is calculated as the cost of capital required to be held against the unexpected losses. The pricing is shown on both a flat fee and an amortised per annum charge basis. The expected loss charge is *contained* within the unexpected loss. In practice, the expected loss is only calculated in order to establish the amount to be treated as an expense in the profit and loss account.

The assumptions used are as follows:

Counterparty Rating	BBB/Baa	BBB/Baa	BBB/Baa
Transaction Final Maturity (Years)	5	5	5
Type Of Transaction	Loan or bond	Interest rate derivative	Currency derivative
Seniority Of Exposure	Senior Unsecured	Senior Unsecured	Senior Unsecured
Interest Rate (% pa)	5.00	5.00	5.00
Cost Of Capital	15.00%	15.00%	15.00%
Face Or Notional Value ($)	1,000,000	1,000,000	1,000,000
Average Credit Exposure ($)	1,000,000	50,000	250,000
Worst Case Credit Exposure ($)	1,000,000	100,000	500,000
Probability Of Counterparty Default			
Cumulative Default Probability (%)	1.95	1.95	1.95
Worst Case Default Probability (%)	5.42	5.42	5.42
Probability Of Positive Exposures (%)	100.00	50.00	50.00
Recovery Rate (%)	36.20	36.20	36.20

The amount of capital required to be held and the capital charge are summarised below:

	Loan or bond	Interest rate derivative	Currency derivative
Expected Loss			
Expected Loss Amount (Pre-Recovery) ($)	19,500	488	2,438
Expected Loss Amount (Post-Recovery) ($)	12,441	311	1,555
Expected Loss Amount (Post-Recovery) (%)	1.24	0.03	0.16
Unexpected Loss			
Unexpected Loss ($)	54,200	5,420	27,100
Economic Capital Requirement ($)	54,200	5,420	27,100
Capital Cost Recovery ($ pa)	8,130	813	4,065
Capital Cost Recovery ($ Present Value)	35,199	3,520	17,599
Unexpected Loss Charge (%)	3.52	0.35	1.76
Total Charge			
Total Charge (%)	3.52	0.35	1.76
Total Charge ($)	35,199	3,520	17,599
Total Charge (% pa)	0.81	0.08	0.41

Exhibit 6.17   Credit Spread Model – CreditMetrics^{TM}

1.   Approach

The basic technique uses historical rating migration information to build a distribution of credit outcomes at a nominated future date that coincides with the nominated risk horizon (CreditMetrics^{TM} assumes a 1 year risk horizon). The key steps are as follows:

1.   A historical transition matrix is derived (usually from ratings data).
2.   Current and implied forward zero rates (incorporating risk free rates and credit spreads) for the relevant rating levels.
3.   The bond is valued as of the forward date using:
   3.1.   Current market values.
   3.2.   Expected values based on the probability of specific rating levels being attained and the bond price based on the implied forward rate and spread levels.

4. The price information is used to derive a distribution of values, allowing the calculation of the economic risk capital required to be held consistent with a nominated confidence level (this is analogous to a credit based value at risk).

2. Example

Assume an investor is holding a BBB rated bond. The bond has a coupon of 6.00% pa and has a 5 year maturity. In order to determine its credit exposure defined in terms of the volatility of a standalone instrument, the investor will need to:

1. Determine the possibility of the issuer's credit quality changing.
2. Establish the value of the instrument held at the relevant risk horizon based on either the forward zero curve for each credit rating category or in case of default, based on the recovery rate that will derive from the seniority of the exposure.
3. The volatility of value due to credit quality changes is then derived by combining the previous two steps.

Assume the credit quality migration (%) is given by the following 1 year transition matrix:

Initial Rating	Rating At Year End (%)							
	Aaa	Aa	A	Baa	Ba	B	Caa-C	Default
Aaa	91.79	7.37	0.81	0.00	0.02	0.00	0.00	0.00
Aa	1.21	90.73	7.67	0.28	0.08	0.01	0.00	0.02
A	0.05	2.49	91.96	4.84	0.51	0.12	0.01	0.01
Baa	0.05	0.26	5.45	88.55	4.72	0.72	0.09	0.15
Ba	0.02	0.04	0.51	5.57	85.50	6.71	0.45	1.19
B	0.01	0.02	0.14	0.41	6.72	83.79	2.58	6.34
Caa-C	0.00	0.00	0.00	0.63	1.63	4.23	69.82	23.69

Source: Hamilton, David T., Cantor, Richard and Ou, Sharon (February 2002) Default And Recovery Rates of Corporate Bond Issues; Moody's Investors Service, New York.

Rating migration data provides information on potential changes in credit quality. The transition matrix is calculated in the same way as default probabilities are determined[40].

---

[40] For discussion of ratings migration issues, see Keenan, Sean C., Fons, Jerome S. and Carty, Lea V "Credit Rating Dynamics: Moody's Watchlist, Rating Migration and Credit Quality Correlation" in Das, Satyajit (Editor) (2001) Credit Derivatives And Credit Linked Notes – Second Edition; John Wiley & Sons, Singapore at Chapter 11.

Based on the probability of the credit quality of the instrument changing, each instrument must be revalued. The revaluation parameters are as follows:

- Revaluation in case of default based on recovery rates – see Table below:

Seniority Class	Mean (%)	Standard Deviation (%)
Senior/Secured Bonds	53.8	24.6
Senior/Unsecured Bonds	44.0	28.0
Senior/Subordinated Bonds	29.0	24.6
Subordinated Bonds	28.5	21.2
Junior/Subordinated Bonds	15.1	18.7

Source: Moody's Investors Service

- Revaluation based on bond values using different rates and credit spreads based on rating levels at the risk horizon. The following 1 year forward zero rates % pa are used:

Rating Category	Year			
	1	2	3	4
AAA	3.60	4.17	4.73	5.12
AA	3.65	4.22	4.78	5.17
A	3.72	4.32	4.93	5.32
BBB	4.10	4.67	5.25	5.63
BB	5.55	6.02	6.78	7.27
B	6.05	7.02	8.03	8.52
CCC	15.05	15.02	14.03	13.52

This information can now be used to determine the possible range of 1 year forward values for the BBB rated bonds. The bond is revalued at the different ratings levels. All cash flows (including the current due coupon) are present valued. This provides the following range of forward bond values:

Rating Category	Price 1 Year Forward
AAA	109.35
AA	109.17
A	108.64
BBB	107.53
BB	102.01
B	98.09
CCC	83.63
Default	44.00

The estimate of the volatility of value can now be derived as follows:

Year End Rating	AAA	AA	A	BBB	BB	B	CCC	Default
State Probability (%)	0.05	0.26	5.45	88.55	4.72	0.72	0.09	0.15
Forward Bond Value ($)	109.35	109.17	108.64	107.53	102.01	98.09	83.63	44.00
Probability Weighted Value ($)	0.06	0.29	5.92	95.22	4.82	0.71	0.08	0.07

The forward bond value distribution is as follows:

Year End Rating	State Probability (%)	Forward Price ($)	Change In Value ($)
Aaa	0.05	109.35	2.20
Aa	0.26	109.17	2.02
A	5.45	108.64	1.49
Baa	88.55	107.53	0.38
Ba	4.72	102.01	−5.14
B	0.72	98.09	−9.06
Caa	0.09	83.63	−23.52
Default	0.15	44.00	−63.15

The credit risk can now be derived from the value (or loss distribution). The bond/credit loss distribution can be used to derive the credit risk by calculating the standard deviation or using percentile measures to generate the risk statistics.

The standard deviation of the bond values is set out below:

Mean Value	$107.15
Standard Deviation	$2.93
Standard Deviation (adjusted for recovery value uncertainty)	$3.67

The mean value of the bond, when compared to the estimated value of the bond (assuming no change in credit quality – that is, no credit risk), can be used to calculate the expected loss. The volatility of loss is calculated from the standard deviation using a nominated confidence level. It is used to derive the unexpected loss. The adjustment for recovery value uncertainty relates to the fact that the recovery rate is not fixed and is quite volatile. This uncertainty adds to the credit risk of holding of the bond. The adjustment uses a mathematical procedure to derive an allowance for this additional risk[41]. An alternative manner in which the risk may be derived uses the calculation of percentile level as a measure of risk. The percentile technique is useful given the asymmetric nature of the distribution.

---

[41] For a description of this methodology, see Gupton, G.M., C.C. Finger and M. Bhatia (2 April 1997) CreditMetricsTM – Technical Document; JP Morgan Inc, New York at Appendix D.

Based on a 99% confidence level, in this case the derived value is $98.60 (a loss of $8.55 relative to the mean projected bond value). This equates to the economic capital requirement against credit risk at a 99% confidence level.

Source: Gupton, G.M., C.C. Finger and M. Bhatia (2 April 1997) Credit-Metrics™ – Technical Document; JP Morgan Inc, New York at 23–33. This version has been updated by Greg Gupton.

9   Credit Modelling – Portfolios

Credit modelling increasingly places an emphasis on the portfolio. This reflects the fact that the loss behaviour of individual firms may be related. In particular, the default of and loss on a number of firms within the portfolio may simultaneously threaten the solvency of the lender. In practice, this dictates that credit modelling is focused on the *overall* risk of the portfolio.

Credit models combine loss exposure, recovery rates, default rates and default rate volatility into a quantification of the risk of a transaction. In the case of credit portfolios, the correlation between the individual components (most significantly, default correlation[42]) must be incorporated. This requires the estimation of default correlation and its incorporation into credit models to generate a loss distribution for the credit portfolio.

10   Default Correlation

10.1   Default Correlation – Rationale

Credit portfolio modelling requires incorporation of credit default correlation. This reflects the joint likelihood of credit quality changes. In effect, it reflects the view that the default/changes in credit quality of different obligors are not independent of each other; that is, there is a correlation relationship between the default events.

Correlation is a statistical measure of the degree to which two variables are related. Correlation may be estimated from historical data. It is generally estimated from historical data using simple linear (ordinary least

---

[42]   Referred to as joint default frequency ("JDF") in Moody'sKMV's EDF model.

squares) regression methodology[43]. Alternative methodologies for estimation of correlation include exponential weighted moving average models[44] or GARCH Models[45].

The correlation coefficient measures the direction and extent of the linear association between the two variables. If the default correlation is 1.00 (100%) then default by one of the two entities will coincide with the default of the second entity. If the default correlation is zero, then a default of one of the two entities will have no effect on the default of the second entity. If the default correlation is −1.00, then a default of one of the two entities will mean that there is absolute certainty that the second entity will not default. In practice, the correlation relationship does not preclude the fact that both entities may be dependent upon a common third factor; for example, macro-economic or industry conditions.

Default correlation is driven intuitively by the following factors:

- Firms within the same industry or country are likely to be affected by common factors that may have similar effects on the credit quality of the firms.
- Firms may also be affected by the fundamental economics of the industry. For example, the default and withdrawal from the industry of a single firm may enhance the survival prospects for other firms within the industry.

The above would argue for some default correlation. Common factors would imply positive default correlation. The case against correlation is that firms are unique and changes in credit quality are driven by events that are specific to the firm. In practice, the research supports the hypothesis that there is some level of *positive* default correlation in markets[46].

---

[43] For a discussion of correlation estimation, see Gillespie, Tom "Mathematical Techniques" in Das, Satyajit (Editor) (1997) Risk Management & Financial Derivatives: A Guide To The Mathematics; LBC Information Services, Sydney; McGraw-Hill, Chicago at Chapter 19; Kritzman, Mark (1995) The Portable Financial Analyst; Probus Publishing: Chicago, Illinois at Chapter 10 or see any standard textbook on statistics.

[44] See Hull, John (2000) Option Futures And Other Derivatives – Fourth Edition; Prentice-Hall Inc., Upper Saddle River, NJ at 382–383.

[45] See Hull, John (2000) Option Futures And Other Derivatives – Fourth Edition; Prentice-Hall Inc., Upper Saddle River, NJ at 382–383; Engle, R. and Mezrich J. "GARCH for Groups" (August 1996) Risk 36–40.

[46] For example, see Lucas, Douglas J. "Default Correlation And Credit Analysis" (March 1995) Journal of Fixed Income 76–87; Erturk, Erakan "Default

Key elements of default correlation in practice include[47]:

- The tendency for higher default correlation between entities within the same industry and the same country/region than the correlation between industries and countries/region[48]. There are limits to these patterns. Within some industries, default correlation between firms is low. This reflects industry structure issues such as high entry barriers, competition factors and specific issues (litigation in the tobacco industry and licensing in certain media industries). Some countries/regions may also show high correlation reflecting economic structures (Europe) and trading patterns (Japan/USA and China and South East Asia).
- Default correlation is sensitive to the time horizon used. Correlation measured over short time periods frequently diverges from that generated from long run data. This reflects several factors. Default correlation generated from short term data is heavily reliant on macro-economic factors. Default correlation generated from long run data is also influenced by sector migration issues and industry factors. Sector migration refers to changes in earnings sources and earnings volatility, reflecting market changes[49]. Industry factors refer to unexpected risk such as litigation[50].

Correlation Among Investment Grade Borrowers" (March 200) Journal of Fixed Income 55–59; Gupton, Greg "CreditMetrics – Assessing The Marginal Risk Contribution Of Credit" in Das, Satyajit (Editor) (2001) Credit Derivatives And Credit Linked Notes – Second Edition; John Wiley & Sons, Singapore Chapter 13 at 572–574; Nagpal, Krishan and Bahar, Reza "Measuring Default Correlation" (March 2001) Risk 129–132.

[47] See During, Alexander and Nassar, Tarek (15 May 2003) Valuing Synthetic CDOs; Deutsche Bank, London at 9–10.

[48] For example, Fitch Ratings found that: (1) correlation within industries was between 18.8% and 27.6%; (2) correlation between industries was 15.8% and 22.7%; and (3) correlation between regions was 4.3% and 18.4%; see Hrvatin, Richard V. and Neugebauer, Matthias (17 February 2004) Default Correlation And Its Effect On Portfolios Of Credit Risk; Fitch Ratings, New York.

[49] Examples include changes in the utility industry as a result of the effect of deregulation or shifts in individual business strategies (Vivendi changing from a utility to a media conglomerate or Mannesmann moving from an industrial company into a mobile phone manufacturer).

[50] Examples include tobacco and asbestos related litigation. For example, Sealed Air was forced to settle asbestos related claims even though it was not directly involved in asbestos related production.

10.2 Incorporating Default Correlation – Framework[51]

Modelling credit portfolios requires incorporation of default correlation or joint default probability. The problem cannot be approached using statistical or actuarial models (such as those used with mortgages, consumer finance or credit card portfolios). This is because typical wholesale credit portfolios do not include a sufficiently large number of entities; that is, the portfolio is not sufficiently diversified. However, a typical portfolio has too many reference entities to use comprehensive scenario analysis to consider all possible loss outcomes. The time to default is also important[52]. This means that static or discrete models cannot be used. Modelling credit portfolios requires the capacity to capture the distribution of the time to default of each reference entity in the portfolio and then combining them to create a joint distribution of correlated defaults.

The standard technique used in modelling credit portfolios is the Gaussian or normal copula function[53]. Copulas are the joint distribution functions of random vectors with standard uniform marginal distributions. **Exhibit 6.18** sets out a general form of copula functions. Copulas are used in statistics to model the marginal distribution of single risks combined to create joint distributions of groups of risks. It is an elegant and convenient method to combine marginal probability distributions given a specified correlation structure. Copulas provide more robust estimates of risk where certain technical assumptions about the form of the joint distribution of risk are not feasible. This makes copulas useful in modelling credit portfolios.

---

[51] See Li, David and Skarabot, Jure "Valuation And Risk Analysis Of Synthetic Collateralised Debt Obligations: A Copula Function Approach" in Gregory, Jon (Editor) (2003) Credit Derivatives: The Definitive Guide; Risk Publications, London at Chapter 14.

[52] This is especially important in tranched portfolio products; see Chapters 2 and 4. The order of default may also be important; see discussion of nth-to-default products in Chapters 2 and 4.

[53] See Li, David X. "On Default Correlation: A Copula Function Approach" (March 2000) Journal of Fixed Income 43–54; Schmitz, Volker and Pier-Ribbert, Erwin "Copulas In Finance" (12 February 2001) Derivatives Week 6–7; Frey, Rudiger, McNeil, Alexander and Nyfeler, Mark "Copulas And Credit Models" (October 2001) Risk 111–114.

Gaussian copulas are relatively easy to calibrate and efficient computationally. Gaussian copulas also exhibit certain characteristics[54]:

- High correlation within a Gaussian copula framework implies increasing functional dependence between default times between firms. It does not imply that firms are likely to default at the same time.
- In Gaussian copula frameworks, the effect of a default of one firm can impact other firms for a significant period after default. This is referred to as the "memory" effect. Some degree of default persistence is consistent with the contagion effect frequently experienced in financial markets. However, within the Gaussian copula framework the memory effect is a non-linear function of credit spread differences between firms and the correlation between them. It is not clear whether that is effective.
- Gaussian copulas also suffer from the problem of stationarity. The combination of Gaussian copulas with credit spread changes means the default of a firm has the effect of large credit spread jumps of surviving firms. This effect is also dependent on time.

Default correlation can be specified in different ways in practice. For example, it could be defined as default over a specified time interval. This approach does not capture the time dependence of default events and the resulting time dependence of default correlation. The use of a discrete model would mean that the default term structure is not incorporated and the time interval used is arbitrary. The alternative approach is to model survival time as a continuous random variable. This approach underlies the use of copulas in that default correlation is defined as the correlation between survival times. The survival time for individual entities is generated from individual credit curves using market credit spreads[55]. This information is then used to create a distribution of survival times for each entity. The marginal distributions derived from the individual credit spread curves are then used to construct a joint distribution of survival times. The construction of the joint distribution uses the default correlation of the two assets that is modelled as the correlation of the individual survival times[56].

---

[54]   See (2002) The Bank of America Guide To Advanced Correlation Products; Bank of America/Risk Publications – Supplement to (July 2004) Risk at 32, 33.
[55]   See discussion earlier in the Chapter.
[56]   See Li, David X. "On Default Correlation: A Copula Function Approach" (March 2000) Journal of Fixed Income 43–54.

Exhibit 6.18 Copula Functions[57]

A Gaussian or normal copula assumes that the marginal distributions of any variable conform to a normal distribution.

A copula of two variables (x and y) is equivalent to a cumulative probability function based on the marginal cumulative probability (defined as the cumulative normal distribution Nd_x and Nd_y) and the assumed correlation between the variables (ρ_{xy}):

$$ND_{x,y}(x, y) = C(Nd_x(x), Nd_y(y), (\rho_{xy}))$$

In order to simulate a distribution of correlated normal variables within a Monte Carlo simulation, the vector of independent random numbers is transformed using a Cholesky algorithm to derive the joint distribution. The bivariate joint probability distribution can be used to derive the survival times for each entity and the joint survival times.

10.3 Default Correlation – Estimation

The default correlation to be incorporated in the portfolio model needs to be estimated. There are a number of choices available to estimate default correlation, including:

- **Uniform constant correlation** – under this approach, constant correlation is assumed. The assumption is subjective and is not independently verifiable. It also defeats the objective of establishing a robust basis for assessing the risk behaviour of the portfolio. In practice, uniform constant correlation is not frequently used.
- **Joint likelihood of credit quality moves** – this approach determines the joint likelihood of default using actual rating and default data available from ratings agencies. It is conceptually similar to compiling a rating transition matrix. The approach does not make assumptions about the underlying process, joint distribution shape or rely on using the data to generate the correlation measure. The approach may not be sensitive to the characteristics of individual firms. This means that the approach may not be able to distinguish below industry or sector level.

---

[57] The copula function described is based on Hrvatin, Richard V. and Neugebauer, Matthias (17 February 2004) Default Correlation And Its Effect On Portfolios Of Credit Risk; Fitch Ratings, New York at 9.

- **Correlation inferred from default rate volatility** – this approach is based on the idea that for a large and homogeneous population of obligors, larger volatility of default rates over time suggests a higher default correlation. The approach is only able to infer one correlation; that is, the effective *average* correlation across all pairs within the population or sector[58].

- **Bond spread correlation** – this approach uses historical time series data of bond price movements to generate default correlation. The approach uses the historical price data and a model relating bond price movements to credit changes to calculate the correlation. The bond price model generally assumes that credit spread behaviour is independent of interest rates and linked to changes in credit quality. The pricing model allows the default probability of a bond to be derived from the observed bond spread[59]. Where there are two or more bonds, the model allows the default correlation to be inferred from the correlation in bond spread changes. The advantage of the approach is that it is market driven and consistent with the valuation of other risky assets. The major problem with the approach is the availability of good quality credit spread information.

- **Equity/asset price correlation** – this approach uses an assumed process (usually the Merton model) as the driver of changes in credit quality. This means that observable changes in equity and asset values can be used to infer changes in credit quality and the relationship between changes in credit quality of different firms. The underlying logic is to link correlation to fundamental factors. This entails using a factor model to improve forecasting accuracy and reduce sampling errors in calculating historical correlation. In practice, this approach is commonly used[60]. **Exhibit 6.19** outlines the process used to derive default correlation under this approach by CreditMetrics™ and Moody'sKMV Corporation[61].

---

[58] This approach is the implicit driver of correlation in the CreditRisk+ framework. It is considered but discarded in the CreditMetrics™ technical document; see Gupton, G.M., C.C. Finger and M. Bhatia (2 April 1997) CreditMetricsTM – Technical Document; JP Morgan Inc, New York at Section 8.1.

[59] See discussion earlier in the Chapter.

[60] Variations on these approaches are also feasible, see Nagpal, Krishan and Bahar, Reza "Modelling Default Correlation" (April 2001) Risk 85–89.

[61] Similar models are also used by Fitch Ratings; see Hrvatin, Richard V. and Neugebauer, Matthias (17 February 2004) Default Correlation And Its Effect On Portfolios Of Credit Risk; Fitch Ratings, New York.

Estimation of default correlation is affected by a number of issues:

- **Computational efficiency** – there is a practical requirement to limit the size of the correlation matrix. For example, a portfolio of 5,000 firms would require a $5,000 \times 4,999$ correlation matrix and 12,497,500 individual pairwise correlations. The methodologies described in **Exhibit 6.19** use multi-factor models of asset returns to reduce the number of correlations.
- **Model issues** – the approaches to estimating default/credit quality change correlation make a number of assumptions. For example, the commonly used models seek to infer the market asset values and correlation based on equity market information. Empirical research indicates that inferring asset correlation from equity correlation may significantly underestimate credit correlation and portfolio risk[62]. This requires the use of factor models that introduce model risk in these calculations.

Exhibit 6.19   Default Correlation – Estimation Approaches

1.   Overview

A common technique for deriving default/credit quality change correlation is to use a structural model where the default/credit quality changes are linked to key factors. The firm's asset returns are assumed to be driven by identifiable systematic and specific risk factors. Specific risk factors are generally firm specific. The impact of specific factors is assumed to be minimal in a well diversified portfolio. The systematic factors are non diversifiable. Asset return correlation is based on systematic risk factors. Within this general framework, a number of possible modelling approaches are feasible. Two approaches (CreditMetrics™ and Moody'sKMV Corporation) are described below.

Advantages of this approach include that it allows the size of the axes of the correlation matrix to be reduced. It also allows correlation to be calculated for certain types of firms such as private firms or illiquid stocks. The approach does not capture specific risks associated with an individual obligor. In essence, the approach is focused on industry and country level risk factors, rather than firm specific risk factors. This means that this approach is best suited to large well diversified risk portfolios.

---

[62]   See Zeng, Bin and Zhang, Jing (2001) Measuring Credit Correlations: Equity Correlations Are Not Enough!; KMV Corporation, San Francisco.

2. CreditMetrics™ Approach[63]

CreditMetrics™ is consistent with the Merton model. Firm asset value is considered as a barometer or index of credit quality (including default). The model establishes a series of thresholds for underlying asset value which correspond to the firm's credit rating level. This allows a distribution of asset values with corresponding credit ratings to be created at a risk horizon of 1 year. The model creates a direct linkage between credit quality and the firm's underlying (asset) value. CreditMetrics™ then uses equity indices as the best available proxy to imply default/credit quality change correlations.

Within this framework, a number of possible approaches to deriving default correlation are feasible. CreditMetrics™ uses equity price correlation at the industry and country level rather than individual firm level correlation. The correlations are generated as follows:

- Individual obligors are mapped to industry and country on the basis of the classification that is most likely to determine its credit performance. There are a number of ways to assign industry and country weights. One approach is to use asset and/or sales percentages in the relevant industry or country. An alternative is to regress the equity price series of the firm against industry and country estimates to determine the key drivers of behaviour.
- Firms are then related to one another via common sensitivity to industry and/or country sectors.

The diagram below shows the approach used.

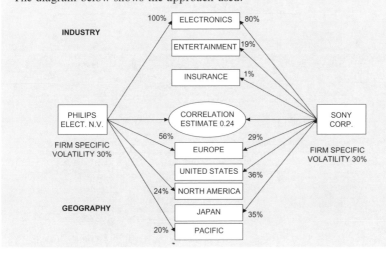

[63] See Gupton, Greg "CreditMetrics™ – Assessing The Marginal Risk Contribution Of Credit" in Das, Satyajit (Editor) (2001) Credit Derivatives And Credit Linked Notes – Second Edition; John Wiley & Sons, Singapore Chapter 13 at 576–580.

All firms are assumed to have a form specific or unique volatility. This refers to the volatility of firm value that is not explained by industry and country factors.

Source: Gupton, Greg "CreditMetrics™ – Assessing The Marginal Risk Contribution Of Credit" in Das, Satyajit (Editor) (2001) Credit Derivatives And Credit Linked Notes – Second Edition; John Wiley & Sons, Singapore Chapter 13 at 579.

3. KMV Approach[64]

Moody'sKMV uses a three layer factor model:

- The first level is company specific factors constructed for individual firms based on country and industry factors.
- The second level is country and industry factors.
- The third level is global, regional and industrial sector factors.

The structure is set out in the diagram below.
The process used is as follows:

- The first level separates the firm specific risk and systematic risk components.
- The systematic risk is captured by a single firm specific index that is constructed as a weighted sum of the firm's exposure to country and industry factors (as defined in the second level). The weighting is based on indicators such as assets and sales.
- The third level decomposes country and industry risk into systematic and specific components (in terms of global economic, regional and sector factor effects).
- The asset correlation is derived from the factor structure.

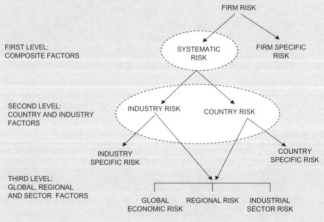

Source: Moody'sKMV Corporation as presented in Crouhy, Michel, Galai, Dan, and Mark, Robert (2001) Risk Management; McGraw-Hill, New York Chapter 9 at 387.

---

[64] See Crouhy, Michel, Galai, Dan, and Mark, Robert (2001) Risk Management; McGraw-Hill, New York Chapter 9 at 384–389.

10.4   Default Correlation – Issues

The Gaussian copula used to model credit portfolios creates practical problems. It is useful in allowing the analysis of relatively simple credit portfolios. It may create problems when used for structured credit products[65].

Collateralised debt obligation ("CDO") tranches on credit indexes[66] are frequently quoted at a constant copula correlation[67]. For example, an equity tranche of a CDO covering the first 3% loss on the Trac-X index may be quoted at a correlation of 20%. The mezzanine tranche covering losses between 3% and 8% may be quoted at a correlation of 15%. Given that the underlying credit portfolio is identical, both tranches should be quoted at the same correlation. Such discrepancies may arise because of inefficiencies in the market. However, it is also consistent with the limitations of the model (that is, insufficient degree of freedom in the default correlation).

Where options on a credit portfolio (such as the Trac-X or equivalent credit index) are traded, the joint effects of default and credit spread changes must be modelled. This is because the value of the option depends upon the sequence of defaults and the credit spread changes of the surviving constituents of the portfolios. Existing models do not allow the correlated changes of default times and credit spreads.

11   Credit Portfolios – Generating the Loss Distribution

Credit modelling of a portfolio relies on generating the portfolio loss distribution using the following parameters:

- Marginal default probabilities for each entity in the portfolio.
- Assumption about recovery rates/loss given default for each entity.
- Default correlation estimates.

The procedure for generating the loss distribution is mathematically and numerically complex. In practice, Monte Carlo simulations are generally

---

[65]   See Duffie, Darrell "Time To Adapt Copula Methods For Modelling Credit Risk Correlation" (April 2004) Risk 77.

[66]   See Chapters 2 and 4.

[67]   For a discussion of some of the issues in using implied correlation, see Chapter 4 where the debate regrading compound and base correlation is outlined: see Mashal, Roy, Naldi, Marco and Tejwani, Gaurav "The Implications Of Implied Correlation" (July 2004) Risk 66–68; Patel, Navroz "Cracking The Correlation Conundrum" (August 2004) Risk 40–42.

used to generate the full distribution of the portfolio values at the relevant time horizon.

The key problem in simulation is speed. The numerical implementation issues increase with the number of values required and individual exposures increase. For example, in the CreditMetrics^{TM} framework, 1 bond and 8 state rating outcomes equates to 8 possible value states that can be observed at the risk horizon. If there are n bonds and 8 state rating outcomes, then this equates to 8^n possible value states that can be observed at the risk horizon. The portfolio of n bonds and 8 state rating outcomes requires estimation of correlation between credit quality migrations to 8^n possible outcomes. The numerical implementation issue is that the number of possible outcomes becomes very large as the number of obligors increases. This means that it is not feasible to use all possible portfolio states to obtain value distribution. For example, the CreditMetrics^{TM} approach concentrates on a reduced set of portfolio values. A reduced set is selected through random sampling to avoid selection bias. The plot of calculated distribution starts to approach the smooth underlying distribution.

Significant efforts have been directed at improving the simulation framework[68]. Commonly used techniques include:

- **Fourier transforms**[69] – this uses a convolution in the frequency domain to aggregate loss distributions. It is faster than Monte Carlo simulations. It also has advantages where the underlying portfolio consists of multi-sector (such as asset backed or structured) securities. It is useful for portfolios with low levels of diversification or a wide spread of credit quality. The disadvantage is that it is a single period model and does not incorporate default timing.

---

[68] See Arvantis, Angelo and Gregory, Jon (2001) Credit: The Complete Guide To Pricing Hedging And Risk Management; Risk Books, London; Smith, Darren "CDOs Of CDOs: Art Eating Itself?" in Gregory, Jon (Editor) (2003) Credit Derivatives: The Definitive Guide; Risk Publications, London at Chapter 13; Li, David and Skarabot, Jure "Valuation And Risk Analysis Of Synthetic Collateralised Debt Obligations: A Copula Function Approach" in Gregory, Jon (Editor) (2003) Credit Derivatives: The Definitive Guide; Risk Publications, London at Chapter 14.

[69] See Debuysscher, A. and Szego, M. (2003) The Fourier Transform Method; Moody's Investors Service.

- **Saddle point techniques**[70] – this entails using moment generating functions of probability distributions and uses a Fourier transform of the probability density function in the relevant tail of the distribution. This is done by finding the saddle point of the probability density function and then using mathematical techniques to approximate the integral. The technique can be used with any distribution (including non normal distributions) where the first and second derivatives are known. It has been used to calculate the credit value-at risk analytically at a specified probability or percentile level. This is accomplished using root finding methods rather than time consuming simulations.

12 Credit Modelling – Portfolio Models

12.1 Overview

Several credit portfolio models have emerged[71]. Key factors that may differ between models include:

- The method for establishing default probability varies. The default probability may be determined from financial statement information, ratings, credit spreads, equity/asset values or macro-economic variables.
- The specification of the default intensity or recovery rate varies. In particular, it may be endogenous or exogenous to the model.
- The process used varies. It may be continuous or discrete, deterministic or stochastic and diffusion based or incorporate jumps.
- The implementation process also varies. Possible implementation frameworks include binomial, finite difference schemes or simulations.

In practice, the models used fall into the following categories:

- **Structural models** – this class of model uses firm specific data and links the default risk to asset value and debt levels. Structural models are all

---

[70] See Martin, Richard, Thompson, Kevin and Browne, Christopher "Taking To The Saddle" (June 2001) Risk 91–94; Martin, R., Thompson, K. and Browne, C. "Taking To The Saddle" in Gordy, Michael B. (Editor) (2003) Credit Risk Modelling; Risk Books, London 137–143.

[71] For an overview, see Gupton, Greg M. "Portfolio Credit Risk Model" in Gregory, Jon (Editor) (2003) Credit Derivatives: The Definitive Guide; Risk Publications, London at Chapter 7.

derivatives of the Merton model[72]. The best known commercial version of the structural model is Moody'sKMV Corporation's EDF™ measure. Proponents of structural models argue that the model provides a robust estimate of credit risk. Opponents argue that the parameters required are difficult to estimate in practice.

- **Reduced form models** – this class of models works directly with market information (credit spreads or rating transition) to derive default risk estimates. The major difference is that the reduced form models bypass firm value and treat default as exogenous. Reduced form models fall into a number of categories including:

  1. *Credit rating models* – these models use credit ratings that are assumed to change over time driven by a Markov process to model default and to create a matrix of ratings transitions[73].
  2. *Credit spread models* – these models use a specified process for the credit spread to generate the loss distribution[74].
  3. *Default models* – these models specify a stochastic process for the default event itself and use this as the basis of modelling credit losses[75]. Default models specify a stochastic process for the default

---

[72] See Black, Fischer and Scholes, Myron "The Pricing Of Options And Corporate Liabilities" (May–June 1973) Journal of Political Economy 81 637–659; Merton, R. "On The Option Pricing Of Corporate Debt: The Risk Structure Of Interest Rates" (1974) Journal of Finance vol 29 449–470; Black, F. and Cox, J. "Valuing Corporate Securities: Some Effects of Bond Indenture Provisions" (1976) Journal of Finance vol 31 no 3 361–367; Bhattacharya, S. and Mason, S. "Risky Debt, Jump Processes and Safety Covenants" (1981) Journal of Financial Economics vol 9 no 3 281–307; Shimko, D, Tejima, N., and Van Deventer, D. "The Pricing of Risky Debt When Interest Rates Are Stochastic" (1993) The Journal of Fixed Income vol 3 58–65; Leland, H. "Corporate Debt Value, Bond Covenants, and Optimal Capital Structure" (1994) Journal of Finance vol 49 1213–1252.

[73] See Jarrow, R, Lando, D, and Turnbull, S "A Markov Model For The Term Structure of Credit Risk Spreads" (1997) Review of Financial Studies vol 10 481–523; Lando, David "On Rating Transition Analysis and Correlation" in (1998) Credit Derivatives: Applications for Risk Management, Investment and Portfolio Optimisation; Risk Books, London at Chapter 11.

[74] See Ramaswamy, K. and Sunderesan, S. "The Valuation of Floating Rate Instruments: Theory And Evidence" (1986) Journal Of Financial Economics 261–272; Das, Sanjiv Ranjan "Credit Risk Derivatives" (Spring 1995) Journal of Derivatives 7–23.

[75] See Jarrow, R. and Turnbull, S. "Pricing Options On Financial Securities Subject To Default Risk" (1995) Journal of Finance vol 50 53–86; Longstaff, F.

event itself and use this as the basis of modelling credit losses. The various default models are differentiated by the process by which the default probabilities are modelled. **Exhibit 6.20** sets out two examples of this type of modelling process.

An issue with reduced form models is the fact that they make no assumptions as to the cause of default[76]. Default is treated as a chance event. The default arrival rate must be estimated in practice from the observed price of the issuer's debt obligations. This assumes the efficiency of the underlying debt market.

A number of other approaches have emerged:

- **Arbitrage free approach**[77] – this approach relies on calculating the implied default rate from spread data for individual issuers and spread data for generic rating groups. Implied spread volatility is generated from volatility of credit spreads in bond markets, spread options and also standby credit facilities in the loan markets. Credit instruments are priced using market data at a specified risk horizon using current and implied values for default and spreads. The arbitrage approach is motivated by the fact that other approaches often generate values whereby the actual and calculated price of credit instruments do not agree. This lack of insistence that the derived price replicate market prices can create significant difficulties in hedging credit derivatives in

---

and Schwartz, E. "A Simple Approach To Valuing Fixed and Floating Rate Debt" (1995) Journal of Finance vol 50 789–819; Das, Sanjiv Ranjan and Tufano, Peter "Pricing Credit-Sensitive Debt When Interest Rates, Credit Ratings and Credit Spreads Are Stochastic" (June 1996) The Journal of Financial Engineering vol 5 no 2 161–198; Duffie, D. and Huang, M. "Swap Rates and Credit Quality" (1996) Journal of Finance vol 51; Duffie, D., Schroeder, M., and Skidas, C. "Recursive Valuation of Defaultable Securities And The Timing Of Resolution of Uncertainty" (1996) Annals of Applied Probability vol 6 1075–1090; Flesaker, Bjorn, Hughston, Lane, Schreiber, Laurence, and Sprung, Lloyd "Taking All The Credit" (September 1994) Risk 104–108; Hughston, L.P. "Pricing Of Credit Derivatives" (March 1996) Financial Derivatives and Risk Management 5 11–16.

[76] This should be contrasted with models based on equity prices (such as the Black-Scholes-Merton approach) where default is assumed to be the insufficiency of assets to meet liabilities rather than a chance event.

[77] See Chaplin, Geoff "The Credit Balance" Financial Products Issue 78 12–13.

the cash markets. The major benefit of the arbitrage free approach is that it avoids the possibility of arbitrage between the credit derivative and the replicating portfolio[78].

- **Macro-economic approach** – an example of this approach is a model developed by McKinsey & Co[79]. The model focuses on the risk of a credit portfolio explicitly linking credit default and credit migration behaviour to the macro-economic factors that are major drivers of the credit quality of the portfolio. The McKinsey approach is also broader in its focus, being designed to be applied to all customer segments and product types. This would encompass liquid loans and bonds (which are the principal focus of the other approaches) but also less liquid classes of credit assets such as mid/small size corporate loans, retail mortgage loans and credit card portfolios.

In practice, the increasingly favoured models are *reduced form models*. The only exception to this is Moody'sKMV Corporation's EDF[TM] measure and its derivatives. The different models are broadly comparable and produce similar results[80]. In the next Sections, a number of models are reviewed.

---

[78] This occurs in other areas of derivative pricing such as interest rate term structure models (e.g. equilibrium type models). In order to overcome this, no arbitrage models may be used to ensure that the model recovers traded market prices through a calibration process. See Das, Satyajit (2004) Swaps/Financial Derivatives 3rd Edition; John Wiley, Singapore at Chapter 8.

[79] See Wilson, Thomas "Portfolio Credit Risk (I)" (September 1997) Risk 111–117; Wilson, Thomas "Portfolio Credit Risk (II)" (October 1997) Risk 56–61.

[80] For a comparison of the different modelling approaches, see Koyluoglu, H. Ugur and Hickman, Andrew "Reconcilable Differences" (October 1998) Risk 56–62; Arvantis, Angelo and Laurent, Jean-Paul "On The Edge Of Completeness" (October 1999) Risk 61–65; Hickman, Andrew "Overview to Credit Risk Modelling" in Das, Satyajit (Editor) (2001) Credit Derivatives And Credit Linked Notes – Second Edition; John Wiley & Sons, Singapore Chapter 12; Crouhy, Michel, Galai, Dan, and Mark, Robert (2001) Risk Management; McGraw-Hill, New York Chapter 11. See also Locke, Jane "Credit Check" (September 1998) Risk 40–44; Letter to the editor (October 1998) Risk 19; Locke, Jane "Off-the-peg, Off-the-mark?" (November 1998) Risk – Credit Risk Special Report 22–27; Paul-Choudhury, Sumit "A Model Combination" (November 1998) Risk – Credit Risk Special Report 18–20.

Exhibit 6.20 Credit Default Models

Model 1[81]

1. Framework

The model assumes that all debt securities can be decomposed into discount (or zero coupon) bonds. A risky bond (one capable of default) consists of a series of risk free zero coupon bonds *plus* a credit spread. The credit spread may be determined by calculating the *risky* zero rates and taking away the risk free zero rates to isolate the credit spread.

Using this term structure of discount securities, and the assumption of a multi factor Brownian motion to generate market randomness and market completeness, it is possible to model the pricing of a risky bond within a Heath-Jarrow-Morton ("HJM") framework[82].

The HJM framework states that the value of a derivative can be stated as:

$$F_a/B_a = E_a[F_b/B_b]$$

Where
F_a is the value of the derivative at time a
B_a is the value at time a for a unit initialised money market interest rate accumulating interest at the instantaneous rate
E_a is the conditional expectation given information up to time a
F_b is the random payoff of an interest rate derivative at time b
B_b is the value at time b for a unit initialised money market interest rate accumulating interest at the instantaneous rate

This Martingale relation allows the determination of a unique pricing measure at time a (which is earlier than b) of an interest rate derivative. The theory also provides suitable general formulae for the money market account process B_b and the bond price P_{ab}.

2. Incorporation of Default Risk

The valuation of risky bonds requires the HJM framework to incorporate the risk of default. This can be done by introducing a jump process (in practice, a Poisson process is used) to incorporate the risk of default. The Poisson process models the

---

[81]   This Exhibit sets out the model described in Hughston, L.P. "Pricing Of Credit Derivatives" (March 1996) Financial Derivatives and Risk Management 5, 11–16.

[82]   See Heath, D., Jarrow, R., and Morton, A. "Bond Pricing And The Term Structure of Interest Rates: A New Methodology For Contingent Claims Pricing" (1992) Econmetrica 77–105.

random arrival of discrete events as (on average) a certain number of events per unit of time determined by the hazard rate, which itself can change randomly over time. The Poisson process models default on a risky bond as the payment of a fixed unit of currency unless there has been default, in which case the bond payment is reduced to zero. The default is modelled as the first arrival time of the Poisson process, the intensity of which can be linked to interest rates in general (even in a path dependent way if desired).

3. Valuing Risky Bonds

Within this framework, the value of a risky bond can be stated as:

$$Q_{ab} = B_a E_a[Q_b/B_b]$$

Where

$$Q_b = 1 + (R_b - 1)n_b$$

The terminology is as above, except as follows:

Q_{ab} is the value of a risky bond with maturity of b at time a
Q_b is the default process as specified above
n_b is the default process indicator that is 1 if default has occurred and 0 if no default has occurred.
R_b is the recovery rate that specifies how much the bond would pay out in the event of default.

The above can be generalised for n_b as the first arrival indicator in a point process with random intensity λ_s where λ_s is adapted to the underlying Brownian motion driving the default free term structure. This allows specification of the conditional probability of default by time b as follows:

$$P[(n_a = 0) \text{ \& } (n_b = 1)] = 1 - \exp_a f^b \lambda_s \, ds$$

Using the fact that at continuous compounded interest earnings the value of the money market investment is the exponential of the integral of the risk free short term interest rate, and assuming constant recovery rates of R, Hughston shows that the value of a risky bond is given by:

$$Q_{ab} = RP_{ab} + (1 - R)E_a[\exp\{ -_a f^b (r_s + \lambda_s) \, ds\}]$$

The above assumes that there is no default at time a. An alternative formulation can be used, allowing an immediate recovery on default based on a function of the value of the claim immediately before the default.

Source: The above is based on Hughston, L.P. "Pricing Of Credit Derivatives" (March 1996) Financial Derivatives and Risk Management 5 11–16. The above represents an abbreviated version of the model and readers are referred to the original for the full exposition.

Model 2[83]

The Jarrow-Turnbull model uses a basic foreign exchange analogy to value credit pricing. The basic approach uses two currencies (US$ and a foreign currency stated in terms of *expected* US$). Both currencies have a term structure of interest rates and therefore a defined present value and are free of default risk *in their own currency*. The exchange rate between US$ and the other currency is stochastic. The exchange rate is, say, 1, but can decrease. This risk of change creates uncertainty, namely exchange rate risk. In the case of credit derivatives, using this analogy, the risk is driven by the risk of *default* rather than changes in currency values.

The approach is as follows:

- Assume a loan to an entity for an amount X.
- The price of the loan is:

$$V_0 = E[P/(1 + R_0)]$$

Where

    V_0 = the present value of the cash flow
    E = an expectations operator using risk adjusted probabilities
    P = the actual payment in terms of the promised payment X
    R_0 = the riskless interest rate over a time period [0, 1]

- Using the above analogy, the actual payment can be restated as:

$$P = eX$$

Where

    e = the exchange rate for agreed $ to *actual* $ where e < 1 in the event of default
    or e = 1 where there is no default.
- The default rate can be elaborated as follows:
    $e = \delta < 1$ if default occurs with probability λ; or
    e = 1 if no default with probability $1 - \lambda$.
Where
    λ = the cumulative risk adjusted probability of default by time 1
    δ = the recovery rate in the event of default
- This allows the value of the loan or bond to be written as:

$$V_0 = E[X\delta/(1 + R_0) \,|\, default]\lambda + E[X/(1 + R_0) \,|\, no\ default](1 - \lambda)$$

The approach states the value of a risky loan or bond is equal to the discounted payoff in default times the probability of default plus the discounted payoff if no

---

[83]   This Exhibit sets out the model developed by Robert Jarrow and Stuart Turnbull, see Jarrow, R "Current Advances In The Modelling Of Credit Risk" (May/June 1998) Journal of Derivatives Taxation & Regulation 196–200.

default occurs times the no default probability. The approach is capable of generalisation covering multiple periods and multiple cash flows.

The key element of this approach is that the use of the foreign exchange analogy assists in the process of hedging and pricing. In essence, the key element of this process is modelling e, which relies on modelling the default probability and the recovery rate.

Source: The above is based on Jarrow, R "Current Advances In The Modelling Of Credit Risk" (May/June 1998) Journal of Derivatives Taxation & Regulation 196–200. The above represents an abbreviated version of the model and readers are referred to the original for the full exposition.

12.2 Rating Transition Models

The rating transition approach models default rate volatility as a discrete variable. Under this approach, the possible default rates are mapped by using historical data of ratings and rating transitions. The underlying logic of this approach is that it captures the distribution of rating changes. When combined with forward rates and credit spreads at different levels, it can be used to capture changes in value of the underlying obligations. The model defines credit risk as uncertainty in values of the instrument at the risk horizon depending on the credit quality state. The credit risk of the portfolio requires correlation between defaults to be used. RMG's CreditMetrics[TM] approach is an example of this type of model[84].

The approach used by CreditMetrics[TM] can be used to illustrate the technique[85]. The basic technique uses historical rating migration information to build a distribution of credit outcomes at a nominated future date that coincides with the nominated risk horizon (CreditMetrics[TM] assumes a 1 year risk horizon). The key steps are as follows:

- A historical transition matrix is derived (usually from ratings data).
- Current and implied forward zero rates (incorporating risk free rates and credit spreads) for the relevant rating levels.
- The bond is then valued as of the forward date using:
  1. Current market values.
  2. Expected values based on the probability of specific rating levels being attained and the bond price based on the implied forward rate and spread levels.

---

[84] For a description of this approach, see Gupton, G.M., C.C. Finger and M. Bhatia (2 April 1997) CreditMetricsTM – Technical Document; JP Morgan Inc, New York.

[85] For an example of the use of the model, see **Exhibit 6.17**.

- The price information is used to derive a distribution of values allowing the calculation of the economic risk capital required to be held consistent with a nominated confidence level (this is analogous to a credit based value at risk).
- For a portfolio, estimates of correlation are then used to aggregate portfolio risks.

The approach can be used to generate the following types of credit risk data:

- For an individual position, a risk estimate based on the loss distribution.
- For a portfolio, it allows marginal risk statistics of the portfolio to be generated to derive both the average risk of the portfolio and the marginal risk contribution of individual transactions.

This allows the model to be used for a variety of applications, including credit portfolio management; risk based exposure limits; risk based pricing; and risk based capital allocation.

This approach is not a structural model. This is because it requires default rates to be input in the form of a transition matrix.

A significant issue with this approach is that the model uses the implied forward spreads to generate the forward credit loss distribution. In practice, forward credit spreads may be poor estimators of actual spot credit spreads. This may bias the model.

12.3 Structural Models

The structural model can be used to derive the probability of default of a company from its equity price and capital structure. This approach is embedded in Moody'sKMV EDF model[86]. The model can be adjusted to derive a portfolio loss distribution. This approach is that underlying Moody's KMV's Portfolio Manager.

The approach is used to calculate a portfolio credit value at risk. The model uses the following inputs:

- Probability of default based on the EDFs of each entity.
- Estimate of the change in debt values based on a continuous scale related to EDF changes over time.

---

[86] See discussion earlier in the Chapter.

- A forecast of the loss given default for an individual exposure based on a predictive model of seniority, firm factors and industry factors.
- Default correlation derived from firm asset values.

The model can be used for private firms by inputting financial statement values into an econometric model to derive EDFs[87].

12.4 Default Rate Volatility Models

These approaches model default rate volatility as a continuous variable. Under this approach, the possible default rate is generated from the default rate and volatility of default rate. This approach is based on a non life insurance approach[88]. CSFP's CreditRisk+ is an example of this approach[89].

Default rate models use a specified process for the default process to generate the loss distribution. The basic approach is analogous to a non life insurance framework whereby claims are assessed on a case by case basis, then losses are combined to form a severity distribution (the Pareto curve[90]). The frequency loss distribution is modelled as a Poisson distribution or a negative binomial distribution[91]. This allows aggregate loss distribution and associated percentiles/summary statistics to be generated for a portfolio. The approach avoids the necessity of a large simulation to produce the full loss distribution.

The distinguishing features of this approach include:

- Default rates are treated as a *continuous* variable and a volatility of default rate is used to capture the uncertainty in the level of default rates. In contrast, the rating migration approach (such as CreditMetrics[TM]) treats default as a discrete variable that is modelled using the rating transition matrix.

---

[87] See discussion earlier in the Chapter.

[88] It is often referred to as a purely actuarial model; see Crouhy, Michel, Galai, Dan, and Mark, Robert (2001) Risk Management; McGraw-Hill, New York at Chapter 10.

[89] For a detailed description, see (1997) CreditRisk+: A Credit Risk Management Framework; Credit Suisse Financial Products.

[90] In theory, the most appropriate curve should be used. The Pareto curve often works but is not always the right curve.

[91] Depending on the nature of the underlying event, insurance events can potentially happen more than once (for example, a motor accident). However, a company can typically default only once. If the probabilities are sufficiently low (which they normally are), then it does not make a significant difference.

• Default correlation is incorporated through the use of default rate
  volatility and sector volatility rather than explicit default correlation.
  This has the merit of avoiding the problems of estimation of default
  correlation. It also avoids issues such as the lack of stability of default
  correlation. It has the advantage of making it easier to perform scenario
  analysis on the default rate volatility.

The model is based on the insurance approach whereby the portfolio
consists of a large number of small risks where each risk has a low
probability of occurring. The model generates the distribution of default
events at a given time (the effective risk horizon). If the volatility of default
rates is ignored, then this distribution approximates a Poisson distribution.
The model incorporates the uncertainty of default rates by specifying a
default rate and a default rate volatility which is then used to generate a
distribution of portfolio losses. **Exhibit 6.21** sets out the typical distribution
of default and losses generated using this approach.

The distribution of losses and defaults has the same level of expected
losses but the distribution incorporating the volatility of default is skewed
with a fatter tail. The distribution of losses differs significantly from the
distribution of defaults in terms of the risk of experiencing large losses. This
reflects the variation in size of exposure. This is based on the fact that the
loss severity on a single default depends on the exposure to that obligor.
The fatter tail of the distribution also dictates that the variance of the
distribution has increased. The increase reflects the default correlation
between borrowers.

In this approach, portfolio diversification is modelled by a factor
sensitivity model whereby the default rate and volatility of default rate on an
individual borrower will reflect specific factors which, overall, explain the
volatility of default rates in the portfolio.

The model is similar to rating transition models in terms of applications.
It can be used for provisioning for credit risk, risk credit limits and credit
portfolio management[92].

Credit Suisse subsequently developed PortfolioRisk+[93]. The model
generates forward looking credit loss distributions for each component

---

[92] For a variation on the basic model which enables it to incorporate ratings
changes, see Rolfes, Bernd and Broeker, Frank "Good Migrations" (November
1998) Risk 72–73.

[93] See Patel, Navroz "PortfolioRisk+ Cracks Tail Risk Conundrum" (March
2002) Risk 10.

within the portfolio. The individual loss distributions are combined to generate a portfolio loss distribution. A technique – saddle point methodology – is used to aggregate the distributions[94]. The advantage of this approach is that a large number of non-normal distributions can be aggregated easily without the use of expensive and time consuming Monte Carlo simulations. The approach allows the construction of an accurate analytical approximation of the tail of a credit loss distribution. This also expedites calculation of marginal risk contributions of individual elements within the portfolio.

Exhibit 6.21   CreditRisk+ – Distribution of Defaults and Losses

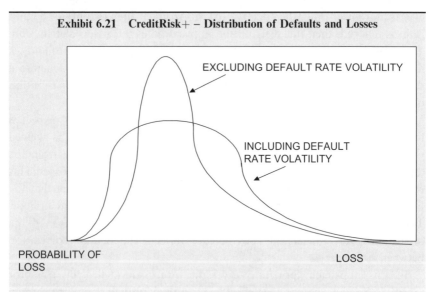

Source: (1997) CreditRisk+: A Credit Risk Management Framework; Credit Suisse Financial Products.

12.5   Credit Portfolio Management

Credit models combine loss exposure, recovery rate, default rates, default rate volatility and default correlation[95] to produce a portfolio loss distribution for the entire portfolio.

---

[94]   See Martin, Richard, Thompson, Kevin and Browne, Christopher "Taking To The Saddle" (June 2001) Risk 91– 94.

[95]   Referred to as joint default frequency ("JDF") in Moody'sKMV's EDF model.

Credit portfolio modelling is designed to provide the following information:

- Risk and capital requirements of a portfolio of credit risk.
- Identification of the level of diversification within and concentration of exposures within the portfolio (components displaying high marginal risk contributions within the portfolio).

Exhibit 6.22 sets out the typical credit loss distribution derived.

The credit loss distribution of the portfolio is used to calculate the expected and unexpected loss on the portfolio. The unexpected loss is calculated at a nominated confidence level. There are two aspects of the unexpected loss calculation that should be noted:

- The confidence level used is high (in excess of 99%). This reflects the shape of the distribution that is characterised by the not insignificant risk of large losses. This means that the difference between the 99% and 99.9% confidence level is frequently large.
- There are several measures of risk. For normally distributed returns, standard deviation is frequently used as a risk measure. For credit loss distributions, the skewed distribution and irregular credit loss tail means that percentile levels are used. The calculation of percentile levels generally requires a simulation. This is time consuming and expensive.

The expected and unexpected loss *for an individual exposure* in a portfolio is calculated as the marginal risk contribution of the exposure to the portfolio risk. This is calculated by simulating the portfolio loss distribution with and without the individual exposure. The increase in expected and unexpected loss on the portfolio is the marginal risk contribution of the individual exposure[96].

The modelling of the credit risk of the portfolio provides the following insights into the portfolio's characteristics:

- **Capital requirements** – the credit loss distributions allow the economic capital required to be held against the portfolio to be determined.

---

[96] For example, CreditMetrics[TM] allows 3 levels of marginal risk analysis:
1. Small size changes to an existing position.
2. Removal of an entire existing position.
3. Change in user defined number of positions simultaneously.

- **Concentration risk** – credit modelling of the portfolio would identify the relative diversification of the portfolio and specific concentration risks within the portfolio. **Exhibit 6.23** sets out a marginal risk analysis of a hypothetical portfolio. The analysis highlights pockets of risk concentration. Traditionally, credit risk managers have sought to control portfolio concentration by a system of credit limits (country, industry and individual obligor). The marginal risk analysis is superior to this approach. This is because credit portfolio modelling incorporates the impact of size of exposure, default probabilities, recovery rates and default correlation in determining concentration risk. In contrast, the traditional form of control is based purely on size of exposure.
- **Portfolio management** – credit modelling also provides a mechanism for understanding risk-return trade offs within the portfolio. This can be at several levels. The aggregate capital requirement of the portfolio can be related to aggregate portfolio returns. This is used to establish whether the portfolio meets overall return benchmarks. A systematic analysis of marginal risk contributions of individual obligors can also be derived. **Exhibit 6.24** sets out a comparison of size of exposure to marginal risk contribution. This allows concentration risk to be managed, accurate risk pricing and limit/portfolio management. For example, the portfolio manager may seek to reduce risk by targeting the obligors that have large marginal risk contributions to the portfolio (large exposure and high marginal risk contributions).

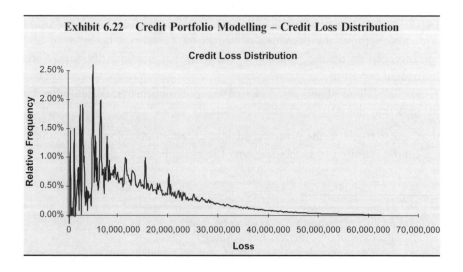

Exhibit 6.22   Credit Portfolio Modelling – Credit Loss Distribution

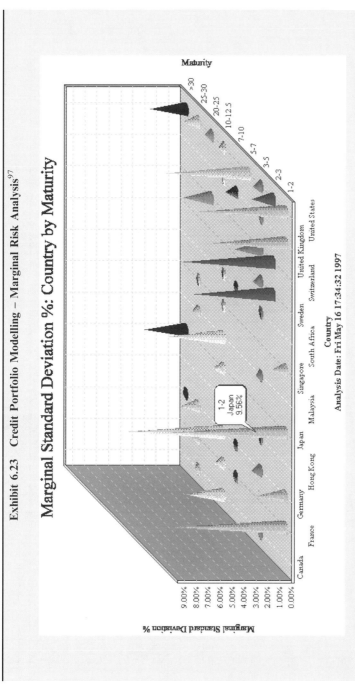

Exhibit 6.23   Credit Portfolio Modelling – Marginal Risk Analysis[97]

Marginal Standard Deviation %: Country by Maturity

Source: Gupton, Greg "CreditMetrics™ – Assessing the Marginal Risk Contribution of Credit" in Das, Satyajit (Editor) (2001) Credit Derivatives & Credit Linked Notes – 2nd Edition: John Wiley & Sons, Singapore Chapter 13 at 583.

[97]   The author would like to thank Greg Gupton and Chris Finger (RMG) for making the screen shots from CreditMetrics™ available for inclusion in the text.

Exhibit 6.24   Credit Portfolio Modelling – Marginal Risk Contribution/Size Of Exposure[98]

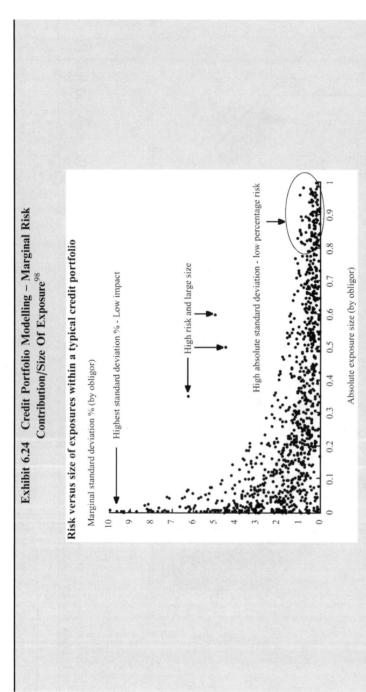

Risk versus size of exposures within a typical credit portfolio

Source: Gupton, Greg "CreditMetrics[TM] – Assessing the Marginal Risk Contribution of Credit" in Das, Satyajit (Editor) (2001) Credit Derivatives & Credit Linked Notes – 2nd Edition: John Wiley & Sons, Singapore Chapter 13 at 584.

[98]   The author would like to thank Greg Gupton and Chris Finger (RMG) for making the screen shots from CreditMetrics[TM] available for inclusion in the text.

13 Credit Modelling – Assumptions/Issues

Credit modelling is based on a number of assumptions. In practice, failure of the assumptions in real markets inevitably weakens the ability to use these models[99]. The assumptions underlying credit modelling include:

- **Market structures** – credit modelling generally assumes some approximation to perfect and efficient markets. This includes an assumption of competitive markets, no transaction costs and no taxes. For credit markets, the assumptions may be less applicable than for other asset markets. This reflects the relative lack of liquidity in trading in non-government debt. It also reflects differences in tax treatment between types of securities in a particular jurisdiction and in transactions between jurisdictions. This may imply that factors such as liquidity risk will need to be specifically encompassed in credit modelling to reduce the risk of model specification errors. The nature of asset trading in credit markets may also be significantly different. For example, the market might be more discontinuous in nature and trading might be more prone to exhibiting greater gaps/discontinuous price changes[100].

- **Data availability** – the availability of accurate data (credit spread changes, defaults, recovery rates and default correlation) is crucial to credit modelling. The relevant data is usually derived from historical information. This process is subject to considerable difficulty. The data weakness is evident at both a theoretical and practical level. At a theoretical level, these include:

    1. There is a paradox in seeking to estimate the likelihood of a particular obligor defaulting or suffering some sort of serious credit event. This is because *that particular firm has not defaulted*. This forces the use of

---

[99] For discussion about the problems of credit modelling, see Jarrow, R "Current Advances In The Modelling Of Credit Risk" (May/June 1998) Journal of Derivatives Taxation & Regulation 196–200; Maurer, Frantz and Pourquery, Pierre "Model Error For Credit Risk" (December 2000) FOW 36–45. See also "Round Table Discussion – Credit Risk" (November 1998) Middle Office III–XV; "The Crisis in Credit Modelling" (1998) Derivatives Strategy 29–34; "Why We Missed The Asian Meltdown" (1998) Derivatives Strategy 16–21; "Modelling Asia: A Roundtable" (1998) Derivatives Strategy 21–23.

[100] For example see Krakovsky, Andrey "Gap Risk In Credit Trading" (March 1999) Risk 65–67.

analogous firms (classified by factors such as ratings levels) to *infer* the default probabilities and recovery rates of the relevant obligor.

2. The difficulty of finding a *representative firm* is significant. This requirement is driven by the need to identify a representative or analogous firm that *has* suffered the credit event to allow derivation through a process of analogy of the data parameters needed. The difficulty is that such a representative firm may not be readily available. Even if available, the firm may not be a very good approximation of the firm whose default risk is being considered. This merely restates that the systematic risk component of credit risk (the component driven by *market wide factors*) is lower than the unsystematic risk component (the component driven by *obligor specific factors*).

The theoretical difficulties make it difficult to apply traditional procedures used in modelling the price behaviour of financial prices (in interest rate, currency, equity and commodity prices) to combine historical and implicit estimation techniques and to calibrate results. Traditional approaches in these markets derive historical estimates based on past price observations that are then calibrated using market prices (implicit estimation or calibration being used to solve for the parameters that equate model price and market prices). At a practical level, the difficulties include:

1. Sample sizes are generally small for default data (particularly at higher credit quality levels).

2. The data samples have inherent geographic biases. The ratings data has historically been skewed in favour of the rated US market. Foreign issuers, as a percentage of Moody's rated universe, constituted only 15% at January 1930 and 18% at January 1990, rising to 35% in 1997[101].

3. The non-stationary nature of many of the estimates (default rates, recovery rates, default correlation) is also problematic. Similarly, the skewed and asymmetric nature of the distribution of these variables, as well as the large standard errors in many of these estimates, creates problems in credit modelling.

---

[101]   See Scott-Quinn, Brian and Walmsley, Julian K. (1998) The Impact of Credit Derivatives On Securities Markets; ISMA, Zurich, Switzerland at 54–55.

The problems identified are even more acute in the case of obligors whose debt is *not publicly traded*. These entities require the use of further inferential techniques to derive estimates that may introduce further errors in the modelling process. Given that the universe of traded obligations of non-government obligors with a large and liquid market in their obligations is small, these data problems are formidable.

- **Numerical implementation** – the numerical implementations of the models are considerable. This complexity derives from the large number of factors, multiple term structures and complex cross correlation (that is, they are typically high dimensional problems). In practice, tree structures (generally non recombinant), implicit and explicit difference models involving the solution of partial differential equations or Monte Carlo simulation techniques are used. The procedure adopted is used to generate a distribution for future cash flows from which the default expectation is inferred. The large scale computational requirements dictate that reduced forms of the models are the only forms that are practical. This introduces a different level of model risk into the process of credit modelling[102].

- **Model validation**[103] – credit models are inherently difficult to validate. For example, market risk models are generally validated through a process of back testing against historical data[104]. This method of back testing is impractical for credit models because default is an infrequent event. The amount of data required to validate credit models is generally not available[105]. This means that model validation relies on other approaches, including:

  1. Reduced form models can be validated by calibrating them to market information (for example, the term structure of credit spreads).

[102] For examples of modelling currently in use by practitioners, see Browne, Christopher, Gregory, Jon, and Martin, Richard "A Credit Risk Toolbox" (December 1998) Risk 50–55.

[103] See Crouhy, Michel, Galai, Dan, and Mark, Robert (2001) Risk Management; McGraw-Hill, New York Chapter 11 at 436–438.

[104] See Das, Satyajit (Editor) (2001) Credit Derivatives And Credit Linked Notes – Second Edition; John Wiley & Sons, Singapore at Chapter 18.

[105] Validation of a credit model based on a 1 year time horizon at 99% confidence level would require 100 years of data; Crouhy, Michel, Galai, Dan, and Mark, Robert (2001) Risk Management; McGraw-Hill, New York Chapter 11 at 439.

2. Models can be tested against cumulative profit and loss of banks[106].
3. Indirect testing by validation of the input (such as default rates) may also be possible.
4. Stress testing to see model performance under abnormal conditions.
5. An emerging trend is for predictive statistical models of credit risk to be validated using the sort of walk forward approach traditionally used to test trading rules[107].

There has been limited work done to date to examine the performance of the credit models identified in order to establish the empirical validity of the models themselves.

There are a number of issues in the management of default risk and modelling credit risk. They include the impact of credit enhancement. The discussion to date assumes that the loss exposure is *clean*; that is, it is not subject to any enhancement. In reality, credit exposures are increasingly enhanced through a variety of measures including:

- Collateralisation.
- Netting of exposures.
- Other techniques, including re-couponing, credit puts, right to break or termination on downgrade provisions[108].

In addition, default exposure may (in theory) be affected by the correlation between market risk factors (embedded in a single transaction), default risk, loss exposure[109] and default correlation.

Credit enhancement would generally lower default losses and alter the exposure. Similarly, the correlation may increase or reduce exposures.

---

[106] See Crouhy, Michel, Galai, Dan, and Mark, Robert (2001) Risk Management; McGraw-Hill, New York, Chapter 6.

[107] See Sobehart, J. R., S.C. Keenan and R.M. Stein (March 2000) "Benchmarking Quantitative Risk Models: A Validation Methodology" Moody's Investors Service; New York (http://riskcalc.moodysrms.com/us/research/crm/53621.asp).

[108] See Das, Satyajit (Editor) (2001) Credit Derivatives And Credit Linked Notes – Second Edition; John Wiley & Sons, Singapore at Chapters 21 and 22.

[109] Anecdotal evidence suggests that lower rated credits make up a significant portion of the payers on fixed rate in interest rate swaps. These entities are more vulnerable to default in a high interest rate environment. However, higher rates equate to low or zero loss exposure under the contract. Therefore, the interaction of market and default risk should reduce the default cost.

In practice, the impact of credit enhancement and *all* the potential correlation is difficult.

Credit modelling must adequately capture the interaction of complex and interdependent variables. The practical econometrics of modelling and estimating the required variables is considerable. Even where the estimates can be generated, the attendant assumptions are difficult to validate. These factors also vary significantly between different segments of the market, such as the investment grade market, the high yield segment, distressed loan assets and emerging market credits.

These factors dictate that the process of credit modelling is at an early stage. Increasing sophistication in modelling is becoming evident. In practice, credit models work better at a portfolio level. These models are less useful for individual risk modelling in terms of marginal contribution for risk.

14 Credit Derivative Pricing and Credit Modelling – Interaction

Credit derivatives are generally priced off the cash market price of credit assets (primarily bonds in the form of asset swaps). Credit derivative pricing takes the market price of assets as a given and derives the derivative value through a process of replication. Credit modelling uses estimates of loss exposure, recovery rates, default rates, default rate volatility and default correlation to derive the loss distribution of a portfolio of transactions. This allows the capital required to be held against the portfolio, and the return required to compensate for the capital held, to be estimated. Individual transactions are assessed on the basis of the marginal risk contribution of each position to the overall risk of the portfolio.

There are a number of issues relating to the two approaches, including:

- Credit derivatives pricing using replication will generally yield a *single* price. The market price will trade close to, though not exactly at, this level (for example, the impact of the cash-credit default swap basis). This is reinforced by the ability of traders to arbitrage price differences.
- Credit modelling will yield a capital charge (in effect, the price of credit risk) for an individual firm that varies from portfolio to portfolio. This is because the capital charges are driven by the marginal risk contribution of an individual position *to the portfolio*. In effect, the capital charge is driven by the structure of the portfolio, including other positions in the

portfolio, the size of the individual exposure and default correlation between exposures. If the level of risk concentration to an individual firm is high, then the capital charge will correspondingly increase. Similarly, if the portfolio has existing high levels of exposure to related firms, industries or countries (positive default correlation), then the capital charge will be higher. This means that the cost of credit (and the corresponding price of credit) will vary significantly between entities.

The market price of credit risk (from the cash or credit derivatives market) and the portfolio charge for credit interact in the following way:

- The portfolio charge for credit relative to the market price of credit will drive the evolution of credit prices. The market price will be the price at which the supply and demand for an individual firm clears.
- Activity in the credit derivative market will be driven by the interaction of the portfolio credit charge/price and the market credit price. In cases where there is a large concentration risk on an individual firm within a portfolio, then the credit charge will potentially exceed the market credit price. This will tend to drive risk managers to purchase protection on the firm to reduce risk within the portfolio. It will also improve the portfolio's risk return performance. Where the portfolio has little or no exposure to the relevant firm, the capital charge within the portfolio will be potentially lower than the market price. This should encourage acquiring credit risk exposure to the firm (for example, through the sale of protection)[110].

---

[110] For discussion of implementation of credit portfolio management in banks, see Lowe, Diana "Concentrating On Credit" (August 1999) Asia Risk 29–32; Lowe, Diana "Pushing Progress In The Credit Process" (October 1999) Asia Risk 28–31; Bedser, Geoff "Indecent Exposure" (October 1999) Risk 28–31; Travers, Paul and Heydenrych, David "Grappling With Credit Risk" (February 2000) Asia Risk 34–35; Keen, Matthew "Two Of A Perfect Pair" (November 2000) FOW 48–53; Aguais, Scott "Credit Risk: Time For Enterprising Management" (April 2001) FOW 49–53; Lee, Peter "Will New Portfolio Managers Save The Banks This Time" (December 2001) Euromoney 44–48; Evans, Jules "Credit Risk And Its Management Raise A Paradox" (March 2002) Euromoney 52–54. For an example, see McNee, Alan "UBS Takes A New Look At Lending" (March 2000) Risk 30–31.

15 Summary

Credit derivatives pricing is based on a replication/arbitrage free pricing approach. In practice, the pricing of credit derivatives is driven off the pricing of debt securities in capital markets (generally the asset swap market). This reflects the necessity of hedging, valuation and price discovery in the spot market. Credit modelling/credit portfolio management is focused on the pricing of credit risk, generally within a portfolio context. This activity is focused on establishing the expected and unexpected credit losses on a portfolio and the amount of capital that must be held against that risk. It is also focused on the return required to compensate for the assumed risk.

Credit modelling is rapidly developing. Increasing research on default risk pricing by academic researchers is increasing the sophistication of credit risk modelling. However, the difficulties of parameter estimation, the instability of relationships, and the problems of efficient numerical implementation, are still formidable. One of the collateral benefits of this increased rigour in the pricing of default risk is that the modelling should ultimately improve the understanding of pricing and management of credit risk in financial services more broadly. Credit derivatives have significantly advanced the measurement and quantification of credit exposures and the return required to compensate for the risk assumed.

7

Credit Derivative Applications

1 Overview

Credit derivatives (including credit linked notes, collateralised debt obligations ("CDOs") and structured credit products) have emerged as an interesting technique for managing credit risk. Credit derivative instruments have also emerged as a mechanism for acquiring/investing in credit risk. In this Chapter, the applications of credit derivatives are described.

The structure of the Chapter is as follows:

- The application opportunities for credit derivatives are considered.
- Specific examples of applications of credit derivatives are described. Applications for banks/financial institutions, investors and corporations are covered. Trading applications are also discussed.

2 Credit Derivatives – Application Opportunities[1]

2.1 Key Drivers

The volume of credit risk within capital markets is very large. The total volume of outstanding bonds and loan transactions undertaken in international markets is in the order of several trillion dollars. In addition,

---

[1] For discussion of applications of credit derivatives, see Gontarek, Walter "Hedging With Credit Derivatives: Practical Applications and Considerations" in (1998) Credit Derivatives: Applications for Risk Management, Investment and Portfolio Optimisation; Risk Books, London at Chapter 2; Tavakoli, Janet M. (1998) Credit Derivatives: A Guide To Instruments And Applications; John Wiley & Sons, Inc., New York; Francis, Jack Clark, Frost, Joyce A., and Whittaker, J. Gregg (Editors) (1999) The Handbook of Credit Derivatives; McGraw-Hill, New York; Nelken, Dr. Israel (1999) Implementing Credit Derivatives; McGraw-Hill, New York; (1999) The JP Morgan Guide To Credit

there is a substantial volume of counterparty credit risk arising from derivative transactions and other off-balance-sheet instruments. There is also substantial credit risk assumed in dealings between non-financial institutions in normal trading operations. This relates to the credit risk in trade receivables, vendor financing, supply and purchase contracts, insurance arrangements, employee share acquisition schemes on a deferred payment basis, and contract prepayments.

Credit risk has historically been regarded as illiquid. The applications of credit derivatives are focused on isolating or unbundling the credit risk (effectively the risk of value changes driven by changes in credit quality) from other risks. The credit risk is structured in a format that allows the risks to be traded in capital markets. This is to facilitate reduction of credit risk through hedging, assumption of credit risk, and trading in credit risk as appropriate.

The application of credit derivatives is predicated on a shift in the *approach* to the management of credit risk. Traditionally, credit risk has been regarded as static in nature. The process of credit risk management has focused on assessing credit risk and matching it with capital or provisions to cover expected losses from default. The principal management techniques

---

Derivatives; Risk Publications, London; Gontarek, Walter "Today's Credit Derivatives Market" in Storrow, Jamie (1999) Credit Derivatives: Key Issues – 2nd Edition; British Bankers' Association, London at Chapter 2; Reoch, Robert "An Introduction To Credit Derivatives" in Storrow, Jamie (1999) Credit Derivatives: Key Issues – 2nd Edition; British Bankers' Association, London at Chapter 3; Tavakoli, Janet M. (2001) Credit Derivatives And Synthetic Structures – Second Edition; John Wiley & Sons, Inc., New York; Das, Satyajit (Editor) (2001) Credit Derivatives And Credit Linked Notes – Second Edition; John Wiley & Sons, Singapore. See also Reoch, Rob and Masters, Blythe "Credit Swaps: An Innovation In Negotiable Exposure" (1995) Capital Market Strategies 7 3–8; Smithson, Charles with Holappa, Hal "Credit Derivatives" (December 1995) Risk vol 8 no 12 38–39; Whittaker, Greg J. and Kumar, Sumita "Credit Derivatives: A Primer" in Konishi, Atsuo and Dattatreya, Ravi (Ed) "The Handbook of Derivative Instruments" (Irwin Publishing, 1996) 595–614; Reoch, Rob "Credit Derivatives And Applications" (March 1996) Financial Derivatives and Risk Management 5 4–10; Theodore, Samuel S and Madelain, Michael "Modern Credit Risk Management and The Use of Credit Derivatives: European Banks' Brave New World (And Its Limits)" (March 1997) Moody's Investors Service- Global Credit Research); Rai, Shaun, Hatstadt, Philippe, Gill, Ala, and Minton, Lyle "Using Credit Swaps To Enhance Credit Portfolio Management" (July 1997) Risk Credit Risk Supplement – Sponsorship Statement.

have been diversification of the credit risk and the use of credit enhancement (for example, collateral) to manage the credit risk incurred.

Credit derivatives allow credit risk to be viewed as a commodity separate from other risks such as interest rate or currency risk. The risk is then capable of being managed dynamically through hedging techniques previously associated with market risk.

The primary advantages of the new approach to the management of credit risk include:

- Credit derivatives increase the liquidity of credit risk and reduce transaction costs and market friction in hedging and trading in credit risk.
- Credit derivatives complete the separation of credit origination and credit investment, increasing opportunities to both diversify credit risk and to assume credit risk. This is done in a format that allows the creation of risk profiles not directly available, or allowing access to credit risk that is traditionally inaccessible for some investors.
- Credit derivatives allow the structuring of credit risk that is not available directly in the market.
- Credit derivatives allow trading in credit risk including arbitrage between different markets (cash/physical versus synthetic) or elements of the capital structure (senior debt versus subordinated debt; debt versus equity).

These factors allow credit derivatives to be used to achieve the following objectives:

- **Hedging credit risk** – this is focused on transferring credit risk. This may be driven by concentration of exposure to a single entity, industry or country. It may also be driven by concern about potential deterioration of the credit quality of the firm or industry.
- **Enhance diversification** – this is focused on the diversification of credit portfolios. This increases efficiency and optimises the risk return performance. It allows reduction in risk exposures to certain firms to whom the lender is over exposed. It simultaneously allows increasing exposure to firms to whom the lender has no or low level of exposure. Credit derivatives may also allow investors to access credit risks that have traditionally been difficult to access.
- **Attract new investment to credit risk** – this is focused on transferring credit risk to investors. Credit derivatives allow a broad range of investors to assume credit risk. It also facilitates investors assuming credit risk to which they previously had no, limited or expensive access.

This assists in broadening the range of institutions that can commit capital to assume credit risk in capital markets[2].

- **Monetisation/trading** – this is focused on trading opportunities. It includes trading expectations of credit pricing or anomalies of credit risk pricing. Forward credit spreads and default risk probabilities are implied by the market price of traded instruments. The forward credit risk parameters imply trading opportunities. There may be inconsistencies in the pricing of credit risk for *the same issuer* (that is, different instruments issued by the same issuer may trade at different prices, implying different credit risks) or for *similar issuers of comparable credit risk*. This may allow trading positions to be created and traded. The implied forward credit spreads or default probabilities may not accord with an investor's expectations, allowing monetisation of the view that *actual credit risk* will vary from the implied forward credit risk[3]. It can also focus on trading between different instruments affected by credit risk. It can also focus on trading aspects of credit risk (default correlation and recovery rate).

The applications of credit derivatives entail using credit derivative structures to create mechanisms to either transfer credit risk or create customised risk-reward profiles. The application opportunities are focused around a number of key dimensions:

- Modification of the credit risk available for investment or trading, including:
  1. Types of credit risk available.
  2. Seniority or credit quality of available risk.
  3. Enhancing the available term structure or currency of credit risk.

---

[2] An example of a market that has traditionally been difficult to access and invest in for institutional investors is the loan market. For discussion of the role of credit derivatives in facilitating access to this market, see Culp, Christopher L. and Neves, Andrea M.P. "Financial Innovations In Leveraged Commercial Loan Markets" (Summer 1998) Journal of Applied Corporate Finance vol 11 no 279–93; Barnish, Keith, Miller, Steve, and Rushmore, Michael "The New Leveraged Loan Syndication Market" (Spring 1997) Journal of Applied Corporate Finance vol 10 no 1 79–88; Mahtani, Arun "Synthetic Structures Facilitate Leveraged Loan Boom" (28 November 1998) International Financing Review Issue 1261 85.

[3] This is conceptually no different to monetisation of expectations that actual spot currency or interest rates will differ from implied forward currency and interest rates.

- Allowing creation of structured exposure profiles and trading in dimensions not available in the cash market, including:
  1. Default correlation.
  2. Recovery rates upon default or loss given default.
  3. Differentiation of relative default risk on different classes of obligations.
  4. Volatility of credit risk and credit pricing.
- Allowing assumption of credit exposure within a framework of structural flexibility.

2.2 Application Opportunities – Credit Risk Structures

Credit derivative structures generally allow flexibility in the creation of different types of credit exposure or particular trading opportunities in credit. The opportunities may not be directly available in the cash or physical market. In effect, the credit derivative structure overcomes the restriction on investment choice or trading resulting from the limited universe of available securities in the cash or physical market.

This affects investment choice. It also affects the ability to transfer or hedge credit risk. In practice, prior to the development of credit derivatives, a bank could not hedge credit exposure without selling or transferring the loan asset. This was difficult (for example, requiring the borrower to consent) and also incurred high transaction costs (including documentation costs). Credit derivative instruments generally avoid the necessity of trading the underlying credit risk directly. This facilitates both hedging and investment.

There are restrictions in the range of available credit assets in any market. The choice of risk in physical bonds/loans is usually delineated by two factors:

- Choice of credit rating or credit quality.
- Seniority or type of obligation.

In practice, there are further constraints in terms of the format of the credit risk. For example, for an investor, the predominant form of credit risk has historically been a bond that is eligible for investment by and capable of sale to the investor. This greatly limits the range of available investments.

Credit derivatives enhance the range of investments for investors, enabling them to access credit assets such as loans or other types of non-traded credit risk. It also enables holders of credit risk to synthetically transfer or hedge credit risk.

Traditional credit markets are also generally difficult to short. This means that investors are limited to be long (exposed to) or flat (no exposure to) credit risk. Credit derivatives allow investors to short credit more readily than traditional credit markets.

Credit derivative technology allows the creation of synthetic credit risk that may not be directly available in the market. This facilitates the flexible assumption of structured credit risks. Examples include:

- **Tranched risk** – an investor may seek to synthetically change the credit quality of its investments. This may be done by taking a single credit or a portfolio and tranching the risk[4]. This can be used to reduce risk or increase risk. The technique allows investors to increase or decrease risk through risk leverage. For example, risk and return may be increased by assuming the risk to the first or second loss on the portfolio of assets. Conversely, purchasing protection on the first or second loss on the portfolio can reduce risk and return. This is valuable in markets where there may be no non-investment grade issuers or high quality issuers. It allows investors to optimise their investments. The tranching also allows the transfer of risk more efficiently and (usually) at a lower cost to the originator. This is because the structure allows supply and demand for each credit risk segment to be precisely matched, increasing pricing efficiency.
- **Seniority Choices** – assume a bank or investor has purchased a loan asset that is a senior obligation of the issuer. In order to increase returns from the investment, it can sell default protection on *subordinated or junior* obligations of the same issuer to alter its risk profile without the necessity of trading in the underlying asset. Alternatively, holders of a subordinated obligation can, through the simultaneous purchase of protection on subordinated obligations and the sale of protection on senior obligations of the issuer, alter their risk within the capital structure. For example, a number of transactions involving convertible preferred shares have been completed where the subordinated nature of the obligations precluded purchase of the securities by some banks and investors. The investments combined with the credit default swaps

---

[4] See Chapter 2 and 4.

produced returns that, even after adjustment for the cost of the conversion in seniority status, provided attractive returns relative to other available fixed interest senior obligations[5].

- **Static Versus Non Static Exposures** – assume a bank is seeking protection on credit exposures under existing derivative transactions with a client. Movements in interest and currency rates have meant that the credit exposure on the transactions has increased to levels in excess of prudential levels. Another bank may offer to sell protection through a credit default swap on the market credit exposure on the derivatives. The rationale of the bank selling the exposure is that the projected exposure on the portfolio, based on its projected exposure of currency and interest rates, is lower than current exposure levels. Given that the bank seeking protection is prepared to pay fees based on higher levels of assumed credit exposure than that anticipated by the second bank, the latter is prepared to assume the exposure, as it believes that it can effectively generate economic profits based on its expectations[6].

- **First-to-Default Baskets** – an investor can create simultaneous exposure to multiple credits by assuming the credit exposure to a basket of reference issuers under a first-to-default structure where it will be required to make a default payment where *any* of the underlying credits defaults[7]. This structure entails an increase in the credit risk to the investor assuming the risk of default, as the credit risk of the first-to-default structure is higher than the individual credits. The higher risk is compensated by a higher return to the investor. In effect, the structure allows trading in default correlation. This specific form of exposure is unavailable in the physical market and can only be created synthetically through credit derivatives.

- **Ratings Protection** – an investor, subject to a minimum credit rating investment constraint, can use credit derivatives to achieve its investment objectives. Assume the investor has a minimum rating constraint of investment grade (BBB−/Baa−). Assume it seeks to purchase the following securities:
  - Issuer A who is BBB− rated (therefore eligible but a downgrade would require liquidation of the investment).

---

[5]   See zero recovery credit default swaps in Chapter 2.
[6]   See Chapters 2 and 4.
[7]   See Chapter 2.

- Issuer B who is BB rated (therefore ineligible).

  The investor seeks to invest in both securities for normal investment reasons, including diversification of industry/issuer risk and perceived attractive returns relative to risk. There are two possible means to structure the investments:

  1. The investor purchases Issuer A's securities while simultaneously purchasing protection through a credit default swap that is triggered on a downgrade, allowing the investor to sell the security at a pre-agreed price. This allows the investor, in return for the cost of purchasing the downgrade protection, to lower its risk of selling the security following the fall in credit rating. The availability of the downgrade protection may allow the investor to purchase these types of securities (close to its credit constraints), rather than avoid such investments to minimise the price risk on a sale after downgrade. The latter problem entails many investors pursuing a policy of only purchasing securities at a rating level well above their minimum criteria (referred to as a *credit gap* or *ratings cushion*) that results in a reduction in returns on the investment portfolio[8].

  2. The investor purchases Issuer B's securities while simultaneously purchasing a credit default swap on Issuer B from a counterparty (within its acceptable credit criteria). This structure allows the investor to acquire assets that would otherwise be unavailable to it. This may be important in allowing investors to participate in certain industry sectors (for example, airlines) where the industry rating average would preclude investment.

  The capacity to customise credit risk allows access to investments that would otherwise be difficult for investors.

Each of the examples discussed highlights the capacity to construct customised exposure to credit risks that are generally not directly available in the market.

2.3 Application Opportunities – Term Structure/Currency

Credit derivatives fundamentally allow the separation of the term or maturity for which credit risk is assumed from the term of *the underlying*

---

[8] In practice, this may be difficult as rating downgrade is rarely used as a credit event in a credit default swap transaction.

credit asset. It also increasingly allows transformation of the currency risk of the cash or physical asset or credit risk.

Bonds or loans have a fixed relationship between the term of the transaction and the term of the credit risk. The disaggregation of risk underlying credit derivatives allows the construction of synthetic maturity credit investments. This has the impact of removing the inherent constraint on an investor that its management of the credit risk of a portfolio is linked to the term of *available* instruments. This allows the following:

- Expression of views on credit sensitive assets for maturities that are different from the maturity of the referenced assets.
- Construction of a complete credit risk term structure.

The application of this concept can be illustrated with the following examples:

- **Specific Credit Duration** – assume an investor is seeking to acquire credit exposure to a particular issuer for a term of 2 years. The maturity is dictated by available credit lines. The issuer in question has no 2 year securities outstanding. The issuer has longer term (say, 5 years or more in remaining maturity) securities outstanding. The investor could acquire the credit exposure it requires by investing in a structured note, where the default risk of the 2 year security is linked to the default risk on the available longer term securities of the target issuer. The investor selling protection under a credit default swap on the relevant issuer for 2 years would achieve a similar result. This structure allows the investor to overcome the lack of availability of the required assets.
- **Forward Start Credit Derivatives** – assume an investor has no term credit lines available to a particular issuer. This reflects that its term credit lines (up to 5 years) are currently being used by existing bonds/loans that mature after 18 months. This use of the credit lines represents a sub-optimal use of credit capital. This is because the returns being obtained against the capital committed reflect the shorter maturity of the credit asset. The available credit capacity is not *fully* utilised. There is a forward gap in utilisation of this line from 18 months to 5 years. In order to optimise the use of its credit capital, the bank or investor can enter into a transaction entailing the sale of credit protection for a period of 3.5 years *commencing in 18 months time* (a forward credit default swap). The transaction would fully utilise the credit capital available. Depending on the pricing of the forward credit

default swap, the transaction may boost the returns on capital over the full term of the transaction.

- **Structured Term Exposure** – an investor willing to assume credit exposure to a particular issuer may only be willing to do so at an increasing cost as the maturity of the risk increases. This can be designed as a structured note where the principal redemption is linked to the default of the reference issuer. The note pays a coupon that increases after an initial period if the note is not called at the end of the period. The note would operate in the following manner. If the credit risk of the issuer improves or if the note issuer's requirement for default risk protection decreases, then the issuer will call the note. If the note issuer still requires default protection at the call date, then it does not call the note but pays the higher coupon rate. The investor in the note will continue to bear the risk of default in the event of the call not being exercised, but will be compensated at a higher rate that presumably adequately covers any risk of loss from default.

The underlying asset or credit risk is generally in a specific currency. The investor may not want the credit risk in that currency. This may be driven by currency risk considerations. In the cash or physical market, the currency risk is difficult to unbundle from the asset. It can be hedged using currency and/or interest rate hedges. Under the hedge, the investor is exposed to the credit contingent mark-to-market or unwind risk on the hedge[9]. Increasingly, quanto credit default swaps (either directly or embedded in a credit linked note or CDO) are used to separate the credit and currency risk[10].

2.4 Application Opportunities – Default Correlation/Recovery Rate Structures

Credit derivatives allow trading in default correlation and recovery rates or loss given default. It is difficult to trade these risk dimensions in the cash market.

Credit derivatives instruments such as tranched CDOs and n^{th}-to-default baskets allow trading in default correlation. Investors in different layers of risk have different exposures to the behaviour of default correlation in the

---

[9]   For a discussion of credit contingent currency risk, see O'Kane, Dominic and Schloegl, Lutz "Cross Currency Credit Explained" (14 May 2002) Lehman Brothers Quantitative Credit Research 53–67.

[10] See Chapter 2.

market[11]. These structures also allow holders of credit portfolios (banks and large credit investors) to monetise *existing* default correlation positions.

Credit derivatives facilitate trading in expectations of recovery rates upon default. The bank or investor providing protection has considerable structural flexibility in nominating the payout due in the event of default, including:

- Cash settlement based on a dealer poll of the post default value of the security.
- Cash settlement based on a pre-agreed payout amount (say, 40–60%) of the nominal face value of the transaction[12].
- Physical delivery of the defaulted securities in exchange for receipt of face value of the transaction.

The availability of the options allows the default payout to be structured to allow the bank or investor to vary the risk reward profile. This facilitates the following types of trading opportunity:

- Selling default protection at recovery levels that are lower than expected recovery rates to allow creation of value through assumption of risks considered unlikely.
- Trading credit risk to maximise return on credit capital allocated to credit risk by using default swaps to adjust expected loss rates on portfolios of credit assets.

Exhibit 7.1 sets out an example of trading in recovery rate risk. Trading recovery rate expectations is only feasible through credit derivatives. This reflects the capacity to isolate the separate aspects of credit risk through credit derivatives.

Exhibit 7.1 Trading Recovery Rates

Assume Bank A is willing to take senior unsecured credit exposure on Company X at a credit spread of 80 bps pa. It expects that in the event of default, the expected loss rate will be 50% of notional value (that is, recovery rate of 50%). Assume another bank (Bank B) prices the equivalent exposure to Company X at the same spread

---

[11] See discussion in Chapters 2, 4 and 6.
[12] For examples of 100% payouts see discussion of zero recovery credit default swaps in Chapter 2.

level. Bank B estimates that in the event of default, its loss rate will be 40% (recovery rate of 60%). The two banks' *pricing* of the credit risk is identical although their *recovery rate expectations* are different.

The difference in recovery rate expectations allows the construction of a credit default swap predicated on the differential recovery rates. Under the proposed transaction, Bank A should rationally be willing to sell a default swap to Bank B on the following terms:

- Bank A will pay a fixed amount in the event of the default of Company X.
- The fixed amount payable will be 50% (that is, the fixed payout option is selected rather than a variable payout option dependent upon the price performance of the defaulted security).

The price paid by Bank B for the purchase of this protection should be 100 bps pa. This is calculated as follows:

$$\text{Credit Spread} \times \text{Loss Rate Assumed by Bank A/Loss Rate Assumed} \\ \text{by Bank B} = 80\,\text{bps pa} \times 50\%/40\% = 100\,\text{bps}$$

Bank A is prepared to sell protection at a return equal to or greater than 80 bps pa. This is because it produces an equivalent or higher return from holding the asset or providing protection under a credit default swap with a variable payout dependent on the actual market recovery rate based on the price of the defaulted security. Bank B should be prepared to pay this amount for the default protection as the default swap offers protection at a higher level than the Bank would receive based on its recovery rate expectations. This would be the case whether the Bank held the credit risk directly or by providing protection under a credit default swap with a variable payout dependent on the price performance of the defaulted security. A transaction between the banks at anywhere between 80 bps pa and 100 bps pa would effectively benefit both counterparties based on individual recovery rate expectations[13].

2.5 Application Opportunities – Structural Flexibility

Credit derivatives provide considerable structural flexibility. These include:

- **Ease in creation of position** – this allows the creation of synthetic credit assets (total return swaps) or credit risk attributes (credit spread or default risk products) on an off-balance-sheet basis without the necessity of trading in the underlying credit markets. This includes the creation of positions not directly available in the credit markets.

---

[13] This transaction is hypothetical and designed to illustrate the opportunity to monetise views on recovery rates. In reality, such structures are difficult to trade because of bid-offer spreads.

- **Capacity to short credit risk** – this allows banks and investors to effectively short sell credit assets. This may be difficult to achieve through direct trading in credit assets. This is, of course, fundamental to being able to hedge existing credit portfolios.
- **Liquidity benefits** – this facilitates trading in credit risk with lower transaction costs and market friction because of the off-balance-sheet form of the instruments.
- **Ease of administration** – this allows investors other than banks to participate synthetically in loan transactions. Credit spread structures allow monetisation of credit spread expectations without the need to trade in the underlying assets. Credit default swaps facilitate the assumption of pure default risk without the need to trade the securities of the reference credit. The synthetic structure allows the separation of credit origination and credit/facilities administration from the credit risk investment itself[14].

2.6   Types of Applications

The major types of applications involving credit derivatives within the identified framework focus on:

- **Credit risk management** – this entails either the transfer of credit risk to reduce the entity's exposure to a particular counterparty. For banks/ financial institutions, it entails the use of the instruments to manage the credit risk of portfolios, reduce risk concentrations, increase portfolio diversification and enhance the risk return characteristics of the portfolio. For non-financial institutions, it entails the ability to isolate and reduce credit exposures incidental to the primary operating activities of the entity. This includes trade receivables and vendor financing. The exposure may be to individual entities or to a geographic region or industry sector. The exposure may arise from the normal course of trading or from a specific project. It will also entail the management of the cost of funding of the entity through the use of credit derivatives to manage new issue credit spreads.
- **Synthetic credit investment** – this entails the use of credit derivatives to synthesise credit assets. This is designed to create credit assets that are not directly available in the market. For banks/financial institutions,

---

[14] See discussion in Chapter 8.

the synthetic assets are substitutes for loans. For investors, the synthetic assets are substitutes for bonds and other tradeable securities.

- **Yield enhancement/Trading** – this focuses on trading and arbitrage in credit markets using credit derivatives. It may take the form of trading expectations about credit risk attributes (credit spreads or default risk) and monetisation of these expectations. This can be done in derivative format off balance sheet or in the form of structured notes. The use of structured notes can allow the gains from the monetisation of these credit risk expectations to be incorporated in the yield or return of the fixed income securities, thereby enhancing portfolio returns. In this context, the investor is allowed access to credit risk in isolation from other risks for the purpose of trading/positioning. This type of activity also increasingly focuses on credit arbitrage. This entails trading the relative value of different types of credit risk (for example, the term structure of credit spreads or different classes of debt) and pricing differences between the cash and synthetic credit markets. It also includes capital structure arbitrage transactions that are focused on differences in valuation of different components of the capital structure of an entity. It also focuses on trading credit market volatility.

Exhibit 7.2 sets out the type of application analysed by user group.

Exhibit 7.2   Credit Derivatives – Types of Applications

Type Of User	Type Of Application
Banks/Financial Institutions	• Credit risk management • Credit portfolio management • Synthetic credit investment • Yield enhancement/Trading[15]
Fixed Income Investors	• Synthetic credit investment • Yield enhancement/Trading
Corporations	• Credit risk management • Management of financing costs

---

[15] Trading in credit markets is covered in the Section on credit derivative applications for fixed income investors. This is despite the fact that both banks/financial institutions and investors (including leveraged investors such as hedge funds) undertake these activities. In these transactions, banks/financial institutions are undertaking proprietary trading activities and are acting as investors risking their own capital.

3   Credit Derivatives – Bank/Financial Institution Applications

3.1   Overview

Applications of credit derivatives by banks/dealers are substantially driven by credit portfolios and client activity[16]. The key areas of activity include:

- **Credit portfolio management** – this is focused on the reduction or acquisition of exposures to individual firms, industries or countries. This entails activity in single name and portfolio based credit derivatives. It is focused on shedding or acquiring credit risk on specific reference entities with a view to improving the risk/return profile of the overall credit portfolio. A key element of this activity includes arbitrage of regulatory credit capital requirements. This is motivated by the desire to align economic capital and regulatory capital required to be held against credit portfolios.
- **Client driven** – this is focused on structuring credit derivatives transactions for clients (other banks, investors and non-financial corporations). It may involve the creation of synthetic forms of credit risk and/or financing/leveraged trades.

Commercial banks or banks with substantial credit portfolios are focused on the use of credit derivatives to manage credit portfolios. Investment banks/dealers are focused on client driven activities.

3.2   Management of Concentration Risk In Credit Portfolios

3.2.1   Concept

A key element of bank/financial institution activity is the use of credit derivatives to manage concentration risk within credit portfolios.

The concept of concentration risk focuses on the additional risk of credit losses in portfolios of credit assets where the portfolios of credit risk are not well diversified. Under portfolio theory, where default correlation between individual obligors is imperfect, a credit portfolio will show reduction in risk

---

[16] See Gontarek, Walter "Hedging With Credit Derivatives: Practical Applications and Considerations" in (1998) Credit Derivatives: Applications for Risk Management, Investment and Portfolio Optimisation; Risk Books, London at Chapter 2; Tierney, John and Misra, Rajeev "The Driving Force Of Credit" (March 2001) Risk – Credit Risk Special Report S22–S24; Gontarek, Walter and Nowell, Peter "A Credit Toolkit" (May 2000) FOW 45–49.

with increases in diversification. An inadequately diversified credit portfolio will generally be characterised by concentration risk that can be measured quantitatively as the excess of expected and unexpected credit loss relative to a well diversified portfolio of similar size and characteristics[17].

3.2.2 Concentration Risk – Key Factors

Concentration risk in credit portfolios of banks/financial institutions is the result of a number of factors, including:

- **Specialisation of banks/financial institutions** – limited resources and competitive forces such as the knowledge and competencies of the institution, relative competitive position and return requirements inevitably force banks to specialise. This specialisation may take the form of industry specialisation, geographic specialisation (country or region) or type of client as classified by credit rating. This specialisation has the consequence of leading to high degrees of concentration in the composition of credit portfolios.
- **Changing structure of credit markets** – several trends in the pattern of capital market activity also create concentration risks:
  1. The trend to direct issuance of securities to investors by higher quality issuers as an alternative to bank financing has resulted in a change in the composition of the credit risk structure of bank loan portfolios. The portfolios now have higher proportionate levels of exposure to lower rated borrowers that do not have access to capital markets.
  2. The trend to large corporations reducing the size of their core banking groups has increased the relative size and scale of bank exposure to individual clients. For example, in recent years, a number of borrowers have raised bank loans of several billions of US$ (say US$5,000 million) from a small group of banks (say, 10 banks). While the loans are often of short duration and are frequently refinanced in other markets quite quickly (for example, acquisitions/merger funding), the substantial size of these exposures can substantially skew the credit portfolio of a particular bank.

  These factors have combined to significantly increase the level of concentration risk in portfolios.
- **Mismatch between origination capacity and diversification objectives** – there is a parallel limitation in the scope of a financial institution being

---

[17] See discussion in Chapter 6.

able to directly originate credit assets outside its natural markets. This reflects the focus of its client relationships, the presence and knowledge requirements of penetrating new markets, and the competitive behaviour of institutions with established market positions in the relevant market segments. This is exacerbated by the increased trend to specialisation that creates higher levels of concentration risk.

- **Incompleteness of credit markets** – credit markets are generally incomplete. The lack of available credit assets with the required term, structure and industry characteristics in the market may increase concentration. A bank or investor located in and focusing on a particular geography is captive to the industrial bias of the region and the borrowing characteristics of the entities active in that region. This creates a natural bias in portfolio structure of credit risk that increases concentration risk.
- **Client relationship pressures** – banks provide individual loan exposures to clients as a primary resource in establishing and maintaining major relationships[18]. This is done in the expectation that the dominant position as a major lender will allow the bank to gain access to other non credit business from the clients. The inability to reduce the direct credit exposures often creates substantial concentration risks within credit portfolios.

The factors identified are collectively referred to as the *credit paradox*. The factors identified have the capacity to significantly increase concentration risk in the credit portfolios of banks/financial institutions to unacceptable levels.

3.2.3 Concentration Risk In Credit Portfolios[19]

The impact of concentration risk within credit risk portfolios is best understood from the viewpoint of portfolio theory. Traditional mean-variance portfolio theory is not directly applicable to credit portfolios. This reflects the characteristics of credit portfolios, including:

- Returns in credit portfolios are skewed in well diversified portfolios.
- Credit risk appears to be non linear in nature.
- Credit risk appears to be exacerbated by the traditional illiquidity of credit risk.

---

[18] For example, see Schack, Justin "The New Battle For The Bulge" (August 2001) Institutional Investor 51–59; Currie, Antony "Brawn Takes On Brains In The Battle For The Corporates" (October 2001) Euromoney 92–99.

[19] See discussion in Chapter 6.

- Increasing the size of the portfolio and increasing diversification can reduce credit risk. The size of portfolio required to reach full diversification is large. It is difficult to achieve in practice.

The quantitative approach to credit portfolio management would indicate that the return on credit assets should be related to the return/ pricing, the size of the exposure and the default correlation between credit assets. This is consistent with the fact that concentration risk arises from an increase in potential credit losses on the portfolio due to large exposures to a particular issuer, industry, region or other grouping of credit assets that have a high default correlation. This analysis indicates that it is desirable, from a risk return perspective, to reduce exposure to issuers to whom the entity is overexposed or increase exposure to issuers to whom the institution is underexposed.

The price that an entity should be prepared to economically pay to achieve this optimisation of portfolio credit risk shows surprising characteristics. To adequately cover the increased risk of concentration, the portfolio manager requires returns that increase in a non linear fashion (at an increasing rate). **Exhibit 7.3** sets out this relationship diagrammatically.

This dictates that an entity that has high levels of exposure to a particular credit should be prepared to pay a *premium* to market returns to reduce the risk of concentration. Similarly, the institution may require a *lower* than market return in increasing its exposure to credits to which it has no or low exposure. This is predicated on the fact that while the returns on individual credits are determined by market prices, the return required to compensate for risk for a particular investor is related to the portfolio structure on an individual entity at the relevant point in time. In effect, the marginal return required is related to the marginal risk contribution to the portfolio risk. This relationship requires increasing returns above market returns where there is already substantial exposure to a particular credit. Traditional methods of managing credit risk based on fixed limits do not necessarily incorporate this return on marginal risk component.

This type of portfolio based approach to management of credit assets is gradually being accepted. The implementation of such approaches forces institutions to address the *management* of concentration risk within credit portfolios to increase the efficiency of returns on capital within a risk-return framework[20].

---

[20] See discussion in Chapter 8.

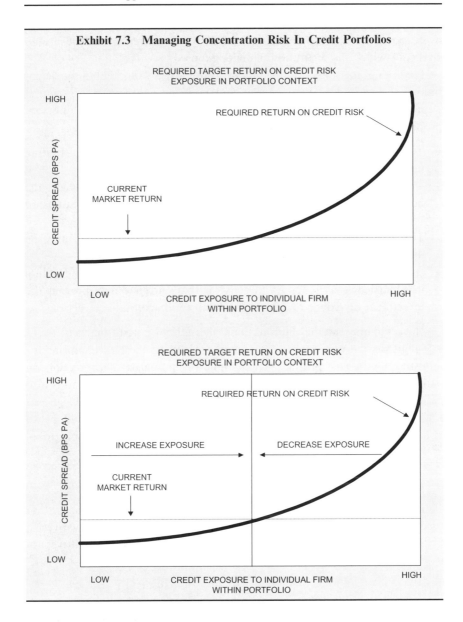

Exhibit 7.3   Managing Concentration Risk In Credit Portfolios

3.2.4   Approaches to Management of Concentration Risk

The recognition of the impact of concentration risk does not dictate the use of credit derivatives. It emphasises the importance of diversification of credit risk and the reduction of exposure to obligors to whom the institution is overexposed. This may be compensated by the increase in exposure to credits to which the institution is under exposed.

Traditional methods of adjusting exposure levels would entail participation in the secondary loan market and boosting credit asset origination efforts in the relevant markets. These approaches have certain inherent problems, including:

- The secondary loan market is not liquid (albeit secondary loan trading has been increasing) and suffers from high transaction costs.
- The sale of loans where the borrower must consent or where the borrower becomes aware of the sale may damage the relationship between the bank and its client.
- The capacity to originate assets in non traditional markets may be difficult and may expose the bank to new risks.
- Even where the asset can be originated, the lack of availability of funding in a particular currency or the cost of that currency may prevent the investment or reduce returns to the bank to unacceptable levels.

These factors underlie the traditional illiquidity of credit markets.

Credit derivatives provide a viable alternative to these mechanisms for adjusting credit risk profiles. This entails the purchase of protection on entities to which the lender is overexposed. Portfolio diversification is also enhanced by acquiring credit risk to entities to which the lender has no or low exposure. The total effect of this set of transactions should be to enhance the overall risk return characteristics of the overall credit portfolio.

3.3 Applications of Credit Derivatives – Bank/Financial Institution Examples

Bank/financial institution applications of credit derivatives are focused on credit portfolio management. This is focused on using credit derivatives to hedge or acquire credit risk[21]. Transactions include credit derivatives on single names or portfolios.

---

[21] See Allen, Robert "Approaches to Bank Credit Diversification: Credit Derivatives and their Alternatives" in (1998) Credit Derivatives: Applications for Risk Management, Investment and Portfolio Optimisation; Risk Books, London at Chapter 1; Gontarek, Walter "Hedging With Credit Derivatives: Practical Applications and Considerations" in (1998) Credit Derivatives: Applications for Risk Management, Investment and Portfolio Optimisation;

Typical transaction structures include:

- **Single name transactions** – this entails credit derivatives based on a single reference entity. Applications include:
  1. *Exposure reduction* – **Exhibit 7.4** sets out an example of using credit derivatives to hedge exposures to an entity.
  2. *Unfunded exposures* – **Exhibit 7.5** sets out an example of using credit derivatives to synthesise an unfunded exposure to an issuer.
  3. *Credit line management* – **Exhibit 7.6** sets out an example of using forward starting credit derivatives to manage credit lines and enhance returns. **Exhibit 7.7** sets out an example of using credit derivatives to manage maturity restrictions for loan participants.
  4. *Credit spread risk management* – **Exhibit 7.8** sets out an example of using credit derivatives to manage credit spread risk within a portfolio.
  5. *Syndications* – **Exhibit 7.9** and **Exhibit 7.10** set out examples of using credit derivatives to manage credit risk in syndications.
  6. *Hedging dynamic exposure on derivatives* – **Exhibit 7.11** and **Exhibit 7.12** set out examples of using credit derivatives to manage credit exposure on derivative transactions.
- **Credit portfolios** – this entails credit derivatives based on a portfolio of reference entities. Typical structures used to transfer or acquire exposure are portfolio default swaps[22], first-to-default baskets[23] and CDO structures[24].

Risk Books, London at Chapter 2; Gontarek, Walter "Today's Credit Derivatives Market" in Storrow, Jamie (Editor) (1999) Credit Derivatives: Key Issues – 2nd Edition; British Bankers' Association, London at Chapter 2; Watzinger, Herman "Credit Derivatives In Bank Loan Portfolio Management – A Practitioner's Approach" in Storrow, Jamie (1999) Credit Derivatives: Key Issues – 2nd Edition; British Bankers' Association, London at Chapter 4. See also Lowe, Diana "Concentrating On Credit" (August 1999) Asia Risk 29–32; Lowe, Diana "Pushing Progress In The Credit Process" (October 1999) Asia Risk 28–31; Travers, Paul and Heydenrych, David "Grappling With Credit Risk" (February 2000) Asia Risk 34–35; McNee, Alan "UBS Takes A New Look At Lending" (March 2000) Risk 30–31; Keen, Matthew "Two Of A Perfect Pair" (November 2000) FOW 48–53; Lee, Peter "Will New Portfolio Managers Save The Bank This Time?" (December 2001) Euromoney 44–48; Evans, Jules "Credit Risk And Its Management Raise A Paradox" (March 2002) Euromoney 52–54.

[22] See Chapter 2.
[23] See Chapter 2.
[24] See Chapter 4.

- **Optimisation of capital utilisation/regulatory arbitrage** – this entails using credit derivatives to minimise regulatory capital/optimise return on credit capital. **Exhibit 7.13**, **Exhibit 7.14**, **Exhibit 7.15** and **Exhibit 7.16** set out examples of using credit derivatives to manage regulatory credit capital[25].

**Exhibit 7.4   Bank/Financial Institution Applications Of Credit Derivatives –
Reducing Credit Exposure**

Assume Bank A has a high level of credit exposure to Company X and the automobile industry generally. Within its portfolio, Bank A considers it would benefit from a reduction in its exposure to both this specific borrower and the sector. The exposure is primarily in the form of medium term loans.

The traditional physical solution for Bank A would be to sell off some of the exposure to Company X in the secondary loan market. The major difficulties may include:

- The lack of liquidity in the secondary loan market.
- The documentary problems in any secondary market asset sale.
- The potential damage to the Bank's relationship with its client (caused by either advising or seeking consent to the sale).

Bank A could use a credit default swap to reduce its exposure. This would entail Bank A entering into a credit default swap where it would purchase protection from a counterparty against the default of Company X. The transaction effectively substitutes the counterparty credit of the counterparty providing protection for its exposure to Company X.

The derivative transaction avoids the difficulty of the physical transaction in the secondary loan market. This is possible because of the fact that the credit default swap does not require the sale of the loan assets. The loan assets continue to remain on the balance sheet of the Bank.

The following aspects of the derivative solution should be noted:

- Bank A can theoretically pay a higher rate of return on the risk of Company X than current market rates. This is because of the improvement in its *portfolio risk*. This is a result of the benefits of the reduction in concentration. This should make it feasible to transfer this exposure to counterparties who will be receiving higher than market returns as an incentive to assume the risk[26].

---

[25]   For additional examples, see Chapters 1, 2, 3 and 4.

[26]   While intellectually tractable, in practice this is difficult, primarily for organisational and income/earnings attribution reasons; see discussion in Chapter 8.

- Bank A can offset any cost of the credit default swap (the fee paid to purchase protection) by taking on credit risk. This entails selling protection on an entity to which the bank has no or low exposure. This reflects the fact that increasing credit exposure to these entities results in a proportionately higher increase in *portfolio* return relative to the increase in *portfolio* risk.
- The credit default swap requires the Bank to assume the credit risk of the counterparty *on the derivative transaction*. It uses credit lines and deploys credit capital against the entity selling it protection on Company X. Alternatively, Bank A could use a funded structure such as a credit linked note to avoid counterparty risk on the credit default swap.

Exhibit 7.5   Bank/Financial Institution Applications Of Credit Derivatives – Unfunded Credit Risk

Assume Bank A has term credit lines available to Company X. The market price for Company X credit is LIBOR plus 40 bps. Bank A's target return on risk for Company X is 45 bps pa on fully funded assets and 35 bps pa on unfunded obligations. Bank A can exceed its target return in US$. The bank funds in US$ at LIBOR *minus* 10 bps. This reflects the bank's strong credit rating (AA) and superior access to US$ funding. The only asset currently available is a Pound Sterling ("GBP") asset. This reflects Company X's current borrowing requirements. Bank A's GBP cost of funds is GBP LIBOR plus 5 bps, reflecting its relatively less advantageous access to GBP funding. This funding cost disadvantage means that Bank A is unable to fund this GBP loan at a level which ensures a return commensurate either with its target returns or the return on US$ assets for the same credit.

The physical solution to this problem would entail trading in the secondary loan market to seek to acquire a US$ loan asset which satisfies Bank A's targets. A credit derivative solution entails Bank A selling protection on Company X under a credit default swap.

This entails Bank A entering into a credit default swap where it sells protection to the counterparty against the default of Company X. If the default swap provides Bank A with a net fee of 35 bps pa, then it meets the Bank's target return levels on unfunded obligations (the default swap is off balance sheet).

The credit default swap transaction in this example is attractive to the counterparty transferring the credit exposure of Company X to Bank A. This reflects the fact that under the transaction, it creates a synthetic AA rated asset (based on the rating of Bank A). This is done through the extension of the GBP loan to Company X, while simultaneously transferring the credit exposure of Company X to Bank A. The return on this asset is approximately LIBOR plus 5 bps that may compare favourably to direct returns on AA rated assets.

**Exhibit 7.6   Bank/Financial Institution Applications Of Credit Derivatives –
Credit Line Utilisation/Forward Start Credit Derivatives**

Assume Bank A has medium term (5 year) credit lines for Company X. The term
structure of credit spreads for Company X is as follows:

Maturity (years)	Company X
1–2	LIBOR + 30 bps pa
3–4	LIBOR + 40 bps pa
5	LIBOR + 50 bps pa

Assume Bank A's target return on its exposure to Company X is around 40 bps pa
for funded exposures and 30 bps for unfunded exposures for maturity up to 5 years.

On a portfolio basis, Bank A's lines to Company X are currently utilised by a
2 year loan that is yielding LIBOR plus 35 bps (this is the remaining term to maturity
of an existing loan). The asset does not meet Bank A's current return criteria.

The physical solution to this problem would entail the sale of the existing loan in
the secondary market and the entry into the longer term loan that meets the return
criteria. The secondary market transactions are subject to the difficulties identified,
while the alternative assets might not be readily available.

The credit derivative solution would entail a forward starting credit default swap.
Bank A enters into a *forward start* credit default swap protecting the counterparty
against default by Company X. The swap covers a period of 3 years *commencing in
2 years from the present*. The structure is identical to Bank A selling protection on
Company X for 5 years and buying protection for 2 years[27]. Over the first 2 years,
Bank A continues to hold its loan exposure to Company X. The default swap does
not operate, allowing the Bank to allocate part of the premium received to enhance
its returns on the loan asset. At the end of year 2 when the existing loan has expired,
Bank A effectively has an unfunded exposure to Company X that is earning a rate of
return above the target rate of return. The total return (combining the existing two
year loan and the 3 year credit default swap commencing 2 years forward) is around
52.2 bps pa over LIBOR over the full 5 year period. This is in excess of its return
target.

The increasing structure of credit spreads creates a natural trading opportunity
for Bank A. At the end of year 2, the value of the credit default swap that has a
remaining term of 3 years out of spot is calculated off the credit margins for *years
1 to 2*. As the spreads are lower than the margin for 5 year risk, assuming no changes
in the credit spread structure, Bank A should be able to reverse its position in the
credit default swap for a gain.

---

[27]   This is exactly how the dealer trading the forward start credit default swap would
hedge.

**Exhibit 7.7 Bank/Financial Institution Applications Of Credit Derivatives –
Loan Maturity Restriction**

Assume Bank A is syndicating a project loan for Company X (the project's principal sponsor) for US$350 million for a term of 12 years (average life 8 years). The complexity of the project makes the syndication difficult. A problem encountered is that some of the banks invited have internal restrictions that prevent them from extending credit beyond a *final* maturity of 10 years. The participation of the banks is important, not only from the point of view of securing the finance, but in providing reassurance to other banks in the syndicate.

Bank A has two choices. The first entails restructuring the project debt repayment schedule. This may be difficult for operational reasons. It may also alter the economics and risk profile of the project. The second is to use credit derivatives to seek to redefine the risk exposure of the relevant banks.

A credit derivative strategy is feasible. A credit default swap covering the final two years exposure could be used to hedge the credit exposure for the banks, subject to the maturity restriction. The transaction would entail the relevant bank purchasing default protection for the final two years from other banks or the sponsor.

The project loan would be undertaken normally, with the relevant banks entering into separate hedges for their exposure with the indemnifying banks or the sponsor. This allows the syndicate and loan structure to be preserved, with the minority lenders' constraints being satisfied separately and without disruption to the project financing.

The hedges can be put in place permanently or for a period of 2 years only. The latter would be designed to ensure that the 10 year constraint was honoured, with the exposure reverting upon the project's remaining term falling within the restriction.

**Exhibit 7.8 Bank/Financial Institution Applications Of Credit Derivatives –
Credit Spread Risk Management**

Assume Bank A has a substantial portfolio of loans to a particular industry. It is concerned that credit spreads to the industry may increase. It is seeking to reduce its exposure to this expected increase in spreads[28].

The only traditional mechanism for reducing this exposure to credit spreads would be to sell off its loan exposures in the secondary market. This may not be feasible on a cost efficient basis.

---

[28] Traditionally, banks would not be concerned about the credit spread exposure as the loan commitment would not be marked to market. There is an ongoing debate as to whether banks should be required to mark loan commitments to market. See Dunbar, Nicholas "The Battle Over Loan Accounting" (July 2001) Risk 26–28; Cass, Dwight and Ferry, John "FASB: Loan Commitments Must Be Treated Like Derivatives" (January 2002) Risk 7.

An alternative mechanism would be for Bank A to enter into a 1 year synthetic lending or standby credit facility. It pays a fee. In return, Bank A has the right, at the end of 1 year, at its option, to require the counterparty to:

- Provide a 3 year revolving credit to a number of leading companies in the relevant industry sector (at pre-agreed spreads over LIBOR).
- Enter into an asset swap (on underlying bonds issued by these companies) at a pre-agreed yield over LIBOR.

The transaction is structured on a cash settlement basis. The payment to be received by Bank A is calculated upon exercise of its rights under the agreement as the difference between the agreed spreads and secondary market spreads (asset swaps) on the reference entities.

The transaction operates as follows:

- Bank A pays the fee.
- At the end of 1 year, if credit spreads on the reference entities have not increased above an agreed level, than the facility expires unused.
- At the end of 1 year, if credit spreads have increased above the agreed level over LIBOR, then the facility is exercised. Bank A receives a cash payment that is designed to offset the loss in value in its portfolio as a result of the increase in credit spreads.

The advantage to Bank A of this structure includes:

- Known cost of the increase in credit spreads as represented by the fee paid.
- Ability to protect its portfolio from erosion in value from increases in credit spreads. This is particularly the case where spreads have declined, and continuing to extend credit or acquire assets at historically low credit spread levels exposes the lenders to high risk from spread changes.

The effectiveness of the hedge is contingent upon the correlation between the reference entities and the underlying portfolio sought to be hedged. The risk that can be hedged using this structure includes individual issuers, industry sectors and country exposures.

**Exhibit 7.9   Bank/Financial Institution Applications Of Credit Derivatives –
Hedging Syndication Risk: Example 1**

Assume Bank A is approached by a major client (Company X) to assist it in raising US$2,000 million to facilitate an acquisition. The loan is to be provided by 4 banks with each committing US$500 million. Each bank will be asked to underwrite US$500 million, of which Bank A plans to syndicate US$250 million, leaving it with a final exposure of US$250 million. The loan will have a term of 3 years. It is anticipated that the loan will be repaid prior to maturity from the proceeds of asset sales planned following the acquisition, or refinanced in the capital markets.

Bank A wishes to meet this client requirement for the following reasons:

- It wishes to support a major client and protect its existing relationship.
- It believes that the transaction will generate significant collateral business (FX, hedging and capital markets transactions associated with the refinancing) which it wishes to position itself for.

It is conscious that entry into this transaction will have the following difficulties:

- The large quantum of the exposure will mean that Bank A will be close to its internal and external prudential limits for exposure to Company X.
- The exposure may in fact prevent Bank A from undertaking the ancillary business that it views as the rationale for entering into this transaction.
- Bank A is aware that Company X will seek to restrict its ability to sell down its exposure on the loan through sub-participation or assignment transactions (by requiring Company X's consent to any such transaction). Company X's reasoning is that it seeks to limit its banking relationship to enable more effective control of its lending groups.

Bank A agrees to provide the loan. It now has two levels of risk (exposure to credit spread changes in the loan market and default risk on the borrower) which it seeks to manage using credit derivatives. The following strategies are available to manage the identified risks:

- **Credit spread risk** – Bank A can seek to hedge the exposure to credit spread risk on its underwriting position[29]. This is through entry into a credit spread forward or through the purchase of a credit spread put. This enables it to effectively short the spread (as it is effectively long the credit spread through the underwriting). The credit spread may be on the specific borrower (in practice, for a large transaction this would be difficult) or on a basket of similar credit quality issuers. The latter does not provide direct protection on changes in the credit spread of Company X. It provides general protection on unexpected changes in the credit spread as a result of changes in credit conditions in the syndication market.
- **Credit default risk** – Bank A can purchase a credit default swap to protect against a default of Company X. This swap will effectively reduce the exposure to the

---

[29] Banks underwriting loan commitments generally insert protection against changes in credit spreads. This is done using the "market flex" clause. Under the provision, the credit spread can be re-priced under certain circumstances. The circumstances generally include: (1) fall in a major market equity index by a specified percentage (say 10%), (2) increase in benchmark government interest rates by a specified amount (say 1.00% pa) and (3) increase in swap spreads by a specified amount (say 50 bps pa). The market flex provisions mean that the underwriter is fully exposed up to the trigger levels.

issuer to a level sought by Bank A while allowing it to undertake the transaction for its clients. The protection can be purchased initially to protect it until syndication is complete. It can also be undertaken following syndication to maintain the credit exposure on the transaction within desired levels.

- **Synthetic syndications** – Bank A can enter into credit default swaps to effectively reduce its exposure on its final participation in this financing by paying the equivalent credit spread on the loan. The bank frees up its credit capacity for the other transactions that it wishes to undertake for the client without the need to syndicate/sell off the loan assets. As it remains the lender of record for the transaction, Company X will not have to deal with the lenders or investors who have effectively acquired the credit exposure, thereby at least partially meeting its objectives.

Several aspects of the credit derivative based hedging strategies should be noted:

- The term of the protection against default is capable of being customised. For example, Bank A may choose to sell down its exposure for a period shorter than the scheduled term of the loan (3 years). This allows it to manage the risk dynamically. It can potentially take advantage of the slope of the credit spread curve to enhance earnings.
- The structure of the transactions allows Bank A pricing flexibility. For example, it may be prepared to pay a premium over the market price of Company X's risk to reduce its risk. This reflects the fact that it may be overexposed in a portfolio sense to the borrower. It also reflects the earnings potential from the ancillary business that it is targeting (for which it needs to free up credit lines).
- Credit derivatives transactions are also attractive to market participants as a means of *acquiring* credit exposure to Company X. The size of the transaction and the minimum participation amounts in syndications has increased. Credit derivatives may be an attractive mechanism for banks to take smaller participation in the transactions, consistent with their risk appetites. This process creates an opportunity for Bank A (as the *wholesaler*) to capture value by way of adjustments in pricing from the banks seeking to participate, but only at levels below the minimum levels in the primary markets (the *retail* buyers). The credit derivative structure may also allow risk to be transferred to non-bank investors. The investors may not be able to participate in a traditional syndication structure. This is because the investors may lack the necessary banking infrastructure to manage the loan commitment.

Exhibit 7.10   Bank/Financial Institution Applications Of Credit Derivatives – Hedging Syndication Risk: Example 2[30]

In 1997, CIBC/CIBC Wood Gundy (the Canadian bank group) in conjunction with co-arranger Ceskoslovenska Obchodni Banka ("CSOB") agreed to arrange a

---

[30]   See Fortune, Mark "Default Swaps Enable Czech Loan" (18 October 1997) International Financing Review Issue 1205 109.

US$500 million loan to Aero Vodochody ("AV"), a Czech aerospace manufacturer. The loan package included import financing, a letter of credit facility and a revolving loan.

A bridge loan of US$100 million became necessary. This is because of a lengthy government process for the approval of the loan. During the process of approval, AV had commitments to make payments on contracts associated with the project to vendors/contractors. The payments were to be financed by the facilities negotiated. CIBC agreed to make a US$100 million bridge loan to meet this interim financing requirement.

However, CIBC needed to reduce its exposure on the bridge loan as soon as possible. This is because of credit concentration issues. In order to hedge its credit risk on the bridge loan, CIBC entered into two credit default swaps for a total of US$50 million. Under the swaps, CIBC pays the two counterparties an agreed fee in return for the counterparties assuming the risk of default. The swaps were for a period of around 1 year. In effect, the credit default swaps reduced CIBC exposure on the bridge loan by 50%.

The reference credit for the default swap was a US$250 million 5 year bond issued by Czech Export Bank and guaranteed by the Czech Republic. The rationale for use of the bond as the reference credit and asset was the fact that AV was also state owned. From a legal and commercial perspective, there was sufficient similarity between the obligor on the loan and the reference credit to provide reasonable protection.

Exhibit 7.11   Bank/Financial Institution Applications Of Credit Derivatives –
Managing Derivative Exposure

Assume Bank A enters into a 12 year cross currency swap with Bank B. The swap is for a notional principal of US$100 million and entails Bank A receiving Yen at a fixed rate of 6.00% pa and paying US$ LIBOR. The exchange rate at commencement is US$1=Yen 160.00. At the time of entry, the expected credit exposure is expected to peak at US$30 million (30% of US$ principal) with an average exposure of around US$20 million (20% of US$ principal). The credit limits and returns on risk capital on this transaction are based on these anticipated credit exposures. The transaction is set out below.

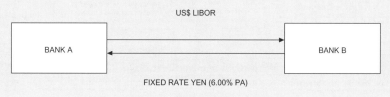

Assume that 4 years have elapsed and the US$/Yen exchange rate is at US$1 = Yen 90 and the Yen interest rate for the remaining term of the swap has fallen to 2.80% pa. The replacement value for the swap (the effective mark to market credit exposure) is US$118 million (118% of US$ principal). This exposure is significantly above that anticipated, reflecting the unexpected volatility and directional change in the exchange and interest rates.

During this period, Bank B, which was AA+ rated at the commencement of the transaction, has been downgraded to A− with a negative credit outlook. This has further exacerbated the credit exposure.

The increase in exposure has the following implications for Bank A:

- The higher than expected credit exposure has worsened the transaction exposure such that the Bank is incurring a loss on the transaction in return on capital terms.
- The increase in exposure may have caused the Bank to sharply increase its utilisation of or breach its counterparty limits to Bank B. It may also have breached its prudential exposures to a single counterparty.
- The increased exposure may have created higher than acceptable concentration risk levels within Bank A's portfolio and also significantly reduced its trading liquidity by tying up inter-bank counterparty/country risk credit lines.

Correcting this exposure problem is difficult for Bank A. This reflects the difficulty and cost of unwinding the swap. It is unlikely that the counterparty will be prepared to unwind the transaction. This reflects the cash impact on the counterparty in unwinding the trade and the inability to re-establish the position because of its lower credit rating. The counterparty may also not be prepared to implement credit enhancement measures (not provided for in the terms of the original documentation covering the swap) such as re-couponing, mark-to-market or cash collateralisation[31].

As an alternative to the termination of the swap or provision of additional credit enhancement, Bank A can purchase protection against default by Bank B. This would take the form of a credit default swap where the counterparty (Bank C) will make a payment to Bank A in the event of a default by Bank B of an amount based on *the mark-to-market value of the swap at the time of default*. The default event may be defined generally or with reference to default on the swap itself. This type of transaction is referred to as a swap guarantee. The transaction is set out below.

---

[31] See Das, Satyajit (2004) Swaps/Financial Derivatives – 3rd Edition; John Wiley & Sons, Singapore at Chapter 21.

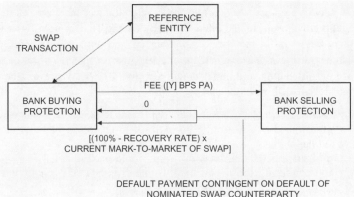

The transaction operates in a manner analogous to a normal credit default swap as follows:

• The bank seeking protection pays a premium (on an upfront or periodic basis).
• The bank providing protection agrees to make a payment if the swap/derivatives counterparty defaults.

The principal distinguishing feature is that the default payment is linked to the *mark-to-market value of the swap/derivatives transaction* at the time of default. The default payout (payable in the case of a credit event affecting Bank B) is specified as:

$$\text{Default payment} = (100\% - \text{Recovery Rate}) \text{ times Current}$$
$$\text{Mark-to-Market Value of the Transaction}$$

The payment made is based on the expected recovery value estimated from the price of traded bonds of the reference entity.

The credit default swap linked to the swap value is different from a normal credit swap in that the amount of the default payment is dynamic and linked to the value of the swap that is a function of *market variables*. Bank A will only suffer a loss if Bank B defaults, there is an amount owing to Bank A under the swap, and the counterparty providing protection under the swap (Bank C) also defaults. This multiple contingency structure significantly enhances the credit quality of the exposure that will generally be superior to that of both Bank B and the credit swap counterparty.

The credit swap linked to the value of the swap is capable of being structured in a number of alternative ways:

1. The default swap may cover *any exposure* under the swap.
2. The default swap may cover exposure up to a pre-agreed amount.
3. The default swap may cover exposure above a minimum amount.

The term of the protection can also be varied, with protection being able to be obtained for periods up to the full remaining term of the swap.

Bank C may be prepared to enter into the swap guarantee where it has a negative mark-to-market exposure to the reference entity (Bank B). The negative mark-to-market may be the result of other transactions entered into between Bank C and Bank B. Where it has a negative mark-to-market, provision of the swap guarantee would not result in any additional credit risk to Bank C where a number of conditions are satisfied, including:

- Bank C is able to net the exposure between it and Bank B. This would require Bank C to assign the swap from Bank A prior to default to allow termination netting to take place.
- Bank C's negative mark-to-market exposure would need to equal or exceed the current and projected exposure to Bank B under the relevant transaction at all times.

In practice, these transactions allow banks with large negative mark-to-market exposures to monetise the implicit value of the "credit asset" represented by the negative credit exposure.

**Exhibit 7.12   Bank/Financial Institution Applications Of Credit Derivatives –
Managing Contingent Interest Rate Exposure**

Assume Company A, an asset finance/leasing company, leases equipment at fixed rentals. The Company raises floating rate funding that is hedged into fixed rate to provide an asset liability match between its funding and the leasing assets. In the event of default, the Company takes possession of the asset and re-leases the equipment. The re-leasing risk is combined with interest rate risk. This interest rate risk derives from the fact that if interest rates fall from the level prevailing when the original lease is undertaken, Company A will be exposed to the risk of loss from the termination of the interest rate swap.

In order to manage its exposure to this contingency, Company A could enter into a credit default swap where the payoff is linked to the mark-to-market exposure on the interest rate swap. The reference credit for the default swap would be the lessee of the equipment. The structure of the transaction would be as follows[32]:

- Company A pays a commitment fee on the overall notional amount. This fee would be lower than the normal fee payable on a default swap.
- Company A would be liable to pay an additional amount (the full premium on a default swap) if the mark-to-market exposure in any period becomes negative (that is, in the event of a default the termination of the swap would result in a loss to Company A). This calculation would typically be done quarterly or monthly.

---

[32] The structure is similar to a credit swaption/an option on a credit default swap; see Chapter 2.

In the event that the mark-to-market exposure under the swap becomes positive, the additional fee is not payable.
- In the event of the lessee defaulting, Company A would receive a payment equal to the mark-to-market value of the swap (provided it is negative).

The structure has the advantage of being more cost effective, as the party seeking protection is only liable to pay the full fee where it requires protection, with its only ongoing cost being the commitment fee. The effect of the structure is to provide default protection only where underlying market movements would result in a termination loss on the swap in the event of default of the lessee.

Exhibit 7.13 Bank/Financial Institution Applications Of Credit Derivatives – Balance Sheet/Funding Arbitrage

Assume Bank A is a lower rated bank. Its higher cost of funding makes it difficult to generate a positive spread on loans to highly rated issuers. In particular, it is difficult to generate a spread that provides its required rate of return on capital. This pressure has forced the Bank to make loans to more risky lower rated borrowers. Lower rated borrowers are a high proportion of its asset portfolio. Bank A is now overexposed to these categories of credit risk.

Bank A may be able to address the difficulties by assuming credit exposures to higher rated credits by entering into credit default swaps where it provides protection against default. This strategy has the following effects:

- The default swap does not need to be funded, thereby minimising the impact of Bank A's unfavourable funding costs.
- Any problems regarding the counterparty risk of Bank A *as a counterparty to the default swap* can be addressed by some form of credit enhancement (collateralisation and periodic mark-to-market provisions).
- The ability to diversify away the concentration to lower credit quality borrowers should allow the overall risk return on the credit portfolio to be significantly enhanced.

There are significant advantages to the counterparty to the default swap obtaining protection against default on the better credit quality assets. These include:

- Maximisation of the advantage of its lower funding cost. This reflects the fact that the premium paid for obtaining the protection against default may be less than the effective spread (asset return less the lower cost bank's funding cost), allowing it to increase its overall returns.
- Where the credit default swap with Bank A is cash collateralised, the counterparty may not be required to hold any capital against the Bank. This will have the effect of enhancing the economic return on the transaction.
- The strategy allows an effective increase in the diversification of its own credit portfolio, but conceivably on economically more attractive terms.

Exhibit 7.14   Bank/Financial Institution Applications Of Credit Derivatives – Credit Capital Arbitrage

Assume Bank A is about to extend credit to a borrower. The loan is to a corporation rated investment grade (BBB/Baa) for 5 years and attracts a spread of 45 bps over LIBOR. The bank has the choice of booking the loan in one of the following ways:

- Extend a traditional loan that is held on the bank balance sheet and fully funded.
- Arrange for the loan to be made by another entity (Bank B), with Bank A assuming the risk of the underlying loan through either a total return swap on the loan or selling credit protection to the loan provider through a credit default swap.

The two transactions are depicted below.

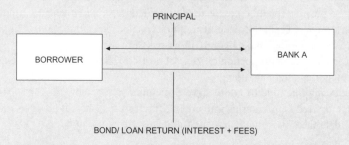

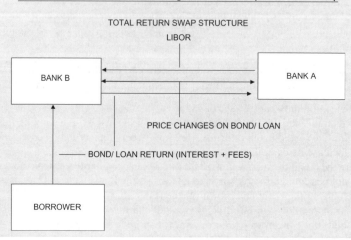

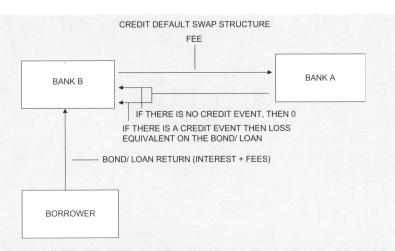

Under each structure, Bank A assumes the credit risk of the bond purchased or loan made to the ultimate borrower. The regulatory capital required against the underlying risk position might be different[33].

Under Basel 1, the bank loan is booked in the banking book and 8% capital must be held against the underlying risk (equivalent to face value multiplied by the counterparty risk weighting (which for a corporate is 100%)). The total return swap or the credit default swap can be booked in the trading book. In order to qualify for trading book treatment, the bank must be able to mark to market the underlying reference asset. If held in the trading book, the capital charge is lower than the banking book for qualifying assets (effectively government or investment grade assets). In the situation described, the capital to be held in the trading book may be as low as 1.60% (80% lower than that required under the banking book treatment).

The return on risk capital is set out in the Table below:

Calculation of Risk Adjusted Return

Nominal Value	$1,000,000
Loan Spread	0.45% pa
Total Return Swap Margin/Credit Default Swap Fee	0.45% pa
Counterparty Risk Weighting	100.0%
Capital Requirement	
Banking Book	8.00%
Trading Book	1.60%

---

[33] For discussion of regulatory treatment of credit derivatives, see Chapters 1, 3 and 4.

	Banking Book	Trading Book
Net Income	$4,500	$4,500
Capital Required	$80,000	$16,000
Return On Capital	5.625%	28.125%
% Increase In Return		500.0%

The calculation of return assumes that Bank A receives the full net spread on the loan. Even where the net spread received is lower than that on the loan, the return to the Bank on a *return on risk capital* basis is greater than for the direct loan. For example, if the net spread received on the total return swap or fee for the credit default swap is 30 bps, then the return on capital to Bank A is 18.75% (an increase of over 3 times).

The decision to take advantage of the trading book treatment requires the bank to mark to market the asset. Any gain or loss is taken to profit and loss. This creates potential volatility in the earnings. Inclusion of the transaction in the trading book may also require market risk capital to be held against the position where the position incurs general market risk (for example, if the asset is not match funded).

Exhibit 7.15   Bank/Financial Institution Applications Of Credit Derivatives – Credit Capital/Funding Arbitrage

Assume a loan to Company X for $10 million for 5 years priced at LIBOR plus 40 bps. There are the following Banks that are prepared to participate in the transaction:

- Bank A rated AA that is able to fund the loan at LIBOR *minus* 20 bps.
- Bank B rated BBB that is able to fund the loan at LIBOR plus 10 bps.

Assume that both banks are subject to regulatory capital requirements where each bank is required to hold capital of 8% against risk weighted assets. The risk weighting for assets is 100% for corporations (the loan to Company X) and 20% for OECD Banks (both Bank A and Bank BBB).

Where both counterparties provided the loan on balance sheet, the resulting return to the Banks is summarised in the Table below:

Loan Returns

Bank	A	B
Interest Income	$640,000	$640,000
Interest Expense	−$533,600	−$561,200
Net Interest Margin	$106,400	$78,800
Capital Held	$800,000	$800,000
Return On Capital	13.30%	9.85%

Notes:

1. The interest calculations assume a LIBOR rate of 6.00% pa.
2. Both banks are assumed to hold capital of 8% exactly against the loan.
3. The funding for the loan is $9,200,000 in loans at an interest expense charged at LIBOR plus/minus the Bank's funding spread and $800,000 in capital is not specifically charged for. The calculation therefore is $9,200,000 × 5.80% (6.00%−0.20%) and $9,200,000 × 6.10% (6.00% +0.10%).
4. Return on capital is calculated as the Net Interest Margin divided by the Capital held ($800,000).

Assume the transaction is restructured as follows:

- The higher rated bank (Bank A) extends the loan.
- Bank A then enters into a default swap where it pays a fee to Bank B in return for Bank B assuming the default risk of Company X.

Economically, the transaction has the effect of allowing Bank B to create exposure to the credit/default risk of Company X, while limiting the funding cost disadvantage suffered by Bank B.

Assuming that the fee paid by Bank A to Bank B for entering into the default swap is equal to the credit spread of 40 bps, the transaction economics are set out in the Tables below:

Return For Bank A

Interest Income	$640,000
Interest Expense	−$570,720
Net Interest Margin	$69,280
Credit Default Swap Fee	−$40,000
Net Income	$29,280
Capital Held	$160,000
Return On Capital	18.30%
Change In Return (%)	38%
Equivalent Loan Margin	0.80%
Incremental Loan Margin	0.400%

Notes:

1. Assumes that the counterparty risk weighting is reduced from 100% to 20% implying a reduction in capital from $800,000 (8% of $10 million times 100%) to $160,000 (8% of $10 million times 20%).
2. The funding for the loan is calculated as $9,840,000 × 5.80% (6.00%–0.20%).
3. Change in Return (%) refers to the percentage change in the return on the credit derivatives based transaction compared to the conventional loan described previously.

4. The concept of equivalent loan margin is based on deriving the margin required to generate the return on capital achieved under a traditional loan structure.

Return For Bank B

Credit Default Swap Fee	$40,000
Interest On Capital	$46,400
Net Income	$86,400
Capital Held	$800,000
Return On Capital	10.80%
Change In Return (%)	10%
Equivalent Loan Margin	0.476%
Incremental Loan Margin	0.076%

Notes:

1. Assumes that the capital required to be held is invested to yield LIBOR-20 bps; that is, $800,000 × 5.80% (6.00%–0.20%).
2. Change in Return (%) refers to the percentage change in the return on the credit derivatives based transaction compared to the conventional loan described previously.
3. The concept of equivalent loan margin is based on deriving the margin required to generate the return on capital achieved under a traditional loan structure.

The transaction enables *both the Banks* to significantly enhance returns on capital as a result of the transaction.

Exhibit 7.16   Bank/Financial Institution Applications Of Credit Derivatives – Synthetic Loan/Credit Capital Arbitrage

Assume Bank A has available credit lines for Company X. The credit lines are for a maturity of (up to) 5 years. Under current market conditions, the pricing for 3 year assets for Company X is around LIBOR plus 30 bps pa. Bank A requires a return of around LIBOR plus 40 bps pa for Company X risk. This return is not available directly in the market.

Bank A may be able to acquire Company X risk through entry into a 1 year (usually 364 days) synthetic lending or standby credit facility. It receives a fee of 17.5 bps flat. Bank A agrees to provide, at the option of the counterparty, at the end of 1 year, a 3 year revolving credit to Company X (spread of LIBOR plus 40 bps pa; undrawn fee of 20 bps pa) or enter into an asset swap (on an underlying security issued by Company X) at a yield of LIBOR plus 40 bps pa.

The transaction operates as follows:

- Bank A receives the fee.
- At the end of 1 year, if credit spreads on Company X have not increased, then the facility expires unused.
- At the end of 1 year, if credit spreads on Company X have increased above LIBOR plus 40 bps, then the facility is exercised by the counterparty placing an asset swap with Bank A at LIBOR plus 40 bps pa.

The advantage to Bank A of this structure includes:

- The transaction meets the target return levels that cannot be met in the direct loan market.
- The transaction may receive favourable regulatory treatment for capital adequacy where the transaction is for maturity less than 1 year.

4 Investor Applications

4.1 Overview

Investors active in credit derivatives include a variety of institutions such as insurance companies, fixed income asset/investment managers, retail investors/high net worth individual investors (either directly or indirectly through private banks) and hedge funds. The risk return profile and portfolio considerations affecting the different investor groups vary significantly. There are several common elements underlying investor activity.

Investor applications of credit derivatives are driven by a number of factors, including:

- **Synthetic investments** – this entails providing investors with access to types of investment not directly available in the market. This may entail providing access to markets that have been traditionally difficult to access such as the loan market. It may also involve providing the structured forms of credit risk that are not directly available in the bond market. It may entail the ability to access large diversified portfolios of credit risk efficiently.
- **Risk management** – this entails using credit derivatives to manage the credit risk of portfolios.
- **Yield enhancement/Trading** – this entails structures designed to enhance the return on credit assets. This entails allowing investors to take positions on, trade and/or monetise different aspects of credit risk. This may also entail the use of leverage to enhance credit spread returns.

In practice, synthetic investments and yield enhancements/trading are the dominant drivers of investor applications.

4.2   Applications of Credit Derivatives – Investor Application Examples

Investor applications are generally focused upon the following areas:

- **Synthetic assets** – this entails the synthesis of credit assets. The synthesis of credit assets is driven by the need to overcome portfolio constraints. **Exhibit 7.17** sets out an example of structuring a synthetic bank loan investment. **Exhibit 7.18** sets out an example of structuring a synthetic portfolio investment. **Exhibit 7.19** sets out an example of structuring a synthetic structured investment. **Exhibit 7.20** entails structuring a synthetic emerging market investment. Other forms of synthetic assets include constructing fixed interest bonds from convertible bonds through "strip" trades/convertible bond arbitrage[34]. In this type of transaction, convertible and fixed income arbitrage traders have looked to unbundle the convertible bond and repackage it through an asset swap or credit default swap/credit linked note[35]. **Exhibit 7.21** sets out an example of convertible arbitrage. Other synthetic assets include the construction of credit portfolios through credit portfolio swaps[36] or credit linked notes/ CDO transactions[37].
- **Exposure reduction** – this is focused on reducing credit risk within investment portfolios. Simple applications would include using credit default swaps to hedge default risk on specific bond issuers. **Exhibit 7.22** sets out an example of default/ratings downgrade protection. **Exhibit 7.23** sets out an example of an emerging market portfolio hedge.
- **Yield enhancement** – this is focused on using aspects of credit risk to enhance returns. **Exhibit 7.24** sets out an example of using default correlations to enhance return in a first-to-default basket. **Exhibit 7.25**, **Exhibit 7.26** and **Exhibit 7.27** set out examples of monetising credit spread expectations to enhance returns. Other structures commonly used

---

[34]   See Mahtani, Arun "Asset Swappers, Bond Investors Target Convertibles" (13 March 1999) International Financing Review Issue 1274 at 75.

[35]   For discussion of convertible arbitrage, see Das, Satyajit (2004) Swaps/Financial Derivatives 3rd Edition; John Wiley, Singapore at Chapter 56.

[36]   See Chapter 2.

[37]   See Chapters 3 and 4.

to enhance returns include the use of tranching (loss layering) in CDOs or recovery rate structures[38].

- **Trading**[39] – this is focused on outright trading of credit spreads or relative value/arbitrage trading opportunities. **Exhibit 7.28** sets out an example of an outright positioning trade. Relative value/arbitrage trading is focused on trading pricing differences between the cash and synthetic credit markets (basis trading), credit spread term structure positions and capital structure arbitrage. **Exhibit 7.29** sets out an example of creating a cheap long or short position using credit default swaps. **Exhibit 7.30** sets out an example of trading the term structure of credit spreads. **Exhibit 7.31** sets out an example of trading the cash-synthetic basis to capture value and assume credit volatility positions. **Exhibit 7.32** sets out an example of trading different components of the debt structure (senior versus subordinated debt). **Exhibit 7.33** sets out an example of debt versus equity relative value trading strategies. **Exhibit 7.34** sets out an example of trading credit default swaps against equity default swaps.

- **Leveraged investments** – leverage can be used to increase the exposure of the investor to changes in the value of the underlying credit assets. The transaction is leveraged by increasing the notional principal of the credit derivative transaction. This increases the sensitivity of the investor's investment return to market price movements. In practice, the credit derivative may be combined with a fixed income instrument as a structured note where the investor does not wish to transact the credit derivative directly or seeks a fully funded cash investment. The ability to use credit derivatives to take leveraged positions on credit risk is attractive to hedge funds[40]. **Exhibit 7.35** sets out an example of a simple leveraged structure. **Exhibit 7.36** sets out an example of a leveraged credit linked note. **Exhibit 7.37** sets out an example of using a first-to-default basket to create leveraged exposure.

---

[38] See Chapters 2 and 4.

[39] Trading in credit markets is covered in this Section despite the fact that both banks/financial institutions and investors (including leveraged investors such as hedge funds) undertake these activities. This classification reflects the fact that in these transactions, banks/financial institutions are undertaking proprietary trading activities and are acting as investors risking their own capital.

[40] See Nowell, Peter "Credit Derivatives Strategies For Hedge Funds" (Spring 2001) FOW/Credit Derivatives 4–9.

**Exhibit 7.17   Investor Applications Of Credit Derivatives –
Synthetic Bank Loan Investment**

Assume Investor M seeks to invest in commercial bank loans for its money market funds. The rationale is to acquire the assets to generate risk adjusted returns in excess of that available from other comparable floating rate investments.

The physical solution would be to directly participate in loans in the primary syndications market or acquire loan participations in the secondary markets. These approaches suffer from a number of inherent difficulties, including:

- The absence of a loan syndication infrastructure making participation in the primary loan market difficult.
- The lack of liquidity in the secondary loan market will also constrain acquiring loan assets.

A credit derivatives based solution would be to acquire this exposure synthetically by entering into the following transactions:

- **Total return swap** – this would entail Investor M entering into a total return loan swap with a counterparty where it receives the total return on the relevant loan(s) in exchange for paying LIBOR plus a margin.
- **Credit default swap** – this would entail Investor M entering into a credit default swap where it would sell protection to the counterparty against the default of the relevant reference entity.

In each case, the credit derivative can be combined with a cash investment equivalent to the face value of the swaps. This is used to fully fund the transaction (in effect, eliminating any leverage). This may be designed as a structured note. This creates a synthetic loan asset investment for the investor.

**Exhibit 7.18   Investor Applications Of Credit Derivatives –
Synthetic Portfolio Investment**

Assume Investor M wishes to invest in a diversified portfolio of high yield bonds. The primary objective is to create a diversified investment in this asset class comparable to the high yield index to which the performance of this portfolio is benchmarked.

The direct physical solution is to replicate the high yield index through direct investment in the underlying assets constituting the index. This approach has a number of problems, including:

- Necessity to trade in a significant number of securities. Some of the issues may not be liquid.
- Requirement for odd lot parcel sizes that might impact on the purchase price.
- Potential lack of liquidity of the portfolio.

- Need for re-balancing if the index composition is altered or where the index weighting is changed.
- Tracking error, where the tracking portfolio of bonds fails to exactly replicate the index, may lead to under performance.

A credit derivative based solution would be to acquire this exposure synthetically by entering into a total return swap based on *the relevant high yield index*. This would entail Investor M entering into a total return loan swap with a dealer where it receives the total return on the relevant index in exchange for paying LIBOR plus a margin.

The transaction, together with a cash investment to effectively fund the LIBOR payments, would effectively replicate the desired exposure to the high yield index. If required, the investment in cash and the swap could be combined into a structured note issued by an acceptable issuer of suitable credit standing to provide the required exposure. This may be more efficient than a physical investment in the index assets. In particular, the problems identified may be substantially reduced, allowing the investor to achieve a diversified exposure to the high yield sector.

In practice, investors increasingly use total return swaps or credit default swaps on the broad index or relevant sub-index of major credit indexes (for example, Trac-X or iBoxx) to synthesise credit portfolio investments[41].

**Exhibit 7.19   Investor Applications Of Credit Derivatives –
Synthetic Structured Investment**

Assume Investor M is seeking to increase its exposure to Yen assets within its fixed income investment portfolio. The investor is subject to the following constraints:

1. It is at the upper limit of its exposure to Japanese sovereign/sovereign guaranteed issuers. It is not able to increase its exposure to Japanese risk.
2. It has credit capacity available to Canadian issuers, in particular to the Canadian provinces. The investor has low exposure to these issuers on a portfolio basis.
3. It has a target maturity of 3 years.

The direct investment solution available would entail the Investor purchasing C$ securities issued by the Canadian provinces and entering into a currency swap to convert the C$ investment into Yen. The direct solution has a number of difficulties, including:

- The available C$ issues are of maturities significantly longer than 3 years.
- The entry into the C$/Yen cross currency swap would require commitment of large counterparty credit limits.

---

[41]   See Chapter 2.

One credit derivative based solution would be to create the following synthetic asset in the form of a credit linked structured note. The final maturity of the note is 3 years (consistent with the investor's target maturity). The note is denominated in Yen (as desired), with the redemption linked to the default of the Canadian provinces (to which the investor wishes to increase exposure).

In this particular case, the transaction is consistent with the investor achieving its investment objectives, with the credit default structured note allowing it to effectively diversify its *credit exposures* within its investment currency and maturity constraints.

**Exhibit 7.20   Investor Applications Of Credit Derivatives –
Synthetic Emerging Market Investment[42]**

Assume Investor M wishes to increase its exposure within its fixed income portfolio to the sovereign debt of an emerging market issuer – Country C. The investor is subject to a number of investment constraints, including:

1. The issuer must be the sovereign itself.
2. The investment must be principal protected.
3. The term of the investment must not exceed 3 years.
4. The investment must have liquidity.

The investor is focusing on Country C's outstanding Brady bonds. The bonds satisfy criteria 1, 2 and 4. However, the Brady bonds have a maturity of 30 years. The bonds violate criteria 3, making them ineligible investments.

A credit derivative based synthetic asset may allow the investor to overcome the maturity constraint. This would entail the creation of a structured note issued by an issuer of acceptable credit quality. The note has a final maturity of 3 years. The note redemption is linked to the Brady Bonds of Country C. The note will perform in a manner consistent with the performance of the under-lying reference securities of the emerging markets issuer. The note allows the disaggregation of the maturity of the investment and the underlying reference asset. This allows the synthetic asset to meet the relevant investment criteria.

---

[42]   This particular type of synthetic asset is suggested in Wheat, Allen "Develop-ments In The OTC Derivatives Markets" (May 1995) Financial Derivatives and Risk Management vol 1 37–44.

Exhibit 7.21 Convertible Bonds – Repackaging/Strip Trade[43]

1. Convertible Arbitrage – Concept

In recent times, there has been increased interest in trading convertible bonds in a form of arbitrage. The transaction entails separation of the equity option and the debt component. The equity option is placed with equity dealers/investors. The debt component is placed with debt dealers/investors as a fixed income investment. This activity is referred to as convertible arbitrage or stripped convertible trading[44].

Convertible bonds combine an equity option and a debt instrument. As the bond can be exchanged for a fixed number of shares, the convertible bond has a parity (conversion) value equal to:

Current stock price multiplied by the conversion ratio adjusted for the foreign exchange rate between the currency of the shares and the currency denomination of the convertible

The performance of the convertible is affected by interest rates, credit spreads, equity prices and equity volatility. As the share price increases, the convertible value becomes dominated by the equity value (the party value). As the share price falls, the equity option loses value and the bond value dominates the valuation of the convertible. The price behaviour is set out below:

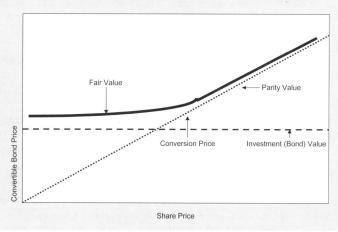

---

[43]   See Calamos, Nick P. (2003) Convertible Arbitrage; John Wiley & Sons, Inc, New Jersey; Francis, Chris, Kakodkar, Atish and Martin, Barnaby (16 April 2003) Credit Derivative Handbook"; Merrill Lynch, London at 53–55.

[44]   See Compton, Paul "Converting Profit" (March 2001) FOW/Equity Derivatives; Calamos, Nick P. (2003) Convertible Arbitrage; John Wiley & Sons, New Jersey. See also Mahtani, Arun "Asset Swappers, Bond Investors Target Convertibles" (13 March 1999) International Financing Review Issue 1274 at 75.

The analysis overstates the value of the floor provided by the value of the bond component of the convertible. This is because there is likely to be some relationship between the equity price and the credit quality/credit spread of the issuer. As the equity value falls, the credit quality of lower rated convertible issuers will generally also decline, resulting in higher credit spreads. This will reduce the value of the bond floor. This is referred to as the falling bond floor problem.

Traditionally, convertible arbitrage activity was undertaken in relation to convertibles where the embedded equity option had little value as a result of a decline in the price of the underlying stock to levels well below the strike price of the option. Under these conditions, the convertible trades as a bond[45]. In these trades, dealers looked to unbundle the security and repackage it through an asset swap[46]. In recent times, convertible arbitrage has been undertaken with issues where the equity option has value. This activity is undertaken in the primary and secondary markets. This reflects the emergence of convertible arbitrage hedge funds as significant investors in equity linked transactions.

This form of trading has taken a number of forms:

- **Convertible arbitrage** – this structure entails a dealer purchasing a convertible and separating the transaction into a conventional fixed income bond and the embedded equity option. The equity option is onsold to an equity dealer. The bond cash flows are re-profiled into a floating rate bond. The dealer holds the bond as a debt investment. The yield achievable is higher than would be available from a direct investment in a comparable bond issued by the underlying issuer.
- **Convertible and credit arbitrage** – this structure is the same as the above form of convertible arbitrage, but with an added feature. The additional feature is that the dealer will transfer the bond risk to a debt investor. This will typically be done using:
  1. An asset swap where the bond is sold to the debt investor and the bond cash flows re-profiled as required by the investor.
  2. A credit default swap where the dealer purchases protection against the risk of default by the issuer. In this case, the dealer continues to hold the convertible. The credit default swap has the effect of creating a fixed income security, where the underlying credit risk is transformed from that of the issuer to that of the counterparty providing credit protection.

The motivation of the convertible and credit arbitrage is pure arbitrage profit. The return to the dealer is that the price of the convertible is less than the total cash received from the sale of the equity option and the sale of the bond/credit risk.

---

[45] These securities are often referred to as "busted" convertibles.

[46] For a discussion of asset swaps, see Das, Satyajit (2004) Swaps/Financial Derivatives – 3rd Edition; John Wiley & Sons, Singapore at Chapter 38.

The major drivers underlying the transactions include:

- **Returns** – the yields available from the transactions have been very attractive on a relative value basis. Relative value groups in dealers and hedge funds drive the activity. The dealers have systematically traded away pricing discrepancies in the conventional fixed income markets. This forced the dealers to focus on the pricing anomalies in equity linked securities. The higher return is, in the case of standard convertible arbitrage, relative to returns available on comparable securities issued by the issuer. In the case of convertible and credit arbitrage, the return is a pure arbitrage profit after adjustment for the counterparty risk on the asset swap or credit default swap. The returns available reflect pricing anomalies related to both the pricing of the bond itself (including any embedded optionality) and also the equity component (low implied volatility on the embedded equity option).
- **Availability of investments** – the lack of availability of fixed income securities issued by the relevant issuer also contributed to the development of this type of transaction. Investors seeking *credit exposure* to a particular issuer may have been constrained by the lack of availability of securities issued by that particular issuer. Where the issuer has outstanding convertibles, the capacity to create a fixed income investor has proved attractive. For example, the lack of European corporate bond issuance in the period 1998–2000 contrasts with the significant volume of convertible and exchangeable bond issuance by European issuers. This created the opportunity to synthesise the credit risk of the issuers through convertible asset swaps. The risk is sold in two possible formats. The first form is as a conventional asset swap. The investor creates a floating rate investment returning a margin relative to LIBOR (in the currency of the investor's choice) by combining the purchase of the convertible, sale of the equity option back to the dealer and entry into an interest rate or currency swap. The second form entails assuming the credit risk indirectly through the sale of credit protection under a credit default swap. Under the second format, the dealer purchases the convertible, sells the equity option to another dealer, and purchases credit protection from the investor wanting to create credit exposure to the issuer. The dealer is left with a substantially hedged position and an arbitrage profit. The investor can assume the credit risk in a funded (credit linked note) or unfunded form (credit default swap).

The transactions are not free of risk. The presence of the equity option and the call features of the convertible (where the drivers are both the equity price and interest rates) all make this type of transaction complex. The risks require the asset swap or credit derivative structure to be customised to the underlying asset to avoid any residual risk of the transaction. For the investor in the asset swap or credit derivative, the major residual issue is the uncertainty regarding the duration of the investment[47].

---

[47] See Das, Satyajit (2004) Swaps/Financial Derivatives 3rd Edition; John Wiley, Singapore at Chapter 4 and 55. See also Das, Satyajit "Pricing & Risk Management of Equity Derivatives Transactions: Part 1" (1998) Financial

2. Convertible Arbitrage – Example

Assume the dealer purchases the following convertible bond:

Issuer	Company X
Maturity	15 November 2010
Face Value Amount	US$10 million
Coupon	3.00% pa payable annually (30/360 bond basis)
Current Price	93.75 plus accrued interest 2.35
Trade Date	22 August 2001
Settlement Date	27 August 2001
Purchase Price	US$9,610,000

The dealer purchases the bond and sells the equity option to an equity dealer. The dealer is now long a bond issued by Company X. The dealer can hold the bond or on-sell the bond (and the accompanying credit risk) to a debt investor. This can be structured as an asset swap or as a credit derivatives transaction. The overall transaction structure is set out below.

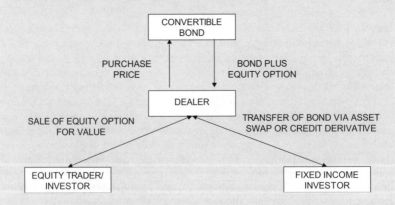

The purchaser of the equity option will generally hedge the equity position as follows:

- Sell an equivalent or similar option in the listed options market or OTC market.
- Delta hedge the position by borrowing and shorting the underlying stock and dynamically managing the position over the term[48].

Products Issue 87 18–23; "Pricing & Risk Management of Equity Derivatives Transactions: Part 2" (1998) Financial Products Issue 89 18–26.

48 See Das, Satyajit (2004) Swaps/Financial Derivatives 3rd Edition; John Wiley, Singapore at Chapters 15 and 16.

In practice, the second option is generally used. This reflects the convertible arbitrage dealer's reluctance to pay away the volatility spread to the equity option dealer[49].

The pure hedge would entail a hedge ratio equal to the number of bonds multiplied by the parity/conversion value of the bond multiplied by the delta of the position[50]. In practice, dealers generally will adjust the hedge using their view on the share price and equity volatility. This means that the hedge ratio may be higher (a "heavy" hedge) or lower (a "lighter" hedge)[51].

In certain markets (primarily emerging markets), equity dealers may purchase a basket of equity options and short the relevant market equity index futures contracts. Under this structure, the dealer runs the basis risk between the basket of equity options and the equity index.

The sale or hedge of the equity option effectively creates a deep discounted bond. Assuming that in this case, the equity option premium is around 12.50% of face value (around US$1,250,000), the effective price paid for the bond is US$8,360,000 (83.60% of face value). This has the effect of increasing the effective return on the bond.

The dealer can hold the bond as a high yielding debt investment. Alternatively, it can be placed with a fixed interest investor. The transaction can be structured as an asset swap or credit derivative transaction.

The asset swap is generally structured as follows:

• The dealer sells the convertible bond to the investor.
• The investor enters into an interest rate swap with the dealer to convert the cash flows into a synthetic floating rate note paying a margin over LIBOR.

The cash flows of the asset swap are as follows:

• **Initial cash flows** – at commencement, the investor pays the face value of the bond to the dealer. There are no initial cash flows under the swap. The investor pays a premium over pure economic value to purchase the convertible bond (effectively, the investor is paying par (100%) where the bond is valued at around 83.60%). The investor receives the value of the premium through the effective payments received under the swap. In effect, the investor pre-pays an amount that is paid back to the investor over the term of the investment as an annuity. This compensates for the low coupon (below current swap rates) and therefore the

---

[49]   In this case, the equity option trader would implement the delta hedge.
[50]   The delta will be based on an appropriate equity option pricing model; see Das, Satyajit (2004) Swaps/Financial Derivatives 3rd Edition; John Wiley, Singapore at Chapters 7 and 55.
[51]   To the extent the position is over or under hedged, the dealer is speculating on and fully exposed to the risk of market changes.

payments to be made by the investor to the dealer[52]. The structure creates a par asset for the investor. The structure also affects the credit risk under the swap. The payment of par substantially reduces the counterparty risk of the investor for the dealer.

- **Periodic payments** – the following exchanges take place over the life of the bond:
  1. On each annual coupon date of the convertible, the investor passes through to the swap counterparty the coupons on the convertible (US$300,000 calculated as 3.00% on US$10 million). Typically, the investor passes through the complete coupon, including the initial full coupon, despite the fact that the swap commences only a short time prior to the first coupon payment. The swap counterparty adjusts for this extra receipt in the margin paid on the floating rate side of the swap.
  2. Every quarter (15 February, 15 May, 15 August and 15 November commencing 15 November 2001 and ending 15 November 2010 unless terminated early), the investor receives a payment equivalent to 3 month US$ LIBOR plus a margin (say 95 bps)[53].

- **Final termination** – unless terminated early, the investor receives the US$10 million face value of the maturing convertible bond.

- **Early termination** – if the bond is converted or called prior to final maturity, the investor receives from the dealer an amount equivalent to face value of the convertible bond underlying the asset swap. The mechanics of early termination (for example, where the equity options are exercised) are as follows:
  1. The holder of the equity option exercises the option.
  2. The dealer terminates the asset swap. This entails the dealer paying the face value to the investor in return for delivery of the convertible bond. The dealer exercises the convertible, exchanging the bond for the underlying shares. The shares are delivered against payment of the strike price by the equity option purchaser. The payment for the shares received by the dealer (under exercise of the option) is used to fund the payment to the investor. The interest rate swap between the dealer and the investor is also terminated. In the case of a call by the issuer, the payment by the dealer to the investor is funded by the payment received from the issuer under the call.

  The investor is compensated for the early termination (pre-payment risk) by the payment of a higher margin. The early termination also creates additional risk for the dealer. This derives from the need to terminate the swap before maturity. There may be a cost of termination reflecting movements in the swap rates between commencement of the asset swap and the termination date.

---

[52]   For discussion of the structuring of asset swaps, see Das, Satyajit (2004) Swaps/ Financial Derivatives 3rd Edition; John Wiley, Singapore at Chapter 38.

[53]   Interest payments can be priced off US$ 3 month LIBOR, swapped into fixed rate or swapped into a currency of the investor's choice.

The result of the transaction is that the investor has synthesised a floating rate investment at a return of US$ LIBOR plus 95 bps. This compares to a return on a conventional bond of comparable maturity issued by the issuer that would swap into US$ LIBOR plus 71 bps. This represents an additional return of 24 bps pa.

Where credit derivatives are used to transfer the debt risk and return to the investor, the structure depends on the form of credit derivatives used. The credit risk can be transferred using a credit default swap or a credit linked note.

Where a credit default swap is used, the structure would be as follows:

- The dealer would continue to hold the convertible bond.
- The dealer would enter into a credit default swap with the investor with the following structure:
  1. The dealer pays the investor the spread (95 bps pa).
  2. The investor assumes the risk of loss on the convertible bond in the event that the issuer defaults on its obligations. If there is a credit event under the convertible bond, then the dealer would deliver the defaulted convertible bond to the investor[54]. The investor would pay the dealer the face value of the convertible bond. This would have the effect of indemnifying the dealer against risk of loss from default by the convertible bond issuer.
  3. The term of the credit default swap would be till maturity or termination by conversion or call.

The transaction could also be structured as a credit linked note issued by the dealer to the investor. The note would be linked to the underlying convertible bond. The structure effectively embeds the credit default swap (on the issuer of the convertible bond) in a note. The economics and mechanics of this structure are similar to that of the credit default swap. A major difference is that the credit linked note provides the dealer with funding. In contrast, the credit default swap only transfers the credit risk but does not provide funding. A further difference is that a credit linked note eliminates credit risk for the dealer on the investor by virtue of the note acting as cash collateral. If a credit linked note structure is used, then the investor has additional risk on the dealer as the issuer of the note.

An advantage of both credit default swaps and credit linked notes is that the transfer of credit risk does not entail an interest rate swap to re-profile the convertible bond cash flows under the asset swap. This means that there is no residual risk from early termination of the interest rate swap. The interest rate risk remains with the dealer and must be managed appropriately.

The dealer will need to make the credit default swap/credit linked note callable to neutralise the early termination risk (conversion/call) on the convertible. This is to ensure a perfect hedge of the credit position.

---

[54] The deliverability of convertible bonds under a credit default swap has been subject to uncertainty, see Chapter 1.

If the convertible has a put date then the credit risk will generally only be hedged with a credit default swap through till the put date.

In practice, the credit hedge is rarely exact. Dealers generally hedge approximately and adjust the hedge for their views on the likely credit risk migration of the issuer and the likelihood of termination through conversion or exercise of any call option. The dealer will hedge on the basis of the credit sensitivity of the position (based on shocking the credit spread by a fixed amount (10 bps pa)). The model hedge will be adjusted for their view on the credit and early termination by increasing or decreasing the credit default swap position. The adjustment of the hedge is dictated in part by the fact that liquidity of the credit default swap market is concentrated in the 5 year maturity[55].

**Exhibit 7.22   Investor Applications Of Credit Derivatives –
Ratings Downgrade Protection**

Assume Investor M is planning to increase its exposure to a specific industry group (say automobiles). The exposure is through the purchase of a basket of bonds issued by companies within the industry. The increase in exposure is predicated on macro economic and business cycle factors. The investor is risk averse and is considering a strategy of protecting its investment. The protection would be through either a hedge of the credit spread or a contingent exit strategy.

The traditional physical solution is to establish the position by investing in the bonds and then exiting the sector by liquidation of the holdings upon default or downgrade. This suffers from a number of difficulties, including:

● Assumptions about market liquidity that may not be reasonable in practice.
● The occurrence of the contingent event is likely to trigger a fall in prices for all the issuers in the basket. This may lead to both price pressures and reduction in liquidity in the non defaulted or non downgraded securities.
● In the absence of liquidity, it may be difficult, under the circumstances considered, to hedge or reduce the credit risk of the portfolio.

The credit spread hedge would focus on the investor buying protection through credit default swaps on the entities whose bonds the investor has purchased. The protection could be bought at the commencement of the investment or at a later date based on the investor's expectation of the industry and the issuers[56].

---

[55] To the extent the position is over or under hedged, the dealer is speculating on and fully exposed to the risk of market changes.

[56] If the investor purchased protection at the time of purchasing the bonds, then it is likely that it would have locked in a negative spread unless the cost of

In this case, the investor would have an investment in the bonds matched against its position in the credit default swaps. If the industry or issuers' credit quality deteriorates, then the credit spread on both the bonds and the credit default swap will increase. This will result in a loss on the bonds and a gain on the credit default swaps. The investor would need to terminate the credit default swaps to realise the value on the credit default swaps to offset the loss on its investment. If the credit quality of the portfolio improves then the credit default swap would expire.

The contingent exit strategy would entail selling the bonds upon the default by or a downgrade of the outstanding debt of *any one* of the issuers. This strategy is based on the logic that the default or downgrade (below a threshold level) of *any* of the issuers within the basket will adversely affect the value of the other bonds (there is a positive correlation between default/credit risks). Two possible credit derivative solutions are feasible:

- **First-to-default note** – as an alternative to purchasing the bonds, the investor invests in a structured note. The note payoff is linked to the default or downgrade of a basket of the underlying issuers[57]. Under this structure, the investor assumes the risk to the issuers included in the basket on a first-to-default basis. In the event of default, the investor suffers a loss based on the loss on the defaulted or downgraded securities, but is effectively repaid the rest of its investment (replicating its exit strategy objectives). In return for this arrangement, the investor pays a premium (in effect, a reduction of the return on the underlying securities) in return for this protection. The major benefit of this arrangement is that the investor achieves an immediate reduction of its exposure to default risk in the industry upon the default of any one of the issuers.
- **First-to-default swap** – the investor purchases the bonds. Simultaneously, the investor enters into a default swap (on a first-to-default basis) where the investor can settle the swap by delivery of the securities included in the basket at pre agreed prices.

Both strategies have the desired effect of achieving a rapid reduction in the exposure to the industry if there is any deterioration in credit quality in the industry.

**Exhibit 7.23   Investor Applications Of Credit Derivatives –
Emerging Market Portfolio Hedge**

Assume Investor M is an emerging market investor with a substantial investment portfolio of Brady bonds. The Investor is seeking to reduce its exposure to this

---

protection was below the spread in the cash market (negative basis; see Chapter 5), or the protection was for a shorter maturity (in which case the investor would be exposed beyond the maturity of the hedge).

[57]   In practice, credit default swaps linked to credit downgrades are rare in practice; see discussion in Chapter 1.

sector. The decision reflects the fall in spreads, prompting Investor M to lock in its capital gains.

Investor M does not wish to sell its holdings (at least not immediately) for a number of reasons:

- The portfolio is large and would create price pressures if rapid liquidation was attempted.
- The physical sale of the securities would also result in the realisation of gains, resulting in acceleration of tax liabilities.

Another factor may be its expectations that US treasury interest rates are likely to decline in the near future.

Against this background, Investor M decides to hedge its Brady bond portfolio for the next 1 year. This is designed to hedge the price risk and allow a systematic sale of the portfolio (if desired) over a longer time period.

The physical hedge would entail shorting the Brady bonds. This may be difficult because of the problems of shorting emerging market debt, including availability of securities for borrowing, the cost of borrowing securities, the term of any such borrowing, and the interest rate uncertainty introduced.

A credit derivative based solution would be to enter into a total return swap where Investor M pays the total rate of return on a reference emerging market index (for example, the IFC Emerging Market Index or a private index published by a financial institution) in exchange for receiving LIBOR.

The transaction would have the following impact:

- Transferring the price risk on the portfolio to the counterparty, creating a hedge against the value of the bonds. This assumes that the underlying portfolio is similar in composition to the index used to hedge (that is, there is limited basis risk).
- The index may well be a more liquid vehicle to effect the hedge, avoiding illiquidity and problems related to short selling.
- The bonds can continue to be held as the price risk has been substantially reduced, allowing the issue of realisation to be deferred.

**Exhibit 7.24   Investor Applications Of Credit Derivatives –
First–To–Default Basket[58]**

Assume Investor M manages a portfolio of bonds subject to a minimum credit rating level of AA/Aa. The investor is seeking opportunities to increase the yield on the portfolio.

---

[58]   For discussion of the economics of first-to-default structures, see Chapter 2. An example outlining the use of first-to-default baskets to create synthetic leverage is discussed later in the Chapter.

Traditional direct approaches require identification of relative value by purchasing undervalued AA/Aa rated assets in the primary or secondary markets to enhance portfolio performance. The capacity to enhance yield in this manner is limited. This is because of strong competition to identify these relative value opportunities.

A credit derivative based solution would focus on investing in a credit default structured note where the default on the note is linked to a basket of 4 AA/Aa credits on a first-to-default basis. In the event that *any one* of the reference credits defaults, then the redemption value of the structured note is reduced by either a pre-agreed fixed amount or the fall in the value of the first defaulted security. For a 5 year maturity, such an investment provides an additional return of around 20 to 30 bps pa relative to the current yield levels on any of the reference securities on an individual basis.

The increased return compensates for the fact that a first-to-default basket is inherently more risky than the individual issuers. In effect, a first-to-default basket of AA/Aa issuers may have a default risk equivalent to lower credit levels, although the individual obligors within the basket satisfy the minimum threshold credit rating level imposed upon the investor.

Exhibit 7.25 Investor Applications Of Credit Derivatives – Monetising Credit Spread Expectations With Spread Forwards Or Collars

Assume Investor M manages a money market portfolio. Authorised portfolio investments are floating interest rate assets that must have a final maturity not exceeding 3 years. The minimum credit rating is A1/P1 or AA/Aa. Investor M is seeking opportunities to enhance the returns on the portfolio in a period of very tight credit spreads.

The investor expects that credit spreads will increase for certain borrowers (one such borrower is Company X). The investor expects that the spread increase will be most marked in longer maturities. For example, assume that Company X's credit spreads for 3 years are around 20 bps pa and for 10 years it is 45 bps pa. Investor M expects that the spreads on the shorter securities will increase to 40 bps pa (an increase of 20 bps) while spreads on the longer maturities will increase to 95 bps pa (an increase of 50 bps). The greater spread duration at the longer maturities, combined with the larger increase, provides greater opportunities to extract value from the 10 year spreads.

Investor M can seek to capture value from this expectation by disaggregating its expectations on changes in credit spreads from other aspects of the underlying securities, such as the term or interest rate exposure.

Examples of the types of transactions that are feasible are set out below. Each example entails a structured note issued by an AA/Aa rated issuer where the redemption is linked to the credit spread on the 10 year securities issued by Company X. The note has a maturity of 2 years. The return on the note is above that available for a conventional security for an equivalent credit quality issuer. This added return is generated from one of the following sources:

- **Sale of the forward spread** – under this structure, the investor sells the 10 year credit spread of Company X two years forward (effectively, a 2 year forward on 8 year credit spreads, reflecting the shortening in the remaining term to maturity). The forward spread is around 49 bps pa. In order to extract value from the transaction, the forward embedded in the note is structured at a forward rate of, say, 54 bps pa. This means that the forward is effectively in the money and the embedded value can be discounted back to the start of the transaction and allocated over the life of the note to increase the yield on the shorter dated transaction. The investor benefits if the credit spreads for Company X widen above 54 bps pa (this is reflected in the adjusted redemption value of the note) or suffers a loss (reflected as a loss of principal) if the spread falls below 54 bps pa.
- **Credit spread collar** – under this structure, the investor purchases a put on the forward credit spread while financing the put through the sale of a call on the spread. The collar created has the effect of allowing the investor to benefit from an increase in the spread. The investor will suffer a loss from a reduction in the spread. The strike prices of the options are structured so that the value received from the sale of the call is higher than that required to purchase the put. For example, in this case, the call could be sold with a strike of 55 bps. The option is in the money based on a forward spread of 49 bps. The put could be purchased at a strike of 70 bps pa that is out of the money. This means that investor M benefits if the spread widens above 70 bps pa, but loses if the spread falls below 55 bps pa. The structure of the strikes is designed to ensure that the collar will provide net premium income that will then be used to enhance the coupon return on the note itself.

The structure allows the investor to seek to improve its returns on its money market investments through monetisation of its expectations on credit spreads. The security is consistent with its investment parameters. The structure allows the investor to obtain exposure to the *spread duration* without altering its overall *interest rate* risk profile. The structure would typically be used to enable the investor to outperform its return benchmark (for example, LIBOR average).

Exhibit 7.26   Investor Applications Of Credit Derivatives – Monetising Credit Spread Expectations With Targeted Put Selling

Assume Investor M manages a portfolio of emerging market bonds. Assume that following a crisis in one of the Latin American emerging markets, there has been a significant sell-off in emerging market debt. The spread for 10 year maturities on an Asian BBB/Baa rated sovereign issuer has widened from 125 bps pa to 155 bps pa over US$ swaps. The rise in credit spreads has been accompanied by a significant increase in volatility.

Investor M expects that this rise in credit spreads is likely to be short lived as the fundamentals assert themselves and the pattern of trading in the Asian emerging market issuer decouples from that of the Latin issuers. It seeks to monetise this expectation through the sale of a put option on the credit spread (relative to a nominated benchmark treasury). The option is for 1 year with a strike yield of 175 bps (some 20 bps above the current spot spread). The investor receives a premium of 1.30% flat of the principal of the transaction.

The investor's payoff profile is as follows:

- If the investor's expectations are realised and the issuer's credit spreads remain at current levels or fall, then the put will not be exercised and the premium received will enhance portfolio returns.
- If the issuer's credit spreads increase to a level above the strike spread of 175, then the put will be exercised. The exercise of the put will, in effect, equate to the purchase of the issuer's 10 year securities (that will have 9 years to go to maturity) at the strike spread. The transaction may in fact be structured to allow the purchaser of the option to sell that security to the investor at the current swap rate at option maturity plus the strike spread. The investor may be prepared to accept the risk on the basis that it considers the securities to represent *value* at these levels. From a purely economic perspective, the premium received equates to providing protection against an increase in the spread of around 22 bps pa. In effect, where the spread increases above around 197 bps pa over the US$ swap rates, the investor suffers an economic loss.

Two aspects of the sale of this covered credit spread put should be noted:

- The transaction may be motivated by the higher volatility of *credit spreads* relative to the volatility of the yield on the securities. This allows extraction of additional value from the sale of the put on the credit spread.
- The option position may benefit from the shortening in the maturity of the underlying securities (from 10 to 9 years) over the life of the option transaction. Assuming a positively shaped credit spread curve, the shortening of the maturity of the underlying securities should assist the investor as it will benefit from the expected fall in the credit spread arising from the fall in maturity.

Exhibit 7.27   Investor Applications Of Credit Derivatives – Monetising Credit Spread Expectations With Digital Options

Assume that Investor M manages a fixed interest portfolio of high credit quality (minimum rating AA/Aa). Contraction in credit spreads means that portfolio returns are below target levels. Assume that the investor has credit lines available to purchase 10 year securities issued by Company X. The reference bond has a coupon of 6.75% pa and a maturity of approximately 10 years. Investor M observes that the credit spread on the securities (currently 40 bps pa to US$ swap rates) has traded in a range of 35 to 50 bps pa relative to US$ swap rates for the previous 12 months. Investor M also expects that the bond will continue to trade within this credit spread range.

Investor M purchases the underlying 10 year bonds issued by Company X. Simultaneously, it enters into a derivative transaction with a dealer where:

- The investor will receive a payment of 35 bps pa.
- In return, the investor will make a payment equivalent to 2.00% to the dealer if the credit spread on the reference security is outside the range 30 bps pa and 55 bps pa at maturity (in 1 year).

The effect of this transaction is the following:

- If the credit spread stays within the nominated range, then the investor enjoys an enhanced yield relative to the return that it would have received on its investment in the bonds. The additional yield is equivalent to the payment received from the dealer.
- If the credit spread moves outside the range, then the investor's return is reduced by around 165 bps pa. The net loss is the amount received of 35 bps pa and the payment due to the counterparty of 200 bps pa. The loss is funded by the allocation of part of the coupon on the reference bonds, effectively reducing the portfolio returns.

The transaction entails the investor selling digital options[59] (both calls and puts) on the credit spread. The fixed payout is the amount (200 bps pa) willing to be foregone by the investor. The structure is identical to range/accrual note structures introduced in the early 1990s[60]. The premium received allows the investor to enhance the return on the portfolio in return for taking on the exposure to potential movements of the spread outside the historical range (the strikes are set slightly outside the historical trading range).

The actual payoffs on the digital options sold can be based on the spread at maturity. Alternatively, the payoff can be calculated on the basis of daily accruals of the payment amount, based on the number of days the spread is outside the range over the full 1 year period. The structure may be varied. For example, by varying the amount of the coupon on the underlying bond that the investor is willing to risk or the strike levels, the level of credit enhancement achieved can be increased or decreased. The structure can also be embedded in a structured note if required by the investor.

The structure captures value from the volatility of credit spreads and their historical performance. The investor achieves enhanced returns if the credit spreads behave consistent with its expectations. The investor does not risk principal and is guaranteed a minimum return as the digital option specifically limits its loss.

---

[59] See Das, Satyajit (2004) Swaps/Financial Derivatives 3rd Edition; John Wiley, Singapore at Chapter 44.

[60] See Das, Satyajit (2004) Swaps/Financial Derivatives 3rd Edition; John Wiley, Singapore at Chapter 53.

Exhibit 7.28   Investor Applications Of Credit Derivatives – Outright Credit Spread Positions

Credit default swaps are frequently used to create positions designed to profit from outright changes in credit spreads. The following strategies are used:

- **Credit spread widening** – assume Investor M expects credit spreads on Company X to widen. This expectation is based on fundamental credit research that indicates that the credit quality of the company is likely to deteriorate. Investor M may monetise this expectation by purchasing protection on Company X using a credit default swap. Under the 5 year credit default swap, Investor M pays a fee (150 bps pa) in return for purchasing default protection on Company X from the dealer. If the credit spread widens as expected in 1 year (to say 200 bps pa), then Investor M can capture value from the spread change by terminating the credit default swap to capture the 50 bps pa gain over the remaining 4 year term of the transaction. If the spread decreases then the investor suffers a mark-to-market loss on the position. The loss would be realised if the transaction is terminated. Alternatively, the loss accrues from the spread paid on the credit default swap through to maturity of the transaction.
- **Credit spread tightening** – assume Investor M expects credit spread on Company X to tighten. This expectation is based on fundamental credit research that indicates that the credit quality of the company is likely to improve over a 1 year risk horizon. Investor M may monetise this expectation by purchasing protection on Company X using a credit default swap. Under the 5 year credit default swap, Investor M receives a fee (150 bps pa) in return for selling default protection on Company X to the dealer. If the credit spread tightens as expected in 1 year (to say 100 bps pa), then Investor M can capture value from the spread change by terminating the credit default swap to capture the 50 bps pa gain over the remaining 4 year term of the transaction. If the spread widens then the investor will suffer a mark-to-market loss on the position. The loss would be realised if the transaction is terminated. If the transaction is not terminated and there is no credit event then the investor will continue to receive the spread on the credit default swap. If the transaction is not terminated and there is a credit event then the investor will suffer a loss on the contract as it has to settle the contract.

The following factors are relevant to both transactions:

- The investor would need to terminate the transaction to capture the value of a favourable spread movement. This would be structured as a reversal/offsetting transaction, assignment/novation or (preferably) cancellation/termination of the original contract[61].
- The value of a credit default swap is equivalent to the difference between the original transaction and the offsetting credit default swap used to terminate the

---

[61]   See Chapter 5.

position. The value of the credit default swap will derive from changes in pricing (the spread on the contract). In order to incorporate the risk of default, the present value of the cash flows is adjusted. Each of the annuity cash flows is weighted by the estimated survival probabilities of the reference entity of the credit default swap[62].

- The credit default swap would need to be terminated reasonably early in its life (that is, with significant remaining term) to capture significant value from the spread change. This reflects the fact that as the unexpired term of the credit default swap shortens, the value of the contract changes. The credit default swap's value behaviour becomes binary – default (pays out loss given default) or no default (zero payout). This reduces the sensitivity to spread movements.

**Exhibit 7.29   Investor Applications Of Credit Derivatives –
Cheap Long/Short Positions[63]**

Credit default swaps can be used to construct simple directional strategies designed to profit from changes in credit spreads (for example, see **Exhibit 7.28**). More complex relative value based strategies designed to trade the cash-synthetic basis are also feasible. These strategies are focused principally on creating higher yielding long positions and lower cost short positions in individual reference entities ("cheap" long or short strategies).

Typical strategies include the following transactions:

- **Cheap long** – assume Investor M already has exposure to Company X or wishes to acquire credit exposure to the company. Assume the cash-synthetic basis is positive (credit default swap spread is 120 bps pa versus asset swap spread of 80 bps pa translating into a + 40 bps pa basis). In this situation, it would be feasible for the investor to earn a higher return on its exposure to Company X by selling protection under a credit default swap (receive 120 bps pa) than in the cash market. Where the investor had an existing position in Company X, it could sell its cash position at 80 bps pa and invest at 120 bps pa via the credit default swap. Where the investor was seeking to establish a new position, it would be more economic to acquire the exposure through the credit default swap market as it offers better returns.
- **Cheap short** – assume Investor M expects a deterioration in the credit quality of Company X and is interested in shorting the credit. A cheap short is available where the basis is negative. For example, where the asset swap spread is 100 bps pa and the credit default spread is 80 bps pa, the negative basis (−20 bps pa) would allow the investor to set up a cheap short by purchasing protection via a credit default swap on Company X.

---

[62] See Chapter 5.
[63] See Francis, Chris, Kakodkar, Atish and Martin, Barnaby (16 April 2003) Credit Derivative Handbook"; Merrill Lynch, London at 44.

The following factors should be considered in any relative value strategy:

- Of itself, a positive or negative basis does not make a position attractive. For example, there may be a number of reasons for a positive basis (cheapest-to-deliver option and different credit events)[64]. These factors may explain the basis, eliminating the value in the transaction.
- Difficulties in shorting in the cash market may make it attractive to set up a short using credit default swaps even where the basis is *positive* (credit default swap spread higher than the asset swap spread). This may be case where there is an expectation of future volatility.
- Cheap long short strategies can be used to create higher yielding or lower cost positions. These positions may be held till maturity. Alternatively, the investor can trade changes in the basis. For example, an investor with a core portfolio position in Company X can trade the basis to seek to generate earnings. For example, the investor would switch to the credit default swap where the basis is positive. If the basis reduces then the investor can terminate the credit default swap and switch back to the asset. Similarly, a cheap short position can be reversed where the basis becomes less negative or more positive. These strategies seek to capture value from the volatility and mean reverting behaviour of the basis between the cash and synthetic markets.

Exhibit 7.30   Investor Applications Of Credit Derivatives – Credit Spread Term Structure Transactions[65]

Credit default swaps are frequently used to trade the term structure of credit spreads. A common transaction focuses on inversion of the credit spread curve in the credit default swap market.

This opportunity generally occurs where there is a deterioration in the credit quality of the reference entity. In practice, this occurs as the issuer's bonds move from being traded on a spread basis to an absolute price basis. This reflects the increased risk of default and the greater emphasis on recovery values. This forces an inversion in the credit default swap curve term structure, with the spread on short dated protection becoming higher than that for longer dated protection[66].

The inversion reflects the following considerations:

- Concern about short term risk of default with hedgers and traders aggressively purchasing short dated protection.

---

[64]   See Chapter 5.

[65]   See Francis, Chris, Kakodkar, Atish and Martin, Barnaby (16 April 2003) "Credit Derivative Handbook"; Merrill Lynch, London at 50–51.

[66]   For example, during 2002, the credit default swap curve for Alcatel became inverted, with the spread between 1 year and 5 years trading between –500/600 bps pa.

- Belief that if the entity survives the immediate crisis then its survival prospects will be greater (a form of survivor bias).
- Increased volatility in shorter dated credit default swap contracts.
- Exacerbation of the inversion in the credit default swap market relative to the cash market because the protection sellers do not have the benefit of owning a security trading below face value[67].

Investors can trade the inversion of the credit spread curve to purchase forward protection at attractive price levels. The structure of the transaction is as follows:

- Investor purchases longer dated protection (5 year at 450 bps pa).
- Investor sells shorter dated protection (1 year at 800 bps pa).

The strategy is equivalent to purchasing 4 year protection 1 year forward at 363 bps pa.

The payoffs of the strategy are as follows:

- If there is a credit event during year 1, the investor is hedged on the default (long and short protection through the two credit default swaps). It also benefits from the carry between the two spreads (350 bps pa) until the credit event.
- If there is a credit event during years 2 to 5, then the investor benefits from the 5 year credit default swap where it has purchased protection on the reference entity. It also benefits from the positive carry during the first year that helps lower the cost of purchasing protection for 5 years.
- If there was no credit event during the entire 5 years, the investor loses the spread paid under the credit default swap. The positive carry during year 1 reduces the cost of the hedge.

Exhibit 7.31   Investor Applications Of Credit Derivatives – Cash-Synthetic Basis Transactions[68]

A common investment strategy is to purchase a bond or asset swap and hedge the credit risk by buying protection under a credit default swap. The strategy is designed to capture value where the cash-synthetic basis is negative[69].

A typical trade would be structured as follows:

- Investor purchases an asset swap on Company ABC 5 year bonds. The asset swap generates a return on LIBOR plus 125 bps pa.
- Investor simultaneously purchases default protection on Company ABC from a dealer. The maturity of the credit default swap is matched to the final maturity of

---

[67]   This may be addressed by using a fees up-front structure on the credit default swap; see Chapter 2.

[68]   See Francis, Chris, Kakodkar, Atish and Martin, Barnaby (16 April 2003) Credit Derivative Handbook"; Merrill Lynch, London at 42–43; 47–50.

[69]   The strategy is often referred to as the protected bond package.

the asset swap. A default under the bond underlying the asset swap would constitute a credit event under the credit default swap. The investor pays a spread of 100 bps pa to the dealer.
- The trade generates a net spread to the investor of 25 bps pa.

The economics of the transaction are complex:

- The transaction offers the investor positive carry.
- The investor is essentially hedged on the underlying credit risk to the reference entity.
- The investor's funding costs are frequently above LIBOR. This means that the net spread may not result in a positive spread to the investor. For example, unless the investor has funding costs below LIBOR plus 25 bps, the transaction would not have positive carry for the investor.
- The investor also has additional costs and risks. For example, the investor has counterparty risk under the credit default swap on the dealer (although this may be cash collateralised). The investors may also incur other capital and administrative costs.

In practice, investors frequently enter into the trade even where the carry is insufficient relative to funding cost or even where the cash-synthetic basis is slightly positive. This reflects the fact that the position allows the investor to benefit from credit market volatility.

The long asset swap/credit default swap hedge position offers the investor the ability to benefit from market volatility with limited downside. This reflects the sensitivity of the position to changes in the basis. The performance of the position will be responsive to the following changes in the credit market:

- **Basis changes** – if the trade is entered into when the basis is negative or slightly positive, then the investor can benefit where the basis becomes positive or more positive. This may allow the investor to unwind both legs (the asset swap and the credit default swap) at a profit.
- **Credit deterioration** – where the underlying credit deteriorates modestly, the position generates profits from the following changes:
  1. The basis tends to become positive where credit spread on a reference entity is widening. An additional factor may be that when a credit deteriorates, the supply of protection on the reference entity becomes scarcer. This makes a position valuable where the investor has purchased protection.
  2. The credit events in the credit default swap are more extensive than the events of default on the bonds and this will enhance the value of the position[70].
  3. The investor is long the cheapest-to-deliver option under the credit default swap and this adds to the value of the position[71].

---

[70] See Chapter 1.
[71] See Chapter 1.

The economics of the position are driven by the interaction of credit market volatility and the cash-synthetic basis. For example, negative basis generally exists where there is a high credit quality issuer whose bonds are trading at tight spreads in the cash market. The basis tends to become positive as the credit quality deteriorates and spreads widen. This relationship reflects the fact that credit spreads, cash-synthetic basis and asset volatility of a firm are related.

The Merton structural model suggests a natural relationship between credit spreads and the entity's equity and asset volatility[72]. Increased equity and asset volatility is reflected in higher credit spreads. This means that investors may benefit from buying credit protection on entities where the equity/asset volatility is high or likely to increase. The high volatility implies that the company's value could take on extreme (very high or very low) values. In particular, if the company's asset value fell sharply then the likelihood of a default/credit event would increase. This would increase the value of a position where the investor was long protection on the entity.

The relationship between credit spreads and equity/asset volatility also affects the basis. A negative or low positive basis indicates that investors are willing to take credit risk on the entity (sell protection under credit default swaps). A strong positive basis indicates that investors are unwilling to assume the credit risk except for a large premium.

This means that the long asset swap/long credit protection transaction is attractive when the basis is low relative to actual or expected equity/asset volatility. Investors can use the position to purchase cheap equity or asset volatility. This is particularly the case where the position can be constructed at positive carry or low net cost.

Other factors that affect the basis trade include:

- **Price sensitivity of the position** – it is important to note that the gain and offsetting loss on the bond/asset swap position and the credit default swap may not be identical. This reflects the fact that the revaluation of the credit default swap will reflect the impact of default on the stream of net payments; that is, the difference between the original credit default swap spread and the current market spread[73]. This means that a widening (tightening) in the credit spread will result in loss (gain) on the asset swap that is larger than the gain (loss) on the credit default swap. The price sensitivity is also affected by the assumed recovery rate. In practice, the credit default swap market tends to price on the basis of approximately a 35% recovery rate. Variations in actual recovery will alter the economics of the position.
- **Documentary issues** – this focuses on nuances of bond documentation. In practice, different bonds have different covenants and other credit conditions. This drives the value of the implicit cheapest-to-deliver options held by the investor under

---

[72]   See Chapters 5 and 6.
[73]   See Chapter 5.

this strategy. For example, the investor benefits where the bond underlying the asset swap has strong covenant protection or where there is a provision for the coupon to step-up if the credit condition of the issuer deteriorates. This is because these conditions will tend to ensure that the price of this bond will deteriorate at a slower rate than other bonds. This will create additional value in the position as the credit default swap will trade to the cheapest to deliver bond.

Exhibit 7.32   Investor Applications Of Credit Derivatives – Senior Versus Subordinated Trading Strategies[74]

Credit default swap trading strategies can be devised to capture value from the relative values of debt with different seniority. The most typical transaction involves senior versus subordinated debt of the same reference entity.

In the market, subordinated debt of an issuer trades at a higher spread than the senior debt of the same issuer with the same maturity. This is also the case in the credit default swap market. The spread difference reflects the following factors:

- The probability of default or credit events should be identical between senior and subordinated debt.
- The spread difference should be directly related to recovery assumptions.

For example, assume subordinated debt spreads are 100 bps pa versus senior debt spreads of 50 bps pa (that is, 2 times). If the assumed recovery rate on senior debt is 60% (loss given default of 40%), then the recovery rate on subordinated debt implied is 20% (loss given default of 80%). Changes in the spread difference between senior and subordinated debt imply changing recovery assumptions. In the above example, if the spread difference tightened to 25 bps (1.5 times), the implied recovery rates are altered. If the assumed recovery rate on senior debt is 60% (loss given default of 40%), then the implied recovery rate on subordinated debt is 40% (loss given default of 60%)[75].

Where there is an active credit default swap market on both senior and subordinated debt of an issuer, then the following trading strategies can be established:

- Where the subordinated/senior ratio is high, investors sell protection on a subordinated basis and purchase protection on a senior basis.

---

[74]   See Francis, Chris, Kakodkar, Atish and Martin, Barnaby (16 April 2003) Credit Derivative Handbook"; Merrill Lynch, London at 52–53.
[75]   Historically, banks have tended to trade at around a 2 times ratio while insurance companies trade at a 1.5 times ratio; see Francis, Chris, Kakodkar, Atish and Martin, Barnaby (16 April 2003) Credit Derivative Handbook"; Merrill Lynch, London at 52–53.

- Where the subordinated/senior ratio is low, investors sell protection on a senior basis and purchase protection on a subordinated basis.

In setting up these transactions, the current ratio is compared to peers in the market or historical patterns. In addition, the transactions are constructed on a cash flow or carry neutral basis. This means that the purchase and sale of protection is undertaken based on the subordinated/senior ratio to ensure that the income on protection sold exactly offsets the expense on the protection purchased.

The transactions are designed to generate earnings from the following market movements:

- If the ratio reverts to the more "normalised" levels, then the investor can unwind the position at a profit.
- If there is a credit event, then the differences in actual recovery between the senior and subordinated debt will generate a profit for the investor.

**Exhibit 7.33   Investor Applications Of Credit Derivatives –
Debt-Equity Trading Strategies.**

1. Capital Structure Arbitrage

Capital structure arbitrage is a generic term that is used to describe a wide variety of trading strategies[76]. It covers a number of strategies including relative value trading between different debt securities (senior versus subordinated debt[77]) and debt-equity trading strategies. It is based on the inherent relationship between credit risk and equity prices[78]. The relationship is commonly based on the Merton or structural credit model[79].

The relationship between debt and equity has been known since the early 1970s. However, practitioners have only begun to use the model actively in recent years. The key driver of debt-equity trading has been hedge funds that have successfully traded equity positions against credit positions to generate attractive returns.

---

[76] See Currie, Antony and Morris, Jennifer "And Now For Capital Structure Arbitrage" (December 2002) Euromoney 38–43.

[77] See **Exhibit 7.32**.

[78] See King, Matt (4 September 2001) Using Equities To Price Credit; JP Morgan, London; Keenan, Sean C., Sobehart, Jorge R. and Benzschawel, Terry L. "The Debt And Equity Linkage And The Valuation Of Credit Derivatives" in Gregory, Jon (Editor) (2003) Credit Derivatives: The Definitive Guide; Risk Publications, London at Chapter 5.

[79] For a discussion of the Merton model, see Chapter 6. See Merton, R. "On The Option Pricing Of Corporate Debt: The Risk Structure Of Interest Rates" (1974) Journal of Finance vol 29 449–470. For a more recent approach using the

2. Debt-Equity Trading Strategy – Example[80]

A typical debt-equity trading strategy may take the following form[81]:

- Investor purchases shares in an entity.
- Investor simultaneously purchases protection on the entity.

The structure and performance of the transaction will be driven by the following factors:

- **Carry** – the purchase of default protection by the investor is funded out of the dividend income from the stock position. The transaction will be structured to have zero carry; that is, the dividend income on the stock must cover the cost of protection. The ratio of the trade (the notional amount of stock to the notional amount of credit protection purchased) is driven by the requirement to have zero carry[82].
- **Profit and loss performance** – the performance of the combined position will be as follows:
  1. If the share price increases sharply, then the gains on the share price will drive the performance of the position. This reflects the fact that the long stock position will show a large gain. The credit spread on the credit default swap will generally tighten, reflecting the credit improvement of the entity. This will generate a loss on the credit default swap position. This loss will generally be smaller than the equity gain. If the position is held through till maturity, then the loss on the credit default swap position will equate to the spread paid away.
  2. If the share price declines, then the equity position will show losses. To the extent that lower equity prices coincide with a deterioration in the credit condition of the entity (higher credit spreads), the credit default swap position will show gains. The gains on the credit default swap should offset the equity

---

traditional option pricing framework, see Crouhy, Michel, Galai, Dan, and Mark, Robert "Credit Risk Revisited" (March 1998) Risk – Credit Risk Supplement 40–44.

[80] See Francis, Chris, Kakodkar, Atish and Martin, Barnaby (16 April 2003) Credit Derivative Handbook"; Merrill Lynch, London at 56–59.

[81] The transaction is referred to as a "wings" trade because it provides positive returns where the underlying shares either outperform of suffer a large decline in value.

[82] For example, if the dividend yield is 4.50% pa and the cost of protection is 1.50% pa then the implied hedge ratio is 3.0 times. This means that for US$10 million of stock position, the investor would purchase US$30 million notional of credit protection.

losses because the notional amount of the credit default swaps is larger than the notional amount of the stock position. For large falls in the equity price (such as the share price going to zero in case of default by the entity), the position may show a profit. This would reflect the fact that gains on the credit default swap position are larger than the loss on the equity position. This will depend on the ratio of the trade and the recovery level on the underlying defaulted debt. At low recovery levels and a high ratio, the position will show a large profit.

3. If the share price does not move significantly, the performance of the portfolio is less predictable. However, the profit and loss will generally be small. The position will have zero carry (as long as dividends continue to be paid). To the extent that small declines in share price are not matched by an increase in credit default swap spreads, the position will show a small loss.

The overall position will produce large returns in the case of large positive or negative changes in share price[83].

- **Holding period** – the positions are generally intended to be held for a period of up to 6 to 12 months. This is despite the fact that the credit default swap will be purchased for 5 years.

The strategy described is generally attractive under certain circumstances:

- Companies where the share price has fallen sharply but the prospects for a recovery in the shares or further sharp declines are high.
- The transaction has a high hedge ratio[84] (that is, the credit default swap notional amount will be large relative to the notional amount of stock). This will generally require a high and reasonably secure dividend stream and relatively tight credit default swap spreads.

A key risk of the strategy is the continuation of dividend payments. This is because the strategy requires the dividends from the stock position to finance the purchase of credit default protection. In practice, the expected dividend can be locked in. This is done by synthesising a long equity position in the equity derivative market. This entails the investor purchasing at-the-money call options and selling at-the-money put options on the stock. The maturity of the options would be set at the intended holding period of the transaction. The expected dividend rate is priced into the option contracts.

---

[83] In practice, the dealer will frequently over hedge or under hedge (that is, deviate from the implied hedge ratio) based on their views of the stock price movements and likely recovery rates.

[84] The ratio is strictly speaking not a hedge.

3. Debt Equity Trading Strategies – Actual Examples

In practice, there are a variety of debt-equity trading strategies available:

- **Hanson** – in November 2002, credit default swap spreads on Hanson were trading at 95 bps pa against model valuation of the spread of 160 bps pa. Dealers and hedge funds purchased Hanson equity and hedged the position by purchasing credit protection using credit default swaps. The hedges were based on an implied equity delta of 12% based on pricing models (that is, the trader would purchase GBP 1.2 million of Hanson stock for GBP 10 million notional of credit default swaps). Subsequently, the market corrected. Hanson shares were relatively unchanged (a small rise) and Hanson credit default swap spreads increased to 140 bps pa. The hedge funds unwound the positions to realise profits[85].

- **Altria** – in April 2003, Altria's debt was downgraded by Standard & Poor's. This was based on litigation concerns. As a result, the 5 year credit default swap spreads on Altria increased to 500 bps pa. The stock price remained stable but the implied volatility on out-of-the-money puts on Altria increased significantly (from 37% to 57%). Bond investors, concerned about potential default, sought to hedge the credit risk of Altria in the credit default swap market. A number of hedge funds specialising in debt-equity arbitrage sold protection to bond investors at the high spread and hedged the position by purchasing out-of-the-money puts. If Altria defaulted, then the hedge funds would have suffered a loss under the credit default swap but this would have been offset by the gain on the equity puts. Subsequently, the credit default swap spreads on Altria tightened to 200 bps allowing the traders to unwind their positions at a profit[86].

- **Household** – in October 2002, credit default swap spreads on Household Finance increased to between 800 bps pa (5 year) and 1,000 pa (3 year). In contrast, Household's share price increased to $26 (a rise of $6). Dealers and hedge funds took this opportunity to purchase Household bonds and shorted Household equity against the position. A typical trade would entail a purchase of US$10 million face value bonds at a price of US$7.5 million and shorting US$2.5 million of shares. The hedge ratio was based on the assumed recovery rate on Household bonds. For example, if the assumed recovery rate is 45%, then the investor would need to protect against a fall in value of 30% (from purchase price of 75% to the assumed recovery rate of 45%). The equity hedge was set up to protect against this decline in value (assuming zero equity value in the case of default). Subsequently, Household's credit default spread

---

[85] See Currie, Antony and Morris, Jennifer "And Now For Capital Structure Arbitrage" (December 2002) Euromoney at 42.

[86] See CitiGroup "Capital Structure Arbitrage: The Past, Present" (November 2003) Risk Sponsors Statement.

tightened sharply, reflecting a takeover bid from HSBC. This resulted in a large gain on the bond position and a smaller loss on the equity position. The traders were able to unwind their transactions at a profit[87].

4. Evaluation of Strategies

Historically, debt-equity trades focused on distressed companies. Increasingly, the focus is on convergence trades and trading correlation between, and relative volatility of, credit and equity markets.

For example, the long equity/long credit protection transaction (described above) is increasingly used to take advantage of high asset volatility, high leverage and leveraged buyout/recapitalisation transactions. Examples of high asset volatility companies are those whose assets are volatile due to litigation concerns from tobacco, asbestos or other product liability. Leveraged companies and potential leveraged buyout/re-capitalisations exhibit binary equity outcome or large differences between equity and debt outlook e.g. positive equity outlook and negative debt outlook. These factors make them ideal for debt-equity trading strategies.

Many strategies are also designed to take advantage of different levels of volatility between credit and debt markets. The long equity/long credit protection strategy is frequently used (when equity volatility is high relative to credit market volatility) to create a payoff that is similar to an equity option straddle. Similarly, long credit (either bonds or sold credit default swap protection)/short equity or long out-of-the-money equity puts seeks to capture value from the higher volatility in credit markets relative to equity markets.

In practice, the strategies are not risk free[88]. The transactions entail significant risks. These risks include:

- Exposure to the correlation of price changes between the credit and equity markets[89].
- Estimation of key inputs such as recovery rates.
- Model risk in calculating hedge ratios and modelling relationships between credit spreads and equity prices.

---

[87] See Currie, Antony and Morris, Jennifer "And Now For Capital Structure Arbitrage" (December 2002) Euromoney at 43.

[88] The term "capital structure arbitrage" is misleading.

[89] For example, for highly rated companies, the correlation between equity prices and credit spreads is low. This means that many of these strategies can be implemented only for lower rated credits (A/BBB or below).

The risk evaluation of these strategies is important. The principal approaches include:

- Using a credit model (structural or reduced form model)[90] to evaluate the relationship between credit and equity market prices and volatility.
- Simulate the transaction using historical correlation (between credit and equity prices) and (implied and realised) asset/equity volatility to assess its performance.
- Stress test the position to assess its performance. For example, in the long equity/ long credit protection strategy, the performance would be evaluated for several scenarios: a large risk in equity price; a large fall in equity price/credit default; and small changes in equity price (with and without corresponding credit spread changes). In addition, the position would be assessed in terms of the separate transactions where the assumed correlation between credit and equity elements breaks down.

The process of analysis and risk evaluation of these strategies is difficult and subjective.

Exhibit 7.34   Investor Applications Of Credit Derivatives – Credit Default Swap Versus Equity Default Swap Relative Value Trading

Assume that the spread on equity default swaps is higher than the spread on credit default swaps for the same reference entity. The higher spread on the equity default swaps implies that there is higher risk of an equity default event (as implied by stock price volatility).

A trader can take advantage of the negative correlation between credit spreads and equity prices to set up the following relative value trade on a specific reference entity:

Position	Spread (bps pa)
Sell protection under equity default swap	+300
Buy protection under credit default swap	−120
Net carry	+180

The positions are for the same notional amount (US$10 million) and same maturity (5 years).

The trader's position is as follows:

- The trader suffers a loss of 50% of notional amount if the share price falls 70% at any time over the 5 years.
- The trader benefits if there is a credit event in relation to the reference entity at any time over the 5 years. The amount of the trader's benefit is not known with

---

[90]   See Chapter 6.

certainty as the amount of any gain depends on recovery values implied by market prices of distressed debt following the credit event.

The position accrues net carry in favour of the trader. The position is relatively low risk where the credit event and equity default event occur simultaneously.

The payoffs of the position are as follows:

1. If the reference entity's credit risk remains the same or improves and the share price does not fall 70%, then the trader earns the net carry on the position.
2. If the reference entity's credit risk deteriorates and the share price falls but there is no credit or equity default event, then the trader earns the net carry on the position.
3. If a credit and equity default event occurs, then the trader earns the net carry on the position until the relevant dates. However, the two positions will only offset each other where the recovery rate on the credit default swap is 50% or lower. This is because in that case, the gain on the credit default swap will be at least equal to the payment required under the equity default swap.
4. If an equity default event takes place but no credit event occurs, then the trader incurs the following losses:
    *   The trader loses the spread on the equity default swap but has to continue paying the spread on the credit default swap. This means there is negative carry of 120 bps pa on the position.
    *   The trader's loss on the equity default swap is not offset by a corresponding gain on the credit default swap.

The risk in 3 above relates to exposure to debt recovery rates. The risk in 4 is more complex relating to the different trigger events of the two contracts.

In practice, the risk in 4 above may be reduced. This reflects the impact of the negative correlation between credit spreads and equity prices. If the share price does fall significantly to trigger the equity default event (a fall of 70%), then it is likely that the credit quality of the reference entity will also have deteriorated and credit spreads increased. This would allow the trader to terminate the credit default swap in the market to capture value from the change in credit spreads. The gain may offset (in part or full) the loss on the equity default swap.

In practice, the risk of these relative value trades is complex. In some cases, traders leverage the credit default swap position to reduce the risk. For example, in the above example, the trader could purchase protection through credit default swaps on 150% of the notional amount of the equity default swap. This would reduce the carry on the trade to 120 bps. The leverage would increase the return on the credit default swap in 3 and 4 above. This leverage can be static or dynamic. In the latter case, the trader would adjust positions over time to maintain parity between the position in the equity default swap.

**Exhibit 7.35   Investor Applications Of Credit Derivatives –
Simple Leveraged Structure**

A total return swap is a purely off-balance-sheet transaction. Where the total return receiver invests in a cash/money market asset, it can create a synthetic on-balance-sheet asset. This transaction structure is set out below.

Funded Total Return Swap

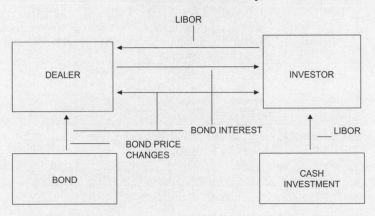

The investor seeking exposure to the underlying bond need not fund the total return swap fully as in the above case. It may choose to undertake the transaction on an unfunded basis. This structure is set out below.

Unfunded/Leveraged Total Return Swap

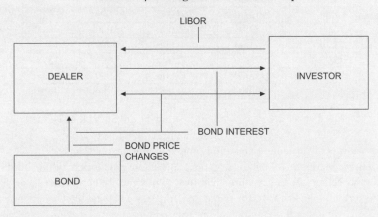

The economics of the leveraged investment can be illustrated with an example. Assume that the investor creates exposure to a high yield asset that is currently yielding LIBOR plus 2.75% pa. The bond is trading at 100% of face value or par.

Assume that in return for receiving the return on the bond, the investor will pay
LIBOR plus 0.80% pa. This reflects a net spread of 1.95% pa accruing to
the investor. The transaction requires the investor to post collateral of 10% of the
nominal face value of the total return swap (assumed to be US$10 million). The
collateral earns interest at 5.50% pa. The swap has a term of 1 year.

The return to the investor is set out in the Table below.

Bond/Loan Price At Maturity (%)	Net Spread On Total Return Swap ($)	Gain (Loss) On Total Return Swap ($)	Collateral Interest ($)	Rate Of Return (% Pa)
105.00	195,000	500,000	55,000	75.00
104.50	195,000	450,000	55,000	70.00
104.00	195,000	400,000	55,000	65.00
103.50	195,000	350,000	55,000	60.00
103.00	195,000	300,000	55,000	55.00
102.50	195,000	250,000	55,000	50.00
102.00	195,000	200,000	55,000	45.00
101.50	195,000	150,000	55,000	40.00
101.00	195,000	100,000	55,000	35.00
100.50	195,000	50,000	55,000	30.00
100.00	195,000	–	55,000	25.00
99.50	195,000	−50,000	55,000	20.00
99.00	195,000	−100,000	55,000	15.00
98.50	195,000	−150,000	55,000	10.00
98.00	195,000	−200,000	55,000	5.00
97.50	195,000	−250,000	55,000	0.00
97.00	195,000	−300,000	55,000	−5.00
96.50	195,000	−350,000	55,000	−10.00
96.00	195,000	−400,000	55,000	−15.00
95.50	195,000	−450,000	55,000	−20.00
95.00	195,000	−500,000	55,000	−25.00

The leveraged structure of returns (on the capital invested; that is, the collateral
posted) is evident from the Table. The structure is attractive to leveraged investors in
credit assets. This includes hedge funds and emerging market banks.

From the viewpoint of the dealer, the transaction generates a return of 80 bps
for a cash collateralised exposure. The swap will typically have ongoing mark-to-
market provisions. The investor is required to post *additional collateral* (over and
above the 10% initial collateral) if the total return swap is out-of-the-money at
specific intervals, or if at any time the swap mark-to-market exposure exceeds a
given trigger amount. This decreases the credit exposure under the transaction for
the dealer.

**Exhibit 7.36   Investor Applications Of Credit Derivatives –
Leveraged Note Structure**

Assume an investor wishes to create a leveraged exposure to a diversified portfolio of securities (either bonds or traded loans). A repackaging vehicle may be used to create diversified exposure to a portfolio of bonds/credits. The transaction is structured as follows:

- The repackaging vehicle issues a structured note to the investor.
- The cash proceeds of the note are used to purchase high quality bond(s).
- The repackaging vehicle enters into total return swaps with a dealer to gain exposure to a variety of bonds/credits. The total return swaps have total notional principal equivalent to the value of the investment in the high quality bonds that are used to fully collateralise the swaps.
- The structured note generates returns to the investor, usually a floating rate return calculated as LIBOR plus a margin. The return is equivalent to the payments received under the total return swaps. The return from the underlying high quality bond investment is used to fund the floating rate payments under the total return swaps.
- At maturity, the structured note pays out the value of the securities underlying the total return swaps. An appreciation in value adds to the pool of funds generated from the liquidation of the high quality collateral pool and is available for distribution to the investor. Any depreciation in the value of the securities underlying the total return swaps is funded by the collateral pool and reduces the payment to the investor in the structured note.

The structure is designed to allow an investor to obtain economic exposure to the diversified portfolio of securities. The major benefits include the higher level of diversification that is obtained as a result of the lower threshold size of total return swaps (versus investment in the bonds) and the elimination of administration costs of managing a portfolio of securities.

The additional element required to engineer leverage is that the total return swaps entered into are for a notional principal *greater than* the face value of the collateral[91]. The leveraged structure will operate as follows:

- As in the unleveraged case, the repackaging vehicle uses the proceeds of the issue of structured notes to purchase high quality securities that are then used to collateralise the total return swaps.
- The collateral will represent approximately 10 to 20% of the notional principal of the total return swaps entered.
- The structured note redeems at maturity as in the previous example. However, the investor can only lose the principal face value of the structured note, *not the notional value of the total return swaps entered into.*

---

[91]   For discussion of the structure, see Chapter 2.

The investor has exposure to both the collateral and the securities underlying the total return swaps.

The rationale for the structure is the higher returns an investor can generate from the leverage embedded in the transactions. Unlike traditional forms of leverage (such as purchasing the underlying securities on margin), the loss that can be suffered by the investor is limited to the face value of the structured notes (effectively the collateral amount).

The structure is set out below.

Leveraged Credit Linked Note Structure

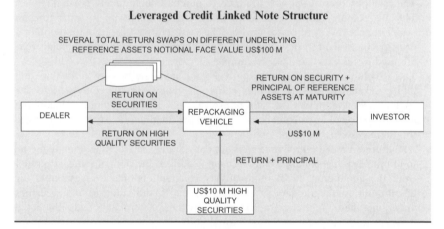

Exhibit 7.37   Investor Applications Of Credit Derivatives – Using First-to-Default Baskets To Create Leveraged Exposure[92]

A less obvious manner in which to create leverage is the first-to-default basket. Assume Investor M manages a portfolio of bonds subject to a minimum credit rating level of AA/Aa. The investor is seeking opportunities to increase the yield on the portfolio.

A credit derivative based solution would focus on investing in a credit default structured note or swap where the default on the note or swap is linked to a basket of 4 AA/Aa credits on a first-to-default basis. If *any one* of the reference credits defaults, then the seller of first-to-default protection is required to purchase the defaulted securities. For a 5 year maturity, such an investment provides an additional return (say around 20 to 30 bps pa) relative to the current yield levels on any of the reference securities on an individual basis.

The rationale for a first-to-default basket is that the combination of credit risks in the structure creates a lower credit quality than the individual credit standing of the credit assets. In effect, a first-to-default basket of AA/Aa issuers may have a default

---

[92]   For discussion of the economics of first-to-default structures, see Chapter 2.

risk equivalent to lower credit levels. However, it satisfies the actual minimum threshold credit rating level for the individual obligors imposed upon the investor. The higher risk reflects low default correlations between the credit assets included in the basket. It also reflects the fact that the structure is inherently leveraged. In a US$50 million transaction on 4 underlying credit assets, the investor provides US$200 million of default protection. This is because it provides protection *on any of the 4 assets* up to a face value of US$50 million on a first-to-default basis. The increased return compensates for the fact that a first-to-default basket is inherently more risky than the individual issuers.

The format for the transfer of credit risk created in the first-to-default basket is attractive for the investors assuming the default risk. The structure provides an elegant mechanism for meeting minimum credit quality limits while allowing the investors to generate incremental *yield*. This provides outperformance relative to the underlying benchmarks against which the performance of the investors is measured. Where the investor has the capacity to purchase the securities *of any of the issuers* included in the basket, the structure of the first-to-default basket allows investors to create leverage through the position on default correlations[93].

5 Corporate/Non-Financial Institution Applications[94]

5.1 Overview

Corporate applications of credit derivatives are still a small part of global credit derivatives activity.

Most firms incur significant credit exposures in the process of conducting day to day normal operations. Credit exposures incurred in normal business

---

[93] For discussion of pricing of first-to default baskets, see Chapter 2.

[94] For an overview, see Buy, Richard, Kaminski, Vincent, Pinnamaneni, Krishnarao, and Shambhogue, Vasant "Actively Managing Corporate Credit Risk: New Methodologies and Instruments For Non-Financial Firms" in (1998) Credit Derivatives: Applications for Risk Management, Investment and Portfolio Optimisation; Risk Books, London at Chapter 5; Reyfman, Alex and Toft, Klaus (6 March 2001) Credit Derivatives – A Risk Management for Nonbank Corporations"; Goldman Sachs – Fixed Income Research; New York; Reyfman, Alex and Toft, Klaus "Default Swap Investment Strategies" (May 2001) Risk – Sponsored Article. See also Ffolkes, Stuart "Credible Credits" (Summer 2000) Power & Energy 9–13; Schenk, Carola and Crabbe, Matthew "A Slow Burning Fuse" (June 2001) Risk 31–32; Petersen, Michael "The Accidental Credit Investors" (August 2001) Euromoney 28–35; Toft, Klaus, Kaye, Melissa and Yoong, Joanne "Credible Protection" (April 2002) FOW 38–41; Thind, Sarfraz "Staying Away In Droves" (July 2003) Risk – Corporate Risk Supplement S2–S3.

operations generally include:

- **Direct credit risk** – this entails credit risk on payments due for goods and services supplied. This includes:
  1. Trade receivables.
  2. Vendor or supplier financing associated with the supply of capital equipment.
- **Prepayments** – this entails credit risk arising from contract prepayments in advance of performance.
- **Business losses** – this includes business losses such as additional set-up or switching costs resulting from the default of a major supplier or customer. The losses generally relate to the disruption of the operations of the enterprise. For example, where a firm has outsourced its computing facilities, the default of the outsourcing firm may result in direct and indirect losses.

The different types of losses are inter-related.

Firms also incur traditional forms of credit risk, primarily to banks/ dealers from financial transactions such as deposits/investments and counterparty exposures on hedges.

Historically, corporations have not separated and managed credit risk in the same way as banks/financial institutions. Credit risk has been seen as "business" risk.

More recently, there has been greater recognition of the credit risk incurred by corporations. This is driven by the following factors:

- **Vendor financing in the telecommunications industry**[95] – during the excesses of the technology boom of the late 1990s, major suppliers of telecommunications equipment financed a significant part of sales. A large portion of the vendor financing was to start-up companies and emerging countries. Following the collapse of the technology boom, several vendor finance portfolios suffered large losses.
- **US energy sector**[96] – a series of defaults in the US energy sector in California and the collapse of Enron resulted in credit driven losses for a number of suppliers.

---

[95] See Schenk, Carola and Crabbe, Matthew "A Slow Burning Fuse" (June 2001) Risk 31–32; Petersen, Michael "The Accidental Credit Investors" (August 2001) Euromoney 28–35.

[96] See Petersen, Michael "The Accidental Credit Investors" (August 2001) Euromoney 28–35; Toft, Klaus, Kaye, Melissa and Yoong, Joanne "Credible Protection" (April 2002) FOW 38–41.

- **Increase in corporate bankruptcies** – the recession in the US and the increase in default rates in 2000/2001 highlighted the credit exposure of corporations. The default/financial distress of a number of well known corporations resulted in significant credit related losses for many corporations. The deterioration in general credit conditions/credit quality has made it difficult for companies to continue to trade with/ expand dealing with some counterparties[97].
- **Emerging market credit risk** – a significant proportion of sales growth for large corporations has been in emerging markets. A series of crises in emerging markets has highlighted the credit risk of counterparties located in emerging markets. The losses suffered have driven corporations to seek to better manage the credit risk arising from normal business operations.

A key factor underlying interest in credit risk from normal operations has been the behaviour of share prices and concern from equity and rating analysts. Share prices have fallen on reports of vendor financing transactions[98]. Credit risk from vendor financing transactions has also been a factor in credit rating downgrades[99].

The identified factors have encouraged corporations to focus on the management of credit risk incurred in trading operations.

The credit risk arising from trading operations has a number of distinctive characteristics:

- **Concentration risk** – the typical credit exposure arising from operations displays a high level of industry and specific counterparty concentration. This reflects the underlying business and industry dynamics. Firms have limited opportunities to diversify credit risks. This means that the risk of credit losses is significantly above that expected in a *diversified portfolio*. The concentration of risk means that on a portfolio basis, corporations should be prepared to pay a premium to reduce credit risk. This is

---

[97] For example, see Goodwin, Scott "Swedish Truckmaker Considers First Credit Derivatives Trade" (25 March 2002) Derivatives Week 1,11.

[98] For example, the Motorola share price fell around 5% when it revealed a potential loss of US$728 million on a loan to Telsim (a Turkish wireless carrier); see Schenk, Carola and Crabbe, Matthew "A Slow Burning Fuse" (June 2001) Risk 31–32.

[99] S & P cited Lucent Technology's vendor financing portfolio as one of the reasons for a downgrade of its debt ratings; see Petersen, Michael "The Accidental Credit Investors" (August 2001) Euromoney 28–35.

because banks/dealers are not constrained in diversifying their credit exposures as they are not subject to the business constraints. This will usually mean that the purchase of credit risk protection will be positive for corporations. It allows firms to free up capital that can be used in their core business. This will be reflected in the lower cost of protection on default purchased externally, relative to the economic cost of maintaining the exposure with provisioning.

- **Type of risk** – the credit risk assumed displays the following characteristics:
  1. *Short term* – a significant portion of the credit risk will be for short terms. This relates to the nature of the underlying transactions. Credit risk on trade receivables is generally for periods of 6 months or less. The major exception would be vendor financing. The nature of the risk means that protection is required on a short term basis. The majority of exposure will be constantly renewed as trading continues. This means that the default protection may need to be renewed at maturity. The level of exposure will need to be continually adjusted.
  2. *Not traded* – the credit risk will generally relate to non traded instruments. The credit derivatives market is generally focused on bonds or loans. Credit risk arising in business operations will generally relate to non-traded trade receivables, contractual obligations and asset based financing. This means it is difficult to precisely hedge the credit risk. There may also be incidental aspects of the transactions such as warranties, performance guarantees and security/asset ownership issues that significantly affect the credit risk.
- **Impact on earnings recognition/cash flow** – the credit risk from operations has the capacity to impact upon the firm's earnings and cash flows. The effects are complex in the following ways:
  1. *Cash flow impact* – the failure to pay for goods and services can significantly stress a firm's cash flow. The firm gains certainty in terms of loss levels and cash flow from hedging credit risk. This may have business benefits in allowing expansion of trading relationships with a counterparty where credit considerations may reduce the capacity to trade.
  2. *Earnings/pricing* – earnings/profits from sales where vendor financing is provided are complex. The expected earnings from the product/services are combined with the earnings from the financing. The earnings are also not realised until the vendor financing

obligations are met. This means that hedging adds a greater degree of pricing precision in a firm's business dealings. The profit margin on sales must cover the known cost of the credit default swap (representing the market cost of the credit risk of the transaction). This allows more accurate quantification of business profitability. It also allows greater discrimination in setting prices.

- **Credit administration** – firms require a credit infrastructure to manage the credit risk arising from operations. This primarily takes the form of a credit function that manages the trade credit process. The use of hedging may generate additional benefits in the form of cost savings in credit administration. The expense of making credit assessments on a business counterparty is reduced where a credit default swap is used to hedge. In effect, the firm gains the benefit of the credit infrastructure of the financial institution providing it with protection.

The nature of the credit risk creates specific issues in hedging:

- **Documentary issues** – the standard structure of credit default swaps[100] may not provide an accurate hedge for credit risk arising from business operations. The primary problems are in the following areas:
  1. *Credit events* – the standard credit events are generally linked to a specified obligation (bond, loan or borrowed money). This may not be appropriate for the credit risk arising from business operations such as trade receivables or service contracts.
  2. *Settlement mechanisms* – the standard form of settlement is by physical delivery of a bond or loan. A fall back is cash settlement based on the market price of a reference bond. This creates significant problems for hedging corporate credit risks. This is because the underlying trade receivables, vendor financing or asset backed lease is unlikely to be deliverable under the credit default swap. Cash settlement based on a public bond may not be closely related to the loss on the firm's credit exposure under trade receivables or vendor financing[101].
  3. *Publicly available information of credit event* – the standard form of credit default swap is triggered through a credit event established through publicly available information. Credit transactions such as

---

[100] See Chapter 1.
[101] For trade receivables, the recovery rate is likely to be higher than for bonds. However, the recovery rate for vendor financing may vary widely from that of public securities.

trade receivables or vendor financing are private bilateral transactions. This means that in practice, the triggering of the credit default swap contract may need to wait upon a credit event on publicly traded debt.

- **Reference Entities** – the range of reference entities traded in the credit derivatives market is limited. The major focus is on large, well known firms. This means that only credit risk incurred in business operations to these entities can be hedged. This significantly limits the scope for hedging.
- **Amount/maturity constraints** – the credit derivatives market trades in amounts of US$5 to 10 million face value. The most liquid maturity is 5 years. This may not be appropriate for hedging the type of credit risk that arises from business operations.

The nature of the credit risk creates specific hedging issues. The single name credit default swap creates significant basis risk. In practice, firms must decide to accept the basis risk or seek customised hedging structures. The customised hedging structures are more expensive and less liquid than standard contracts.

This means that in practice, credit derivatives coexist with a range of other credit risk management approaches, including:

- **Securitisation** – this is focused on traditional securitisation of receivables or vendor financing receivables[102]. For example, US and European car manufacturers are issuers of large volumes of bonds backed by automobile loans[103]. Similarly, many corporations have established trade receivables backed commercial paper programs. Banks also operate commercial paper conduits that purchase receivables from smaller companies (too small to set up their own programs)[104].
- **Forfaiting/trade receivables discounting** – this is focused on traditional trade finance arrangements such as letters of credit/guarantees and discounting trade bills/receivables/forfaiting[105]. The firm assuming credit risk in a business relationship transfers this directly to a bank/financial institution using these instruments.

---

[102] See Rosenthal, James A. and Ocampo, Juan M. (1988) Securitisation Of Credit; John Wiley & Sons, New York; Hill, Claire A. "Securitisation: A Financing Strategy For Emerging Markets Firms" (Fall 1998) Journal Of Applied Corporate Finance 55–62.

[103] See Delhanty, Thomas and Waldman, Michael (November 1986) Certificates For Automobile Receivables (CARS); Salomon Brothers Inc., New York. See also Waldman, Michael and Delhanty, Thomas (August 1986) Introduction to Credit Card-Backed Securities; Salomon Brothers Inc., New York.

- **Credit insurance** – this is focused on traditional forms of trade credit insurance or credit insurance available from monoline insurers, specialist trade credit insurers or government/supranational agencies (for emerging market transactions). The insurance is used to provide protection from the underlying credit risk.
- **Structured credit products** – this is focused on non-standard credit default swap structures. The most important of these was a structure referred to as a bankruptcy credit default swap[106]. The structure differed from standard credit default swaps in that the only credit event was bankruptcy and the payout was a pre-agreed fixed sum (digital payout). The advantage of the structure is that it is suited to hedging exposure arising from business operations[107].
- **Dual trigger credit hedges** – this type of transaction has generally been used with commodity suppliers. It is structured as a commodity linked credit derivative contract[108]. Assume a commodity supplier has a long term contract to supply a commodity, minerals or power to a purchaser at a fixed price. If the commodity price falls, then the supplier's fixed price supply contract is in-the-money. If the purchaser defaults on the contract, then the supplier would suffer a loss. This loss would be the difference between the market price and fixed price under the contract. The supplier has a credit exposure on the purchaser under these circumstances. The dual trigger credit hedge operates to protect the supplier from this event. Under the contract, the provider of protection agrees to purchase the commodity at the fixed price in the event the purchaser goes bankrupt[109].

---

[104] See Wood, Jack and Mason, Sarah "Securitisation Via Multi-Seller Vehicles" in (1994) Corporate Finance Guide To Securitisation 6–11; "Securitisation And Multi-seller Conduits" (1996) Capital Market Strategies 3 25–32. See also Cutler, Stewart L. "Asset Backed CP Poised For Exponential Growth" (August 1994) Corporate Finance 17–19.

[105] See Gmur, Charles J. (1986) Trade Financing – Second Edition; Euromoney Publications, London.

[106] The structure was developed by Enron; see Bergin, Tom "Enron Launches Credit Derivative Business Offering Bankruptcy Swaps" (29 February–6 March 2000) Financial products 3; "Enron Brings Real-Time Hedging" (April 2000) Corporate Finance 4. A similar product was offered by Swiss Re New Markets; see Ferry, John "Swiss Re Puts Credit Derivatives On The Net" (July 2001) Risk 18.

[107] The digital bankruptcy credit swap had limited acceptance and success.

[108] The structure was developed by Enron.

5.2 Applications of Credit Derivatives –
Corporate/Non-Financial Institution Examples

Corporate applications of credit derivatives focus on the following:

- **Management of credit risk** – this is focused on managing credit risk under trade receivables, vendor financing and other trading contracts. **Exhibit 7.38** sets out an example of managing trade receivables exposure to a financially distressed firm. **Exhibit 7.39** sets out an example of hedging/managing the credit risk on a vendor financing. **Exhibit 7.40** sets out an example of managing credit exposure of a supplier. **Exhibit 7.41** sets out an example of hedging credit risk to a lessee in the context of a property financing.
- **Management of country/project risk** – this is similar to the management of credit risk generally. It is focused on the specific management of sovereign or country risk in the context of cross border investments or projects. **Exhibit 7.42** sets out an example of hedging country risk in a project. **Exhibit 7.43** sets out an example of hedging funds transfer/convertibility risk.
- **Managing funding** – this is focused on management of credit spread risk on new funding or the cost of liabilities. **Exhibit 7.44** sets out an example of using credit spread products to manage new issue/funding spread risk[110].

---

[109] See Petersen, Michael "The Accidental Credit Investors" (August 2001) Euromoney 28–35.

[110] In 2004, Dresdner Kleinwort Wasserstein launched a credit spread warrant to hedge the credit spread risk for a French corporation (Casino). The warrants were based on Euro 400 million of bonds of unissued bonds. Each warrant allowed the holder to purchase Euro 1,000 of Casino bonds at a yield of 85 bps over the Euro swap mid-rate. The warrants were issued in May 2004 with a maturity of December 2004. The warrants had a European exercise structure. Warrant buyers paid 54 bps of the underlying notional value. If spreads decrease between May and December 2004, then the warrants will be exercised requiring Casino to issue the bonds at the agreed spread. If spreads increase then the warrant will not be exercised. Casino will be required to issue at a higher spread. The company's cost will be reduced by the amount of premium received. The structure was more attractive to the company then pre-funding the financing requirement. See Wolcott, Rachel "Bets On For Credit Spread Warrants" (July 2004) Risk 47–49; Brown, Mark "Timing The Pounce On Tight Credit Spreads" (July 2004) Euromoney 38–42.

Exhibit 7.45 sets out an actual example of using credit default swaps to reduce the effective cost of debt.

- **Investment in credit derivatives** – this entails the sale of credit protection to generate earnings to enhance investment returns. **Exhibit 7.46** sets out an example of providing protection to enhance returns on cash investments. **Exhibit 7.47** sets out an example of a synthetic buyback of debt using a credit linked note.

There has been controversy in relation to self referenced credit default swaps[111]. This entails a corporation selling protection on itself. This is usually structured as the purchase of a credit linked note by the company. The note has the self referenced credit default swap embedded within the note[112]. The note structure is used to eliminate counterparty risk in the transaction. For example, the synthetic debt buyback (see **Exhibit 7.47** above) uses self referenced credit linked notes.

The controversy relates to the following potential problems:

- The use of credit default swaps by the company to seek to manipulate the credit spread on its own debt.
- The fact that the cash and liquid assets reported by the company may be misleading, as in case of default by the company, the triggering of the self referenced credit default swap would reduce its cash resources.

These concerns have led rating agencies to scrutinise transactions entailing self referenced credit default swaps[113].

**Exhibit 7.38   Corporate Applications Of Credit Derivatives –
Managing Exposure To Credit Impaired Buyer**[114]

Assume Company X sells a significant amount of its products to a retailer. The sales are on 45 day credit terms. The retailer experiences financial difficulties and files for Chapter 11 bankruptcy. The effect of this is to significantly increase the credit risk to Company X on its receivables. The inability to extend credit terms will have the effect of resulting in a substantial loss of sales to the retailer.

---

[111]   See Douglas-Jones, Jane "Credit Derivatives" (January 2003) FOW 41.
[112]   See Chapter 3.
[113]   See (13 January 2004) Self Referenced CLNs Raise Questions And Concerns; Fitch Ratings, New York; "Fitch Adjusts Measures For CLNs" (February 2004) Risk 6.
[114]   For an example in practice, see "Credit Risk Hedge For Corporations" (March 1999) Global Finance 27.

Company X has two courses of action available to it:

- **Continue to transact with the retailer** – this would mean that Company X will incur additional credit risk. This may ultimately result in bad debt losses that will impact upon Company X's financial position.
- **Continue to transact but hedge credit risk** – this would mean that Company X will incur the additional risk but will simultaneously hedge its credit risk through the credit derivatives market.

The credit derivative entails the purchase of protection by Company X using a credit default swap. The reference entity is the retailer. The face value amount of the transaction is the amount of trade receivables. Company X pays a fee and in return, the seller of protection agrees to pay Company X 100% of the face value of receivables in the case where a credit event occurs.

Credit event in these circumstances is defined to include:

- Failure to pay receivables that are due after a grace period of say, 30 days.
- Plans to cease operations or liquidate assets under Chapter 11 are approved.
- Chapter 11 bankruptcy is converted into full bankruptcy under Chapter 7 bankruptcy.

The effect of this transaction is to enable Company X to estimate the cost of any losses and continue to trade with the retailer.

Exhibit 7.39   Corporate Applications Of Credit Derivatives – Vendor Financing

Assume Company X is a manufacturer of telecommunications equipment. It wins a contract to supply US$500 million of equipment to a wireless telephone operator in an emerging country. The contract requires Company X to provide finance for the purchase. The operator will pay for the equipment in the form of an initial payment of US$100 million and 5 annual payments payable in arrears.

Company X assumes the credit risk of the operator in the transaction. The operator and the country have a weak credit rating. Company X is reluctant to provide the financing because of concerns about the credit risk entailed. However, failure to provide financing will result in the loss of the sale. Company X agrees to provide vendor financing subject to the credit risk to the operator being hedged.

Assume the following market rates/prices:

US$ 5 year swap rate:	6.00% pa
Company X 5 year credit spread:	1.00% pa
Operator 5 year credit spread[115]:	3.50% pa

---

[115]   Assume the credit spreads are derived from the credit default swap market.

Based on the above information, the 5 annual payments should be set at US$106.9 million per annum. This reflects the payments required to amortise the US$400 million financing over 5 years at a funding rate of 10.50%. The funding rate is based on the 5 year swap rate, Company X's credit spread and the operator's credit spread. This payment then compensates Company X for the cost of funding the extension of credit and assuming the credit risk of the operator.

Company X then enters into a credit default swap where the operator is the reference entity[116]. Company X pays a fee of 3.50% pa to the seller of protection. In return, the seller of protection agrees to indemnify Company X from losses on the vendor financing contract.

Several aspects of the credit default swap contract require careful consideration:

- The face value of the credit default swap contract is amortising, reflecting the structure of the vendor financing.
- The credit events will need to reflect the nature of the underlying credit risk. The credit events could be either generic (bankruptcy, failure to pay or restructuring) or linked to the specific vendor financing contract. In practice, if the credit event is linked to the vendor financing contract, then the ability to use publicly available information to establish the occurrence of a credit event may be compromised. This reflects the bilateral and private nature of the financing. This may create timing issues about the specific time of the credit event.
- The settlement mechanism also needs to reflect the nature of the underlying transaction. The vendor financing itself is unlikely to be a deliverable obligation. This means that the contract will have to be structured in one of the following ways:
  1. *Conventional settlement by delivery of bond or loan* – this would require Company X to assume the basis risk. In the event of default, Company X would need to purchase a bond or loan that would be delivered into the credit default swap contract to realise the value. The gain would offset the loss on the vendor financing. There would be potential differences between the gain on the credit default swap and the loss on the vendor financing. This may be positive for Company X. This is because the loss on the vendor financing may be lower than losses on comparable bonds/loans, reflecting the underlying asset security. It reflects the impact of the cheapest-to-deliver option implicit in the credit default swap.
  2. *Cash settlement* – this would entail linking the settlement to a nominated reference bond. The payment in case of default would be the change in value of the bond on the outstanding balance of the vendor financing. This again entails basis risk for Company X.

---

[116] In emerging market transactions, if the underlying credit risk is not specifically traded, then a credit default swap on the sovereign is often used to provide a proxy hedge. This is particularly the case where the entity is owned (partially or fully) by the country.

3. *Documenting the vendor financing as a loan* – this would entail documenting the vendor financing as a bond/loan (say, in the form of a series of promissory notes). The bonds/loan would be normal debt obligations and may be deliverable obligations for the purpose of the credit default swap. This reduces but does not eliminate the basis risk. This is because the asset security issues remain.

The issues identified highlight the practical difficulty of using conventional credit default swaps to hedge this type of credit exposure. Hedging the credit risk entails Company X assuming the basis risk or paying the dealer to assume the basis risk relative to a standard credit default swap contract.

The use of the approach described has collateral benefits. For example, it enables Company X to understand and attribute the *true* profitability of the contract.

For example, assume that the original contract price of US$500 million included a 10% (US$50 million) profit margin. If Company X agreed to provide the vendor financing *without incorporating the credit spread of the operator*, then it would not have been compensated for potential credit losses and overstated earnings. For example, if the payments are based on the funding cost of Company X (7.00% pa), then the annual payments are US$97.6 million. In present value terms, this entails an underpricing of the risk of around US$34.9 million (the lower payments discounted back at the rate reflecting the operator's credit risk). This is a significant portion of the profit on the contract. In effect, the profit on the contract is largely made up of the credit risk on the vendor financing. This creates interesting issues of income recognition for Company X regarding the profit on the contract.

**Exhibit 7.40   Corporate Applications Of Credit Derivatives –
Managing Exposure Of Supplier**

Assume Company X is a copper producer. It has a contract to provide US$25 million of copper per annum to a smelter. The copper is provided in 4 quarterly shipments. The smelter is of low credit risk. The trade terms are payment in 90 days after delivery. The payment is based on open account with no credit enhancement. This means that Company X has credit exposure to the buyer. Company X is concerned about the impact on earnings and probability of default by the smelter.

Company X can hedge its credit exposure by purchasing protection using a credit default swap on the smelter. The hedge would protect the earnings and cash flow of Company X from default by the smelter.

Several aspects of the hedge should be noted:

- **Structure** – the protection could be purchased on a rolling basis for 3 months to cover any specific payment obligations.
- **Basis risk** – the issues identified in **Exhibit 7.39** regarding the definition of credit events and settlement are relevant.

- **Cost** – the fee payable under the credit default swap contract may be high. This reflects the low credit quality of the smelter. It may also be high relative to the profitability of the underlying commodity contract.

In practice, the cost of the hedge can be managed in a number of ways[117]:

- **Basket trades** – this entails the purchase of protection on a basket of entities to which Company X has credit exposures. This can be structured as a first-to-default basket where the default correlations can be used to reduce the cost of hedging[118]. In practice, Company X's exposure may be highly correlated (same industry), which lowers the benefit of the structure. In addition, Company X will only be protected against the first entity in the basket to default.
- **Credit switches** – this entails financing the purchase of protection *with the simultaneous sale of protection on another reference entity*. The entity on which protection is sold is generally unrelated to the entity on which protection is purchased. This can be used to diversify the credit risk of Company X and lower the cost of hedging. Company X assumes credit risk to a second entity with which it has potentially no trading relationship. This assumes that Company X has the credit skills to evaluate the risk of default of that entity and is willing to assume this risk.

Exhibit 7.41 Corporate Applications Of Credit Derivatives – Managing Exposure To Lessee

Assume Company X is a property company. It has developed a site and is now seeking to finance the commercial development with debt. The debt is to be secured over the cash flows from the lease of the property. Company X has secured a long term tenant for the premises. The lease rentals will sustain a high level of debt finance.

The lenders are concerned about the credit quality of the lessee (a well known but non-investment grade firm) and are unwilling to provide the required level of debt. They are also seeking a higher margin on the financing. This is because the lenders see the transaction as relying on the underlying value of the property and potential remarketing of the premises. This is because of the credit driven uncertainty regarding the lessee.

Company X can manage the exposure to the lessee by entering into a credit default swap with a highly rated dealer. Under the credit default swap, Company X pays a fee to the dealer in return for an indemnity from the dealer against loss arising from default by the lessee.

---

[117] For example, see Toft, Klaus, Kaye, Melissa and Yoong, Joanne "Credible Protection" (April 2002) FOW 38–41.

[118] See discussion in Chapter 65.

The financing for the development is secured by the lease itself and the implicit guarantee of the lease through the credit default swap. The credit quality of the lessee is replaced by the credit quality of the dealer.

Several aspects of the structure should be noted:

- **Basis risk** – the issues identified in **Exhibit 7.39** regarding the definition of credit events and settlement are relevant.
- **Structure** – the protection could be purchased to cover a shorter period than the full lease term (say, 5 years of a 15 year lease). This is because the lenders risk to a lessee default is greatest during this period. After the initial period, the balance of the loan is reduced sufficiently to reduce the loan to property value ratio to more acceptable levels.
- **Cost** – the fee payable under the credit default swap contract is offset by the following:
  1. The reduction in debt cost as the credit risk of the transaction is enhanced.
  2. The amount of debt funding obtained is increased.
- **Settlement** – the issues identified in **Exhibit 7.39** regarding the settlement mechanism under the credit default swap are relevant.

**Exhibit 7.42   Corporate Applications Of Credit Derivatives –
Project Finance Country Risk**

Assume Company X is committed to undertake a major investment in an emerging market country. The company believes the political environment is uncertain. It is possible that the country risk may deteriorate in the near term. The company is confident that the project will provide above average returns over the longer term. The short term potential for deterioration may have a deleterious impact on Company X. This effect is in terms of credit ratings and market perception.

The planned investment is significant in relation to the size of the company. The company wishes to isolate the political risk and hedge it to the maximum extent possible. While it is not feasible to hedge the risk of the *project* itself, the company believes that the risk of the project is reasonably correlated with the performance of the country itself. It is willing to accept the correlation risk between the risk of sovereign debt and the project risk (the basis risk).

The physical solution would entail shorting or purchasing a put option on the sovereign debt of the relevant country. This assumes that the emerging market nation has outstanding internationally traded securities that can form the basis of the transaction. The physical solution has a number of difficulties, including:

- The cost of creating the hedge may be high, reflecting difficulties in borrowing the securities for the purpose of shorting and the difficulty in managing the short position.

- The risk of losses on price fluctuations in the security resulting in losses on the hedge where these are caused by factors *which are unrelated to changes in the political risk*.

The credit derivatives based alternative would entail Company X entering into a credit default swap where it pays a fee in return for which it receives protection against any default on the sovereign's outstanding foreign currency debt. In the event of default, the issuer receives a payment based on the price performance of the sovereign bonds. The structure provides protection to the Company from a potential loss resulting from political risk. The credit default swap does not have the problems noted above in relation to the physical solution.

The following aspects of the transaction should be noted:

- The hedge will only be effective where there is a credit event (as specified) under the sovereign debt. If the increase in political risk affects the *project* (for example expropriation) without default on the relevant sovereign obligations, then the hedge will not be effective.
- The actual loss suffered by Company X as a result of its political risk must be similar to the change in the value of the bonds for the hedge to be effective. In practice, a fixed pre-estimate may be preferred; for example, an amount equating to the equity investment in the project or some portion thereof is used. The issues are symptomatic of the basis risk of the hedge.

The credit default swap allows Company X to isolate and manage its political risk using market based instruments and prices. This approach provides an alternative or supplement to traditional insurance based approaches to political risk management in cross border investments.

**Exhibit 7.43 Corporate Applications Of Credit Derivatives –
Hedging Currency Convertibility Risk**

Assume Company X has a subsidiary located in an Asian country. The subsidiary operates purely within the country and all cash flows are in local currency. Profits of the subsidiary are paid out each year to Company X (the parent company) in the form of dividends. Assume an emerging market crisis occurs and extreme market volatility is experienced. The local currency falls sharply in value as international investors withdraw capital. The country experiences balance of payments difficulties. There is increasing risk that the country may impose foreign exchange controls restricting the convertibility of the currency and/or restrict foreign currency remittances to overseas entities.

Company X can hedge its exposure to the imposition of foreign exchange controls through entry into a currency inconvertibility hedge with a dealer. Company X pays a fee to the dealer based on the expected dividend remittance to be hedged. In return, the dealer agrees to the following payments:

• If foreign exchange controls are not imposed, then there is no payment.
• If foreign exchange controls are imposed and the remittance of dividends to the parent is prevented, then the dealer will pay the US$ equivalent of the dividend amount to Company X in New York. In return, Company X will deliver the equivalent in local currency (calculated at the then prevailing spot exchange rate) in the Asian country where the subsidiary is domiciled.

The transaction has the effect of hedging Company X's currency conversion risk. The transaction does not hedge its currency risk on the dividend. The currency risk must be managed separately.

**Exhibit 7.44   Corporate Applications Of Credit Derivatives –
Credit Spread Risk On New Borrowing**

Assume Company X expects to issue new 5 year debt in 1 year's time. Corporate credit spreads have declined significantly. The current credit structure is set out in the Table below:

Maturity (years)	Credit Spread (bps pa)
1	25
5	50
6	50

The company is concerned that credit spreads might rise above implied forward spreads (the implied forward spread is 55 bps pa). Company X therefore seeks to lock in the credit spread on its expected borrowing. The company seeks to isolate its exposures on its credit spreads as it is of the view that the underlying benchmark rates (the US$ swap rates) are unlikely to be above the current implied forward rate.

The physical solution would require Company X to issue debt immediately and invest the proceeds in cash or other liquid securities until the funds are required in 1 year's time. This approach has a number of problems, including:

• The transaction may significantly increase the size of the balance sheet as both the borrowing and the cash investment would utilise the balance sheet. It would also increase the gearing of the company where gross debt is utilised.
• There would be an earnings impact. In this case, the impact would be around 1.00% pa or US$1 million pa on a borrowing of US$100 million. This would reduce *current earnings*. The cost is from the following sources:
    1. The credit spread between borrowing and investment for Company X (in this case 50 bps pa).

2. The shape of the yield curve where a positive yield curve would result in a cost to Company X. This is equal to the difference between the 1 year and 6 year rates. In the current case, this equates to an additional cost of 50 bps pa.

- The necessity to borrow for longer maturities than the actual financing required. In the above case, the borrowing would be for 6 years rather than for the required 5 years. This has the impact of forcing up the cost (potentially, both the interest rate and the spread) and also may create access issues, particularly for lower rated entities where longer maturities may be less readily available or only at higher rates.

An alternative to the physical transactions would be for Company X to enter into a credit spread forward with a dealer to lock in the current implied forward credit spread. The credit spread would be at the current implied forward spread level of 55 bps pa to a forward date of 1 year.

The hedge would operate as follows:

- If spreads increased, then the credit spread forward would increase in value, resulting in a positive cash flow settlement. For example, assuming a spread duration of 4.08, an increase in the 5 year credit spread to 70 bps pa would result in a payment received of 61.2 bps on the forward. This would offset the lower receipts on the issue of debt or higher cost as a result of the widening of the spread.
- If spreads decreased, then Company X would incur a loss on the credit spread forward. This loss would be offset by higher receipts or lower cost on the issue of the debt.

Some aspects of the hedge should be noted:

- The efficiency on the hedge will be affected by changes in the absolute level of the spread and underlying rates. For example, if the 5 year swap rate is 6.45% pa and the corresponding 5 year rate for Company X is 7.15% pa (a credit spread of 70 bps pa), then the loss on the borrowing from the wider spread is around 61.5 bps. This compares to a gain on the credit spread forward of 61.2 bps. The small slippage reflects the changing spread duration (that is, convexity). Changes in the underlying interest rates may exacerbate this problem. Assume that the 5 year swap rate falls to 6.25% pa, implying an issue cost of 6.95% pa. The higher spread equates to a loss of 61.8 bps. This is not exactly offset by the gain on the credit spread forward. The convexity effect of rates and spreads will typically create hedging errors that will lower but not eliminate the risk exposure[119].
- In practice, Company X may not have a large universe of outstanding traded securities of sufficient liquidity available. In this case, it may be necessary to undertake the transaction on a very liquid equivalent security issued by another issuer or on a basket of such issuers. This will reduce the efficiency of the hedge because of the inherent basis risk.

---

[119] See discussion in Chapter 65.

An alternative to the above strategy would entail the purchase of a put option on the spread to hedge any increase in the credit spread. A further alternative would be to purchase protection on itself under a credit default swap. The credit default swap would be reversed in the market at the time the company financed to lock in the spread.

**Exhibit 7.45   Corporate Applications Of Credit Derivatives –
Reducing Cost Of Borrowings[120]**

Increasingly, credit derivatives are being used to reduce the cost of corporate borrowing.

In 2002, Kepco, the South Korean electricity utility, issued a US$650 million bond swapping the proceeds into Yen. The objective was to refinance an existing yen borrowing. A credit contingent element was introduced into the currency swap. The swap was referenced to the Republic of Korea. If Korea experiences a credit event, then the currency swap terminates, leaving Kepco with a US$ liability. In the case of a credit event, then the defaulted Korean bonds are delivered to Kepco.

The effect of the credit contingent element is to reduce the cost to Kepco. It is equivalent to reinvesting the issue proceeds into a Korean bond that is trading above LIBOR. This is captured by the credit default swap spread that reduces the borrower's costs. The risk to Kepco is complex. It assumes the risk of the sovereign (Korea) defaulting. It also assumes the mark-to-market risk on its underlying US$ liability. It also assumes the inherent correlation risk between the credit risk of Korea and currency rate (specifically the difference between the US$/Won and Yen/Won rate). Given that the Won is likely to depreciate in case of a sovereign default against all currencies, the major exposure is to changes in the value of the US$/Yen exchange rate.

**Exhibit 7.46   Corporate Applications Of Credit Derivatives –
Investment In Credit Default Swaps**

Corporations can *provide* credit protection through credit default swaps where the company agrees to make an agreed payment on default in return for receipt of a fee. This type of activity is based on the following factors:

- Acting as a financial investor seeking additional return on its cash surpluses through assumption of credit risks on a diversified portfolio of credit exposures.

---

[120] The description of the transaction is based on Sawyer, Nick "House Of The Year And Credit Derivatives House Of The Year – JPMorgan" (October 2002) AsiaRisk 10–11; Sawyer, Nick "Dabbling With Credit" (February 2004) Treasury – Supplement To AsiaRisk S28–S29.

It is similar to investment in commercial paper or other short term obligations of the issuer.

• Selling default protection on entities where the default risk assumed is poorly correlated on an industry or individual basis to credit exposures in its existing business operations. This would allow the generation of income that would reduce the potential credit losses on its existing credit exposures.

• Selling default protection on competitors within the industry in the sense that this would provide a competitive hedge. For example, default by a competitor may have a favourable earnings impact on the company. The gain would offset any loss on the default swap where the Company has assumed default risk[121].

Companies with available capital resources additional to their business requirements may be attracted to deploying it to assume certain credit risks which either diversify their existing, usually concentrated credit exposures, or are related to their industry positions.

Exhibit 7.47   Corporate Applications Of Credit Derivatives –
Synthetic Debt Repurchase

Assume Company X has a significant amount of outstanding long term debt. The debt is in the form of public bonds with a remaining life of 8 years. The bonds are non-callable. Company X has sold some assets as part of a corporate reorganisation. It would like to use this cash to retire its bonds.

Retirement of the outstanding debt poses significant challenges for Company X. A cash market solution would be to repurchase the bonds in the open market. In practice, this has a number of difficulties, including:

• The repurchase is expensive. The company would generally have to pay a premium to the market price to effect the repurchase.

• The repurchase is unlikely to be 100% successful. This means that some debt will remain outstanding, forcing the company to incur ongoing costs of servicing the bonds[122].

A possible synthetic solution is for Company X to purchase a credit linked note, where the payoff is based on a credit default swap where *Company X is the reference entity*. In effect, the Company is selling protection *on itself* (often referred to as a

---

[121]   In practice, this would be very unusual.

[122]   There may be a "clean up" provision if the level of outstanding debt falls below a threshold level. This would allow the issuer to compulsorily acquire any remaining debt.

"self referenced" credit default swap). This is acceptable from a credit viewpoint because the embedded credit default swap is fully cash collateralised through the credit linked note[123].

The impact of the transaction is as follows:

- Company X receives a stream of payments based on market rates plus a fee (based on its credit spread). The earnings on the credit linked note offset the servicing cost of its existing bonds. This assumes that the bonds are floating rate or, if fixed rate, then interest rates have not decreased since issue. This also assumes that the credit spread of the company has not decreased. This has the effect of reducing the earnings impact of the outstanding bonds.
- The bonds are not retired. Company X's balance sheet will show both the bonds (as a liability) and the credit linked note (as an asset).

6 Summary

Credit derivative structures offer interesting mechanisms for the isolation or disaggregation of credit exposures. This allows the effective trading of this type of risk between counterparties, facilitating the hedging and assumption of risk.

The application of credit derivatives is in its relatively early stages of development. The principal applications to date have focused on:

- Banks/financial institutions seeking to hedge credit risk, improve portfolio diversification and improve returns on available credit capital.
- Fixed income investors prepared to assume credit risk as a mechanism for return enhancement or exposure management.

The application of credit derivatives by corporations to manage the credit risks incurred in the course of normal trading is also feasible and is developing.

Increasingly, credit derivatives are also used to trade credit risk and establish complex trading strategies encompassing different elements of a firm's capital structure.

---

[123] Self referenced credit default swaps have created controversy. For example, there are suggestions that some borrowers have used this structure to seek to manipulate the firm's credit spread in the debt market.

The development of additional applications is likely as understanding of credit derivative structures increases, markets in these instruments gain in liquidity, and pricing becomes increasingly transparent. The enhancement of credit pricing and increased understanding of credit portfolios and the risk of credit concentration is also likely to be a major factor in the evolution of applications.

8
Credit Derivative Markets

1 Overview

The credit derivatives market is of relatively recent origin. Since inception, the credit derivatives market has grown at a rapid rate. The growth reflects the fundamental value of credit derivatives in creating a new mechanism for transferring/hedging and assuming credit risk.

This Chapter describes the market for credit derivatives. The structure of the Chapter is as follows:

- The origin and key phases of market development are considered.
- The estimated size of the market is then examined.
- The structure of the market, in particular the nature of the participants, is analysed.
- Special sub-sectors of the market – the role of credit derivatives in the US leveraged loan market and credit derivatives in emerging markets – are described.
- Some key developmental problems are identified.
- Potential areas of development in the market are considered.

2 Credit Derivatives – Origins And Key Factors In Development

2.1 Market Origins

The origins of the market for credit derivatives are not clear. The market appears to have evolved out of the market for secondary loan trading that developed in the early 1990s. The earliest transactions appear to have been completed around 1991/92[1]. The early transactions entailed total return

---

[1] For a view of the development of the credit derivatives market, see Falloon, William "Freundian Analysis" (December 1997) Risk 60–62.

swap transactions modelled on equity total return swaps. The basic motivation driving the development of the market was the desire to reduce credit risk to a *specific* counterparty to free up credit lines. This spawned the use of first-to-default baskets as a mechanism for transferring the risk on a basket of obligors to investors. It also drove the creation of total return swaps as a mechanism for shifting the economic risk of the asset without the necessity for trading in the asset itself.

2.2 Key Factors In Development

The key factors underlying the development of the market include:

- Concern about concentration of credit risk in bank asset portfolios.
- Developments in the management of credit risk.
- Focus on overcoming the inefficiency and illiquidity of available structures for transferring and trading credit risk.
- Incompleteness of the credit risk spectrum.
- Recognition of the need to develop structures that would facilitate attracting new investment risk capital into assumption of credit risk.

Concern about concentration of credit exposures has developed gradually. The deterioration of credit quality in the asset portfolios in the early 1990s served to emphasise the importance of credit risk and the often poorly diversified structure of bank credit portfolios. The concentration problems became evident in loan portfolios and credit risk on derivative portfolios. The concentration of exposures to certain industries (real estate and cyclical industries) became apparent. These industries were adversely affected by the global recession. The problem of credit concentration was not confined to problem credits at the lower levels of credit ratings. There was increased scrutiny of credit concentration *to higher quality counterparties*.

The scrutiny of credit exposures highlighted the large concentrations of exposures to a number of prominent sovereigns and multinational entities. The exposures derived from traditional lending transactions and long term derivatives transactions (interest rate and currency swaps), often completed in connection with capital market issues. The exposures to individual counterparties were, in many cases, extremely large. This forced financial institutions to examine mechanisms for managing this exposure. A prime concern in this regard was the ability to continue to deal with the counterparties but *without significantly increasing the credit exposure to the parties*.

The problems of concentration of credit exposure relating to derivatives and other market risk sensitive instruments became evident around 1992/93. A combination of market factors (the appreciation of the yen and falling yen interest rates) and credit factors (the decline in the credit quality of a number of Japanese banks evidenced by credit rating downgrades) resulted in a sharp increase in credit risks in these portfolios. In certain cases, internal credit limits and absolute prudential limits on exposures to individual counterparties were reached, and in some cases exceeded.

The problems of concentration risk were reinforced in the 1997–2002 period with the rapid deterioration in the credit quality of a number of major emerging market obligors. A combination of weaker local currency values, high interest rates, asset quality problems in local bank portfolios and the flight of foreign capital from emerging markets caused severe solvency problems for emerging markets obligors. The high level of exposure to emerging markets and corporate obligors in the emerging countries became evident in the portfolios of major banks/dealers. The problem of rapid changes in the *level* of exposure in certain derivative contracts also emerged as a serious problem. For example, the mark-to-market credit exposure on currency swaps undertaken with Thai, Korean and Indonesian counterparties, where the local entity was paying US\$ and receiving the local currency (Baht, Won or Rupiah), increased dramatically. As the local currency devalued (often by 100% or more), the currency swap counterparty's credit risk to the local obligor increased rapidly to levels often *in excess of the notional principal value of the swap*[2].

The problems of concentration risk were reinforced again in the late 1990s and early 2000s. The collapse of the technology based investment boom, crises in the Californian electricity industry, a number of high profile bankruptcies (for example, Enron, WorldCom and Parmalat) and a number of emerging market crises (for example, Argentina) highlighted the problems of credit risk concentration.

The increase in credit concentration risk is, in part, structural. Mergers and acquisitions amongst banks/financial institutions and bank clients have exacerbated concentration risk. In the period commencing from the late

---

[2]   These swaps have come to be known as "wrong way" swaps; see Das, Satyajit (2004) Swaps/Financial Derivatives 3rd Edition; John Wiley, Singapore at Chapter 21.

1990s, a number of major bank mergers occurred as the financial services industry consolidated. In many cases, the merging banks had common clients, particularly major corporations and large borrowers. The mergers had the effect of creating significant concentration risk to these clients. The mergers also created concentration in inter-bank transactions. The reduced number of counterparties in inter-bank trading (for example, derivatives/financial products trading) contributed to an increase in concentration risk to banks/financial institutions[3]. Consolidation among clients also contributes to concentration risk. Major consolidation in industries such as energy, mining, automobiles, pharmaceuticals and insurance has created significant concentration risk in credit portfolios.

The increasing concern about the level of credit risk and concentration risk in credit portfolios was paralleled by increasing focus on risk adjusted performance measurement in banks and financial institutions. Implementation of these approaches rapidly highlighted the risk and relative returns on credit risk/credit portfolios. The result of these processes served to highlight the dynamic nature of credit risk and the need to manage it actively. The inefficiency and illiquidity of the traditional mechanisms for credit trading prompted focus on credit derivatives as a mechanism for active management of these types of risks.

As credit derivative products started to become available, several factors added to the impetus for growth. The ability to develop products that extended the range of credit risks available created new applications. A further factor related to the flexibility of the structures and the ability to allow participation by *non bank investors*. This reflected the fact that the synthetic nature of the instruments allowed institutions with little or none of the traditional infrastructure of banks to assume credit risk.

The participation of non bank investors (for example, fixed income investors and insurance companies) coincided with a period of low nominal interest rates and low credit spreads. This encouraged investors to identify new sources of return and yield enhancement. The new markets that developed in response to investor demand were the emerging market

---

[3]   For example, the merger between JPMorgan and Chase Manhattan led to significant concentration. In certain segments of inter-bank derivatives trading, the combined entity had a market share of around 20–30% of total market volumes.

segment and the bank loan market (in particular, the leveraged loan market)[4]. Credit derivatives rapidly developed as a flexible mechanism for packaging and distributing the credit risk of both these market segments to investors.

The early stages of the market emphasised the following types of transactions:

- Ability to isolate and transfer credit risk on specific assets, allowing banks to hedge credit risks.
- Opportunity to access new classes of credit assets (such as bank loans and emerging market assets) that had traditionally not been directly available to non bank investors.
- Interest in investors generating yield enhancement through investment in credit risks through loans and derivative exposures.

As the market evolved, other factors and types of transactions that extend the range and focus of applications have emerged, including:

- Credit risk became recognised as a unique and specific investment asset class.
- Transactions focused on opportunities to increase the spectrum of credit risks, including the maturity structure, types of credit risk assumed and specific combinations of risks. This included the ability to trade structured credit risk including default correlation and recovery rate risk.
- Use of credit derivatives to manage credit risk within portfolios in order to reduce risk concentrations, improve management of credit capital to optimise returns on available credit lines and generally seek to enhance risk adjusted returns on credit assets *on a portfolio basis.*

---

[4] In mid 1997, institutional investor participation in the US domestic market totalled around 40 to 50% of the bank loan market, and was focused particularly on the lower credit rated and leveraged loan markets. This included prime rate mutual funds, crossover investors from the high yield market and special purpose asset repackaging vehicles (such as CDOs). Institutional investment in bank loans continues to be a component of the market. However, CDO investors have emerged as the dominant form of institutional investor participation in the bank loan market. The trend is most evident in the US. Similar activity is increasingly apparent in Europe. See Peter Lee "Hybrids Take Root" (September 1997) Euromoney 12; Evans, Nick "Loan Market Opens Up To New Investors" (July 2002) Euromoney 126–128.

2.3 Key Phases In Market Development[5]

The development of the market was, to a large degree, spasmodic. At each phase, particular factors and types of transaction appear to have dominated the evolution of the market[6]. The market development can be loosely divided into the following phases:

- **To 1992** – a period dominated by banks, primarily seeking to reduce exposures to particular counterparties, developing credit derivatives as a mechanism for transferring credit risk.

---

[5] The author wishes to thank Paul Hattori for drawing aspects of market evolution to his attention and some of the ideas discussed here draw on Hattori, Paul "Credit Derivatives – A View Of The Market" A speech given to a Seminar on Credit Derivatives (Lanesborough Hotel, London, March 1997).

[6] For discussion of the evolution of the market, see Smith, Terry "The New Credit Derivatives" (March 1993) Global Finance 109–110; Falloon, William "Credit Where Credit's Due" (March 1994) Risk 9–11; "A Wealth of Stealth" (July 1993) Risk 29–33; van Duyn, Aline "Credit Risk For Sale. Any Buyers?" (April 1995) Euromoney 41–43; "Taking Credit" (17 August 1995) IFR Swaps Issue 82 1,10; "Credit Without Charity" (6 September 1995) IFR Financial Products Issue 25 14–16; Parsley, Mark "Credit Derivatives Get Cracking" (March 1996) Euromoney 28–34; "Regulating Credit Derivatives" (3 April 1996) IFR Financial Products Issue 39 16–17; Irving, Richard "Credit Derivatives Come Good" (July 1996) Risk vol 9 no 7 22–26; Banks, Jim "Comfy With Credit?" (July 1996) Futures & Options World 30–33; "Credit Where It's Due" (4 September 1996) IFR Financial Products Issue 49 1–3; Murphy, David "Keeping Credit Under Control" (September 1996) Risk vol 9 no 9 123–126; McDermott, Robert "The Long Waited Arrival of Credit Derivatives" (December/January 1997) Derivatives Strategy 19–26; Ghose, Ronit (Editor) Credit Derivatives: Key Issues (1997, British Bankers' Association, London); Lee, Peter "Masters of Credit or Hype" (July 1997) Euromoney 44–49; Beder, Tanyo Styblo, and Iacono, Frank "The Good, The Bad – And The Ugly" (July 1997) Risk Credit Risk Supplement 30–33; "Credit Derivatives – Five Years Out" (July–August 1997) Derivatives Strategy 48–55; Covill, Laura "Getting Hooked On Credit Derivatives" (February 1999) Euromoney 31–32; Storrow, Jamie (Editor) (1999) Credit Derivatives: Key Issues – 2nd Edition; British Bankers' Association, London; "Credit Derivatives Conference 1999: New Alternatives In Credit Management" (February 2000) Derivatives Strategy 34–39; McNee, Alan "The Search For Credit End-Users" (June 1999) Risk 38–39; Sandiford, Jane "Credit: Restructuring The Global Market" (January 2001) FOW 30–34; Sandiford, Jane "Constructing Credit" (March 2001) FOW 39–43; Cappon, Andre "Credit Derivatives: Opportunities

- **1993 to 1994** – a period dominated by funding arbitrage exploited by total return investors (such as hedge funds) to take highly leveraged views on certain credits and markets (particularly emerging markets) and specific transactions, such as Italian tax arbitrage transactions.
- **1995 to 1996** – a period dominated by:
  1. Low interest rates and low/falling credit spreads, forcing investors to leverage their positions to earn satisfactory returns.
  2. Increased investment interest in emerging markets using credit derivative formats.
  3. Increased interest in leveraged loan markets using credit derivatives.
- **1997 to 1998** – the collapse of asset values in emerging markets, the Long Term Capital Management crisis and the liquidity crisis in capital markets generally.
- **Post 1999** – the mature phase of the market with the incorporation of credit derivatives into the mainstream of capital markets including:
  1. Use of credit derivatives/credit linked notes/collateralised debt obligations ("CDOs") to manage bank credit portfolios.
  2. Emergence of credit risk as a specific investment asset class and widespread interest from investors in assuming/trading credit risk using credit derivatives/CDOs.

There is a lack of delineation and substantial overlap between the market phases. The division into the identified phases highlights the nature of the development of the market for credit derivatives.

In Phase 1 (to 1992), the driving factor was the *internal* requirement for certain major banks to reduce the credit exposure to certain counterparties. The counterparties included a number of Scandinavian and European sovereign entities that had been active borrowers in international markets. Another prominent group was the Japanese banks as the "bubble economy" of the late 1980s came to an end, heralding a period of concern about the credit quality of the banking system.

For Exchanges And Clearing Houses" (September 2001) FOW 36–40; Rule, David "The Credit Derivatives Market: Its Development And Possible Implications For Financial Stability" (June 2001) Financial Stability Review 117–140; Evans, Nick "Maturity Of Hot New Market Faces Its Sternest Test" (December 2001) Euromoney 34–42; (10 March 2003) Global Credit Derivatives: Risk Management Or Risk?; FitchRatings; (24 September 2003) Global Credit Derivatives: A Qualified Success; FitchRatings.

The transactions were structured in a number of ways. These included total return swaps, credit default swaps and credit linked notes. The structured notes included first-to-default basket structures with a fixed payout in case of default, where the investor was rewarded by an enhanced return over LIBOR. The value dynamics were dictated by the cost of reduction in the credit exposures to the banks and the enhanced returns to investors seeking higher return in a period of low rates and low credit spreads.

Phase 2 (1993 to 1994) was driven by two groups of investors. The first – total return investors – were seeking exposure to certain types of credit risks. The risks sought were to the domestic US high yield market and emerging markets. The investments were driven by the objective of both positive carry on the investment and the prospect of capital appreciation. The capital appreciation was driven by expectations of spread tightening (resulting from economic recovery) for the domestic high yield market, or the re-rating of emerging market sovereign issuers. Credit derivatives, in the form of total return swaps, offered the investors the capacity to both fund the assets at a competitive cost and significantly leverage their positions. Credit derivatives competed with the repo market in providing funding for the investors. The total return swaps (usually collateralised by around 5 to 10% and providing funding at around 80 bps over LIBOR) became a prominent part of the market.

The second group of investors was driven by a tax anomaly in the Italian tax system (involving withholding tax). The tax factors, combined with anomalies in the bond and swap market, allowed investors to purchase Italian domestic bonds that were then swapped to an attractive margin over LIBOR[7]. The transactions were undertaken in significant size (in the order of US$ billions[8]).

The problem with the arbitrage transaction was the increasing concentration of credit risk and the lack of availability of credit limits to keep exploiting this anomaly. This prompted the use of credit default swaps to shield the purchaser of the assets from the underlying Italian credit risk.

---

[7] For discussion of the Italian bond arbitrage, see Das, Satyajit (2004) Swaps/ Financial Derivatives 3rd Edition; John Wiley, Singapore at Chapter 38.

[8] For an insight into activity in this type of trade by certain hedge funds, see Muehring, Kevin "John Meriwether By The Numbers" (November 1996) Institutional Investor 50–63.

The typical structure that evolved entailed a credit default swap on one designated Italian BTP to maturity in return for the payment of a fee (usually around 20/25 bps pa). Even after incorporating the credit default swap (usually to generate a AAA rated asset), investors were able to generate earnings of around US$ LIBOR plus 25–30 bps[9].

Phase 3 (1995 to 1996) was fuelled by the sharp decline in credit spreads that took place in 1995/96. This spread contraction was evident in both developed and emerging markets. This led to traders wanting to continue to be exposed to spreads but wanting to fund positions off balance sheet. This was due to the fact that at low spreads, it was more and more difficult to fund the positions profitably, and to also limit the exposure to a widening of spreads. At the same time, investors were unable to achieve target return levels at current spread levels and were willing to take some additional risk in order to increase returns to more acceptable levels. Investors increasingly sought higher returns from either sale of hidden optionality on credit risk (credit spreads), or taking default risk in formats that allowed them to incorporate leverage to enhance returns. Investors also increased their credit risk by investing in emerging markets and/or leveraged loan markets.

In this environment, a number of products evolved. The first group entailed selling the investor assets (either securities or asset swaps) at a higher than market spread in return for the investor having *an option* to repurchase the asset at par within 12 months (callable asset swaps). If spreads continued to decrease, then the dealer exercised the call option to repurchase the asset that could be sold at a tighter spread. Investors were able to enhance returns through the sale of optionality. The second group was essentially structured as protection against increasing spreads. They took the form of asset swaptions, synthetic lending facilities or volume/size options. The essential feature of all of the trades was the ability to place asset swaps with the seller of the option at a pre-agreed spread in the event of rises in credit spreads. The dealers obtained protection on their positions. The investors received a yield which, when the option premium was incorporated, was acceptable[10].

Investors also began to aggressively trade credit default correlation with first-to-default baskets and use total return swaps to leverage credit views.

---

[9]   See Irving, Richard "Credit Derivatives Come Good" (July 1996) Risk 22–26
      at 26.
[10] For discussion of these structures, see Chapter 2.

The entry into emerging and leveraged bank loan markets was driven (as noted above) by an altered risk return profile. The *format* of the investment was driven by the increasing availability of credit derivative structures[11]. This reflected a variety of structural considerations. In emerging markets, the considerations included:

- **Maturity** – the available emerging market assets were generally of long duration, while investor demand was for shorter term risk. Total return swaps and credit default swaps were used to synthesise shorter tenor assets for investors.
- **Regulatory factors** – the complex regulatory factors and investment mechanics discouraged foreign *direct* investment in many emerging markets. They included regulations preventing foreign ownership, withholding taxes, high transaction costs (stamp taxes, custody costs, high foreign exchange transaction margins), lack of liquidity of the asset market and currency convertibility risk. Total return swaps and, to a lesser extent, credit default swap structures, were used to overcome these issues.
- **Trading factors** – trading strategies such as the desire to trade the credit spread of emerging market paper or short emerging market issues were difficult to implement. This reflected the absence of well developed repo markets to finance assets or borrow securities. In addition, the requirement for leveraged transaction structures to further enhance returns also became a major driving factor. Total return swaps, credit default products and credit spread forwards/options rapidly emerged as the vehicle for investment in emerging market issues.

Credit derivatives use among banks/dealers and emerging market traders was also important. The major driver was the need to manage credit exposures at a sovereign and individual counterparty level. As activity in emerging markets developed, banks and traders active in these market segments rapidly increased their exposure to individual countries and counterparties. This exposure rapidly increased to significant levels. This drove the need to hedge some of the economic credit risk. This became a major factor in allowing banks/dealers to continue to transact business

---

[11] See "Credit Derivatives Come Alive In Asia" (22 January 1997) Financial Products Issue 58 10–12; Crossman, Alex "Credit Notes Harvest Asian Interest" (15 November 1997) International Financial Review Issue 1209 40.

with counterparties in the relevant jurisdiction. Total return swaps and credit default swaps rapidly emerged as a mechanism for this hedging.

In leveraged loan markets, the factors driving the use of the credit derivative format included all of the above factors, as well as the following additional factors:

- **Structural flexibility** – the investor often sought to assume one or other part of often complex packages of loans. The actual loan participations were sometimes structured as *strips* – that is, lenders had to participate in more than one tranche[12]. The investors were frequently interested only in a specific component of the overall risk of the transaction. In addition, initial participation amounts may have been well above the optimal investment amount for individual investors in the context of an overall diversified portfolio. In some cases, restrictions on assignments/loan sales may also have limited the scope for risk transfer. The use of total return swaps and credit default swaps was adapted to the identified investor objectives and to overcome some of the barriers to risk transfer.
- **Administrative flexibility** – institutional investors typically did not possess the loan administration infrastructure to participate directly in loans. The total return swaps, credit default swaps and synthetic lending facility/asset swaption structures were ideally suited to transferring the risk, while allowing the originating or participation bank to remain the lender of record for the transaction.

The use of credit derivatives in both emerging markets and leveraged loan markets is specifically considered below.

Phase 4 (1997 to 1998) was dominated by the crisis in emerging markets and the flow on into capital markets generally[13]. The crisis had its origins

---

[12] For example, a lender might have to take a participation in the senior secured, unsecured and mezzanine (subordinated) debt facilities. This structure is designed to align lender and equity investor interests and lower the agency costs of the transaction.

[13] For discussion of the impact of the emerging market crisis, see Clow, Robert "Past Due" (December 1997) Institutional Investor 159–163; Wilson, Neil "Credit Derivatives" (January 1998) Futures & Options World 51; Paul-Choudury, Sumit "Strength Through Adversity" (March 1998) Risk – Credit Risk Supplement 6–9; Elliot, Margaret "Waking Up To Credit Risk" (April 1998) Derivatives Strategy 32–38; Louis, Jack "Tonic For The Troops" (February 1999) Risk 18–23. For discussion of the Asian crisis, see Backman, Michael (1999) Asian Eclipse; John Wiley & Sons, Singapore.

in Asia. In July 1997, the Thai Baht was decoupled from the US$ to which it had been pegged. The Baht promptly plunged in value. The situation was repeated in quick succession in a series of other Asian economies such as Korea, Indonesia and Malaysia. The situation also affected, to varying degrees, other regional economies such as the Philippines, Taiwan, India, Hong Kong and Singapore. The rapid depreciation in the value of the local currency was accompanied by a series of events, including:

- Unhedged foreign currency borrowing (in US$, DEM and yen) by issuers in these countries showed significant foreign exchange losses. Both sovereign and corporate borrowers in Asia had large amounts of unhedged foreign currency debt. The transactions had been undertaken to capitalise on large favourable interest rate differentials in the belief that the local currency was effectively linked to the US$ and unlikely to depreciate significantly.
- There was a sharp decline in local currency stock markets and in asset prices generally.
- Local currency interest rates increased to very high levels.
- There was a flight of capital from these markets. This reflected withdrawal of short term financing lines by foreign lenders as well as liquidation of portfolio investments.

The combination of these events triggered a collapse in economic activity and a recession in these countries. The solvency of many borrowers was completely undermined by these events, with the default risk rising sharply. The crisis triggered intervention by the International Monetary Fund in several countries.

The crisis rapidly affected other markets. The immediate effect was in other emerging markets. Russia and Eastern Europe were affected first. Russia defaulted on its rouble obligations in the second half of 1998[14]. Latin America was also affected, with Brazil being forced to float the Real. The currency promptly fell sharply in value[15].

---

[14] For analysis of the Russian default, see Stoakes, Christopher "Ways Out Of Russia's Big Freeze" (November 1998) Euromoney 20; Dyson, Jack "Every Man For Himself" (March 1999) Euromoney 25–28.

[15] For analysis of the behaviour of the market for emerging debt, see Kulesz, Javier "Contagion: Did The Market Discriminate?" (19 November 1998) Financial Products Issue 102 14–15; Currie, Antony "Back To The Age Of Defaults" (November 1998) Euromoney 60–63.

The crisis in emerging markets rapidly affected capital markets more generally. The key transmission mechanism was a general reduction in liquidity, a contraction in available capital (particularly for other than the highest credit quality categories), and a sharp increase in credit spreads. These factors triggered major problems for banks and investors. The most serious victim of the spreading crisis was Long Term Capital Management (a very large and well known hedge fund). The hedge fund had to seek (unsuccessfully) an infusion of new capital to survive serious erosion in the net asset value of the fund[16].

The impact on the banking system was immediate and massive. Bank credit losses rose sharply, reflecting large provisions against credit exposures to emerging market and hedge fund counterparties. In addition, banks active in emerging markets sustained serious trading losses as emerging market financial assets fell sharply in value.

This period, with its unprecedented volatility, had an impact on the development of credit derivatives markets. Major problems arose because the credit derivative format had begun to become established as a favoured method for taking on emerging market exposure. For example, investment in the Russian GKO market was substantially structured in the form of credit linked notes[17].

As the crisis developed, credit default swaps were triggered and total return swaps were terminated. This resulted in cash or physical settlement of the transactions. Initially there was considerable confusion about the actual mechanics of the transactions. There was also acrimony about the economic effect. This included counterparties seeking to disown transactions. This was on the basis that they had not understood the transaction and its risks. It also included concern about the mismatch between the actual loss suffered and the payout under the default hedge. The problems encountered created significant negative publicity and also concern about the actual efficacy of credit derivatives.

As the initial problems with existing transactions were resolved, the credit derivatives market received considerable impetus from the

---

[16] See discussion in Das, Satyajit (2004) Swaps/Financial Derivatives 3rd Edition; John Wiley, Singapore at Chapter 24.

[17] See Chapter 3.

effects of the crisis[18]. This impetus came from a number of sources, including:

- **Need for credit risk management** – the crisis served to highlight the need for active management of credit risk. At a macro level, this reinforced interest in the use of credit derivatives to hedge/manage credit risk, particularly concentration risk within portfolios. At a micro level, as limits to emerging countries and individual obligors were reduced, there was an immediate need to seek mechanisms for hedging existing positions to ensure compliance with limits. Credit derivatives markets (total return swaps and credit default swaps) rapidly became a means for achieving these objectives.
- **Emerging market debt portfolio management** – in the aftermath of the crisis, traders in emerging market debt were faced with large inventory positions that were both illiquid and also showing large mark-to-market losses. Traders seeking to liquidate positions found it necessary to develop new and innovative mechanisms for selling down this risk. Structures such as total return swaps and credit linked notes (CDOs and basket structures) were used to seek to repackage and liquidate the positions. The motivation was both to increase the value received and also to access liquidity.
- **Access to liquidity** – for borrowers in emerging markets, financing and access to cash was an urgent issue. The prospect of selling prime marketable assets (such as equities and bonds) at distressed prices was unattractive. Total return swaps emerged as a means for accessing cash while maintaining the desired price exposure to the underlying assets. The structures often allowed access to funding at more economic costs than direct funding (if available)[19].
- **Repatriation on investment to home markets** – as investors disinvested from emerging markets, the liquidity was directed into other assets. After

---

[18]   See Quist, Robert "Credit Derivatives Ease Asia's Debt Crisis" (February 1998) Risk 4–5; Horsewood, Rachel, Gailey, Colin, and Yu, Daniel "Back To Basics" (March 1998) AsiaMoney 20–24; Rhode, William "Brave New World" (August 1998) Asia Risk 10–13; Abed, Kamal "It Ain't What You Do…" (November 1998) Futures & OTC World 55.

[19]   For example, see discussion on the use of equity swaps to achieve similar objectives, see Das, Satyajit (2004) Swaps/Financial Derivatives 3rd Edition; John Wiley, Singapore at Chapters 55 and 60.

the initial period, markets such as the leveraged loan market and the domestic US high yield market attracted investment. The increase in spreads, the robust state of the US economy and the perception that investment returns were in excess of the *expected* default risk drove this investment. Credit derivative formats were again extensively used to access these markets. In addition, some investors began to seek re-investment opportunities in emerging markets on a selective basis. This included purchase of financial assets as well as distressed bonds. Credit derivative structures were often used to create the appropriate format for these investments that primarily focused on recovery rates and credit spread movements.

- **Portfolio liquidation** – the capital losses suffered by banks forced some banks to seek to adjust their balance sheets. For example, Japanese banks (already weakened by credit losses in Japan) suffered large credit losses on their significant loan portfolios to Korean, Thai and Indonesian obligors. These banks used credit derivatives in a number of ways. Japanese banks used credit derivatives to shed risk over key balance dates to "window dress" balance sheet and risk profiles. More fundamentally, Japanese banks undertook the securitisation of loan assets (through credit linked notes/CDOs) or sought economic hedges through credit default swaps. This was primarily to free up regulatory capital.
- **Concern about currency transferability risk** – the imposition of currency controls by Malaysia served to reinforce already evident concerns about currency convertibility risk in emerging markets. Interest in currency conversion protection increased during this period from both investors (both portfolio and direct) as well as emerging market traders[20].

In essence, the crisis was important to the evolution of the credit derivatives market in a number of ways, including:

- It served to highlight that the hedges actually functioned as intended, albeit with some problems. The triggering of defaults and the need to settle default payments served to highlight key issues in the operation of the structures. This led to significant enhancements and improvements in documentation, structuring and design of transactions.

---

[20] See Kirby, James "Capital Controls Raise Risk" (October 1998) Asia Risk 9.

- It highlighted the necessity of active credit risk management in a dramatic manner.
- It illustrated that credit derivatives could assist in the management of credit risks. Credit derivatives emerged as part of the way in which the crisis was dealt with rather than as a causal factor in the crisis.

It is arguable that this phase of activity in credit derivatives was pivotal in establishing these instruments as a significant factor in capital markets.

Phase 5 (1999 to the present) represents the mature phase of the credit derivatives market. It is characterised by increasing maturity at both a product level and in the application of the products to credit risk management.

Following the emerging market crisis, credit derivatives have become accepted at several levels within capital markets:

- For banks/financial institutions, the various structures have become a more accepted means to manage credit risk. This covers managing tactical credit risk to individual counterparties. It also covers strategic portfolio management (primarily in the form of portfolio securitisation structures such as CDOs).
- For investors, the instruments have come to be seen as an alternative means for synthesising investment assets. The development of credit linked notes/CDO structures is driven by interest in assuming credit risk and trading relative value positions in credit risks.
- For both banks/financial institutions, investors and traders, credit derivatives have emerged as the preferred mechanism for trading credit risk and certain credit risk dimensions unavailable directly in the cash market (default correlation and recovery rates).

Key drivers have included the increased standardisation of structures, terminology and documentation. Increased pricing transparency and the availability of information on pricing techniques has also assisted this process. Increased liquidity and the rise in volumes of transactions outstanding have contributed to the acceptance of the products. An additional driver for banks has been their increased focus on regulatory and economic capital management. The presence of significant regulatory capital arbitrage opportunities has also been a factor.

The discussion of the points of focus in the evolution of the market in credit derivatives highlights the eclectic pattern of the market's development. It also highlights the intricate manner in which specific imperatives that have prevailed in different guises at different times have gradually allowed the development of the products and elicited the participation of banks/dealers and investor groups.

3 Credit Derivatives Market – Size And Activity Levels[21]

The size of the market and activity levels is difficult to gauge. The difficulties are the result of a number of factors:

- Absence of specific survey data on these types of transactions until recently.
- The wide variety of transaction structures used including structured notes, off-balance-sheet derivative transactions and other forms (insurance structures). This has prompted significant debates as to the types of transactions that should be treated as credit derivatives.
- The lack of standardisation of credit derivative structures that creates inherent difficulties of characterisation and collation of data.
- The generally secretive nature of this market and its lack of transparency which impedes assessment of the market size.

At end 2004, the market was estimated to be in excess of US$6,000 billion. Growth in the market has been very rapid. The key characteristics of the market include:

- The predominant instrument is credit default swaps. The second most important instrument is credit linked notes/CDOs.
- The credit default swaps are focused around a maturity of 5 years. The majority of activity is in less than 5 years. The market is heavily focused on North American and European credit risk. The major part of the market is focused around investment grade credit risk.

---

[21] See Smithson, Charles with Holappa, Hal and Rai, Shaun "Credit Derivatives (2)" (June 1996) Risk 47–48; (1996) BBA Credit Derivatives Report 1996; British Bankers' Association; "BBA Counts Up Credit Trades" (8 October 1998) Financial Products Issue 99 7; Storrow, Jamie (Editor) (1999) Credit Derivatives: Key Issues – 2nd Edition; British Bankers' Association, London at 127; Smithson, Charles and Hayt, Gregory "Credit Derivatives Go From Strength To Strength" (December 1999) Risk 54–55; Hargreaves, Tim "Default Swaps Drive Growth" (March 2000) Risk – Credit Risk Special Report S2–S3; Patel, Navroz "Credit Derivatives: Vanilla Volumes Challenged" (February 2001) Risk 32–34; Patel, Navroz "The Vanilla Explosion" (February 2002) Risk 24–26.

- The major users of credit derivatives to hedge are banks/dealers. Investors (primarily asset managers, hedge funds and insurance/reinsurance companies) use credit derivatives to acquire credit risk.
- The market is concentrated, with a few dealers dominating the market activity.
- Major trading centres continue to be London (focused on European and international transactions) and New York (focused on the large domestic US market).

4 Credit Derivatives Market – Participants

4.1 Overview

The range of participants in the credit derivatives market is broad. It covers commercial banks, investment banks, fixed interest investors, insurance/reinsurance companies and non-financial corporations. Each group is motivated by different requirements. The range of transactions for each group, both current and potential, is different.

Underlying the different applications are the isolation of the underlying credit risk, the attempt to increase the liquidity of/ability to trade credit risk, and the transformation of credit into a more generic asset class. The ability to use the standard ISDA agreement and the resultant standardisation of documentation is also an important factor in the participation of individual types of organisations.

4.2 Commercial Banks

Commercial bank activity is predicated on the fact that these organisations are holders of substantial credit risk through their normal operations. In this regard, the market for credit derivatives is regarded as an adjunct to both traditional methods of management of credit exposures and loan asset trading/distribution activities. **Exhibit 8.1** sets out a comparison of credit derivatives (primarily, total return swaps and credit default products) and more traditional methods of transferring credit risk.

The major focus of applications will typically emphasise:

- **Transferring credit risk** – this is an alternative to traditional forms of selling down credit risk.
- **Hedging credit risk** – this takes the form of purchasing default protection.

- **Synthetic credit assets** – this uses credit derivatives to originate/assume credit risk of different counterparties.
- **Credit portfolio management** – this focuses on reducing portfolio credit concentration and improving the utilisation of credit capital.

Banks exhibit a specific pattern of activity in the credit derivatives market[22]:

- In aggregate, banks are significant net buyers of protection in the credit derivatives market. This is consistent with the role of banks as originators of credit risk. In effect, the banking industry uses the credit derivative market to transfer credit risk to other sectors of the capital market that lack credit origination capacity.
- The behaviour of individual banks varies significantly. Major buyers of protection include large and sophisticated banks. The remainder of the banking sector (primarily, smaller regional banks in North America, Europe, Asia and Australasia) are net sellers of protection. These banks appear to use the credit derivative market as a mechanism to originate and invest in credit risk.
- The major products used by banks are single name credit default swaps and (to a lesser extent) credit linked notes/CDOs. There is also increasing use of portfolio credit products.
- The volume of credit derivative transactions varies significantly between a bank's banking and trading books[23]. For major banks (especially those with significant trading/investment banking operations), the trading book volumes are large relative to banking book volumes. For smaller banks, the trading book volumes are less significant. This is consistent with major dealers using credit derivatives (particularly credit default swaps) to trade credit risk. It is also consistent with smaller banks using credit derivatives to hedge credit risk and acquire synthetic credit risk (as an alternative to traditional types of credit risk such as loans). These banks tend to hold positions through to maturity.

---

[22] See (24 September 2003) Global Credit Derivatives: A Qualified Success; Fitch Ratings, New York.

[23] For a discussion of the distinction between a bank's banking and trading books, see Das, Satyajit (2004) Swaps/Financial Derivatives 3rd Edition; John Wiley, Singapore at Chapters 33 and 34. See also Chapter 1.

Exhibit 8.1   Credit Derivatives Versus Conventional Credit Risk Sale Transactions[24]

Instrument	Credit Derivatives	Loan Sale	Participation	Guarantee/Letter of Credit
Impact				
Type of risk	Deliverable obligations (bonds and assignable/consent required loans)	Loans	Loans	Varied
Financing	No financing (as off balance sheet)	Funding achieved	Funding achieved in case of funded sub-participations	No financing
Pricing	Market driven (based on securities/loan traded prices)	Private without transparency	Private without transparency	Private without transparency
Counterparty credit risk	On credit derivative	No	Yes	Yes
Default costs	Low	Loan recovery costs	Loan recovery costs	Loan recovery costs
Accounting	No impact	Realisation of gain or loss	Realisation of gain or loss	No impact
Ongoing costs	Minimal	Present	Present	Minimal
Documentation	Standard ISDA	Customised	Customised	Customised
Confidentiality	Confidential	Requires involvement of borrower	May require involvement of borrower	Confidential

[24] This Table draws on but is not identical to Hattori, Paul "Credit Derivatives – A View Of The Market" A speech given to a Seminar on Credit Derivatives (Lanesborough Hotel, London, March 1997).

4.3 Investment Banks/Dealers

Investment bank/dealer participation in the market for credit derivatives is driven by a broad range of factors. Investment banks traditionally are not long term holders of *credit* risk. The bulk of the risk assumed is market risk from inventory holdings of bonds/securities and trading with financial institutions. In recent times, investment banks have assumed higher levels of credit exposure from the following primary sources:

- Entry into term derivative transactions as an adjunct to new issues of securities.
- Entry into loan/credit syndications and increased emphasis on loan trading (reflecting in some part, the increased liquidity of these markets).

The credit risk arising from traditional sources has also undergone a metamorphosis. This is the result of the increased importance of trading and distribution of non investment grade securities and emerging market paper. These types of securities have higher levels of credit risk than more traditional government and investment grade corporate securities. This increases the level of credit risk in inventories of securities held by dealers.

Against this background, investment bank applications of credit derivatives have evolved into the following distinct areas of activity:

- Hedging credit exposures in the dealer's portfolio or arising from its activities.
- Trading in credit derivatives as a new activity complementing trading activities in other assets.

The hedging activity has focused on hedging both default risk and credit spread risk. Default risk hedging by investment banks can be illustrated by the following examples:

- Assume an investment bank has a large counterparty credit exposure to a sovereign issuer (AA/Aa rated). The exposure arises under term swap contracts (final maturity 10 years; average maturity 5 years) associated with securities issues underwritten by the bank. The current exposure is at the limit that the bank can prudently assume. The inability to either increase the credit exposure limits or free up the existing credit lines will constrain further new issue business with this issuer. Under these circumstances, the investment bank can purchase default protection through a credit default swap to reduce its credit exposure to the issuer. The protection would typically be bought for short terms and rolled as required, with the level of protection being adjusted to the run off of existing positions.

- Assume an investment bank has a large holding of the debt securities of an emerging market sovereign issuer (BB/Ba rated) in connection with an underwriting. The position is difficult to liquidate quickly without creating significant losses. The holding has the effect of increasing the credit exposure to this issuer and to the country beyond prudential limits. The credit exposure can be hedged using a default swap to allow the credit risk to be reduced to acceptable levels until the securities are distributed.

The other source of risk is the significant credit spread risk incurred by investment banks in their securities inventories and underwriting activities. Credit spread products can be used to hedge these risks.

The trading focus is more straightforward in objective. As credit has emerged as a more liquid commodity, investment banks have perceived opportunities to trade in and distribute credit risk in a manner analogous to trading in other asset classes such as debt, equities, foreign exchange and commodities. A significant factor in this focus has been the demand for credit linked products (including CDO's) from fixed income investors that constitute a significant client base for dealers. Trading volumes generated from these activities are significant and a multiple of the volumes generated by credit hedging.

4.4 Fixed Income Investors

Fixed income investors have traditionally assumed credit risk in a variety of forms. The largest component of credit risk assumed has been in the form of bonds/debt securities issued by obligors. Credit derivatives provide investors with the capacity to isolate and separate credit risk (both default and spread risk) and to either hedge this risk away or assume specific risk as desired.

The participation of investors has been motivated by a variety of factors that varies between types of institutions. Traditional investors (insurance companies, pension funds and investment managers) view credit derivatives as a mechanism for more completely and efficiently disaggregating credit risk and allowing trading in this risk attribute. Other investors such as special purpose funds (for example, prime rate funds) and hedge funds view credit derivatives as providing the capacity to participate in certain market segments that traditionally would have excluded their participation. The inherent leverage potential in the derivative format has been particularly attractive for hedge funds, enabling them to create leveraged credit views.

Investors are attracted by the inefficiencies in credit pricing both between credits of similar default characteristics and between market segments *for the same issuer* (bank loan market, securities/bond markets and the convertible markets). The fact that credit derivatives allow effective arbitrage between the markets has motivated participation.

The primary applications to emerge for fixed income investors include:

- **Replication applications** – focused on creating synthetic exposure to the investment grade loan markets and high yield/non investment grade or emerging markets to overcome barriers to or the high costs of direct access.
- **Yield enhancement** – primarily generated by assuming spread risk or the risk of credit default in return for higher income. This includes the creation of structured credit risk and the use of leverage (for example, CDOs).
- **Trading** – emphasising trading in credit risk and credit market volatility. This includes targeted buying or selling of securities at defined spread levels to capture premium income from sale of options, trading spread expectations and assuming specific types of default exposures on a risk return basis.

The nature of participation of fixed income investors is different between jurisdictions. Most investor participation has been opportunistic, predicated on the above factors. However, there are significant differences between market segments.

4.5   Non-Financial Corporations

The participation of non-financial corporations to date has been limited. This reflects the poorly developed framework for credit risk management within corporations. The major applications currently include:

- **Credit risk management** – this focuses primarily in the context of vendor financing, trading with distressed entities and in international projects (located in emerging markets).
- **Synthetic investments** – this focuses on non-financial corporations providing protection on other corporations to enhance returns on cash/ liquid assets. It also includes the sale of protection on the corporation itself (self referenced credit default swaps) as investment of surplus funds or part of synthetic debt repurchases.

4.6   Insurance/Reinsurance Companies

Insurance/reinsurance companies have emerged as significant participants in the credit derivatives market[25]. This group has become a significant seller of credit protection in the market over a relatively short period of time.

The global insurance sector has emerged as a large seller of protection. In effect, the banking sector has transferred significant volumes of credit risk to the insurance sector. Participants in the insurance sector include life insurance companies, property and casualty insurance companies and the reinsurance sector. It also includes the financial guarantors/monoline bond insurers. This trend has been a part of the insurance sector's diversification into alternative asset classes and alternative risk transfer ("ART")[26].

The involvement of insurance companies has exhibited the following patterns[27]:

- The major products used are CDOs, portfolio products and structured credit transaction.
- The major proportion of participation has come from North American and European insurers.
- The average credit quality of exposure assumed by insurance companies has been relatively high (A or better). This is true of financial guarantors/ monoline bond insurers who have increasingly focused on highly rated credit risk (higher attachment points in portfolio products/CDO tranches).

The participation of insurance companies is driven by a number of factors, including[28]:

- **Risk underwriting** – insurance companies have historically underwritten credit risk. This has traditionally taken the form of credit insurance,

---

[25] See Cass, Dwight "Insurers Cash In On Credit Market" (December 1999) Risk 47–48; Dunbar, Nicholas "Insurers Surge Into Credit Derivatives" (July 2000) Risk 8; Teague, Solomon "Has Insurance Credit Risk Transfer Been Over-played?" (July 2004) Risk – Credit Risk Supplement 64–65.

[26] See Das, Satyajit (2004) Swaps/Financial Derivatives 3rd Edition; John Wiley, Singapore at Chapter 70.

[27] See (24 September 2003) Global Credit Derivatives: A Qualified Success; Fitch Ratings, New York.

[28] See Gontarek, Walter and Nowell, Peter "Insurable Risks" (March 2000) FOW 45–49; Gontarek, Walter and Sirr, Jeffrey "Hungry For Credit Returns"

trade credit and surety bonds. Some insurance companies (financial guarantors/monoline bond insurers) have specialised in assuming credit risk. In recent years there has been increased focus on direct assumption of credit risk through the credit derivatives market. This is driven by these factors:

1. Insurance premiums (particularly in the reinsurance sector) are highly cyclical. During periods when insurance premiums offer poor risk adjusted returns, insurers have sought to underwrite alternative risks such as credit risk.

2. Credit risk offers attractive risk adjusted returns in its own right. The capital market frequently offers large premiums for liquidity risks that further enhance the risk adjusted returns.

3. Credit risk is also poorly correlated with traditional property and casualty risk. This reduces the volatility of the underwriting port-folio, allowing lower capital reservation and generating attractive returns on capital.

- **Investment** – insurance companies invest capital/reserves and premiums received to cover potential liabilities under insurance policies written. Credit derivatives provide insurance companies with attractive invest-ment opportunities to enhance returns on investment portfolios. This is similar to the factors driving investor participation in credit derivatives generally. There are several aspects to this activity, including:

1. The use of credit derivatives allows separation of credit and liquidity risk. The insurance company can invest in high quality cash assets to ensure liquidity in order to meet insurance contract payouts. The credit derivatives can be overlaid on the cash portfolio to synthetically capture the additional return from credit spreads.

2. In markets such as Europe, the range of corporate credit risk available in the bond market has historically been limited. The use of credit derivatives allows insurers to create well diversified portfolios of credit risk more efficiently.

- **Regulatory capital** – there are significant differences in the regulatory capital requirements of banks and insurance companies. Banks are subject to the global Basel regulatory framework[29]. In contrast, state

---

(October 2000) Risk – Credit Risk Special Report S2-S8; Schaumann, Hilmar "Optimal Credit" (February 2001) FOW 28–31.

[29] See Das, Satyajit (2004) Swaps/Financial Derivatives 3rd Edition; John Wiley, Singapore at Chapters 33 and 34.

and national regulators regulate insurance companies. In the case of some types of insurers (reinsurance companies and monoline insurers), there may be limited regulation, with capital adequacy being driven by rating agencies and rating considerations. Insurance regulations frequently dictate lower capital requirement for credit risk than for a comparable regulated bank. This reflects a more flexible capital adequacy framework. It also reflects the fact that insurance company capital takes into account certain factors (credit quality, seniority of claim, maturity and portfolio diversification) that is not currently recognised under the bank capital adequacy framework[30]. This means that insurance companies are more efficient holders of credit risk than banks.

The use of credit derivatives to structure and transfer credit risk to insurance companies also has some additional elements:

- **Origination capacity** – insurance companies lack the credit origination capacity of banks/dealers. This makes credit derivatives an ideal form of risk transfer mechanism. The bank originates credit risk that is then transferred to the most efficient long term holder of that risk.
- **Risk culture** – insurance companies have a well defined risk culture. This entails using capital and investments to cover sequential claims on cash flows. Traditional insurance company risk finance emphasises constructing different risk layers. Some layers are retained while other layers are hedged or transferred. This approach, when applied to credit risk, allows the stratification of credit risk in a new way, with specific defined types of risk being created and traded. The approach has prompted the development of different types of transactions (particularly the tranched trades/CDOs). Credit derivatives are well suited to these types of credit risk trading.

The major focus of insurance companies is high quality, well diversified investment grade assets. The major structures used to transfer credit risks to insurance/reinsurance companies include:

- **Conventional credit derivatives** – insurers assume credit risk in a variety of conventional formats, including single name credit default swaps and

---

[30] Basel 2 seeks to incorporate some of these factors into the bank capital adequacy framework; see discussion in Das, Satyajit (2004) Swaps/Financial Derivatives 3rd Edition; John Wiley, Singapore at Chapter 33.

portfolio credit default swaps. For example, reinsurance companies have been prominent in assuming the super senior exposure in unfunded synthetic securitisations. Insurance companies are also major investors in tranched trades (both off balance sheet and funded). This includes investment in tranches of CDO transactions.

- **Transformer vehicles** – a key issue in insurance company participation in credit derivatives is the capacity to enter into derivative contracts. In order to facilitate participation, a number of banks have established insurance transformer vehicles[31]. The transformer vehicle is usually a special purpose captive insurance company that enters into credit default swaps with the dealer and hedges itself with a matching credit insurance contract with an insurance company. **Exhibit 8.2** sets out the structure of an insurance transformer vehicle. The use of transformer vehicles requires that the contracts be carefully structured to eliminate any basis risk or risk of characterisation of the ISDA agreement into an insurance contract[32]. **Exhibit 8.3** sets out a number of differences between traditional insurance contracts and credit derivatives.

The factors driving the participation of insurance companies are both cyclical (reflecting the state of the insurance market) and secular.

In 2002/2003, the credit exposures of monoline insurers (under CDOs) came under close scrutiny. The concern related to deterioration in the credit quality of certain CDO investments and unexpected earnings volatility from credit investments[33]. This concern led to a reduction in the involvement of these insurers in credit derivatives (particularly CDO markets). This suggests that future growth of insurer participation will grow at a slower rate. However, insurers will continue to be involved in credit markets as they are seen as an attractive area of growth.

---

[31] For example, Deutsche Bank uses a vehicle called GCRe (Global Credit Reinsurance); see Misra, Rajeev and van Doorn, Alarik "Securitisation Or Insuritisation?" (December 2000) Risk – Alternative Risk Strategies Special Report – Sponsors Statement. Other dealers also have similar vehicles; see Smith, Corrine "JP Morgan Moves Into Insurance Transformation" (February 2002) FOW 22.

[32] See discussion in Chapter 1.

[33] This related to the mark-to-market accounting treatment of some of these credit investments under the US accounting standard (FASB 133). For a discussion of the accounting standards, see Das, Satyajit (2004) Swaps/Financial Derivatives 3rd Edition; John Wiley, Singapore at Chapter 31.

Exhibit 8.2   Insurance Transformer Vehicles

The basic objective of an insurance transformer vehicle is to repackage credit default swaps into an equivalent credit insurance policy. This is done with the objective of transferring the credit risk, using the credit insurance policy, to an insurance company.

The basic structure is set out below:

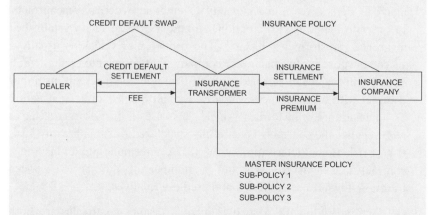

The basic elements are as follows[34]:

- The insurance transformer is set up as an insurance entity. The common structure is to establish a Bermudan insurance vehicle. The vehicle is not owned by the dealer and is separately managed. The dealer procures transactions for the vehicle and hedges its risks. The shares of the company are owned by a charity and held by a share trustee. The vehicle generally has independent directors, administrators, external auditors and legal counsel.
- The transformer enters into a credit default swap with the dealer.
- The risk assumed is simultaneously hedged with a back-to-back insurance policy entered into with an insurance company.
- The dealer pays a fee under the credit default swap to the transformer. The transformer uses the fee to make premium payments to the insurer.
- If there is no credit event under the credit default swap, then there are no further payments.
- If there is a credit event under the credit default swap, then the settlement under the credit default swap (cash or physical) matches the settlement under the insurance contract.

---

[34] The basic concepts used are similar to those used with repackaging vehicles generally; see Chapter 3. See also Das, Satyajit (2004) Swaps/Financial Derivatives 3rd Edition; John Wiley, Singapore at Chapter 38.

Two other aspects of the structure should be noted:

- The transformer operates in the same way as a program issuer[35]. This entails the *same* vehicle entering into multiple matched trades. Each trade is segregated into an individual "cell". Each cell is based on an individual insurance policy secured over a specific credit default swap. This is designed to separate the individual transactions from other transactions entered into by the transformer.
- The transformer enters into a master insurance policy with each insurance company. The details of individual trades undertaken are documented as a sub-policy that accedes to the master policy agreement.

Exhibit 8.3   Insurance Contracts Versus Credit Derivatives Contracts[36]

	Credit Default Swap	**Credit Insurance Policy**
Documentation	Standardised terms documented under ISDA Master	Standalone contract with no standard industry documentation
Credit events	Specific events (bankruptcy, failure to pay, restructuring) as defined applicable to the reference entity	Based on a specific bond or obligation
Settlement	• Payment based on credit event as notified in a credit event notice based on publicly available information • Physical delivery or cash settlement • Payment/settlement at a fixed time after credit event	• Payment based on evidence of loss event provided by insured party • Cash payment • Payment after waiting period (generally 90–120 days)
Governing law	England or New York	Various, depending upon location of insurer
Netting	Applicable	Not applicable
Exposure to reference entity	No requirement for protection buyer to have exposure to reference entity	Insured party must have an insurable interest (exposure) to reference entity

---

[35] See Chapter 3.   See also Das, Satyajit (2004) Swaps/Financial Derivatives 3rd Edition; John Wiley, Singapore at Chapter 38.

[36] The Table is based on Gontarek, Walter and Nowell, Peter "Insurable Risks" (March 2000) FOW 45–49 at 48.

5 Credit Derivatives – Trading

The market for credit derivatives is increasingly becoming a highly liquid and fully tradable market in credit risk. The level of trading in the secondary market is growing rapidly. There are relatively liquid markets with reasonably tight bid-offer spreads in a number of entities (primarily major global banks, frequent issuers (including automobile finance companies), well known global corporations and major sovereign entities).

Most trading is conducted on a closely *matched basis* with some warehousing of positions. The warehousing of positions is integrated with the institution's overall credit risk management and/or credit risk trading. The limit on credit trading is driven by difficulties in hedging/risk management[37].

The market is likely to become more liquid as time elapses. This increase will reflect a variety of factors, including:

- The entry of new dealers, expanding the range of traders and participants. In recent years, a number of major banks have made significant commitments to the credit derivatives business by making key hires to establish and operate substantial credit trading operations. While the market difficulties experienced in 1997 and 1998 have affected some of these dealers, resulting in some retrenchment of trading capacity, the activity levels have continued to increase steadily.
- There is general acceptance of credit derivatives and credit hedging. Most banks have begun to *use* these instruments to manage their credit risk to individual counterparties and the credit portfolio. This has meant increases in trading volumes and overall enhancement of market liquidity/trading volumes.
- The entrance of a number of inter-bank brokers seeking to facilitate trading in these products. At least two electronic trading platforms focused on credit derivatives have emerged – CreditTrade and Creditex[38]. These are relatively new and are evolving rapidly to combine a mix of voice and electronic broking services.

---

[37] See discussion in Chapter 5.
[38] See Abed, Kamal "Credit Brokers Plan To Counter Threat Of Online Intermediation" (19–25 October 1999) Financial Products 1, 10; Abed, Kamal "Battle For e-Credit Begins" (November 1999) Futures & OTC World 14; Falloon, William "Creditex And The Internet Revolution" (November 1999) Risk 33–35; Polyn, Gallagher "Credit Derivatives Platforms Turn To Structured Products" (March 2002) Risk – Credit Risk S14–S15.

- The continued standardisation of documentation and product structures will facilitate trading by increasing the homogeneity of the underlying assets traded[39].

Trading in credit derivatives exhibits the following characteristics:

- The principal traded product is single name credit default swaps. Most major dealers have a "flow trading" desk focused on trading single name credit default swaps. Volumes are driven by client demand, structured credit products and proprietary trading. A significant source of volume is structured products and CDO transactions that require trading in single name credit default swaps to acquire or manage credit risk. A further significant source of volume is the integrated credit trading "books" established by dealers to structure products (for example, n^{th}-to-default baskets and single tranche CDOs). The risk management of these books require continuous trading to dynamically hedge existing positions[40].
- Trading strategies are relatively straightforward with a focus on assuming long or short positions on credit spreads. Increasingly, there is interest in trading default correlation and recovery rates. In addition, there is increasing interest in trading the relationship between equity and credit markets. This has resulted in focus on so-called capital structure arbitrage trading strategies[41].

A central issue to trading is the need for most dealers to optimise the location of the credit trading function and its relationship to the credit function more generally. To date, the credit derivatives function has been either located within derivatives trading or the securities trading/capital markets areas. It is often combined with asset swaps or structured products (essentially less liquid or non standard products). In some dealers, it is located within the bank's loan syndication/loan or asset sales area.

The lack of familiarity with credit risk and the unavailability of natural hedges in a lot of cases makes the use of the derivatives desks to trade credit derivatives problematic. Similarly, the use of securities trading as the focus of credit trading activity is also not ideal, as it tends to bias activity to traded securities. In reality, the credit trading function has a more central role

---

[39] See Chapter 1.
[40] See Chapters 2 and 4.
[41] See Chapters 4, 5 and 7.

in financial institutions. Until the location issue is resolved, the integration of credit trading to the *credit risk management of the entity* is likely to be incomplete[42]. This manifests itself in lower liquidity and lower trading levels in these products.

6 Credit Derivatives – Market Sectors

6.1 Overview

The market for credit derivatives is capable of dissection in a number of ways, including the type of underlying assets, the liquidity of underlying assets, specific types of credit risk (investment grade, non investment grade, distressed credits and emerging market credits) and geographically.

6.2 Liquidity Of Underlying Assets

It is important in dissecting the market for credit derivatives to separate the universe of underlying reference credit obligations into liquid and illiquid assets.

Liquid assets refer primarily to bonds. It includes tradable loans (sometimes in the form of Transferable Loan Certificates ("TLCs") or loan assignments, novation and risk and sub participation agreements)[43]. Illiquid assets encompass all other credit obligations, including non traded loans and non static exposures (arising from derivatives). The illiquidity is a function of the *form* of the obligations (such as the exposure on a derivative), conditions impacting upon the issuer or obligor (such as distressed credits), or the lack of trading interest in the type of obligations (due to size or the limited range of investors in emerging markets). Estimates typically classify approximately 5% of outstanding credit risk as liquid. The remaining 95% are treated as substantially illiquid.

---

[42] See discussion later in this Chapter.

[43] There is an increasingly liquid secondary loan market in the US, particularly in leveraged loans. There is a parallel market developing in Europe. Volume traded is significant, with dealers making prices and active participation from loan investors; see Lee, Peter "Hybrids Take Root" (September 1997) Euromoney 12; McNee, Alan "Commercial Debt Trading Takes Off" (December 1999) Risk 12; "Secondary Loan Market Takes Off" (July 2000) Euromoney 124; Verma-Console, Bobby "First-Rate Secondary Loan Market" (January 2001) 52–55; Evans, Nick "Loan Market Opens Up To New Investors" (July 2002) Euromoney 126–128.

Originally, the credit derivatives market was focused on liquid credit assets. This reflected the ease of obtaining prices, marking positions to market, the need to establish payouts on the transactions in case of a credit event, and the ease in dealer hedging of positions. As the market has evolved, there is much greater interest in the larger and more interesting illiquid market segments. The fact that it is in illiquid credit markets that the advantages of credit derivatives are greater has come to be appreciated. The advantages include creation of liquidity by allowing trading in these assets, reduction in transaction costs and market frictions, and enhancing efficiency in the management of portfolios containing these types of assets.

The distinction is also reflected in both the nature of the participation and the types of products favoured. The liquid market sector has attracted investment banks/securities dealers. This reflects the fact that the credit derivatives business is a natural extension of the trading and distribution business in the underlying securities. It is also most relevant to their traditional client bases, particularly fixed income investors. The illiquid asset sectors have attracted interest from commercial banks. This reflects the fact that their own balance sheets contain significant volumes of these illiquid assets. Credit derivatives are a natural extension of traditional methods of managing these risks within their portfolios.

Developments in documentation (such as the concept of deliverable obligations including consent required loans) have assisted in allowing the risk on traditionally illiquid credit assets to be traded.

6.3   Types Of Exposure – Static Versus Non Static

The early phase of the market emphasised traditional static credit exposures such as bonds, loans and other credit extension transactions. The obligations were fully funded and had no market price sensitivity. As the market has developed, credit derivatives, particularly default swaps linked to non static exposures such as those generated by derivatives, have emerged. The differentiating factors of these types of exposures include:

- Non funded exposures.
- Market price sensitivity of the credit exposure.
- The *actual* credit exposure is not capable of exact estimation at the commencement of the transaction.

The factors create major problems for the management of credit exposures in financial institutions. The problems arise from the fact that while the *expected* credit exposure is estimated prior to entry into the transaction and appropriate limits are established, changes in market rates could result in the exposure being significantly different from that forecast. The changes in the level of credit exposure have a number of implications, including:

- Causing a breach of internal credit limits.
- Creating concentration of credit risk within the entity's credit portfolios.
- Reducing trading liquidity through increased utilisation of counterparty credit limits, thereby potentially increasing the market risk of the entity.

The fact that this is more than a theoretical possibility was graphically illustrated during 1994/95. The appreciation of the Yen and the drop in Japanese interest rates led to a dramatic change in the mark-to-market values of currency swaps and long dated forward foreign exchange positions, dramatically increasing the counterparty credit risk. The fact that this market rate change coincided with a decline in the credit rating of Japanese financial institutions served to highlight the dynamic nature of credit exposure in these types of transactions. The experience was repeated in 1997/98 when the sharp depreciation in the value of some Asian currencies had a similar impact on existing derivative positions. Similar conditions occurred in 2003/2004 when the Euro appreciated significantly against the US$, causing rapid and large changes in counterparty credit risk on some transactions.

The issues identified above, combined with the dramatic growth in the volume of derivatives and other off-balance-sheet transactions sensitive to market risk, have created increased interest in credit derivatives to manage the exposure of these types of transactions.

6.4 Market Sectors

The credit derivatives market can also be divided into sectors based on the credit quality of the underlying reference assets or obligations. The usual categories are as follows:

- **Investment grade credit** – this category covers higher quality credits. Lower grade investment credits (BBB/Baa), while technically investment grade, are generally closer to the non investment credits in terms of credit derivative activity[44]. The risk of default is relatively low in this market

---

[44]   They are referred to as "cross over" credits.

segment. The primary motivations for transactions in this segment include:

1. Managing regulatory capital required to be held against credit risk.
2. Management of concentration risk and credit lines to counterparties.
3. Reducing the impact of market friction, such as withholding taxes and regulatory factors.
4. Creating customised or structured forms of exposure.
5. Completing the available credit spectrum in terms of currency and maturity.

The types of products most frequently encountered include:

1. Credit default swaps.
2. Credit linked notes/CDOs focusing on yield enhancement (for example, through tranching/risk leverage or default correlation (first-to-default structures)) or diversification of credit.

- **Non investment grade credit** – the dynamics of lower rated investment grade/non investment grade credits is significantly different to that of investment grade credits. The higher default risk and the higher level of barriers to participation in this investment sector are significant factors in this market segment. The primary motivations in this sector include:

1. Hedging default risk.
2. Facilitating access to credit assets where direct exposure is otherwise difficult.
3. Reduction in transaction costs.
4. Yield enhancement applications, including assumption of credit exposures.
5. Facilitating funding to overcome market imperfections such as the absence of a liquid repo market in these securities.

The products most frequently used include:

1. Total return loan swaps, including structures indexed to individual loans/bonds or high yield index products.
2. Credit spread products.
3. Credit default swaps.
4. Credit linked notes/CDOs to provide specific types of credit exposure.
5. Structured credit exposure, including capital structure arbitrage (as between secured, senior and subordinated tranches of transactions) and recovery rates plays.

- **Distressed credits** – this market sector focuses on obligations where the issuer has defaulted/is in financial distress and/or where the underlying obligations are being rescheduled/restructured. The primary motivation for transactions in this sector include:

1. Credit exposure or problem loan management.
2. Opportunistic loan trading driven by high risk trading, leveraged distressed loan plays and/or industry, sector or geographic plays based on anticipated macro-economic cycle transactions.
3. Recovery rate expectations driven transactions.
4. The capacity to finance positions off balance sheet.

The activity in this sector is an extension of loan/asset trading where credit derivatives provide a more efficient *mechanism* for creating or reducing exposure to the underlying credit[45]. The products likely to be encountered in this sector include total return swaps, credit default swaps (where default has not occurred) and structured credit transactions.

- **Emerging markets**[46] – this market sector focuses on obligations where the issuer is domiciled in emerging markets (primarily Latin America, Eastern Europe and Asia). The dynamics of this market segment are dictated by the predominant role of sovereign credit risk in these sectors and the difficulties of or inefficiencies in obtaining direct exposures to the underlying credit assets. The nature of investment risk (higher political risk and regulatory risks; for example, currency inconvertibility) in these markets is also different. The primary motivation for transactions in this sector include:

1. Risk management, including management of country risk or cross border limits.
2. Attempts to isolate and capture returns from instruments without *direct* exposure to the underlying credit risk of the exposure (for example, through an emerging market index or securities where the

---

[45] For discussion of distressed debt trading, see Denniston, Karol K. (2000) Distressed Debt Trading; Euromoney Books, London.

[46] For discussion of credit derivatives in an emerging market context, see Watzinger, Hermann "Credit Derivatives In Emerging Markets" in Ghose, Ronit (Editor) Credit Derivatives: Key Issues (1997, British Bankers' Association, London); van der Maas, Paul and Naqui, Nabeel "Credit Derivatives Structures Within An Emerging Markets Framework" in Storrow, Jamie (Editor) (1999) Credit Derivatives: Key Issues – 2nd Edition; British Bankers' Association, London.

return is indexed to the price performance of a reference underlying bond).

3. Lowering transaction costs, particularly those arising from taxation and other regulations (for example, using total return swaps to synthesise direct investments to avoid withholding taxes).

4. Capturing value from spread movements that can often be very dramatic (through credit spread products).

5. Relative value performance strategies.

6. Creating customised risk reward profiles (for example, through targeted put selling and covered call writing).

7. Managing aspects of the political and regulatory risk of these operating environments.

The full range of products is likely to be encountered in this sector.

6.5 Geographic Structure

An interesting aspect of the market is its geographic structure. The most noteworthy aspect of the geographical structure is the proliferation of credit derivative products across *all* the market segments.

The key market sectors are the US/North American market and the European market. The volumes from these markets dominate the global credit derivatives market. The other markets that are significant include Japan and Australia/New Zealand.

The emerging markets component of credit derivatives is focused on Latin America, Eastern Europe, Asia and South Africa. Credit derivatives on emerging market issuers are a significant component of the market. This continues to be the case, albeit at more subdued levels, after the 1997/98 crisis and Argentine default. The bulk of activity is undertaken between investors, corporations and banks based outside the emerging market. Local activity (local banks and/or investors) is a relatively modest part of the market.

There are a number of significant differences in the pattern of development between the market segments. Commercial banks, investment banks/dealers and investors dominate activity in the US market. The banks are primarily involved in managing their credit portfolios or selling down loan positions acquired in the primary markets. Management of regulatory capital and return on credit risk is a major driver of credit derivative activity. Investors are primarily involved in order to acquire indirect exposure to certain sectors such as the non investment grade loan markets.

Other participants like hedge funds have emerged as significant contributors of capital to credit risk based on specific credit views based on individual issuers, sectors or economy wide views. The US market contains several unique sectors. One such sector where credit derivatives have emerged as a significant factor is the leveraged loan market[47].

The European market[48] is primarily focused on banks, including smaller banks. The banks are concerned with the management of portfolio credit concentration (arising from strong market positions in their home markets) and either funding cost advantages or disadvantages. The opportunities to acquire credit exposure synthetically to diversify their credit risks, while maximising their returns relative to their funding cost positions, has provided a strong impetus to growth. Investor participation in Europe has also been a major factor. The capacity to trade credit spreads and invest in credit risk has increasingly been a centre of focus. Bank capital management has also emerged as a significant factor, albeit at a slower pace than in corresponding organisations in the USA.

Factors that have impeded the rate of development of credit derivatives in Europe include:

- The higher degree of bank intermediation in most European markets has the effect of reduced amounts of available traded bonds. This is compounded by a higher proportion of loans to small to middle market clients in many European countries relative to North America.
- The absence of meaningful historical data on European loan portfolios and a lower portion of rated obligors reduces the ability to price and trade credit risk generally.

European market development has been affected by the impact of the introduction of the Euro[49]. Initially, the surge of trading on the convergence of interest rates between the countries destined to become part of "Euroland" created credit derivative opportunities. This reflected the often very large positions assumed by investors in government and sovereign

---

[47] See discussion later in the Chapter.
[48] See Theodore, Samuel S. and Madelain, Michel (March 1997) Modern Credit Risk Management And The Use Of Credit Derivatives: European Banks' Brave New World (And Its Limits); Moody's Investors Service; Morris, Jenny "An Unfinished Credit Revolution" (August 2001) Euromoney 36–41.
[49] See Paul-Choudhury, Sumit "New Tricks For The Old World" (November 1998) Risk – Credit Risk Special Report 8–9.

securities of particular countries in anticipation of convergence in interest rates. The resulting concentration in credit exposure forced some investors to use synthetic structures (credit spread transactions) or use credit default swaps to manage credit concentration risk and credit limit utilisation.

In the longer term, the advent of the Euro had significant implications for the development of credit derivatives. The elimination of currency risk between 11 European nations had the inadvertent effect of creating not only a large single and unified market, but one where credit differentiation (as expressed by spread to the strongest credit quality issuer) is the dominant market variable. In effect, the Euro creates a large bond/securities market. The use of credit spread derivative structures to trade and monetise credit expectations (effectively the spread to the German Euro securities yield) between Euroland countries have grown[50]. In addition, the creation of a unified single bond market has the potential to create a market comparable to the US domestic market. The emergence of an embryonic high yield and leveraged loan market in Europe is the initial step in that direction[51]. These factors are likely to allow the development of credit derivatives products in Europe similar to the US markets.

The credit derivatives market in Japan is less developed than in the US or Europe. Japanese banks are active in credit derivatives[52]. The nature of the activity is narrowly focused in a number of specific areas.

Japanese banks have been active in using credit derivative structures (total return swaps, credit default swaps and credit linked notes/CDOs) to manage the risk on foreign loan portfolios. The major driver of activity has been the need for Japanese banks to reduce credit risk to improve their regulatory capital ratios. An additional factor has been the high US$ funding cost payable by Japanese banks (the "Japan premium"). The Japanese banks have focused on their good quality portfolios of foreign

---

[50] See Nicholls, Mark "Credit Plays In Vogue As Europe Mulls EMU" (November 1997) Risk 8.

[51] See Adams, Jeremy and Ball, Matthew "The Banks Behind The High Yield Hype" (August 1997) Corporate Finance 33–38; Paul-Choudhury, Sumit "Jewels In The Junk" (April 1998) Risk 32–34; Brewis, Janine "Growing Gains And Pains Of The High Yield Market" (May 1998) Corporate Finance 38–42.

[52] See Reed, Nick "Credit Products Come To The Fore In Japan" (December 1995) Risk 15–17; Westlake, Melvyn "Escape Route For Troubled Banks" (March 2001) Risk – Japan Risk 23–24; Sawyer, Nick "Striking The Right Balance" (November 2001) Risk – Japan Risk S26–S30.

credit assets. This is because the assets are readily tradable. Structured sales have been used to reduce risk weighted assets to improve capital ratios.

This activity has primarily used credit default swaps and CDO structures[53]. Japanese banks have also used credit derivatives to manage the risk of the distressed credit portfolios. This includes credit exposures in the domestic market and emerging market (particularly in Asia). This activity uses credit default swaps and credit linked notes to manage credit risk. This type of activity has entailed genuine economic risk transfer but also frequently balance date "cosmetic" transactions. This frequently entails risk management over balance dates (for example, step up callable credit linked structures[54]).

Japanese banks and investors have also been aggressive investors in foreign credit risk. This has consisted of investment in high yield/non investment grade credit risk and mezzanine/equity tranches of CDOs. The activity is driven by low rates of growth in borrowing by Japanese companies during the protracted recession/low economic expansion in the Japanese domestic market. The activity is also driven by the need of the Japanese banks/investors to diversify their credit portfolios with non-Japanese credit risk. It is driven by the need to enhance return and earnings. The sharp decrease in Japanese credit spreads in 2003/2004 has been a significant factor driving this activity[55]. This type of trading has been particularly important for banks seeking to improve returns to improve capital ratios.

There has been activity in the credit risk *of the Japanese banks themselves*. A large part of that activity has focused on non Japanese counterparties seeking to shed credit risk to Japanese banks. This reflects the deterioration in the credit quality of the Japanese banks/dealers. This has taken traditional forms, including credit default swaps and credit linked notes. A significant aspect of this activity is non bank Japanese counterparties (highly rated corporations and insurance companies, particularly fire and marine insurance companies) selling default protection on Japanese banks. An element of this activity is the arbitrage of information or knowledge gaps between the Japanese entities and non Japanese banks.

---

[53] See Rutter, James "Selling The Securitisation Story" (May 1998) Euromoney 8–10.

[54] See Chapter 3.

[55] See Trinephi, Mia "Avoiding The Crush" (June 2004) AsiaRisk 30–31.

The market for credit derivatives in non-Japan Asia has developed. The major markets include Australia/New Zealand, Korea and Hong Kong. A significant credit derivatives market has developed in Australia[56]. Key components of this have been a well developed domestic financial market, the presence of a number of internationally known companies and a large domestic investor market. Australian/New Zealand reference entities form a small but significant component of global portfolio transactions. This has helped provide impetus to the domestic market. The other markets in Asia are relatively small, but developing[57].

The development of credit derivatives in emerging markets has been primarily linked to the difficulties faced by banks/dealers, investors and to a lesser extent, non-financial corporations in managing their growing sovereign risk exposures. For banks/dealers and investors, the use of default swaps to manage exposures to individual credits has provided a significant impetus to the market. For investors, the opportunity to capture value from the change in emerging market credit spreads has also been a factor in their participation. Some special factors in relation to the role of credit derivatives in emerging markets are considered in the next section.

6.6 Emerging Markets – The Role Of Credit Derivatives[58]

Credit derivatives play an important role in emerging markets. The primary motivation for transactions in this sector include the ability to create *indirect* exposure to the underlying credit risk, lowering transaction costs, tax/ regulatory efficiency, and managing aspects of the political and regulatory risk of emerging market operating environments.

Investment in/trading with emerging market counterparties entails assuming both traditional risks and certain risks that are unique to this market sector. **Exhibit 8.4** sets out a classification of the risks of emerging

---

[56] See Katerdijian, Pierre "Aussie Rules In Credit" (March 2002) FOW 30.

[57] See Sawyer, Nick "A New Twist To ABS" (February 2002) Asia Risk 27–29; "Banks Look To Synthetic CDOs" (April 2002) Asia Risk 4.

[58] For perspectives on the use of credit derivatives in emerging markets, see Gheerbant, Mark "Managing Country Risk Using Credit Derivatives" in (1998) Credit Derivatives: Applications for Risk Management, Investment and Portfolio Optimisation; Risk Books, London at Chapter 3; Van Der Maas, Paul and Naqui, Nabeel "Credit Derivatives Within An Emerging Market Framework" in Storrow, Jamie (Editor) (1999) Credit Derivatives: Key Issues – 2nd Edition; British Bankers' Association, London at Chapter 6.

markets. Transactions involving emerging market counterparties tend, in general, to be characterised by higher degrees of credit risk (often reflecting the lower credit rating of the country and its impact on the rating of individual counterparties), regulatory and sovereign risk. Credit derivative applications have increasingly been used to manage these risks.

Typical applications have included:

- Use of credit default swaps and total return swaps to hedge counterparty risk, reflecting the lower credit capacity available to be deployed in these markets as well as the volatile outlook of the markets.
- Use of total return swaps to replicate emerging market investments and leverage risk.
- Use of currency inconvertibility protection structures to manage this aspect of sovereign risk.

Some special types of applications warrant mention:

- **Credit derivatives in repackaging emerging market securities** – these transactions focused historically on repackaging Brady bonds (with their high yield and irregular cash flows) using an asset repackaging vehicle. The cash flows of the Brady bond were then swapped into European currencies. The objective was to create a higher yielding emerging market security for European investors. The structure was designed to arbitrage the pricing of emerging market debt issued directly in the Eurobond market. The structures created a contingent exposure in relation to default on the Brady Bonds for the swap counterparty. The residual value of the Brady bonds may not be sufficient to cover any loss resulting from the termination of the cross currency swap used to re-profile the cash flows. Credit default swaps, where the default payment is linked to the current mark-to-market value of the swap, were used to reduce this risk. There are few counterparties capable of evaluating the joint probability of market and default risk and then assuming this risk for a fee. This limited the scope for the arbitrage to be executed. The transactions were opportunistically executed.
- **Default protection in financing transactions** – **Exhibit 8.5** sets out an example of a typical emerging market structured transaction. The transaction highlights the use of credit derivatives in repackaging credit risk to facilitate access to certain types of investments.
- **Funding transactions** – emerging market companies often use the sale of assets combined with a total return swap (where the borrower receives

the return on the asset and pays an interest rate amount) to raise funds at a cost which is lower than that available in other markets. Similar transactions entailing the use of equity swaps are also common[59]. The structure enables the borrower to continue to maintain exposure to the underlying asset (including any potential price application) while generating lower cost funding. The lower borrowing cost derives from the fact that the lender effectively extends credit secured by the assets and the reduction in counterparty risk to the exposure on the swap (which is a fraction of the face value of the transaction). The lender also benefits from the lower joint default probability of the counterparty and the underlying asset. This allows the spread charged to be often significantly lower than the normal credit spread charged to the borrower.

Exhibit 8.4 Emerging Markets – Risk Hierarchy	
Type of Risk	**Definition**
Asset price risk (interest rate; currency; equity)	Exposure to changes in the value of the underlying variable
Credit Risk	Exposure to risk of counterparty default
Regulatory Risk	Exposure to changes in the regulations applicable to the transaction (securities legislation, tax regulations etc)
Sovereign Risk	Exposure to political risk, including risk of currency inconvertibility or non transferability, expropriation/confiscation etc

Exhibit 8.5 Emerging Market Financing Structure Incorporating Credit Derivatives

In the period 1997–98, a number of financing structures evolved that embedded credit default swaps. The transaction set out below, involving Korean won denominated bonds, was typical of these structures[60].

---

[59] See Das, Satyajit (2004) Swaps/Financial Derivatives 3rd Edition; John Wiley, Singapore at Chapters 55 and 60.

[60] See Rhode, William "Banks Face Losses On Esoteric Korean Notes" (February 1998) Asia Risk 8–9.

The diagram below sets out the basic structure:

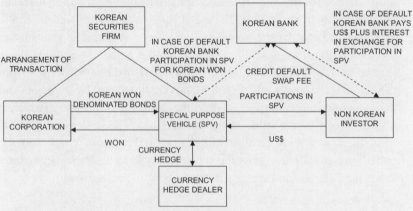

The transaction structure operates as follows:

- A Korean securities firm typically arranged the transaction.
- Korean corporations issued won denominated bonds in the domestic market.
- The bonds were transferred via the arranger to a special purpose vehicle ("SPV"). The SPV used was a unit trust based in Dublin, Ireland. The use of Dublin was predicated on the double taxation treaty between Korea and Ireland.
- The SPV issued participations collateralised by the assets of the SPV. The trust issued units in the trust collateralised by the won denominated bonds. The units were issued in US$ and were structured to be serviced and redeemed in US$.
- The structure exposed the investor in the SPV to two risks: credit risk to the Korean Corporation and the won/US$ currency risk. Each of these was hedged in separate transactions.
- In order to manage the credit risk, the investor in the SPV entered into a credit default swap with a bank (typically, a Korean bank). The credit default swap operated in the following manner. The investor in the SPV pays a fee to the bank selling default protection. In the case of default, the bank providing default protection makes a payment equal to the face value of investment and interest. In return, the investor transfers the participation in the SPV to the bank. In effect, it is a physical settlement of the credit default swap. The bank providing credit default protection can then exchange the participation in the SPV for the underlying won denominated bonds (which are presumably in default).
- The currency risk is managed by a currency hedge entered into by the SPV with a bank. The hedge was structured as a cross currency swap where the SPV pays won denominated cash flows and in return, receives US$ cash flows.

The basic rationale of this structure was facilitating fund raising by Korean corporations and allowing foreign investors to access investment opportunities in the Korean *domestic* bond market. Factors favouring this structure included:

- The applicable regulations at the time prevented foreign investor access to the domestic won bond market[61].
- The structure avoided the 27.5% withholding tax on bond interest because of the Ireland-Korea double taxation treaty.

Some risk aspects of the structure merit comment:

- The use of Korean banks to provide protection ultimately created problems. Given the high credit risk of the underlying won bond issuer, in reality the investor was heavily reliant on the credit default swap. As proved to be the case, the risk of a *Korean* bank defaulting in that situation was high. This reflected both broad macro-economic inter-relationships and the often complex ownership/ business relationships between Korean companies (within the chaebol groupings). In effect, the default correlation was high. This increased the risk of credit risk loss to the investor.
- The credit risk on the currency hedge is interesting. The bank providing the hedge is paying US$ and receiving Won. This means that in a domestic crisis, the swap may not expose the bank to credit risk. This is because the payments to be received are of lower value (reflecting the decline in the value of the local currency) relative to payments to be made (the US$ payments)[62].

6.7 Leveraged Loan Market –
The Role of Credit Derivatives[63]

The role of credit derivatives in relation to the high yield or non investment grade credit market in the US has already been identified. In a parallel development, a market in leveraged loans has emerged. This market overlaps significantly with and complements the high yield *bond* market[64]. The role of credit derivatives in the leveraged loan market is significant.

---

[61] The structure was based on similar equity financing transactions that had previously been completed. Subsequently, under the IMF imposed reform scheme, access to the domestic won bond market for foreign investors was allowed.

[62] This is an example of a "right way" currency swap; see Chapter 21.

[63] See Asarnow, Elliot "Credit Derivatives: Linking Loan Portfolio Management and Bank Loan Investment Programs" in (1998) Credit Derivatives: Applications for Risk Management, Investment and Portfolio Optimisation; Risk Books, London at Chapter 6.

[64] See Barnish, Keith, Miller, Steve, and Rushmore, Michael "The New Leveraged Loan Syndication Market" (Spring 1997) Journal of Applied Corporate Finance vol 10 no 1 79–88; Culp, Christopher, and Neves, Andrea M.P. "Financial

The leveraged loan market was historically defined as loans priced at LIBOR plus 150 bps or more. This market has developed as a non investment grade bank loan market providing funding for lower credit rated organisations. The market has existed since the late 1980s, but has assumed increased importance in recent years. The key factor in the leveraged loan market is its evolution as a *public capital market* exhibiting the characteristics of *bond markets* rather than the *traditional bank loan market*. Importantly, the leveraged loan market has attracted greater investment from institutional investors than traditional loan markets. It also features greater levels of secondary market trading, independent credit ratings and credit research than conventional loan markets. It has also attracted greater credit derivatives activity.

The driving force in this market has been institutional investor participation. This has been driven by a number of factors:

- **Attractive returns relative to risk** – compared to the investment grade loan market where surplus liquidity saw a progressive fall in credit spreads until the sharp reversal in 1997, the leveraged loan market provided high returns. The returns were attractive on a risk adjusted basis in view of the covenant protection incorporated in these loans. The protection includes seniority in capital structure, collateral and mandatory repayments from excess cash flows and asset sales. The fact that such loans are often pre-paid prior to maturity also serves to lower the risk profile.
- **Loans as a separate asset class** – participation has been based, at least in part, on the emergence of loan assets as a specific and distinct asset class. **Exhibit 8.6** sets out the performance of bank loan indexes. The analysis highlights the higher returns available and the modest risk of bank loans as a fixed interest asset class. In particular, the higher recovery rates in case of default and low volatility (in part, because of the floating rate structure of loans that minimises interest rate risk) means that such assets are attractive. The fact that investment in bank loans (effectively in a portfolio context) can enhance return on a risk adjusted basis on fixed income portfolios has attracted institutional investor interest[65].

Innovations In Leveraged Commercial Loan Markets" Journal of Applied Corporate Finance vol 11 no 2 79–94.

[65] See Asarnow, Elliot "Corporate Loans As An Asset Class" (Summer 1996) Journal of Portfolio Management; Marker, Jim and Rapoport, Michael R. (1996) Historical Performance of Corporate Loans: An Update; Citibank's Corporate Loan Market Review And Outlook – 1st Quarter 1996.

- **Ratings of loans** – the major credit rating agencies now provide credit ratings for *loans*. Importantly, the credit rating process is different for loans and reflects risk analysis of the loan's structural characteristics (security, covenants etc) and differential recovery rates[66]. Significant differences (up to 2 to 3 rating levels) may exist between loans and bonds issued by the same obligor. The ratings have developed in response to investor demand as both participation and trading have increased.
- **Alternative to high yield market** – the leveraged loan market has emerged as an alternative to the high yield market and provided investment assets even when the high yield market has been less active[67].
- **Liquidity** – secondary market liquidity has also grown rapidly[68].

A further factor influencing US institutional participation in loan asset markets is the increasing involvement of *investment banks* in the origination, syndication and distribution of loan assets. This development is driven by a number of factors. In the early 1990s, the market for leveraged finance (for LBO/MBOs and other corporate restructuring) came to be dominated by the high yield bond market. In an effort to compete, banks expanded their loan activities to gradually encompass these types of leveraged financing (by increasing their risk appetite and becoming involved in leveraged loans). This development resulted in bank loans and high yield bonds essentially becoming close substitutes for each other in these types of transactions, blurring the previous distinction between bank and bond markets.

The investment banks reacted to this development by increasingly committing their own capital to financing leveraged transactions, but also setting up loan origination/distribution activities. However, the investment banks remain reluctant to commit *long term funding* to such transactions. In order to economise on using their own capital, the investment banks set up

---

[66] See Carty, Lea V., Hamilton, David T., Keenan, Sean C., Moss, Adam, Mulvaney, Michael, Marshela, Tom and Subhas, M.G. (June 1998) Bankrupt Loan Recoveries; Moody's Investors Service Global Credit Research.

[67] Leveraged loan volume has, on occasion, outstripped high yield bond issuance. For example, in 1996, leveraged loans totalled US$135 billion against US$60 billion in high yield issuance. See Barnish, Keith, Miller, Steve, and Rushmore, Michael "The New Leveraged Loan Syndication Market" (Spring 1997) Journal of Applied Corporate Finance vol 10 no 1 79–88 at 85.

[68] See Garman, M. Christopher, and Fridson, Martin S. (13 April 1998) Highlights of Loan Trading: 1997 Review; Merrill Lynch Global Securities Research & Economic Group.

a number of funds, usually combining their capital with that of institutional investors to provide this term loan capital. The development of the vehicles allowing investors to indirectly participate in the bank loan market attracted increased institutional interest. For the investment banks, it has provided a large and efficient funding source for loan capital[69]. Over time, CDOs structured by investment banks using leveraged or bank loan assets have come to fulfil a similar role.

The institutional investment has, in the main, been synthetic, entailing the use of credit derivatives. This is due to barriers to direct participation. In particular, total return swaps, credit default swaps and credit linked notes/CDO structures have been important in allowing this investment to be channelled into this sector[70]. The use of credit derivatives is driven by the ability to introduce leverage to enhance returns and reduce administrative burdens (processing loan repayment, prepayments etc). Some credit linked note structures are driven by the necessity to create baskets of loans that have an investment grade rating that are required by insurance companies (to avoid higher capital requirements under insurance guidelines) and mutual funds (with minimum credit quality requirements). For the investors, the credit derivative format provides an attractive and liquid manner to obtain exposure to this type of asset.

Exhibit 8.6 Leveraged Loans As An Asset Class – Comparative Performance Monthly Returns June 1992 to 1997			
Asset Class	Average Monthly Return (%)	Standard Deviation	Sharpe Ratio
3 month Treasury Bills	0.38	0.09	Not Applicable
Leveraged Loans	0.73	0.51	0.68
Mortgage Backed Securities	0.61	0.95	0.24
10 Year Treasury Notes	0.62	1.94	0.14
High Grade Corporate Bonds	0.74	1.4	0.25
High Yield Bonds	0.95	1.08	0.52
Small Stocks	1.34	3.65	0.26
Big Stocks	1.53	3	0.38

[69] For discussion of these developments, see Atlas, Riva "You Gotta Have Leverage" (February 1997) Institutional Investor 134–142.

[70] See Mahtani, Arun "Synthetic Structures Facilitate Leveraged Loan Boom" (28 November 1998) International Financing Review Issue 1261 85.

Correlation of Monthly Returns June 1992 to 1997

	Leveraged Loans	High Yield Bonds	Mortgage Backed	10 year T-Bonds	3 Month T Bills	Big Stocks	Small Stocks	High Grade Corporates
Leveraged Loans	1.000							
High Yield Bonds	0.148	1.000						
Mortgage Backed	0.040	0.805	1.000					
10 year Treasuries	0.054	0.751	0.887	1.000				
3 month Treasuries	−0.145	0.276	0.357	0.294	1.000			
Large Stocks	0.077	0.598	0.527	0.511	0.289	1.000		
Small Stocks	0.052	0.387	0.156	0.147	0.108	0.652	1.000	
High Grade corporate	0.087	0.764	0.900	0.985	0.276	0.537	0.151	1.000

Notes: Leveraged Loans are calculated as the LPC Leveraged Loan Index. Mortgage Backed securities are calculated as the Merrill Lynch Mortgage Backed Master Index. High grade corporate bonds are calculated as the Merrill Lynch High Grade Corporate Master Index. High yield bonds are calculated as the Merrill Lynch High Yield Master Index. Small stocks and big stocks are calculated as the Russell 2,000 index and the Standard & Poor's Index of 500 common stocks.

Source: Garman, M. Christopher, and Fridson, Martin S. (13 April 1998) Highlights of Loan Trading: 1997 Review; Merrill Lynch Global Securities Research & Economic Group at 4, 5.

7   Credit Derivatives Market – Developmental Issues

The credit derivatives market is currently experiencing strong and rapid growth. The rapid growth in the market reflects a number of factors:

- **Advantages of credit derivatives** – credit derivatives have been successful in facilitating the diversification of credit risk and improving the liquidity of credit markets. The credit events that have occurred (such as Enron and WorldCom) suggest that the availability of credit derivatives is effective in allowing credit risk to be efficiently distributed. Similarly, credit derivatives have increased the liquidity of credit markets. This has facilitated access to credit risk and also allowed the shorting of credit risk to hedge portfolio positions.
- **Documentation** – the ISDA standard form confirmation and Credit Derivatives Definitions have assisted in standardising the documentation of credit derivative transactions. There are still some significant issues relating to key documentary terms (such as the definition of certain credit events (restructuring) and the settlement mechanism (specifically for consent required loans)). Importantly, the documentation has proved relatively robust and efficient during a number of market crises. This has provided dealers and users of credit derivatives with significant comfort. **Exhibit 8.7** sets out the major credit events experienced in the credit default swap market. **Exhibit 8.8** sets out some information on credit disputes relating to credit default swaps. It appears that the documentation has operated reasonably effectively and the level of disputes is modest.
- **Regulatory treatment** – the current position falls short of a unified framework for treating credit derivatives. Regulators have generally exhibited a positive attitude to the market developments. In reality, under current regulatory capital guidelines, a reduction in capital held against exposures *is achievable* in most circumstances. The impact of Basel 2 upon credit derivative activity is unclear.
- **Default experience** – this has been at a theoretical and practical level. Credit risk modelling has greatly increased the understanding of credit risk *generally*. At a practical level, the experience of default/financial distress (particularly as a result of the emerging market crises and the collapse of the technology investment boom) has served to enhance participants' understanding of the value of credit hedging. This has encouraged the active use of these instruments.

A number of important issues remain which continue to affect the development of the market. The issues include:

- **Range of available credit** – the range of credit risk/reference entities available in the credit derivative markets remains relatively limited. **Exhibit 8.9** sets out the major reference entities traded in the credit default swap market. In developed markets, the major entities traded are sovereigns, major financial institutions and well known global corporations. In emerging markets, trading is concentrated on the sovereign and a small number of financial services/corporate entities. This has limited the growth of the market. It also creates concentration risk in structured products (portfolio products and CDOs), inhibiting the development of the market. The market has gained in liquidity. However, concerns about liquidity remain, especially under conditions of stress[71].

- **Market concentration issues** – trading in credit derivatives is heavily concentrated amongst a small group of dealers[72]. The leading dealer has around 20% market share. The top 10 probably have a combined market share of around 70–80%[73]. The high level of concentration makes the market vulnerable to deterioration in the credit quality of a major dealer or the withdrawal of a dealer for strategic or other reasons.

- **Pricing** – the lack of an accepted pricing model (such as Black-Scholes-Merton for options) creates an inherent lack of transparency. This discourages participation and trading. In addition, the difficulties in modelling parameters like default risk, recovery rates and default correlation (for portfolios) remains significant[74].

- **Suitability/moral hazard issues**[75]– the credit derivatives market facilitates transfer of risk from major banks to smaller regional banks and insurance companies/fixed income investors. There remains concern that the entities assuming this risk are not adequately equipped to assess

---

[71]   See (7 June 2004) Liquidity In The Credit Default Swap Market: Too Little Too Late; Fitch Ratings, New York.

[72]   See (24 September 2003) Global Credit Derivatives: A Qualified Success; Fitch Ratings, New York.

[73]   It is not clear if the level of concentration is higher than in other financial products.

[74]   For example, some dealers and software vendors have teamed up to provide benchmark prices for credit default swaps; see Cass, Dwight "CreditGrades.com To Offer Free Credit Derivatives pricing" (April 2002) Risk 9.

[75]   See (24 September 2003) Global Credit Derivatives: A Qualified Success; Fitch Ratings, New York.

the risk assumed. This is allied to the inherent information asymmetry between originators of credit risk and the ultimate protection sellers. This concern is particularly marked in relation to complex structured credit products and CDOs where the investor is assuming significant default correlation risk[76]. The separation of credit origination and credit risk assumption may also create a moral hazard where credit originators apply lower standards to new transactions. In addition, the ability to transfer credit risk may alter behaviour in the case of financial distress (for example, the incentive to restructure or institute bankruptcy proceedings). This may impact upon rates of default and recovery rates in the credit markets.

- **Model risk issues**[77] – the development of credit trading and establishment of integrated trading operations significantly increases model risk. Trading in credit risk and dynamically hedging credit positions entails significant reliance on credit pricing models and parameter estimates (default probabilities, recovery rates and default correlation)[78]. The models are not proven and may well be unable to accurately capture the full complexity of credit market behaviour[79]. This exposes the dealers to risk of loss. The model risk in practice is exacerbated by illiquidity (the inability to always trade to adjust hedges) and transaction costs (large bid offer spreads). It is also exacerbated by the inability to directly trade certain key parameters such as default correlation or recovery rates. This means that a dealer must frequently be prepared to hold an exposure to maturity or use weak proxy hedges as a result of the lack of availability of counterparties to hedge the risk.

---

[76] See Chapters 2 and 4.

[77] For a discussion of model risk, see Das, Satyajit (2004) Swaps/Financial Derivatives 3rd Edition; John Wiley, Singapore at Chapter 25.

[78] See discussion in Chapters 4 and 6.

[79] It is generally agreed that the commonly used Merton structural credit model has significant weakness. Fundamental assumptions of the model are not satisfied in practice. The model does not frequently capture the relationship between debt and equity market prices. In particular, so-called "arbitrage" opportunities in credit markets may reflect the use of mis-specified models with inaccurate inputs. See Keenan, Sean C., Sobehart, Jorge R. and Benzschawel, Terry L. "The Debt And Equity Linkage And The Valuation Of Credit Derivatives in Gregory, Jon (Editor) (2003) Credit Derivatives: The Definitive Guide; Risk Publications, London at Chapter 5.

- **Organisation** – credit occupies a central role in most organisations. It transcends *product* or *geographic* boundaries, creating significant difficulties in developing an organisation for the credit derivatives trading function within the institution. This prevents the maximisation of the capability to manage credit risk within the firm. It may also generate inefficiency in interaction between units that further reduces the utility of these products. The issues of organisation and operations are particularly important for banks and financial institutions and are considered below.
- **Systems issues** – the limited availability of appropriate technology and systems to deal with credit risk also impedes development.
- **Operations** – the nature of the products (the primacy of *credit* issues) means that traditional *derivative* operations areas are not always well equipped to manage the settlement and payment determination aspects of these products. This also creates impediments to growth.
- **Financial disclosure** – the level of financial disclosure of credit derivative activity is variable. There are limited guidelines of disclosure[80]. Major banks/financial institutions active in credit derivatives provide reasonably comprehensive disclosure in their financial statements. Financial disclosure is weakest amongst non bank participants in the credit derivatives market, in particular investors and corporations. Major areas of concern include extent and type of credit exposure, concentration risk (to individual entities or industries), capital adequacy, leverage and off-balance-sheet exposures. For banks, concerns would also include adequacy of loan loss reserves/provisions and efficiency of hedges[81].

Exhibit 8.7   Credit Derivatives Market – Credit Events

Adelphia Comm.
Air Canada
Armstrong
Argentina
AT&T Canada
Comdisco

---

[80] Accounting and financial disclosure issues are complicated by the fact that different credit risk transfer mechanisms (loan syndications, loan sales/ assignment, guarantees, securitisation and credit derivatives/CDOs) may have different treatment despite similar economic results.

[81] See (24 September 2003) Global Credit Derivatives: A Qualified Success; Fitch Ratings, New York.

Conseco
Enron
Finova
Global Crossing
K-Mart
Marconi
NRG Energy
Owens Corning
Pacific Gas & Electric
Parmalat
Railtrack
Solutia
Southern California Edison
Swissair
Telecom Argentina
Teleglobe
TXU/TXU Europe
Warnaco
WorldCom
Xerox

Source: Adapted from (24 September 2003) Global Credit Derivatives: A Qualified
Success; Fitch Ratings, New York at 5.

Exhibit 8.8   Credit Derivatives Market – Disputes Over Credit Events

Number of Credit Events	339
Number of Institutions Reporting Credit Events	52
Number Of Institutions Reporting Disputes	12

Notes:
1. Many institutions reported multiple credit events.
2. Disputes most frequently cited related to Xerox, Railtrack and Marconi.

Source: (24 September 2003) Global Credit Derivatives: A Qualified Success; Fitch
Ratings, New York at 5.

Exhibit 8.9   Credit Derivatives Market – Major Reference Entities

Top 25 Reference Entities

Reference Entity	Debt Outstanding (US$ billion)
France Telecom	52
DaimlerChrysler	55
Ford Motor Corp./Ford Motor Credit Corporation	121
General Motors/GMAC	114

Reference Entity	Debt Outstanding (US$ billion)
General Electric/GECC	187
Citigroup	116
Deutsche Telekom	50
Japan	1,168
Philip Morris	10
ABN Amro	44
Deutsche Bank	105
Household Finance	101
Amgen	4
AOL Time Warner	101
Bank of America	53
BNP Paribas	37
Greece	93
Italy	971
JP Morgan Chase	57
Verizon	39
Vodafone Group	21
Walt Disney	12
Freddie Mac	524
Merrill Lynch	65
Portugal	201

Notes: Commonly quoted reference entities based on frequency of occurrence.

Top Reference Entity By Region

North America	Europe/Asia
General Motors/GMAC	DaimlerChrysler
Ford Motor Corp./Ford Motor Credit Corporation	France Telecom
General Electric/GECC	Deutsche Bank
France Telecom	Ford Motor Corp./Ford Motor Credit Corporation
AOL Time Warner	JP Morgan Chase
Household Finance	ABN Amro
Amgen	BNP Paribas
DaimlerChrysler	Citibank
Philip Morris	Deutsche Telekom
Verizon	General Electric/GECC
Walt Disney	General Motors/GMAC
Japan	Italy

Notes: Reference entities quoted by institutions in each region based on frequency of occurrence.

Source: (24 September 2003) Global Credit Derivatives: A Qualified Success; Fitch Ratings, New York at 3.

Exhibit 8.9   Credit Derivatives Market – Major Dealers

Counterparty	Rating
JP Morgan Chase	A+
Merrill Lynch	AA−
Deutsche Bank	AA−
Morgan Stanley	AA−
Credit Suisse First Boston	AA−
Goldman Sachs	AA−
UBS	AA+
Lehman Brothers	A+
Citigroup	AA+
Commerzbank	A−
Toronto Dominion	AA−
BNP Paribas	AA
Bank Of America	AA−
Bear Stearns	A+
Societe Generale	AA−
Royal Bank of Canada	AA
Barclays	AA+
Dresdner	A−
Royal Bank of Scotland	AA
ABN Amro	AA−
CIBC	AA−
Rabobank	AA+
WestLB	AAA
HVB	A
AIG	AAA

Notes: Commonly quoted counterparties based on frequency of occurrence.

Source: (24 September 2003) Global Credit Derivatives: A Qualified Success; Fitch Ratings, New York at 6.

8   Credit Derivatives Function – Organisation

8.1   *Potential Applications of Credit Derivatives*

A significant problem in the growth and development of credit derivatives trading within a bank/financial institution is the proper location of this function *within the organisation*[82].

---

[82]   For example, see Drzik, John P. and Kuritzkes, Andrew "Credit Derivatives: The Tip Of The Iceberg" (July 1997) Risk Credit Risk Supplement Sponsor's Statement; Nason, Rick, Cromarty, Christine, and Maglic, Stevan "Credit Derivatives: An Organisational Dilemma" (March 1998) Risk Credit Risk Supplement Sponsor's Statement; Varotsis, Paul "Where Do Credit Derivatives

Most organisations have a number of areas that have a legitimate claim to (and do in reality) trade credit derivatives. The areas include:

- Fixed income desks
- High yield/non-investment grade desks
- Emerging market desks
- Repo or finance desks
- Asset swaps desks
- Syndication/asset sales desks
- Distressed debt trading
- Securitisation desks
- Equity desks (particularly convertible trading)
- Individual credit officers/account managers
- Credit portfolio management
- Problem loan management.

The potential users of the products cross product and functional boundaries. **Exhibit 8.10** sets out a summary of the purposes and products traded. The complexity of the relationships is evident from the range of motivations of individual desks in their use of credit derivative structures. This makes it difficult to optimally structure the credit derivatives unit from an operational perspective.

8.2 Organisational Options[83]

8.2.1 Overview

The required organisation of the credit derivative function within an entity requires consideration of a banking process model. Traditionally, credit risk has been regarded as illiquid. The *classical paradigm* of credit risk management has focused on assessing credit risk and matching it with

---

Fit In" in Storrow, Jamie (Editor) (1999) Credit Derivatives: Key Issues – 2nd Edition; British Bankers' Association, London at Chapter 8; Lowe, Diana "Concentrating On Credit" (August 1999) Asia Risk 29–31; Bedser, Geoff "Indecent Exposure" (October 1999) Risk 28–31 Travers, Paul and Heydenrych, David "Grappling With Credit Risk" (February 2000) Risk 34–35; Keen, Matthew "Two Of A Perfect Pair" (November 2000) FOW 48–53.

[83] For discussion of this issue, see Das, Satyajit "The Credit Revolution" (September 1999) Futures & OTC World 52–61. See also Robinson, Andrew and Mockett, Warren (1999) Commercial Lending Transforming The Business Model For Japanese Banks; PricewaterhouseCoopers, Japan.

Exhibit 8.10 Potential Users Of Credit Derivatives Within A Financial Institution

DESK	PURPOSE	PRODUCTS			
		TOTAL RETURN SWAPS	CREDIT DEFAULT SWAPS	CREDIT SPREAD PRODUCTS	OTHER
Fixed Income	• Trading • Risk Management • Client driven products (including those not available directly)	• To finance positions for clients	• Trade/manage credit risk assumed • Synthesise fixed income products for clients	• Trade/manage spread risk • Synthesise credit spread products for clients	• Structured credit products • Credit linked notes • CDOs
High Yield	• Trading • Risk Management • Client driven products (including those not available directly)	• To finance positions for clients	• Trade/manage credit risk assumed • Synthesise fixed income products for clients	• Trade/manage spread risk • Synthesise credit spread products for clients	• Structured credit products • Credit linked notes • CDOs
Emerging Markets	• Trading • Risk Management • Client driven products (including those not available directly)	• To finance positions for clients	• Trade/manage credit risk assumed • Synthesise fixed income products for clients	• Trade/manage spread risk • Synthesise credit spread products for clients	• Structured credit products • Credit linked notes • CDOs • Trade currency inconvertibility protection for clients/own account
Repo/Finance	• Finance inventory • Assist clients fund assets	• To finance position synthetically (non government obligations) • Arbitrage against repo rates			

DESK	PURPOSE	PRODUCTS			
Asset Swaps	• Trading • Risk management of asset swap inventory • Client driven products (including those not available directly) • Use as hedge against credit derivative products	• Leveraged/unfunded asset swap products for clients	• Manage credit risk of inventory • Synthetise from asset swaps • Arbitrage against asset swap pricing	• Manage spread risk of inventory • Synthetise from asset swaps • Arbitrage against asset swap pricing	• Embed credit spread optionality in asset swaps
Syndications/ Loan Sales	• Selling down/acquiring loan risk	• Utilise as de facto unfunded risk participations	• Utilise as de facto unfunded risk participations	• Manage syndication spread risks	• Use synthetic lending facilities/ asset swaptions to synthesise revolving credit facilities for investors
Distressed Debt	• Trading distressed debt • Funding distressed debt position	• To finance position synthetically	• Assume risks (identical to selling puts on the distressed debts) • Assume recovery rate positions		
Securitisation	• Securitising credit portfolios • Enhancing the credit of securitised assets		• Alternative to monoline insurers as a form of credit enhancement		• Credit linked notes • CDOs
Equity (Convertible) Trading	• Funding convertible positions • Repackaging the credit risk of convertibles	• To finance position synthetically	• Hedging/managing the risk of convertible portfolios • Synthetise fixed income products for clients		

(continued)

Exhibit 8.10   Continued

DESK	PURPOSE	PRODUCTS			
		TOTAL RETURN SWAPS	CREDIT DEFAULT SWAPS	CREDIT SPREAD PRODUCTS	OTHER
Individual Account Managers	• Manage exposure to individual credits	• Sell down/acquire exposure to clients as part of maximising client revenues	• Sell down/acquire exposure to clients as part of maximising client revenues		
Credit Portfolio Management	• Manage aggregate portfolio risk characteristics • Manage concentration risk • Manage return on economic credit capital • Manage regulatory credit capital	• Sell down/acquire exposure to clients as part of maximising client revenues	• Sell down/acquire exposure to clients as part of maximising client revenues		• Use of structured credit products/credit linked notes/CDOs to manage total portfolio in terms of economic returns and regulatory capital • Trade credit risk
Problem loan management	• Hedge/transfer the risk of distressed loans	• Sell down exposure to clients	• Sell down exposure to clients		• Recovery rate management

capital or provisions to cover expected losses from default. The principal management techniques have been diversification of the credit risk and the use of credit enhancement (for example, collateral). The *modern paradigm* views credit risk as a separate asset capable of being managed dynamically through hedging techniques (such as risk syndication, securitisation and credit derivatives) in a manner analogous to the management of market risk.

8.2.2 *Classical Credit Model*

Exhibit 8.11 sets out the classical banking model and credit risk management paradigm. The key elements in the process depicted are as follows:

- The origination function identifies and seeks to enter into a transaction with a client. The transaction can be a simple loan, purchase of a security, derivative transaction or underwriting of risk (for example, a debt issue). The entry into the transaction generates credit risk for the bank/financial services entity.
- The origination function seeks credit approval from the credit function. This will usually take the form of a credit limit request.
- The credit function processes this request. This takes the form of identification of the credit exposure assumed (from analysis of the transaction terms) and assessment of the risk of default of the obligor/counterparty. The process may involve the senior management/board of the bank (through the mechanism of a credit committee or commitment committee).
- The credit function then either approves or refuses the credit request. The approval takes the form of a credit limit that is established for the counterparty to encompass the transaction to be entered into.
- The credit function may provide the credit limit, subject to conditions which may include:
  1. Credit or documentation conditions such as collateral or financial covenants that must be arranged.
  2. Pricing guidelines.
  Credit or documentary conditions attached to the credit approval are common. Pricing guidelines are less common. In practice, the credit conditions are mandatory, while the pricing guidelines are (in reality) suggestions that do not need to be adhered to by the origination function.
- The transaction is then completed. The credit risk assumed is recorded. It may be subject to periodic review (usually annual). There may also be

various forms of credit administration arising from the documentation underlying the transaction. These would include reviewing financial information provided and ensuring compliance with credit conditions. There would also be internal credit limit administration.

Exhibit 8.12 sets out the credit analysis and assessment process underlying the classical banking paradigm.

Credit risk is managed within the classical paradigm using the following mechanisms:

- Avoidance of risk exposures by denying credit limits to obligors/counter-parties considered likely to be at risk of failing to perform obligations.
- Provisioning against risk of loss on transactions entered into periodically on a subjective basis, usually based on past credit performance of individual or portfolio.
- Maintaining capital against credit risk (usually based on regulatory capital requirements).

Credit risk is not intended to be traded or transferred. Some risk (particularly arising from large individual transactions) may be syndicated to other banks and there may be limited asset sales (assignments, risk participations etc).

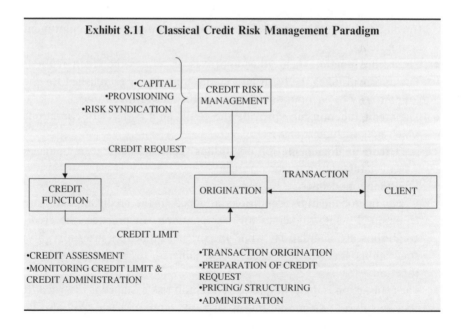

Exhibit 8.11   Classical Credit Risk Management Paradigm

Exhibit 8.12 Classical Credit Risk Management Paradigm – Credit Analysis Process

Phase	Tasks	Comments
Credit Approval Request	Preparation of request for credit limit encompassing: • Transaction terms • Documentation • Financial and business information on obligor/counterparty • Industry information • Overall relationship between bank and obligor/counterparty	
Credit Analysis – Transaction	Analysis of transaction risk including: • Settlement exposure • Counterparty risk (for loan equivalents this is the face value; for derivatives/financial products, it is based on the *expected* projected future credit exposure ("PFCE") based on a simulation model) • Documentary risk arising from unique features of the transaction.	
Credit Analysis – Counterparty Risk	Analysis of default risk of obligor/counterparty including: • Specific credit quality and capacity to perform obligations • Industry factors • Level of current credit exposure	This may be entirely internal or rely on a mixture of external (rating agencies) and internal analysis. The process may or may not encompass explicit consideration of default probabilities and recovery rates.

(continued)

Exhibit 8.12   Continued

Phase	Tasks	Comments
Credit Risk Assessment	Assessment of credit risk based on: • Risk of failure to perform transaction obligation. • Establishment of credit conditions to safeguard exposures.	The process is focused on: • Exposure to individual entity rather than the impact on a diversified exposure. • Avoidance of credit losses rather than creating a linkage between risk and return (pricing) • The process is subjective rather than objective. The process may rely solely on internal assessment or may rely on a mixture of internal and external assessment (credit ratings).
Limit Establishment	Credit request is approved or denied. Approval may be subject to conditions (typically documentation requirements such as collateral, covenants, mark-to-market, netting etc).	There may be pricing guidelines but these are generally non-binding.
Limit Administration	Credit limit must be periodically monitored to ensure compliance. For static (loan equivalent) exposures, this focuses on drawings not exceeding the limit and documentary conditions. For non static exposures (derivatives/financial products), this also includes ensuring that the *actual* mark-to-market exposure does not exceed the projected exposure.	
Credit Reviews	The obligor/counterparty risk is reviewed periodically (annually) to review changes in credit quality and ability to perform transaction.	

The implications of the classical credit risk management paradigm include:

- **Credit risk assumption** – the classical credit risk paradigm is inherently binary. A particular credit risk limit is either approved (the risk accepted and assumed) or denied (the risk is not accepted). This means that there is no implicit risk reward trade-off within the credit risk management framework.
- **Credit pricing** – there is no *explicit* linkage between the pricing of credit risk and the quantum of credit risk assumed in a transaction. The only linkage is that created by the *market* price of credit risk at a given time. This means that the pricing of credit may not necessarily fully reflect the *credit risk to the individual institution*. For example, specific factors such as the extent of exposure to an obligor/counterparty or industry (concentration risk) or the structure of a credit portfolio are not reflected in credit risk pricing. This creates potential inconsistencies of pricing of different transactions within the same organisation. In addition, it is difficult to explicitly link pricing, credit risk and credit capital within a risk-return framework.
- **Credit capital management** – as there is no explicit consideration of capital committed to the transaction and no explicit linkage of pricing to credit approval, it is difficult within the classical credit risk paradigm to manage the utilisation of and return on *economic* credit risk capital.
- **Credit risk focus** – the classical credit risk management paradigm is focused on *individual* obligors and counterparties and the risk of non-performance of contractual obligations. There is less emphasis on the overall *portfolio* of credit risk.
- **Changes in credit conditions/credit quality** – the classical credit risk management paradigm implicitly assumes that the majority of credit risk is to be *held to maturity*. The static framework for risk management does not specifically handle changes in individual credit quality, changes in industry or country credit risk, and changes in credit risk pricing. In addition, changes in value of obligations from changes in credit quality *short of default* are substantially ignored.
- **Performance attribution of originators** – as there is no explicit credit charge to the origination function, it is difficult to determine the full costed profitability of individual transactions or a relationship with a specific client organisation. This creates the risk of cross subsidisation. It also creates significant difficulties in accurate performance attribution to, and performance measurement of, origination functions.

- **Performance attribution of credit functions** – the classical credit risk management paradigm does not facilitate accurate performance attribution to and performance measurement of credit functions. The model is consistent with the credit function being a cost centre. This creates adverse incentives. Originators who bear no credit risk and may not be explicitly charged for the full credit risk assumed are encouraged to take higher risks. In contrast, the credit function is explicitly encouraged to disallow credit risk requests where there is a risk of default. This may prevent credit risk losses but may sub-optimise return on credit risk capital through inefficient risk assumption policies.

8.2.3 Modern Credit Model

Exhibit 8.13 sets out the modern banking model and corresponding credit risk management paradigm. The key elements in the process depicted are as follows:

- The origination function identifies and seeks to enter into a transaction with a client. The transaction can be a simple loan, purchase of a security, derivative transaction or underwriting of risk (for example, a debt issue). The entry into the transaction would generate credit risk for the bank/financial services entity.
- The originator seeks approval from the credit function.
- The credit function would not base its approval on the traditional binary approval process. It would indicate to the originator the *price* it would charge the *originator* as a credit capital charge for allocating lines to undertake the transaction. This explicit cost would be charged against the profit and loss account of the originator of the transaction (whether it is a relationship manager, trader or capital markets desk).
- The credit function would be required to price the credit charge against the transaction as *the lower* of:
  1. *Internal* – this would be based on the *marginal contribution* to *portfolio risk* of the proposed transaction. The return would equate to that required to cover the incremental expected loss (provision) and unexpected losses (capital charge) of the portfolio resulting from the transaction.
  2. *External* – this would be based on the market price for purchasing default protection (through a credit default swap) from or otherwise hedging the credit risk with an acceptable financial counterparty.

- If the transaction were undertaken, then the credit risk would be treated *internally* as a credit default risk swap written between the credit function (the seller of protection) and the transaction originator (the buyer of protection).
- The credit function would then have the responsibility for managing the credit risk assumed. This may take the following forms:
  1. Creating provisions and holding capital against the risk.
  2. Syndication of credit risk or asset sales.
  3. Purchasing protection against the risk through a credit derivative transaction.
  4. Aggregation of selected credit risks and selling them down through securitisation structures (CDOs) or by issuing credit linked notes.

Exhibit 8.14 sets out the process of handling credit risk internally within the institution. In essence, the approach requires the creation of a central "credit warehouse" to centralise and manage the credit risk incurred by the institution.

Exhibit 8.15 sets out the credit analysis and assessment process underlying the modern banking paradigm.

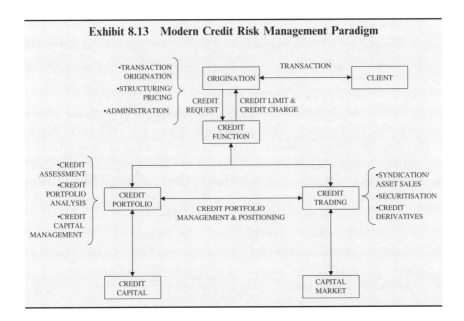

Exhibit 8.13   Modern Credit Risk Management Paradigm

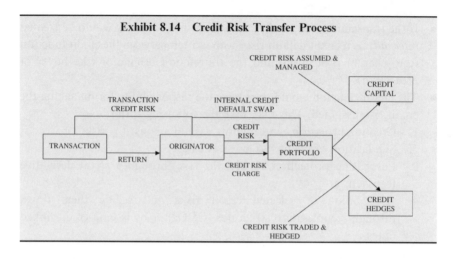

Exhibit 8.14   Credit Risk Transfer Process

The implications of the modern credit risk management paradigm include:

- **Credit risk assumption** – there is an explicit risk reward trade-off within the credit risk management framework. The essential element of this process is that there is a price at which any transaction can be done, at least in terms of credit risk. This price is never higher than the market price for the credit risk adjusted for counterparty risks on the credit derivative transaction. This is achieved in practice through the ability to enter into a transaction that is then specifically hedged through a back-to-back credit default swap. This enables the conduct of financial transactions with minimal credit risk being incurred. This means that in effect, no organisation is ever full on its credit limit with a specific individual obligor/counterparty. It can continue to do business with a particular entity but hedge its credit risk where it is no longer able to assume additional exposure economically (because of concentration risk), or does not (for other reasons) want to assume a specific credit risk.
- **Credit pricing** – there is an *explicit* linkage between the pricing of credit risk and the credit risk assumed in a transaction. The linkage is at the *market* price of credit risk at a given time. This means that the pricing of credit fully reflects the *credit risk to the individual institution*. The concept of the central credit warehouse creates consistency in pricing of credit risk on different transactions within the same organisation.
- **Credit capital management** – there is explicit consideration of capital committed to the transaction and explicit linkage of pricing to credit

Exhibit 8.15 Modern Credit Risk Management Paradigm – Credit Analysis Process

Phase	Tasks	Comments
Credit Request	Preparation of request for credit limit encompassing: • Transaction terms • Documentation	
Credit Analysis – Transaction	Analysis of transaction risk including: • Settlement exposure • Counterparty risk (for loan equivalents this is the face value; for derivatives/financial products it is based on the *expected* projected future credit exposure ("PFCE") based on a simulation model). • Documentary risk arising from unique features of the transaction.	
Credit Analysis – Counterparty Risk	Analysis of default risk of obligor/counterparty including: • Specific credit quality and capacity to perform obligations • Industry factors • Level of current credit exposure	This relies substantially on external (rating agencies) analysis. Internal analysis is focused on mapping credit data into a rating type framework to generate *shadow* or internal ratings. The process will encompass explicit consideration of default probabilities and recovery rates.
Credit Risk Assessment	Assessment of credit risk based on: • Risk of failure to perform transaction obligation. • Establishment of credit conditions to safeguard exposures.	This process is focused on exposure to an individual entity *in a total credit risk portfolio context*. Risk is specifically measured in terms of: • Marginal contribution to portfolio risk. • Expected losses. • Capital required to be committed to support unexpected losses.

(continued)

Exhibit 8.15 Continued

Phase	Tasks	Comments
Limit Establishment	Credit request is approved or denied. Approval is subject to: • Explicit credit charge for credit capital • Conditions (typically documentation requirements such as collateral, covenants, mark-to-market, netting etc).	There is an explicit link between pricing and the credit risk assumed.
Limit Administration	Credit limit must periodically be monitored to ensure compliance. For static (loan equivalent) exposures, this focuses on drawings not exceeding the limit and documentary conditions. For non static exposures (derivatives/financial products), this also includes ensuring that the *actual* mark-to-market exposure does not exceed the projected exposure.	
Credit Reviews	The credit position is marked to market using external market prices or model generated prices. This is used to: • Review strategy towards individual obligors/counterparties, industries and countries. • Portfolio management strategies. • Establish provisioning policies and manage credit risk capital.	The credit portfolio manager may hedge/sell the credit risk if it chooses to optimise returns.

approval. This facilitates the utilisation of *economic* credit risk capital and management of returns on capital.

- **Credit risk management** – the modern credit risk management paradigm is focused on the overall *portfolio* of credit risk. The credit risk of individual obligors/counterparties is important in so far as it affects the overall portfolio risk and return. This necessitates a shift from *individual* credit analysis to *portfolio* risk analysis. The process of managing the credit risk of the institution becomes more rigorous. This covers provisioning policy and managing returns on risk capital. It also covers management of regulatory capital.

- **Changes in credit conditions/credit quality** – the modern credit risk management paradigm does not implicitly assume that the majority of credit risk is to be *held to maturity*. It explicitly assumes that credit risk can and may be traded. The structure separates the transaction from the credit risk inherent in the transaction. Both are then managed separately. This dynamic framework for risk management allows explicit management of changes in individual credit quality, changes in industry or country credit risk, and changes in credit risk pricing. Changes in value of obligations from changes in credit quality *short of default* are incorporated. In effect, the structure creates positive incentives to trade credit risk held in the portfolio to maximise returns or minimise losses.

- **Integration of market and credit risk** – the modern paradigm allows a greater degree of integration of market risk and credit risk. For example, when a currency swap or any market sensitive instrument is traded, the *credit exposure* is dynamic. The exposure is modelled and limits established. Changes in market rates beyond those forecast can rapidly lead to the *actual exposure* exceeding the *forecast exposure*. This risk is inherent in all credit risk management of market value instruments, but is not explicitly and systematically managed. In the new process model, the exposure could be managed by the credit risk function estimating worst case and average exposures, and then purchasing protection against movements in rates beyond the forecast levels. This protection would be in the form of out-of-the-money options purchased from the relevant market risk desk. It would allow the accurate quantification of the risks and the capital costs of assuming the risks. This would in turn allow more accurate pricing of the risks.

- **Performance attribution of originators** – as there is an explicit credit charge to the origination function, it is feasible to determine the full costed profitability of individual transactions or a relationship with a specific client organisation. The specific risk charge to the origination function allows the *relationship dividend* to be measured. For example, an originator willing to do the transaction at an economic loss (in terms of compensation for credit risk) would immediately see the negative impact on his or her profit and loss account. The extent to which other transactions compensate for this loss leading transaction can now be explicitly measured.

- **Performance attribution of credit function** – the modern credit risk management paradigm facilitates accurate performance attribution to, and performance measurement of, credit functions. The credit function becomes essentially a credit trading desk *with its own profit and loss*. It manages its risk dynamically based on its portfolio and its evolving expectations on default risk, default correlation and recovery rates. For example, it may short credit risk *in anticipation* of a change in the credit cycle by buying protection. It may seek to originate exposures to particular entities, industries or geographic sectors either through the origination teams (primary credit markets) or through the credit derivative markets (secondary credit market). It will also actively manage the portfolio to maximise returns.

The modern credit management paradigm also has implications for both transaction origination and credit risk management. In terms of transaction origination, the client base can be effectively bifurcated into two segments:

- **Core clients** – these are the key target market for the institutions and consist of clients with whom the entity has a wide ranging and broadly based relationship.
- **Non core clients** – these are clients with whom the institution has no major relationship, but a credit relationship provides profitable returns relative to risk and aids in diversification of the credit risk portfolio.

The separation of clients into the two groups drives the strategy for covering/servicing individual clients. The core clients will continue to be serviced in a traditional manner. This will entail maintenance of direct relationships using relationship/account coverage staff and/or product specialists. There may be a degree of cross-subsidisation across products for core clients. Profitability, consistent with a broad ranging relationship covering multiple products, would generally be considered at both a product and relationship level. The non-core client group creates different challenges. It is conceivable that traditional methods of providing coverage may be superseded by a new approach for non-core clients. The new approach is predicated on the credit trading function originating credit risk *directly through the secondary markets* (securitisation and credit derivatives trading)[84].

In the modern banking/credit risk management paradigm, credit risk is managed dynamically. Credit risk is managed using the following mechanisms:

- Provisioning against risk of loss on transactions entered into periodically on a subjective basis and based on the market price of individual credits.
- Maintaining capital against credit risk (usually based on *economic* capital requirements).

Credit risk management is predicated on the credit risk being traded or transferred. The principal techniques for shifting risk include:

- Syndication of credit risk and asset sales (assignments, risk participation etc).
- Securitisation of credit risk using CDO structures.
- Credit derivatives trading (credit default swaps and total return swaps).

8.2.4 Summary

The modern credit risk management paradigm embeds credit derivatives activity firmly within the framework of credit risk management generally. A significant impact of the change of the modern credit risk management paradigm is the migration of the credit derivative function from the derivative to the credit desk within the institution. It also requires a shift in the philosophy of credit risk management.

The process described above relates to the overall restructure of the capture and management of credit risk within the institution. Credit derivative instruments become generic building block tools for financial engineering across the entire business unit. In effect, credit derivatives will be embedded in the organisation structure at two distinct levels as follows:

- A centralised credit trading and management function that manages the *total credit risk* of the institution's portfolio in an integrated fashion.

---

[84] For an example of implementing this approach; see Desantes, Robert "Credit Derivatives: An End User Perspective" in Gontarek, Walter "Hedging With Credit Derivatives: Practical Applications And Considerations" in (1998) Credit Derivatives: Applications For Risk Management, Investment and Portfolio Optimisation; Risk Books, London at 34.

- The instruments will increasingly be homogenous and absorbed into the trading or financial engineering disciplines across all business activities.

In essence, this process is not radically different from that which has and continues to take place in other assets and market risk. In these areas, derivatives trading is gradually being merged with the cash markets for the underlying assets.

Changes in the management of credit risk generally are fundamental to the optimal utilisation of credit derivatives. A number of organisations have made this transition, at least in part.

9 Operational Issues

The use of credit derivatives also requires major re-engineering of financial institutions and their credit functions. The major operational issues include:

- **Credit portfolio management models** – this is the focus on managing the credit portfolio as an integrated whole. This requires implementation of credit portfolio management approaches and supporting systems.
- **Systems** – the availability of credit risk management systems currently lags market risk management systems. The availability of software to price and trade credit risks and credit derivatives as well as manage credit portfolios is an important factor in enabling the market to develop further. **Exhibit 8.16** sets out a schematic view of the systems/data elements needed to support credit risk trading and management in a bank.
- **Middle office and operational structures** – the ability of *traditional* middle offices or operations areas to settle and monitor credit derivative transactions is questionable. The complexity of credit event language, the options for calculating the default payments, and the very different demands on counterparties in such transactions (as compared to traditional market risk derivatives) means that traditional middle offices or operations are not equipped to deal with these trades. The lack of transparency and difficulty in marking to market individual transactions also creates problems. Approaches currently being used include establishment of a separate middle office function for credit derivatives, merging credit derivatives operations with loan administration, or re-engineering the credit monitoring function to encompass these products.

Exhibit 8.16 Credit Risk Management – Systems Requirements

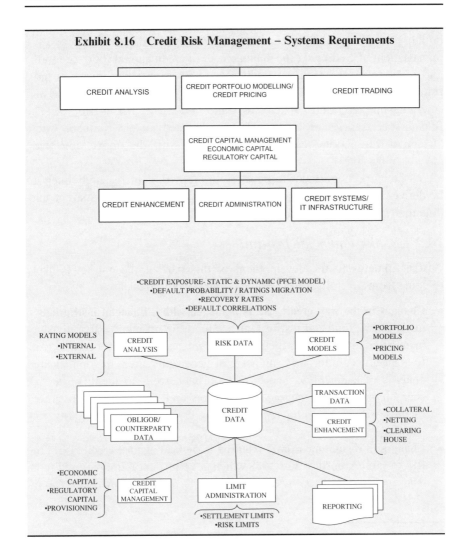

10 Potential Areas of Development

10.1 Overview

The market for credit derivatives to date has evolved in response to the requirements of two primary groups of participants – banks/financial institutions and fixed income investors.

The primary objective of the banks/financial institutions to date has been to reduce the concentration of credit risk in the portfolio and increase liquidity of credit risk. This has been driven by the desire to improve the management of credit risk, the management of credit capital (both economic and regulatory) and transfer credit risk to investors. The investors have primarily sought synthetic access to markets (loan markets, high yield and emerging markets) and capacity to trade *pure* credit risk attributes. The pricing inefficiencies of credit risk have created an environment where attractive transaction possibilities, consistent with the above objectives, have been feasible.

As the market continues to develop, the growth is increasingly likely to be derived from additional sources and the credit derivatives market may potentially evolve in a number of directions.

10.2 Banks/Financial Institutions

Further impetus to the development of this part of the market is likely to come from several sources. The most important areas are:

- **Changes in the way credit risk is managed within financial institutions** – increasingly, financial institutions are focusing on more active management of credit exposures incurred. This ranges from concentration risks to a specific counterparty, industry or geographic area, to sophisticated analysis of a *portfolio*. The latter approach seeks to identify the risk characteristics of the *aggregate* exposures and relate the return earned *to the credit risk capital required to be dedicated to the specific risks taken*[85].
- **Changes in regulatory capital required to be held against credit risk** – the BIS Capital Accord of July 1988 which governs the capital required to be held against credit risk is due to be superseded by a new bank capital

---

[85] For discussion of implementation of credit portfolio management in banks, see Lowe, Diana "Concentrating On Credit" (August 1999) Asia Risk 29–32; Lowe, Diana "Pushing Progress In The Credit Process" (October 1999) Asia Risk 28–31; Bedser, Geoff "Indecent Exposure" (October 1999) Risk 28–31; Travers, Paul and Heydenrych, David "Grappling With Credit Risk" (February 2000) Asia Risk 34–35; Keen, Matthew "Two Of A Perfect Pair" (November 2000) FOW 48–53; Aguais, Scott "Credit Risk: Time For Enterprising Management" (April 2001) FOW 49–53; Lee, Peter "Will New Portfolio Managers Save The Banks This Time" (December 2001) Euromoney 44–48; Evans, Jules "Credit Risk And Its Management Raise A Paradox" (March 2002) Euromoney 52–54. For an example, see McNee, Alan "UBS Takes A New Look At Lending" (March 2000) Risk 30–31.

regulatory standard (Basel 2)[86]. Basel 2 addresses the inconsistencies of the existing framework to some degree. The most logical solution is to "*harness for supervisory purposes the market oriented models already in use by banks for management purposes*"[87]. Basel 2 does not allow the use of full credit modelling and credit portfolio management models. The changes will create a more favourable environment for credit portfolio management and (indirectly) activity in credit derivatives.

The current focus of applications of credit derivatives is the transfer and hedging of credit risk and credit portfolio management. The applications are capable of extensions in a number of areas, including:

- Using credit derivatives for the purpose of credit risk enhancement in structured finance projects (for example, securitisation, project finances etc). This would be as a substitute to other forms of credit enhancement.
- Allow assumption of credit risks outside normal risk criteria.

There is significant potential for application of credit derivatives beyond these types of applications.

The shift in structure and processing models for credit risk will dictate that the growth in credit derivatives will increasingly be derived from additional sources (particularly for commercial banks), including:

- A more unified and consistent methodology for pricing credit risk *uniformly* across markets, allowing increasing efficiency of credit pricing. Credit derivatives may emerge as a synthetic measurement tool.
- Banks/financial institutions may separate out the process of credit origination from the assumption and management of credit risk. Banks may shift focus from the *assumption* of credit risk to the *origination* and *distribution* of credit risk.
- The emergence of credit risk as *a separate asset class* for investors that is traded in a manner similar to trading in other assets.
- Systematic arbitrage across capital markets to assume credit risk in the *most efficient form* (either direct or indirect) based on optimisation of transaction costs, market friction, and regulatory factors.

---

[86] See Das, Satyajit (2004) Swaps/Financial Derivatives 3rd Edition; John Wiley, Singapore at Chapter 33.

[87] The words in italics are those of Alan Greenspan, Chairman of the US Federal Reserve Board.

The use of credit derivatives as a synthetic measurement tool focuses on a number of separate elements. The use of credit derivatives to *value* credit risk within financial institutions allows increased accuracy of, and consistency in, default risk pricing. Combined with portfolio management concepts, it allows measurement and management of credit concentration issues within loan portfolios.

The development of more accurate measures of credit risk within financial institution portfolios allows improved credit risk management in the following respects:

- Credit loss performance can be benchmarked against the cost of obtaining default protection through a default swap.
- Improved capital management, allowing credit capital allocation on a more accurate risk-reward basis.
- Improved performance measurement and management as return on capital committed against default risk becomes transparent.

A major impetus to these potential applications is the implementation of Risk Adjusted Performance Measurement ("RAPM") systems within banks such as RAROC[88]. The implementation of these systems requires accurate estimates of credit capital and the risk of credit losses to be effective. The use of credit derivatives as a synthetic measure of credit risk assists in overcoming some of these problems.

There is increasing interest in using credit derivatives to actively *trade* credit risk. This entails taking views on and positions in credit spreads or default risks of issuers. This entails taking positions on the risk of default, the recovery rate and the correlation between default risks in portfolios. The risk is compared to the return for that risk. The net result is that credit risks (where the return provides excess compensation for the estimated credit risk) are assumed, and credit risks (where the return is lower than the risk) are sold. In essence, it is designed to convert credit from a *necessary consequence* of financial transactions to a specific market parameter that can be traded.

The objective of trading can be either for profit from correctly predicting market movements, or for broader competitive positioning. The latter could take the form of (for example) selling forward low spreads against future

---

[88]   See discussion in Das, Satyajit (2004) Swaps/Financial Derivatives 3rd Edition; John Wiley, Singapore at Chapter 28.

underwriting of risk. It can also entail hedging default risk at attractive cost levels to enable aggressive market expansion at a future date without exposure to the credit risk.

The ultimate potential application entails a shift in emphasis for financial institutions from *holders* of credit risk to *originators* and *distributors* of credit risk. The primary analogy here is to the impact of securitisation on asset portfolios of banks and other financial institutions. The advent of securitisation has enabled the conversion of assets traditionally considered illiquid, such as mortgages and credit card receivables, into tradable securities. The change has altered the role of financial institutions into one of asset originators and asset distributors rather than classical take-and-hold investors in the loans. **Exhibit 8.17** sets out a number of possible models of banking practice.

Credit derivatives have the potential to convert the role of financial institutions to that of *originators of credit risk*. Under this altered paradigm, banks/financial institutions would originate the credit risk in on-balance-sheet form (loan or bond), or off-balance-sheet form (derivative). The credit risk would then be distributed to other parties. The distinction between this process and that of classical securitisation is the unbundling of credit and liquidity risk, and the separation of the decision to sell down the individual elements.

The process could entail two separate types of activity as follows:

- The transfer of credit risk to *other financial institutions*. This would overcome the credit paradox, allowing banks to diversify their credit portfolios beyond their own credit origination capabilities in order to reduce concentration risks as well as improve their risk return characteristics.
- The transfer of credit risk to *non-bank investors*. This would be similar to the securitisation of loans through capital market instruments for distribution to direct investors. This would enable new capital to be attracted to support credit risk as well as facilitating arbitrage between credit pricing in different market sectors.

The major advantages of this change in credit emphasis include:

- The capacity for banks to leverage their existing credit infrastructure more effectively.
- Allowing liquefaction of bank balance sheets.
- Improve the efficiency of credit risk pricing.
- Optimise investment in credit risk.

Exhibit 8.17   Models of Banking Practice

MODEL 1 – CLASSICAL BANKING MODEL

LOAN TRANSACTION   DEPOSIT TRANSACTION

| BORROWER | → | BANK | — | DEPOSITOR |

BANK ORIGINATES, FUNDS, ADMINISTERS
AND RETAINS CREDIT RISK OF BORROWER

MODEL 2 – INVESTMENT BANKING / SECURITIES MODEL

ISSUE OF SECURITIES   DISTRIBUTION OF SECURITIES

UNDERWRITING OF PLACEMENT OF SECURITIES
AND SYNDICATION OF UNDERWRITING RISK

OTHER BANKS

BANK ORIGINATES TRANSACTION AND MAY ADMINISTER IT AS
PAYMENT AGENT. FUNDING ANDCREDIT RISK OF BORROWER IS
TRANSFERRED TO INVESTOR. PRIMARY RISK IS UNDERWRITING
WHICH IS SYNDICATED TO REDUCE RISK LEVEL.

MODEL 3 – SECURITISATION MODEL

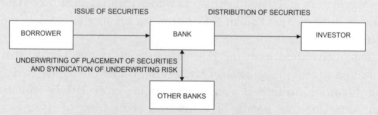

LOAN TRANSACTION   SALE OF LOAN BACKED
SECURITIES

SALE OF LOAN TO
SECURITISATION VEHICLE

BANK ORIGINATES AND ADMINISTERS THE LOAN. BANK SELLS LOAN TO
SECURITISATION VEHICLE WHICH ISSUES LOAN ASSET BACKED SECURTIES. FUNDING
AND CREDIT RISK OF BORROWER IS BORNE BY INVESTOR. BANK RISK IS CONFINED
TO CREDIT RISK PRE-SALE TO SECURITISATION VEHICLE AND ANY UNDERWRITING
RISK ON THE PLACEMENT OF THE LOAN ASSET BACKED SECURITIES

MODEL 4 – ECONOMIC RISK TRANSFER MODEL

LOAN TRANSACTION   CREDIT DEFAULT SWAP OR
CREDIT LINKED NOTE

BANK ORIGINATES, FUNDS AND ADMINISTERS THE LOAN. CREDIT RISK OF
BORROWER IS TRANSFERRED TO INVESTORS OR OTHER BANKS. BANK
CREDIT RISK IS PRE ECONOMIC HEDGE ONLY. WHERE A CREDIT LINKED
NOTE IS ISSUED, THE INVESTOR/ OTHER BANK ALSO PROVIDES FUNDING.

10.3 Investors

Investor applications have focused primarily on using credit derivatives for the purpose of yield enhancement or credit diversification. The investors have primarily been fixed income portfolios.

The potential extension of applications for investors focuses on the evolution of credit and default risk as a separate asset class. While definitive research evidence is not available, separate investment in credit or default risk may add returns to portfolios in excess of that required to compensate for the additional risk, based on the low correlation of default risk to other market risk factors.

The addition of credit risk as a separate asset class would encourage investors to deploy capital to take on credit risk, increase trading in credit risk and allow the development of both new generations of credit derivative products and applications[89].

10.4 Non-Financial Corporations

Existing applications of credit derivatives among non-financial corporations are narrowly focused on management of credit risk associated with vendor financing, trade receivables or investments/projects (particularly, sovereign risk in emerging countries). The potential for further applications for non-financial corporations focuses on the operational integration of credit risk within the overall financial and strategic/economic risk framework of these organisations.

To understand the potential for these additional applications, it is necessary to categorise the credit risks inherent in the normal operations of *any*

---

[89] The introduction of credit indices designed as an index of the market's valuation of pure credit risk (stripped of interest rate risk and swap spread movements) may assist this development. These indices were introduced as a vehicle for investment, active management and benchmarking of corporate credit exposure. They offer investors access to a more diversified, liquid and better balanced (less skewed to high grade credit) portfolio of credit risk relative to corporate cash bond indices. The index is based on the prices of credit default swaps and investors can use credit default swaps and/or credit linked notes to replicate exposure to the index or components thereof. Exchange-traded futures and options as well as OTC derivative structures on the ECSI are also feasible. See Chapter 2; see also Patel, Navroz "A Cautious Embrace" (June 2003) Risk Management For Investors – Risk S6–S7.

non-financial corporation as follows:

- **Financing risk** – this relates primarily to the cost of new funding for the issuer.
- **Default risk on financial counterparties** – this covers both financial transactions (counterparty exposures on derivative transactions) as well as extensions of credit either directly (receivables, vendor finance) or indirectly (pre-payments).
- **Default risk of major business relationships** – this covers the business and strategic impact of the financial distress of a major supplier of inputs, purchaser of products, or distributor on the organisation.

The first two types of exposure are relatively easy to quantify. They are similar to the types of credit risk already discussed and to the types of exposures encountered by banks/financial institutions or investors. The last risk is more difficult to measure. It is likely, in reality, to be the most important of the credit exposures encountered by corporations.

A review of most corporations tends to reveal a high degree of concentration of credit risk. As in the case of financial institutions, business or strategic considerations drive this concentration risk. This concentration has the potential to create problems for the entity by either limiting the potential for expansion of the business relationships (because they represent unacceptable increases in credit exposure) or expansion of the trading relationship which exposes the entity to higher overall risk levels. The latter may ultimately impact upon the rating of the company itself.

Against this background, an understanding of the potential of credit derivatives, where there is an operational integration of credit risk, allows the development of the following range of applications:

- Increasing the range of clients with whom the organisation can trade (as the default risk can be hedged at a known cost), allowing reduction of concentration as well as expansion of business relationships.
- Hedging against the potential losses to the company resulting from the default of a major supplier, client or distributor.
- Use of credit derivatives to disaggregate the profitability/earnings of commercial transactions and attribute sources of earnings, allowing improved analysis of risk reward attributes of transactions. For example, a sale of capital equipment on deferred payment terms to a lower credit quality entity may seem superficially profitable, but part of the earnings are directly attributable to the credit risk assumed in the vendor

financing provided. Disaggregation of each element of profitability is important in allowing appropriate pricing decisions to be made.

The concentrated nature of credit risk in corporate portfolios dictates that these entities will generally benefit from both purchasing and selling protection against default risk. In addition, for large well capitalised entities, entry into credit swaps, where they sell protection against default, may emerge as an attractive investment for surplus liquidity of these organisations.

11 Summary

The market for credit derivatives is still relatively new. It is growing rapidly and maturing. Given the central role played by credit risk in financial markets, the potential for this market is undoubted, and it would be surprising if the market did not ultimately rival derivative markets in other assets.

There are significant issues in the current development of the market, including:

- The limited range of credits available, in particular, the concentration on traded bonds and loans.
- The lack of underlying price discovery, reflecting a lack of liquidity in these instruments.
- The absence of standardised default risk models.

It is clear that many of these issues reflect the emergent nature of the products. Many of the issues identified are being dealt with and, as the market develops, the barriers to participation will become increasingly less significant.

The emergence of credit derivatives has the potential to change banking and credit risk management in a profound manner. The obvious parallel in this regard is the way in which the emergence of derivatives has generally altered the markets for debt, foreign exchange, equities and commodities. The ultimate structure and size of the market for credit derivatives is, to an extent, less consequential than probably imagined. The process of development and analysis prompted by the emergence of credit derivatives in the areas of credit risk pricing, portfolio concentration and management of credit risk, will in itself profoundly affect capital markets.

INDEX

ALTS, 283

Applications, 1, 23, 32, 172, 198, 218, 239, 306, 309, 611, 630–636, 639, 642–644, 652–654, 704–707, 726, 750, 764, 785

Banks/Financial Institutions, 6, 203, 241, 247, 308, 611, 623, 624, 626, 627, 688, 706, 712, 724, 761, 787, 790

  Corporations, 13, 624, 752

  Insurance companies, 310, 735

  Investors, 6, 13, 17

  Trading, 23, 27

Asian markets, 105

Asset backed loan CDOs, 368, 380

Asset backed securities ("ABS"), 310, 316, 692

Asset backed securities ("ABS") CDOs, 380, 381–385

Asset class, credit risk as, 7, 652, 706

Asset class, loans as, 243, 754

Asset swaps, 154, 172, 173, 192–194, 205, 277, 461–463, 470, 489, 490, 497, 504, 607, 636, 657, 765

Asset swaptions, 154, 201, 202, 206, 717, 767

Assignments, 309, 354, 719, 740, 770, 781

Balance sheet management, 308, 316, 329

Bankruptcy, 4, 15, 33, 66, 77–79, 92–94, 120, 133, 141, 163, 167, 182, 194, 209, 224, 248, 253, 257, 265, 300, 311, 326, 349, 353, 379, 482, 501, 502, 545, 693, 695–697, 737

Bankruptcy remote, 281, 311, 324, 343, 385

Bank of International Settlement ("BIS"), 125, 126, 128, 135, 784

Banking book, 126, 134, 135, 139, 146, 147, 150, 151, 200, 451–453, 455, 645, 646, 727

Basel, 1 126, 128, 129, 135, 137, 139, 143, 148, 150, 200, 244, 373, 451, 645

Basel, 2 108, 126, 128, 138, 140, 141, 144, 146–149, 152, 200, 455–458, 758, 785

Basis (see Cash-synthetic basis), 476, 651, 670, 672–674

Basis trading, 480, 486, 651

BIS Credit Capital Guidelines, 138, 140, 144, 451

BIS Market Risk Capital Guidelines, 128, 130, 135

BISTRO, 328–333, 335, 336, 338–342, 366

Black-Scholes-Merton model, 526, 759

Brady bonds, 27, 261, 262, 654, 663, 664, 750

Callable asset swaps, 206, 207, 717

Callable credit linked notes, 748

Capital management, 308, 364, 404, 715, 721, 724, 746, 773, 776, 786

Capital structure arbitrage, 154, 505, 510, 624, 651, 676, 743

Cash collateralisation, 264, 301, 640
Cash flow structures, 314, 315, 382
Cash synthetic basis, 476, 670, 672–674
  Behaviour, 484, 486
  Causes, 477–484
  Concept, 463
  Negative, 476, 478–481
  Positive, 476–482
CDO equity, 423, 424, 427, 429, 431,
  433, 434, 443, 444, 450
CDO mezzanine, 391, 392, 427, 431,
  435, 437
Client relationships, 308, 317, 627
Collateral, 11, 12, 15, 17, 80, 142, 148,
  149, 248, 249, 264, 277, 281, 282,
  286–297, 300–304, 311, 314,
  317–319, 322, 323, 325–328,
  330–333, 339, 348–352, 368, 369,
  371, 373, 374, 376, 396, 400–405,
  434, 436, 452, 453, 457, 504, 609,
  661, 684–686, 698, 754, 772, 778
Collateralised Bond Obligations
  ("CBOs"), 307
Collateralised Loan Obligations
  ("CLOs"), 307
Collateralised Debt Obligations
  ("CDOs"), 154, 183, 239, 305, 535,
  611, 715
  Assets underlying, 284, 385, 452
  Concept, 307–309
  Evolution of, 306, 343, 417
  Hedging, 218, 428
  Investments, 219, 306, 367, 413, 418,
  419, 421, 440, 446, 735
  Investment performance, 443
  Pricing, 354, 381, 382, 419
  Rating, 347, 348, 354
  Structure, 199, 341, 444, 448, 631,
  724, 748, 781
  Variations, 368, 372
Collateralised Fund Obligations
  ("CFOs"), 394
Collateral quality tests, 351
Commercial banks, 475, 511, 557, 625,
  726, 741, 745, 785
Confidentiality, 17, 18, 96, 97, 323, 728

Constant Maturity Credit Spread
  Swaps, 154
Constant Maturity Credit Default
  Swaps, 154, 207–209
Coverage tests, 352, 383, 417
Convertible arbitrage, 111, 174, 398,
  483, 484, 486, 508, 650, 655–659
Corporate credit exposures, 328
Corporations, 141, 244, 308, 345, 369,
  386, 479, 624–626, 646, 688–690,
  704, 731, 745, 749, 752, 759, 761,
  789, 790
Correlation, 24, 140, 147, 148, 154, 192,
  193, 195, 196, 199, 219, 227, 360,
  385, 398, 503, 514, 528, 537, 539,
  566, 569, 663, 680–682, 757, 786,
  789
Credit concentration risk, 711, 747
Credit capital treatment – CDOs, 134
Credit capital treatment – credit default
  swaps, 7, 28–33, 58–61, 84, 85, 159,
  209
Credit capital treatment – credit linked
  notes, 129, 229, 239, 322, 323,
  326–330, 695, 706, 743, 756
Credit capital treatment – credit spread
  products, 7, 18, 19, 22–24, 130,
  207, 460, 528, 730
Credit capital treatment – total return
  swaps, 7
Credit default notes, 263, 269
Credit Default Swaps, 7, 8, 11, 28, 33,
  58–61, 81, 84–86, 100, 110–114,
  144, 154–159, 174, 176, 182,
  207–209, 211–217, 222, 224–229,
  243, 345, 352, 373, 393, 403,
  405–407, 416, 417, 421, 428,
  460–462, 471, 480, 490, 492,
  496–500, 502–505, 623, 638,
  639, 643, 653, 661–663, 669–672,
  681, 693, 704, 718, 725, 727,
  731, 736, 739, 743, 747, 750,
  751, 758
  Applications, 64–67
  Benefits of, 115, 155, 256
  Confirmation for, 28, 59, 117

Key Terms, 61
Rationale, 158
Structure, 7, 28, 154
Term sheet, 10, 223
Credit delta, 189, 409–411, 421–423,
    427, 428, 431
Credit derivative versus loan sale, 309,
    719, 728
Credit enhancement applications, 743
Credit exposure, 29, 59, 156, 297, 299,
    322, 326, 332, 336, 371, 378, 379,
    413, 480, 494, 503, 533, 543, 570,
    615, 617, 619, 623, 632, 633,
    638–640, 657, 689, 698, 729, 742,
    771, 777
Credit exposure reduction, 612
Credit Event, 29–31, 33, 76, 78, 79, 83,
    84, 86, 97, 98, 100, 101, 103, 108,
    160, 177, 178, 182, 216, 265, 266,
    270–272, 274, 288, 471, 473, 500,
    502, 672
Credit Exchange Agreement, 192,
    193
Credit Indexes, 162, 192, 210–216, 219,
    220, 255, 367, 392, 421, 430, 510,
    585, 653
  Applications, 219
  Concept, 210
  Products, 219
  Structures, 392
Credit Linked Notes, 213, 216, 235,
    239, 241, 245–250, 275, 287, 298,
    299, 322, 325–328, 365, 766
  Definition, 239
  Rationale, 239, 241
  Repackaged notes, 287
  Types, 249
  Utilisation, 239, 307
Credit Linked Repackaged Notes, 250,
    287, 290
Credit Linked Structured Notes,
    247, 249–251, 275, 276, 299, 303,
    307
Credit migration models, 173, 398, 510,
    590
Credit paradox, 627, 787

Credit Portfolio Management, 458, 532,
    595, 597, 598, 609, 624, 625, 628,
    630, 727, 765, 782, 785
Credit portfolio models, 587
Credit Portfolio Securitisation, 250,
    307
Credit rating models, 588
Credit risk, 1, 3–7, 32, 125, 129, 130,
    152, 236, 237, 241–250, 287, 302,
    307–309, 329, 341, 343, 363, 364,
    371, 372, 457, 458, 474, 490,
    534–540, 612, 613–631, 688–698,
    710, 713, 724–734, 738, 748, 753,
    758, 760, 769, 773–791
Credit risk as options, 779
Credit risk management, 308, 309,
    364, 404, 537, 612, 623, 624, 692,
    722, 724, 731, 738, 740, 765,
    769, 771, 773, 774, 776, 779–782,
    786, 791
Credit risk versus market risk, 779
Credit Spreads, 18–20, 23–25, 204,
    206, 208, 410, 411, 422, 514–
    518, 553, 554, 555, 636, 665–667,
    674
  Calculation, 18
  Definition, 18
  Forward, 24
  Volatility, 520
Credit Spread Forwards, 2, 24, 25, 27,
    31, 514, 529, 531, 718
Credit spread models, 550, 555, 588
Credit spread notes, 259
Credit Spread Swaps, 20, 25, 208, 293,
    294
  Benefits of, 203, 227
  Described, 2
  Examples of, 19, 26
  Key Terms, 203
  Rationale, 293
  Structure, 20, 208, 259
Credit Spread Option, 21, 26, 172, 201,
    520, 529
  Applications, 23–28
  Examples of, 26
  Structure, 172, 520

Credit Swaptions, 154, 161–163,
  172–176, 216
  Applications, 172–174
  Documentation, 161
  Pricing, 89, 202
  Structure, 161, 163
Credit value at risk, 595
CreditMetrics, 569, 571, 581–584, 586,
  594, 596, 601, 602
CreditRisk +, 596
Cross acceleration, 266, 269, 270, 274
Cross default, 81, 133, 141, 180, 266,
  269, 270, 274
Currency convertibility risk, 701, 718,
  723
Currency in Convertibility Agreement,
  231–234

Dealer Poll, 11, 14, 15, 87, 162, 215,
  253, 257, 300, 621
Default, 2–8, 11–18, 29, 30, 31, 33, 58,
  77, 81, 98–116, 131, 133, 146,
  154–163, 172–201, 221–231,
  263–274, 291, 296–298, 380,
  357–360, 365, 368–381, 423–432,
  460–462, 470–494, 496–505,
  535–538, 540–570, 572–583,
  614–625, 669–675, 716–731,
  747–754, 773–777, 789–791
Default correlation, 153, 181, 183,
  186–190, 192, 193, 196, 198, 199,
  243, 293, 297, 343, 369, 381, 385,
  387, 391, 394, 396, 406, 409–412,
  417, 423–429, 434–436, 440, 445,
  447, 503, 504, 533, 536, 537, 566,
  569, 575–582, 585, 596–598, 600,
  603, 604, 606–608, 615, 617, 620,
  621, 625, 650, 687, 699, 713, 717,
  724, 739, 743, 753, 759, 760, 780
  Base correlation, 430, 431
  CDOs, 152, 179, 183, 306, 307
  Compound correlation, 430
  Concept, 315
  Estimation, 576
  Nth-to-default products, 181, 199
  Trading, 218, 308

Default payments, 377, 723, 782
Default prediction models, 556, 568
Default probability, 143, 195, 349, 350,
  357–360, 419, 424, 429, 440,
  489–492, 497, 498, 535, 536, 540,
  550, 551, 553, 555, 556, 558–562,
  565–567, 570, 578, 581, 587, 594,
  751
Default products, 146, 718, 726
Default risk, 3, 5, 191, 269, 428, 461,
  503, 515, 533, 535, 569, 791
Definition of credit derivatives, 377,
  388, 698, 700
Development of market, 380, 414, 709,
  714, 746, 758
Digital (Binary) options, 226, 667, 668
Distressed debt, 89, 227, 298, 550, 682,
  765, 767
Distribution of credit losses, 536, 537
Diversification of credit risk, 246, 629,
  758

Economic capital, 125, 132, 323, 343,
  344, 571, 575, 599, 625, 724
Efficient markets, 426, 603
Eisberg, 331, 367
Emerging markets, 7, 78, 191, 205, 206,
  230, 241, 246, 262, 268, 444, 654,
  659, 666, 689, 708, 711, 715–723,
  731, 740, 744, 745, 749, 751, 759,
  784
Emerging market applications of
  credit derivatives, 650, 654, 663,
  664, 666
Equity-to-credit (E2C) models, 460,
  504, 505, 509, 510
Equity default swaps, 154, 221–227,
  229, 230, 380, 402, 403, 651, 681
  Applications, 227, 229–230
  Concept, 221
  Pricing, 224, 230
  Products, 229
  Structure, 222, 229
European Market, 745, 746
Evolution of Market, 310, 364, 714,
  723, 724

Expected Default Frequency ("EDF")
Model, 557–560, 562–564
Expected loss, 199, 247–249, 336,
357–358, 536, 566, 571, 621

First-to-default baskets, 182, 183, 186,
188, 190–193, 199, 200, 617, 631,
686, 710, 717
Concept, 181
Hedging, 186
Pricing, 186, 188, 189
Structure, 181, 192, 200, 617, 631
Variations, 192
Fixed income investors, 243, 244,
624, 706, 712, 730, 731, 741,
759, 783
Fixed payout structure, 86, 402, 622
Forward start credit derivatives, 619,
634
Funding applications, 32, 141
Funding arbitrage, 643, 646, 715

GKOs, 100, 273
Glacier, 322, 324–328

Hazard model, 458
Hedging credit default swaps, 115, 140
Hedging credit spread products, 23
Hedging default risk, 743, 787
Hedging derivatives credit risk, 6, 145,
152
Hedging total return swaps, 513
High yield bond markets, 755

iBoxx, 213, 214, 220, 392, 653
Index linked notes, 210, 368, 380, 392
Integrated credit trading, 739
Internal credit models, 321, 327, 340,
455, 711, 742, 770
Investment banks, 190, 191, 212, 277,
280–282, 284, 308, 343, 367, 389,
475, 625, 726, 729, 730, 741, 755,
756
Investment grade markets, 607

ISDA, 15, 28, 59–62, 70, 73, 74, 84, 85,
95, 99, 104, 110, 112–117, 119, 124,
163–165, 225, 244, 354, 377–379,
726, 728, 735, 737, 758

Japanese market, 229
Jarrow, Robert, 534, 591, 593, 594, 603

KMV Corporations (see Moody's
KMW), 557, 558, 560–562, 564,
581, 582

Leverage, 9, 17, 154, 181, 192, 198, 204,
228, 252, 254–259, 267, 296,
341–343, 383, 387, 397, 398, 400,
406, 413, 431–438, 444, 446, 447,
450, 480, 482, 515, 538, 545, 550,
559, 561, 651, 652, 682–687, 708,
713, 715–719, 723, 756, 761, 787
Leveraged notes, 254
Leveraged applications, 651, 680, 683,
686
Leveraged loan markets, 715, 717, 719
Liquidity, 3, 5, 19, 59, 134, 146, 176,
178, 211, 213, 217, 219, 234, 241,
242, 276, 277, 380, 393–397, 400,
478, 479, 490, 603, 623, 662, 733,
740, 755, 758, 791
Liquidity risk, 351, 441, 603, 733, 787
Loan Participation, 70, 71, 91, 92, 163,
170, 652, 719
Loss exposure, 540, 541, 543, 544, 565,
566, 569, 575, 598, 606, 607
Loss given default, 129, 248, 349, 357,
359, 369, 410, 419, 420, 424, 489,
491, 497, 535, 536, 538, 544, 546,
556, 585, 596, 615, 620, 670, 675

Management of concentration risk, 32,
625, 629, 743
Management of currency convertibility
risk, 223, 268, 271, 701, 718, 723
Management of financing cost
applications, 437
Management of return on risk, 324,
537, 633, 645, 646

Management of syndication risk, 636, 638
Market for credit risk, 213, 474, 476, 481, 484, 485
Market participants, 103, 105, 107, 113, 152, 176, 212, 421, 480, 638
Market risk contingent credit default swaps, 157
Market sectors, 6, 173, 740, 742, 745, 787
Market value structure, 314, 315, 366
Master trust structure, 314
Materiality Requirement, 98, 132, 300, 457
MECS, 278
Merton, Robert, 221, 505–507, 556, 557
Merton structural model, 674
Models of banking practice, 787, 788
Modelling CDOs, 410
Modelling credit risk, 532, 606
Modelling credit portfolios, 578
Monetisation of credit spread expectations, 623
Moody's KMW, 557, 558, 560, 561, 562
Multiple issuance structures, 283
Multiple issuer or umbrella programs, 284–286

Non static exposures, 617, 740, 741
Nth-to-default baskets (see also First-to-Default Baskets), 154, 181, 187, 192, 195, 196, 198, 199, 210, 421, 429, 430, 535, 620, 739

Off-balance sheet, 7, 17, 24, 32, 316, 317, 480
Operational aspects of credit derivatives, 102, 396
Optimising balance sheet management, 308, 316, 329
Option based default prediction models, 568
Organisation of credit derivatives, 765
Origins of market, 709

Participations, 70, 72, 92, 123, 163, 170, 309, 317, 320, 652, 719, 728, 752, 767, 770
Payment timing, 14, 27, 29, 33, 65
Phases of market development, 708
Physical Settlement, 82
Points up front structure (see Upfront credit default swap), 30, 31
Portfolio management/diversification applications, 533, 537, 538
Portfolio products, 732, 759
Pricing credit default swaps, 458, 462
Pricing credit spread forwards, 514
Pricing credit spread option, 520
Pricing default risk, 609
Pricing framework, 221, 505, 557, 677
Pricing in practice, 490
Pricing Models, 489, 503, 535, 679, 760
Pricing Models, types of, 503
Pricing total return swap, 511, 512
Product hierarchy of credit derivatives, 8
Product variations, 220, 229, 252, 261, 267
Program Issuers, 284
Project finance applications, 700
Prospects for credit derivatives, 230, 510, 576, 678
Proxy hedges, 512, 760
Publicly available information, 66, 83–86, 97, 300, 691, 697, 737
Putable asset swaps, 172, 204, 205

Quanto credit default swaps, 154, 176, 178, 620

Range Notes, 235
Rating agencies, 199, 244, 248, 280, 286, 298, 322, 324, 327, 348, 354, 356, 357, 371, 384–387, 395, 396, 403, 406, 419, 440–442, 544, 545, 551, 695, 734, 755, 771
Rating criteria, 404
Rating downgrade, 203, 389, 689, 711
Rating migration, 386, 437, 571, 572, 594, 596

Rating migration model, 348, 349
Rating protection structures, 234, 750
Recovery rate, 30, 89, 179, 187, 297,
    360, 482, 491, 503, 540, 544, 545,
    555, 556, 622, 675, 679, 691
Recovery rate structures, 154, 179, 620,
    651
Reduced form models, 588–590, 605
Reference asset/reference bond or loan/
    reference security, 29, 75, 130, 132,
    134, 136, 140, 255
Reference Entity, 28–31, 33, 61, 64,
    73–76, 79–81, 88, 97, 110, 116, 123,
    157, 159–163, 176, 188, 196–198,
    208–210, 226–228, 236, 243,
    263–265, 269–271, 274, 288, 298,
    304, 422, 491, 496, 497, 501, 503,
    504, 673, 681, 682, 697, 737, 763
Regulatory capital, 2, 103, 108, 125,
    126, 128–130, 132, 133, 152, 200,
    243, 244, 306, 308, 309, 316, 323,
    330, 331, 343–345, 347, 362, 441,
    450, 455, 478, 512, 625, 632, 645,
    646, 723, 724, 733, 743, 745, 747,
    758, 768, 770, 779, 784
Regulatory capital arbitrage, 724
Repackaged credit linked notes, 238,
    247, 250, 275, 287, 290, 292, 298,
    299, 301, 307
Repackaging vehicles, 275–278,
    280–283, 298, 301
Replication products, 7
Replication in the asset market, 8, 513,
    533, 535, 607
Repo markets, 212, 472, 718
Restructuring credit event, 101–104,
    106–108, 113, 124, 141, 217,
    500–502
Risk decomposition, 3
R.O.S.E. transaction, 319

Securitised asset swaps, 277
Securitisation, 152, 200, 238, 250, 306,
    307, 309, 315, 328–332, 337, 338,
    340–341, 344, 346, 347, 361, 362,

    366–369, 371–375, 403, 451–458,
    692, 765, 781, 787
Single tranche CDOs, 306, 367, 405,
    406, 408, 421, 422, 428, 739
Applications, 422
Concept, 405
Hedging, 409, 413, 428
Pricing, 405
Structure, 405, 406, 408, 412
Size of market, 725
SME (Small and Medium Enterprises)
    CDOs, 367–370, 371, 373–375
Sovereign credit risk, 268, 744
Spread duration, 22, 23, 25, 665, 703
Static exposure, 569, 617, 740, 741
Structured Finance CDOs, 381–389
Super senior investment, 441
Super senior swap, 417
Super senior tranche, 329–331,
    338–341, 346, 426, 436, 440–442,
    453–455, 457
Swap guarantees, 154, 156, 372
Syndication applications, 635, 636, 638
Synthetic assets, 276, 463, 467, 624, 650
Synthetic bonds, 250, 298, 299, 301, 302
Synthetic CLOs, 452
Synthetic credit assets, 287, 289, 292,
    483, 622, 727
Synthetic credit portfolio securitisation,
    250, 307, 724
Synthetic emerging market structured
    notes, 268, 273, 274
Synthetic lending facilities, 201, 204,
    206, 717
Synthetic syndications, 638
Systematic risk, 537, 582, 584, 604

Term structure of credit risk, 514
Timing of default payment, 160, 188
Total Return Credit Linked Notes
Total Return Swaps, 2, 7, 8, 10, 13, 15,
    17, 31, 130, 134, 144, 146–148, 152,
    213, 216, 254, 255, 294–296, 421,
    511–513, 685, 686, 710, 716–719,
    722, 750
Applications, 15–18

Total Return Swaps (*continued*)
   Documentation, 10–15
   Key Terms, 10
   Rationale, 15–18
   Structure, 7–11, 251, 252
Total Rate of Return Swaps, 9
Trac-X, 213, 214, 220, 392, 585, 653
Trading book, 126, 128, 130, 131, 134,
      135, 138, 146, 147, 150–152, 201,
      404, 406, 407, 451, 455, 478, 645,
      646, 727
Trading in credit derivatives, 113, 729,
      739, 759
Triangle, 322
Turnbull, Stuart, 106, 107, 460, 489,
      500, 501, 588, 593

Unexpected loss, 129, 536, 543,
      565–571, 574, 599, 774, 777
Unsystematic risk, 537, 604
Upfront credit default swap, 154,
      158–161, 672
US market, 18, 76, 107, 179, 314, 604,
      726, 745–747

Value at Risk (VAR), 128, 135, 149,
      492, 569, 572, 587, 595
Volume or size options, 204, 206, 207,
      717

Wal Mart synthetic bond, 299

Yield enhancement applications, 743